STRATEGIC MANAGEMENT
Text, Readings, and Canadian Cases

T H I R D   E D I T I O N

STRATEGIC MANAGEMENT
Text, Readings, and Canadian Cases

Mark C. Baetz

Associate Professor
School of Business and Economics
Wilfrid Laurier University

Paul W. Beamish

Associate Professor
Western Business School
The University of Western Ontario

Burr Ridge, Illinois
Boston, Massachusetts
Sydney, Australia

To our wives: Jeanie and Maureen

© RICHARD D. IRWIN, INC., 1987, 1990, and 1993

Vice president: Sarah Iles
Senior sponsoring editor: Roderick T. Banister
Marketing manager: Kurt Messersmith
Project editor: Margaret Haywood
Production manager: Bette K. Ittersagen
Cover designer: Mercedes Santos
Art manager: Kim Meriwether
Compositor: Graphic World, Inc.
Typeface: 10/12 Times Roman
Printer: R. R. Donnelley & Sons Company

ISBN 0-256-10799-8

Library of Congress Catalog Number: 92-072849

Printed in the United States of America
2 3 4 5 6 7 8 9 0 DOC 9 8 7 6 5 4 3

Mark Baetz is currently Associate Professor of Business at the School of Business and Economics at Wilfrid Laurier University (WLU) in Waterloo, Ontario. He has been a professor at WLU since 1980. He has coauthored two textbooks and has written several case studies and articles dealing with strategic management and business-government relations. Dr. Baetz has a Ph.D. and an MBA from The University of Western Ontario and a BA from the University of Toronto. He has received numerous scholarships and awards including the Gold Medal in the MBA Program at Western. Dr. Baetz has been a consultant to several large corporations, dealing with such issues as the development of a strategic plan and the establishment of a government relations department. He is currently teaching courses on strategic management and business-government relations. He worked for IBM Canada Ltd and Bell Canada before joining the faculty at WLU.

Paul Beamish holds the William G. Davis Chair in International Business at the Western Business School, The University of Western Ontario. Effective July 1, 1992, he was appointed editor-in-chief of the *Journal of International Business Studies (JIBS)*. He is the author or coauthor of 8 books, 40 articles, contributed chapters, or published conference papers, and 36 case studies. His articles have appeared in such journals as *Strategic Management Journal*, *JIBS*, and *Columbia Journal of World Business*. His consulting and management training activities have been in both the public and private sector for such organizations as the World Bank, the Canadian Foreign Service Institute, Northern Telecom, and Valmet. He has received Best Research Awards from the Academy of Management and the Administrative Sciences Association of Canada and research grants from groups in Canada and the United States. He worked for the Procter and Gamble Company of Canada and Wilfrid Laurier University before joining Western's faculty in 1987.

As with the second edition, this book was possible only because of the academic and intellectual support from colleagues at The University of Western Ontario (UWO), Wilfrid Laurier University (WLU), and across the country. The primary stimulus for this book was our own ongoing need for new Canadian material.

Having made the decision to produce a book of Canadian cases in strategic management, a number of other decisions were made: (1) to bring together Canadian cases written not only by ourselves but by faculty across North America; (2) to include only decision-oriented cases, which we believe provide the best training for future managers; (3) to include cases dealing with international business and business-government relations, which are aspects of general management particularly important to managers in Canada, a country with a small domestic market and extensive levels of government involvement in business; (4) to provide text material including a basic conceptual framework for use with all the cases; and (5) to include a section on how to do case and financial analysis.

We solicited and received much useful feedback on the second edition from colleagues at the more than 40 institutions in Canada and the United States where the second edition has been used. From this feedback, we have decided to retain the basic structure of the second edition but have changed the vast majority of the cases. This package contains 23 new cases and three new readings. In addition, 4 cases have been revised or condensed.

We are indebted to several groups of people for assisting in the preparation of this book. First, we are grateful to the case contributors from UWO, WLU, and other institutions. At UWO, we wish to thank Chris Albinson, Mary Crossan, Nick Fry, John Hulland, Bud Johnston, Peter Killing, Allen Morrison, Don Thain, and Rod White, and research assistants Charles Blair, Fred Chan, Steven Cox, Pamela Jeffrey, John McCready, Kerry McLellan, Jennifer McNaughton, Joyce Miller, Ian Sullivan, and Adam Twarog. At WLU we wish to thank Ken Harling, Peter Kelly, and Ray Suutari for assisting in the development of cases. Cases were also contributed by colleagues from 15 other institutions:

John Barnett, University of New Hampshire
Bill Blake, Memorial University
Robert Blunden, Dalhousie University
James Bowey, Bishop's University
Jonathan Calof, University of Ottawa
Brooke Dobni, University of Saskatchewan
Jonathan Foster, London School of Economics
Raymond Gaudette, Concordia University
Walter Good, University of Manitoba
Harold Gram, Concordia University

Louis Hebert, Concordia University
Diane Hogan, Memorial University
Louise Jones, Memorial University
Thomas Poynter, Transitions Group
Peter Richardson, Queen's University
Gordon Shillinglaw, IMD
Guy Stanley, Pace University
Charles Summer, University of
    Washington in Seattle
Stephen Tax, University of Manitoba

From the above list it is clear that the effort to produce the book has been both a national and international effort.

With regard to the textual material, the footnotes at the end of each chapter indicate the source of the material in the chapter. We wish to acknowledge, in particular, the assistance of Art Thompson and A.J. Strickland on Chapters 2, 7, and 9, Ken Harling on Chapters 4 and 5, and Ray Suutari on Chapter 5 and the reading on "Doing Business in the United States."

Others who provided helpful comments on the outline of the third edition included J. Charmard, Dalhousie University; Brooke Dobni, University of Saskatchewan; Clement Hobbs, Carleton University; David Rutenberg, Queen's University; and John Usher, University of Alberta.

We are indebted to the strategy area teaching groups at UWO and WLU. Our special thanks to John Banks, Ruth Cruikshank, Elliott Currie, Ken Harling, Peter Kelly, and Ray Suutari.

We are also grateful for the secretarial assistance. At WLU we wish to thank Elsie Grogan and her staff, and Helen Hillier; and at Western, Jeannette Weston.

Another group that was instrumental in the preparation of this book was the group of reviewers used by our publisher. These included colleagues across the country too numerous to mention. They helped ensure that quality standards were achieved.

Financial assistance for case writing at Western was received through the Plan for Excellence. Our thanks to Jim Hatch. At WLU, the Case Studies Grant Program was vital.

In addition, we wish to thank the various executives who gave us the required access to complete the cases in this book. Finally, we wish to recognize our students on whom we tested the cases for classroom use. Some students served as research assistants; their contributions are duly noted in each case.

Any errors or omissions in this book remain our responsibility. We look forward to feedback from its various users.

Mark C. Baetz
Paul W. Beamish

C O N T E N T S

I TEXT

1 STRATEGIC MANAGEMENT— AN OVERVIEW

Most battles are won—or lost—before they are engaged, by men who take no part in them; by their strategists.

Carl von Clausewitz, *On War* (1832)

Luck affects everything.

Ovid

Businesses are successful for a variety of reasons: some are lucky, some are the first to do something, and some do well the one or two things most critical for success without realizing how important the particular activities are. Finally, some devise strategies that take into account environment, managerial resources, and values; develop an organization that fits their strategy; and revise both whenever competitive conditions require it. A business may be successful because of one or more of these reasons, which may take place only once or regularly. The assumption behind any book on *strategic management* is that the only sustainable basis for organizational success is the final one—a well-formulated, implemented, and controlled strategy.

Strategic management/business policy is the capstone course in most university and college business administration programs in North America. Management schools teach strategic management—which integrates the material about the functional areas—in order to prepare students as administrators capable of seeing important relationships at a strategic level.

The study of strategic management has been steadily evolving. Original emphasis was on the functions of the general manager—still an integral part of the field. More recently, the strategic management field has broadened to include the study of

> the organizational systems and processes used to establish overall organizational goals and objectives and to formulate, implement, and control the strategies and policies necessary to achieve these goals and objectives.[1]

3

This text reflects this broadening in scope by providing case studies dealing with most of the major subfields of strategic management. Eighteen major subfields are summarized in Exhibit 1–1 under five headings: major reference groups, conceptualizing strategic management, elements of strategy formulation, elements of strategy implementation and review, and organizations.

The common element in discussions of strategic management is an emphasis on strategy. The word *strategy* has become one of the most debased terms in recent years, often indiscriminately used in an attempt to add importance or significance to a variety of topics.

Derived from the ancient Greek *strategos* or "the art of the general,"[2] strategy has military roots. In fact, not surprisingly, strong similarities exist between the responsibilities of the military general and the general manager of an organization. Their definitions of strategy overlap as well. In a military context, strategy has been defined as "the employment of the battle as the means to gain the end of the war."[3] In a corporate setting, strategy can be defined as the implementable management scheme for achieving corporate ends. Alternately, corporate strategy has been viewed as "the pattern in the organization's important decisions and actions, and consists of a few key areas or things by which the firm seeks to distinguish itself."[4] Finally, in a broader context, strategy

---

EXHIBIT 1–1 Some Major Subfields of Strategic Management/Business Policy

Groups
  1. Board of directors.
  2. General management.
  3. Stakeholder analysis.
Conceptualizing strategic management.
  4. The strategy-structure-performance linkage.
  5. Corporate-level strategy (including mergers, acquisitions, and divestitures).
  6. Business-level strategy.
Elements of strategy formulation.
  7. Organizational goals.
  8. Corporate social policy and management ethics.
  9. Macroenvironmental analysis.
10. Strategic decision making (choice of strategy).
Elements of strategy implementation and review.
11. The design of macroorganizational structure and systems.
12. Strategic planning and information systems.
13. Strategic control systems.
14. Organizational culture.
15. Leadership style for general managers.
Organizations.
16. The strategic management of small businesses and new ventures.
17. The strategic management of not-for-profit organizations (including governments).
18. The strategic management of international business.

SOURCE: Reprinted by permission from *West Series in Strategic Management*, Charles W. Hofer, consulting ed. (St. Paul, Minn.: West Publishing, 1986). Copyright © 1986 by West Publishing Co. All rights reserved.

has been defined as "that which has to do with determining the basic objectives of an organization and allocating resources to their accomplishment."[5]

Understanding the role of resource allocation in the strategic management process is critical. Resource allocations serve to interpret and apply the firm's strategy. In fact, the essence of the strategy of an organization is how and where it allocates resources.

A firm grasp of the resource allocation process is necessary to appreciate its role in the strategic management process. As the matrix in Exhibit 1–2 indicates, the resource allocation process has three phases and three subprocesses. The first phase is the initiating phase—where many product/market ideas and proposals originate. This is the level where many new business graduates will spend their first years of employment. The other two phases are corporate (senior management level) and integrating. It is through the integrating phase—or what might be called the middle-management level—that the goals and plans defined by corporate management will be conveyed down through the organization. It is also through the integrating phase that operational proposals (from the initiating phase) will be first screened and, if deemed promising, conveyed up through the organization to the corporate level.

Exhibit 1-2 The Resource Allocation Process

Process ⟍ Phase	Definition *Goal/Plan/Result Definition and Measurement*		Commitment *Project/Plan Impetus*		Organization *Determination of Organizational Context*	
Corporate (senior management)	Macro strategy Company environment aggregate system		Terminal decision, yes or no		Design of corporate context Overall structure, personnel assignment and development, incentive and control systems, style	
Integrating (middle management)	Financial aggregate goals Strategic thrust ↓	↑ Product-market strategies	Filtered company needs (the company "wants") ↓	↑ Filtered product/ market needs (the businesses "want')	Corporate needs Implementation (differentiation integration) ↓	↑ Subunit needs Interpretation, adaptive needs
Initiating (operating level)	Product-market strategies Operational plans and execution		Competing plans/proposals I've got a "great" idea		Product/market not served by structure	

The three subprocesses in the resource allocation process are definition, commitment, and organizational context. In the definition process, the underlying economic and technical considerations of a proposed investment (resource allocation) are determined. In order to understand how proposals that have already been defined move toward funding, the second of the three subprocesses—commitment or impetus—comes into play. It is at this stage that a senior manager must commit (or not) to sponsor a project. Because the general manager's reputation for good judgment may rise or fall depending on the outcome of the investment, the required commitment will be given only after careful consideration of the various demands at the corporate and operational levels. Not surprisingly, this second subprocess can be viewed primarily as a political one.[6]

The final subprocess is context, which is the set of organizational elements—including formal structure, information and control systems, and reward systems—which influence both definition and impetus. This flow from the definition or formulation of a potential resource allocation through commitment to how it will ultimately affect, and be affected by, the organization begins to move us toward an understanding of the basic framework which underlies the study of strategic management.

According to Mintzberg,[7] there are three functional roles of the general manager: interpersonal, informational, and decision related. The interpersonal roles can be further subdivided into figurehead, liaison, and leader roles. The informational roles can be divided into monitor, disseminator, and spokesman roles. Finally, the decision-related roles would include acting as innovator, resource allocator, negotiator, and disturbance handler. It is a rare general manager who is equally effective in all roles. General managers who are able to acknowledge this reality will often try to develop a staff with complementary skills.

Before examining the underlying paradigm, the components of business strategy will be discussed.

The Major Components of Strategy

Every firm has a strategy. Implicit or explicit, effective or ineffective, as intended or not—whenever a firm allocates the resources of people or capital, it is making a statement about its strategy.

Three components are present in a strategy: (1) goals and objectives, (2) product/market emphasis, and (3) basis of competition.

Goals/Objectives

In many of the more successful organizations there is a clear sense of who we are and where we are going. In deriving a notion of mission or purpose, managers must confront questions such as: What kind of organization/business is it? What will it become if it stays on its present path? What does it want to be? What should it be?

The organization's mission or purpose can be translated into specific measurable performance targets. These objectives typically relate to profitability, growth, return on investment, market share, technological strength, and so forth. In addition, there are "soft" goals and objectives. These might include such things as benefits to society, employee welfare, and management autonomy. Knowledge of the existence of a "soft" counterpart to "hard" terms is essential if one is to have a more complete understanding of an organization.

Product/Market Emphasis

A second component of strategy is the product/market emphasis. Both the existing and potential range and focus of product/service and market alternatives must be considered (see Exhibit 1–3).

The term *market* refers to both geographic and customer groups. Geographic markets can be local, regional, national, or international in scope. An important subsegment in any discussion of domestic versus international markets is the mode of involvement. Whether inside or outside of Canada, various modes of activity may be utilized. The principal modes include licensing, trade, joint ventures, and wholly owned operations. Too often we ignore the potential impact of the first three of these modes on strategy.

As the Canadian economy becomes more international, both the inward- and outward-looking elements of market scope must be recognized. International business is not solely business which takes place in markets outside

EXHIBIT 1-3 Product/Service and Market Alternatives

		Market Alternatives			
		Reduced Market	*Existing Market*	*Expanded Market*	*New Market*
	Reduced Products/Services				
Product/ Service Alternatives	Existing Products/Services				
	Modified Products/Services				
	New Products/Services				

Exhibit 1-4 Strategy and Modes of Involvement

Mode	Outward Perspective	Inward Perspective
Licensing orientation	Licensor	Licensee
Trade	Exporting	Importing
Joint ventures	Outside Canada	In Canada
Wholly owned operations	Establishing or acquiring a business outside Canada	Managing a business in Canada: either Canadian or foreign controlled

Canada. A Canadian-Japanese joint venture in Canada may well be more international in its scope than, for example, a Canadian-American joint venture set up (outside Canada) in the United States. Exhibit 1–4 summarizes the principal modes and the related considerations.

There are any number of ways to define *customer* scope and focus. One view is that a business can be more accurately defined by focusing on the customer.[8] Specifically, the view holds that a business can be defined in terms of (1) customer groups (who is being satisfied?), (2) customer needs (what is being satisfied?), and (3) alternative technologies (how are customer needs satisfied?).

Basis of Competition

The third component of strategy is basis of competition. The five elements of industry structure, discussed in greater detail in Chapter 3 (see Exhibit 3–1), show that the competitive forces that shape strategy arise from suppliers, customers, substitute products, new entrants, and the moves and countermoves of rival firms.[9] This framework for analyzing competitors (and industries) is useful for understanding how a firm presently and potentially can compete. With this background on the components of strategy complete, it is now possible to place it in the context of a conceptual framework for understanding strategic management.

A Conceptual Framework for Strategic Management

All organizations are concerned with performance. Whether it is a not-for-profit organization, a multinational corporation, or the corner store, all must act in such a way as to remain viable. The strategies that organizations adopt in an attempt to achieve satisfactory performance are varied. Similarly, the organizational structures that are chosen to reflect these strategies differ as well.

The underlying paradigm in the strategic management area for the past 30 years has been the strategy-structure-performance relationship.[10] This relationship tells us two things—one which is immediately obvious and one which is not.

EXHIBIT 1-5 The Underlying Paradigm in Strategic Management

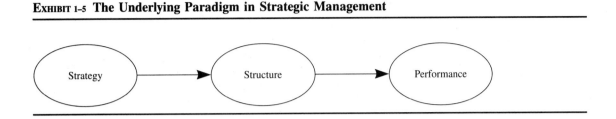

The first and obvious point is that strategy affects performance. Whether one is attempting to organize a fund-raiser, increase sales, start a business, or allocate resources in a large organization—strategy matters.

The second, perhaps less obvious point is that organizational structure matters also, as it can support or hamper the strategy. To implement any strategy, certain organizational actions must be taken: certain tasks must be carried out; reward and information systems put in place; people hired, trained, and managed; and reporting relationships established. An unlimited number of potential organizational actions exist. However, they are not all equally appropriate in all situations. Depending on the strategy chosen, some organizational structures are more appropriate than others. In fact, possibly the greatest challenge in the strategic management area is fitting an appropriate organization to the strategy which has been formulated.

In the balance of this chapter, we review several well-accepted strategic management models which form the basis for the conceptual framework used in this text. Keep in mind that all of these models have as part of their origins the same underlying paradigm, depicted in Exhibit 1–5.

Exhibit 1–6 details one of the dozens of published models of strategic management. Like most approaches, this model is divided into sections on strategy formulation and implementation. Although formulation and implementation are inextricably linked, for analytic purposes they can be considered individually.

The major variables influencing strategy are *(a)* the preferences, personal values, and aspirations of top management, *(b)* the external environment, including competitive opportunities and risks, *(c)* the internal environment which focuses on the organization's managerial, financial, and technical resources and capabilities, and *(d)* organizational responsibility to society. The conceptual framework used in this text includes the first three of these variables. These will be examined in detail in Chapters 3, 4, and 5. Acknowledgment of noneconomic responsibility to society is subsumed here under managerial preferences and values.

In Exhibit 1–6 there are a large number of arrows between the variables used to illustrate the interrelationships which exist. While in the general case strategy influences structure, certainly in many instances the relationship can be in the other direction or, in fact, in both directions.

EXHIBIT 1-6 **Strategic Management Model**

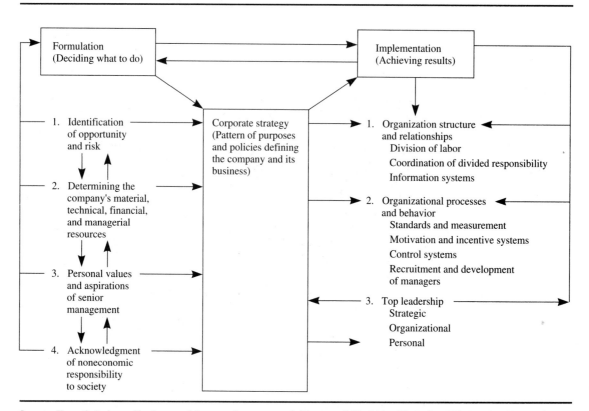

SOURCE: Kenneth Andrews, *The Concept of Corporate Strategy*, rev. ed. (Homewood, Ill.: Richard D. Irwin, 1980). Reprinted by permission.

The strategy implementation half of the model in Exhibit 1–6 is composed of a separate group of variables. Typically, the major organization design variables are *(a)* information and control systems, *(b)* reward systems, *(c)* people, which includes leadership style, *(d)* organizational structure, and *(e)* resource allocation task. This last variable, task, is sometimes viewed as a bridge between formulation and implementation. In this text, all five of these variables are included as part of strategy implementation, although using a slightly different configuration. The role of these variables in the strategic management process will be discussed in detail in Chapters 7 and 8. An overview of the key variables used in the conceptual framework in this text is provided in Exhibit 1–7. As the arrows in this exhibit suggest, a constant review process takes place.

Some of the key questions which should be asked as part of the process of reviewing and evaluating a strategy include:[11]

1. Is there internal consistency between the components of the strategy? (i.e., Do the goals/objectives, product/market scope, and basis of competition all fit together?)

EXHIBIT 1-7 The Strategic Management Process: Basic Conceptual Framework

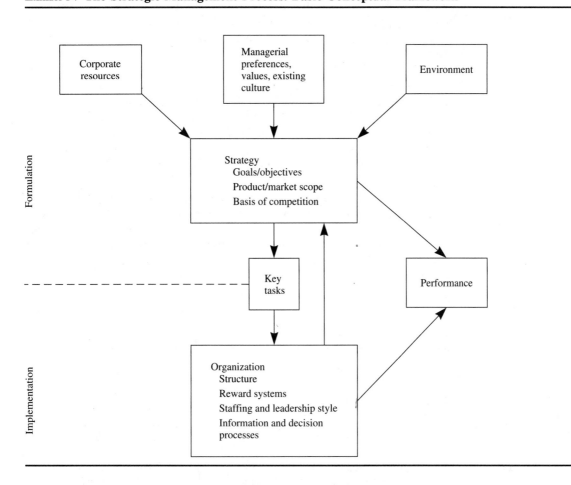

2. Is the strategy appropriate in light of threats and opportunities in the environment?
3. Is the strategy appropriate in light of available resources?
4. What level of risk is associated with the strategy?
5. To what extent does the strategy satisfy managerial preferences and values?
6. What are the key tasks arising out of the strategy and has the organization been designed so that these tasks are performed?

The last question concerns the link between strategy formulation and implementation. Arising out of the corporate strategy are the key tasks the organization has to perform. For example, if the strategy is to compete on the basis of price, one of the key tasks will be cost control. As a result, the organization must be designed with cost control in mind; that is, people should be rewarded on the basis of cost control, and the information system must provide adequate information about costs. If any organization design variables are inconsistent with cost control, then the strategy may not be implemented effectively.

The case studies in this text were chosen to illustrate the impact/role of some or all of the variables in the conceptual framework. These case studies are all decision oriented, requiring a decision as to a course of action for the organization. Achievement of a defensible overall strategy for the organization means that errors in tactics (the specific means of exercising the strategy) may not be fatal. Although the perspective we employ here is that of the general manager, it is important to acknowledge that effective functional managers are also called upon to adopt a strategic orientation. All functions in an organization include both strategic and nonstrategic activities (nonstrategic activities would be made up of the more routinized activities that require little attention from the general manager or other senior managers). Wherever possible, the effective functional manager will approach tasks strategically rather than operationally. Exhibit 1–8 provides an example of how a particular function can be characterized as strategic rather than operational.

Exhibit 1-8 Purchasing as a Strategic Function

Characteristics	Operational Approach	Strategic Approach
Organization structure	Low visibility, lengthy reporting chain.	High visibility, direct reporting to top management.
Organization perception	Isolated ineffective clerks. A necessary administrative expense.	Active, effective material supply managers. Possible source of additional profit.
Information access	Limited exposure to critical reports and meetings; added only occasionally to distribution lists of key material.	Access to a library of material, some of which is generated at the request of purchasing.
Decision issues	Makes decision based on price.	Provides expert analysis of forecasting, sourcing, price, availability, delivery and supplier information; and even outsourcing recommendations.
Supplier network and relationships	Works superficially with many suppliers. Arm's-length, often adversarial, relationships.	Focuses on fewer suppliers. Cooperative relationships.
Frame of reference	Local, provincial, or at best national.	International, with regular investigation of nondomestic sources.
Strategic management	No direct input to the strategy process.	Provides critical input to strategy process.

SOURCE: Adapted by P.W. Beamish from John N. Pearson and Karen J. Gritzmacher, "Integrating Purchasing into Strategic Management," *Long Range Planning*, 23, no. 3 (1990) pp. 91–99.

In Chapter 2, a detailed framework for conducting a case study analysis—including the financial analysis—is provided. This material is included in order to provide some direction in developing "better" case analyses.

Notes to Chapter 1

1. From Charles W. Hofer, consulting ed., *West Series in Strategic Management* (St. Paul, Minn.: West Publishing, 1986), Common Foreword, p. xi.
2. Jay R. Galbraith and Robert K. Kazanjian, *Strategy Implementation: Structure, Systems and Process,* 2nd ed. (St. Paul, Minn.: West Publishing, 1986), p. 3.
3. Carl von Clausewitz, *On War,* originally published in 1832. Translation published by Routledge and Kegan Paul, Ltd., 1908 (Middlesex, England: Pelican [Penguin] Books, 1968).
4. Michael Kamis, *Strategic Planning for Changing Times* (Dayton, Ohio: Cassette Recording Co., 1984).
5. William Curry, "A Condensed Version of Business Policy," mimeographed (Waterloo, Ont.: Wilfrid Laurier University, 1980).
6. See Ian C. McMillan and Patricia E. Jones, *Strategy Formulation: Power and Politics,* 2nd ed. (St. Paul, Minn.: West Publishing, 1986).
7. See Henry Mintzberg, *The Nature of Managerial Work* (New York: Harper & Row, 1973), pp. 91–93.
8. Derek F. Abell, *Defining a Business: The Starting Point of Strategic Planning* (Englewood Cliffs, N.J.: Prentice Hall, 1980), p. 169.
9. See also Michael E. Porter, *Competitive Strategy: Techniques for Analyzing Industries and Competitors* (New York: Free Press, 1980).
10. See Alfred D. Chandler, *Strategy and Structure* (Cambridge, Mass.: MIT Press, 1962).
11. Some of these questions were derived from Seymour Tilles, "How to Evaluate Corporate Strategy," *Harvard Business Review,* July–August 1963.

2   CASE ANALYSIS

The general who wins a battle makes many calculations before the battle is fought. The general who loses a battle makes but few.

Sun Tzu, *The Art of War* (480 B.C.)

Management is an action-oriented activity. It requires doing to achieve proficiency. Managers succeed or fail not so much because of what they know as because of what they do. A person cannot expect to succeed as a manager and become a "professional" simply by studying excellent books on management—no matter how thoroughly the text material is mastered nor how many A's are earned at exam time. Just as a skater needs to practice at being a better skater, a person who aspires to become a manager can benefit from practicing at being a manager.

Practicing Management via Case Analysis

In academic programs of management education, students practice at being managers via case analysis. A case sets forth, in a factual manner, the events and organizational circumstances surrounding a particular managerial situation. It puts the readers at the scene of the action and familiarizes them with the situation as it prevailed. A case can concern a whole industry, a single organization, or even just a part of an organization; the organization involved can be either profit seeking or not-for-profit. Cases about business organizations usually

This chapter has been adapted by the authors *or* incorporates material from Arthur A. Thompson and A. J. Strickland, *Strategic Management: Concepts and Cases* (Plano, Tex.: Business Publications, 1984), pp. 272–89. Used with permission.

include descriptions of the industry and its competitive conditions, the organization's history and development, its products and markets, the backgrounds and personalities of the key people involved, the production facilities, the work climate, the organizational structure, the marketing methods, and the external environment, together with whatever pertinent financial, production, accounting, sales, and market information was available to management.

The essence of the student's role in the case method is to diagnose and size up the situation described in the case and to think through what, if any, actions need to be taken. The purpose is for the student, as analyst, to appraise the situation from a managerial perspective, asking: What factors have contributed to the situation? What problems are evident? How serious are they? What analysis is needed to probe for solutions? What actionable recommendations can be offered? What facts and figures support my position?

It should be emphasized that most cases are not intended to be examples of right and wrong, or good and bad management. The organizations concerned are selected neither because they are the best or the worst in their industry nor because they present an interesting and relevant analytical situation. The important thing about a case is that it represents an actual situation where managers were obligated to recognize and cope with the problems as they were.

Why Use Cases to Practice Management?

Charles I. Gragg's classic article, "Because Wisdom Can't Be Told,"[1] illustrates that the mere act of listening to lectures and sound advice about management does little for anyone's management skills. He contended it was unlikely that accumulated managerial experience and wisdom could effectively be passed on by lectures and readings alone. Gragg suggested that if anything has been learned about the practice of management, it is that a storehouse of ready-made answers does not exist. Each managerial situation has unique aspects, requiring its own diagnosis and understanding as a prelude to judgment and action. In Gragg's view and in the view of other case-method advocates, cases provide aspiring managers with an important and valid kind of daily practice in wrestling with management problems.

The case method is, indeed, *learning by doing.* The pedagogy of the case method of instruction is predicated on the benefits of acquiring managerial "experience" by means of simulated management exercises (cases). The best justification for cases is that few, if any, students during the course of their university education have an opportunity to come into direct personal contact with different kinds of companies and real-life managerial situations. Cases offer a viable substitute by bringing a variety of industries, organizations, and management problems into the classroom and permitting students to assume the manager's role. Management cases, therefore, provide students with a kind of experiential exercise in which to test their ability to apply their textbook knowledge about management.

Objectives of the Case Method

As the foregoing discussion suggests, using cases as an instructional technique is intended to produce four student-related results:[2]

1. Helping you to acquire the skills of putting textbook knowledge about management into practice.
2. Getting you out of the habit of being a receiver of facts, concepts, and techniques and into the habit of diagnosing problems, analyzing and evaluating alternatives, and formulating workable plans of action.
3. Training you to work out answers and solutions for yourself, as opposed to relying upon the authoritative crutch of the professor or a textbook.
4. Providing you with exposure to a range of firms and managerial situations (which might take a lifetime to experience personally), thus offering you a basis for comparison when you begin your own management career.

If you understand that these are the objectives of the case method of instruction, then you are less likely to be bothered by something that puzzles some students: "What is the answer to the case?" Being accustomed to textbook statements of fact and supposedly definitive lecture notes, students often find that discussions and analyses of managerial cases do not produce any hard answers. Instead, issues in the case are discussed pro and con. Various alternatives and approaches are evaluated. Usually, a good argument can be made for more than one course of action. If the class discussion concludes without a clear consensus on what to do and which way to go, some students may, at first, feel frustrated because they are not told "what the answer is" or "what the company actually did."

However, cases where answers are not clear-cut are quite realistic. Organizational problems whose analysis leads to a definite, single-pronged solution are likely to be so oversimplified and rare as to be trivial or devoid of practical value. In reality, several feasible courses of action may exist for dealing with the same set of circumstances. Moreover, in real-life management situations when one makes a decision or selects a particular course of action, there is no peeking at the back of a book to see if you have chosen the best thing to do. No book of provably correct answers exists; in fact, the first test of management action is *results.* The important thing for a student to understand in case analysis is that it is the managerial exercise of identifying, diagnosing, and recommending that counts rather than discovering the right answer or finding out what actually happened.

To put it another way, *the purpose of management cases is not to learn authoritative answers to specific managerial problems but to become skilled in the process of designing workable action plans through evaluation of the prevailing circumstances.* The aim of case analysis is not for you to try to guess what the instructor is thinking or what the organization did but, rather, to see whether you can support your views against the counterviews of the group or, failing to do so, join in the sense of discovery of different approaches and perspectives. Therefore, *in case analysis you are expected to bear the strains of thinking actively, of making managerial assessments which may be vigorously challenged, of offering your analysis, and of proposing action plans—this is how you are provided with meaningful practice at being a manager.*

Analyzing the case yourself is what initiates you in the ways of thinking "managerially" and exercising responsible judgment. At the same time, you can use cases to test the rigor and effectiveness of your own approach to the practice of management and to begin to evolve your own management philosophy and management style.

Use of the Socratic method of questioning-answering-questioning-answering, where there is no single correct answer but always another question, is at the heart of the case process. A good case can be used with student groups of varying qualifications. With the more highly experienced qualified groups, the other questions become tougher.

Preparing a Case for Class Discussion

Given that cases rest on the principle of learning by doing, their effectiveness hinges upon *you* making *your* analysis and reaching *your* own decisions and then in the classroom participating in a collective analysis and discussion of the issues. If this is your first experience with the case method, you may have to reorient your study habits. Since a case assignment emphasizes student participation, it is obvious that the effectiveness of the class discussion depends upon each student having studied the case *beforehand.* Consequently, unlike lecture courses where there is no imperative of specific preparation before each class and where assigned readings and reviews of lecture notes may be done at irregular intervals, *a case assignment requires conscientious preparation before class.* You cannot, after all, expect to get much out of hearing the class discuss a case with which you are totally unfamiliar.

Unfortunately, though, there is no nice, neat, proven procedure for conducting a case analysis. There is no formula, no fail-safe, step-by-step technique that we can recommend beyond emphasizing the sequence: *identify, evaluate, consider alternatives,* and *recommend.* Each case is a new situation and has its own set of issues, analytical requirements, and action alternatives.

A first step in understanding how the case method of teaching/learning works is to recognize that it represents a radical departure from the lecture/discussion/problem classroom technique. To begin with, members of the class do most of the talking. The instructor's role is to solicit student participation and guide the discussion. Expect the instructor to begin the class with such questions as: What is the organization's strategy? What are the strategic issues and problems confronting the company? What is your assessment of the company's situation? Is the industry an attractive one to be in? Is management doing a good job? Are the organization's objectives and strategies compatible with its skills and resources? Typically, members of the class will evaluate and test their opinions as much in discussions with each other as with the instructor. But irrespective of whether the discussion emphasis is instructor-student or student-student, members of the class carry the burden for analyzing the situation and for being prepared to present and defend their analyses in the classroom. Thus, you should expect an absence of professorial "here's how to do it," "right answers," and "hard knowledge for your notebook"; instead, be prepared for a discussion involving your size-up of the situation, what actions you would take, and why you would take them.[3]

Begin preparing for class by reading the case once for familiarity. An initial reading should give you the general flavor of the situation and make possible preliminary identification of issues. On the second reading, attempt to gain full command of the facts. Make some notes about apparent organizational objectives, strategies, policies, symptoms of problems, root problems, unresolved issues, and roles of key individuals. Be alert for issues or problems that are lurking beneath the surface. For instance, at first glance it might appear that an issue in the case is whether a product has ample market potential at the current selling price; on closer examination, you may see that the root problem is that the method being used to compensate salespeople fails to generate adequate incentive for achieving greater unit volume. Strive for a sharp, clear-cut size-up of the issues posed in the case situation.

To help diagnose the situation, put yourself in the position of some manager or managerial group portrayed in the case and get attuned to the overall environment facing management. Try to get a good feel for the condition of the company, the industry, and the economics of the business. Get a handle on how the market works and on the nature of competition. This is essential if you are to come up with solutions which will be both workable and acceptable in light of the prevailing external constraints and internal organizational realities. Do not be dismayed if you find it impractical to isolate the problems and issues into distinct categories which can be treated separately. Very few significant strategy management problems can be neatly sorted into mutually exclusive areas of concern. Furthermore, expect the cases (especially those in this book) to contain several problems and issues, rather than just one. Guard against making a single, simple statement of the problem unless the issue is very clear-cut. Admittedly, there will be cases where issues are well defined and the main problem is figuring out what to do; but in most cases you can expect a set of problems and issues to be present, some of which are related and some of which are not.

Next, you must move toward a solid evaluation of the case situation, based on the information given. Developing an ability to evaluate companies and size up their situations is the core of what strategic analysis is all about. The cases in this book, of course, are all strategy related, and they each require some form of strategic analysis, that is, analysis of how well the organization's strategy has been formulated and implemented.

Uppermost in your efforts, strive for defensible arguments and positions. Do not rely upon just your opinion; support it with evidence! Analyze the available data and make whatever relevant accounting, financial, marketing, or operations calculations are necessary to support your assessment of the situation. Crunch the numbers! If your instructor has provided you with specific study questions for the case, by all means make some notes as to how you would answer them. Include in your notes all the reasons and evidence you can muster to support your diagnosis and evaluation.

Last, when information or data in the case are conflicting and/or various opinions are contradictory, decide which is more valid and why. Forcing you to make judgments about the validity of the data and information presented in the case is both deliberate and realistic. It is deliberate because one function of the case method is to help you develop your powers of judgment and inference. It is realistic because a great many managerial situations entail conflicting points of view.

Once you have thoroughly diagnosed the company's situation and weighed the pros and cons of various alternative courses of action, the final step of case analysis is to decide what you think the company needs to do to improve its performance. Draw up your set of recommendations on what to do and be prepared to give your action agenda. This is really the most crucial part of the process; diagnosis divorced from corrective action is sterile. But bear in mind that proposing realistic, workable solutions and offering a hasty, ill-conceived "possibility" are not the same thing. Don't recommend anything you would not be prepared to do yourself if you were in the decision maker's shoes. Be sure you can give reasons that your recommendations are preferable to other options which exist.

On a few occasions, some desirable information may not be included in the case. In such instances, you may be inclined to complain about the lack of facts. A manager, however, uses more than facts upon which to base his or her decision. Moreover, it may be possible to make a number of inferences from the facts you do have. So be wary of rushing to include as part of your recommendations the need to get more information. From time to time, of course, a search for additional facts or information may be entirely appropriate, but you must also recognize that the organization's managers may not have had any more information available than that presented in the case. Before recommending that action be postponed until additional facts are uncovered, be sure that you think it will be worthwhile to get them and that the organization can afford to wait. In general, though, try to recommend a course of action based upon the evidence you have at hand.

Again, remember that rarely is there a "right" decision or just one "optimal" plan of action or an "approved" solution. Your goal should be to develop what you think is a pragmatic, defensible course of action based upon a serious analysis of the situation and appearing to you to be right in view of your assessment of the facts. Admittedly, someone else may evaluate the same facts in another way and thus have a different right solution, but since several good plans of action can normally be conceived, you should not be afraid to stick by your own analysis and judgment. One can make a strong argument for the view that the right answer for a manager is the one that he or she can propose, explain, defend, and make work when it is implemented. This is the middle ground we support between the "no right answer" and "one right answer" schools of thought. Clearly, some answers are better than others.

The Classroom Experience

> Take notes on the spot, a note is worth a cart-load of recollections.
>
> Ralph Waldo Emerson

In experiencing class discussion of management cases, you will, in all probability, notice very quickly that you will not have thought of everything in the case that your fellow students think of. While you will see things others did not, they will see things you did not. Do not be dismayed or alarmed by this. It is normal. As the old adage goes, "Two heads are better than one." So it is to be expected that the class as a whole will do a more penetrating and searching job of case analysis than will any one person working alone. This is the power of group effort, and one of its virtues is that it will give you more insight into the variety of approaches and how to cope with differences of opinion. Second, you will see better why sometimes it is not managerially wise to assume a rigid position on an issue until a full range of views and information has been assembled. And, undoubtedly, somewhere along the way, you will begin to recognize that neither the instructor nor other students in the class have all the answers, and even if they think they do, you are still free to present and hold to your own views. The truth in the saying, "there's more than one way to skin a cat" will be seen to apply nicely to most management situations.

For class discussion of cases to be useful and stimulating, you need to keep the following points in mind:

1. The case method enlists a maximum of individual participation in class discussion. It is not enough to be present as a silent observer; if every student took this approach, then there would be no discussion. (Thus, do not be surprised if a portion of your grade is based on your participation in case discussions.)
2. Although you should do your own independent work and independent thinking, don't hesitate to discuss the case with other students. Managers often discuss their problems with other key people.
3. During case discussions, expect and tolerate challenges to the views expressed. Be willing to submit your conclusions for scrutiny and rebuttal. State your views without fear of disapproval and overcome the hesitation of speaking out.
4. In orally presenting and defending your ideas, strive to be convincing and persuasive. Always give supporting evidence and reasons.

5. Expect the instructor to assume the role of extensive questioner and listener. Expect to be cross-examined for evidence and reasons by your instructor or by others in the class. Expect students to dominate the discussion and do most of the talking.

6. Although discussion of a case is a group process, this does not imply conformity to group opinion. Learning respect for the views and approaches of others is an integral part of case analysis exercises. But be willing to "swim against the tide" of majority opinion. In the practice of management, there is always room for originality, unorthodoxy, and unique personality.

7. In participating in the discussion, make a conscious effort to *contribute* rather than just talk. There *is* a big difference between saying something that builds the discussion and offering a long-winded, off-the-cuff remark that leaves the class wondering what the point was.

8. Effective case discussion can occur only if participants have the facts of the case well in hand; rehashing information in the case should be held to a minimum except as it provides documentation, comparisons, or support for your position. In making your point, assume that everyone has read the case and knows what "the case says."

9. During the discussion, new insights provided by the group's efforts are likely to emerge. Don't be alarmed or surprised if you and others in the class change your mind about some things as the discussion unfolds. Be alert for how these changes affect your analysis and recommendations (in case you are called on to speak).

10. Although there will always be situations in which more technical information is imperative to the making of an intelligent decision, try not to shirk from making decisions in the face of incomplete information. Wrestling with imperfect information is a normal condition managers face and is something you should get used to.

Preparing a Written Case Analysis

From time to time, your instructor may ask you to prepare a written analysis of the case assignment. Preparing a written case analysis is much like preparing a case for class discussion, except that your analysis, when completed, must be reduced to writing. Just as there was no set formula for preparing a case for oral discussion, there is no iron-clad procedure for doing a written case analysis. With a bit of experience, you will arrive at your own preferred method of attack in writing up a case, and you will learn to adjust your approach to the unique aspects that each case presents.

Your instructor may assign you a specific topic around which to prepare your written report. Common assignments include: (1) Identify and evaluate company X's corporate strategy. (2) In view of the opportunities and risks you see in the industry, what is your assessment of the company's position and strategy?

(3) How would you size up the strategic situation of company Y? (4) What recommendation would you make to company Z's top management? (5) What specific functions and activities does the company have to perform especially well in order for its strategy to succeed?

Alternatively, you may be asked to do a comprehensive written case analysis. It is typical for a comprehensive written case analysis to emphasize four things:

1. Identification.
2. Analysis and evaluation.
3. Discussion of alternatives.
4. Presentation of recommendations.

You may wish to consider the following pointers in preparing a comprehensive written case analysis.[4]

Identification.   It is essential that your paper reflect a sharply focused diagnosis of strategic issues and key problems and, further, that you demonstrate good business judgment in sizing up the company's present situation. Make sure you understand and can identify the firm's strategy (see Chapters 1, 3, 4, and 5). You would probably be well advised to begin your paper by sizing up the company's situation, its strategy, and the significant problems and issues which confront management. State problems/issues as clearly and precisely as you can. Unless it is necessary to do so for emphasis, avoid recounting facts and history about the company (assume your professor has read the case and is familiar with the organization!).

Analysis and Evaluation.   Very likely, you will find this section the hardest part of the report. Analysis is hard work! Study the tables, exhibits, and financial statements in the case carefully. Check out the firm's financial ratios, its profit margins and rates of return, and its capital structure and decide how strong the firm is financially. (Exhibit 2–1 contains a summary of various financial ratios and how they are calculated.) Similarly, look at marketing, production, managerial competences, and so on, and evaluate the factors underlying the organization's successes and failures. Decide whether it has a distinctive competence and, if so, whether it is capitalizing upon it. Check out the quality of the firm's business portfolio.

Check to see if the firm's strategy at all levels is working and determine the reasons why or why not. Appraise internal *strengths* and *weaknesses* and assess external *opportunities* and *threats;* to do a "SWOT analysis," see Exhibit 2–2 for suggestions of what to look for. Decide whether a competitor analysis is needed to clarify competitive forces (you may want to draw up a strategic group map as in Exhibit 3–3 and/or do an industry analysis as in Exhibit 3–1, in Chapter 3). Decide whether and why the firm's competitive position is getting stronger or weaker. Review the material in Chapters 1, 3, 4, and 5 to see if you have overlooked some aspect of strategy evaluation. Try to decide whether the main

Exhibit 2–1 A Summary of Key Financial Ratios, How They Are Calculated, and What They Show

Ratio	How Calculated	What It Shows
Profitability Ratios		
1. Gross profit margin	$$\dfrac{\text{Sales} - \text{Cost of goods sold}}{\text{Sales}}$$	An indication of the total margin available to cover operating expenses and yield a profit.
2. Operating profit margin	$$\dfrac{\text{Profit before taxes and before interest}}{\text{Sales}}$$	An indication of the firm's profitability from current operations without regard to the interest charges accruing from the capital structure. (Helps to assess impact of different capital structures.)
3. Net profit margin (or return on sales)	$$\dfrac{\text{Profits after taxes}}{\text{Sales}}$$	After-tax profits per dollar of sales. Subpar-profit margins indicate that the firm's sales prices are relatively low or that its costs are relatively high or both.
4. Return on total assets	$$\dfrac{\text{Profits after taxes}}{\text{Total assets}}$$ or $$\dfrac{\text{Profits after taxes} + \text{interest}}{\text{Total assets}}$$	A measure of the return on total investment in the enterprise. It is sometimes desirable to add interest to after-tax profits to form the numerator of the ratio since total assets are financed by creditors as well as by stockholders; hence, it is accurate to measure the productivity of assets by the returns provided to both classes of investors.
5. Return on stockholders' equity (or return on net worth)	$$\dfrac{\text{Profits after taxes}}{\text{Total stockholders' equity}}$$	A measure of the rate of return on stockholders' investment in the enterprise.
6. Return on common equity	$$\dfrac{\text{Profits after taxes} - \text{Preferred stock dividends}}{\text{Total stockholders' equity} - \text{Par value of preferred stock}}$$	A measure of the rate of return on the investment that the owners of common stock have made in the enterprise.
7. Earnings per share	$$\dfrac{\text{Profits after taxes} - \text{Preferred stock dividends}}{\text{Number of shares of common stock outstanding}}$$	The earnings available to the owners of common stock.
Liquidity Ratios		
1. Current ratio	$$\dfrac{\text{Current assets}}{\text{Current liabilities}}$$	The extent to which the claims of short-term creditors are covered by assets expected to be converted to cash in a period roughly corresponding to the maturity of the liabilities.
2. Quick ratio (or acid-test ratio)	$$\dfrac{\text{Current assets} - \text{inventory}}{\text{Current liabilities}}$$	A measure of the firm's ability to pay off short-term obligations without relying upon the sale of its inventories.
3. Inventory to net working capital	$$\dfrac{\text{Inventory}}{\text{Current assets} - \text{Current liabilities}}$$	A measure of the extent to which the firm's working capital is tied up in inventory.

EXHIBIT 2–1 *(continued)*

Ratio	How Calculated	What It Shows
Leverage Ratios		
1. Debt-to-assets ratio	$\dfrac{\text{Total debt}}{\text{Total assets}}$	A measure of the extent to which borrowed funds have been used to finance the firm's operations
2. Debt-to-equity ratio	$\dfrac{\text{Total debt}}{\text{Total stockholders' equity}}$	Another measure of the funds provided by creditors versus the funds provided by owners.
3. Long-term debt-to-equity ratio	$\dfrac{\text{Long-term debt}}{\text{Total stockholders' equity}}$	A widely used measure of the balance between debt and equity in the firm's long-term capital structure.
4. Times-interest-earned (or coverage) ratios	$\dfrac{\text{Profits before interest and taxes}}{\text{Total interest charges}}$	A measure of the extent to which earnings can decline without the firm becoming unable to meet its annual interest costs.
5. Fixed-charge coverage	$\dfrac{\text{Profits before taxes and interest} \div \text{Lease obligations}}{\text{Total interest charges} \div \text{Lease obligations}}$	A more inclusive indication of the firm's ability to meet all of its fixed-charge obligations.
Activity Ratios		
1. Inventory turnover	$\dfrac{\text{Sales}}{\text{Inventory of finished goods}}$	When compared to industry averages, it provides an indication of whether a company has excessive or inadequate finished goods inventory.
2. Fixed-assets turnover	$\dfrac{\text{Sales}}{\text{Fixed assets}}$	A measure of the sales productivity and utilization of plant and equipment.
3. Total-assets turnover	$\dfrac{\text{Sales}}{\text{Total assets}}$	A measure of the utilization of all the firm's assets. A ratio below the industry average indicates that the company is not generating a sufficient volume of business given the size of its asset investment.
4. Accounts-receivable turnover	$\dfrac{\text{Annual credit sales}}{\text{Accounts receivable}}$	A measure of the average length of time it takes the firm to collect the sales made on credit.
5. Average collection period	$\dfrac{\text{Accounts receivable}}{\text{Total sales} \div 365}$ or $\dfrac{\text{Accounts receivable}}{\text{Average daily sales}}$	The average length of time the firm must wait after making a sale before it receives payment.
Other Ratios		
1. Dividend yield on common stock	$\dfrac{\text{Annual dividends per share}}{\text{Current market price per share}}$	A measure of the return to owners received in the form of dividends.
2. Price-earnings ratio	$\dfrac{\text{Current market price per share}}{\text{After-tax earnings per share}}$	Faster growing or less risky firms tend to have higher price-earnings ratios than slower growing or more risky firms.

EXHIBIT 2–1 *(concluded)*

Ratio	How Calculated	What It Shows
3. Dividend-payout ratio	$\dfrac{\text{Annual dividends per share}}{\text{After-tax earning per share}}$	The percentages of profits paid out as dividends.
4. Cash flow per share	$\dfrac{\text{After-tax profits} + \text{Depreciation}}{\text{Number of common shares outstanding}}$	A measure of the discretionary funds over and above expenses available for use by the firm.
5. Break-even analysis	$\dfrac{\text{Fixed costs}}{\substack{\text{Contribution margin/unit} \\ \text{(Selling price/unit} - \\ \text{Variable cost/unit)}}}$	A measure of how many units must be sold to begin to make a profit; to demonstrate the relationship of revenue, expenses, and net income.

NOTE: Industry-average ratios against which a particular company's ratios may be judged are available in the following:
1. Statistics Canada, Corporation Financial Statistics (15 ratios for 182 industries).
2. *Key Business Ratios*, published by Dun and Bradstreet Canada (11 ratios for 166 lines of business).
3. *Market Research Handbook*, published by Statistics Canada (7 ratios for 17 industries).

EXHIBIT 2–2 The SWOT Analysis–with Suggestions of What to Look For

Internal

Strengths	Weaknesses
Adequate financial resources?	No clear strategic direction?
Well thought of by buyers?	Obsolete facilities?
An acknowledged market leader?	Lack of managerial depth and talent?
Well-conceived functional area strategies?	Missing any key skills or competencies?
Access to economies of scale?	Poor track record in implementing strategy?
Insulated (at least somewhat) from strong competitive pressure?	Plagued with internal operating problems?
Proprietary technology?	Falling behind in R & D?
Cost advantages?	Too narrow a product line?
Product innovation abilities?	Weak market image?
Proven management?	Below-average marketing skills?
Other?	Unable to finance needed changes in strategy?
	Other?

External

Opportunities	Threats
Serve additional customer groups?	Likely entry of new competitors?
Enter new markets or segments?	Rising sales of substitute products?
Expand product line to meet broader range of customer needs?	Slower market growth?
Diversify into related products?	Adverse government policies?
Add complementary products?	Growing competitive pressures?
Vertical integration?	Vulnerability to recession and business cycle?
Ability to move to better strategic group?	Growing bargaining power of customers or suppliers?
Complacency among rival firms?	Changing buyer needs and tastes?
Faster market growth?	Adverse demographic changes?
Other?	Other?

problems revolve around a need to revise strategy, a need to improve strategy implementation, or both. In appraising the quality of strategy implementation, you should review Chapters 7–9.

In writing your analysis and evaluation, bear in mind:

1. You are obliged to offer supporting evidence for your views and judgments. Do not rely upon unsupported opinions, overgeneralizations, and platitudes as a substitute for tight, logical argument backed up with facts and figures.

2. If your analysis involves some important quantitative calculations, then you should use tables and charts to present the data clearly and efficiently. Don't just tack the exhibits on at the end of your report and let the reader figure out what they mean and why they were included. Instead, in the body of your report, cite some of the key numbers and summarize the conclusions to be drawn from the exhibits and refer the reader to your charts and exhibits for more details.

3. You should indicate you have command of the economics of the business and the key factors which are crucial to the organization's success or failure. Check to see that your analysis states what the company needs to concentrate on in order to be a higher performer.

4. Your interpretation of the evidence should be reasonable and objective. Be wary of preparing a one-sided argument which omits all aspects not favourable to your conclusion. Likewise, try not to exaggerate or overdramatize. Endeavour to inject balance into your analysis and to avoid emotional rhetoric. Strive to display good business judgment.

Discussion of Alternatives.   There are typically many more alternatives available than a cursory study of the case reveals. A thorough case analysis should include a discussion of all major alternatives. It is important that meaningful differences exist between each alternative. In addition, the discussion of alternatives must go beyond the following:

- Do nothing.
- Something obviously inappropriate.
- The alternative to be recommended.

Each alternative discussed should be analyzed in terms of the associated pros and cons.

Recommendations.   The final section of the written case analysis should consist of a set of definite recommendations and a plan of action. Your set of recommendations should address all of the problems/issues you identified and analyzed. If the recommendations come as a surprise or do not follow logically from the analysis, the effect is to weaken greatly your suggestions of what to do. Obviously, your recommendations for action should offer a reasonable prospect of success. State what you think the consequences of your recommendations will be and indicate how your recommendations will solve the problems you identified. *Be sure that the company is financially able to carry out what you recommend.* Also check to see if your recommendations are workable in terms of acceptance by the persons involved, the organization's competence to implement them, and prevailing market and environmental constraints. Unless you feel justifiably *compelled* to do so, do not qualify, hedge, or weasel on the actions you believe should be taken.

Furthermore, state your recommendations in sufficient detail to be meaningful—get down to some definite nitty-gritty details. Avoid such unhelpful statements as "the organization should do more planning" or "the company should be more aggressive in marketing its product." State *specifically* what should be done and *make sure your recommendations are operational.* For instance, do not stop with saying, "The firm should improve its market position." Continue on with exactly *how* you think this should be done. And, finally, you should say something about how your plan should be implemented. Here you may wish to offer a definite agenda for action, stipulating a timetable and sequence for initiating actions, indicating priorities, and suggesting who should be responsible for doing what. For example, "Manager X should take the following steps: (1) _____, (2) _____, (3) _____, (4) _____." One way to organize your recommendations is in a one-page summary according to the chart in Exhibit 2–3.

A key element in the recommendation summary is to assess the financial implications of each recommendation. Any proposed strategy must be feasible, which means, among other things, that the organization must be able to afford it. In addition, when there are major uncertainties, particularly in the medium to long term, contingency plans should be specified, that is, "If such and such transpires, then do X."

In preparing your plan of action, remember there is a great deal of difference between being responsible, on the one hand, for a decision that may be costly if it proves in error and, on the other hand, expressing a casual opinion as to some of the courses of action that might be taken when you do not have to bear the responsibility for any of the consequences. A good rule to follow in making your recommendations is to avoid recommending anything you would not yourself be willing to do if you were in management's shoes. The importance of learning to develop good judgment in a managerial situation is indicated by the fact that while the same information and operating data may be available to every manager or executive in an organization, the quality of the judgments about what the information means and what actions need to be taken do vary from person to person.[5] Developing good judgment is thus essential.

It should go without saying that your report should be organized and written in a manner that communicates well and is persuasive. Great ideas amount to little unless others can be convinced of their merit—this takes effective communication.

EXHIBIT 2-3 Organizing Recommendations

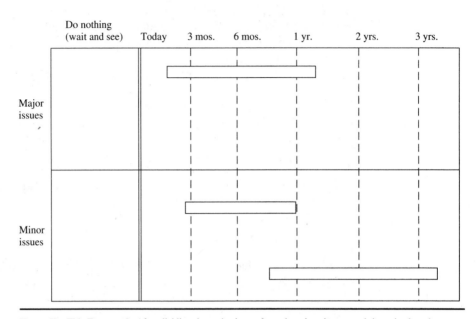

How to Use This Framework. After dividing the major issues from the minor issues, each issue is plotted according to timing. The closed hollow bar indicates over which period this issue will be resolved. Inside each hollow bar should be noted the title of the issue and the cost (financial, managerial, and so forth) of implementation. This framework allows us to assess on one page the reasonableness of whatever organizational recommendations are being made.

Keeping Tabs on Your Performance

Every instructor has his or her own procedure for evaluating student performance, so, with one exception, it is not possible to generalize about grades and the grading of case analyses. The one exception is that grades on case analyses (written or oral) almost never depend entirely on how you propose to solve the organization's difficulties. The important elements in evaluating student performance on case analyses consist of *(a)* the care with which facts and background knowledge are used, *(b)* demonstration of the ability to state problems and issues clearly, *(c)* use of appropriate analytical techniques, *(d)* evidence of sound logic and argument, *(e)* consistency between analysis and recommendations, and *(f)* ability to formulate reasonable and feasible recommendations for action. Remember, a hard-hitting, incisive, logical approach will almost always triumph over a seat-of-the-pants opinion, emotional rhetoric, and platitudes.

One final point. You may find it hard to keep a finger on the pulse of how much you are learning from cases. This contrasts with lecture/problem/discussion courses where experience has given you an intuitive feeling for how well you are acquiring substantive knowledge of theoretical concepts, problem-solving techniques, and institutional practices. But in a case course, where analytical ability and the skill of making sound judgments are less apparent, you may lack a sense of solid accomplishment, at least at first. Admittedly, additions to one's managerial skills and powers of diagnosis are not as noticeable or as tangible as a loose-leaf binder full of lecture notes. But this does not mean they are any less real or that you are making any less progress in learning how to be a manager.

To begin with, in the process of hunting around for solutions, very likely you will find that considerable knowledge about types of organizations, the nature of various businesses, the range of management practices, and so on has rubbed off. Moreover, you will be gaining a better grasp of how to evaluate risks and cope with the uncertainties of enterprise. Likewise, you will develop a sharper appreciation of both the common and the unique aspects of managerial encounters. You will become more comfortable with the processes whereby objectives are set, strategies are initiated, organizations are designed, methods of control are implemented and evaluated, performance is reappraised, and improvements are sought. Such processes are the essence of strategic management, and learning more about them through the case method is no less an achievement just because there is a dearth of finely calibrated measuring devices and authoritative crutches on which to lean.

Notes to Chapter 2

1. Charles I. Gragg, "Because Wisdom Can't Be Told," in *The Case Method at the Harvard Business School,* ed. M. P. McNair (New York: McGraw-Hill, 1954), p. 11.
2. Ibid., pp. 12–14; and D. R. Schoen and Philip A. Sprague, "What Is the Case Method?" in McNair, *The Case Method at the Harvard Business School,* pp. 78–79.
3. Schoen and Sprague, "What Is the Case Method?" p. 80.
4. For some additional ideas and viewpoints, you may wish to consult Thomas J. Raymond, "Written Analysis of Cases," in McNair, *The Case Method at the Harvard Business School,* pp. 139–63. In Raymond's article is an actual case, a sample analysis of the case, and a sample of a student's written report on the case.
5. Gragg, "Because Wisdom Can't Be Told," p. 10.

3   STRATEGY FORMULATION AND ENVIRONMENT

No army can withstand the strength of an idea whose time has come.
V. Hugo

Welcome to the global village.
Marshall McLuhan

Making strategic decisions or choices is the critical function of the general manager. Strategic choices can be categorized in a number of ways. For example, they can relate to the extent of product line diversification, the extent of vertical integration, and the choice of cooperative strategy.

The process of making strategic decisions is known as *strategy formulation.* In formulating a strategy, the effective general manager makes strategic choices which are consistent with environmental threats and opportunities, organizational resources, and managerial preferences and values.

The Influence of Environment on Strategy Formulation

In Canada, six environments are of particular relevance to firms as they make strategic choices. The first is the industry environment.

The Industry Environment

The key concerns in the industry environment are as follows:

1. The elements of industry structure (see Exhibit 3–1).
2. The stage in the life cycle of products in the industry (see Exhibit 3–2).

EXHIBIT 3–1 Elements of Industry Structure

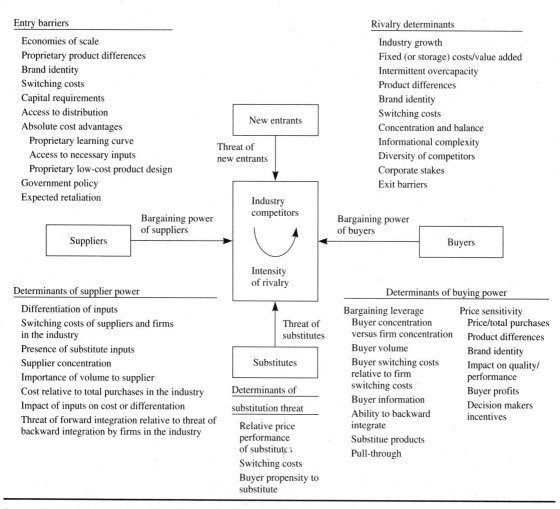

Entry barriers

Economies of scale
Proprietary product differences
Brand identity
Switching costs
Capital requirements
Access to distribution
Absolute cost advantages
  Proprietary learning curve
  Access to necessary inputs
  Proprietary low-cost product design
Government policy
Expected retaliation

Rivalry determinants

Industry growth
Fixed (or storage) costs/value added
Intermittent overcapacity
Product differences
Brand identity
Switching costs
Concentration and balance
Informational complexity
Diversity of competitors
Corporate stakes
Exit barriers

New entrants

Threat of new entrants

Industry competitors

Intensity of rivalry

Bargaining power of suppliers

Suppliers

Bargaining power of buyers

Buyers

Determinants of supplier power

Differentiation of inputs
Switching costs of suppliers and firms in the industry
Presence of substitute inputs
Supplier concentration
Importance of volume to supplier
Cost relative to total purchases in the industry
Impact of inputs on cost or differentation
Threat of forward integration relative to threat of backward integration by firms in the industry

Threat of substitutes

Substitutes

Determinants of substitution threat

Relative price performance of substitutes
Switching costs
Buyer propensity to substitute

Determinants of buying power

Bargaining leverage
  Buyer concentration versus firm concentration
  Buyer volume
  Buyer switching costs relative to firm switching costs
  Buyer information
  Ability to backward integrate
  Substitue products
  Pull-through

Price sensitivity
  Price/total purchases
  Product differences
  Brand identity
  Impact on quality/performance
  Buyer profits
  Decision makers incentives

SOURCE: Reprinted with permission of The Free Press, a Division of Macmillan, Inc., from *Competitive Advantage: Creating and Sustaining Superior Performance*, by Michael E. Porter. Copyright © 1985 by Michael E. Porter.

3. The direction the industry is headed (for example, overcapacity, requiring rationalization).

4. The forces (for example, political, social, economic, technological) driving the industry in a particular direction.

5. The underlying economics and performance of the business (for example, cost structures, profit levels).

6. The key success factors (for example, cost, delivery).

7. Demand segments and strategic groups. (See Exhibit 3–3)

Exhibit 3–2 Product/Market Life-Cycle Stages

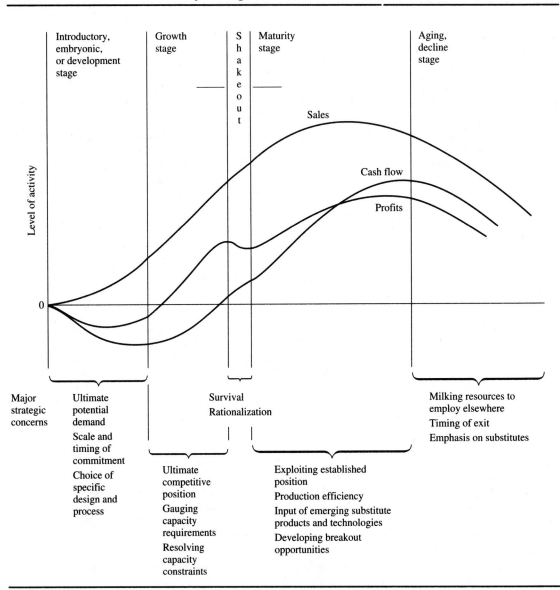

SOURCE: Adapted with permission from L. A. Digman, *Strategic Management* (Plano, Tex.: Business Publications, 1986); and Joseph N. Fry and J. Peter Killing, *Strategic Analysis and Action,* 2nd ed. (Scarborough, Ont.: Prentice-Hall Canada, 1989).

The first two concerns—industry structure and stage of the life cycle—require further explanation. As noted in Exhibit 3–1, each industry has a number of competitors, and their intensity of rivalry, which affects the potential for profitability, is determined by four major elements: (1) the threat of new entrants, (2) the threat of substitutes, (3) the bargaining power of buyers, and (4) the bargaining power of suppliers. Each of these elements, in turn, is influenced by various factors as outlined in the exhibit. For example, entry barriers in the industry, which include such elements as economies of scale, determine the extent to which new entrants are a threat.

Another major element of the industry environment is the product/market life cycle which assumes that all products, and, therefore, industries, move through stages of a life cycle. The cycle begins at the development stage, moving to a growth stage, then shakeout, then maturity, and finally, the decline stage. It is important to note that while the sales of a particular product—and collectively the sales of similar products making up a particular industry—may follow these stages, the cash flow and profits are likely to follow somewhat different cycles. Furthermore, the major strategic concerns at each stage vary quite considerably. For example, at the introductory or embryonic stage, the concerns are the ultimate potential demand and the scale and timing of commitment, while at the decline stage, the concerns are milking resources to employ elsewhere, timing of a possible exit, and emphasis on substitutes (see Exhibit 3–2).

In analyzing an industry, it is also useful to determine if the industry is a global industry, that is, an industry that requires global operations to compete effectively.[1] An industry can be considered global if the product/service has worldwide demand, production economies of scale exist, there is no complex segmentation within markets, and few trade barriers exist. Firms in global industries must generally be true multinationals (that is, production and marketing in several foreign countries) in order to compete successfully. Examples of globally oriented Canadian firms are Northern Telecom, Alcan, and Bombardier.

The Competitive Environment

The second environment to consider is the competitive environment. The key concerns in the competitive environment are as follows:

1. The forces driving competition in the industry (which is a function of industry structure—see Exhibit 3–1).
2. The differences in the competitive approaches of rival firms (for example, price competition, advertising battles, increased customer service).
3. Strategies, positions, and competitive strength of market leaders and close rivals.
4. Why some rivals are doing better than others.

The value chain is an important tool for analyzing how a company is faring relative to its competitors. The significance of this tool is described below.

Value Chain.   Porter's generic value chain contains primary activities (inbound logistics, operations, outbound logistics, marketing and sales, and service) and secondary activities (firm infrastructure, human resource management, technol-

EXHIBIT 3-3 Illustrative Strategic Group Map of Competitors in the Canadian Furniture Retail Business

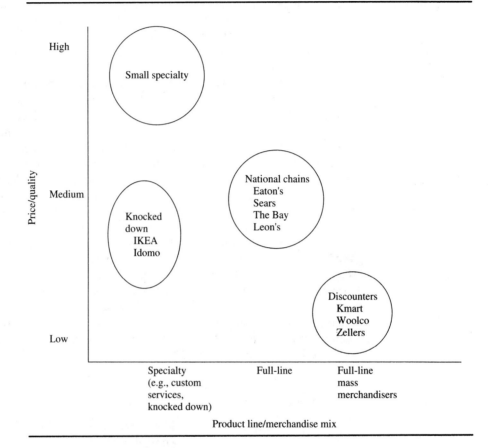

ogy development, and procurement). Organizations can and do compete at any place on the value chain. For example, in terms of the primary activities in a generic value chain for oriental carpet retailers (see Exhibit 3–4), firms can attempt to attain competitive advantage by adding value at one or more locations, *or* in terms of certain dimensions within particular activities. *Value* can be defined as attainable selling price and is measured by total revenue. Profits result when the attainable selling price exceeds product/service costs (that is, when a margin exists).

Not all firms strive for cost leadership in their quest for profits. Some firms emphasize differentiation as a means of achieving greater profitability. For example, automakers will deliberately add a vast array of "options" to the cars they produce in the hope that customers will pay for these high-margin items. These options will normally increase the attainable selling price (value). As a consequence, to analyze competitive position, value, not cost, must be used.

EXHIBIT 3–4 Primary Activities in Generic Value Chain for Oriental Carpet Retailers

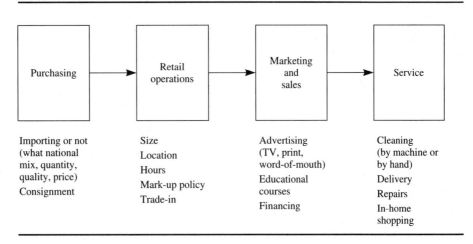

Purchasing	Retail operations	Marketing and sales	Service

Importing or not (what national mix, quantity, quality, price)

Consignment

Size

Location

Hours

Mark-up policy

Trade-in

Advertising (TV, print, word-of-mouth)

Educational courses

Financing

Cleaning (by machine or by hand)

Delivery

Repairs

In-home shopping

Having made this distinction between cost and value, the balance of this analysis will nonetheless focus primarily on cost since cost is the most tangible component of the value equation.

For a company to be competitively successful, its costs must be in line with those of rival producers, after taking into account, of course, that product differentiation creates justification for some cost differences. The need to be cost competitive is not so stringent as to *require* the costs of every firm in the industry to be *equal,* but as a rule, the more a firm's costs are above those of the low-cost producers, the more vulnerable its market position becomes. Given the numerous opportunities for there to be cost disparities among competing companies, it is incumbent upon firms to be alert to how their costs compare with rivals' costs and how they can remain cost competitive over the long run. This is where *strategic cost analysis* comes in.

Strategic cost analysis focuses on a firm's relative cost position vis-à-vis its rivals. The primary analytical tool of strategic cost analysis is the construction of a total industry value or *activity-cost chain* showing the makeup of costs all the way from the inception of raw materials and components production to the end price paid by ultimate customers.[2] The activity-cost chain thus includes more than just a firm's own internal cost structure; it includes the buildup of cost (and thus the "value" of the product) at each stage in the whole market chain of getting the product into the hands of the final user, as shown in Exhibit 3–5. Constructing an integrated activity-cost chain is more revealing than restricting attention to just a firm's own internal costs. This is because a firm's overall ability to furnish end-users with its product at a competitive price can easily depend on cost factors originating either *backward* in the suppliers' portion of the activity-cost chain or *forward* in the distribution channel portion of the chain.

Exhibit 3–5   Generic Activity-Cost Chain for a Representative Industry Situation

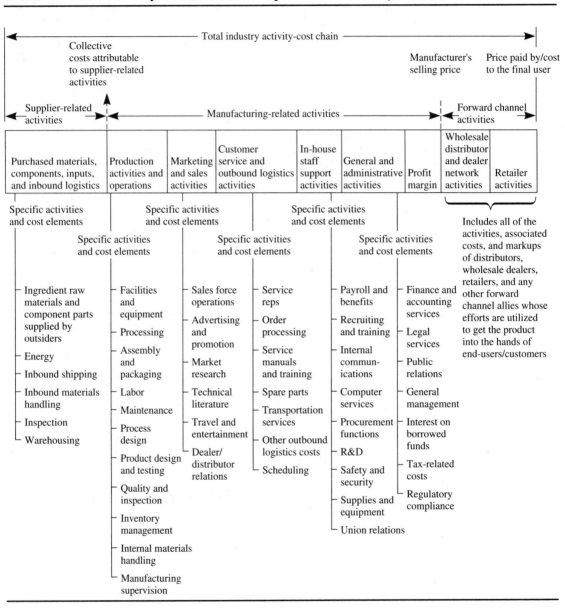

The task of constructing a complete cost chain is not easily accomplished. It requires breaking a firm's own historical cost accounting data out into several principal cost categories and developing cost estimates for the backward and forward channel portions of getting the product to the end-user as well. And it requires estimating the same cost elements for one's rivals and estimating their cost chains—an advanced art in competitive intelligence in itself. But despite the tedium of the task and the imprecision of some of the estimates, the payoff in exposing the cost competitiveness of one's position and the attendant strategic alternatives makes it a valuable analytical tool.

In Exhibit 3–5 observe that there are three main areas in the cost chain where important differences in the *relative* costs of competing firms can occur: in the suppliers' part of the cost chain, in their own respective activity segments, or in the forward channel portion of the chain. To the extent that the reasons for a firm's lack of cost competitiveness lie either in the backward or forward sections of the cost chain, then its job of reestablishing cost competitiveness may well have to extend beyond its own in-house operations. When a firm has a cost disadvantage in the area of purchased inputs and inbound logistics, five strategic options quickly emerge for consideration:

1. Negotiate more favorable prices with suppliers.
2. Integrate backward to gain control over material costs.
3. Try to use lower-priced substitute inputs.
4. Search out sources of savings in inbound shipping and materials logistics costs.
5. Try to make up the difference by initiating cost savings elsewhere in the overall cost chain.

When a firm's cost disadvantage occurs in the forward end of the cost chain, there are three corrective options:

1. Push for more favourable terms with distributors and other forward channel allies.
2. Change to a more economical distribution strategy, including the possibility of forward integration.
3. Try to make up the difference by initiating cost savings earlier in the cost chain.

It is likely, of course, that a substantial portion of any relative cost disadvantage lies within rival firms' own activity-cost structures. Here, five options for restoring cost parity emerge:

1. Initiate internal budget-tightening measures aimed at using fewer inputs to generate the desired output (cost-cutting retrenchment).
2. Invest in cost-saving technological improvements.
3. Innovate around the troublesome cost components as new investments are made in plant and equipment.
4. Redesign the product to achieve cost reductions.
5. Try to make up the internal cost disadvantage by achieving cost savings in the backward and forward portions of the cost chain.

The construction of activity-cost chains is a valuable tool for competitive diagnosis because of what it reveals about a firm's overall cost competitiveness and the relative cost positions of firms in the industry. Examining the makeup of one's own activity-cost chain and comparing it against the chains of important rival firms indicates who has how much of a cost advantage/disadvantage vis-à-vis major competitors and pinpoints which cost components in the cost chain are the source of the cost advantage or disadvantage. Strategic cost analysis adds much to the picture of the competitive environment, particularly concerning who the low-cost producers are, who is in the best position to compete on the basis of price, and who may be vulnerable to attack because of a poor relative cost position.

The Political Environment

The political environment of Canadian business is particularly important given the scale and scope of government activity in Canada.[3] Governments act in a wide variety of ways to create both opportunities and threats for business (see Exhibit 3–6). Among the most important government actions are (1) *regulation,* which can increase costs but also control competition or even give a competitive advantage (if firms have adapted to particularly stringent regulations in one location and are therefore better able to handle such regulations elsewhere); (2) *taxation,* which can reduce returns but also increase competitive advantage if a firm faces lower taxation than its competitors; (3) *expenditure,* which can create competitive disadvantage or advantage depending on whether government grants and subsidies received are larger than what competitors receive; (4) *takeover* creating a crown corporation, which can be an unfair and unpredictable competitor but also a deep-pocket customer; (5) *privatization,* which can increase competition but also result in a more level playing field; (6) *consultation,* which can become an opportunity for business to influence government policy but also provides government an opportunity to manipulate (i.e., co-opt) business by using the consultative process to justify decisions already made.

Given the variety of threats and opportunities facing business because of government actions, it is essential that each firm formulate and implement a

EXHIBIT 3–6 Opportunities and Threats from Government Actions

Threats	*Government Actions*	*Opportunities*
Increase costs	← Regulation→	Control competition
Reduce ROI	← Taxation →	Competitive advantage
Competitive disadvantage	← Expenditure→	Subsidies, grants, customer
Unfair/unpredictable competitor	← Takeover (Crown Corp.) →	Deep-pocket customer
Increased competition	← Privatization →	Level playing field
Co-opt	← Consultation →	Influence policy

political strategy (see Exhibit 3–7). In formulating such a strategy, the following elements need to be considered: (1) objective(s) (e.g., obtain favourable legislation/interpretation of legislation); (2) issue(s) (e.g., current, emerging); (3) stakeholders to determine allies, opponents, targets; (4) position/case (in terms of "public interest"). In implementing a political strategy, the following elements need to be considered: (1) timing; (2) technique(s) (i.e., direct—e.g., negotiation, litigation—or indirect—e.g., advocacy advertising, political contributions); (3) vehicle(s) (e.g., trade association, government relations (GR) department, GR consultant, coalition); and (4) style (e.g., confrontation, conciliation).

Social Environment

The following are some of the key concerns in the social environment:

1. Ecology (e.g., pollution, global warming, acid rain).
2. Demographics (e.g., population growth rates and unequal distribution of population, aging work force in industrialized countries, high education requirements).
3. Quality of life (e.g., safety, health care, education, standard of living).
4. Noneconomic activities (e.g., volunteerism, charities).

As with all of the various environments, one of the tasks of the general manager is the ability to identify significant environmental forces, to understand them in the context of the organization, and create (when necessary) responses to these pressures and opportunities. The relationship between the social environment and any organization's viability is increasingly intertwined.

Organizations vary widely in the postures they adopt regarding their dealings with environmental issues. These postures[4] can range from reactive (rules cost us

---

EXHIBIT 3–7 Political Strategy: Formulation and Implementation

Political Strategy

Formulation

- Objective(s)
- Issue(s)
- Stakeholders (allies, opponents, targets)
- Position/Case ("public interest")

Implementation

- Timing
- Technique(s) — Direct (negotiate, litigate)
                 — Indirect (advocacy advertising, political contributions)
- Vehicle(s)   (e.g., coalition, GR department, consultants)
- Style   (e.g., confrontation or conciliation)

money), to defensive (rules are OK, but), to accommodative (obey the rules), to proactive (environment comes first).

The principles of corporate strategy are often useful in developing approaches involving issues in the social environment. For example, IMAGINE, a national program to encourage giving and volunteering, suggests a strategy for deciding between charities (see box).

Be Picky

Do you ever feel overwhelmed by all the good causes that ask for donations? You'd like to help every one, but it's just not possible. Local Heroes know that the answer is to be picky.

- Review the causes you already support and be sure that your experience with each of them is rewarding.
- Then think about other issues you feel are critical to you and your community.
- Now look for the organizations that work in these areas. Call them up, visit their offices, or write for their brochures and find out all you can about what they do. The more involved you get, the more satisfaction you'll get back.
- Nobody expects you to say yes all the time, but you can be a Local Hero by making some causes "Your Causes." So be picky. And be a Local Hero.

Technological Environment

Technological developments have reshaped the ability of many firms to compete. The key concerns in the technological environment involve building the organizational capability to (1) forecast and identify relevant developments—both within and beyond the industry, (2) assess the impact of these developments on existing operations, and (3) define opportunities. Development of such an organizational capability should result in the eventual creation of a technological strategy. Technological strategy deals with "choices in technology, product design and development, sources of technology and R&D management and funding."[5]

International Environment

The sixth and final environment relevant to firms in Canada is the international environment. Given Canada's open economy, high levels of foreign ownership, and relatively small domestic market, Canadian firms, as seen in many of the cases in this book, are forced to be aware of the trends and market opportunities in countries outside Canada, particularly the United States. For 200 large U.S. and European multinational enterprises (MNEs), higher performance is associated with a greater degree of internationalization.[6] The implication of this for many Canadian firms is that internationalization is something which can be welcomed rather than feared.

Some of the many differences between the environment in Canada and the international environment concern such variables as currencies (which differ in value and stability), political and economic stability, data availability and its reliability, types of regulatory (legal and accounting) systems, market homogeneity, stage of economic development, and language and cultural mores.

There are, then, at least six environments that are important to strategic decision making in Canada: (1) industry, (2) competitive, (3) political/governmental, (4) social, (5) technological, and (6) international. Each of these must be considered in making strategic choices since analysis of these environments will indicate various opportunities and threats facing the organization. The objective in assessing the various environments is to formulate a strategy which best fits these environments. This is an ongoing challenge, given that environments change continually.

Notes to Chapter 3

1. Michael E. Porter, *Competitive Strategy: Techniques for Analyzing Industries and Competitors* (New York: Free Press, 1980), chap. 11.
2. The ins and outs of strategic cost analysis are discussed in greater length in Michael E. Porter, *Competitive Advantage: Creating and Sustaining Superior Performance* (New York: Free Press, 1985), chap. 2. What follows is a distilled adaptation by Thompson and Strickland of the approach pioneered by Porter. See Arthur A. Thompson, Jr., and A. J. Stickland III, *Strategy Formulation and Implementation,* 3rd ed. (Plano, Tex.: Business Publications, 1986), pp. 135–37.
3. See, for example, Mark C. Baetz and Donald H. Thain, *Canadian Cases in Business-Government Relations* (Toronto: Methuen Publications, 1985).
4. These categories are from Max B. Clarkson, "Defining, Evaluating and Managing Corporate Social Performance: The Stakeholder Management Model," *Research in Corporate Social Performance and Policy,* vol. 12 (Greenwich, Conn.: JAI Press, 1991).
5. See R. A. Burgelman and M. A. Maidique, *Strategic Management of Technology and Innovation,* (Homewood, Ill.: Richard D. Irwin, 1988).
6. See J. M. Geringer, Paul W. Beamish, and R. da Costa, "Diversification Strategy and Internationalization: Implications for MNE Performance," *Strategic Management Journal* 10, no. 2 (March/April 1989), pp. 109–19.

4 STRATEGY AND RESOURCES

Analysis of resources is a crucial consideration when both formulating and implementing a strategy. If the strategy is not supported by the business's resources, the strategy will be unsuccessful. And when a strategy changes, accompanying changes in resources are usually necessary. The questions that then arise are whether these changes are possible and how they can best be brought about. In this chapter, the analysis of resources and their relationship with strategy are considered.

Strategy's Fit with Resources

The relationship between resources and strategy is two-way (Exhibit 4–1). Strategy affects resources and resources affect strategy.

Two questions must be kept in mind when determining the specific resources required to pursue a strategy: Do the resources allow the strategy to be performed? Do they support a basis of competition? Starting with resources held, the strategist determines the unique characteristics of the firm's current resources that differentiate it from what its competitors do or could do. These differences are called *distinctive competencies* when they account for the success of the business over its competition. Having established what these distinctive competencies are, a strategy is then developed that makes good use of them. The overall resource requirements of this strategy are then examined.

Resource gaps are the differences between the resources required and the resources held. If the gaps can be reduced, the strategy makes sense from the perspective of resources. If the gaps cannot be filled, the strategy has to be revised so that the gaps between resources required and those held are surmountable.

Exhibit 4-1 **The Relationship between Strategy and Resources**

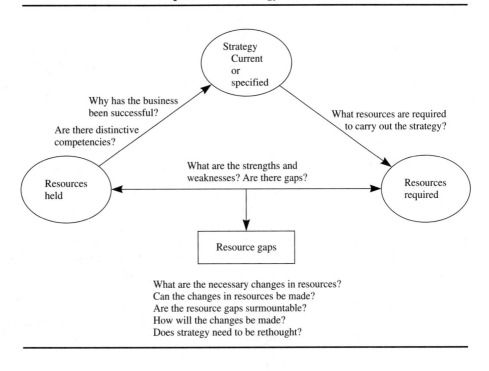

Evaluating Resources Held and Determining Resources Required

Resources can be evaluated from several different perspectives. The most prevalent way of evaluating them is **by functional areas:** finance, research and development, human resources, operations, marketing. For each function, functionally related questions, samples of which appear in Exhibit 4–2, are answered. When a functional perspective is taken, the strategist also needs to consider the context within which the functions operate. The contribution of each function to the business's strategy needs to be addressed as some functions may be more important to the strategy than others. The interrelationships among the functions also need to be addressed as what is done in one function can have a bearing on what can or cannot be done in another function.

A second way of evaluating resources is **by type:** financial, physical, human, and organizational. Financial resources are the funds that the company has or can raise. They are the most basic and flexible resources of the business, and can be converted into other resources. Converting other resources into financial resources is less certain and more difficult. Physical resources are the buildings, raw material, and equipment that the company has to work with and what it can do with them. Human resources are the people in the firm and what they are able to do. Organizational resources are the procedures and techniques the firm has developed that are necessary for success in the business.

A third way of evaluating resources is in terms of their **tangibility.** Tangible resources, such as a plant or the number of employees, can be observed and measured. Less tangible resources are also important though their characteristics and importance are harder to evaluate. Examples of less tangible resources are a recognized corporate name that may allow the company to command a premium price in the market, long-term contracts with suppliers that ensure availability of inputs, and the loyalty and dedication of employees that can determine their productivity.

A fourth way of evaluating resources is in terms of their **breadth.** A resource is essentially broad/wide when it is easily transferred to other situations and narrow/specialized when it is not. Sales staff with knowledge of many different products is an example of a broad resource, while specialized product knowledge is an example of a narrow resource. A broad resource facilitates a business's expansion of its product, market, and industry scope, while a narrow resource serves to limit change of scope.

A final way of evaluating resources is in terms of the **activity cost chain.** Within each activity, different kinds of resources are required as indicated by the different cost elements that were identified in Exhibit 3–5.

EXHIBIT 4–2 An Overview of the Functional Perspective

Function	A Partial List of Questions to Answer
Finance	What is the apparent capacity of the firm to generate internal and external funds?
	What funds are required for each strategic alternative?
Research and development	How important is technology to the firm's processes and products?
	What percentage of the firm's resources are devoted to research and development?
Human resources	What is the ambition, depth, drive, loyalty, and skill of the managerial/administrative group in the firm?
	What is the cost, flexibility, motivation, productivity, and skill of the work force?
Procurement	How important is the procurement function to the firm?
	Does the firm have good relations with suppliers?
Operations	What is the capacity, cost, and productivity of operations?
	What is the age, condition, and flexibility of the plant and equipment?
	What is the quality of the products produced?
Marketing	Does the firm command a premium price and, if so, why?
	How well does the firm know its customers and its competitors?

Resource Gaps

Rarely is the precise combination of resources needed to pursue a strategy in place. With a new strategy, resource requirements can be considerably different from current resources, thus creating resource gaps. When assessing the resource gaps, a useful approach is to construct a table with entries down the side for the various tasks or functions and with headings across the top for (1) current resources, (2) projected resources, (3) gaps between those two, and (4) how the gaps might be filled (Exhibit 4–3). The body of this table is then filled in with the analytical details.

A new strategy is not the only situation in which resource gaps occur. Just maintaining an ongoing strategy may create resource gaps. New resources must be developed when existing resources deteriorate, depreciate, or turn over. In addition, success with the existing strategy can create resource gaps when additional resources are required for growth. On occasion, more resources are generated than can be employed profitably in a business. Underutilization of existing resources is a form of resource gap which is unrecognized in many organizations. Another dilemma, for example, is when a firm generates more cash than it can use in the business and makes itself an attractive takeover target.

Identifying the Gaps

Resource gaps are identified through strength-and-weakness analysis as part of the SWOT analysis described in Chapter 2. Determination of strengths and weaknesses involves a relative comparison and must be done for each strategic alternative since each alternative has its own peculiar resource requirements. Tied to each strength or weakness is a gap between the resource held and the

---

EXHIBIT 4-3 Assessing Resource Gaps

Functional Area	Current Resources	Required Resources	Resource Gaps	Filling the Gaps: Tactics and Risk
Finance R&D Human resources Procurement Operations Marketing				

resource required to pursue the strategy. Each gap can be described in terms of magnitude, direction of change, and time by which it has to be reduced.

Reducing the Gaps

The ability of the business to reduce the gaps identified is influenced by the nature of the changes required and the ability of the business to make these changes. The gaps can be reduced by reallocating, developing, buying, and selling resources. Depending on how the gap is reduced, cost, ease, and timing will differ. Resources can be acquired from the outside, but their high market cost can make it more desirable to develop them internally. Developing resources is usually cheaper, but slower. It can have other positive benefits, however, such as providing for the development of managers. Moreover, development of resources may be required if sufficient quantities or qualities are not available, either elsewhere in the business or in the marketplace. Obviously, many tactical issues have to be addressed when considering how gaps might be filled.

It should also be noted that the ability to reduce a resource gap will depend on the particular country in which the firm is located. As Michael Porter has noted,[1] a firm's resource base is not simply a function of its own past investments but is also determined by the supply of resources such as capital and labour in the country. In other words, there is an interaction between firm-level and country-level sources of competitive advantage.

Reducing gaps presents the business with risks. The risk associated with filling a gap is greater when the gap is larger, when the resource has to be increased rather than decreased, and when the gap has to be filled sooner. Risk is also greater when there are more gaps to be filled, since it is less likely that the company will be able to fill them all. If the risk posed by the gaps is acceptable while the strategy appears effective, then a fit has been found between resources and strategy.

Summary

Finding an acceptable fit between the strategy and the resources available to the business is a major step in formulating strategy.[2] First, the resource situation must be examined in terms of what is available and what is needed. Resources can be evaluated in several ways: by functional area, by type, by tangibility, by breadth, and by activity costs. Resource gaps must be identified and evaluated to determine the likelihood of their being overcome. Whether they can be overcome depends on the gaps' size, number, and nature; the ways in which the gaps can be reduced; and the time available. When the likelihood of filling the resource gaps poses too great a risk to be acceptable, the strategy has to be modified in order to bring its resource requirements closer to current resources.

Note to Chapter 4

1. See M. E. Porter, *The Competitive Advantage of Nations* (New York: The Free Press, 1990).
2. For more discussion on the analysis of resources, see R. B. Buchele, "How to Evaluate a Firm," *California Management Review,* Fall 1962; J. H. Grant and W. R. King, *The Logic of Strategic Planning* (Boston: Little, Brown, 1982), chaps. 4–7; M. E. Porter, *Competitive Advantage: Creating and Sustaining Superior Performance* (New York: Free Press, 1985); W. E. Rothschild, *Putting It All Together: A Guide to Strategic Thinking* (New York: AMACOM, 1976), chap. 6; R. S. Sloma, *How to Measure Managerial Performance* (New York: Macmillan, 1980); and H. H. Stevenson, "Defining Corporate Strengths and Weaknesses," *Sloan Management Review,* Spring 1976, pp. 51–68.

5 STRATEGY AND MANAGERIAL PREFERENCES/VALUES

Fortune favours the bold.
Juvenal

Every absurdity has a champion to defend it.
Oliver Goldsmith

Strategy formulation may seem to be a highly rational and reasoned process of analysing environmental opportunities and threats, and resource strengths and weaknesses. However, managers of a business may have different assessments of the firm's environment and resource base. They may also use different criteria when evaluating strategic alternatives, and have different perceptions of the need for change. These differences are often due to managerial preferences and values. Such differences can lead to major conflicts. Conflict is frequently re-solved with a strategy that represents a negotiated compromise. Strategy formu-lation is thus heavily influenced by forces derived from personal attributes, preferences, and values.

In this chapter, the role of managerial preferences/values in strategy formu-lation is considered. The chapter will also describe the concept of corporate culture and stakeholder pressures since these influence, and are influenced by, managerial preferences/values.

Managerial Preferences/Values

Every manager has individual preferences or values that influence his or her thoughts and behavior. Preferences are derived from the individual's basic needs. These needs are modified through the manager's personal goals, beliefs, attitudes, and competencies.[1]

Personal preferences need to be transformed into group preferences for management to have a set of consistent managerial preferences to guide strategic decision making. This transformation is accomplished through a complex process in which power plays an instrumental role.[2] Power enables certain individuals in management to dominate the formation of managerial preferences (should they so desire) such that the group's preferences closely reflect their personal preferences. For this reason, any assessment of managerial preferences must consider who the powerful people in the management team are, how they see the situation, and what they think should be done.

Certain preferences are directly related to the components of strategy itself. Managers have preferences for the types and levels of goals, and where and how the company competes. Managerial preferences are important to strategy in other ways as well. Risk preferences influence the trade-off between risks and rewards, and determine the margin of safety sought to ensure competitive success, financial continuity, and organizational survival. Preferences about self-sufficiency influence the degree of independence sought from key stakeholders. And finally, preferences about how to lead and manage will influence the culture of the firm as these preferences shape decisions about how to keep employees committed, motivated, and loyal, and decisions about how to best use employees' talents.

The Relationship between Strategy and Managerial Preferences/Values

Managerial preferences/values influence strategy. For example, a preference for growth to satisfy a need for achievement or recognition can encourage managers to follow a strategy of diversification. However, the firm may lack the resources, or there may not be environmental opportunities to follow such a strategy. As a result, the managers' preferences and values are not satisfied. This leaves a gap between the preferences/values the manager holds and what preferences/values can be satisfied (Exhibit 5–1).[3] Sometimes a gap arises from moral or ethical standards. For example, some managers may be against the consumption of liquor because of religious background. They would likely face a moral dilemma if asked to support or implement a strategic decision to acquire a liquor company.

When there is a major gap between the preferences/values held and preferences/values satisfied, a change in either strategy or preferences/values is required. However, it may be very difficult to change either to close the gap. A change in strategy may not be possible without negatively affecting strategy's fit with the environment and/or resources. A change in preferences/values may be resisted because of strongly held beliefs based on a particular educational, employment, or religious background. For example, in terms of employment background, managers who have worked most of their lives in a particular industry may have a preference for staying in that industry since they know and understand it. For such managers, a strategic decision to move into another industry is likely to create a gap between preferences/values held and preferences/values satisfied.

EXHIBIT 5–1 Relationship between Strategy and Managerial Preferences/Values

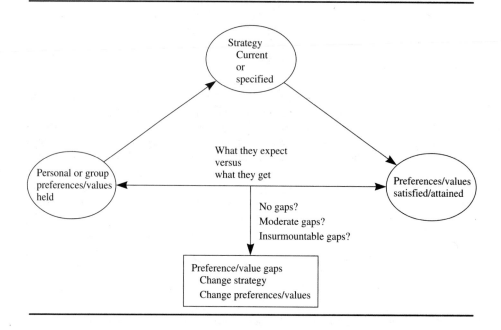

When a management group rather than an individual is setting a firm's strategy, there can be additional complications in assessing the fit between managerial preferences/values and strategy. In particular, when managers in the group have conflicting preferences, it becomes a problem of determining whose preferences are relevant. In most cases, the relevant preferences are those of the managers with the greatest power.

Corporate Culture

Corporate culture is defined as the common preferences/values held by those working in the firm about the way things are done. It gives rise to norms and informal rules that people follow. It also provides them with a common understanding of what is considered important, and a standard for performance in areas that preserve the firm's distinctiveness (see box).

From the strategic perspective, a corporate culture closely linked to an effective business strategy can mean the difference between success and failure for a business.[4] The reason is that the culture often has a direct impact on how well a particular strategy is or can be implemented. Consequently, when the culture accounts for a business's success, strategy can be expected to build on it. And when the strategy requires a change in culture, pursuit of the strategy is constrained, sometimes to the extent that a strategy cannot be pursued.

Pack Your Own Chute

On the evening of January 18, 1992, the passengers on Delta Airlines' scheduled flight from Atlanta, Georgia, to Columbia, South Carolina, received an object lesson on corporate culture. That day two centimetres of snow fell across the southern United States. Unaccustomed to snow, this resulted in flight delays and cancellations. Delta's scheduled 8:30 P.M. flight left the gate at 11:00 P.M. and joined the queue for de-icing. After more than a four-hour wait on the tarmac, the plane departed for Columbia, arriving at 4:00 A.M..

In Columbia, the airport appeared empty except for security guards—no Delta ground crew personnel to help passengers and no apparent baggage handlers. The only taxi service had shut down hours earlier.

What solution did the flight crew—the only available Delta personnel at the airport—have? They smiled, silently walked past all the passengers, and climbed into the private van that had been arranged to take them to their hotel.

Culture in an organization can range between strong and weak. A strong culture greatly influences the behavior of organizational members, while a weak one is irrelevant in determining the actions of most members. Evidence for the strength of a culture is found in Exhibit 5–2. In general, businesses with strong cultures are likely to have better performance.[5] However, a strong culture is not a sure road to success. A culture that has been a strength may become a weakness if it does not fit with the requirements of a new strategy. Nor is a strong culture necessarily self-sustaining. It can break down when rapid growth brings in new people faster than they can be socialized to the culture.

The compatibility between culture and strategy, sometimes called *cultural risk,* can be examined using a simple process. First, the key tasks arising from the strategy are determined. Next, the behavior required to perform the tasks satisfactorily is determined. This is compared with the behavior arising out of the current corporate culture. If required behavior is similar to actual behavior, culture poses no risk to the implementation of strategy. If it is different, culture can present so much risk that it is a barrier to the pursuit of a strategy.

The strategist can deal with cultural risk in several ways. One approach is to ignore culture and plunge ahead. Since a good fit is needed between culture and strategy, this approach nearly always invites disaster. Another approach is to manage around culture, either by performing the tasks in ways more in line with the current culture, or, more drastically, by modifying the strategy so that different tasks are required. A third approach is to change the selected components of culture that affect performance of specific tasks that are identified as areas of risk. A simple example of a change in culture to meet the needs of strategy is as

Exhibit 5-2 Evidence of the Strength of a Culture

Character of the Culture	Evidence of Character
Strong	Members share preferences or values about how to succeed.
	Members know the activities the business must carry out well to be successful.
	Standards of achievement are well established.
	"Heroes" in the organization personify values, and provide tangible role models to follow.
Weak	Members have no clear preferences or values about how to succeed.
	Members do not agree on the beliefs or values that are important.
	Different parts of the business have different beliefs or values.
	"Heroes" of the business are destructive or disruptive.
	Rituals are disorganized, with organizational members either "doing their own thing" or working at cross-purposes.

follows. A company facing a more competitive environment found that it needed to improve its relationships with customers. It reoriented the culture to this end by using the slogan "the customer is always right" and by training employees to respond courteously and promptly to customer requests.

Stakeholders

Managers are increasingly expected to consider a growing number of stakeholders when formulating strategy. A stakeholder is an individual or a group with a "stake" in the business. Each stakeholder depends on the business in order to realize goals, while the business depends on each stakeholder for something each provides the business. Management is most likely to satisfy critical stakeholders if it takes their preferences into account when formulating the strategy.

General classes of stakeholders who influence strategic decisions are shareholders, management, employees, financiers, suppliers, customers, community, and government. Illustrative preferences/values of these stakeholders and how they encourage managers to meet them are presented in Exhibit 5–3. Managers often reflect the preferences/values of stakeholders they see as important to the performance of their job. Thus, the marketing manager will tend to reflect customer interests, and the financial manager will tend to reflect financiers' interests. Stakeholders sometimes share certain common interests, as do shareholders and managers who hold stock options.

Some stakeholders are "self-appointed" yet have the potential to reshape an entire company's or industry's status. For example, at the industry level, pressure groups in Europe were able to convince politicians there to ban selected fur imports from Canada to reduce the annual Canadian seal hunt. Rational arguments were put forth in support of the seal hunt. The benefits noted included (1) the traditional employment created for otherwise seasonal workers and

Exhibit 5-3 The Interests of Stakeholders

Stakeholder	Preferences, Values, Expectations	Ways They Exert Influence on the Business
Shareholders	Appreciation in the value of stock dividends Social responsibility	Buying and selling stock Election of directors Proxy fights Public expression of satisfaction or discontent through the press or at annual meetings
Managers	Participation in decisions Authority/power Compensation (salary, bonuses, benefits) Opportunity for advancement Job security	Taking/leaving jobs in the firm Commitment to work Quality of work
Employees	Compensation (wages, benefits, profit sharing) Participation in workplace decisions Safe working conditions Opportunity for advancement Job security	Taking/leaving jobs in the firm Strikes Absenteeism Workplace grievances Quality of work Union activity
Financiers	Orderly repayment of principal and interest Further opportunities for sound investment of monies Timely disclosure of events	Willingness to lend additional funds Covenants in the loan agreements Enforcement of covenants Credit rating/interest rates charged
Suppliers	Continued, consistent orders Prompt payment	Prices charged Credit terms Delivery performance Willingness to meet special demands Supply priority during periods of shortage Technical assistance Recommendations to other suppliers
Customers	Satisfactory products or services Satisfactory price/quality relationship Fair adjustment practices (warranties, responses, etc.)	Amount purchased Word of mouth advertising Complaints, returns, claims Product liability suits New product ideas
Community	Continuity of employment Continuity of payment of taxes Environmentally sound activities Actions socially sound Employee participation in community activities	Boycotts, protests, demonstrations Awards by community groups Pressure on government
Government	Continuity of employment Continuity of payment of taxes Environmentally sound activities Advance national objectives (R&D, exports, job creation) Satisfy regulations	Subsidies, tax concessions Regulations Licenses, permits Awards by government Enforcement of regulations

(2) increasing the available fish stocks (seals consumed large quantities). Rational arguments were no match, however, for pictures of "cute" baby seals.

Which stakeholders' preferences management seeks to satisfy involves difficult choices, sometimes including ethical issues; trade-offs need to be made among the competing preferences of stakeholders, and the decision is often influenced by the stakeholders' power. Factors influencing the potential power of stakeholders are outlined in Exhibit 5–4. When top executives were asked "who is really important to the business?" customers were seen as most important, followed by oneself, subordinates, employees, and bosses. Those who were least important, in order of declining importance, were stockholders, elected public officials, and government bureaucrats.[6]

EXHIBIT 5–4 Potential Power Held by Stakeholders When Seeking to Influence Strategic Decisions

	Degree of Potential Power	
Stakeholder	*Is High If:*	*Is Low If:*
Shareholders	Controlling block of shares with an active interest in the company.	Shares are widely held by uninterested shareholders.
	Many shareholders who have a common interest in what the company does.	Shares are widely held by shareholders with heterogeneous interests.
	Shareholders hold stock so they can exert influence over management decisions.	A dominant CEO strongly influences elections to the board.
Managers	Management is led by a dominating CEO.	The board of directors dominates decision making.
	The management team has been in place for a long time.	
	Compensation is heavily influenced by performance-based bonuses.	
Employees	Belong to a strong union.	Unskilled labour force.
	The company has a tradition of good employee relations.	High unemployment.
Financiers	The company is highly leveraged.	The company generates the investment money it needs internally.
	The company has defaulted on the covenants in the loan agreements.	
Suppliers	Limited sources of supply.	Many alternative suppliers.
	Switching costs are high.	
Customers	Few possible customers.	Many possible customers.
	A few customers buy a significant proportion of the output.	The company's product is unique.
	Customers possess a credible threat for backward integration.	
Community	A single-industry town.	The company has facilities in many locations.
Government	Regulations provide government with control over company activities.	
	Government approval is required for mergers and acquisitions.	
	The government can provide grants, licenses, and special tax benefits.	

The following questions are relevant when determining the influence of stakeholder interests:

1. Which stakeholders' interests are most important?
2. To which stakeholders should management give its loyalty?
3. Will any stakeholders be injured by the proposed decisions?
4. Should strategy be changed to meet stakeholder expectations?
5. Is it possible to negotiate a compromise?
6. Should certain stakeholders be replaced?

These questions also raise ethical considerations about "what is right" and "what is wrong."[7]

Summary

This chapter has emphasized the human element in the strategy formulation process. What seemed to be a highly rational and analytical process up to this point no longer seems so with the introduction of managerial preferences/values, corporate culture, and stakeholder pressures. Corporate culture reflects preferences/values shared by all in the firm. A culture in which many preferences/values are shared is said to be a strong culture and may be a major source of success for the firm. Every firm has stakeholders who exert power in varying degrees in order to get the firm to satisfy their preferences, values, and expectations.

Notes to Chapter 5

1. Discussion of the personal system in relation to needs and behaviour is found in most texts dealing with organizational behaviour. One good example is A. R. Cohen, S. L. Fink, H. Gadon, and R. Willets, *Effective Behavior in Organizations,* 4th ed. (Homewood, Ill.: Richard D. Irwin, 1988), chaps. 7 and 8.
2. Additional coverage of this topic can be found in I. C. MacMillan and P. E. Jones, *Strategy Formulation: Power and Politics,* 2nd ed. (St. Paul, Minn.: West Publishing, 1986).
3. Additional sources of information on managerial preferences are G. Donaldson and J. W. Lorsch, *Decision Making at the Top* (New York: Basic Books, 1983), chaps. 5 and 6; J. N. Fry and J. P. Killing, *Strategic Analysis and Action,* 2nd ed. (Scarborough, Ont.: Prentice-Hall Canada, 1989), chap. 8; and C. R. Schwenk, "Management Illusions and Biases: Their Impact on Strategic Decisions," *Long-Range Planning* 18, no. 5 (1985), pp. 74–80.

4. The role of culture in successful business organizations has been popularized in Great Britain by W. Goldsmith and D. Clutterback, *The Winning Streak* (Harmondsworth, Middlesex, England, Penguin Books, 1985) and in the United States by T. Peters and R. H. Waterman, *In Search of Excellence* (New York: Harper & Row, 1982). Additional sources of information on corporate culture are J. Barney, "Organizational Culture: Can It Be a Source of Sustained Competitive Advantage?" *Academy of Management Review,* July 1986, pp. 656–65; S. Davis, *Managing Corporate Culture* (Cambridge, Mass.: Ballinger, 1984); and T. Deal and A. Kennedy, *Corporate Cultures* (Reading, Mass.: Addison-Wesley, 1982).

5. According to T. Deal and A. Kennedy, a strong culture has almost always been the driving force behind continuing success in American business. In *Corporate Cultures* (Reading, Mass.: Addison-Wesley, 1982), p. 5.

6. B. Z. Posner and W. H. Schmidt, "Values and the American Manager: An Update," *California Management Review,* Spring 1984, p. 206.

7. Additional sources of information on ethical questions are R. E. Freeman and D. R. Gilbert, Jr., *Corporate Strategy and the Search for Ethics* (Englewood Cliffs, N.J.: Prentice Hall, 1988); S. W. Gellerman, "Why 'Good' Managers Make Bad Ethical Choices," *Harvard Business Review,* July–August 1986, pp. 85–90; and L. L. Nash, "Ethics without a Sermon," *Harvard Business Review,* November–December 1981, pp. 79–90.

6 CATEGORIZING STRATEGIC DECISIONS

Having now described the key variables—environment, resources, and managerial preferences and values—that general managers must consider in making strategic choices, the next task is to examine the major ways of categorizing these strategic choices. There are literally dozens of ways of categorizing strategic decisions. Not all are appropriate for each organization. Nonetheless, there are typically more viable alternatives available than are actually considered by most managers.

This chapter will describe the following basic categories of strategic choices:

1. Diversification.
2. Integration.
3. Cooperation.
4. Generic approaches.
5. Retrenchment.

The chapter will conclude by outlining the characteristics of strategic management decisions at different levels.

Diversification

Based on the extent of product line diversification, Leonard Wrigley identified the following four types of firms: single-product, dominant-product, related-product, and unrelated-product. Each type represented a distinct corporate strategy, with measurable differences between each type in terms of their deviation from an original product technology or marketing emphasis.

In turn, the original product technology or marketing emphasis suggests an underlying skill base within the firm. This skill base or "core skill" was defined by Wrigley as "the collective knowledge, skills, habits of working together, as well as the collective experience of what the market will bear, that is required in the cadre of managerial and technical personnel if the firm is to survive and grow in a competitive market."[1]

Wrigley's four categories of firms were subsequently subdivided by Rumelt into a total of nine types, each of which was then related to performance. Significantly, firms adopting a single-business, dominant-constrained, related-constrained, or active-conglomerate strategy were observed to have above-average profitability. This held true in both a domestic context (United States, Canada) and international context (United States multinational, European multinational).[2]

The higher performance associated with firms having a single-product, dominant-constrained, or related-constrained product diversification is intuitively consistent with the "core skill" concept. It has been frequently emphasized that successful firms "stick to their knitting."[3] The above-average profitability associated with active conglomerates—the exception to the core-skill concept—must be understood in their portfolio nature. Here, unrelated-product firms are actively bought and sold primarily on the basis of their short-term financial contribution to overall corporate profits. There are important implications for general managers of differences in the profitability levels associated with the degree of product diversification. Internally, whether a firm is considering an acquisition, a merger, or simply a change in product emphasis, the likely impact of the change upon profits can be now better assessed. External to the firm, product diversification strategy represents another tool which bankers, accountants, and investment dealers can use to assist them in assessing a firm's future profitability. The notion of relatedness of product/service has been combined with "newness" of market to produce a variety of strategic choices as illustrated in Exhibit 6–1.

Market penetration involves seeking increased market share for present products or services in present markets through greater marketing efforts. It is appropriate when:[4]

Exhibit 6–1 Product/Market Strategic Choices

Product/ Service		Market/Customer Base	
		Existing	*New*
Product/ Service	Existing	Market penetration	Market development
	Modified/improved	Product development	
	New but related	Concentric diversification	
	New and unrelated	Horizontal diversification	Conglomerate diversification

- Current markets are not saturated with your particular product or service.
- The usage rate of present customers could be significantly increased.
- The market shares of major competitors have been declining while total industry sales have been increasing.
- The correlation between dollar sales and dollar marketing expenditures has historically been high.
- Increased economies of scale provide major competitive advantages.

Market development involves the introduction of present products or services into new geographic areas. It is appropriate when:

- New channels of distribution are available that are reliable, inexpensive, and of good quality.
- An organization is very successful at what it does.
- New untapped or unsaturated markets exist.
- An organization has the needed capital and human resources to manage expanded operations.
- An organization has excess production capacity.
- An organization's basic industry is rapidly becoming global in scope.

Product development involves seeking increased sales by improving or modifying present products or services, for either existing or new customers. This strategy is appropriate when:

- An organization has successful products that are in the maturity stage of their life cycles; the idea here is to attract satisfied customers to try new (improved) products as a result of their positive experience with the organization's present products or services.
- An organization competes in an industry that is characterized by rapid technological developments.
- Major competitors offer better quality products at comparable prices.
- An organization competes in a high-growth industry.
- An organization has especially strong research and development capabilities.

Concentric diversification involves the addition of new, but related, products or services for either existing or new customers. This strategy is appropriate when:

- An organization competes in a no-growth or a slow-growth industry.
- Adding new, but related, products would significantly enhance the sales of current products.
- New, but related, products could be offered at highly competitive prices.

- New, but related, products have seasonal sales levels that counterbalance an organization's existing peaks and valleys.
- An organization's products are currently in the decline stage of their life cycles.
- An organization has a strong management team.

Horizontal diversification involves the addition of new, unrelated products or services for present customers. It is appropriate when:

- Revenues derived from an organization's current products or services would significantly increase by adding the new, unrelated products.
- An organization competes in a highly competitive and/or a no-growth industry, as indicated by low industry profit margins and returns.
- An organization's present channels of distribution can be used to market the new products to current customers.
- The new products have countercyclical sales patterns compared to an organization's present products.

Conglomerate diversification involves the addition of new, unrelated products or services for new customers. It is appropriate when:

- An organization's basic industry is experiencing declining annual sales and profits.
- An organization has the capital and managerial talent needed to compete successfully in a new industry.
- The organization has the opportunity to purchase an unrelated business that is an attractive investment opportunity.
- There exists financial synergy between the acquired and acquiring firm; note that a key difference between concentric and conglomerate diversification is that the former should be based on some commonality in markets, products, or technology; whereas the latter should be based more on profit considerations.
- Existing markets for an organization's present products are saturated.
- An organization that has historically concentrated on a single industry could be charged for violating Canada's Competition Act.

To create shareholder wealth with any form of diversification, Porter[5] suggests the need to meet three essential tests:

1. *Industry Attractiveness Test.*   The industry chosen for diversification must be an attractive one.
2. *Cost-of-Entry Test.*   The cost of entry must not capitalize future profits.
3. *Better-Off Test.*   Either the acquiror or acquiree must gain competitive advantage.

Based on a sample of the diversification records of 33 large U.S. companies, Porter found that companies had ignored at least one or two of these tests, and "the strategic results were disastrous."[6] Most of the 33 companies had divested many more acquisitions than they had kept.

Integration

There are two basic types of integration: vertical and horizontal. Vertical integration involves a choice of integrating backward to the original supplier of goods or services, and/or integrating forward to the ultimate customer. Horizontal integration means seeking ownership or increased control over competitors in very similar markets.

Some advantages of vertical integration are to reduce vulnerability by securing supply and/or markets, or to reduce transaction costs and absorb more of the value in the chain of stages of integration. In general, vertical integration helps a business to protect profit margins and market share by ensuring access to consumers or material inputs. Some of the advantages and disadvantages of vertical integration are summarized in Exhibit 6–2.

Backward integration, that is, seeking ownership or increased control over suppliers, is appropriate when:

EXHIBIT 6-2 Some Advantages and Disadvantages of Vertical Integration

Advantages	Disadvantages
Internal benefits:	**Internal costs:**
Integration economies reduce costs by eliminating steps, reducing duplicate overhead, and cutting costs (technology-dependent).	Need for overhead to coordinate vertical integration increases costs.
Improved coordination of activities reduces inventory and other costs.	Burden of excess capacity from unevenly balanced minimum-efficient-scale plants (technology-dependent).
Avoid time-consuming tasks such as price shopping, communicating design details, or negotiating contracts.	Poorly organized vertically integrated firms do not enjoy synergies that compensate for higher costs.
Competitive benefits:	**Competitive dangers:**
Avoid foreclosure to inputs, services, or markets.	Obsolete processes may be perpetuated.
Improved marketing or technological intelligence.	Creates mobility (or exit) barriers.
Opportunity to create product differentiation (increased value-added).	Links firm to sick adjacent businesses.
Superior control of firm's economic environment (market power).	Lose access to information from suppliers or distributors.
Create credibility for new products.	Synergies created through vertical integration may be overrated.
Synergies could be created by coordinating vertical activities skillfully.	Managers integrated before thinking through the most appropriate way to do so.

SOURCE: Reprinted by permission of the publisher from *Strategic Flexibility: A Management Guide for Changing Times,* by Kathryn Rudie Harrigan (Lexington, Mass: Lexington Books, D. C. Heath and Company). Copyright © 1985, D. C. Heath and Company.

- An organization's present suppliers are especially expensive, or unreliable, or incapable of meeting the firm's needs for parts, components, assemblies, or raw materials.
- The number of suppliers is few and the number of competitors is many.
- An organization competes in an industry that is growing rapidly; this is a factor because integrative-type strategies (forward, backward, and horizontal) reduce an organization's ability to diversify in a declining industry.
- An organization has both the capital and human resources needed to manage the new business of supplying its own raw materials.
- The advantages of stable prices are particularly important; this is a factor because an organization can stabilize the cost of its raw materials and the associated price of its products through backward integration.
- Present suppliers have high profit margins, which suggests that the business of supplying products or services in the given industry is a worthwhile venture.
- An organization needs to acquire a needed resource quickly.

Forward integration, that is, gaining ownership or increased control over distributors or retailers, is appropriate when:

- An organization's present distributors are especially expensive, or unreliable, or incapable of meeting the firm's distribution needs.
- The availability of quality distributors is so limited as to offer a competitive advantage to those firms that integrate forward.
- An organization competes in an industry that is growing and is expected to continue to grow markedly; this is a factor because forward integration reduces an organization's ability to diversify if its basic industry falters.
- An organization has both the capital and human resources needed to manage the new business of distributing its own products.
- The advantages of stable production are particularly high; this is a consideration because an organization can increase the predictability of the demand for its output through forward integration.
- Present distributors or retailers have high profit margins; this situation suggests that a company could profitably distribute its own products and price them more competitively by integrating forward.

Horizontal integration, that is, seeking ownership or increased control over competitors, is appropriate when:

- An organization can gain monopolistic characteristics in a particular area or region without being challenged by the federal government for "tending substantially" to reduce competition.

EXHIBIT 6-3 Four Acquisition Postures

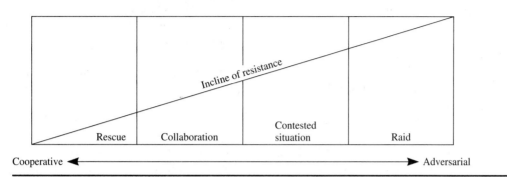

SOURCE: Price, Pritchett, Pritchett and Associates, Inc., *After the Merger: Managing the Shockwaves* (Homewood, Ill.: Dow-Jones Irwin, 1985). Reprinted by permission.

- An organization competes in a growing industry.
- Increased economies of scale provide major competitive advantages.
- An organization has both the capital and human talent needed to successfully manage an expanded organization.
- Competitors are faltering due to a lack of managerial expertise or a need for particular resources which your organization possesses; note that horizontal integration would not be appropriate if competitors are doing poorly because overall industry sales are declining.

A frequently observed method of horizontal integration is through acquisition or merger. In any acquisition or merger, four acquisitional postures exist: rescues, collaborations, contested situations, and raids (see Exhibit 6-3). The most adversarial acquisition is the raid; the most cooperative, the rescue. The degree of resistance rises steadily from rescues through to raids. The need to consider carefully how to integrate a newly acquired business is often overlooked. Numerous stresses exist which, if not managed, can result in failure.

Cooperation

One of the predominant trends in the past decade has been the increased use of cooperative strategies. Whether in the domestic or international market, more frequent use of joint ventures, licensing, countertrade, and technology/R&D collaboration has been observed. Characterizing these collaborative arrangements has been a willingness to either share or split managerial control in a particular undertaking.

Several opportunities for sharing can come from a cooperative strategy. These include sharing a sales force, advertising activities, manufacturing facilities, and management know-how.[7] A number of potential competitive advantages are associated with each type of opportunity for sharing, but sometimes the fit can be more illusory than real. For example, salespersons may not be as effective as expected in representing a new product. Despite the difficulties that can arise, a recent trend is the increase in cooperative arrangements between hitherto competing organizations.

Some cases in this book provide specific examples of cooperative strategies. These include cases on licensing (Edison Price), joint ventures (Russki Adventures), and technology sharing (IKEA).

The existence of so many potential cooperative strategies dramatically increases the opportunities available to Canadian businesses. There are conditions, however, which would suggest the use of one form of cooperation over another. Some of the considerations before deciding on the form of cooperation would include assessments of:

- Level of risk.
- Synergies/complementary skills to be gained.
- Regulations influencing type of involvement.
- Managerial and financial resources available to go it alone.
- Speed of innovation required.

The advantages to be gained by licensing depend on the technology, firm size, product maturity, and extent of the firm's experience. A number of internal and external circumstances may lead a firm to employ a licensing strategy:

1. The licensee has existing products or facilities but requires technology, which may be acquired more cheaply or quickly from third parties (licensors) than by internal R&D; the need may be of limited extent or long duration.
2. The licensor wishes to exploit its technology in secondary markets that may be too small to justify larger investments; the required economies of scale may not be attainable.
3. The licensee wishes to maximize its own business by adding new technologies.
4. Host-country governments restrict imports and/or foreign direct investment (FDI), or the risk of nationalization or foreign control is too great.
5. Prospects of "technology feedback" are high (that is, the licensor has contractually assured itself of access to new developments generated by the licensee and based on licensed knowledge).
6. Licensing is a way of testing and developing a market that can later be exploited by direct investment.
7. The licensee is unlikely to become a future competitor.
8. The pace of technological change is sufficiently rapid that the licensor

can remain technologically superior and ahead of the licensee, who is a potential competitor.

9. Opportunities exist for licensing auxiliary processes without having to license basic product or process technologies.

10. A firm lacks the capital and managerial resources required for exporting or FDI but wants to earn additional profits with minimum commitment.

Joint ventures are appropriate when:

- A privately owned organization is forming a joint venture with a publicly owned organization. There are some advantages of being privately held, such as close ownership; there are some advantages of being publicly held, such as access to stock issuances as a source of capital. Therefore the unique advantages of being privately and publicly held may sometimes be synergistically combined.

- A domestic organization is forming a joint venture with a foreign company; joint venture can provide a domestic company with the opportunity for obtaining local management in a foreign country and the local managers' knowledge of the foreign economy, politics, and culture. This may also have the residual advantage of reducing risks such as expropriation and harassment by host country officials.

- The distinctive competencies of two or more firms complement each other especially well.

- Some project is potentially very profitable, but requires overwhelming resources and risks.

- Two or more smaller firms have trouble competing with a large firm.

- There exists a need to introduce a new technology quickly.

Generic Approaches

Following from the work of Michael Porter among others,[8] strategies can be viewed broadly as falling into one of these three categories: (1) overall cost leadership, where the firm strives to be overall cost leader in the industry by using a range of functional policies compatible with industry economics; (2) differentiation, where the firm strives to be distinctive across the industry in some aspect of its products or services that is of value to the customer, such as quality or style; (3) focus, where a firm concentrates its efforts at serving a distinctively defined market segment, which may include some combination of a portion of a product line, particular customer segment, limited geogrpahic area, or particular distribution channel. The firm choosing a focus or niche strategy may be able to achieve either or both cost leadership or differentiation; however, it is unable to be the low-cost producer or differentiated across the entire industry.

Each of the three generic strategies involves risks. Cost leadership is vulnerable to imitation by competitors or technology changes (for example, "technological leapfrogging"). Differentiation will not be sustained if the bases for differentiation become less important to buyers or if competitors imitate. A focus strategy is vulnerable to imitation, or the target segment can become unattractive if demand disappears or if broadly targeted competitors overwhelm the segment. Subsequently, Porter changed his generic categories so that strategic advantage could be based on either low cost or differentiation, and be targeted at a broad, industry-wide and/or narrow segment. To Deming, a critical element of both the low cost and differentiation strategies is quality. Improved quality can result in lower costs due to "less rework, fewer mistakes, fewer delays or snags, better use of machine time and materials."[9]

Retrenchment

When a business is in trouble—whether it be the result of such factors as strong, sometimes unexpected competition, technological turbulence, or escalating interest rates—a different set of strategic choices faces the general manager. An attempt can be made to turn the business around, or the business can be immediately divested or liquidated. The business can also be "harvested," which involves optimizing cash flows through such tactics as curtailing all new investments, cutting advertising expenditures, or increasing prices, until the business is sold or liquidated.

The decision of whether to attempt a turnaround depends on the kind of turnaround strategy which is likely to be successful and then whether the firm is willing to bear the risks, devote the resources, and make the management commitment associated with this particular turnaround strategy.

Turnaround strategies can be classified as follows:[10]

1. Efficiency oriented.
    a. Asset reduction (for example, disposal of assets).
    b. Cost cutting (for example, cutbacks in administrative R&D, marketing expenses).
2. Entrepreneurial.
    a. Revenue generation (for example, increase sales by product reintroduction, increased advertising, increased selling effort, lower prices).
    b. Product/market refocusing (for example, shift emphasis into defensible or lucrative niches).

Turnarounds can follow definite stages: (1) change in management, (2) evaluation, (3) emergency, to "stop the bleeding" or "unload," (4) stabilization, emphasizing organization, that is, building, and (5) return-to-normal growth.

Turnarounds are appropriate when an organization:

· Has a clearly distinctive competence, but has failed to meet its objectives and goals consistently over time.

- Is one of the weakest competitors in a given industry.
- Is plagued by inefficiency, low profitability, poor employee morale, and pressure from stockholders to improve performance.
- Has failed to capitalize on external opportunities, minimize external threats, take advantage of internal strengths, and overcome internal weaknesses over time; that is, when the organization's strategic managers have failed (and possibly been replaced by more competent individuals).
- Has grown so large so quickly that major internal reorganization is needed.

Divestiture, that is, selling a division or part of an organization, is appropriate when:

- An organization has pursued a turnaround strategy and it failed to accomplish needed improvements.
- A division needs more resources to be competitive than the company can provide.
- A division is responsible for an organization's overall poor performance.
- A division is a misfit with the rest of an organization; this can result from radically different markets, customers, managers, employees, values, or needs.
- A large amount of cash is needed quickly and cannot be reasonably obtained from other sources.

Liquidation, that is, selling all of a company's assets, in parts, for their tangible worth, is appropriate when:

- An organization has pursued both a turnaround strategy and a divestiture strategy and neither has been successful.
- An organization's only alternative is bankruptcy; liquidation represents an orderly and planned means of obtaining the greatest possible cash for an organization's assets. A company can legally declare bankruptcy first and then liquidate various divisions to raise needed capital.
- The stockholders of a firm can minimize their losses by selling the organization's assets.

Characteristics of Strategic Management Decisions at Different Levels

Strategic decisions have also been categorized by level, with the levels differentiated according to a wide variety of characteristics (see Exhibit 6–4). At least three levels of strategy can be identified: (1) corporate, (2) business, and (3) functional/operating. The characteristics which differentiate these levels vary widely as follows: (1) type of decision, (2) measurability of decision, (3) frequency of decision, (4) adaptability, (5) relation to present activities, (6) risk, (7) profit potential, (8) cost, (9) time horizon, (10) flexibility, (11) cooperation required, (12) applicability, and (13) focus.

EXHIBIT 6–4 Characteristics of Strategic Management Decisions at Different Levels

	Level of Strategy		
Characteristic	*Corporate*	*Business*	*Functional/Operating*
Type of decision	Conceptual	Mixed	Operational
Measurability of decision	Value judgments dominant	Semiquantifiable	Usually quantifiable
Frequency of decision	Periodic or sporadic	Periodic or sporadic	Periodic
Adaptability	Low	Medium	High
Relation to present activities	Innovative	Mixed	Supplementary
Risk	Wide range	Moderate	Low
Profit potential	Large	Medium	Small
Cost	Major	Medium	Modest
Time horizon	Long range	Medium range	Short range
Flexibility	High	Medium	Low
Cooperation required	Considerable	Moderate	Little
Applicability	Multibusiness organizations	All organizations	All organizations
Focus	Which businesses and their interrelationships	How to compete most effectively	Functional and operational business-unit support
Examples	*Choice of business*	*Plant location*	*Inventory levels*

SOURCE: Adapted from John A. Pearce II and Richard B. Robinson, Jr., *Formulation and Implementation of Competitive Strategy,* 2nd ed. (Homewood, Ill.: Richard D. Irwin, 1985), fig. 1–2, p. 10; and Lester A. Digman, *Strategic Management* (Plano, Tex.: Business Publications, Inc. 1986), tab. 1–2, p. 27. Reprinted by permission.

In conclusion, there are many ways to categorize the strategic choices facing a general manager. The general manager's objective is to make choices which are most consistent with three variables: (1) environment, (2) resources, and (3) managerial preferences and values. This process can be extremely challenging, given that the variables to be co-aligned are multifaceted and continually changing.

Notes to Chapter 6

1. Leonard Wrigley, "Divisional Autonomy and Diversification" (doctoral dissertation, Harvard University, 1970).
2. For more details, see J. M. Geringer, Paul W. Beamish, and R. da Costa, "Diversification Strategy and Internationalization: Implications for MNE Performance," *Strategic Management Journal* 10, no. 2 (March/April 1989).

3. See Thomas J. Peters and Robert H. Waterman, *In Search of Excellence* (New York: Harper & Row, 1982).

4. The conditions for the various strategic choices outlined in Exhibit 6–1 and outlined in the integration, cooperation, and retrenchment sections of this chapter have been reprinted by permission from F. R. David, "How Do We Choose among Alternative Growth Strategies?" *Managerial Planning* 33, no. 4 (January–February 1985), pp. 14–17, 22.

5. For more details see Michael E. Porter, "From Competitive Advantage to Corporate Strategy," *Harvard Business Review,* May–June 1987.

6. Ibid., p. 46.

7. For more examples, see Michael E. Porter, *Competitive Advantage: Creating and Sustaining Superior Performance* (New York: Free Press, 1985), chap. 9.

8. See Michael E. Porter, *Competitive Strategy: Techniques for Analyzing Industries and Competitors* (New York: Free Press, 1980), chap 11.

9. See W.E. Deming, *Out of the Crisis* (Cambridge, Mass.: MIT, 1986), p. 31.

10. For a more complete analysis of these turnaround strategies, see Donald C. Hambrick and Steven M. Schecter, "Turnaround Strategies for Mature Industrial-Product Business Units," *Academy of Management Journal,* June 1983, pp. 231–48.

CHAPTER

7 ORGANIZATION DESIGN

Power tends to corrupt, absolute power corrupts absolutely.

Lord Acton

If a general is ignorant of the principle of adaptability, he must not be entrusted with a position of authority. The skillful employer of men will employ the wise man, the brave man, the covetous man, and the stupid man. For the wise man delights in establishing his merit, the brave man likes to show his courage in action, the covetous man is quick at seizing advantages, and the stupid man has no fear of death.

Su Ma Ch'ien (100 B.C.)
The Art of War

An army of sheep led by a lion would defeat an army of lions led by a sheep.

Arab Proverb.

To implement any strategy, certain organizational actions must be taken. In this chapter, we review the major components for the design of organizations.

The major organization design variables significant in implementing strategy are structure, information and decision processes, reward systems, and staffing and leadership style (see Exhibit 7–1).

Structure

Structure can be viewed as "the design of organization through which the enterprise is administered."[1] Structure is more than an organization chart. Here it is viewed as having three elements: division of labour (amount of role differentiation), shape (span of control and number of layers), and distribution of

---

EXHIBIT 7-1 Major Organization Design Variables

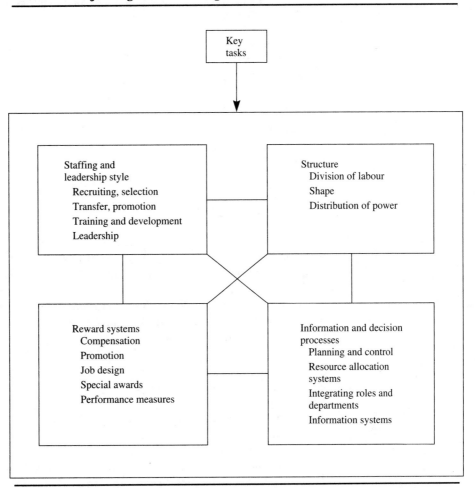

power (both vertical and horizontal, explicit and implicit). One writer commented on organizational structure as follows:

> The best organizations in terms of morale and productivity are those whose structure follows what might be called the natural hierarchy: one-day time-frame workers report to a foreman who can organize at least the next three months; he follows the dictates of a manager who can plan a year or longer; he reports to a general manager with a two-year time frame; he answers to a vice president capable of charting strategy over five years. Atop it all sits a chief executive who can cast his mind forward to encompass the next ten or more years. In common parlance, this ability,

much sought after in executives, is called vision. For a rough handle on where you fit, think about the most distant deadline you feel comfortable with.[2]

Information and Decision Processes

"Across the structure, processes are overlaid to allocate resources and coordinate activities not handled by the department structure."[3] These information and decision processes include planning and control systems (for such things as budgets, schedules, and forecasts), integrating mechanisms (particularly necessary when the task context is one of high interdependence between the functional areas), and information systems (be they computerized, statistical, or informal).

Reward Systems

Perhaps the most easily understood element of organization design is reward systems. Decisions on compensation packages (however they are composed), on promotions (accompanied with any combination of such things as bigger offices, more status, a free parking space, increased holidays, a private secretary, and so forth), on ways of awarding outstanding performance, and on the design of jobs (and who gets the more interesting or high-profile assignments), all can be designed in such a way as to reinforce desired behaviour.

Staffing and Leadership Style

People will make or break most organizations. Getting (recruiting, selecting), grooming (training and developing), and retaining (transfering, promoting) personnel are critical parts of every organization.

A key variable related to people is style. "Managers have personal styles of operation. They come to be identified as entrepreneurial, bureaucratic, hands on, authoritarian, or paternalistic."[4] Since leadership styles are not easily changed, the choice of leader style is made with the choice of individual, and it is important to choose a style that fits the needs of the organization. Yet in some organizations, these style and "people" decisions are not given enough consideration.

Skill development can occur during university and employment. As the Making the Match project identified (see box), the focus of skill development by educators compared to employers often differs.

Probably the greatest failing when organizations are designed is the lack of attempt at achieving consistency between *(a)* the organization design variables themselves and *(b)* those variables and the strategy as formulated. Also, if the strategy changes, all of the design variables may need to be adjusted to maintain the desired consistency and fit.

In 1984 the Corporate-Higher Education Forum commissioned the Making the Match project. It grew out of concerns raised by Canadian employers about the adequacy of university education in relation to the human resources requirements of corporations.

In 1986, Phase II was initiated.

- The objective was to map the skill development process during university and employment within the context of changing organizational structures.

  Where are the skills valued by employers developed? MTM Phase II data confirm the notion that learning is a multi-source life-long process.

- Concrete, practical skills such as problem solving/analytic, technical, written communication, and personal organization/time management are largely developed through university courses and on-the-job experience.

- Softer skills, such as conflict management and interpersonal, are not being developed through university courses to any great degree but rather are developed prior to university or on-the-job.

- Students find extra-curricular activities important in the development of leadership skills, and primary/secondary school important for oral communication.

Source: J. C. Rush, F. T. Evers, Presentation to the Annual Meeting of the Corporate-Higher Education Forum, Halifax, Nova Scotia, 1991.

Specific examples of recommended configurations of strategy and organizational variables that constitute a fit are shown in Exhibit 7–2 for three broad strategies: single or dominant business, related diversified, and unrelated diversified.

How Structure Evolves as Strategy Evolves: The Stages Model[5]

In a number of respects, the strategist's approach to organization building is governed by the size and growth stage of the enterprise, as well as by the key success factors inherent in the organization's business. For instance, the type of organization structure that suits a small specialty steel firm relying upon a concentration strategy in a regional market is not likely to be suitable for a large, vertically integrated steel producer doing business in geographically diverse areas. The organization form that works best in a multiproduct, multitechnology,

---

EXHIBIT 7-2 Strategy-Organization Fit

Strategy	• Dominant business • Vertically integrated	• Unrelated diversified • Growth through acquisition	• Related diversified • Growth through internal development, some acquisition
Strategic focus and task focus	• Degree of integration • Market share • Product line breadth	• Degree of diversity • Types of business • Resource allocation across discrete businesses • Entry and exit businesses	• Realization of synergy from related products, processes, technologies, markets • Resource allocation • Diversification opportunities
Structure and decision-making style	• Centralized functional • Top control of strategic decisions • Delegation of operations through plans and procedures	• Highly decentralized product divisions/profit centers • Small corporate office • No centralized line functions • Almost complete delegation of operations and strategy within existing businesses • Control through results, selection of management, and capital allocation	• Multidivisional/profit centers • Grouping of highly related business with some centralized functions within groups • Delegated responsibility for operations • Shared responsibility for strategy
Information and decision process	• Coordination and integration through structure, rules, planning, and budgeting • Use of integrating roles for project activity across functions	• No integration across businesses • Coordination and information flows between corporate and division levels around management information systems and budgets	• Coordinate and integrate across businesses and between levels with planning, integrating roles, integrating departments
Rewards	• Performance against functional objectives • Mix of objective and subjective performance measures	• Formula-based bonus on ROI or profitability of divisions • Equity rewards • Strict objective, impersonal evaluation	• Bonus based on divisional and corporate profit performance • Mix of objective and subjective performance measures
People and careers	• Primarily functional specialists • Some interfunctional movement to develop some general managers	• Aggressive, independent general managers of divisions • Career development opportunities are primarily intradivisional	• Broad requirements for general managers and integrators • Career developments cross-functional, interdivisional, and corporate-divisional

---

SOURCE: Reprinted by permission from *Strategy Implementation,* 2nd ed., pp. 116–17, by Jay Galbraith and Robert Kazanjian. Copyright © 1986 by West Publishing Company. All rights reserved.

multibusiness corporation pursuing unrelated diversification is, understandably, likely to be different yet again. Recognition of this characteristic has prompted several attempts to formulate a model linking changes in organizational structure to stages in an organization's strategic development.[6]

The underpinning of the stages concept is that enterprises can be arrayed along a continuum running from very simple to very complex organizational forms and that there is a tendency for an organization to move along this continuum toward more complex forms as it grows in size, market coverage, and product-line scope and as the strategic aspects of its customer-technology-business portfolio become more intricate. Four distinct stages of strategy-related organization structure have been singled out.

Stage I. A Stage I organization is essentially a small, single-business enterprise managed by one person. The owner-entrepreneur has close daily contact with employees and each phase of operations. Most employees report directly to the owner, who makes all the pertinent decisions regarding objectives, strategy, daily operations, and so on. As a consequence, the organization's strengths, vulnerabilities, and resources are closely allied with the entrepreneur's personality, management ability and style, and personal financial situation. Not only is a Stage I enterprise an extension of the interests, abilities, and limitations of its owner-entrepreneur but also its activities are typically concentrated in just one line of business. For the most part, Stage I enterprises are organized very simply with nearly all management decisions and functions being performed by the owner-entrepreneur.

Stage II. Stage II organizations differ from Stage I enterprises in one essential respect: An increased scale and scope of operations create a pervasive strategic need for management specialization and force a transition from one-person management to group management. However, a Stage II enterprise, although run by a team of managers with functionally specialized responsibilities, remains fundamentally a single-business operation. This is not to imply, though, that the categories of management specialization are uniform among large, single-business enterprises. In practice, there is wide variation. Some Stage II organizations prefer to divide strategic responsibilities along classic functional lines—marketing, production, finance, personnel, control, engineering, public relations, procurement, planning, and so on. In vertically integrated Stage II companies, the main organization units are sequenced according to the flow from one vertical stage to another. For example, the organizational building blocks of a large oil company usually consist of exploration, drilling, pipelines, refining, wholesale distribution, and retail sales. In a process-oriented Stage II company, the functional units are sequenced in the order of the steps of the production process.

Stage III. Stage III embraces those organizations whose operations, though concentrated in a single field or product line, are large enough and scattered over a wide enough geographical area to justify having *geographically decentralized* operating units. These units all report to corporate headquarters and conform to corporate policies, but they are given the flexibility to tailor their unit's strategic plan to meet the specific needs of each respective geographic area. Ordinarily, each of the semiautonomous operating units of a Stage III organization is structured along functional lines.

The key difference between Stage II and Stage III, however, is that while the functional units of a Stage II organization stand or fall together (in that they are built around one business and one end market), the operating units of a Stage III firm can stand alone (or nearly so) in the sense that the operations in each geographic unit are not rigidly tied to or dependent on those in other areas. Characteristic firms in this category would be breweries, cement companies, and steel mills having production capacity and sales organizations in several geographically separate market areas.

Stage IV.   Stage IV is typified by large, multiproduct, multiunit, multimarket enterprises decentralized by line of business. Their corporate strategies emphasize diversification—related and/or unrelated. As with Stage III companies, the semiautonomous operating units report to a corporate headquarters and conform to certain firm-wide policies, but the divisional units pursue their own respective line-of-business strategies. Typically, each separate business unit is headed by a general manager who has profit-and-loss responsibility and whose authority extends across all of the unit's functional areas except, perhaps, accounting and capital investment (both of which are traditionally subject to corporate approval). Both business-strategy decisions and operating decisions are thus concentrated at the line-of-business level rather than at the corporate level. The organization structure within the line-of-business unit may be along the lines of Stage I, II, or III types of organizations. A characteristic Stage IV company would be Canadian Pacific.

Movement through the Stages.   The stages model provides useful insights into why organization structure tends to change in accordance with product-customer-technology relationships and new directions in corporate strategy. As firms have progressed from small, entrepreneurial enterprises following a basic concentration strategy to more complex strategic phases of volume expansion, vertical integration, geographic expansion, and line-of-business diversification, their organizational structures have evolved from unifunctional to functionally centralized to multidivisional decentralized organizational forms. Firms that remain single-line businesses almost always have some form of a centralized functional structure. Enterprises predominantly in one industry but slightly diversified typically have a hybrid structure; the dominant business is managed via a functional organization, and the diversified activities are handled through a decentralized divisionalized form. The more diversified an organization becomes, irrespective of whether the diversification is along related or unrelated lines, the more it moves toward some form of decentralized business units.

However, it is by no means imperative that organizations begin at Stage I and move in irreversible lockstep sequence toward Stage IV.[7] Some firms have moved from a Stage II organization to a Stage IV form without ever passing through Stage III. And some organizations exhibit characteristics of two or more stages simultaneously. Furthermore, some companies have found it desirable to revert to more centralized forms after decentralizing.

Still, it does appear that as the strategic emphasis shifts from a small, single-product business to large, dominant-product businesses and then on to broad diversification, a firm's organizational structure evolves, in turn, from one-person management to large group functional management to decentralized, line-of-business management. About 90 percent of the Fortune 500 firms (nearly all of which are diversified to one degree or another) have a divisionalized organization structure with the primary basis for decentralization being line-of-business considerations.

Exhibit 7–3 summarizes some of the common organizational changes required in the transition from Stage I to Stage IV.

One final lesson that the stages model teaches is worth iterating. A reassessment of organization structure and authority is always useful whenever strategy is changed.[8] A new strategy is likely to entail new or subtly different skills and key activities. If these changes go unrecognized, especially the subtle ones, the resulting mismatch between strategy and organization can pose implementation problems and curtail performance.

EXHIBIT 7–3 Common Organizational Changes Required in Transitions

	Entrepreneurial Single Business *Stage I*	*to:*	*Professional Single Business* *Stage II*	*to:*	*Professional Multibusiness* *Stages III and IV*
Structure			Move from ill-defined functional specialization to well-articulated functions. Almost total centralization converted to substantial functional responsibility, authority. Integration by entrepreneur gives way to various integrating devices.		Move from functional to product/ market (business unit) specialization. Development of corporate functions to manage business unit portfolio. Delegation of operating and some strategic discretion to units. Integration across units by corporate functions.
Business-decision processes			Move planning and resource allocation from an extension of entrepreneurial preferences to more objective processes. Increasing use of functional (sales, costs to budget) performance criteria		Move planning and resource allocation focus from functional departments to business units. Strategic goals (market share, profits) used to assess and control businesses.
Personnel-decision processes			Move to more systematic procedures and objective criteria for staffing, training, and assessing individual performance. Rewards less subject to personal relationships, paternalism.		Further development of systematic procedures with broadening to emphasize the development of general managers. Rewards variable in relation to business unit performance.
Leadership style			Move from a personally oriented, hands-on domination of operations to a less-obtrusive style emphasizing leadership and integration of functional units relative to strategic needs.		Senior management further distanced from operations. Symbolic and context-setting aspects of style become more critical. Leadership in relation to corporate/business unit strategic needs.

SOURCE: Adapted from J. N. Fry and J. P. Killing, *Strategic Analysis and Action*, 2nd ed. (Scarborough, Ont.: Prentice-Hall Canada, 1989), fig. 10.8, p. 226. Used with permission.

Notes to Chapter 7

1. A. D. Chandler, *Strategy and Structure* (Cambridge, Mass.: MIT Press, 1962), p. 14.
2. *Fortune,* February 4, 1985.
3. Jay R. Galbraith and Robert K. Kazanjian, *Strategy Implementation,* 2nd ed. (St. Paul, Minn.: West Publishing, 1986), p. 114.
4. Joseph N. Fry and J. Peter Killing, *Strategic Analysis and Action* (Scarborough, Ont.: Prentice-Hall Canada, 1986), p. 202.
5. This section has been adapted in part from Arthur A. Thompson, Jr., and A. J. Strickland III, *Strategy Formulation and Implementation,* 3rd ed. (Plano, Tex.: Business Publications, 1986), pp. 330–34.
6. See, for example, Malcolm S. Salter, "Stages of Corporate Development," *Journal of Business Policy,* Spring 1970, pp. 23–27; Donald H. Thain, "Stages of Corporate Development," *Business Quarterly,* Winter 1969, pp. 32–45; Bruce R. Scott, "The Industrial State: Old Myths and New Realities," *Harvard Business Review,* March–April 1973, pp. 133–48; and Chandler, *Strategy and Structure,* chap. 1.
7. For a more thorough discussion of this point, see Salter, "Stages of Corporate Development," pp. 34–35.
8. For an excellent documentation of how a number of well-known corporations revised their organization structures to meet the needs of strategy changes and specific product/market developments, see E. R. Corey and S. H. Star, *Organization Strategy* (Boston: Division of Research, Harvard University Graduate School of Business Administration, 1971), chap. 3.

8 ORGANIZATION FORMS

So much of what we call management consists in making it difficult for people to work.

Peter Drucker

There are essentially four strategy-related approaches to organization: (1) functional specialization, (2) geographic organization, (3) decentralized business/product divisions, and (4) matrix structures featuring *dual* lines of authority and strategic priority. Each form relates structure to strategy in a different way and, consequently, has its own set of strategy-related pros and cons. Each of these forms will now be discussed.

The Functional Organization Structure

A functional organization structure tends to be effective in single-business units where key activities revolve around well-defined skills and areas of specialization. In such cases, in-depth specialization and focused concentration on performing functional area tasks and activities can enhance both operating efficiency and the development of a distinctive competence. Generally speaking, organizing by functional specialties promotes full utilization of the most up-to-date technical skills and helps a business capitalize on the efficiency gains to be had from using specialized personnel, facilities, and equipment. These are strategically important considerations for single-business organizations, dominant-product enterprises, and vertically integrated firms and account for why they usually have some kind of centralized, functionally specialized structure.

However, just what form the functional specialization will take varies according to customer-product-technology considerations. For instance, a technical instruments manufacturer may be organized around research and development, engineering, production, technical services, quality control, marketing, personnel, and finance and accounting. A municipal government may, on the other hand, be departmentalized according to purposeful function—fire, public safety, health services, water and sewer, streets, parks and recreation, and education. A university may divide up its organizational units into academic affairs, student services, alumni relations, athletics, buildings and grounds, institutional services, and budget control. Two types of functional organizational approaches are diagrammed in Exhibit 8–1.

The Achilles' heel of a functional structure is getting and keeping tight strategic coordination across the separated functional units. Functional specialists, partly because of how they are trained and the technical "mystique" of jobs, tend to develop their own mindset and ways of doing things. The more functional specialists differ in their perspectives and their approaches to task accomplishment, the more difficult it becomes to achieve both strategic and operating coordination between them. They neither "talk the same language" nor have an adequate understanding and appreciation for one another's strategic role, problems, and changed circumstances. Each functional group is more interested in its own "empire" and promoting its own strategic interest and importance (despite the lip service given to cooperation and "what's best for the company"). Tunnel vision and empire building in functional departments impose a time-consuming administrative burden on a general manager in terms of resolving cross-functional differences, enforcing joint cooperation, and opening lines of communication. In addition, a purely functional organization tends to be myopic when it comes to promoting entrepreneurial creativity, adapting quickly to major customer-market-technological changes, and pursuing opportunities that go beyond the conventional boundaries of the industry.

Geographic Forms of Organization

Organizing according to geographic areas or territories is a rather common structural form for large-scale enterprises whose strategies need to be tailored to fit the particular needs and features of different geographical areas. As indicated in Exhibit 8–2, geographic organization has its advantages and disadvantages, but the chief reason for its popularity is that, for one reason or another, it promotes improved performance.

In the private sector, a territorial structure is typically utilized by chain store retailers, power companies, cement firms, railroads, airlines, the larger paper-box and carton manufacturers, and large bakeries and dairy products enterprises. In the public sector, such organizations as the Canadian Red Cross and religious groups have adopted territorial structures in order to be directly accessible to geographically dispersed clienteles.

EXHIBIT 8-1 Functional Organizational Structures

A. The building blocks of a "typical" functional organization structure

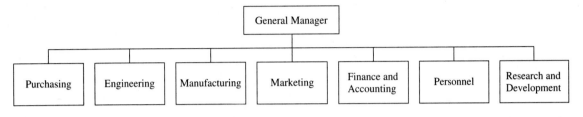

B. The building blocks of a process-oriented functional structure

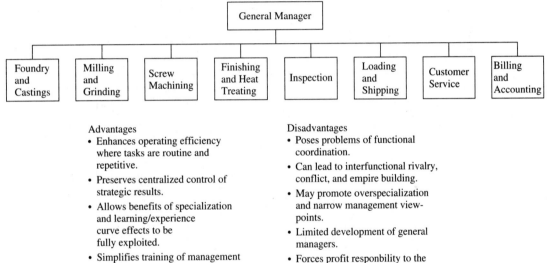

Advantages
- Enhances operating efficiency where tasks are routine and repetitive.
- Preserves centralized control of strategic results.
- Allows benefits of specialization and learning/experience curve effects to be fully exploited.
- Simplifies training of management specialists.
- Promotes high emphasis on craftmanship and professional standards.
- Well suited to developing distinctive competencies in one or more functional areas.
- Structure is tied to key activities within the business.

Disadvantages
- Poses problems of functional coordination.
- Can lead to interfunctional rivalry, conflict, and empire building.
- May promote overspecialization and narrow management viewpoints.
- Limited development of general managers.
- Forces profit responbility to the top.
- Functional specialists often attach more importance to what is best for the functional area than to what is best for the whole business.
- May lead to uneconomically small units or underutilization of specialized facilities and manpower.
- Functional myopia often works against creative entrepreneurship, against adapting to change, and against attempts to restructure the activity-cost chain that threatens the status of one or more functional departments.

EXHIBIT 8–2 A Geographic Organization Structure

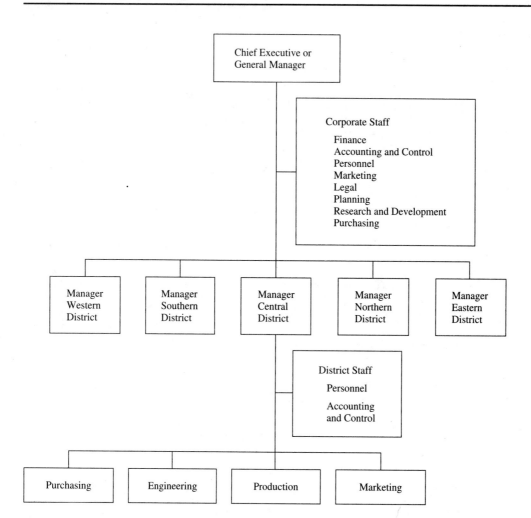

Advantages

- Allows tailoring of strategy to needs of each geographic market.
- Delegates profit/loss responsibility to lowest strategic level.
- Improves functional coordination within the target geographic market.
- Takes advantage of economies of local operations.
- Area units make an excellent training ground to higher level general managers.

Disadvantages

- Greater difficulty in maintaining consistent and uniform companywide practices.
- Requires a larger management staff, especially general managers.
- Leads to duplication of staff services.
- Poses a problem of headquarters control over local operations.

Decentralized Business Units

Grouping activities along business and product lines has been a clear-cut trend among diversified enterprises for the past half century, beginning with the pioneering efforts of Du Pont and General Motors in the 1920s. Separate business/product divisions emerged because diversification made a functionally specialized manager's job incredibly complex. Imagine the problems a manufacturing executive and his or her staff would have if put in charge of, say, 50 different plants using 20 different technologies to produce 30 different products in 8 different businesses/industries. In a multibusiness enterprise, the needs of strategy virtually dictate that the organizational sequence be corporate to line of business to functional area within a business rather than corporate to functional area (aggregated for all businesses). The latter produces a nightmare in making sense out of business strategy and achieving functional area coordination for a given business.

From a business strategy implementation standpoint, it is far more logical to group all the different activities that belong to the same business under one organization roof, thereby creating line-of-business units (which, then, can be subdivided into whatever functional subunits suit the key activities/critical tasks makeup of the business). The outcome not only is a structure that fits strategy but is also a structure that makes the jobs of managers more doable. The creation of separate business units (or strategic business units—SBUs—as they are sometimes called) is then accomplished by decentralizing authority over the unit to the business-level manager. The approach, very simply, is to put entrepreneurially oriented general managers in charge of the business unit, giving them enough authority to formulate and implement the business strategy that they deem appropriate, motivating them with incentives, and then holding them accountable for the results they produce. However, when strong strategic fit exists across related business units, it can be tough to get autonomy-conscious business-unit general managers to cooperate in coordinating and sharing related activities; each GM tends to want to argue long and hard about "turf" and about being held accountable for activities not totally under his or her control.

A typical line-of-business organization structure is shown in Exhibit 8–3, along with the strategy-related pros and cons of this type of organization form.

Matrix Forms of Organization

A matrix form of organization is a structure with two (or more) channels of command, two lines of budget authority, two sources of performance and reward, and so forth. The key feature of the matrix is that product (or business) and functional lines of authority are overlaid (to form a matrix or grid), and mana-

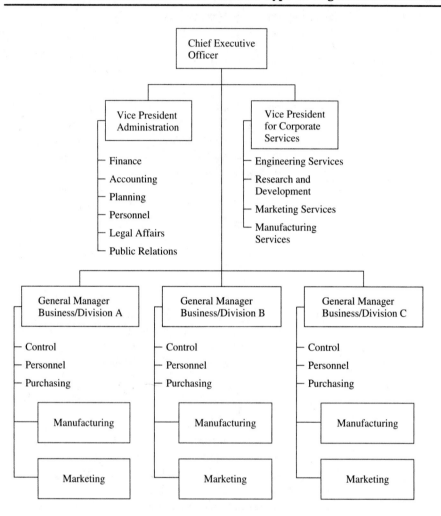

Advantages

- Offers a logical and workable means of decentralizing responsibility and delegating authority in diversified organizations.
- Puts responsibility for business strategy in closer proximity to each business's unique environment.
- Allows critical tasks and specialization to be organized to fit business strategy.
- Frees CEO to handle corporate strategy issues.
- Creates clear profit/loss accountability.

Disadvantages

- Leads to proliferation of staff functions, policy inconsistencies between divisions, and problems of coordination of divisional operations.
- Poses a problem of how much authority to centralize and how much to decentralize.
- May lead to excessive divisional rivalry for corporate resources and attention.
- Raises issue of how to allocate corporate-level overhead.
- Business/division autonomy works against achieving coordination of related activities in different business units thus blocking to some extent the capture of strategic fit benefits.

gerial authority over the activities in each unit/cell of the matrix is shared between the product manager and the functional manager—as shown in Exhibit 8–4. In a matrix structure, subordinates have a continuing dual assignment: to the business/product line/project and to their base function.[1] The outcome is a compromise between functional specialization (engineering, R&D, manufacturing, marketing, accounting) and product line or market segment or line-of-business specialization (where all of the specialized talents needed for the product line/market segment/line of business are assigned to the same divisional unit).

A matrix-type organization is a genuinely different structural form and represents a "new way of life." One reason is that the unit-of-command principle is broken; two reporting channels, two bosses, and shared authority create a new kind of organization climate. In essence, the matrix is a conflict resolution system through which strategic and operating priorities are negotiated, power is shared, and resources are allocated internally on a "strongest case for what is best overall for the unit" type basis.[2]

The impetus for matrix organizations stems from growing use of strategies that add new sources of diversity (products, customer groups, technology, lines of business) to a firm's range of activities. Out of this diversity come product managers, functional managers, geographic-area managers, new-venture managers, and business-level managers—all of whom have important *strategic* responsibilities. When at least two of several variables (product, customer, technology, geography, functional area, and market segment) have roughly equal strategic priorities, then a matrix theoretically can be an effective structural form. A matrix arrangement promotes internal checks and balances among competing viewpoints and perspectives, with separate managers for different dimensions of strategic initiative. A matrix approach thus allows *each* of several strategic considerations to be managed directly and to be formally represented in the organization structure. In this sense, it helps middle managers make trade-off decisions from an organizationwide perspective.[3] Most applications of matrix organization are limited to certain important functions rather than spanning the whole of a large-scale diversified enterprise.

A number of companies shun matrix organization because of its chief weaknesses.[4] It is a complex structure to manage; people often end up confused over to whom to report for what. Moreover, because the matrix signals that everything is important and, further, that everybody needs to communicate with everybody else, a "transactions logjam" can emerge. Actions turn into paralysis, since with shared authority it is hard to move decisively without first considering many points of view and getting clearance from many other people. Sizable transactions costs and communications inefficiency can arise, as well as delays in responding. Even so, there are situations where the benefits of conflict resolution and consensus building outweigh these weaknesses.

EXHIBIT 8-4 A Matrix Organization Structure

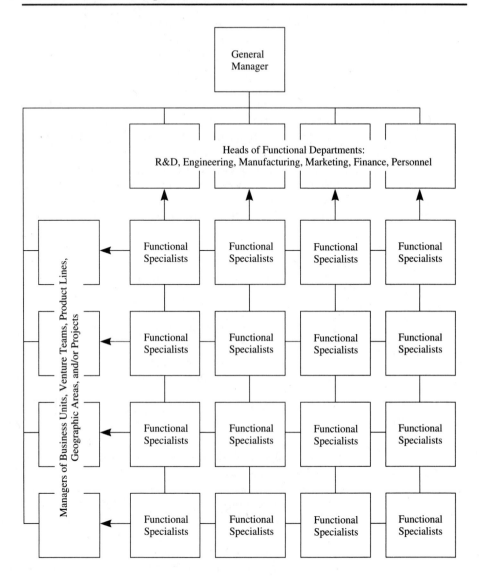

Advantages

- Permits more attention to each dimension of strategic priority.
- Creates checks and balances among competing viewpoints.
- Facilitates simultaneous pursuit of different types of strategic initiative.
- Promotes making trade-off decisions on the basis of "what's best for the organization as a whole."
- Encourages cooperation, consensus-building, conflict resolution, and coordination of related activites.

Disadvantages

- Very complex to manage.
- Hard to maintain "balance" between the two lines of authority.
- So much shared authority can result in a transactions logjam and disproportionate amounts of time being spent on communications.
- It is hard to move quickly and decisively without getting clearance from many other people.
- Promotes an organizational bureaucracy and hamstrings creative entrepreneurship.

Combination and Supplemental Methods of Organization

A single type of structural design is not always sufficient to meet the requirements of strategy. When this occurs, one option is to mix and blend the basic organization forms, matching structure to strategy, requirement by requirement, and unit by unit. Another is to supplement a basic organization design with special-situation devices such as project manager/project staff approaches, task force approaches, or venture teams.

Minicase: Illustration of Structure–Strategy Linkages

The following minicase can be used to assess alternative organizational structures. Suggested discussion questions follow this case.

T. G. Bright and Co., Limited—1986*

In 1977, T. G. Bright and Co., Limited (Brights) of Niagara Falls, Ontario, sold a wide range of wine products in Ontario in eight categories—sparkling, rosé, white table, port, sherry, appetizer, red table, and other (which included such diverse products as Muscatel, Mazel Tov, and sacramental wine). Through wholly owned subsidiaries, Brights also offered additional selections in many of these eight categories in other provinces.

It was a small firm ($14 million in sales) with over half its sales volume in Ontario (see Table 1), most of its manufacturing in Ontario, and a product line which had not digressed from wine. Its 1977 organization is reflected in Exhibit 1.

By 1980, Brights' organization was modified to include a second regional operations manager (see Exhibit 2). A third production facility in Quebec had been acquired in 1979. With this acquisition, the proportion of sales in Quebec—27 percent in 1979—was expected to increase so that Brights would have the largest nongovernment operation in Quebec.

TABLE 1: **Percentage Share of Canadian Wine Market**

	Ontario	*Quebec*	*Rest of Country*
Brights sales	55%	27%	18%
Total Canadian market	34	32	34

---

*This case was prepared by Professor Paul W. Beamish as a basis for classroom discussion. Copyright © 1986 by Paul W. Beamish.

Exhibit 1 1977 Organization

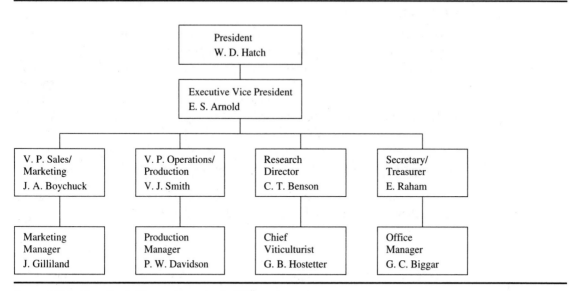

SOURCE: Derived from list of officers and executives in 1977 annual report.

Exhibit 2 1980 Organization

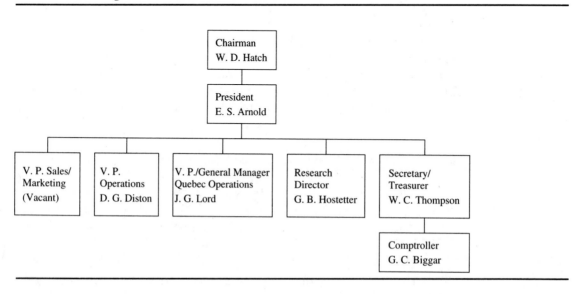

Two other organization changes were made:

1. Hatch became chairman and Arnold became president, with the position of executive vice president dropped.
2. The position of vice president, sales/marketing, had been filled for a few months but of late had been vacant and was being managed by the president.

In late 1980, Brights formed a joint venture with the Inkameep Indian Band of Oliver, British Columbia, to establish a winery in B.C.'s Okanagan Valley. In 1984 and 1985, small winery operations were established in Manitoba and Nova Scotia, respectively. Sales in 1984 were nearly $38 million, net of excise and sales tax.

In 1985 a limited import operation in wines and spirits under the name of Wines of the Globe was established. (In 1984 the Province of Quebec modified its regulations to permit the bottling of imported wines by local wineries.)

Brights' nonrestaurant sales were through provincial government outlets, small grocery stores (in Quebec), and company-owned retail outlets. The company operated over 20 retail outlets in Ontario, with perhaps half being located in Toronto.

In order to keep pace with changing consumer tastes, Brights' product mix had been steadily shifting away from fortified wines to those with lower alcohol levels. In addition, a greater proportion of sales was in white rather than red wines. With the purchase of a Quebec cider company in 1978, Bright acquired the ability and license to produce cider. Brights had also introduced a wine cooler, which combined specially fermented wine and pure spring water.

Grapes were supplied from three sources—company-owned vineyards, purchases from other grape growers, and concentrate and bulk purchases from other countries. Grapes purchased from local growers in Southern Ontario (and, to a lesser extent, the Okanagan region in B.C.) were the primary source of supply.

By 1985, Brights had once again modified its organization structure (see Exhibit 3).

The chairman, W. D. Hatch, died in 1985. The chairman's position was not reflected in the 1985 annual report list of officers and executives. In lieu of a vice president, sales/marketing, a staff director of marketing was appointed to work with the regional vice presidents. The previous vice president/general manager of Quebec Operations had left the company. His replacement held the title of vice president/general manager Eastern Division.

In 1986, W. C. Thompson resigned and G. C. Biggar became secretary. The designation for the three vice president/general managers changed from being in charge of Operations, Quebec Operations, and B. C. Operations to being in charge of the Central Division, Eastern Division, and Western Division, respectively.

Exhibit 3 1985 Organization

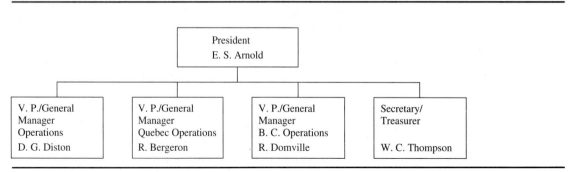

SOURCE: List of officers and executives from 1985 annual report.

Carling O'Keefe Limited, Toronto, Ontario, announced on June 26, 1986, that its wholly owned subsidiary, Jordan & Ste-Michelle Cellars Ltd., had been sold (including substantially all of its assets) to T. G. Bright and Co., Limited.

The purchase price was approximately $30 million. It was estimated that the transaction resulted in a loss to Carling O'Keefe Limited of approximately $7,750,000 after tax, or 36 cents per common share. The business had been unprofitable in 1986.

Jordan & Ste-Michelle Cellars Ltd. had wineries in St. Catharines, Ontario, and Surrey, British Columbia, and, until September 1985, had operated a winery in Calgary, Alberta. Except for 33 company-operated retail stores in Ontario, all sales were made through outlets operated by provincial liquor boards. The company had recently entered into a joint venture to manufacture and distribute cider products for the U.S. market.

At the time of the sale, the gross income for Jordan & Ste-Michelle Cellars Ltd. was almost identical to that of Brights. The acquisition meant that Brights was now the largest winery in Canada by a large margin.

Discussion Questions

1. In 1986, Brights had a regional structure. What alternative forms could it have adopted?
   a. Why, then, did it adopt a regional structure?
   b. How big does a company have to be to justify a regional structure?
2. Why did Brights have a functional structure in 1977, given the arguments for a regional?
3. Why was the position of executive vice president eliminated in 1980? Why was the position of vice president, marketing, kept vacant in 1980/81? Why

was the position of vice president, marketing, ultimately eliminated and replaced with a staff director of marketing?

4. What might occur now that the acquisition has occurred?

Notes to Chapter 8

The text in this chapter has been adapted in part from Arthur A. Thompson, Jr., and A. J. Strickland III, *Strategy Formulation and Implementation,* 3rd ed. (Plano, Tex.: Business Publications, 1986), pp. 334–45.

1. A more thorough treatment of matrix organization forms can be found in Jay R. Galbraith, "Matrix Organizational Designs," *Business Horizons,* February 1971, pp. 29–40.

2. An excellent critique of matrix organizations is presented in Stanley M. Davis and Paul R. Lawrence, "Problems of Matrix Organizations," *Harvard Business Review,* May–June 1978, pp. 131–42.

3. Ibid., p. 132.

4. Thomas J. Peters and Robert H. Waterman, Jr., *In Search of Excellence* (New York: Harper & Row, 1982), pp. 306–7.

9 MANAGING CHANGE

Ability is nothing without opportunity.
Napoleon

Change is not progress.
H. L. Mencken

Organizations must constantly deal with change. Managers wishing to make changes in their organization must often be both effective champions and implementers of the particular change-plan. The ability to commit to a change and see that it is adopted is a highly valued skill. Such a skill may, however, be overvalued, for it neglects important steps in the change process. Such steps both precede and follow the commitment-adoption phase of strategic change.

The Three Phases of Strategic Change

In broad terms, the process of strategic change can be thought of as having three phases. The first phase is awareness and capability building; the second, commitment and adoption; and the third, reinforcement and recycling (see Exhibit 9–1). The most exciting phase for most managers, and certainly the one which receives the greatest emphasis in the popular press, is the second one. Managing this phase well is necessary but not sufficient for overall organizational success.

Phase One: Awareness and Capability Building

The first phase in the strategic change process is awareness and capability building. Without widespread awareness of the need for change, most managers will resist the change. Such a reaction is both understandable and unfortunate.

Exhibit 9-1 Achieving Readiness for and Implanting Strategic Change

Change Target Development	*Potential Obstacles*	*Common Management Tactics*
Awareness understanding:		
Establishing a general appreciation of the need for and direction of change	Ambiguous change requirements	Informal contact, lobbying
	Inertial resistance	Loosening up exercises—target exposure, involvement
	Information bottlenecks	Short-term task forces
Building a greater depth of knowledge of the situation, its consequences and potential remedies	Limited capacity to understand	
Capability:		
Developing capacity to perform new tasks	Personnel bottlenecks—inadequate training and experience	Training programs
		Support systems development
	Support systems bottlenecks	Personnel changes
	Behavioral resistance	Direct coaching
Commitment:		
Developing genuine agreement about and support for the required changes	Displacement of the problem	Involvement activities
	Behavioral resistance	Partial solutions and demonstrations
	Inadequacies, inconsistencies in support and incentive systems	Negotiations
	Weak position of power	Coalition building
		Coercion
		Personnel changes
Adoption:		
Achieving change in behaviour, effective performance	Tangible risk	Close monitoring
	Lagging resistance, support factors	Intensification and recycling of readiness efforts
	Poor readiness	Mop-up action
Reinforcement:		
Sustaining effort and diligence in performing new tasks	Loss of commitment	Rewards for new behavior
	Resource and organizational inconsistencies	Adjustment of resource and organizational factors
Recycling:		
Defining and implementing improvements and new directions	Problems in linking a series of changes	Training and structuring for flexibility
	Complacency	Continuous challenges for improvement

Source: J. N. Fry and J. P. Killing, *Strategic Analysis and Action*, 2nd ed. (Scarborough, Ont.: Prentice-Hall Canada, 1989), figs. 13.5 and 13.6. Reprinted by permission.

Even when there exists wide awareness of the need for change, there may not be a shared view of the appropriate direction of change. For example, everyone may be dissatisfied with the firm's performance and recognize the need for change. But should the solution be to retrench, or to take an aggressive, growth-oriented approach? Developing commitment to a particular change will be extremely difficult if the organization cannot first resolve fundamental questions about the firm's direction.

Assuming that widespread awareness of the need for, and agreement on the direction of, change does exist—and this is a big assumption—management can then proceed with examining whether it has (or can develop) the necessary capabilities to permit the change to take place. Building capabilities through staff or systems development can be a time-consuming and (in the short term) not immediately gratifying process. Nonetheless, it is absolutely essential. Just as a hockey coach needs players who know how to skate and who possess hockey sticks, managers must ensure that the organizational capability for change exists.

Phase Two: Commitment and Adoption

With the proper groundwork laid, the manager-as-change-agent can begin placing greater effort on the development of widespread support and enthusiasm for the proposed change. Organizational champions cannot enact changes themselves, particularly in larger firms. Through negotiations and coalition building they need to get other managers to "sign on," or if this is unsuccessful or too slow, they need to consider such tactics as coercion or personnel changes. As at many points in the strategic change process, resistance may exist.

Having developed wider commitment (and mitigated where possible the principal sources of resistance) attention can then turn to actual adoption of the change. Construction of a facility can begin, people can be hired or moved, money can be spent, people can agree to take on new responsibilities.

What characterizes the commitment and adoption phase is an escalating sense of irrevocability. Decisions are being made and acted upon. In contrast, during the awareness and capability phase—even though some resources were being allocated—management still had the option to change their mind, or slow the process.

Phase Three: Reinforcement and Recycling

Even with the change having been adopted, the change process does not end. Follow-up effort and reinforcement are typically required. It may be a less glamourous phase, but it is no less important. Just as a newly purchased automobile will subsequently require scheduled maintenance, service, and parts, so also does a company change require ongoing attention. This ongoing attention is necessary both to reinforce change and to ensure that the organization keeps pace with changes in the environment. Only through a process of ongoing reassessment can the organization improve overall prospects for success.

Types of Change

One of the most significant influences on the way in which the three phases of the change process are managed is the degree of urgency required. When the impact of urgency on change is considered, we are left with four principal types of change: imperative change, contrived crisis, responsive change, and foreseeable change (see Exhibit 9–2).

Imperative Change

When the necessity for change is urgent, comprehensive action is required, and little slack exists with respect to timing. Action is required now. Imperative change may or may not constitute a crisis. A true crisis would be a situation where the viability of the organization, or a significant portion of it, is in jeopardy. For example, a competitor may have made a significant technological advance which threatens sales or the bank may be demanding immediate repayment.

Organizations may confront many imperative change situations that are not crises. With abrupt changes in legislative or competitive environments, opportunities may present themselves according to a timetable not of the company's making. Or perhaps an attractive acquisition candidate is suddenly available and requires a bid decision now. When such opportunities occur, the company's ability to move quickly will determine its success—or failure.

Contrived Crisis

"Of Boxes, Bubbles, and Effective Management,"[1] details the unique response of a group of Canadian managers to a true crisis. The issue for these managers was not so much one of opportunities, but of surviving. Three years after the crisis—when the crisis was no longer present—their proposed solution to avoid stagnant management was "if there isn't a crisis, we create one."

EXHIBIT 9–2 Pressure for Change

	Type of Change			
	Imperative	*Contrived Crisis*	*Responsive*	*Foreseeable*
Necessity for Change	Pressing	Questionable	Tangible, but not pressing	Forecast
Action Required	Comprehensive	Comprehensive	Diagnostic, plus some clear needs	Uncertain, but diagnostic at a minimum
Timing for Required Change	Immediate	Immediate	Soon	Uncertain
Range of Options Available	Limited	Limited	Mid-level	Wide

The use of a contrived crisis is inherently risky. The nature of crisis manage-ment—whether of a true or contrived crisis—is that rapid action, based on incomplete analysis, is required now. In a contrived crisis, however, the need for change may be questionable, and managerial resistance may develop. As well, the general manager who throws his or her organization into a crisis, and is seen to have contrived it, runs a serious risk of losing credibility. A contrived crisis may help to energize a tired or complacent work force, test the quality of existing management, or "engage an entire organization"[2] toward a particular challenge. The risk is that because events happen so quickly in any crisis, it may not be possible to direct this pool of energy to where it is desired.

Responsive Change

Unlike with imperative change, in a responsive change situation the necessity for change is not as pressing. Action is clearly required, but sufficient time is available to permit the organization to respond to conditions in a more planned fashion. Abrupt realignments of a firm's strategy or organization are not required.

Foreseeable Change

The characteristics of foreseeable change are a forecast need for change but with the required actions and the timing both uncertain. This type of change tends to have the longest term perspective. Here one can identify the need for some sort of change in the future, but without knowing precisely the extent and timing. Not surprisingly it is sometimes more difficult to develop awareness and understand-ing around this type of change.

Given the uncertainty which surrounds it, the method of change tends to be incremental. Managers edge toward their goals with small steps.

There is a view in some circles that change typically results primarily from a long-range planning process—a process in which a presumably omniscient stra-tegic planner lays out precisely what is needed. Omniscience is in short supply in all organizations, and most managers will readily admit their knowledge is finite. Realistically then, change tends to take place in a more incremental fashion.

Most good managers recognize the value of gaining practice with change through small, logical incremental steps rather than major one-time realign-ments. As one writer noted:

> An organization that is used to continuous small changes and that has balanced strategic expertise at the top with operating expertise and entrepreneurship at the bottom is probably better prepared for a big leap than is any organization that has gone for several years without any change at all.[3]

Further, these managers recognize that dealing with change will always create some level of stress in an organization, and too much stress all at once can be fatal. The process of logical incrementalism[4] necessarily contains a large number of steps due to its contingent reinforcing behavioral nature.

EXHIBIT 9-3 Key Stakeholder Perceptions of Type of Change Situation

	Type of Change				
Stakeholder	*No Change*	*Foreseeable*	*Responsive*	*Contrived Crisis*	*Imperative*
A					
B					
C					
D					

The General Manager and Change

The general manager (GM) is the person most responsible for managing change. His or her task is influenced by:

- Experience in the organization and industry.
- Political position in the organization.
- Preferences and values.
- Style.
- Urgency.
- Available resources.

The obvious implication of such a complex list is that key stakeholders may very well hold different perceptions about what type of change situation exists. As Exhibit 9–3 suggests, by plotting an estimate of how each stakeholder may perceive the change situation, it is possible to focus on areas of potential disagreement. The specific type of change which is obvious to you may not be obvious to someone else, and vice versa. Further, others may not perceive the need for any change.

Tactics for Change

The general manager has a variety of tactics available for implementing change. These will depend in part on the level and preference for the use of power, and whether this power can or should be exerted directly or indirectly. Exhibit 9–4 lays out four basic tactics for change—giving orders, changing the context, persuasion, and opening channels. Each has advantages and disadvantages and unique characteristics.

EXHIBIT 9–4 Tactics for Change

High Use of Power

Direct Action: Giving Orders	*Indirect Action: Changing Context*
Characteristics: Forceful, top-down, unambiguous, power based	*Characteristics:* Formal or informal, power driven; if the organization or resources are changed as a means of driving a change in direction or behavior, great attention must be placed on implementation
Pros: Fast Desired direction clear Requires little senior management time *Cons:* Low organization commitment High resistance possible Places heavy reliance on abilities of the GM	*Pros:* Fast (but not as quick as Giving Orders) Useful approach when management power cannot be used directly on principal targets *Cons:* High resistance possible Risky since action is indirect but power driven Timing important

Lower Use of Power

Direct Action: Persuasion	*Indirect Action: Opening Channels*
Characteristics: Less formal; time-intensive, participative, negotiated; may require information to "educate" the employees and/or to permit employees to see that change is in their self-interest	*Characteristics:* Subtle, evolutionary, informal; slower; consensus oriented
Pros: Higher organization commitment likely Greater motivation *Cons:* Slower implementation Requires a lot of GM time for communications May require compromise	*Pros*: High commitment likely Draws ideas from maximum number of people *Cons:* Very slow implementation Requires a GM with foresight, patience, tolerance for ambiguity Will require compromise

---

Giving Orders

This approach is characterized by the forceful, top-down unambiguous issuance of orders. It has the advantage of being fast, and requiring little senior management time. However, low organization commitment and high resistance may result from such an approach. As well, it places heavy reliance on the abilities of the GM to have correctly surmised what change is needed. Not surprisingly, "giving orders" is a tactic frequently observed in an imperative change situation.

Persuasion

Persuasion is a less formal and more time-intensive tactic than "giving orders." It involves negotiation and is more participative in nature. It is a tactic employed by GMs who either do not have a great deal of power, or prefer not to use it. In order to persuade, additional information may have to be collected in order to educate the target group on the advantages of the change. If the target groups or individuals see the change as being in their self-interest, greater motivation and commitment will result. The problems associated with this change tactic are that it may require a lot of GM time, is much slower than giving orders, and may require more compromise.

Opening Channels

The most subtle of the tactics for change has been called "opening channels." It is characterized by a low use of power and by indirect actions. It is slow, informal, consensus oriented, and takes an evolutionary approach. The objective is to open the channels of communication and interaction in such a way that employees are guided in a particular general direction. The task of the GM is to put in place the conditions (through resource means such as task forces and training programs) that will enable the organization to more openly consider a particular change.

Realistically, the GM will be unable to exert a great deal of control or precision over the pace at which the change occurs. This is not typically a problem, however, since here the GM has a longer-term focus. Not surprisingly, this tactic for change is often associated with foreseeable change.

The principal benefits of opening channels are that high commitment is likely, and input will be received from the maximum number of people. It has the disadvantages of being slow and requiring a GM with foresight, patience, tolerance for ambiguity, and a willingness to compromise.

Changing Context

Changing context as a tactic for implementing change is characterized by high use of power and by indirect action. Changing the organization and/or resources are the principal methods employed. Some of the advantages of this tactic are that it is fast (but not as fast as giving orders) and useful when management power cannot be exerted directly on the change target. For example, a GM wishing to make an important acquisition may wish to make the acquisition with the support of senior management. While he has wide support, he faces some resistance, particularly from one key head office manager who would likely be involved if the acquisition was made. One organizational solution would be to transfer the resisting manager to an unrelated or distant division. *Then,* the acquisition can proceed with support of management. The GM exerts his or her power by moving the resisting manager, and by this indirect action achieves the GM's acquisition objective. While moving a manager is a direct action, this tactic is considered indirect because it was not strictly a requirement of achieving the principal change—the acquisition. The organization context was changed so as to facilitate achievement of the prime change.

There are inherent risks to this tactic for change. Changing context may not eliminate all the intended resistance, and may create new sources of resistance. Consequently, the GM must give great attention to implementation and timing issues.

Conclusion

This chapter has provided an introduction to managing change. The process of a strategic change has three phases: awareness and capability building, commitment and adoption, and reinforcement and recycling. As Exhibit 9–1 noted, there are potential obstacles and common management tactics for each phase.

A significant influence on how the change process is managed is the degree of urgency required. In this context there are four main types of change: imperative change, contrived crisis, responsive change, and foreseeable change.

A strategy has not been implemented until the target behavior has changed. In most instances, the task of installing the new strategy and seeing that the behaviour of people in the organization changes is a formidable one for the GM. Yet with creativity and determination it is possible.

The tactics available for implementing change will depend in part on the GM's status and degree of preference for the use of power, and on whether or not this power should be applied directly. Exhibit 9–4 noted four basic tactics for achieving change: giving orders, persuasion, opening channels, and changing the context.

Notes to Chapter 9

1. David K. Hurst "Of Boxes, Bubbles and Effective Management," *Harvard Business Review*, May–June 1984.
2. Gary Hamel and C. K. Prahalad, "Strategic Intent," *Harvard Business Review*, May–June 1989, p. 67.
3. Robert A. Hayes, "Strategic Planning—Forward in Reverse?" *Harvard Business Review*, November–December 1985, p. 117.
4. For further discussion, see James Brian Quinn, *Strategies for Change: Logical Incrementalism* (Homewood, Ill.: Richard D. Irwin, 1980).

II READINGS

Reading 1
A Manager's Guide for Evaluating Competitive Analysis Techniques

John Prescott and John Grant

Virtually all managers acknowledge the importance of understanding their industries and their competitors. As a result, interest has grown rapidly in the use of various competitive analysis techniques to help formulate and implement strategy. However, managers who want to conduct competitive analyses are faced with perplexing choices among a wide variety of techniques with different strengths and weaknesses, an abundance of internal and external data sources, an array of computer software packages, and constraints in terms of time, money, information, and personnel. Many managers are asking, "Where do I start?"

The efficient selection of appropriate techniques for a particular situation depends on a three-phase process of awareness and choice. First, what relevant techniques are available and how do they relate to one another? Second, what is the focus and scope of the competitive arena of interest? Third, what constraints on time and other resources limit the extent of analyses that can be undertaken? Our extensive review of the literature and of applications in several industries can help managers and analysts complete these three phases effectively.

Utilization Profiles

In order to assist managers to select and apply competitive analysis techniques, we developed a reference guide consisting in part of profiles describing various competitive analysis techniques (Exhibit 1). These profiles can assist managers in several ways. We chose a broad array of techniques to illustrate the increasing variety of analytical options available. The key characteristics of each technique have been highlighted along with their typical advantages and limitations. This should help managers to identify the techniques best suited to their situations. Few competitive analyses can be successfully completed using a single technique; the guide can help managers to choose the combination of techniques that will address the issue most effectively and efficiently. We provide references that present additional operational details for each technique.

SOURCE: "A Manager's Guide for Evaluating Competitive Analysis Techniques." *Interfaces* 18, no. 3 (May–June 1988). Copyright © 1988, The Institute of Management Sciences, 290 Westminster Street, Providence, Rhode Island, 02903, USA. Reprinted by permission of John Prescott and John Grant.

Exhibit 1: Utilization Profiles of Competitive Analysis Techniques

Twenty-one techniques are evaluated along 11 important dimensions. To use the table, locate the technique and evaluative dimension of interest. In the row and column intersection (cell), our assessment of a technique's characteristics as they apply to the dimension will be summarized.

| Techniques | Resource Needs | | | | Data Needs | | |
| | Time | | | | | | |
	Development	Execution	Costs	Managerial Skills	Sources	Availability	Timeliness
(1) Political and country risk analysis	Long	Long	High	Conceptual Analytical Diagnostic	Literature search Informants Personal interviews	From analysis	Historical Current
(2) Industry scenarios	Long	Long	High	Conceptual Analytical Diagnostic	Focus groups Literature search Personal interviews	Customized	Future
(3) Economists' model of industry attractive-ness	Moderate	Long	Medium	Technical Conceptual Diagnostic	Case study Personal interviews Literature search	Off-the-shelf but basically derived from analysis	Current
(4) BCG industry matrix	Short	Moderate	Medium	Technical Conceptual Diagnostic	Literature search Personal interviews	From analysis	Current
(5) Industry segmentation	Moderate	Moderate	Medium	Conceptual Diagnostic Analytical	Case study Personal interviews Literature search	From analysis	Current
(6) PIMS	Moderate	Short	Medium	Technical Analytical	Data bases	Off-the-shelf	Current

The techniques are arranged in descending order from a broad industry level to a narrower functional level. Multiple entries for the managerial skills and sources and evaluative dimensions are in descending order of importance and priority, respectively.

Accuracy Constraints	Updating Requirements		Advantages	Limitations	References
	Frequency	Difficulty			
Availability	Periodic	Reanalyze	Understand other cultures or political positions and potential problem areas	Often evaluated using own norms Language problems Data often difficult to evaluate and can change rapidly if power positions change	Desta [1985] Hofer and Haller [1980]
Assumption of sources	Ad hoc	Reconceptualize	Sensitize management to the need to adapt to industry evolution	Based upon assumptions subject to change Costs	Wack [1985a, b] Porter [1985]
Managerial skills	Ad hoc	Reconceptualize	Structured approach to examining industries Identifies competitors Basis for other in-depth analysis	Basic assumption that economic structure of industry is root of competition Drawing of industry boundaries	Porter [1980]
Managerial skills	Ad hoc	Reanalysis	Primarily a diagnostic tool for identifying profitable industry segments	Needs to be used in conjunction with other techniques such as industry analysis and CSFs	Pekar [1982]
Conceptual skills	Ad hoc	Reanalysis	Identifies pockets of opportunity Identifies pockets of future profits or areas under attack	Choosing segmentation dimensions Piecemeal approach to competition	Bonoma and Shapiro [1983] Porter [1985]
Representativeness of businesses in data base	Periodic	Repetitive	Flexibility of use Variety of operations	Lack of organizational variables	Wagner [1984] Schoeffler, Buzzell, and Heaney [1974] Ramanujam and Venkatraman [1984]

EXHIBIT 1 *(continued)*

Dimensions / Techniques	Resource Needs				Data Needs		
	Time		Costs	Managerial Skills	Sources	Availability	Timeliness
	Development	Execution					
(7) Technological assessment	Long	Long	High	Technical Conceptual Analytical	Direct observation Participant observation Data bases Documents	From analysis Sometimes Customized	Future
(8) Multipoint competition	Short	Moderate	Low to Medium	Conceptual Diagnostic	Literature search Personal interviews	From analysis	Current
(9) Critical success factors	Short	Moderate	Medium	Conceptual Diagnostic Analytical	Literature search Case study	From analysis	Current
(10) Strategic group analysis	Moderate	Short	Low	Conceptual Diagnostic	Literature search Personal interviews Case study	From analysis	Current
(11) Value-chain analysis and field maps	Short	Long	High	Technical Diagnostic	Case study Personal interviews Literature search	Customized	Current
(12) Experience curve	Short	Moderate	Medium	Technical Diagnostic	Documents Personal interviews Direct observation	From analysis	Current
(13) Stakeholder analysis and assumption surfacing and testing	Short	Moderate to High	Medium	Conceptual Diagnostic Analytical	Personal interviews Focus groups Literature search	Customized	Past Current
(14) Market signaling	Moderate to Long	Continuous	Low	Conceptual Diagnostic Analytical	Documents Personal interviews Direct observation	From analysis	Future

Accuracy Constraints	Updating Requirements		Advantages	Limitations	References
	Frequency	Difficulty			
Financial support	Continuous	Reconceptualize	Keep abreast of key technological drivers	Expensive, continuous, difficult process	Petrov [1982] Hayes and Wheelwright [1979a, b]
Sources	Ad hoc	Reanalysis	Identifies areas where a competitor may retaliate (vice versa)	Typically ignores motives, skills, etc., of competitor	Karnani and Wernerfelt [1985]
Managerial skills	Periodic	Reanalysis	Fast, inexpensive method for focusing efforts	Often is superficial	Rockart [1979] Leidecker and Bruno [1984]
Managerial skills	Periodic	Reanalyze	Fast, cheap, easy way to understand key competitors	Superficial; ignores firms outside industry	McGee and Thomas [1986] Porter [1980]
Sources	Ad hoc	Reanalyze	Best techniques for understanding operating details of a competitor or one's self	Data often difficult to obtain Slow, expensive	Kaiser [1984] Porter [1985]
Sources	Ad hoc	Repetitive	Provides an understanding of cost and thus pricing dynamics Gives a picture of whether to compete on basis of costs	Based upon history which may not carry through to future	Hall and Howell [1985] Hax and Majluf [1984]
Managerial skills	Periodic	Reanalyze	Introspection Attempts to get at underlying causes of behavior	Subject to misinterpretation	Freeman [1984] Rowe, Mason, and Dickel [1985]
Managerial skills	Continuous	Reconceptualize	Early warning indicator	Misinterpretation Get off on the wrong direction	Porter [1980]

EXHIBIT 1 (*concluded*)

Dimensions / Techniques	Resource Needs				Data Needs		
	Time						
	Development	*Execution*	*Costs*	*Managerial Skills*	*Sources*	*Availability*	*Timeliness*
(15) Portfolio analysis	Moderate	Short	Low	Technical	Literature search Case study Personal interviews	From analysis	Current
(16) Strength and weakness analysis	Short	Long	High	Interpersonal Technical Diagnostic	Personal interviews Direct observation Case study	Customized	Current
(17) Synergy analysis	Moderate	Long	High	Technical Diagnostic Conceptual	Documents Case study Personal interviews	Customized	Current
(18) Financial statement analysis	Short	Short	Low	Technical Analytical	Documents Historical records Data bases	Off-the-shelf From analysis	Historical
(19) Value-based planning	Long	Moderate to Long	Medium	Technical	Historical records Data bases	From analysis	Historical
(20) Management profiles	Short	Short	Low	Interpersonal Technical	Personal interviews Informants Documents	From analysis	Current
(21) Reverse engineering	Short	Varies	Varies	Technical	Product purchasing	Off-the-shelf	Current

Accuracy Constraints	Updating Requirements		Advantages	Limitations	References
	Frequency	Difficulty			
Sources	Periodic	Reanalyze	Visual summary Requires managers to think systematically about industry and competitive position Heuristic method of decision making	Superficial Assumes cash flow/ profit drives decision	Hax and Majluf [1984] Grant and King [1982]
Sources	Ad hoc	Reanalyze	Provides in-depth understanding of entire business's capabilities Provides feedback for remedial action	Costly; long; cooperation of personnel essential Hierarchical position of manager influences perception	Stevenson [1985, 1976]
Sources	Ad hoc	Reanalyze	Shows cost or differentiation advantage as a result of sharing—staying power, exit decisions, response times	Data difficulties Time-consuming	Porter [1985]
Sources	Periodic	Repetitive	Fast, easy, cheap handle on financial picture	Data problems Usually limited to public corporations	Hax and Majluf [1984] Hofer and Schendel [1978]
Sources	Periodic	Repetitive	Simplicity—ability to compare alternatives and competitors	Basic assumption that maximizing stock price is primary goal Difficult to implement for individual business units of multidivision company (private firm)	Reimann [1986] Kaiser [1984] Fruhan [1979]
Recency of sources	Continuous	Repetitive	Development of management profiles and manpower (succession) charts Managers do not always act in a rational manner	Past is good predictor of future	Ball [1987]
Managerial skills	Ad hoc	Reanalyze	Best way to understand a competitor's product characteristics and costs	Can be time-consuming May not be critical success factor	—

Competitive Analysis Techniques

The utilization profiles array a diverse set of 21 techniques and evaluate them along 11 important dimensions. The techniques described below are sequenced beginning with broad industry-level techniques and moving to narrower functional area techniques. However, most of the techniques are applicable at either the corporate or the business-unit level. Detailed descriptions of the techniques can be found in Hax and Majluf [1984], Grant and King [1982], Porter [1980], and Prescott [1987].

Political and country risk analysis assesses the types (asset, operational, profitability, personnel) and extent of risks from operating in foreign countries.

Industry scenarios develop detailed, internally consistent descriptions of what various future structures of the industry may be like.

The economists' model of industry attractiveness analyzes the five basic forces (bargaining power of suppliers and customers, threat of substitute products, threat of entry, and industry rivalry) driving industry competition.

BCG industry matrix identifies the attractiveness of an industry based on the number of potential sources for achieving a competitive advantage and the size of the advantage that a leading business can achieve.

Industry segmentation identifies discrete pockets of competition within an industry. The bases of segment identification are often product variety, buyer characteristics, channels of distribution, and geography.

PIMS is an ongoing data base of the Strategic Planning Institute which collects data describing business units' operating activities, their industries and competitors, their products and customers. The purpose is to assist planning efforts of the participating businesses.

A technological assessment develops an understanding of the technological relationships and changes occurring in an industry.

Multipoint competition analysis explores the implications of a situation in which diversified firms compete against each other in several markets.

Critical success factor analysis identifies the few areas in which a business must do adequately in order to be successful.

A strategic group analysis identifies groups of businesses which follow similar strategies, have similar administrative systems, and tend to be affected by and respond to competitive moves and external events in similar ways.

A value chain analysis and field maps identify the costs, operating characteristics, and interrelationships of a business's primary activities (that is, inbound logistics, operations, outbound logistics, marketing and sales, service) and supporting activities (that is, firm infrastructure, human resource management, technological development, procurement).

Experience curves show that the costs of producing a product (service) decrease in a regular manner as the experience of producing it increases. The decrease in costs occurs over the total life of a product.

Stakeholder analysis and assumption surfacing and testing identify and examine any individual or group goals that affect or are affected by the realization of the businesses' goals.

Market signaling is any action by a competitor that provides a direct or indirect indication of its intentions, motives, goals, or internal situation.

Portfolio analysis locates a corporation's businesses along dimensions of industry attractiveness and competitive position to help managers to make resource allocation decisions and to evaluate future cash flows and profitability potential.

Strengths and weaknesses analysis identifies advantages and deficiencies in resources, skills, and capabilities for a business relative to its competitors.

Synergy analysis examines tangible (raw material, production, distribution) and intangible (management know-how, reputation) benefits of shared activities among business units.

Financial statement analysis assesses both the short-term health and long-term financial resources of a firm.

Value-based planning evaluates strategies and strategic moves in light of their probable stock market effects and financing implications. (It does not refer to managerial values in our usage.)

Management profiles examine the goals, backgrounds, and personalities of the individuals making strategic decisions in a competing firm or institution.

Reverse engineering is purchasing and dismantling a competitor's product to identify how it was designed and constructed so that costs and quality can be estimated.

Dimension Descriptions

For each of the 11 dimensions developed to evaluate the techniques, we selected criteria to enhance its meaningfulness. The criteria reflect our experience and understanding of what considerations are important for evaluating a particular technique. While firms often use external consultants for some aspects of competitive analysis, we assume that internal personnel will be conducting all phases of the analyses.

Time: The time required to implement a technique can be separated into development and execution phases. The developmental phase involves specifying objectives and determining any initial constraints that will be imposed on the project. The execution phase involves the collection of data, analysis, and dissemination of the findings to the appropriate individuals.

Financial Resources: The financial resources required to conduct an analysis with a given technique can be categorized as low (under \$10,000), medium (\$10,000 to \$50,000), or high (over \$50,000).

Managerial Skills: To complete an assignment a manager may need a number of specific skills; these may be classed in five groups: technical, interpersonal, conceptual, diagnostic, and analytic. Technical skills are those necessary to accomplish specialized activities. Interpersonal skills involve the ability to communicate with, understand, and motivate both individuals and groups. Conceptual skills are the abilities of a manager to think in the abstract and understand cause-and-effect relationships. Diagnostic skills allow a manager to study the symptoms of a problem and determine the underlying causes. Analytical skills involve the ability to identify the key variables in a situation, understand their interrelationships, and decide which should receive the most attention.

Sources: Sources are persons, products, written materials, anything from which information is obtained. Sources are of two primary types, "learning-curve" and "target" [Washington Researchers, 1983]. Learning-curve sources are those that provide general rather than specific knowledge; they are used when time is not critical and to prepare for a target source. For example, industry studies and books are typical learning-curve sources. Target sources, on the other hand, contain specific information and provide the greatest volume of pertinent information in the shortest period of time. Trade associations, company and competitor personnel are typical target sources. They are often one-shot sources that cannot be used repetitively.

The sites from which one obtains information can be classified as either "field" or "library." By combining the sources and sites of information, we developed a typology of data collection techniques. Exhibit 2 contains 15 data collection techniques that can be used for competitive analysis assignments [Miller, 1983]. For each, we have recommended the most appropriate sources. If a particular technique presents problems in availability or application, then nearby techniques in the exhibit should be considered. For example, if product purchasing is desired but is too expensive or unavailable, then direct observation or a literature search should be used.

Availability: While data can be obtained for almost any project for a price, the ease with which one can secure data can be classified. Three categories we have found useful are "off-the-shelf," "derived from analysis," and "customized." Off-the-shelf refers to data in the form the manager needs. If the essential raw data are available but require some analyses to put them in the desired form, then we classify the availability as "derived from analysis." When the information for a study must be developed, we call it "customized."

Timeliness: Data, analysis, and implications that deal primarily with the past are historical; those that address the present or future, we call current or future.

Accuracy Constraints: The value of a particular technique is limited by the quality of the resources and validity of the data used. Using the above dimensions, we identified the key constraint that would potentially hinder the usefulness of the given technique. This dimension is analogous to a warning label for the user.

EXHIBIT 2   A Typology of Data Collection Techniques

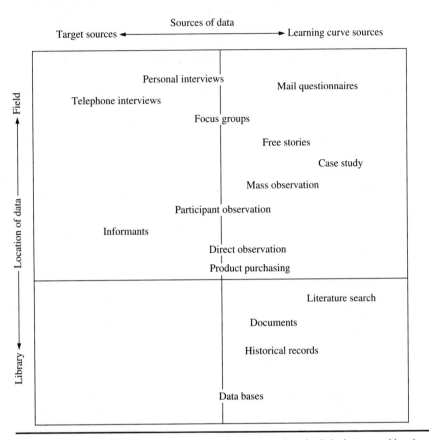

NOTE: The exhibit shows the options available for collecting data, given the desired source and location. A source of data can either provide specific target information or general learning-curve information. The location of the data can reside in a field setting or in a library.

Updating Requirements: Competitive analyses are seldom one-time phenomena. In order to understand the updating requirements for each technique, two useful dimensions are "frequency" and "difficulty." The frequency dimension can be divided into ad hoc (when the need arises), periodic (according to an established schedule), and continuous.

The difficulty dimension addresses the extent and nature of skills that may be required during an update. If the same analysis can be performed again with no modifications, then we have labeled it repetitive. If modifications must be made because the format or content of the information has changed, we describe it as reanalysis. If the assumptions of the analysis need to be challenged or changed, then the updating requires a reconceptualization.

Advantages and Limitations: The final two dimensions summarize the major advantages and limitations of the technique. While these assessments are implicit once the preceding criteria have been applied to a specific analytical assignment, they are intended to underscore special considerations. Examples of advantages could be insight into cultural constraints or an industry's evolution; whereas limitations could be communications difficulties or conflicting assumptions, either of which may lead to misunderstandings.

References: The publications chosen are from a much broader list of strategic management references. We based our choice on their availability, managerial orientation, and relative recency. Most contain bibliographies that further extend the resources.

While these evaluation dimensions vary in importance across competitive analysis assignments, recognizing them can greatly facilitate choices when groups of managers and analysts are working together.

Selecting and Using the Techniques

The transition from a description of techniques to their selection for application is best conveyed by an actual example.

The competitive environment of an electric utility company has recently been undergoing significant changes. A great many industrial customers, the utility's "bread-and-butter," have been closing or reducing operations. Other industrial and commercial customers have been threatening partial backward integration into cogeneration systems. Residential customers have been voicing concerns before the public utility board because they pay some of the highest rates in the country. Because of potentially low returns and increasingly high risks, the investment community seems less willing to finance the large capital expenditures necessary in this industry. The utility's geographic service area, vigorously engaged in attracting new businesses, is looking for high-technology and service businesses, which typically consume modest amounts of electricity.

To further complicate its competitive problems, a variety of governmental bodies is openly discussing the benefits of deregulation. Since electricity can be distributed cheaply over wide geographical areas, the need to restrict the boundaries of each utility is being questioned. Deregulation, some argue, would benefit consumers by allowing them to choose among a wider set of competitors.

The managers in the company are faced with an internal situation of severe financial constraints, top management's desire to take immediate corrective action, and a lack of skills in formal strategic planning. The newly hired planners charged with addressing the above issues need a method for organizing their competitive analysis efforts. They must choose techniques for understanding their industry and competitors.

Selecting Techniques

Many competitive analysis assignments begin when top executives become dissatisfied with their firm's prevailing emphasis and understanding of the competitive environment. This was the case in the electrical utility company described above. Management initiated a series of meetings which focused on the strategic planning efforts at the firm. One of the outcomes was an assignment to conduct an analysis of the industry and competitors. The planners, facing the constraints of a limited budget, perceived urgency, and after a series of meetings, an inexperienced support staff decided to focus on two fundamental issues: first, to understand the contemporary dynamics of the broadly defined electrical utility industry; second, to address the strategic position of the firm relative to its key existing and potential competitors. The managers needed to identify those competitive analysis techniques that would best answer their questions within their existing constraints. The outcome is shown in Exhibit 3.

Exhibit 3 also illustrates several important aspects of the process of initiating a competitive analysis assignment. Even the most basic assignments, like those described in the table, present the manager with a variety of choices. The firm in this case concentrated its efforts on basic analyses that would lay the foundation for later in-depth studies. As a result, several possible alternatives were rejected because they were too costly, time-consuming, complicated, or not relevant to the circumstances at that time. For example, industry scenarios were deferred for two interrelated reasons. The team needed to understand the industry better before it could address more sophisticated issues. Second, developing industry scenarios would have been too costly and time-consuming. Techniques, such as political and country risk analysis, multipoint competition, synergy analysis, and market signaling were viewed as not relevant to the immediate issues. The competitive analysis team examined each of the 21 techniques and chose those which best suited the assignment and the constraints imposed on the project.

The team applied three interrelated techniques in order to better understand the industry. First, the economists' model of industry attractiveness provided a comprehensive picture of the industry. It revealed that competition should be viewed from both a regional and a national perspective. Further, deregulation (a concern of top management) was not likely to occur for another three to five years, and then the transmission systems of electrical utilities would be the first area to be deregulated. Finally, while the bargaining power of

EXHIBIT 3   A Competitive Analysis at an Electrical Utility Company

	Techniques	
Needs	*Chosen*	*Rejected/Deferred*
To understand the dynamics of the industry	Economists' model of industry attractiveness Strategic group analysis Critical success factors	Industry scenarios Industry segmentation Stakeholder analysis
To identify its strategic position relative to its key competitors	Financial analysis Management profiles Strengths and weaknesses analysis	Value-based planning Value-chain analysis

electrical utilities is not strong, their profitability was expected to increase over the next five years due in part to a construction cycle coming to an end.

Second, using the industry analysis as a foundation, strategic group analysis identified those key competitors important in identifying the firm's relative position. Strategic groups were developed on a national level using publicly available operating and financial data for a set of about 70 firms. On a regional level, a group of eight electrical and gas utility firms were selected, which were either in the firm's transmission grid or which competed in their geographical territory.

Third, critical success factors were identified at two levels. During the industry analysis, CSFs were identified for the industry as a whole. Then CSFs were identified for the strategic groups. The layering or combining of techniques within an analysis allows managers to address multiple aspects of a question.

Having narrowed the field of competitors to a manageable number through the strategic group analysis, the team turned to the second issue. It sought to build profiles of the competitors to depict the relative positions of the firms. The choices were to conduct a financial analysis of the firms, to examine their management teams' profiles, and to analyze their strengths and weaknesses. These methods were chosen because the data were easily available, the time for the analysis was relatively short, and the result would be a set of reports that other managers in the firm could use easily. This last point was very important. Since most managers were not really convinced that it was necessary to consider the competition, the competitive analysis team felt it extremely important to choose those techniques that were understood by virtually all managers. When the managers saw the usefulness of these analyses, the team would then move to other analyses that were less familiar but which could provide additional intelligence. Most of the techniques rejected or deferred (Exhibit 3) fit in this category.

From this example, it is clear that even seemingly simple competitive analysis assignments pose important issues and questions. In this case, questions concerning the relative position of the firm could not be tackled until the managers understood the industry as a competitive arena. This new perspective on the environment required customer feedback, technical appraisals, and regulatory understanding.

The assignment in this case took approximately three months to complete, with approximately one-third of the time being spent on the developmental aspects of the study.

Conclusions

Growing competitiveness in many markets and along many combinations of dimensions is increasing the complexity of competitive analysis problems facing managers. Our descriptions of techniques, evaluation dimensions, and information types should provide managers with helpful guidance in making competitive analyses.

References

Ball, Richard. 1987, "Assessing your competitor's people and organization," *Long-Range Planning*, vol. 20, no. 2, pp. 32–41.

Bonoma, Thomas V., and Shapiro, Bensen P. 1983, *Segmenting the Industrial Market*, Lexington Books, Lexington, Massachusetts.

Desta, Asayehgn. 1985, "Assessing political risk in less developed countries," *Journal of Business Strategy*, vol. 5, no. 4, pp. 40–53.

Freeman, R. Edward. 1984, *Strategic Management: A Stakeholder Approach*, Pitman Publishing Company, Boston, Massachusetts.

Fruhan, William E., Jr. 1979, *Financial Strategy: Studies in the Creation, Transfer and Destruction of Shareholder Value*, Richard D. Irwin, Homewood, Illinois.

Grant, John H., and King, William R. 1982, *The Logic of Strategic Planning*, Little, Brown, Boston, Massachusetts.

Hall, Graham, and Howell, Sydney. 1985, "The experience curve from the economist's perspective," *Strategic Management Journal*, vol. 6, no. 2, pp. 197–212.

Hax, Arnoldo C., and Majluf, Nicolas S. 1984, *Strategic Management: An Integrative Perspective*, Prentice Hall, Englewood Cliffs, New Jersey.

Hayes, Robert H., and Wheelwright, Steven C. 1979a, "The dynamics of process-product life cycles," *Harvard Business Review*, vol. 57, no. 2 (March–April), pp. 127–36.

Hayes, Robert H., and Wheelwright, Steven C. 1979b, "Link manufacturing process and product life cycles," *Harvard Business Review*, vol. 57, no. 1 (January–February), pp. 133–40.

Hofer, Charles W., and Haller, Terry. 1980, "Globescan: A way to better international risk assessment," *Journal of Business Strategy*, vol. 1, no. 2, pp. 41–55.

Hofer, Charles W., and Schendel, Dan. 1978, *Strategy Formulation: Analytical Concepts*, West Publishing, St. Paul, Minnesota.

Kaiser, Michael M. 1984, *Understanding the Competition: A Practical Guide to Competitive Analysis*, Michael M. Kaiser Associates, Inc., Washington, D.C.

Karnani, Aneel, and Wernerfelt, Birger. 1985, "Multiple point competition," *Strategic Management Journal*, vol. 6, no. 1, pp. 87–96.

Leidecker, Joel K., and Bruno, Albert V. 1984, "Identifying and using critical success factors," *Long-Range Planning*, vol. 17, no. 1 (February), pp. 23–32.

McGee, John, and Thomas, Howard. 1986, "Strategic Groups: Theory, research and taxonomy," *Strategic Management Journal*, vol. 7, no. 2, pp. 141–60.

Miller, Delbert C. 1983, *Handbook of Research Design and Social Measurement*, Longman, New York.

Pekar, Peter P. 1982, "The strategic environmental matrix: A concept on trial," *Planning Review*, vol. 10, no. 5, pp. 28–30.

Petrov, Boris. 1982, "The advent of the technology portfolio," *Journal of Business Strategy*, vol. 3, no. 2, pp. 70–75.

Porter, Michael E. 1980, *Competitive Strategy*, Free Press, New York.

Porter, Michael E. 1985, *Competitive Advantage: Creating and Sustaining Superior Performance*, Free Press, New York.

Prescott, John E. 1987, "A process for applying analytic models in competitive analysis," in *Strategic Planning and Management Handbook*, eds. David I. Cleland and William R. King, Van Nostrand Reinhold, New York, pp. 222–51.

Ramanujam, Vasudevan, and Venkatraman, N. 1984, "An inventory and critique of strategy research using the PIMS data base," *Academy of Management Review*, vol. 9, no. 1, pp. 138–51.

Reimann, B. C. 1986, "Strategy valuation in portfolio planning: Combining Q and VROI ratios," *Planning Review*, vol. 14, no. 1, pp. 18–23, 42–45.

Rockart, John F. 1979, "Chief executives define their own data needs," *Harvard Business Review*, vol. 5, no. 2 (March–April), pp. 81–92.

Rowe, Alan J.; Mason, Richard O.; and Dickel, Karl E. 1985, *Strategic Management and Business Policy*, 2nd ed., Addison-Wesley Publishing, Reading, Massachusetts.

Schoeffler, Sidney; Buzzell, Robert D.; and Heany, Donald F. 1974, "Impact of strategic planning on profit performance," *Harvard Business Review*, vol. 52, no. 2, pp. 137–45.

Stevenson, Howard H. 1976, "Defining corporate strengths and weaknesses," *Sloan Management Review*, vol. 17, no. 3 (Spring), pp. 51–68.

Stevenson, Howard H. 1985, "Resource assessment: Identifying corporate strengths and weaknesses," in *Handbook of Business Strategy*, ed. William D. Guth, Warren, Gorham and Lamont, Boston, Massachusetts, chap. 5, pp. 1–30.

Wack, Pierre. 1985a, "Scenarios: Shooting the rapids," *Harvard Business Review*, vol. 63, no. 6, pp. 139–50.

Wack, Pierre. 1985b, "Scenarios: Uncharted waters ahead," *Harvard Business Review*, vol. 63, no. 5, pp. 73–89.

Wagner, Harvey M. 1984, "Profit wonders, investment blunders," *Harvard Business Review*, vol. 62, no. 5, pp. 121–35.

Washington Researchers. 1983, *Company Information: A Model Investigation*, Washington Researchers Ltd., Washington, D.C.

READING 2
CRAFTING STRATEGY

Henry Mintzberg

Tracking Strategy

In 1971, I became intrigued by an unusual definition of strategy as a pattern in a stream of decisions (later changed to actions). I initiated a research project at McGill University, and over the next 13 years a team of us tracked the strategies of 11 organizations over several decades of their history. (Students at various levels also carried out about 20 other less comprehensive studies.) The organizations we studied were Air Canada (1937–1976), Arcop, an architectural firm (1953–1978), Asbestos Corporation (1912–1975), Canadelle, a manufacturer of women's undergarments (1939–1976), McGill University (1829–1980), the National Film Board of Canada (1939–1976), *Saturday Night* magazine (1928–1971), the *Sherbrooke Record*, a small daily newspaper (1946–1976), Steinberg Inc., a large supermarket chain (1917–1974), the U.S. military's strategy in Vietnam (1949–1973), and Volkswagenwerk (1934–1974).

As a first step, we developed chronological lists and graphs of the most important actions taken by each organization—such as store openings and closings, new flight destinations, and new product introductions. Second, we inferred patterns in these actions and labeled them as strategies.

Third, we represented graphically all the strategies we inferred in an organization so that we could line them up to see whether there were distinct periods in their development—for example, periods of stability, flux, or global change. Fourth, we used interviews and in-depth reports to study what appeared to be the key points of change in each organization's strategic history.

Finally, armed with all this strategic history, the research team studied each set of findings to develop conclusions about the process of strategy formation. Three themes guided us: the interplay of environment, leadership, and organization; the pattern of strategic change; and the processes by which strategies form. This article presents those conclusions.

Imagine someone planning strategy. What likely springs to mind is an image of orderly thinking: a senior manager, or a group of them, sitting in an office formulating courses of action that everyone else will implement on schedule. The keynote is reason—rational control, the systematic analysis of competitors and markets, of company strengths and weaknesses, the combination of these analyses producing clear, explicit, full-blown strategies.

Now imagine someone *crafting* strategy. A wholly different image likely results, as different from planning as craft is from mechanization. Craft evokes traditional skill, dedication, perfection through the mastery of detail. What springs to mind is not so much thinking and reason as involvement, a feeling of intimacy and harmony with the materials at hand, developed through long

SOURCE: Reprinted by permission of *Harvard Business Review*. "Crafting Strategy," by Henry Mintzberg (July–August 1987). Copyright © 1987 by the President and Fellows of Harvard College. All rights reserved.

experience and commitment. Formulation and implementation merge into a fluid process of learning through which creative strategies evolve.

My thesis is simple: the crafting image better captures the process by which effective strategies come to be. The planning image, long popular in the literature, distorts these processes and thereby misguides organizations that embrace it unreservedly.

In developing this thesis, I shall draw on the experiences of a single craftsman, a potter, and compare them with the results of a research project that tracked the strategies of a number of corporations across several decades. Because the two contexts are so obviously different, my metaphor, like my assertion, may seem farfetched at first. Yet if we think of a craftsman as an organization of one, we can see that he or she must also resolve one of the great challenges the corporate strategist faces: knowing the organization's capabilities well enough to think deeply enough about its strategic direction. By considering strategy making from the perspective of one person, free of all the paraphernalia of what has been called the strategy industry, we can learn something about the formation of strategy in the corporation. For much as our potter has to manage her craft, so too managers have to craft their strategy.

At work, the potter sits before a lump of clay on the wheel. Her mind is on the clay, but she is also aware of sitting between her past experiences and her future prospects. She knows exactly what has and has not worked for her in the past. She has an intimate knowledge of her work, her capabilities, and her markets. As a craftsman, she senses rather than analyzes these things; her knowledge is "tacit." All these things are working in her mind as her hands are working the clay. The product that emerges on the wheel is likely to be in the tradition of her past work, but she may break away and embark on a new direction. Even so, the past is no less present, projecting itself into the future.

In my metaphor, managers are craftsmen and strategy is their clay. Like the potter, they sit between a past of corporate capabilities and a future of market opportunities. And if they are truly craftsmen, they bring to their work an equally intimate knowledge of the materials at hand. That is the essence of crafting strategy.

In the pages that follow, we will explore this metaphor by looking at how strategies get made as opposed to how they are supposed to get made. Throughout, I will be drawing on the two sets of experiences I've mentioned. One, described in the insert, is a research project on patterns in strategy formation that has been going on at McGill University under my direction since 1971. The second is the stream of work of a successful potter, my wife, who began her craft in 1967.

Strategies Are Both Plans for the Future and Patterns from the Past

Ask almost anyone what strategy is, and they will define it as a plan of some sort, an explicit guide to future behavior. Then ask them what strategy a competitor or a government or even they themselves have actually pursued. Chances are they will describe consistency in *past* behavior—a pattern in action over time. Strategy, it turns out, is one of those words that people define in one way and often use in another, without realizing the difference.

The reason for this is simple. Strategy's formal definition and its Greek military origins notwithstanding, we need the word as much to explain past actions as to describe intended behavior. After all, if strategies can be planned and intended, they can also be pursued and realized (or not realized, as the case may be). And pattern in action, or what we call realized strategy, explains that pursuit. Moreover, just as a plan need not produce a pattern (some strategies that are intended are simply not realized), so too a pattern need not result from a plan. An organization can have a pattern (or realized strategy) without knowing it, let alone making it explicit.

Patterns, like beauty, are in the mind of the beholder, of course. But anyone reviewing a chronological lineup of our craftsman's work would have little trouble discerning clear patterns, at least in certain periods. Until 1974, for example, she made small, decorative ceramic animals and objects of various kinds. Then this "knickknack strategy" stopped abruptly, and eventually new patterns formed around waferlike sculptures and ceramic bowls, highly textured and unglazed.

Finding equivalent patterns in action for organizations isn't that much more difficult. Indeed, for such large companies as Volkswagenwerk and Air Canada, in our research, it proved simpler! (As well it should. A craftsman, after all, can change what she does in a studio a lot more easily than a Volkswagenwerk can retool its assembly lines.) Mapping the product models at Volkswagenwerk from the late 1940s to the late 1970s, for example, uncovers a clear pattern of concentration on the Beetle, followed in the late 1960s by a frantic search for replacements through acquisitions and internally developed new models, to a strategic reorientation around more stylish, water-cooled, front-wheel-drive vehicles in the mid-1970s.

But what about intended strategies, those formal plans and pronouncements we think of when we use the term *strategy?* Ironically, here we run into all kinds of problems. Even with a single craftsman, how can we know what her intended strategies really were? If we could go back, would we find expressions of intention? And if we could, would we be able to trust them? We often fool ourselves, as well as others, by denying our subconscious motives. And remember that intentions are cheap, at least when compared with realizations.

Reading the Organization's Mind

If you believe all this has more to do with the Freudian recesses of a craftsman's mind than with the practical realities of producing automobiles, then think again. For who knows what the intended strategies of a Volkswagenwerk really mean, let alone what they are? Can we simply assume in this collective context that the company's intended strategies are represented by its formal plans or by other statements emanating from the executive suite? Might these be just vain hopes or rationalizations or ploys to fool the competition? And even if expressed intentions exist, to what extent do others in the organization share them? How do we read the collective mind? Who is the strategist anyway?

The traditional view of strategic management resolves these problems quite simply, by what organizational theorists call attribution. You see it all the time in the business press. When General Motors acts, it's because Roger Smith has made a strategy. Given realization, there must have been intention, and that is automatically attributed to the chief.

In a short magazine article, this assumption is understandable. Journalists don't have a lot of time to uncover the origins of strategy, and GM is a large, complicated organization. But just consider all the complexity and confusion that gets tucked under this assumption—all the meetings and debates, the many people, the dead ends, the folding and unfolding of ideas. Now imagine trying to build a formal strategy-making system around that assumption. Is it any wonder that formal strategic planning is often such a resounding failure?

To unravel some of the confusion—and move away from the artificial complexity we have piled around the strategy-making process—we need to get back to some basic concepts. The most basic of all is the intimate connection between thought and action. That is the key to craft, and so also to the crafting of strategy.

Strategies Need Not Be Deliberate— They Can Also Emerge

Virtually everything that has been written about strategy making depicts it as a deliberate process. First we think, then we act. We formulate, then we implement. The progression seems so perfectly sensible. Why would anybody want to proceed differently?

Our potter is in the studio, rolling the clay to make a waferlike sculpture. The clay sticks to the rolling pin, and a round form appears. Why not make a cylindrical vase? One idea leads to another, until a new pattern forms. Action has driven thinking: a strategy has emerged.

Out in the field, a salesman visits a customer. The product isn't quite right, and together they work out some modifications. The salesman returns to his company and puts the changes through; after two or three more rounds, they finally get it right. A new product emerges, which eventually opens up a new market. The company has changed strategic course.

In fact, most salespeople are less fortunate than this one or than our craftsman. In an organization of one, the implementor is the formulator, so innovations can be incorporated into strategy quickly and easily. In a large organization, the innovator may be 10 levels removed from the leader who is supposed to dictate strategy and may also have to sell the idea to dozens of peers doing the same job.

Some salespeople, of course, can proceed on their own, modifying products to suit their customers and convincing skunkworks in the factory to produce them. In effect, they pursue their own strategies. Maybe no one else notices or cares. Sometimes, however, their innovations do get noticed, perhaps years later, when the company's prevalent strategies have broken down and its leaders are groping for something new. Then the salesperson's strategy may be allowed to pervade the system, to become organizational.

Is this story farfetched? Certainly not. We've all heard stories like it. But since we tend to see only what we believe, if we believe that strategies have to be planned, we're unlikely to see the real meaning such stories hold.

Consider how the National Film Board of Canada (NFB) came to adopt a feature-film strategy. The NFB is a federal government agency, famous for its creativity and expert in the production of short documentaries. Some years back, it funded a filmmaker on a project that unexpectedly ran long. To distribute his film, the NFB turned to theaters and so inadvertently gained experience in marketing feature-length films. Other filmmakers caught onto the idea, and eventually the NFB found itself pursuing a feature-film strategy—a pattern of producing such films.

My point is simple, deceptively simple: strategies can *form* as well as be *formulated*. A realized strategy can emerge in response to an evolving situation, or it can be brought about deliberately, through a process of formulation followed by implementation. But when these planned intentions do not produce the desired actions, organizations are left with unrealized strategies.

Today we hear a great deal about unrealized strategies, almost always in concert with the claim that implementation has failed. Management has been lax, controls have been loose, people haven't been committed. Excuses abound. At times, indeed, they may be valid. But often these explanations prove too easy. So some people look beyond implementation to formulation. The strategists haven't been smart enough.

While it is certainly true that many intended strategies are ill conceived, I believe that the problem often lies one step beyond, in the distinction we make between formulation and implementation, the common assumption that thought must be independent of (and precede) action. Sure, people could be smarter—but not only by conceiving more clever strategies. Sometimes they can be smarter by allowing their strategies to develop gradually, through the organization's actions and experiences. Smart strategists appreciate that they cannot always be smart enough to think through everything in advance.

Hands and Minds

No craftsman thinks some days and works others. The craftsman's mind is going constantly, in tandem with her hands. Yet large organizations try to separate the work of minds and hands. In so doing, they often sever the vital feedback link between the two. The salesperson who finds a customer with an unmet need may possess the most strategic bit of information in the entire organization. But that information is useless if he or she cannot create a strategy in response to it or else convey the information to someone who can—because the channels are blocked or because the formulators have simply finished formulating. The notion that strategy is something that should happen way up there, far removed from the details of running an organization on a daily basis, is one of the great fallacies of conventional strategic management. And it explains a good many of the most dramatic failures in business and public policy today.

We at McGill call strategies like the NFB's that appear without clear intentions—or in spite of them—emergent strategies. Actions simply converge into patterns. They may become deliberate, of course, if the pattern is recognized and then legitimated by senior management. But that's after the fact.

All this may sound rather strange, I know. Strategies that emerge? Managers who acknowledge strategies already formed? Over the years, our research group at McGill has met with a good deal of resistance from people upset by what they perceive to be our passive definition of a word so bound up with proactive behavior and free will. After all, strategy means control—the ancient Greeks used it to describe the art of the army general.

Strategic Learning

But we have persisted in this usage for one reason: learning. Purely deliberate strategy precludes learning once the strategy is formulated; emergent strategy fosters it. People take actions one by one and respond to them, so that patterns eventually form.

Our craftsman tries to make a freestanding sculptural form. It doesn't work, so she rounds it a bit here, flattens it a bit there. The result looks better, but still isn't quite right. She makes another and another and another. Eventually, after days or months or years, she finally has what she wants. She is off on a new strategy.

In practice, of course, all strategy making walks on two feet, one deliberate, the other emergent. For just as purely deliberate strategy making precludes learning, so purely emergent strategy making precludes control. Pushed to the limit, neither approach makes much sense. Learning must be coupled with control. That is why the McGill research group uses the word *strategy* for both emergent and deliberate behavior.

Likewise, there is no such thing as a purely deliberate strategy or a purely emergent one. No organization—not even the ones commanded by those ancient Greek generals—knows enough to work everything out in advance, to ignore learning en route. And no one—not even a solitary potter—can be flexible enough to leave everything to happenstance, to give up all control. Craft requires control just as it requires responsiveness to the material at hand. Thus deliberate and emergent strategy form the end points of a continuum along which the strategies that are crafted in the real world may be found. Some strategies may approach either end, but many more fall at intermediate points.

Effective Strategies Develop in All Kinds of Strange Ways

Effective strategies can show up in the strangest places and develop through the most unexpected means. There is no one best way to make strategy.

The form for a cat collapses on the wheel, and our potter sees a bull taking shape. Clay sticks to a rolling pin, and a line of cylinders results. Wafers come into being because of a shortage of clay and limited kiln space in a studio in France. Thus errors become opportunities, and limitations stimulate creativity. The natural propensity to experiment, even boredom, likewise stimulate strategic change.

Organizations that craft their strategies have similar experiences. Recall the National Film Board with its inadvertently long film. Or consider its experiences with experimental films, which made special use of animation and sound. For 20 years, the NFB produced a bare but steady trickle of such films. In fact, every film but one in that trickle was produced by a single person, Norman McLaren, the NFB's most celebrated filmmaker. McLaren pursued a *personal strategy* of experimentation, deliberate for him perhaps (though who can know whether he had the whole stream in mind or simply planned one film at a time?) but not for the organization. Then 20 years later, others followed his lead and the trickle widened, his personal strategy becoming more broadly organizational.

Conversely, in 1952, when television came to Canada, a *consensus strategy* quickly emerged at the NFB. Senior management was not keen on producing films for the new medium. But while the arguments raged, one filmmaker quietly went off and made a single series for TV. That precedent set, one by one his colleagues leapt in, and within months the NFB—and its management—found themselves committed for several years to a new strategy with an intensity unmatched before or since. This consensus strategy arose spontaneously, as a result of many independent decisions made by the filmmakers about the films they wished to make. Can we call this strategy deliberate? For the filmmakers perhaps; for the senior management certainly not. But for the organization? It all depends on your perspective, on how you choose to read the organization's mind.

While the NFB may seem like an extreme case, it highlights behavior that can be found, albeit in muted form, in all organizations. Those who doubt this might read Richard Pascale's account of how Honda stumbled into its enormous success in the American motorcycle market. Brilliant as its strategy may have looked after the fact, Honda's managers made almost every conceivable mistake until the market finally hit them over the head with the right formula. The Honda managers on site in America, driving their products themselves (and thus inadvertently picking up market reaction), did only one thing right: they learned, firsthand.[1]

---

[1]Richard T. Pascale, "Perspective on Strategy: The Real Story behind Honda's Success," *California Management Review,* May–June 1984, p. 47.

Grass-Roots Strategy Making

These strategies all reflect, in whole or part, what we like to call a grass-roots approach to strategic management. Strategies grow like weeds in a garden. They take root in all kinds of places, wherever people have the capacity to learn (because they are in touch with the situation) and the resources to support that capacity. These strategies become organizational when they become collective, that is, when they proliferate to guide the behavior of the organization at large.

Of course, this view is overstated. But it is no less extreme than the conventional view of strategic management, which might be labeled the hothouse approach. Neither is right. Reality falls between the two. Some of the most effective strategies we uncovered in our research combined deliberation and control with flexibility and organizational learning.

Consider first what we call the *umbrella strategy*. Here senior management sets out broad guidelines (say, to produce only high-margin products at the cutting edge of technology or to favor products using bonding technology) and leaves the specifics (such as what these products will be) to others lower down in the organization. This strategy is not only deliberate (in its guidelines) and emergent (in its specifics), but it is also deliberately emergent in that the process is consciously managed to allow strategies to emerge en route. IBM used the umbrella strategy in the early 1960s with the impending 360 series, when its senior management approved a set of broad criteria for the design of a family of computers later developed in detail throughout the organization.[2]

Deliberately emergent, too, is what we call the *process strategy*. Here management controls the process of strategy formation—concerning itself with the design of the structure, its staffing, procedures, and so on—while leaving the actual content to others.

Both process and umbrella strategies seem to be especially prevalent in businesses that require great expertise and creativity—a 3M, a Hewlett-Packard, a National Film Board. Such organizations can be effective only if their implementors are allowed to be formulators because it is people way down in the hierarchy who are in touch with the situation at hand and have the requisite technical expertise. In a sense, these are organizations peopled with craftsmen, all of whom must be strategists.

Strategic Reorientations Happen in Brief, Quantum Leaps

The conventional view of strategic management, especially in the planning literature, claims that change must be continuous: the organization should be adapting all the time. Yet this view proves to be ironic because the very concept of

---

[2]James Brian Quinn, "IBM (A) case," in *The Strategy Process: Concepts, Contexts, Cases,* ed. James Brian Quinn, Henry Mintzberg, and Robert M. James (Englewood Cliffs, N.J.: Prentice Hall, 1988).

strategy is rooted in stability, not change. As this same literature makes clear, organizations pursue strategies to set direction, to lay out courses of action, and to elicit cooperation from their members around common, established guidelines. By any definition, strategy imposes stability on an organization. No stability means no strategy (no course to the future, no pattern from the past). Indeed, the very fact of having a strategy, and especially of making it explicit (as the conventional literature implores managers to do), creates resistance to strategic change!

What the conventional view fails to come to grips with, then, is how and when to promote change. A fundamental dilemma of strategy making is the need to reconcile the forces for stability and for change—to focus efforts and gain operating efficiencies on the one hand, yet adapt and maintain currency with a changing external environment on the other.

Quantum Leaps

Our own research and that of colleagues suggest that organizations resolve these opposing forces by attending first to one and then to the other. Clear periods of stability and change can usually be distinguished in any organization; while it is true that particular strategies may always be changing marginally, it seems equally true that major shifts in strategic orientation occur only rarely.

In our study of Steinberg Inc., a large Quebec supermarket chain headquartered in Montreal, we found only two important reorientations in the 60 years from its founding to the mid-1970s: a shift to self-service in 1933 and the introduction of shopping centers and public financing in 1953. At Volkswagenwerk, we saw only one between the late 1940s and the 1970s, the tumultuous shift from the traditional Beetle to the Audi-type design mentioned earlier. And at Air Canada, we found none over the airline's first four decades, following its initial positioning.

Our colleagues at McGill, Danny Miller and Peter Friesen, found this pattern of change so common in their studies of large numbers of companies (especially the high-performance ones) that they built a theory around it, which they labeled the quantum theory of strategic change.[3] Their basic point is that organizations adopt two distinctly different modes of behavior at different times.

Most of the time they pursue a given strategic orientation. Change may seem continuous, but it occurs in the context of that orientation (perfecting a given retailing formula, for example) and usually amounts to doing more of the same, perhaps better as well. Most organizations favor these periods of stability because they achieve success not by changing strategies but by exploiting the ones they have. They, like craftsmen, seek continuous improvement by using their distinctive competencies in established courses.

While this goes on, however, the world continues to change, sometimes slowly, occasionally in dramatic shifts. Thus gradually or suddenly, the

---

[3]See Danny Miller and Peter H. Friesen, *Organizations: A Quantum View* (Englewood Cliffs, N.J.: Prentice Hall, 1984).

organization's strategic orientation moves out of sync with its environment. Then what Miller and Friesen call a strategic revolution must take place. That long period of evolutionary change is suddenly punctuated by a brief bout of revolutionary turmoil in which the organization quickly alters many of its established patterns. In effect, it tries to leap to a new stability quickly to reestablish an integrated posture among a new set of strategies, structures, and culture.

But what about all those emergent strategies, growing like weeds around the organization? What the quantum theory suggests is that the really novel ones are generally held in check in some corner of the organization until a strategic revolution becomes necessary. Then as an alternative to having to develop new strategies from scratch or having to import generic strategies from competitors, the organization can turn to its own emerging patterns to find its new orientation. As the old, established strategy disintegrates, the seeds of the new one begin to spread.

This quantum theory of change seems to apply particularly well to large, established, mass-production companies. Because they are especially reliant on standardized procedures, their resistance to strategic reorientation tends to be especially fierce. So we find long periods of stability broken by short disruptive periods of revolutionary change.

Volkswagenwerk is a case in point. Long enamored of the Beetle and armed with a tightly integrated set of strategies, the company ignored fundamental changes in its markets throughout the late 1950s and 1960s. The bureaucratic momentum of its mass-production organization combined with the psychological momentum of its leader, who institutionalized the strategies in the first place. When change finally did come, it was tumultuous: the company groped its way through a hodgepodge of products before it settled on a new set of vehicles championed by a new leader. Strategic reorientations really are cultural revolutions.

Cycles of Change

In more creative organizations, we see a somewhat different pattern of change and stability, one that's more balanced. Companies in the business of producing novel outputs apparently need to fly off in all directions from time to time to sustain their creativity. Yet they also need to settle down after such periods to find some order in the resulting chaos.

The National Film Board's tendency to move in and out of focus through remarkably balanced periods of convergence and divergence is a case in point. Concentrated production of films to aid the war effort in the 1940s gave way to great divergence after the war as the organization sought a new raison d'être. Then the advent of television brought back a very sharp focus in the early 1950s, as noted earlier. But in the late 1950s, this dissipated almost as quickly as it began, giving rise to another creative period of exploration. Then the social changes in the early 1960s evoked a new period of convergence around experimental films and social issues.

We use the label "adhocracy" for organizations, like the National Film Board, that produce individual, or custom-made, products (or designs) in an innovative way, on a project basis.[4] Our craftsman is an adhocracy of sorts too, since each of her ceramic sculptures is unique. And her pattern of strategic change was much like that of the NFB's, with evident cycles of convergence and divergence: a focus on knick knacks from 1967 to 1972; then a period of exploration to about 1976, which resulted in a refocus on ceramic sculptures; that continued to about 1981, to be followed by a period of searching for new directions. More recently, a focus on ceramic murals seems to be emerging.

Whether through quantum revolutions or cycles of convergence and divergence, however, organizations seem to need to separate in time the basic forces for change and stability, reconciling them by attending to each in turn. Many strategic failures can be attributed either to mixing the two or to an obsession with one of these forces at the expense of the other.

The problems are evident in the work of many craftsmen. On the one hand, there are those who seize on the perfection of a single theme and never change. Eventually the creativity disappears from their work and the world passes them by—much as it did Volkswagenwerk until the company was shocked into its strategic revolution. And then there are those who are always changing, who flit from one idea to another and never settle down. Because no theme or strategy ever emerges in their work, they cannot exploit or even develop any distinctive competence. And because their work lacks definition, identity crises are likely to develop, with neither the craftsmen nor their clientele knowing what to make of it. Miller and Friesen found this behavior in conventional business too; they label it "the impulsive firm running blind."[5] How often have we seen it in companies that go on acquisition sprees?

To Manage Strategy is to Craft Thought and Action, Control and Learning, Stability and Change

The popular view sees the strategist as a planner or as a visionary, someone sitting on a pedestal dictating brilliant strategies for everyone else to implement. While recognizing the importance of thinking ahead and especially of the need for creative vision in this pedantic world, I wish to propose an additional view of the strategist—as a pattern recognizer, a learner if you will—who manages a process in which strategies (and visions) can emerge as well as be deliberately conceived. I also wish to redefine that strategist, to extend that someone into the

---

[4]See Henry Mintzberg, "Organization Design: Fashion or Fit?" *Harvard Business Review,* January–February 1981, p. 103; also see Mintzberg, *Structure in Fives: Designing Effective Organizations* (Englewood Cliffs, N.J.: Prentice Hall, 1983). The term *adhocracy* was coined by Warren G. Bennis and Philip E. Slater in *The Temporary Society* (New York: Harper & Row, 1964).

[5]Danny Miller and Peter H. Friesen, "Archetypes of Strategy Formulation," *Management Science,* May 1978, p. 921.

collective entity made up of the many actors whose interplay speaks an organization's mind. This strategist *finds* strategies no less than creates them, often in patterns that form inadvertently in its own behavior.

What, then, does it mean to craft strategy? Let us return to the words associated with craft: dedication, experience, involvement with the material, the personal touch, mastery of detail, a sense of harmony and integration. Managers who craft strategy do not spend much time in executive suites reading MIS reports or industry analyses. They are involved, responsive to their materials, learning about their organizations and industries through personal touch. They are also sensitive to experience, recognizing that while individual vision may be important, other factors must help determine strategy as well.

Manage Stability.   Managing strategy is mostly managing stability, not change. Indeed, most of the time senior managers should not be formulating strategy at all; they should be getting on with making their organizations as effective as possible in pursuing the strategies they already have. Like distinguished craftsmen, organizations become distinguished because they master the details.

To manage strategy, then, at least in the first instance, is not so much to promote change as to know *when* to do so. Advocates of strategic planning often urge managers to plan for perpetual instability in the environment (for example, by rolling over five-year plans annually). But this obsession with change is dysfunctional. Organizations that reassess their strategies continuously are like individuals who reassess their jobs or their marriages continuously—in both cases, people will drive themselves crazy or else reduce themselves to inaction. The formal planning process repeats itself so often and so mechanically that it desensitizes the organization to real change, programs it more and more deeply into set patterns, and thereby encourages it to make only minor adaptations.

So-called strategic planning must be recognized for what it is: a means, not to create strategy, but to program a strategy already created—to work out its implications formally. It is essentially analytic in nature, based on decomposition, while strategy creation is essentially a process of synthesis. That is why trying to create strategies through formal planning most often leads to extrapolating existing ones or copying those of competitors.

That is not to say that planners have no role to play in strategy formation. In addition to programming strategies created by other means, they can feed ad hoc analyses into the strategy-making process at the front end to be sure that the hard data are taken into consideration. They can also stimulate others to think strategically. And of course people called planners can be strategists too, so long as are creative thinkers who are in touch with what is relevant. But that has nothing to do with the technology of formal planning.

Detect Discontinuity.   Environments do not change on any regular or orderly basis. And they seldom undergo continuous dramatic change, claims about our "age of discontinuity" and environmental "turbulence" notwithstanding. (Go tell people who lived through the Great Depression or survivors of the siege of

Leningrad during World War II that ours are turbulent times.) Much of the time, change is minor and even temporary and requires no strategic response. Once in a while there is a truly significant discontinuity or, even less often, a gestalt shift in the environment, where everything important seems to change at once. But these events, while critical, are also easy to recognize.

The real challenge in crafting strategy lies in detecting the subtle discontinuities that may undermine a business in the future. And for that, there is no technique, no program, just a sharp mind in touch with the situation. Such discontinuities are unexpected and irregular, essentially unprecedented. They can be dealt with only by minds that are attuned to existing patterns yet able to perceive important breaks in them. Unfortunately, this form of strategic thinking tends to atrophy during the long periods of stability that most organizations experience (just as it did at Volkswagenwerk during the 1950s and 1960s). So the trick is to manage within a given strategic orientation most of the time yet be able to pick out the occasional discontinuity that really matters.

The Steinberg chain was built and run for more than half a century by a man named Sam Steinberg. For 20 years, the company concentrated on perfecting a self-service retailing formula introduced in 1933. Installing fluorescent lighting and figuring out how to package meat in cellophane wrapping were the "strategic" issues of the day. Then in 1952, with the arrival of the first shopping center in Montreal, Steinberg realized he had to redefine his business almost overnight. He knew he needed to control those shopping centers and that control would require public financing and other major changes. So he reoriented his business. The ability to make that kind of switch in thinking is the essence of strategic management. And it has more to do with vision and involvement than it does with analytic technique.

Know the Business.   Sam Steinberg was the epitome of the entrepreneur, a man intimately involved with all the details of his business, who spent Saturday mornings visiting his stores. As he told us in discussing his company's competitive advantage: "Nobody knew the grocery business like we did. Everything has to do with your knowledge. I knew merchandise, I knew cost, I knew selling, I knew customers. I knew everything, and I passed on all my knowledge; I kept teaching my people. That's the advantage we had. Our competitors couldn't touch us."

Note the kind of knowledge involved: not intellectual knowledge, not analytical reports or abstracted facts and figures (though these can certainly help), but personal knowledge, intimate understanding, equivalent to the craftsman's feel for the clay. Facts are available to anyone; this kind of knowledge is not. Wisdom is the word that captures it best. But wisdom is a word that has been lost in the bureaucracies we have built for ourselves, systems designed to distance leaders from operating details. Show me managers who think they can rely on formal planning to create their strategies, and I'll show you managers who lack intimate knowledge of their businesses or the creativity to do something with it.

Craftsmen have to train themselves to see, to pick up things other people miss. The same holds true for managers of strategy. It is those with a kind of peripheral vision who are best able to detect and take advantage of events as they unfold.

Manage Patterns.   Whether in an executive suite in Manhattan or a pottery studio in Montreal, a key to managing strategy is the ability to detect emerging patterns and help them take shape. The job of the manager is not just to preconceive specific strategies but also to recognize their emergence elsewhere in the organization and intervene when appropriate.

Like weeds that appear unexpectedly in a garden, some emergent strategies may need to be uprooted immediately. But management cannot be too quick to cut off the unexpected, for tomorrow's vision may grow out of today's aberration. (Europeans, after all, enjoy salads made from the leaves of the dandelion, America's most notorious weed.) Thus some patterns are worth watching until their effects have more clearly manifested themselves. Then those that prove useful can be made deliberate and be incorporated into the formal strategy, even if that means shifting the strategic umbrella to cover them.

To manage in this context, then, is to create the climate within which a wide variety of strategies can grow. In more complex organizations, this may mean building flexible structures, hiring creative people, defining broad umbrella strategies, and watching for the patterns that emerge.

Reconcile Change and Continuity.   Finally, managers considering radical departures need to keep the quantum theory of change in mind. As Ecclesiastes reminds us, there is a time to sow and a time to reap. Some new patterns must be held in check until the organization is ready for a strategic revolution, or at least a period of divergence. Managers who are obsessed with either change or stability are bound eventually to harm their organizations. As pattern recognizer, the manager has to be able to sense when to exploit an established crop of strategies and when to encourage new strains to displace the old.

While strategy is a word that is usually associated with the future, its link to the past is no less central. As Kierkegaard once observed, life is lived forward but understood backward. Managers may have to live strategy in the future, but they must understand it through the past.

Like potters at the wheel, organizations must make sense of the past if they hope to manage the future. Only by coming to understand the patterns that form in their own behavior do they get to know their capabilities and their potential. Thus crafting strategy, like managing craft, requires a natural synthesis of the future, present, and past.

Author's note: Readers interested in learning more about the results of the tracking strategy project have a wide range of studies to draw from. Works published to date can be found in Robert Lamb and Paul Shivastava, eds., *Advances in Strategic Management,* vol. 4 (Greenwich, Conn.: JAI Press, 1986), pp. 3–41; *Management Science,* May 1978, p. 934; *Administrative Science Quarterly,* June 1985, p. 160; *Canadian Journal of Administrative Sciences,* June 1984, p. 1; *Academy of Management Journal,* September 1982, p. 465; Robert Lamb, ed., *Competitive Strategic Management* (Englewood Cliffs, N.J.: Prentice Hall, 1984).

READING 3
DOING BUSINESS IN THE UNITED STATES

Ray Suutari

The United States is Canada's natural trading partner. Geographically close, with a similar culture and no barrier arising from a difference in the basic language of business, English, it is not surprising that approximately 75 percent of Canadian trade is with the United States. In 1990, Canadian exports to the United States totaled $110 billion. Canadian exports are, however, concentrated in resources, resource-based products, and automobiles, all which have had virtually duty-free entry into the United States for some time.

The relatively low proportion of exports of nonresource-based goods, despite the natural advantage of exporting to the U.S. market, is not due to the existence of tariffs, because they have been relatively low. More likely, it is due to the Canadian attitude toward the need to export. Canada enjoys one of the highest standards of living in the world, and as a result, there have been no overwhelming pressures to export. However, in the early 1990s this attitude has started to change as new markets have had to be found to offset increasing competition from U.S. companies entering the Canadian market. Further rationalization of production to a North American basis under the Free Trade Agreement has resulted in some Canadian branch plants being closed, so that replacement customers have to be found.

A limited number of Canadians are also concerned about their ability to compete. One tongue-in-cheek indication of Canadian perceptions of themselves is provided by a survey of attitudes reflected in Canadian business textbooks as shown in Exhibit 1. These perceptions are, of course, wrong. Canadians have no inherent barriers to doing business in the United States, provided that they recognize certain facts:

1. There are significant differences between Canadian and U.S. business arising from the Canadian environment. These must be understood.
2. These differences create both competitive advantages and disadvantages which must be recognized in developing export strategies.
3. Implementation requires considerable effort to establish distribution capability, as well as sensitivity to U.S. buying practices.

The sections to follow will review each of these aspects in more detail.

SOURCE: This reading was prepared by Ray Suutari, © 1992 Ray Suutari, School of Business and Economics, Wilfrid Laurier University.

EXHIBIT 1 Survey of Canadian Business Perceptions in Relation to the United States

---

1. The fact that Canada is not like the United States is cause for shame and sadness.
2. The fact that we have more government institutions than the United States is evidence that something is wrong with the country.
3. Canadians, Canadian managers, Canadian customers, and definitely Canadian entrepreneurs all compare poorly with their American counterparts.
4. The fact that we have many foreign-owned firms is evidence that there is something wrong with all of us personally as well as the country.
5. Our early resource-based economy is a thing to be ashamed of. It would have been better if we had big manufacturing industries in 1880. Why this did not occur is a mystery.
6. The government in Canada "controls" business.
7. Canadian firms that venture into the United States do so because there is something wrong with Canadians.
8. Foreign firms that set up business in Canada do so because there is something wrong with Canadians.
9. The fact that an American firm succeeds is always evidence of that management's superior personal qualities; it is never due solely to huge domestic markets.
10. There is no risk capital in Canada. All the capital in the United States is risk capital.
11. R&D is something Americans and Japanese do well all the time. R&D, if done in Canada, is always too little or just plain bad.
12. My colleagues will laugh at me if I write positive things about Canadian business.

SOURCE: John W. Redston, "The Canadian Business Context: Conclusions from a Survey of Canadian General Business Texts 1960–1987," Working Paper, Red River Community College, Winnipeg, September 1988. Reprinted by permission.

The Canadian Environment

Canadian business structures, their strategies, attitudes, and practices have evolved in response to the Canadian environment. The differences in the Canadian environment from the United States must be recognized in order to understand the adjustments which must be made in order to successfully do business in the United States.

The characteristics of the Canadian environment can be defined in terms of demographics, geography, the labour force, the commercial/industrial structure, and the role of the government. These can be summarized as follows:

1. Demographically, Canada has a very small population which is culturally fragmented.
2. Geographically, the Canadian population is broadly dispersed in a narrow band close to the U.S. border. Further, Canada has a relatively harsh climate.
3. The Canadian labour force is highly unionized, and the unions have a left wing political bias.
4. Overall business activity is concentrated in relatively few companies with a significant but declining degree of foreign control.

Exhibit 2 **Demographic Characteristics**

Canadian Situation
Small domestic population of 26 million versus 246 million in the United States.
Culturally segmented, with Francophone component constituting one quarter of the population.
Immigration patterns have changed. Far more new Canadians are of Asian descent than European
  descent.

Underlying Reasons
The United States has been the preferred destination of immigrants due to image, dynamic
  economy, climate, and so on. More recently, restrictive immigration policies have limited
  population growth.
Historic cultural segmentation centered in Quebec has been perpetuated and reinforced by special
  political status.

5. The governments, federal and provincial, play a significant role in the
   economy, though this intervention is frequently in favour of business.

Demographics

The Canadian demographic situation and the underlying reasons are shown in
Exhibit 2.

The main implication of the small domestic market is the difficulty in
achieving economies of scale, particularly in manufacturing. Diseconomies tend
to be present at the product level (short production runs), plant level (smaller
plants which cannot justify the use of highly productive, specialized machinery),
and the corporate level (ability to afford R&D, product development, and
specialized staff). These disadvantages in secondary manufacturing had been
substantially offset by high tariffs which are now disappearing under free trade.

Cultural segmentation further fragments the relatively small market with
special product needs and imposes the costs of bilingual labeling, instructions,
and so on. The United States also has a substantial cultural segment in its
Hispanic population. However, this is a smaller proportion of its population
(officially 7 percent), is geographically dispersed, and it does not enjoy special
political status protecting its culture.

The Canadian market is also regionally segmented by geography, different
economic bases, and cultural traditions. However, the differences between Canadian regions are likely no greater than occur in the United States, where
lifestyle and climate can create the differences as exist between the Northeast
and the Southwest.

The relatively small Canadian market has resulted in some Canadian industries outgrowing the Canadian market. For example, the Canadian commercial
real estate development companies, having rebuilt the central areas of virtually
every major Canadian city, logically moved into the U.S. market in the 1970s
where they have become a major force. Unfortunately, for political reasons, the

industry blamed excessive government interference for the move, and this likely contributed to the perception that Canadian firms venture into the United States because there is something wrong with Canada, as indicated in Exhibit 1.

Geography

In terms of population distribution, as set out in Exhibit 3, Canada is a country approximately 5000 km long by 200 km wide. In contrast, a distance of only 800 km along the Atlantic seaboard from Boston to Washington contains a population of 25 million in the major metropolitan centres alone. Of course, not all of the United States is this densely populated, but the major concentrations on the Atlantic, Midwest, and Pacific coast each are far larger than the total Canadian market. For example, the population of the New England and Mid-Atlantic states alone (New York, New Jersey, Pennsylvania) totals over 50 million, almost twice the size of the Canadian domestic market.

The northern United States is also exposed to the same climate as Canada, but this area contains a relatively small proportion of the total population. A large proportion of the United States has the advantage of a more moderate climate.

The broad implications of Canadian geography as a consequence of the population distribution and climatic factors are

1. Costs are higher in virtually every segment of the economy.
    - For manufacturing, buildings must be more substantial and heating costs incurred.
    - Distribution distances are longer and frequently require regional warehousing.
    - More government infrastructure is required for highways and their maintenance, postal service, and so on.
    - Consumers face nondiscretionary costs for heating and clothing, reducing discretionary income.
2. Merchandising is fragmented by four well-defined seasons which increases risks due to short selling periods. For example, a cool early

---

EXHIBIT 3 Geographic Factors

Canadian Situation
Long distances between population concentrations.
Population concentrated along U.S. border.
Relatively cold climate with well-defined seasons.

Underlying Reasons
Distances between major population concentrations are the result of the breadth of the country and natural geographic barriers such as the Gulf of St. Lawrence, the Pre-Cambrian Shield, and the Rocky Mountains.
Population concentration along southern border results from historic transportation routes (St. Lawrence River and the Great Lakes), the location of the best agricultural land, and the more moderate climate.

---

summer can slow down apparel sales to the point that markdowns are required to dispose of inventory to make room for the next season due within several months.

3. The very large proportion of population living near the U.S. border is exposed to U.S. media and cultural influence by receipt of U.S. television signals. This has contributed to cultural similarity and standardization of consumer products between Canada and the United States . On the other hand, the U.S. population living within the reach of a Canadian TV signal (about 100 km) is relatively small, with only a few major cities such as Detroit and Cleveland within this area.

The implications of the Canadian geographic environment are not entirely negative. It is the basis for a major tourist industry, and the solutions to transportation and communications problems have placed Canada in the forefront of the telecommunications industry and railway operations.

Labour

The Canadian labour relations environment is highly confrontational as a result of the high degree of unionization and the militancy of the unions, as indicated in Exhibit 4. As a result, the incidence of strikes and their duration is significantly higher than the United States and among the worst of the seven major industrialized nations, except for Italy.

Apart from the difficulties of organizing labour in the United States, the U.S. record also reflects the fact that their labour leadership appears to believe in the free enterprise system and is ready to work within it. In contrast, this belief does not exist in many Canadian unions, as reflected by demands for

---

Exhibit 4 Labour Force Situation

Canadian Situation
- The nonagricultural labour force is highly unionized at 34.5 percent versus 18 percent in the United States.
- Canadian unions are highly militant with a left wing political bias.

Underlying Reasons
- Labour laws (provincial) are favourable to union organization and certification. This has included unionization of the civil service which contributes 5.7 percent to the overall Canadian unionization rate.
- There are no Canadian nonunion havens as exist in the U.S. South and the "right-to-work" states.
- Canadian industry is more concentrated in large companies which have been easier to unionize.
- Canadian union leadership has contained a high proportion of immigrants from the United Kingdom who appear to have brought with them British attitudes of class conflict.
- Unions in Canada have direct political representation via the New Democratic Party. U.S. unions must moderate their views in order to remain compatible with the Democratic or Republican party platforms.

government intervention and calls for nationalization of major companies involved in long strikes. Also, Canadian unions often resist wage concessions even when the survival of the company or plant is at stake.

The general implications of the Canadian situation are:

- Labour relations are confrontational, with strikes relatively common, including in the public sector.
- Wage rate increases are not tied to productivity increases.
- There are major distortions in the value of service versus wage levels extracted by powerful unions. As a result, relatively low-skilled postal workers represented by a militant union are paid about the same as highly skilled nurses who have major responsibilities.

Another characteristic of the Canadian labour force is its relatively small size arising from the small population. As a result, specialized skills may be in short supply, especially during boom periods.

Industrial/Commercial Structure

The extent of industrial concentration in Canada is the natural consequence of the relatively small economy. There is, after all, only room for a limited number of large operations, and the Combines Act does not significantly inhibit mergers, as has the Sherman Anti-Trust Act in the United States. See Exhibit 5.

Canadians are often characterized as being adverse to taking risks leading to the high degree of foreign ownership. This is, however, unfair. A foreign

---

EXHIBIT 5 Industrial/Commercial Structure

Canadian Situation
- Economic activity is concentrated in a relatively smaller number of companies compared to the United States.
- Foreign control is extensive, with 129 of the largest 250 industrial companies being foreign controlled.
- Ownership by Canadians is also highly concentrated. Companies controlled by the Bronfman, Reichmann, Weston, Thompson, and Desmarais families have sales equivalent to about 8 percent of the Canadian gross domestic product. In contrast, the U.S. auto industry accounts for only about 4 percent of that country's GDP.
- The five largest banks control 60 percent of total assets of the 50 largest financial institutions in Canada.
- Deregulation is proceeding more slowly than in the United States.

Underlying Reasons
- The relatively small domestic market limits the number of competitive units that can have reasonable economies of scale.
- Relatively lenient combines laws have not discouraged concentration.
- The proximity of the United States and the absence of language barriers have made Canada the logical area for U.S. expansion.

company, drawing on its domestic resources, can start a branch operation at relatively little risk in comparison with a stand-alone Canadian plant. However, this foreign control does result in product designs being imported, limiting Canadian contribution opportunities and research and development activities.

The overall implication of the degree of industrial concentration in Canada is that the level of competition is significantly lower in Canada than the United States. For example, off-price retailing and merchandising and "factory outlet" malls have shown rapid growth in the United States, while going nowhere in Canada. This may be attributable to the high degree of concentration of the retail sector, which the rather fragmented producing sector does not want to antagonize by supplying discount outlets. The high degree of buying power of the major companies therefore tends to inhibit competition across the economic spectrum.

The Government Role

A broad illustration of the difference in the role of government between Canada and the United States is provided by their underlying national philosophies. For Canada, the role of government as set out in the British-North America Act is to provide "peace, order and good government." In the United States, the Declaration of Independence sets the goal as "life, liberty and the pursuit of happiness." In general, Canadians are more tolerant of government intervention than are Americans, and Canada is regarded as a more caring society with extensive social programs in such areas as medical care, unemployment insurance, and old age security.

The implication of government involvement is not necessarily bad for business as is generally believed (Exhibit 6). In certain cases it is quite favourable, such as in the reduction of fringe benefit costs made possible by the Medicare system and the availability of subsidies or loans for establishing major new plants. However, the adverse impacts are:

- The extent of provincial jurisdiction multiplies regulation and fragments certain industries such as brewing and trucking.
- The use of public money to promote economic development such as in the petroleum industry contributes to the perpetuation of government deficits.

Some Other Differences

The relatively large size of the U.S. market and the intensity of the competition have led to differences in consumer behaviour. Some key differences are:

- Shoppers are accustomed to a much wider range of choice than in Canada. Six or seven brands of a product are not unusual as compared with two or three in Canada.

Exhibit 6 The Government Role

Canadian Situation
- Canadian governments (federal and provincial) actively intervene in the business sector via regulation, crown corporations, and subsidization.
- Government power is fragmented between the federal and provincial levels, with the provincial government having substantial jurisdiction.
- Six of the 100 largest industrial companies in Canada are crown corporations with Ontario Hydro, Petro Canada, and Hydro-Quebec ranking 11th, 12th, and 14th, respectively (1988 figures).

Underlying Reasons
- The relatively small economy has forced government to provide infrastructure which would not support private initiatives, particularly in more remote areas. This has involved the governments in transportation (railway, airline) and in electric power.
- The relatively high degree of jurisdiction vested in the provinces was a condition of confederation in which relatively mature, established provinces required the dilution of the central government role.
- Existence of relatively undeveloped areas requires active subsidization of economic development under the government policy of equalizing social service standards between provinces.

- Retailing tends to be much more specialized than in Canada, with stores targeting specific market segments. This too is attributable to the large market which can support specialized chains of the size necessary to achieve economies of scale.
- Shopping malls and free-standing stores account for 48 percent of U.S. shoppers as compared with only 20 percent in Canada, where shopping centres are dominant.

The U.S. situation requires highly sophisticated marketing management. Retailers try to develop special relationships with their market segments in order to create and sustain a loyal customer following. Canadian retailers cannot therefore expect to enter the U.S. market by merely transplanting a concept which has been successful in Canada. Marketing at any level in the United States requires more specialized expertise.

Overall Conclusions

As indicated by the discussion of the various elements of the Canadian environment, the Canadian situation is, in many respects, substantially different from the United States. The major factors which must be recognized in the development of a strategy for doing business in the United States can be summarized as follows:

1. Canada is a relatively high-cost country. The combination of reasons creating this includes the small scale of operation, high labour rates,

climatic factors, and distances in supply and distribution. The cost disadvantages may be partially offset by currency exchange rates.

2. Canadians are generally conditioned to a much less competitive domestic environment than exists in the United States in virtually all areas of activity. However, Canadians have proportionately more experience than Americans when operating outside of North America.

3. Concepts which are effective in Canada cannot necessarily be successfully transplanted to the United States, and vice versa. This is due to the overall differences in the environments and applies particularly to retailing.

Successful entry into the U.S. market cannot therefore be undertaken on the basis that the markets are similar. To the contrary, an entry strategy must be planned on the basis that the environments are considerably different, with weaknesses to overcome, and strengths leveraged.

Entry Strategy

The U.S. market can be entered by way of direct investment in a U.S. facility or by exporting. The primary consideration in the decision is obviously the need to be cost competitive. Exporting is usually a logical first step as it usually requires less investment and can provide increased sales volume with a high marginal profit contribution.

Export Strategy

As a first step to planning an export program, the company's potential as an exporter should realistically be assessed by asking the questions provided in Exhibit 7. If potential is indicated to exist, an export strategy should be developed, containing the following elements:

1. Compete on the basis of "value," not "price." In the face of the high-cost Canadian environment, competing solely on the basis of price, while not impossible, is obviously difficult. The factor which reduces price sensitivity is "value," which can consist of:
   a. Superior performance or durability, either in general or in some specific function.
   b. More attractive or unique design or styling.
   c. Extended warranties.

2. Target specific rather than broad markets. This follows directly from the "value" approach, as differentiated products usually appeal only to specific market segments. These markets must be identified, and the

---

EXHIBIT 7 Something to Sell
A Checklist to Assess Your Potential as an Exporter

Assess your potential as an exporter by realistically examining your products or services in a global framework. Begin by asking the following questions:

1. Who already uses your product or service? Is it in broad general use or is it limited to a particular group because of socioeconomic factors? Is it particularly popular with a certain age group?
2. What modifications are required for it to appeal to customers in a foreign market?
3. Is its use influenced or affected by climatic or geographic factors? If so, what are they?
4. What is its shelf life? Will it be affected by time in transit?
5. Does your product or service involve operating costs? If so, what complementary equipment or services must the customer buy?
6. Does it require professional assembly or other technical skills?
7. What special packaging or literature is required? These costs must be added to the unit cost to determine whether or not you can export at a competitive price.
8. What are the technical or regulatory requirements? They may differ from country to country.
9. What after-sales service is needed? Is it locally available or is it up to you to provide it? If you need to provide it, do you have the resources?
10. How easily can the product be shipped? Would shipping costs make competitive pricing a problem?
11. Will you be able to serve both your domestic customers and your new foreign clients?
12. If domestic demand increases, can you still handle the requirements of your export customers?

SOURCE: Adapted from "How To Do Business in the U.S.," Ministry of Industry, Trade and Technology, Province of Ontario, 1987.

product or approach tailored or modified to appeal to these markets. It is in this area where the basis of success in Canada must be reexamined in the context of the U.S. market in order to establish the extent to which it can be transplanted, or how it must be modified to be effective. While the niches may constitute only a relatively small proportion of the U.S. market, they are still large in comparison with the Canadian market, and being small may not be as intensely competitive as the mass markets.

3. Give close attention to distribution. Value must be sold, that is, the features which provide competitive advantage must be brought to the potential buyers' attention. This means that the distributor must be capable of providing this sales effort through the combination of direct selling, promotional material, follow-up, and so on. This requires the careful selection of the distribution channel and the organization which will be representing you in the United States, as well as the incentives necessary to do a good job.

4. Recognize that there are differences between Canadian and U.S. channels of distribution and selling practices. Specifically:

    a. U.S. manufacturers make greater use of independent sales representatives. About 70 percent of manufacturers use agents on a commission basis which can be as low as 3 percent. In Canada, manufacturers rely on in-house sales forces with only 30 percent using independent representatives.

b. The wholesale function is less important in the United States where its revenue equals 32.7 percent of GNP versus 41.1 percent in Canada. The smaller average size of the Canadian retailer and distribution distances likely account for the difference.

5. Exploit the Canadian image if possible. For example, the Canadian brewing industry has developed a substantial export market in the United States, assisted by the fact that Canadian beer has a favourable image. Similarly, Canadian winter recreational products such as snow-mobiles, hockey equipment, and so on, have gained significant positions in the U.S. market. Where applicable, the ability to withstand and operate in a "Canadian" winter can be used to emphasize durability.

6. Support the strategy with adequate resources, both financial and management. The process of identifying markets, recruiting distributors, providing them with support material (catalogues, brochures), training the sales staff in your product's characteristics (seminars, plant visits), advertising, and even establishing inventories in regional warehouses can be expensive. If viewed solely as an expense, the effort may be incomplete and risk failure or disappointing results. It should be kept in mind that being established in any market with a strong distributor relationship and customer base can provide consistency in sales volume and growth potential over a long time. This is an asset of enduring value and like all assets of enduring value, the outlays and effort to establish it should be treated like an investment rather than an expense.

To summarize, strategies to export to the United States should be highly specific, that is, planned to capture highly targeted markets with well-defined appeals. This requires not only careful development of the strategy but close attention to implementation.

The implementation effort must also recognize that the U.S. market is different and that it must be approached with recognition of its characteristics and its sensitivities. The following suggestions are based upon exporters' experiences:

1. Where U.S. management or services are required, such as a regional sales manager or product managers, hire experienced U.S. people. Canadians sent to the United States must initially learn about the idiosyncrasies of the U.S. market, its regulations, tax structures, hiring and training, and so on, which distracts from the basic job, particularly in the very important early phase.

2. Set price on the basis of delivered cost including any duties (Delivered Duty Paid), or as a minimum, DDP at port of entry. This avoids the

confusion and uncertainty of these items. The U.S. price list should be separate and *not* show prices in both U.S. and Canadian dollars. In pricing for the United States, it should be remembered that the Canadian Goods and Services Tax is not applicable on exported products. Imported raw materials used in manufacture are entitled to duty drawback. (Appendix A provides a summary of the components of export pricing.)

3. Catalogues, display, or promotional material should not emphasize Canadian content, unless there is a specific image advantage. In particular, bilingual (French/English) sales literature is not well received in the United States. American importers often believe that Canadian-made goods are better than those from offshore suppliers since they consider Canada to be part of the North American domestic economy. As a result, the appearance of "foreignness" should be deemphasized. The image of proximity may be further enhanced by having a U.S. postal address (via a U.S. mail agency) and a toll-free 800 phone line.

4. The product must conform to American standards and requirements. This can include labeling for country of origin and "care" standards (not bilingual), flammability standards, Food and Drug Administration Standards for food and cosmetic products, electrical product approvals, and product liability requirements.

5. Use Canadian government assistance, which is readily available. The governments, both federal and provincial, have very active export promotion programs. The range of assistance available includes:
   a. Assistance in identifying potential markets from provincial departments and consulates in major U.S. cities.
   b. Publications and seminars on various export-related issues.
   c. Assistance in participating in trade missions, trade fairs, and exhibitions.
   d. Ensuring supplier credit programs via the Export Development program.
   e. Financing export development programs via grants or loans (varies from province to province).

In addition, the Canadian Manufacturers Association and Canadian Export Association provide assistance via various publications.

The principle underlying the implementation suggestions is "know your market," a basic axiom for both domestic and export marketing.

Direct Investment Strategy

When a market base has been established in the United States, and expansion of capacity is required, the question as to where additional capacity should be built must be considered. This is mainly an issue of where costs are lowest, after recognizing costs arising from the duplication of infrastructures.

While U.S. wage rates and taxes are generally lower than in Canada, these may not be the only determinants of the economics of production. The following must also be taken into consideration:

- Certain energy costs, particularly hydro, are lower in Canada.
- The overall quality of labour tends to be low in the low-wage geographic areas of the United States as the result of low levels of education. Thus, both worker productivity and the ability to handle more sophisticated tasks may be limited.
- Medical insurance if provided to employees as a fringe benefit is both expensive and highly variable in cost. As an indication of the level of cost, the major automobile manufacturers estimate that medical insurance costs them $300 per car produced in their U.S. plants versus $60 per car in Canada. In the United States, smaller companies trying to keep their costs down often place coverage with limited preferred risk pools if they qualify by way of the age and general health of the employees. However, it takes only a few serious illnesses on the part of the employees to drastically raise premiums, making year-to-year estimation of costs difficult.

In addition to operating cost advantage, financing for new plants may be available on better terms than in Canada. Counties and municipalities are able to offer attractive financing by way of locally issued revenue bonds to attract new industry. These provide a combination of low interest rates and extended repayment terms, or are used to build a plant and lease it to the company. Many municipalities also offer tax concessions to the new company.

Summary

1. The United States is a natural export market for Canadian business because of its size, proximity, common language, and similarity of cultures.
2. Despite these advantages, there are substantial differences between the Canadian and U.S. environments which result in Canada being a relatively high-cost country with a less competitive environment. As a result of the differences, concepts successful in Canada may not be effective in the United States.
3. Strategies for exporting to the United States should be based on reducing price sensitivity by selling "value" to specific target markets via carefully chosen distributors. The high cost of entry on any significant scale should be regarded as an investment.
4. Implementation requires knowledge of the idiosyncracies of the U.S. market, clear pricing, as well as meeting their product and labeling standards.

Government programs at both the federal and provincial levels are available to assist U.S. export development programs.

References

"Annual Report of the Ministry of Supply and Services Canada under the Corporations and Labour Unions Returns Act, Part II—Labour Unions, 1986," Statistics Canada 71–202.

Arnold, J.R., "Exporting to the United States—Costing Products" Appendix II, Selecting and Using Manufacturers Agents in the United States.

Brown, P.B., "Matters of Impact," *Inc.,* October 1988, pp. 115–18.

"Diversions," *Report on Business Magazine, The Globe and Mail,* July/August 1985.

The Financial Post 500, *Financial Post Company Ltd.,* Summer 1982.

"The Fortune 500," *Fortune,* April 25, 1988.

"How to Do Business in the U.S.," Ministry of Industry, Trade and Technology, Province of Ontario, Queen's Printer for Ontario, 1987.

Kidd, Kenneth, "Price Gaps that Drive Canadians to U.S. Shops Start in the Far East," *The Globe and Mail,* April 23, 1991.

Leighton, David S.R., "Doing Business in the U.S.: Canada's Challenge," *Business Quarterly,* Fall 1987, pp. 80–84.

Marfels, Christian, "Aggregate Concentration in International Perspective: Canada, Federal Republic of Germany, Japan and the United States," in *Mergers, Corporate Concentration and Power in Canada,* ed. R.S. Khemani, D.M. Shapiro, and W.T. Stanbury (Institute for Research on Public Policy, 1988), chap. 3.

Saffer, Morris, "Canadian Retailers: How to Succeed in U.S. Markets," *Business Quarterly,* Winter 1989, pp. 38–41.

Tigert, D.D., "Canada Versus the U.S.: The Growing Economic Gap," *The Financial Post,* March 21, 1984.

APPENDIX A:
HOW TO WORK OUT EXPORT PRICES[1]

One of the early steps in campaigning for export markets is working out realistic export prices—or "costing," as it is sometimes called. Too often, goods are priced for export merely on the basis of domestic price plus freight and insurance. Sometimes the resulting price is unrealistically high; occasionally it is too low. The would-be exporter should remember that foreign buyers usually have quotations from many countries to compare and will seek the best possible prices. Export quotations should therefore be kept as low as possible commensurate with a reasonable profit—and certainly a profit no higher than on domestic sales. Manufacturers who want eventually to make volume foreign sales should bear in mind that these will result from good quality offered at a fair price and should keep their profit to a minimum.

Federal sales tax does not apply to exports, and if any charge for advertising is made in domestic prices, it should be deducted from the base price before calculating export prices.

The following worksheet may serve as a sample guide to assist you in arriving at a realistic export price for your products.

More detailed information about export financing is available in the External Affairs publication *Export Guide—A Practical Approach.*

---

[1] J. R. Arnold, Export Consultant, Lasqueti, B.C. VOR 2JO. Reprinted by permission.

An Export Pricing Worksheet (C.I.F.)

Ref: 6243
Name of customer: Mr. Buyer, Importers Inc.
Address: 162 Overseas Blvd., Foreign Country
Product: WIDGET
Special terms or conditions quoted:
Unit quoted: 1,000
Gross weight: 64 kg
Cubic measure: 140 m^3

Item	(Can. $)
Cost and freight	
1. Cost of unit before profit	10,000
2. Profit at 10% (for example)	1,000
3. Overseas agent's commission at 7½% (for example)	825
4. Export packing	75
5. Labelling cost	10
6. Stencil marking cost	0
7. Strapping cost	5
8. Cartage	2
9. Freight to seaboard cost: $6.00 per 1,000; Type of carrier: rail	6
10. Unloading charges	2
11. Terminal charges	1
12. Longload or heavy loading charges	0
13. Consular documents charges	N/A
14. Other charges (cable, phone)	4
15. Ocean freight cost	30
16. Forwarding agent's fee	10
17. Export credit insurance at 1% (for example)	100
18. Financing charges for credit sales	400
Total of cost and freight	12,470
Insurance	
19. Marine insurance (add 10% to total of cost and freight) 13,717	
Approximate premium +137	
Amount to be insured 13,854	
20. Type of insurance: All risks; Rate: 1%; Premium: 138.54	139
Grand Total (C.I.F.)	12,609
Convert Canadian $ to export market currency	104,208

READING 4
CANADA AT THE CROSSROADS

The Reality of a New Competitive Environment

Michael E. Porter and Monitor Company

CANADA AND INTERNATIONAL COMPETITION: THEORY AND EVIDENCE

Setting the Context

The principal economic goal of a country is to provide a high and rising standard of living for its citizens. By this yardstick Canada's economy has performed well over the last 30 years. It has achieved one of the world's highest standards of living while creating and maintaining a generous and socially progressive state. Adjusted for purchasing power, Canada ranked second among Organization for Economic Cooperation and Development (OECD) countries in per capita gross domestic product (GDP) in 1989, up from fourth in 1960.

We believe, however, that Canada today is at an economic crossroads and that the core of its economic prosperity is at risk. Canada's rich natural resource endowments, its proximity to the United States, and a history of insulation from international competition have combined to allow Canadian industry to achieve an enviable economic performance. These same advantages, however, have led to an array of policies, strategies, and attitudes on the part of governments, business, labour, and individual Canadians that leave the economy in many respects ill-equipped to respond to a rapidly changing competitive environment.

Canadian industry now is undergoing a rapid structural change. As this process continues, signs are already accumulating that Canadian industry is encountering difficulties as it confronts a changed and more competitive environment. If the current trajectory continues, the standard of living of Canadians seems destined to fall behind. Yet there is nothing inevitable about this outcome; Canadians have in their own hands the power to change it.

Threats to Prosperity

The underpinning of competitiveness, and thus of a country's standard of living, is productivity. Productivity is the value of output produced by a day of work or a dollar of capital invested. In the long run, productivity determines the standard of living by setting wages, profits, and, ultimately, the resources available to meet

SOURCE: Excerpts from a study prepared for the Business Council on National Issues and the government of Canada, October 1991, by Michael E. Porter, Harvard Business School, and Monitor Company.

social needs. To achieve sustained productivity growth, an economy must continually *upgrade* itself. An upgrading economy is one that relentlessly pursues greater productivity in existing industries by improving products, utilizing more efficient production processes, and migrating into more sophisticated and higher-value industry segments. It is also an economy that has the capability to compete in entirely new industries, absorbing the resources made available from improved productivity in existing industries. The capacity of an economy to upgrade—its competitive potential—depends on underlying structural and institutional characteristics, such as its work force, its infrastructure, its postsecondary educational institutions, and its public policies. Cyclical factors, such as shifts in world commodity prices or exchange rates, can create the illusion of prosperity, but in reality yield only temporary advantages.

The Changing Competitive Environment

Traditionally, Canadians have lived in a relatively insulated environment brought about by paternalistic government policies, a history of market protection, and the accumulated attitudes and experiences of both individuals and businesses.

This old economic order, as we call it, was a system where many prospered. However, because the old order generally provided insulation from external pressures and fostered limited internal pressures, many of the critical requirements for upgrading to more sophisticated and sustainable competitive advantages in Canadian industry have been missing or are only weakly present.

Increasing globalization of trade and investment, accelerating technological changes, rapidly evolving company and country strategies, and—more recently—the Free Trade Agreement with the United States, represent significant discontinuities in the nature of international competition confronting Canadian-based industry. Together, these forces are pushing Canada away from the "comfortable insularity" of the old order. They will both magnify long-standing competitive weaknesses and hasten the pace of structural adjustment to a new competitive reality. What is most troubling is the fact that in essential areas such as science, technology, education, and training, significant barriers stand in the way of effective upgrading.

Owing to Canada's extensive trading relationship with the United States and its unusually high degree of foreign ownership, the shifting character of international competition poses particularly daunting challenges for Canadian firms and public policymakers. Many companies are currently in the process of determining how to reconfigure their North American and international activities, including deciding where to locate what we describe as their "home bases" for individual product lines and even their entire corporate operation. Typically, a company's home base is where the best jobs reside, where core research and development is undertaken, and where strategic control lies. Home bases are important to an economy because they support high productivity and productivity growth. In the context of the changing global economy, we believe that Canada is in danger of losing much of its capacity to attract and retain home bases.

So far, many industries and sectors show few signs of upgrading. In addition, as we discuss below, macroeconomic indicators have begun to manifest the weaknesses that exist at the industry level. Though Canada's status as a wealthy country is not in doubt, the risk is of a slowly eroding standard of living over the coming years.

Worrisome Performance Trends

Over the 1980s, Canada's economy performed quite well. Real economic growth between 1983 and 1989 was second only to Japan among the seven leading industrial countries (the G7). Canada also enjoyed the second fastest rate of employment growth among the G7 over the same period (the United States was first). Yet despite these favourable macroeconomic indicators, there is mounting evidence that Canada suffers from underlying economic weaknesses that could undercut its ability to achieve a higher standard of living in the future.

• The most serious weakness is *low productivity growth.* Since the early 1970s, Canada has ranked near the bottom of all major industrial countries in productivity growth. From 1979 to 1989, total factor productivity (TFP)—which measures the growth in productivity of both labour and capital inputs—rose by a mere 0.4 percent per year, tying Canada with the United States as the worst performer among the G7 countries. Over the same period, manufacturing labour productivity growth in Canada was the lowest among the G7 countries, averaging only 1.8 percent per annum.

• A second and closely related concern is Canada's record in the area of *unit labour costs.* Unit labour costs measure labour costs adjusted for productivity. They are a key indicator of competitiveness, especially for industries and firms that produce tradeable goods and services. Between 1979 and 1989, Canada's unit labour costs in the manufacturing sector rose more quickly than those in most other industrialized countries, and increased more than twice as fast as costs in the United States, which is the most important competitive benchmark for Canadian industry.

• *Unemployment* is a third danger signal. Despite robust employment growth over the past two decades, the unemployment rate in Canada has exceeded that in most other industrialized countries. In recent years, long-term unemployment has become more of a problem, and the average duration of unemployment has risen. Although the unemployment trend is a separate issue from that of productivity growth, growing numbers of workers with marginal or intermittent attachments to the labour force, and the rising average duration of unemployment, point to underlying problems that could affect Canada's capacity to upgrade its economy and respond successfully to changes in technology and global markets.

• *Lagging investments in upgrading skills and technology.* Canada's poor record in productivity growth and unemployment is disturbing. More worrisome in many ways, however, is that the investments that will drive productivity and employment growth in the future have been lagging. While aggregate investment growth has been quite strong, Canada trails competitor countries in private sector investments linked directly to enhanced productivity. Between 1980 and 1989, investment in machinery and equipment as a percentage of GDP was lower in Canada than in most other major industrialized countries. Similarly, Canadian private sector investment in research and development as a percentage of GDP is the second lowest among the G7 countries (slightly ahead of Italy). Moreover, investments by Canadian firms in worker training fall well short of levels registered in the United States, Germany, Japan, and many other advanced countries.

• Finally, the *macroeconomic environment* is not sufficiently supportive of investment. The ability of government to create a stable macroeconomic environment is being hampered by chronic government deficits and rapidly growing public debt. Combined federal and provincial government debt has been growing more quickly than the economy for a decade and now exceeds 70 percent of GDP. Among the G7 countries, only Italy has a higher government debt level. Servicing these massive government debt obligations lowers Canadian income and places constraints on the ability of Canadian governments to maintain an environment that encourages investment and the upgrading efforts of Canadian industry.

Canada's Position in International Competition

This study provides a detailed examination of Canada's position in international competition between 1978 and 1989 and how this compares with the positions of other industrialized countries. Here, we can only summarize the key findings and conclusions that flow from this in-depth analysis.

Focus on the Traded Sector

A country's performance in the traded sector provides a unique window into the sources of national economic prosperity. The traded sector is a large and increasingly important component of the economies of all industrialized countries. It has particular leverage for productivity growth, especially in smaller and mid-size countries such as Canada, where the ability to trade frees productive local industries from the constraints of the domestic market. Thus freed, these industries can grow and absorb resources from less productive industries, whose products can then be imported. In addition, the traded sector is where firms from a multiplicity of countries compete. It is the place where one can best analyze the ways in which the economic context in different countries creates advantages or disadvantages for firms.

This study takes a detailed look at Canada's export sector. It explores Canada's position in international competition, both over time and relative to other industrialized countries. The basis for our statistical analysis is the United Nations Standard International Trade Classification (SITC) statistics. These trade statistics, which measure exports and imports in approximately 4,000 narrowly defined industries, allow us to compare the trade performance of many countries over time at the level of strategically distinct industries. The UN trade statistics were also used in the original 10-nation research reported in *The Competitive Advantage of Nations.*

The export sector is a vital component of Canada's economy, representing 25.2 percent of GDP in 1989. Among the G7 countries, Canada is second only to Germany in the importance of trade to its economy. Canada's share of world market economy exports has varied between 4 and 5 percent over the past three decades. The trend for the period as a whole has been one of slow decline. More important than the trend in Canada's world export share, however, is how the composition of Canadian exports has evolved.

The remainder of this section summarizes the main characteristics of Canada's exports—a subject explored at much greater length in the full study report.

Significant Natural Resource Dependence

Perhaps the most striking feature of Canada's export profile is the prominent role of natural resource-based exports. These accounted for 45.8 percent of Canada's total exports in 1989. In fact, Canada's share of world resource exports rose from 5.0 percent in 1978 to 8.3 percent in 1989. Of nine major trading countries, Canada has by far the largest share of country exports based on unprocessed and semiprocessed natural resources; these comprised more than one third of all Canadian exports in 1989, compared to 20 percent in the United States and 11 percent in Sweden.

Exports of natural resource-based products are by no means undesirable—indeed, they have done much to make Canada wealthy. However, a high proportion of exports concentrated in relatively *unprocessed* resources suggests that, on the whole, Canadian industry has failed to upgrade or extend its competitive advantage into processing technology and the marketing and support of more sophisticated resource-based products. Dependence on semi- and unprocessed resources also leaves Canada vulnerable to commodity price shifts, technology substitution, and the emergence of lower-cost competitors, often in less developed countries. Why this pattern exists and what it means for the future is therefore a critical issue.

Exports Concentrated in Five Broad Clusters

Understanding the underpinnings of Canada's competitive advantage is aided by examining the nature of its industry *clusters.* To do this, all export industries are grouped into distinct clusters defined by end-use applications. Each cluster contains a number of distinct industries (with forest products, for example, consisting of market pulp, newsprint, sawmilling, and many other industries related to the forest sector). *Upstream industries* produce inputs used by many other industries. Most upstream industries are resource-based, with the exception of semiconductors/computers. There are six broad sectors connected to *industrial and supporting functions.* Industries at this level typically compete on the basis of technology and are often the industrial core of the economy. Another six sectors are associated with *final consumption goods and services.* Industries at this level are connected to end consumer needs. Resource-rich countries typically begin at the top level of upstream industries, while resource-poor countries start from the bottom level of labour-intensive final consumption goods. Most gradually grow toward the middle (industrial and supporting) level as they upgrade and lay the foundation of an industrial core.

Canadian exports are highly concentrated in three of the 16 clusters—materials/metals, forest products, and transportation—which together account for nearly 62 percent of Canada's exports. These three clusters, along with petroleum/chemicals and food/beverages, represented more than 82 percent of total Canadian exports in 1989. Looked at by end-use application, Canadian exports are concentrated at the level of upstream industries, where three of the five main clusters are located. At the level of industrial and supporting goods, Canadian exports consist largely of transportation equipment. Here we see the effect of the Canada–United States Auto Pact, which has had a profound influence on Canada's manufacturing sector (and, especially, its manufacturing exports). In 1989, fully 79 percent of transportation sector exports were from industries related to the Auto Pact. (Other cluster exports included aircraft and related parts and urban mass transit equipment.) Final consumption goods and services represent a relatively small share of Canada's exports (15 percent in 1989), the most significant cluster being food/beverage products, which consists largely of minimally processed products such as fish and grain.

Key Role of Foreign-Controlled Companies

Foreign ownership is relatively high in Canada, although it has been declining since the 1960s. In the manufacturing sector, for example, approximately 45 percent of assets in Canada are foreign controlled. Foreign ownership is quite widespread in most of Canada's five leading export clusters. Exhibit 1 shows the share of corporate assets controlled by foreign firms in selected industries within the various clusters. Among Canada's five main export clusters, foreign ownership is highest in transportation equipment and lowest in forest products. Many of the strategic decisions in important Canadian sectors are made outside of Canada, based on the overall global strategies of parent companies. How the choices made by these parent companies with respect to the location of home base activities for all or segments of their businesses will evolve in response to changes in international competition is a critical issue for the Canadian economy.

Very Limited Machinery Exports

Canada has few internationally competitive machinery industries. In total, machinery exports accounted for just 3.4 percent of all Canadian exports in 1989, up

Exhibit 1 Foreign-Controlled Share of Assets of Selected Canadian Industries, 1987

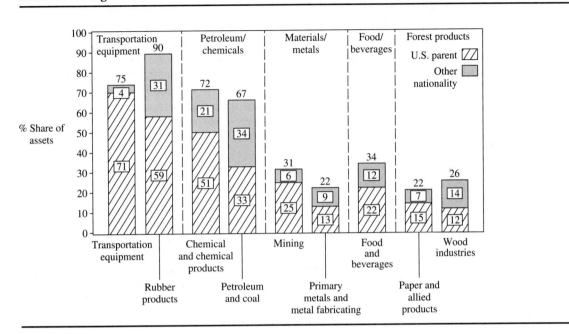

Source: Statistics Canada; Calura

slightly from 3 percent in 1978, but substantially lower than in other major industrialized countries. In fact, Canada's share of competitive machinery exports fell from 1.3 percent of world exports in 1978 to 0.7 percent in 1989.[1] In addition, Canada's trade deficit in machinery increased 31 percent in real terms since 1978, to U.S. $3.3 billion.

Machinery industries are a sign of healthy economic upgrading. They give a country's core industries quicker access to and more control over fast-changing process technologies. Superiority in machinery and related and supporting industries can help to sustain competitive advantage in primary goods. Primary goods producers can often work closely with machinery firms located in their home country to upgrade and improve productivity. This relationship tends to be more difficult to build with foreign suppliers. In short, with few competitive machinery industries, many Canadian businesses are deprived of the dynamic interactions that foster process innovation and upgrading.

---

[1]The definition of international competitiveness employed in this study was consistent with that of the 10-nation study: a world export market share greater than Canada's overall share of market economy exports in 1989.

Principal Clusters Exhibit Limited Breadth or Depth

In looking in more detail, we find that even the most significant export clusters exhibit limited breadth or depth. For instance, in the forest products cluster, three industries—sawn wood, newsprint, and market pulp—account for 75 percent of total exports. There is almost no export position in more sophisticated segments such as fine paper. Most significantly, in analyzing the patterns of change in export composition from 1978–1989, we see little evidence to suggest exports have shifted into more sophisticated industry segments within these clusters.

Few Service Industries Are Internationally Competitive

Services represent about 68 percent of Canada's GDP and account for upwards of 70 percent of total employment. Among the G7 countries, Canada is second only to the United States in the relative size of the service sector. Although most services are not traded, they do represent a significant portion of the inputs of all goods exported by Canada. Uncompetitive domestic service industries can undermine the competitive position of a country's goods-producing sectors. The need for constant productivity improvements and upgrading thus applies equally to service industries, regardless of whether the output of such industries directly enters international trade.

International trade in services has been growing rapidly and now amounts to more than U.S. $700 billion per year (out of total world trade of $3.3 trillion). However, relatively few industries in the Canadian services sector have reached international standing and Canada's service exports as a percentage of total exports are the lowest of the G7.

Deteriorating Trade Balances Outside of Resource Sectors

Canada's overall mix of exports has remained quite consistent in the recent past, with resource-dependent industries maintaining a 45–46 percent share of total exports between 1978 and 1989. Four out of Canada's five dominant export sectors enjoy positive trade balances—materials/metals, forest products, petroleum/chemicals, and food/beverages. Canada's strength in resource-based sectors is reflected in its growing positive trade balance in upstream industries, reaching $23 billion in 1989 (measured in U.S. dollars), up sharply from $9 billion in 1978. A rising trade surplus in the forest products sector (from $5.3 billion in 1978 to $16.4 billion in 1989) largely accounts for Canada's strengthening position in upstream industries.

Canada's trade balance is negative, however, in most of 16 industry clusters. Overall, Canada has recorded growing trade surpluses in resource-dependent goods, and rising trade deficits in nonresource sectors. Higher deficits in most nonresource industries point to weaknesses in Canada's competitive profile. Imports are fulfilling Canadian demand in a growing range of sophisticated industry segments. Canada remains extremely dependent on exports of resource-based products (and transportation equipment) to sustain its wealth and standard of living.

Export Economy Divided into Four Main Categories

Looking closely at Canada's trade patterns suggests another way of picturing the Canadian economy. In particular, it is possible to divide the export sector into four broad industry groupings:

1. *Resource-based industries.* These are industries in which Canadian exports are derived wholly or largely from natural resource advantages. Pulp and paper, lumber, and copper are examples.

2. *Market access-driven industries.* These consist of industries where Canadian exports come from plants established by foreign companies primarily to gain access to the Canadian market. Indicators used to identify such industries in our research were a high share of assets controlled by foreign companies and/or historically high tariffs. Auto Pact industries are the most important example and currently represent about 60 percent of all exports from market access-driven industries. Other industries in this category are rubber products, commercial refrigeration, office and business machines, electrical appliances, and some areas of industrial chemicals.

3. *Innovation-driven industries.* These are defined as either Canadian-owned indigenous industries or foreign-owned industries where competitiveness has been driven largely by Canadian-based innovation. Manufacturing industries in this category include telecommunications equipment, aircraft and aircraft parts, and electronic components.

4. *Other industries.* These represent the balance of Canada's export sector. Industries falling into this group tend to be uncompetitive or marginally competitive based on world export share. Industries in this group consist mainly of foreign-controlled firms with modest exports or indigenous industries involved in trade solely with bordering states of the United States.

To approximate how Canadian exports are divided into these groups, we used UN trade data. Unfortunately, this data covers goods-producing industries but not services. Canadian goods-producing industries were classified using the above categories, and the industries in each category were then aggregated (as measured by shipments). Exhibit 2 displays the trends by category in terms of exports and balance of trade. (Note that exports are valued in 1989 U.S. dollars.) The estimates are crude, but they are consistent with earlier data. As shown, the most significant growth in Canadian exports of goods between 1978 and 1989 was in the resource sector, which markedly increased its exports and its trade surplus over the decade. In the innovation-driven industries, exports have increased slightly and the trade balance is slightly negative, while in the market access sector, exports are up and the trade balance relatively steady. However, the size and trajectory of the "other industries" category is troubling. It is a significant part of the economy but has been contributing to worsening trade balances. This

EXHIBIT 2   Canadian Goods-Producing Export Economy by Type of Industries

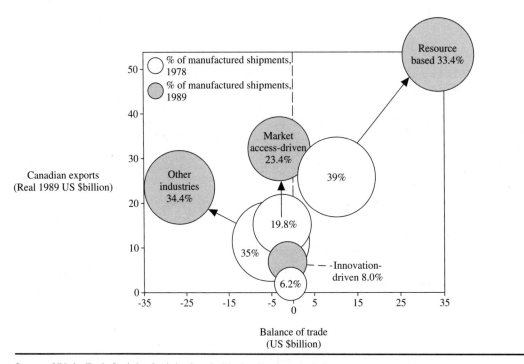

SOURCE: UN sitc Trade Statistics; Statistics Canada; Monitor Company Analysis.

again underscores the fact that the resource sector is the strongest part of the export economy.

Canada's International Competitive Position: Conclusion

This brief overview of Canada's position in international competition and its export economy highlights a number of real or potential weaknesses. Canada's high dependence on exports of relatively unprocessed natural resource-based products signals a lack of breadth even in the country's most prominent export clusters. Likewise, Canada's very weak position in machinery indicates a lack of depth within key industry clusters. Most importantly, our analysis found little evidence that either the breadth or the depth of Canada's major export clusters is increasing. Taken together, this evidence is consistent with the brief macroeconomic picture, previously presented, which points to an economy that shows limited signs of upgrading, and suggests that productivity growth—the critical driver of prosperity—may be increasingly difficult to achieve.

Determinants of National Competitive Advantage: The "Diamond"

Competitiveness has emerged as a preeminent issue for firms and government policymakers in every industrialized country. Most efforts to explain national competitiveness have taken an aggregate perspective, focusing on factor endowments, macroeconomic indicators, or government policies. Patterns of international trade have traditionally been explained within the framework of comparative advantage. The best-known variant of this theory begins with the premise that all countries employ equivalent technologies but differ in their endowments of so-called factors of production—land, labour, natural resources, and capital—which are the basic inputs of production. The traditional theory holds that particular countries gain advantage in those industries that make the most intensive use of the productive factors they have in abundance.

Recently, however, there has been a growing realization that traditional comparative advantage theory is no longer sufficient to understand the patterns of trade in modern international competition. Competition is becoming increasingly global in character. More and more firms are adopting a global perspective when making decisions about where to source raw materials, manufacture, and sell their products or services. This has the effect of "de-coupling" the firm from the factor endowments of a country. Raw materials, components, machinery, and many services are now available to firms in most countries on increasingly comparable terms. The success of a firm is thus less and less dependent on endowments of basic factors in its home country.

With the trend toward globalization of industry, it is tempting to think that the individual country is no longer important to the international success of its firms, or even that countries have become irrelevant to international competition. Results from the 10-nation study, as well as from our study of Canadian competitiveness, strongly suggest that this view is mistaken. Leading international competitors in a given industry are often located in the same country and often in the same city or region. The positions of countries in international competition tend to be surprisingly stable, stretching over several decades or even longer. This suggests that competitive advantage is created and sustained through a highly localized process, and that the attributes of particular countries *do* shape patterns of competitive success.

The Diamond of National Advantage

What is needed is a new paradigm that presents a consistent and holistic explanatory framework. This paradigm must explain several empirical facts. First, no one country is competitive in all or most industries; rather, countries are competitive in particular industries and industry segments. Second, each country exhibits distinct patterns of international competitive success and failure. Third, countries tend to succeed in clusters of industries rather than in isolated industries, and the pattern of competitive clusters differs markedly from country to country.

The principal conclusion from the 10-nation study is that sustained international competitive advantage results from ongoing improvement and innovation, not from static advantages. Here, innovation is defined very broadly, to encompass technology and the full spectrum of activities relevant to competing in the marketplace. Creating competitive advantage requires that its sources be relentlessly upgraded and broadened.

Against this backdrop, the critical questions then become: What is it about a country that supports high and rising levels of productivity in individual industries? In what ways does a country provide a dynamic environment for its firms? How do countries differ in the competitive environment created for their industries? The results of the 10-nation study suggest that the answer to these questions lies in four broad attributes of a country that, individually and as a system, constitute the "diamond of national advantage." This can be thought of as the playing field that each country establishes for its industries and companies (see Exhibit 3). The four attributes are

- *Factor conditions.* The country's position in basic factors of production such as labour, land, natural resources, and infrastructure. Also included

EXHIBIT 3 National Determinants of Competitive Advantage: "The Diamond"

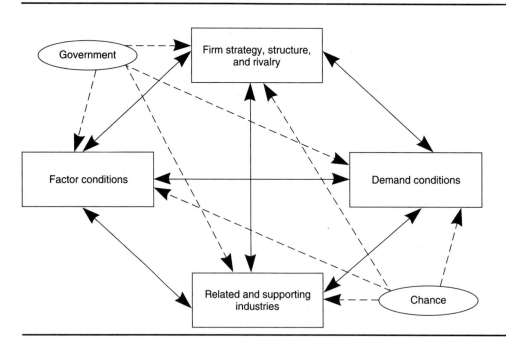

are highly specialized and advanced pools of skills, technology, and infrastructure tailored to meet the needs of particular industries.

- *Demand conditions.* The nature of home-market demand for the output of local industries. Particularly important is the presence of sophisticated and demanding local customers who pressure firms to innovate and whose needs anticipate needs elsewhere.

- *Related and supporting industries.* The presence (or absence) in the country of supplier industries and other related industries that are internationally competitive. This determinant includes local suppliers of specialized inputs (e.g., machinery, components, and services) that are integral to innovation in the industry, as well as innovative local companies in industries related by technology, skills, or customers.

- *Firm strategy, structure, and rivalry.* The conditions in the country affecting how companies are created, organized, and managed, as well as the nature of domestic rivalry.

Two additional variables, government and chance, also influence the national competitive environment in important ways. *Government policy* is best understood by examining how it has an impact on each of the four determinants of competitive advantage included in the diamond. The role of government is analyzed by looking at its effects on factor creation and the goals and behaviour of individuals and firms, its role as a buyer of goods and services, and its influence on the competitive environment through competition policies, regulation, and government ownership of enterprises.

Chance events are developments outside of the control of the country's government and its firms, but which affect the competitive environment. Examples include breakthroughs in basic technologies, external political, economic and legal developments, and international war and conflict. Chance events can create opportunities for a country's firms to acquire or strengthen competitive advantage.

The Diamond as a System

Each of the four determinants of competitiveness influences the capacity of a country's industry to innovate and upgrade. Together they constitute a dynamic system that is more important than its parts.

The ability to benefit from one attribute in the diamond depends on the state of others. The presence of sophisticated and demanding buyers, for example, will not result in advanced products or production processes unless the quality of human resources enables firms to respond to buyer needs. There must also be a climate that supports sustained investment to fund the development of these products and processes. At the broadest level, weaknesses in any one determinant will constrain an industry's potential for advancement and upgrading.

The four determinants are also mutually reinforcing. For example, the development of specialized supporting industries tends to increase the supply of specialized factors that also benefit an industry. Vigorous domestic rivalry also stimulates the development of unique pools of specialized factors. This is particularly likely if the rivals are all located in one city or region.

The diamond also bears centrally on a country's ability to attract mobile factors of production, a final form of mutual reinforcement. Mobile factors, particularly ideas and highly skilled individuals, are becoming increasingly important to international competitiveness. Mobile factors tend to be drawn to the location where they can achieve the greatest productivity, because that is where they can obtain the highest returns. The same features that make a country an attractive home base also help it attract mobile factors.

Advantages in the entire diamond may not be necessary for competitive advantage in low-skill or inherently resource-dependent industries. Firms may also be able to penetrate the standardized, lower technology segments of more advanced industries without broad advantages in the diamond. In such instances, basic factor costs may be decisive. Competitive advantage in more sophisticated industries and industry segments, on the other hand, rarely results from strength in a single determinant. Sustained success in these industries and segments usually requires the interaction of favourable conditions in several of the determinants and at least parity in the others.

Geographic concentration also elevates and magnifies the interaction of the four determinants. It enhances the pressure from local rivalry and the frequency of spin-offs, works to stimulate and raise the sophistication of local customers, stimulates the formation of related and supporting industries, triggers greater local investment in specialized factor creation, and provides a magnet for mobile factors.

These same forces explain another important finding of the 10-nation study with particular relevance to Canada. There is often a marked disparity between the economic success of regions within countries. The striking difference between the industrial success of northern and southern Italy, northern and southern Germany, and eastern and central Canada are three such examples.

One manifestation of the systemic nature of the determinants is in the phenomenon of clustering. Clusters involve supplier industries, customer industries, and related industries that are all competitive. Such clusters are characteristic of every advanced economy—American entertainment, German chemicals, Japanese electronics, Danish foods. Countries tend to be successful in clusters of linked industries. It is rare that an isolated industry or firm achieves international success.

Clusters grow and transform themselves through spin-offs and diversification of firms into upstream, downstream, and related industries and activities. The fields where several clusters overlap are often fertile grounds for new business formation. In Japan, for example, the interstices among electronics and new materials are spawning new competitive strengths in fields as diverse as robotics and displays.

Vital clusters of industries are often at the heart of a country's economic development, and especially its capacity to innovate. As suggested by the earlier trade analysis, however, the creation of more dynamic industry clusters represents a major challenge facing the Canadian economy.

Applying the Diamond in a Canadian Context

In applying this framework to Canada, four features of the Canadian economy must be addressed: the prominence of natural resource industries in Canada's exports, the role of rivalry in the relatively small Canadian market, the high degree of foreign ownership of Canadian industry, and the effects of Canada's location next to the huge U. S. market.

1. *Natural resources.* Canada's economy, and especially its export economy, is heavily based on natural resources. Some argue that resource industries are inherently less desirable than manufacturing or "high-tech" industries. This logic is flawed. There is nothing inherently undesirable about resource-based industries, provided they support high levels of productivity and productivity growth. Such industries can make a country wealthy if its resource position is highly favourable, as has been the case for Canada during most of its history. If resource-based industries continually upgrade their sophistication through improvements in their processes and products, competitive positions can be sustained and productivity growth assured. In many resource-based economies, however, resource abundance contributes to a set of policies, attitudes, and institutions that reduce incentives to upgrade and make it difficult to move beyond the factor-driven stage of development. This can leave resource-based economies vulnerable to adverse shifts in technology, markets, and international competition. The key test we must apply in appraising Canada's resource-based industries is their record in upgrading competitive advantage and their capacity for upgrading in the future.

2. *Domestic rivalry.* Domestic rivalry is critical to innovation and to the development of competitive advantage. Yet some commentators contend that Canada's relatively small market precludes the coexistence of strong Canadian-based rivals. Others argue that the proximity of the United States—and thus of U. S.–based competition in the form of imports of American goods—can compensate for limited rivalry at home. Previous research, however, has shown that vigorous domestic rivalry encourages international success not just in large countries, but also in small and mid-sized economies such as Denmark, Sweden, Switzerland, and Taiwan. The number of local firms needed for effective local competition will vary by industry, depending on economies of scale and other factors. In every country studied in the 10-nation research, some firms were found that had achieved a measure of international success without the benefit of local rivalry. Sometimes government policy has limited local competition in virtually all countries (as in telecommunications). Local rivalry may also be less important to competitive advantage in pure commodity businesses in which advantage derives from factor costs rather than innovation. However, the great preponderance of evidence suggests that local rivalry plays a powerful role in competitive advantage. Weak domestic rivalry in many industries in Canada,

then, will tend to diminish the odds of achieving sustained international success.

3. *Foreign investment.* There are three main types of foreign investment. Factor-sourcing investment typically seeks access to a country's natural resources, labour, or other basic factors. Foreign firms making such investments have their home bases outside of the host country. Market access foreign investment arises when companies are required—for example, by tariffs or government regulations—to develop a presence in a country in order to gain access to its domestic market. In these cases, too, the home base remains in the country of the parent firm. Most foreign investments in Canada have been motivated by a desire to source Canadian resources or gain access to the Canadian market.

The third, and most beneficial, type of foreign investment is that which establishes or acquires a home base for a particular business or business unit in the host country. In these cases, the management and other core activities are located in the host country, which signals that that country possesses true international competitive advantage in the industry. The home base is where the firm normally contributes the most to the local economy in a particular industry, by establishing the most productive jobs, investing in specialized factor creation, acting as a sophisticated buyer for other local industries as well as a sophisticated related and supporting firm for other industries, and helping to create a vibrant local competitive milieu.

Canada has witnessed a good deal of debate on the issue of foreign investment and its impact on the country's economy. Much of this debate has been wide of the mark. We believe that in most circumstances, a country is better off with foreign investment than without it. And Canada, in our view, has been a net beneficiary. Foreign companies bring to the host country capital, skills, and technology—all of which boost productivity. Yet the pattern of foreign activities in Canada also signals circumstances that create vulnerabilities for the future. Though there are exceptions, few foreign-controlled firms have made Canada a home base for product lines.

As competition becomes more global and trade and investment barriers fall, the location of firm activities will reflect true economic advantage. The key challenge then is to create the conditions under which foreign—and Canadian—firms will *want* to locate home bases, and perform sophisticated activities, in Canada.

4. *The importance of Canadian diamonds given North American and global competition.* Canada and the United States share a lengthy, easily permeable border as well as many social and cultural attributes. Why, then, should we focus our attention on the Canadian diamond? Wouldn't it make more sense to look at the larger North American diamond, and ask how Canadian firms can take advantage of circumstances in the United States to achieve competitive success? The most basic reason to be concerned about the Canadian diamond is that Canada's standard of living largely depends on the activities that take place in Canada. The location of the most productive economic activities, especially home base activities, is determined by the health of the Canadian diamond in any given industry compared to other locations. And while there are many

similarities between Canada and the United States, there are also significant differences—in institutions, trading patterns, tax policies, customer behaviour, economic structure, and labour force composition, among other areas. It is these differences that serve to create distinctive Canadian diamonds in industries. Although the Canada–United States Free Trade Agreement is likely to lessen some of the differences between the two countries, it will also magnify the competitive impact of those that remain.

Competitive advantage tends to be highly localized within countries. Locations differ in the environment they provide for innovation and upgrading. Proximity to customers, suppliers, rivals, and sources of specialized factors is crucial to the innovation process. The geographic locus of competitive advantage can cross national borders. In the case of Canada, the relevant arena of competitive advantage for a particular industry may encompass adjacent parts of the United States. In addition, it makes sense for Canadian firms to reach into the U. S. diamond to strengthen their competitive position or overcome weaknesses in the Canadian diamond—for example, by selling to and getting feedback from more sophisticated American customers. But Canadian firms can only take advantage of the U. S. diamond selectively. Basic factors and demand are easiest to access. In contrast, industry-specific infrastructure, a highly skilled workforce, and certain types of supplier and customer relationships are difficult for a country's firms—including Canada's—to source at a distance.

In short, there is no single North American diamond in industries which allows us to ignore Canadian circumstances. Our attention must therefore be directed to the strength of Canadian determinants.

DIRECTIONS FOR CHANGE

The Comfortable Insularity of the Old Order

The preceding section presents a picture of an economic system that had served Canada well in many respects but leaves the economy ill-equipped for the future. This old economic order was an internally consistent system in which the determinants were mutually consistent and reinforcing. This makes change exceedingly difficult.

Canada's abundant factor resources have been the bedrock of the economy. In many cases, these resources allowed Canadian firms to be profitable by exporting relatively unprocessed commodities rather than through upgrading. Strategies based on basic factor advantages often limited the demand for advanced technology. This in turn constrained investment in R&D and demand for highly skilled employees, which was reflected in enrolment patterns in universities and in the nature of educational programs. The virtual absence of leading-edge related and supporting industries inhibited another possible source of technology.

These tendencies spilled over into other sectors of the economy where Canada did not have such advantages. Many firms, insulated from external and internal rivalry, were content to exploit the profitable home market. The rate of innovation was slow. What emerged was a tendency to administer existing wealth rather than to invest vigorously to create new wealth.

Canada's wealth also provided little incentive for labour, management, and government to work together to improve national competitiveness. Significant chasms now exist between the three constituencies and within government itself. The relationship between labour and management has often been confrontational. At the same time, management has seldom treated labour as partners. Labour and government have also not worked well together, with labour often taking on an adversarial role with respect to many aspects of economic policy, while governments' relations with their own work force have also sometimes been strained.

Canadian companies have sought government assistance in export promotion, investment in specialized infrastructure, government procurement, and other forms of support. They rarely have cooperated, however, with governments in areas that have important impacts on international competitiveness, such as R&D, training, and education. The federal and provincial governments have struggled over roles and mandates. This has led to conflicting and overlapping programs that have worked to the detriment of the economy.

These attitudes and behaviours reflect the old competitiveness paradigm. Business acted as if economic rents would go on forever and moved to exploit the sheltered Canadian market. Labour acted as if jobs and high and rising wages could be taken for granted, because business profits were high and secure. Governments held the view that ample resources would continue to exist to fund social needs.

Government's Overall Effect on the Old Economic Order

Government's proper role is to challenge and raise the sights of industry by improving the quality of the inputs that firms draw upon, and creating a competitive context that promotes upgrading. Effective government policies create an environment which stimulates companies to gain competitive advantage, rather than involving government directly in the process.

As we have discussed, government policies in Canada have often not measured up. Those policies that have most hampered competitiveness in the Canadian economy can be grouped into a small number of major themes that are outgrowths of the old economic order.

1. *Insulation from external and internal competition.* Historically, considerable effort has been directed at insulating the Canadian economy from external pressures by protecting firms from international competition and safeguarding

national autonomy. Similarly, weak competition policies were a natural outgrowth of the view that companies had to be large to compete with foreign firms.

2. *Forestalling the need for upgrading.* Canadian government policies have often sought to remove the need for upgrading rather than encourage it. Artificially constrained factor input costs—in industries as diverse as transportation, hydroelectric power, and agriculture—lessen pressures for upgrading and reflect a static, cost-based conception of competition. In fact, it could be argued that the current Canadian preoccupation with bringing down exchange rates is a reflection of the same mindset.

3. *Direct intervention instead of business action.* Canadian governments have had a strong tendency to intervene directly in competition rather than stimulate upgrading by industry itself. In many policy areas, particularly in science and technology, and education and training, private sector participation has not been well leveraged. Direct intervention in the form of subsidies and bailouts has also been a prominent feature of the Canadian economic landscape.

4. *Programs to distribute wealth and improve welfare needlessly undermine the economy.* There is a strongly held belief in Canada that all citizens have a right to essential services such as health care and education, a minimum standard of living maintained by social welfare programs, and the opportunity to be employed. Yet the implementation of programs has often proven counterproductive. Canada's commitment to employment has frequently been used to justify protective strategies that preserve jobs in the short term but simultaneously distort rivalry and delay necessary adjustment. In addition, the effectiveness of the substantial resources devoted to the task of narrowing regional economic disparities has often been undermined by programs which emphasize diversification rather than building on regional strengths.

5. *Conflicting government policies and objectives.* No one level of government in Canada controls a full set of variables in any given policy area, which complicates the process of policy development and implementation. A high level of policy coordination is necessary to make Canada's decentralized system work, but such coordination has been lacking. For example, in labour market programs, the provinces set and enforce employment standards, while the federal government maintains responsibility for training and unemployment compensation. Furthering Canada's science and technology capabilities has also been hampered by a lack of coordination between federal and provincial research bodies. Jurisdictional overlap has often added a layer of complexity and compounded the level of uncertainty that firms face in anticipating changes in the business environment.

Forces of Change

As we have seen in our discussion of the determinants of competitive advantage, the Canadian economy is coming under increasing external pressures. Forces of change are disintegrating the old order. New competitive realities—including globalization of production, finance and markets, accelerating technological change, lower tariffs worldwide, and free trade between Canada and the United States (and perhaps Mexico)—call for a more dynamic and flexible set of responses than those typical of the old Canadian order. Canada's future competitiveness, therefore, must be driven by a new paradigm, based on productivity and innovation.

Major structural adjustment in Canada is inevitable. The question is whether the adjustment is positive or whether it leads to an erosion in the standard of living. Also at issue is how long and painful the restructuring process will be, even if business, labour, and government move in the right direction. How long will it take for Canada to transform itself from the old paradigm to a new one? And how much will it cost?

As external pressures are increasing, Canadian firms are beginning to experience greater internal pressures. This is due partly to a number of government policies that are increasingly oriented toward providing a more challenging competitive domestic environment, and partly as a result of positive initiatives taken by firms themselves.

At the federal level, positive government steps include the recently strengthened competition laws, privatization of crown corporations, and efforts to deregulate industries, including energy and transportation. Government is also beginning to employ policies that encourage, and even pressure, firms to upgrade. Tax reform has reduced past distortions, and generous R&D incentives are in place. Increasing the private sector's commitment to training is at the heart of the federal government's new Labour Force Development Strategy. Reform of unemployment insurance has improved incentives to upgrade skills and return to the workforce, though more must be done. In the area of science and technology, a rising number of government programs are being oriented to priorities driven by the private sector.

In response to the significant external and internal pressures facing the economy, we have also seen signs of positive change in a number of industries studied, including industries in the resource sector. For example, Inco has taken significant steps to upgrade its mineral extraction and smelting technologies and improve labour-management relations. A number of companies in the pulp and paper sector are beginning modernization programs. Other firms have begun to reposition their activities in light of intensified competition by becoming more focused and effective producers.

Systemic Barriers to Change

With increasing external pressures and some positive internal initiatives, one might be tempted to believe that Canada's weaknesses will be corrected naturally. However, the vestiges of the old economic order in Canada have imposed significant barriers to upgrading. These barriers are systemic, not isolated. They reside in policies, institutions, and attitudes that permeate the economy. The challenge is heightened by the fact that the diamond is an interdependent system, in which the weakest link constrains progress.

While some necessary steps are being taken, the current extent of change is inadequate. Our analysis of the determinants of competitive advantage in Canada revealed both tangible and intangible barriers to upgrading. Though each industry has a unique diamond, the strength of which is driven by features specific to that industry, virtually all industries we have examined are affected by at least some of these barriers.

Canada's workforce is not well equipped for upgrading and change. The basic skill levels of many citizens are inadequate, in spite of high per capita spending on education. Shortages exist or are looming in skill- and technology-related occupations. Specialized skill development is lagging due to poor vocational apprenticeship training and weak links between educational institutions and industry. Finally, company investments in training are low compared to other industrialized countries.

Canada's R&D infrastructure is not well aligned with requirements for upgrading. Too much R&D spending takes place through government laboratories. The links between publicly funded research institutes and industry are poorly developed. The supply of highly qualified personnel may be inadequate for future research needs.

The level of sophistication of Canadian home demand also works against upgrading. Weak related and supporting industries, as well as inadequate cluster development, constrain innovation and new business formation in Canada. The lack of Canadian process equipment manufacturers is particularly striking and contributes to the weakness in process technology development and adoption in this country.

Firm strategies and structure and the extent of local rivalry in Canada have done little to enhance domestic productivity. Too many Canadian firms continue to maintain an insular focus, concentrated almost exclusively on the domestic market. Finally, a number of Canada's "safety net" programs continue to diminish personal incentives to upgrade skills.

In many ways, however, the most significant barriers to upgrading are attitudinal. Too often, the old mindsets are still in place in business, labour, and government. Canadians still see competitiveness in terms of the old paradigm, which points to inappropriate responses to the current difficulties.

Threats to Canadian Industries

The forces we have described in general terms can be translated into specific threats in the broad categories of Canadian industries identified earlier. These individual threats differ from group to group, though their underlying causes and implications are similar.

Resource-Based Industries

Given its abundant factor endowments, Canada's heavy emphasis on resources is not surprising. Yet the sustainability of these industries' competitive advantage is in question. Depletion of resources is a threat to both renewable resource industries, such as fisheries, where a number of factors can upset projected equilibrium levels, and nonrenewable resource industries, where new sites are often more remote and therefore more expensive to exploit.

Canada's biggest problem is likely the emergence of lower cost competitors. Basic factor advantages are increasingly replicated by countries such as Venezuela in aluminum or Brazil in pulp and paper. Apart from the resource costs themselves, Canada does not generally have strong cost positions in activities that are driven by labour rates, productivity, or the age and efficiency of capital stock. In these areas, Canada has often failed to make the necessary investments, such as upgrading process technology to increase the efficiencies in production, that would yield a stronger position. Unless Canada upgrades its resource-based industries, it will be trapped in segments where investments tend to be inflexible and where its marginal costs are higher than major competitors'.

Market Access-Based Industries

Many of Canada's market access-based industries, initially spawned to overcome high tariff barriers, are seriously threatened by the increasingly open trading environment. As trade barriers continue to fall, market access no longer requires a major production base in Canada. Many firms are now in the process of reconfiguring their North American and, in some cases, global operations. Some have made decisions to move production out of Canada, taking with them not only jobs but also valuable skills and expertise.

One particularly unattractive aspect of many Canadian industry diamonds is interprovincial barriers to trade: By moving to the United States, firms may encounter virtually no penalty in terms of access to other Canadian provinces, given present trade barriers between provinces. Clearly, if effective barriers remain, firms that choose to stay in Canada are unlikely to invest as much in upgrading their existing domestic facilities than if these barriers were removed.

Innovation-Driven Industries

Canada's innovation-driven industries are tangible proof that Canada can achieve an innovation-driven economy. Yet these industries may also be at risk. Firms that have prospered in spite of weak Canadian clusters may find this weakness increasingly eroding their competitiveness. Firms in such industries may move their home bases outside of Canada to take advantage of more favourable diamonds elsewhere. Even those Canadian industries within strong clusters are at risk because of systemic barriers to upgrading discussed earlier.

Moving to a New Order

We believe Canada is at an economic turning point. Its old economic order is outmoded and in the process of being dismantled. Canadians can respond in one of two ways. One path is to cling to the old order and actively resist the process of change. The other is to continue building on recent economic reforms and seek to further the process of systemic adjustment in the economy. We are convinced that this second path will better ensure Canada's continued prosperity in the fast-changing global economy. Moving to a new economic order will be uncomfortable for many and actively resisted by some. Inevitably, it will involve short-run costs. Yet we are persuaded that these costs are less than might be supposed. It is not that Canadian business and government must spend more, but that they must act and spend differently. More importantly, however, the shift to a new economic order will require a different mindset on the part of government, business, labour, and many individual citizens, one which recognizes and adopts a new paradigm of competitiveness.

The mandate of this study has been to diagnose the state of competitiveness in Canadian industry and highlight key priorities for change. We have not sought to generate detailed policy recommendations. The task of fashioning specific policies and responses must fall to Canadian policymakers and private sector leaders themselves. The final part of this study seeks to provide some guidance by outlining a new economic vision for firms, labour, and governments. We begin, however, by briefly reviewing Canada's major economic strengths.

Strengths to Build On

As it faces a shifting competitive environment, Canada is in the favourable position of having a solid foundation on which to build. In particular, Canada is in many respects better placed to respond to changing global competition than other resource-rich countries such as Australia and New Zealand. Canada has a large export sector that accounts for more than one quarter of GDP and represents a significant share of world trade. It also enjoys preferred access to the world's largest and richest economy, the United States. Canada has a large, diversified natural resource base and ranks among the world's leaders in a range of renewable and nonrenewable resources. It also benefits from having a relatively young and well-educated labour force.

Many Canadian firms have proven that they can compete in global industries. Canada's success in a number of highly contested global industries—including telecommunications, consulting engineering, and nickel—illustrates the intrinsic potential for continued prosperity. Canadian firms have proven that they can compete on the basis of innovation. Northern Telecom, CAE Electronics, Inco, and Canstar are a few examples of firms examined in our research which are at the leading edge of technological sophistication in their industries. They have built and sustained internationally competitive positions through a commitment to R&D and technology adoption. They have created and drawn upon strengths in their home diamonds to achieve international success. Innovation and upgrading are at the core of their business strategies.

There is, in short, a foundation in place in Canada that should allow more firms and industries to achieve sustained advantage in international competition. Canadian industry enjoys a good basic infrastructure, a core of university and other research capability, and an educated human resource base with demonstrated potential. The challenge is to redirect government policies and company strategies to develop and build upon these strengths. Free trade will play a positive role here. With the advent of the Canada-United States Free Trade Agreement, Canadian firms can increasingly benefit from proximity and ready access to the U. S. market. The United States represents not only a significant and growing export market but also a source of products, technology, and ideas. Free trade will hasten the process by which the Canadian economy specializes in those areas where it performs best, thereby boosting productivity. At the same time, Canadian firms will be able to tap selectively into stronger U.S. diamonds to overcome weaknesses in Canada's competitive context in areas such as home demand conditions and related and supporting industries—although, as we have stressed, this is not a panacea.

Elements of an Economic Vision

We believe that a new vision for the Canadian economy is needed, one in which Canada's natural resource abundance is fully exploited, in which firms and governments focus on creating advanced skills and technology, in which sophisticated home demand drives more firms to create advanced products and processes, in which many more Canadian firms compete globally, and in which competition provides a key stimulus for continual upgrading. This does not mean that Canadian firms must compete in different industries than they do today. But it does suggest that they will have to compete in different ways. Firms in Canada need to employ different and more effective strategies, rely on more advanced methods and technologies, and migrate into more sophisticated segments of their industries. In cases where industries cannot be upgraded, resources should flow to more productive uses.

While many specific steps are necessary to raise productivity and improve the dynamism of the economy, we believe that a new economic vision for Canada is best defined in terms of a small number of overarching imperatives:

• *Become an innovation-driven economy.* Innovation—in its broadest sense—is the critical requirement for economic upgrading and increased prosperity. Canadian enterprises in all sectors must move to develop innovation-based advantages. This includes firms in nontraded service industries as well as in the traded sector. Governments must align their policies to support this strategic objective.

• *Increase the sophistication of the natural resource sector.* Resource-based industries have been and will remain a mainstay of Canada's economy. But threats exist to the sustainability of Canada's position in many resource-based industries—threats such as declining real commodity prices, the emergence of low-cost foreign suppliers, and technologically driven changes in end-markets. In the future, Canadian resource producers will be under unprecedented pressure to increase productivity, use more sophisticated technology and specialized skills, and develop more sophisticated and differentiated products.

• *Tackle barriers to upgrading throughout the economy.* Eliminating barriers to upgrading productivity must be a priority for firms and governments. Strategies to develop more advanced and specialized factors must be implemented. Incentives must be shifted, wherever possible, to encourage a greater focus on work, investment, and skill building.

• *Build on Canada's regional strengths.* Many government policies in Canada have put a higher priority on economic diversification than on competitive advantage. A different concept of regional and industrial development is needed, one that focuses on building industry clusters where they already have established or nascent strengths.

• *Move quickly and decisively to achieve complete free trade within Canada.* The fruits of greater specialization will not be fully realized unless Canada becomes a true single market. Competitiveness in a variety of industries has been hindered by the existence of internal nontariff barriers to trade, investment, and labour mobility. These have worked against the development of sufficient scale in some industries and dulled the rivalry necessary to achieve competitive advantage. It is encouraging that the federal government's recent proposals for constitutional reform promise to move toward internal free trade and a strengthening of the Canadian economic union.

• *Transform foreign subsidiaries into home bases.* Given its high levels of foreign investment and large number of branch plants (especially in manufacturing industries), transforming foreign subsidiaries into home bases is one of the most critical challenges facing Canada in the 1990s. Branch plants whose sole raison d'être has been to serve the Canadian market will relocate if their productivity does not match or exceed operations elsewhere. Multinationals will make choices about where to make investments in new skills, technologies, and product lines according to whether or not the Canadian environment is conducive to innovation and productivity growth.

• *Create and maintain a supportive and stable macroeconomic climate.* Finally, sound macroeconomic policies are central to any vision of a competitive, dynamic Canadian economy. Fiscal, monetary, tax, and regulatory policies should all be geared to attaining low inflation, balanced and manageable public finances, and a stable overall economic climate. This will result in a lower cost of capital, encourage investment, and neutralize the tendency for companies to be distracted by exchange rates and interest rates instead of concentrating on the true underpinnings of long-term competitiveness.

Implications for Canadian Firms

Business, labour, governments, and other public sector institutions must all play a role in responding to these imperatives. A particularly heavy responsibility, however, falls on companies and their managers. Firms, not governments, are on the front lines of international competition. Forced to compete in a more global, open, and fast-changing environment, Canadian firms must focus on setting strategies that will allow them to create and sustain competitive advantage. They should move now to reexamine their strategies, not wait for government or outside forces to intervene. While each Canadian industry will present different challenges, many firms will need to take steps in several important areas.

Assess the Canadian Diamond

Canadian firms must begin by understanding their competitive position by product area as well as how their Canadian home bases create competitive advantages and disadvantages. In analyzing their competitive position, the most formidable international competitors in an industry should be the key reference points. Internationally successful firms, as well as the national diamonds in which they are based, provide the benchmarks against which Canadian conditions must be assessed. Canadian companies should be addressing the following questions:

  • *The boundaries of the home diamond.* What are the geographic boundaries of the "home" diamond? Does it appear to cross the border with the United States and, if so, what are the key differences for firms operating on either side?

  • *Sustainability of basic factor advantages.* How sustainable are Canadian advantages in raw materials, electricity, or other natural endowments? To what extent does the firm rely on explicit or implicit subsidies rather than real factor advantages? How are evolving international trade rules and foreign circumstances likely to alter existing advantages?

  • *Quality of human resources.* How does Canada compare in terms of specialized skills relevant to the firm's industry? Are Canadian workers as well trained and well motivated as their foreign counterparts?

  • *Technology access.* Where does Canada stand in specialized technologies related to the industry? Are there research institutes or programs in Canada that will assist Canadian firms to innovate?

  • *Infrastructure access.* How supportive is Canada's basic and specialized infrastructure in terms of the requirements for competitive advantage in the firm's industry? How does Canada compare with other countries?

  • *Canadian demand sophistication.* Is Canadian demand for the firm's products/services sophisticated? Does it anticipate international needs?

  • *Supplier access.* Compared to foreign rivals, does the Canadian firm have better or inferior access to local suppliers in important technologies?

  • *Related industries.* What are the related industries that will most influence industry competition? What strengths does Canada have in these industries?

• *Competitor diamonds.* Who are the most significant foreign competitors in the industry? What is the state of their diamonds?

• *Potential entrants.* Who are the emerging potential entrants? What is their cost position? How dependent are they on low-cost natural resources, inexpensive labour, or government support?

• *Capacity for differentiation.* What are the sources of differentiation relative to rival firms? Are there products or segments in which the Canadian firm is more innovative?

Move toward Innovation-Driven Advantages

Many Canadian firms have long pursued static, cost-based strategies in which they produce "me-too" products and depend on factor costs or pure scale to provide advantages. A large number of such firms are now under pressure from foreign rivals with more efficient processes or cheaper basic factors. To respond to these challenges, firms need to compete in more sophisticated ways. A broader, more dynamic view of cost makes sense for many firms. More investments must be channeled into efficient and innovative processes to increase productivity. Firms facing low-cost foreign competitors may need to reorient their strategies from producing unprocessed and semiprocessed products (where competition is necessarily based on cost) to more highly processed and differentiated products in related segments.

Focus on Areas of True Competitive Advantage

After looking at these issues and questions, many Canadian firms will conclude that they should adopt more focused strategies. In a world of soft economic competition and tariff protection, the proliferation of product lines and businesses may have made sense. The new imperative is to focus on those product lines, market segments, and businesses where Canadian firms can achieve sustainable advantage. Often, this will call for a rationalization of product lines and a concentration on lines that draw on unique competitive strengths. A number of firms in Canada have begun this process. GE Canada, for instance, has narrowed its Canadian product line and increased production of selected products to supply other GE operations worldwide. Similarly, Culinar, a Quebec-based consumer snack food producer, has moved to reduce the breadth of its core product line, divest weaker peripheral businesses, and focus on areas of advantage.

In addition to rationalizing product lines, many businesses will need to reevaluate their degree of vertical integration and exit from products where vertical integration does not provide advantage vis-à-vis rivals. For some companies, a reevaluation of growth-through-diversification strategies will also be required. In a world of more open trade and tougher competition, a greater focus on core businesses will make sense for most firms.

Upgrade the Canadian Diamond

Upgrading the Canadian diamond takes on special importance as firms move toward more sophisticated business strategies. Canadian firms need to act in several areas:

• *Increase investment in specialized human resource development.* Like any asset, employees at all levels require investment to keep them up-to-date. In an environment characterized by more open competition, Canadian firms will have to rely more on advanced skills and improved labour force productivity and less on traditional basic factor advantages.

• *Forge closer ties with educational institutions.* Canadian firms must take a more pro-active approach if they want educational institutions to produce employees with both the general and specialized skills required for competitiveness. Canadian business, like its counterparts in Germany and several other countries, should be providing more direct input into course development at universities, colleges, and technical institutes. Business in Canada should be looking at ways to enhance the status of community colleges to ensure they are not viewed as "second-best" alternatives. Firms should also actively promote and participate in more cooperative educational programs where students work part-time or alternate periods of work and schooling. More businesses are becoming involved with co-op programs. For example, Inco entered into a partnership with Cambrian College in Sudbury to develop an innovative 48-week course that combines academic studies with training at Inco.

• *Improve technology development and adoption.* Firms should also be playing a more active role in ensuring that work conducted at university research institutes or centres and government laboratories is commercially relevant. Many successful firms contract out a great deal of their basic research and perform applied and developmental research in-house. Unfortunately, Canada has few specialized "centres of excellence" within its universities or community colleges where leading-edge research takes place, where the world's best professors come to teach, and where students are attracted from around the world. Firms should consider jointly funding and influencing the research conducted in such centres through trade associations, with related industries, and with government.

• *Transform trade associations into factor-creating mechanisms.* For the small- and mid-sized enterprises that dominate in many sectors of the Canadian economy, the need to upgrade in the areas of human resources and technology development and adoption may appear to pose daunting challenges. Cooperative ventures can be a fruitful path to upgrading factor capabilities for such companies. For example, firms can expand technical assistance and provide more funds to trade associations to develop training programs relevant to their industry. They can support the development of training consortia in which labour and government may participate as partners to industry—as has recently taken place in the electrical/electronics industry. Trade associations can also be a critical liaison between industry and educational institutes in helping to ensure the relevance of curricula discussed above. Finally, in the area of technology development and adoption, trade associations can also represent a valuable clearing house for dissemination of precompetitive research into common areas of concern such as the environment.

• *Nurture Canadian supplier industries.* The absence of dynamic clusters of competitive industries in Canada has been detrimental to innovation. Many firms have sourced abroad, while others have backward-integrated to compensate for the lack of indigenous supporting industries. Canadian companies should be taking steps to strengthen domestic supplier industries. Encouraging domestic suppliers, through local sourcing and the transferring of technology and skills, has become integral to the strategies of prominent Canadian companies such as IBM Canada and Nova Corporation.

• *Strive to develop and serve demanding Canadian buyers.* Firms should strive to serve the most sophisticated and demanding buyers in their home market. Selling to demanding local buyers will strengthen their ability to compete in global markets.

• *Establish links with Canadian-based firms in related industries.* Related industries are those linked to an industry by common technologies, distribution channels, skills, or customers. Canadian firms should strive to develop links with Canadian-based firms in related industries in order to increase technical interchange and information flows in a variety of areas.

• *Develop labour-management relations centered on productivity.* To improve productivity, many Canadian firms will have to adopt less authoritarian approaches to work force management and a broader view of employees' potential to contribute to firm goals. Labour should be treated as a partner, not an adversary. Employees should be rewarded for productivity growth but should also expect to share the pain in periods of economic adversity.

• *Rely more on performance-related compensation.* In structuring compensation schemes, Canadian companies should move toward making both individual and company performance a significant part of remuneration at all levels.

Adopt More Global Strategies

More than 70 percent of Canadian manufacturers do not serve any export markets, and the majority of those that do export sell solely to the United States. Canada's reliance on the United States as an export market has grown over the past decade, at a time when globalization of many industries has increased. Given a more open global trade and business environment, firms in Canada need to develop global strategies if they are to compete successfully against foreign rivals in many industries. Competing globally means competing beyond North America. First and foremost, it means penetrating foreign markets both through trade and, ultimately, foreign investment. To succeed in international markets, Canadian firms must move more aggressively to satisfy the needs of foreign buyers and establish foreign sales and service channels. They must have the patience to make the investments necessary to build foreign market positions.

Northern Telecom's recent acquisition of STC, a U.K.-based supplier of switches and transmission equipment, should enhance Northern's ability to sell into the post-1992 European market.

Competing globally can bring many advantages aside from increased sales. No country has a unique advantage in all the determinants of competitive advantage. Firms can selectively tap into sources of advantage in foreign diamonds, both to compensate for deficiencies at home and to exploit unique characteristics abroad. Canadian firms will benefit by serving the most sophisticated and demanding buyers in foreign countries. Given the ease of access to the U.S. market and the cultural similarities between the two countries, Canadian companies have an unusual ability to benefit from American buyers. The essential foundations for innovation must be present in the home base, however.

Define a North American or Global Mandate

Many foreign-owned or -controlled subsidiaries in Canada are today faced with urgent questions about their future role. Foreign subsidiaries in the manufacturing sector tend to be the firms with the broadest product lines, which overlap with those of subsidiaries in other countries. They also face the need to conform to their parents' global strategy. The potential consequences of a weak Canadian diamond are particularly acute for these firms given the ease and speed with which Canadian operations can be downsized and operations in other countries reconfigured to compensate.

Canadian subsidiaries must try to define a new role that is consistent with the evolving nature of the global strategies being pursued by many of the world's most advanced multinationals. This role is to have the Canadian operation become a North American or global headquarters for a particular product line or business segment in order to exploit particular advantages and strengths in the Canadian diamond. A number of foreign firms operating in Canada have moved in this direction. IBM Canada, for example, has the worldwide mandate for hardware power supplies. Hewlett-Packard Canada's Edmonton-based Idacom division manufactures computer-based protocol analyzers for the worldwide market, while its Calgary operation has the world mandate for supervisory control and data acquisition software. Campbell Soup is reconfiguring its Canadian operations to fit a North American manufacturing strategy. Canada is taking responsibility for a series of small-batch, specialty product lines that are especially well suited to the small yet flexible Canadian plants. The British firm ICI, after taking full control of its Canadian subsidiary ICI Canada, located the world headquarters for its industrial explosives business in Canada.

Redefine the Relationship with Government

Canadian firms must reevaluate their expectations of government and place different demands on government than in the past. First, they should insist that government activity not substitute for business initiative. Second, they should no longer look to government to provide traditional forms of assistance—subsidies, artificial cost structures, lax regulations, guaranteed procurement. Third, Canadian firms should pressure government to contribute to competitiveness through the provision of high-quality infrastructure, advanced factor creation, and appropriate incentives. Government-assisted R&D centres and training programs, for example, can be significant assets for firms. More generally, Canadian firms should promote government policies that promise to improve the home diamond in the industry or industries in which they compete.

Implications for Labour

With some 37 percent of the labour force unionized, organized labour in Canada plays a significant role in the country's economy as well as in a host of individual industries (especially in the resource and manufacturing sectors). Unions also exercise influence by adopting strategies and objectives that affect workplace relations in the broader private sector. The attitudes, policies, and approaches of organized labour can either help or hinder competitiveness. Far-sighted union leaders understand that efforts to increase productivity, upgrade skills, and facilitate shifts into more sophisticated jobs are the best guarantee of good wages in the long term.

In the old Canadian economic order, breakdowns in labour-management relations generally carried little cost. Large resource rents were there to be divided. Market protection and weak rivalry allowed cost increases to be passed on. Companies could prosper without paying much attention to their workforce. Finding themselves in a comfortable competitive environment, many companies accepted wage demands unconnected to productivity performance and tolerated work practices that impeded innovation. These behaviours and attitudes no longer fit the new competitive realities facing Canadian industry. New approaches to labour-management relations are needed. For organized labour, several implications follow from this:

• *Focus on productivity.* Canadian unions have sometimes been hostile to the imperative of productivity improvement, seeing it as a threat to jobs or a veiled attempt to reduce wages and benefits. To varying degrees, they have resisted developments geared to achieving higher productivity—such as workforce reorganization, multiskilling, and compensation systems more closely tied to performance. Today more than ever before, the future viability of many Canadian industries and firms depends on their success in upgrading productivity. Unions can make an important contribution by assisting firms to identify and remove obstacles to productivity improvement by pressing for job enhancement and flexibility and by supporting advancement based on training and merit.

• *Skills upgrading.* Broadening and increasing workers' skills should be a central objective of labour. In recent years, there have been encouraging signs that unions have come to accept the inevitability of technological change and the necessary skills upgrading that accompanies it. Most of the onus for developing a "training culture" within Canadian business, however, must fall on managers, not workers or their unions.

• *More cooperative labour-management relations.* Shifts in production technologies and increasing competition call for a deeper reevaluation of the traditional labour-management framework. A more collaborative approach is essential. For their part, unions should embrace opportunities to participate in firm planning and encourage more information exchange. If Canadian industry is to compete successfully in the future, labour must move beyond its traditional and deeply rooted inclination to see management as the "opposing team."

Implications for Governments

Both the 10-nation study and our Canadian research have demonstrated that government can improve or detract from national competitive advantage. The question is not whether government should have a role, but what that role should be. Government's role in shaping competitiveness is inherently partial. Government policies in a particular area will generally fail unless they work in tandem with other determinants of competitive advantage. Government policy should be directed to building the skills, research infrastructure, and other inputs on which all firms draw. Through regulations, tax legislation, competition policies, and policies in other areas, government should seek to fashion an environment that supports upgrading and productivity growth. In this section, we summarize the broad implications of our findings for Canadian policymakers. We begin by outlining several general principles for sound policy and then focus on a number of specific areas in which changes are needed.

Some General Principles

Canadian governments should be guided by a limited number of principles as they seek to develop policies to assist Canadian industries and companies achieve international competitive success:

1. *Encourage adjustment and upgrading.* Competitive success grows out of dynamism, not static advantages such as cheap labour or subsidized input costs. Too often, government policy reflects a static mindset. In the next several years, many industries in Canada will be forced to restructure and refocus—rationalizing product lines, exiting from peripheral businesses, shifting away from some industries and segments and toward others. Government should facilitate these adjustments, not stand in the way. This will involve a government commitment to retraining, building infrastructure appropriate to changed circumstances, and providing an overall environment conducive to restructuring.

2. *Minimize direct interventions.* Direct interventions in the economy often have unfortunate consequences. Ineffective use of expenditures results in wasted resources. In addition, direct intervention frequently leads to an unhealthy dependence on government by industry. Federal and provincial governments

should be using indirect means rather than direct interventions to promote competitiveness. Indirect policies encompass programs designed to improve infrastructure and human resources, as well as economic policies that encourage investment and upgrading.

3. *Rely on incentives instead of grants.* Subsidies and grants to specific firms rarely translate into durable competitive advantage. There is little evidence that governments can successfully "pick winners" by targeting support to particular enterprises. Broader incentives that encourage individuals and firms to upgrade skills, or that create advanced factor pools and improved infrastructure, are more effective policy tools.

4. *Reengineer social policies.* In the long run, competitiveness and social goals tend to be mutually reinforcing. More productive industries lead to a stronger national economy, which in turn is better able to meet diverse social policy objectives. At the same time, an effective social infrastructure helps to underpin economic success. The design of social programs can have profound and often unanticipated consequences for the economy. In New Zealand, for example, a noncontributory pension scheme reduced national savings, while the structure of social assistance payments encouraged young people to drop out of school and militated against skill upgrading. Aggregate social spending in Canada is not out of line compared to most other industrialized countries. However, to create an attractive environment for competitive advantage, it is crucial that social goals be pursued in a way that does not sacrifice incentives, upgrading, and productivity growth. Consideration must be given to redesigning social programs that do not meet this test.

5. *Improve intergovernmental policy coordination.* Government imposes an increasingly heavy burden on Canada's economy. This burden is magnified by inadequate coordination of federal and provincial government policies in areas such as economic management, tax policy, training, education, the environment, and procurement. Canadians today are paying a high price to maintain elaborate bureaucracies at both the federal and provincial levels, yet are not receiving the benefits of either strong central control or effective decentralized decision making. The ultimate structure of a potentially reformed Canadian confederation is now under active discussion. This subject lies outside the scope of our study. However, we are convinced that improving Canada's international competitiveness will necessitate a substantially greater degree of collaboration and coordination between Ottawa and the provinces than has been typical in the past.

6. *Maintain an open policy toward foreign investment.* We strongly believe that efforts to restrict foreign investment in Canada, or to legislate foreign company behaviour, should be avoided. Except in rare cases, foreign investment contributes to the economy through new products, processes, assets, and skills that boost productivity. A substantial body of Canadian research supports this view. Foreign-owned companies are often more efficient and more technologically advanced than domestic firms; many invest as much, if not more, in R&D as their Canadian counterparts. However, while Canada is better off with foreign investment than without it, the existing pattern of foreign activity in the economy

reflects weaknesses that are cause for concern. Because of deficiencies in Canadian industry diamonds, foreign operations in Canada are too often limited to sourcing raw materials or performing the minimum activities needed to gain access to the local market. An important objective of government economic policy must be to improve the Canadian economic environment so that foreign companies will, over time, change and broaden the nature of their Canadian activities.

7. *Promote a sound and stable macroeconomic environment to complement other initiatives.* While a stable macroeconomic environment assists in achieving international competitiveness, it does not create or ensure it. Devaluing Canada's currency also does not provide a long-term solution to the country's underlying competitiveness problems. There is, however, little doubt about the types of macroeconomic goals that governments should be setting in order to support competitiveness: low inflation, which works to lower the real cost of capital; a high rate of national saving; and balanced public sector finances. The size of government deficits, and the rapid growth of government debt which has resulted from many years of large deficits, is perhaps the most critical macroeconomic problem facing Canada today. Chronic public sector deficits contribute to higher inflation, interest rates, and taxes. Determined action to reduce government deficits is imperative if Canada is to compete successfully through the 1990s and beyond.

Priorities in Specific Policy Areas: Factor Conditions

The number of government policies that affect the competitiveness of a country's industries and firms is almost limitless. Based on our Canadian research, we have identified some specific priorities for improvement in each part of the Canadian diamond. Because Canadian competitiveness has been mainly rooted in factor advantages, government policies bearing on factor conditions are particularly important.

Investment in Education and Specialized Skills.   Upgrading human resources will be critical to Canadian firms' ability to become more competitive. Canada has a relatively well-educated workforce, but its education and training systems have failed to respond adequately to the challenges posed by the contemporary global economy. Ensuring that the education system does a better job imparting basic skills is one priority. Improving and expanding private sector training is another. Governments should be considering new initiatives in several areas:

• *Provide more training for the unemployed.* Recent moves by the federal government to direct a larger share of labour market program funding to training the unemployed are a promising beginning, but more must be done to shift from passive income support to "active" labour market programs that encourage adjustment and skill upgrading.

• *Promote private sector training.* Canadian firms, in general, spend significantly less on workforce training than their counterparts in other industrialized countries. Governments should consider providing incentives to stimulate more training. One option might be to give UI premium rebates to firms that undertake training (possibly targeted at small and mid-sized firms). Another option would be to develop tax exemptions or credits to encourage training.

• *Set high national educational standards.* Canada's relatively generous spending on education has not translated into superior performance. Canada is virtually alone among advanced countries in having no national education standards of any kind. In other countries, such standards are an important ingredient in fostering high achievement. National standards are not inconsistent with a decentralized education system. In Germany, for instance, national standards coexist with an education system administered by the states, not the central government. A national standard need not require a full-fledged national system for testing, provided an appropriate level of intergovernmental cooperation exists. Provincial governments should move quickly to collaborate in developing agreed standards and testing mechanisms.

• *Put more emphasis on practical curricula and science skills.* Compared to other countries examined in our research, Canada has relatively few scientists, engineers, and technical workers in its labour force. Evidence points to declining interest in the sciences among elementary and high school students, declining enrollment in trade and vocational programs at the postsecondary level, and flat or falling enrollment in college-based technology-oriented programs. School curricula should be redesigned to put more emphasis on science, mathematics, and technology disciplines.

• *Expand apprenticeship programs and update curricula.* Many apprenticeship programs in Canada suffer from limited access, lack of standardized certification criteria, and high drop-out rates. Cooperative efforts on the part of governments, industry, and labour to update apprenticeship programs and extend such training into more occupations are urgently needed if Canada is to expand its pool of highly skilled workers.

• *Work more closely with trade associations.* As discussed above, trade associations represent a potentially high leverage mechanism for upgrading Canadian factors, particularly in the areas of education and training. Governments at all levels should seek to work more closely with these associations to strengthen factor conditions.

• *Promote cooperative education.* Cooperative education programs have proven to be an excellent vehicle for linking education to the workplace and for facilitating the transition from school to the labour force. Participation in these programs should be broadened.

• *Align university funding to support competitiveness.* As currently structured, government funding mechanisms for universities may not adequately underwrite the cost differentials that exist between science- and technology-related courses and other fields of study. Governments should reevaluate existing funding mechanisms and take steps to ensure that adequate resources are available for programs directly linked to competitiveness. Provincial governments should also reexamine the appropriate role of tuition in the overall university funding mix and the potential for school autonomy in setting tuition fees. The privatisation of some programs or even institutions should be seriously considered.

More Focused Technology Development and Faster Adoption.   Technology development and adoption are areas where Canada suffers from significant weaknesses. The problem lies more with the private sector than with government, however. Stimulating more research and development and faster adoption of technology in the private sector must be a priority objective of government. Among the specific steps we recommend are the following:

  • *Improve coordination of government R&D programs.* Our research revealed a number of areas where excessive fragmentation of government expenditures has limited the effectiveness of science and technology programs. Duplication of research between universities and government labs is also of concern given the overall scarcity of government resources. Expenditures and research efforts in federal and provincial government research organizations must be better coordinated and tied more closely to university research activities.

  • *Forge stronger links among government laboratories, provincial organizations, universities, and the private sector.* Government policy on science and technology has attached a high priority to advancing science and to training qualified personnel. While these goals are important, in the future, government policy in this area should put a greater emphasis on fostering more intimate linkages with industry.

  • *Increase the proportion of government-funded R&D performed in the private sector.* While government R&D spending has increasingly emphasized private sector and university performance, federal laboratories still accounted for 55 percent of government expenditures of $2.7 billion in 1990, while provincial laboratories accounted for 41 percent of provincial government expenditures of $664 million. Given the funding issues which currently exist within the university system in terms of science and technology infrastructure, as well as the issues of ensuring commercial relevance and technology diffusion associated with government labs, we believe governments at the federal and provincial levels should continue to reduce the proportion of their funds spent internally, in addition to increasing the linkages with industry with respect to the activities that remain.

  • *Encourage greater specialization among universities.* Current government policies and funding mechanisms often discourage specialization among Canadian universities. To create the specialized skills and other advanced factors necessary to achieve competitive advantage, more specialization in university programs and research activities should be encouraged.

  • *Expand information available on intellectual property.* Intellectual property laws, and the information infrastructure that supports them, play an important role in fostering technology diffusion. The federal government should move rapidly to complete the automation of the patent search process.

Increase the Pace of Regulatory Reform in Infrastructure Sectors.   Regulatory reform in Canada has generally lagged the pace set in the United States. This has resulted in higher service costs to Canadian producers of many goods and services. Canada should continue to move ahead with regulatory reforms in key infrastructure areas such as transportation and communications. In addition, the federal and provincial governments should renew efforts to achieve a greater degree of harmonization of policies that restrict interprovincial competition and rationalization in areas such as trucking.

Strengthen Resource Conservation and Renewal Policies. Effective natural resource conservation is vital to sustaining the competitiveness of resource-based industries. Canada's record to date has been mixed, although improvements are evident in areas such as forest replantation. With close to half of Canada's goods sector exports dependent on natural resources, governments must ensure that their resource policies promote long-term conservation, not short-term exploitation.

Priorities in Specific Policy Areas: Demand Conditions. Governments have a significant impact on a country's home demand conditions. Their leverage over demand is greatest in the areas of government procurement, regulation of product safety and standards, and environmental standards. The aim of government policy should be to encourage home demand that is early and sophisticated and that anticipates international needs and trends.

Restructure Government Procurement. The effectiveness of government procurement policy in spurring innovation and competitive advantage in Canada has been undermined by several factors: blurred policy objectives, provincial government restrictions on out-of-province bidding, and a common preference for off-the-shelf products. Only infrequently have governments acted as a sophisticated buyer and sought to pressure Canadian companies to upgrade or created an early market for new products. While some progress in reforming procurement practices has been made in recent years, further efforts are required:

• *Encourage more open competition for government contracts.* Discriminatory purchasing practices, especially at the provincial level, have resulted in significant economic costs. All governments should strive to ensure that competition is open to out-of-province and out-of-country bidders.

• *Use challenging performance specifications.* Use of "make to blueprint" design specifications still appears to be widespread in government procurement in Canada. Wherever possible, governments should move toward performance-based specifications in order to encourage suppliers to develop and proliferate innovative products and processes.

Adopt Stringent and Forward-Looking Regulatory Standards. Strict, anticipatory regulatory standards can be a potent force for spurring upgrading in industry, provided they are designed and administered effectively. Strict product quality and safety standards pressure firms to improve products in ways that are eventually demanded by international markets. High regulatory standards in areas such as construction, telecommunications, and transportation can stimulate early and sophisticated home demand. Tough standards for energy efficiency and environmental impact trigger innovations in products and processes that are highly valued elsewhere. In all of these areas, governments in Canada should be continuing to move toward more stringent standards and regulations.

Priorities in Specific Policy Areas: Related and Supporting Industries

Our research has found that the presence of home-based related and supporting industries is often critical in stimulating and facilitating innovation and productivity growth. The lack of depth and breadth in most Canadian industry clusters represents a significant weakness as the country and its industries seek to respond to a new competitive environment. Canadian government policy in areas such as regional and industrial development has frequently worked against the objective of building strong, geographically concentrated clusters. Government policies should be tailored to meet the following guidelines:

- *Ensure that programs and policies in all areas are consistent with the development of stronger industry clusters.* Governments should critically examine the full range of policies to determine whether these policies support the growth of clusters.
- *Employ policies that build on existing regional strengths.* The presence of an industry or cluster in a region is generally a sign that some competitive advantage already exists. Government policies should be geared to enhancing clusters rather than—as has so often been the case in Canada—subsidizing existing, inefficient industries and activities or trying to create industries unrelated to local economic strengths.
- *Focus on promoting the development of specialized factors.* The most effective way for governments to reinforce cluster development is to focus on investments that assist in creating specialized factors such as technical institutes, training centres, and other infrastructure related to the needs of specific industries. Importantly, many of the policies and programs that most effectively promote specialized factors are provincial or local in origin.

Priorities in Specific Policy Areas: Firm Strategy, Structure, and Rivalry

Governments can strengthen the competitiveness of their industries by fostering a stable economic environment and creating incentives for investment, skill upgrading, and risk-taking, and by ensuring that a healthy degree of competition prevails in the home market.

Create Stronger Individual and Corporate Incentives for Investment and Upgrading.   Through tax policies and its actions in other policy areas, government helps to structure the incentives for individuals to work, save, and invest in skill building. Government policies also influence the goals and strategies of firms. To strengthen this important determinant of competitive advantage, governments in Canada should be looking at initiatives such as the following:

• *Reengineer "safety net" programs to ensure they are well targeted to those in need and provide appropriate incentives.* Some existing social programs should be restructured so that clear incentives always exist for individuals to work and improve skills. In particular, consideration should be given to reforming social assistance programs to allow recipients to keep a greater portion of earnings from employment, thereby encouraging them to participate in the labour force and upgrade their skills.

• *Encourage stronger linkages between performance and compensation.* Canada currently trails a number of competitor countries in linking compensation to productivity or firm performance at both the managerial and worker levels. Governments can assist in promoting compensation linked to performance through its policies toward its own work force and also by encouraging appropriate behaviour in the private sector. Providing further incentives for employees to invest in their companies would be one way to strengthen linkages between pay and performance in the private sector.

• *Provide more favourable tax treatment for long-term equity investment.* To increase its international competitiveness, Canada must invest heavily in training, technology, machinery, and equipment. Yet the payoff from such investments is often realized only over the long term. There is concern in Canada (and the United States) that investors—individual, corporate, and institutional—are often guided by a shorter-term outlook. Current tax policy may contribute to a short-term view. While the tax treatment of capital gains in Canada is somewhat more favourable than that in the United States, this is largely offset by higher marginal tax rates. In addition, a number of other countries have introduced measures specifically designed to encourage long-term investment. We believe that Canada should also be exploring ways to restructure capital gains taxation in order to increase incentives for long-term investment in productive assets.

Extend Efforts to Increase Rivalry. Canada has made significant strides in recent years toward instituting policies that enhance domestic rivalry. Freer trade, deregulation, and the modernization of competition laws are all important steps that have moved the country in the right direction. Now the federal and provincial governments must make an extraordinary effort to eliminate interprovincial barriers as expeditiously as possible. The federal government's recent constitutional initiative should provide a useful impetus to achieve progress in this field.

Move Aggressively to Restore a Favourable Macroeconomic Environment. All levels of government must share in the burden of bringing deficits and debt under much better control, by reevaluating spending programs and increasing the effectiveness of dollars spent. The underlying philosophy of the federal government's recent proposals, contained in its report *Canadian Federalism and*

Economic Union, which calls for increased fiscal coordination among the federal and provincial governments, is a sound one and the proposals deserve serious consideration. Finally, despite recent proposals by some, devaluing Canada's currency is not a long-term solution to Canada's competitiveness problems, even if it might temporarily improve the competitive position of some Canadian industries.

Implications for Canadian Citizens

Perhaps the most important factor in Canada's ability to move forward is the attitudes and the mindset of individual Canadians. Unless individual citizens can accept and internalize the new reality, positive programs will be undermined. Canadians must better understand the foundations of their past prosperity and the fact that the comfortable old order is disintegrating. They must also recognize that the sources of Canadian competitiveness are at risk. Most importantly, Canadians must understand that they cannot return to the old order. Instead of looking longingly at the past, Canadians must adopt the new paradigm for what will determine future Canadian competitiveness. They must respond to this new paradigm in their roles as employees, as managers, as voters, and as members of their communities.

READING 5
SUSTAINABLE COMPETITIVE ADVANTAGE—WHAT IT IS, WHAT IT ISN'T

Kevin P. Coyne

> I shall not today attempt to define the kinds of material to be embraced within that shorthand description; and perhaps I could never succeed in intelligibly doing so. But I know it when I see it.
>
> Supreme Court Justice Potter Stewart
> *(Jacobellis v. State of Ohio)*

Although it was pornography, not sustainable competitive advantage, that the late Justice Stewart doubted his ability to define, his remark neatly characterizes the current state of thinking about the latter subject as well. Explicitly or implicitly, sustainable competitive advantage (SCA) has long occupied a central place in strategic thinking. Witness the widely accepted definition of competitive strategy as "an integrated set of actions that produce a sustainable advantage over competitors."[1] But exactly what constitutes sustainable competitive advantage is a question rarely asked. Most corporate strategists are content to apply Justice Stewart's test; they know an SCA when they see it—or so they assume.

But perhaps an SCA is not always so easy to identify. In developing its liquid hand soap, Minnetonka, Inc., focused its efforts on building an advantage that was easily copied later. In the wristwatch market, Texas Instruments attempted to exploit an advantage over its competitors that turned out to be unimportant to target consumers. RCA built barriers to competition in the vacuum tube market in the 1950s only to find these barriers irrelevant when transistors and semiconductors were born. CB radio producers built capacity to fill a demand that later evaporated. In each case, the companies failed to see in advance that, for one reason or another, they lacked a sustainable competitive advantage.

Perhaps it is because the meaning of "sustainable competitive advantage" is superficially self-evident that virtually no effort has been made to define it explicitly. After all, it can be argued that the dictionary's definitions of the three words bring forth the heart of the concept. But every strategist needs to discover whether an SCA is actually or potentially present, and if so, what its implications are for competitive and business strategy.

Therefore, this article will describe a number of established strategic concepts and build on them to develop a clear and explicit concept of SCA.

---

[1]*Competitive strategy*, as the term is used in this article, is exclusively concerned with defeating competitors and achieving dominance in a product/market segment. It is thus—in concept, and usually in practice—a subset of business strategy, which addresses the broader goal of maximizing the wealth of shareholders.

SOURCE: Reprinted from *Business Horizons* (January–February 1986). Copyright © 1986, by the Foundation for the School of Business at Indiana University. Used with permission.

Specifically, we will examine:

· **The conditions for SCA.**

When does a producer have a competitive advantage? How can the strategist test whether such an advantage is sustainable?

· **Some implications of SCA for strategy.**

Does having SCA guarantee success? Can a producer succeed without an SCA? Should a producer always pursue an SCA?

Conditions for SCA

Any producer who sells his goods or services at a profit undeniably enjoys a competitive advantage with those customers who choose to buy from him instead of his competitors, though these competitors may be superior in size, strength, product quality, or distribution power. Some advantages, however, are obviously worth more than others. A competitive advantage is meaningful in strategy only when three distinct conditions are met:

1. Customers perceive a consistent difference in important attributes between the producer's product or service and those of his competitors.
2. That difference is the direct consequence of a capability gap between the producer and his competitors.
3. Both the difference in important attributes and the capability gap can be expected to endure over time.

In earlier strategy work, these conditions have been jointly embedded in the concepts of "key factors for success" (KFS), "degrees of freedom," and "lower costs or higher value to the customer." In the interest of clarity, however, they deserve separate consideration.

Differentiation in Important Attributes

Obviously, competitive advantage results from differentiation among competitors—but not just any differentiation. For a producer to enjoy a competitive advantage in a product/market segment, the difference or differences between him and his competitors must be felt in the marketplace: that is, they must be reflected in some *product/delivery attribute* that is a *key buying criterion* for the market. And the product must be differentiated enough to win the loyalty of a significant set of buyers; it must have a *footprint in the market*.

Product/Delivery Attribute

Customers rarely base their choice of a product or service on internal characteristics of the producer that are not reflected in a perceived product or delivery difference. Indeed, they usually neither know nor care about those characteristics. Almost invariably, the most important contact between the customer and the producer is the marketplace—the "strategic triangle" where the producer meets his customers and competitors. It is here that the competitive contest for the scarce resource, the sales dollar, is directly engaged.

Just as differences among animal species that are unrelated to scarce resources do not contribute to the survival of the fittest, so producer differences that do not affect the market do not influence the competitive process. Differences among competitors in plant locations, raw material choices, labor policies, and the like matter only when and if those differences translate into product/delivery attributes that influence the customers' choice of where to spend their sales dollars.

"Product/delivery attributes" include not only such familiar elements as price, quality, aesthetics, and functionality, but also broader attributes such as availability, consumer awareness, visibility, and after-sales service. Anything that affects customers' perceptions of the product or service, its usefulness to them, and their access to it is a product/delivery attribute. Anything that does not affect these perceptions is not.

Having lower costs, for example, may well result in significantly higher margins. But this *business* advantage will become a *competitive* advantage only if and when the producer directly or indirectly recycles the additional profits into product/delivery attributes such as price, product quality, advertising, or additional capacity that increases availability. Only then is the producer's competitive position enhanced. Two examples illustrate this point.

1. For years, the "excess" profits of a major packaged goods company—the low-cost producer in its industry—have been siphoned off by its corporate parent for reinvestment in other subsidiaries. The packaged goods subsidiary has therefore been no more able to take initiatives or respond to competitive threats than if it did not produce those excess profits. Thus, business advantage may exist, but competitive advantage is lacking. If risk-adjusted returns available from investments in other business exceed those of additional investment in the packaged goods subsidiary, the corporate parent may be making the best business decisions. However, the packaged goods subsidiary has gained no competitive advantage from its superior position.

2. The corporate parent of a newly acquired, relatively high-cost producer in an industrial products market has decided to aggressively expand its subsidiary. This expansion is potentially at the expense of the current market leader, an independent company occupying the low-cost position in the industry. The resources that the new parent is willing to invest are far larger than the incremental profits generated by the market leader's lower costs. Because the new subsidiary can invest more than the market leader in product design, product

quality, distribution, and so forth, it is the subsidiary that has, or soon will have, the competitive advantage.

In short, it is the application, not just the generation, of greater resources that is required for *competitive* advantage.

Key Buying Criterion

Every product has numerous attributes that competitors can use to differentiate themselves to gain some degree of advantage. To be strategically significant, however, an advantage must be based on positive differentiation of an attribute that is a *key buying criterion* for a particular market segment and is not offset by a negative differentiation in any other key buying criterion. In the end, competitive advantage is the result of all net differences in important product/delivery attributes, not just one factor such as price or quality. Differences in other, less important attributes may be helpful at the margin, but they are not strategically significant.

Key buying criteria vary, of course, by industry and even by market segment. In fact, because market segments differ in their choice of key buying criteria, a particular product may have a competitive advantage in some segments while being at a disadvantage in others. Price aside, the elaborate technical features that professional photographers prize in Hasselblad cameras would baffle and discourage most of the casual users who make up the mass market.

In any one product/market segment, however, only a very few criteria are likely to be important enough to serve as the basis for a meaningful competitive advantage. These criteria are likely to be basic—that is, central to the concept of the product or service itself, as opposed to "add-ons" or "features." For example, in the tubular steel industry, there are just two key product/delivery attributes: a single measure of quality (third-party testing reject rate) and local availability on the day required by the customer's drilling schedule.

Texas Instruments (TI) apparently did not fully understand the importance of differentiation along key buying criteria when it entered the wristwatch market. Its strategy was to build upon its ability to drive down costs—and therefore prices (the product attribute)—beyond the point where competitors could respond. But this competitive strategy, which had worked in electronic components, failed in wristwatches because price, past a certain point, was no longer a key buying criterion: customers cared more about aesthetics. TI had surpassed all of its competitors in an attribute that did not matter in the marketplace.

"Footprint in the Market"

To contribute to an SCA, the differences in product/delivery attributes must command the attention and loyalty of a substantial customer base; in other words, they must produce a "footprint in the market" of significant breadth and depth.

Breadth.   How many customers are attracted to the product above all others by the difference in product attributes? What volume do these customers purchase?

Depth.   How strong a preference has this difference generated? Would minor changes in the balance of attributes cause the customers to switch?

Breadth and depth are usually associated in marketing circles with the concept of "branding." Branding can indeed be a source of competitive advantage, as shown by Perrier's spectacular advantage in a commodity as prosaic as bottled mineral water.

But the importance of breadth and depth are not limited to branding strategies. Even a producer who is pursuing a low-price strategy must ensure that his lower price will cause customers to choose his product and that changes in nonprice attributes by competitors would be unlikely to lure them away.

Durable Differentiation

Positive differentiation in key product/delivery attributes is essential to competitive advantage. However, a differentiation that can be readily erased does not by itself confer a meaningful advantage. Competitive advantages described in such terms as "faster delivery" or "superior product quality" are illusory if competitors can erase the differentiation at will.

For example, Minnetonka, Inc., created a new market niche with "Softsoap." As a result, its stock price more than doubled. Before long, however, 50 different brands of liquid soap, some selling for a fifth of Softsoap's price, appeared on the market. As a result, Minnetonka saw its earnings fall to zero and its stock price decline by 75 percent.

An advantage is durable only if competitors cannot readily imitate the producer's superior product/delivery attributes. In other words, a gap in the *capability* underlying the differentiation must separate the producer from his competitors; otherwise no meaningful competitive advantage exists. (Conversely, of course, no meaningful advantage can arise from a capability gap that does not produce an important difference in product/delivery attributes.)

Understanding the capability gap, then, is basic to determining whether a competitive advantage actually exists. For example, an attribute such as faster delivery does not constitute a real competitive advantage unless it is based on a capability gap such as may exist if the company has a much bigger truck fleet than its competitors can afford to maintain. Higher product quality does not in itself constitute a competitive advantage. But unique access to intrinsically superior raw materials that enable the producer to deliver a better-quality product may well do so.

A capability gap exists when the function responsible for the differentiated product/delivery attribute is one that only the producer in question can perform, or one that competitors (given their particular limitations) could do only with maximum effort. So defined, capability gaps fall into four categories.

1. **Business system gaps** result from the ability to perform individual functions more effectively than competitors and from the inability of competitors to easily follow suit. For example, differences in labour union work rules can constitute a capability gap resulting in superior production capability. Superior engineering or technical skills may create a capability gap leading to greater precision or reliability in the finished product.

2. **Position gaps** result from prior decisions, actions, and circumstances. Reputation, consumer awareness and trust, and order backlogs, which can represent important capability gaps, are often the legacy of an earlier management generation. Thus, current competitive advantage may be the consequence of a past facilities location decision. BHP, the large Australian steel maker, enjoys important production efficiencies because it is the only producer to have located its smelter adjacent to its iron ore source, eliminating expensive iron ore transportation costs.

3. **Regulatory/legal gaps** result from government's limiting the competitors who can perform certain activities, or the degree to which they can perform those activities. Patents, operating licenses, import quotas, and consumer safety laws can all open important capability gaps among competitors. For example, Ciba-Geigy's patent on a low-cost herbicide allowed it to dominate certain segments of the agricultural chemical market for years.

4. **Organization or managerial quality gaps** result from an organization's ability consistently to innovate and adapt more quickly and effectively than its competitors. For example, in industries like computers or financial services, where the competitive environment is shifting rapidly, this flexibility may be the single most important capability gap. In other industries, the key capability gap may be an ability to out-innovate competitors, keeping them always on the defensive.

Note that only the first category, business system gaps, covers actions that are currently under the control of the producer. Frustrating as it may be to the strategist, competitive advantage or disadvantage is often the result of factors he or she is in no position to alter in the short term.

The broad concept of a capability gap becomes useful only when we succeed in closely specifying a producer's *actual* capability gap over competitors in a *particular* situation. Analysts can detect the existence of a capability gap by examining broad functions in the business system, but they must then go further and determine the root cause of superior performance in that function.

Individual capability gaps between competitors are very specific. There must be a precise reason why one producer can outperform another, or there is no competitive advantage. The capability gap consists of specific, often physical, differences. It is likely to be prosaic and measurable, not intangible. Abstract terms, such as "higher labor productivity" or "technological leadership," often serve as useful shorthand, but they are too general for precise analysis. Moreover, they implicitly equate capability gaps with marginal performance superiority, rather than with discrete differences—such as specific work rule differences or technical resources capacity—that are not easily imitated.

For example, if marginal performance superiority constituted competitive advantage, one would expect "focus" competitors—those who have no capability advantage but excel in serving a particular niche through sheer concentration of effort—to win out over more general competitors who decide to invade that niche. But as American Motors learned when Detroit's "Big Three" began producing small cars, and as some regional banks are learning as money center banks enter their markets, "trying harder" is no substitute for the possession of unique capabilities.

Only by understanding specific differences in capability can the strategist accurately determine and measure the actions that competitors must take to eliminate the gap and the obstacles and costs to them of doing so.

Lasting Advantage (Sustainability)

If a meaningful advantage is a function of a positive difference in important attributes based on an underlying capability gap, then the sustainability of the competitive advantage is simply a function of the durability of both the attributes and the gap.

There is not much value in an advantage in product/delivery attributes that do not retain their importance over time. Manufacturers of CB radios, video games, and designer jeans saw their revenues decline and their financial losses mount not because their competitors did anything to erode their capability advantages, but because most of their customers simply no longer valued those products enough to pay the price. In each case, industry participants believed that they had benefited from a permanent shift in consumer preferences and began to invest accordingly. In each case they were wrong.

Whether consumers will continue to demand a product over time, and how they can be influenced to prefer certain product attributes over time, are essentially marketing issues, subject to normal marketing analytical techniques. How basic is the customer need that the product meets? How central to its function or availability is the attribute in each question? These may be the key questions to ask in this connection.

The sustainability of competitive advantage is also a function of the durability of the capability gap that created the attractive attribute. In fact, the most important condition for sustainability is that existing and potential competitors either cannot or will not take the actions required to close the gap. If competitors can and will fill the gap, the advantage is by definition not sustainable.

Obviously, a capability gap that competitors are unable to close is preferable to one that relies on some restraint. Unfortunately, a producer cannot choose whether a particular capability gap meets the former or the latter condition.

Consider the two cases more closely.

Case 1. *Competitors cannot fill the gap.* This situation occurs when the capability itself is protected by specific entry and mobility barriers such as an important product patent or unique access to a key raw material (for example,

DeBeer's Consolidated Mines). In a Case 1 situation, sustainability is assured at least until the barrier is eroded or eliminated (converting the situation to Case 2). Barriers can erode or be eliminated over time, unless they are inherent in the nature of the business.[2]

A more significant danger to Case 1 advantages, however, probably lies not in the gradual erosion of barriers, but in the possibility that competitors may leapfrog the barriers by a new game strategy.

For example, the introduction of the transistor in 1955 did nothing to erode the barriers that RCA had created in vacuum tubes; it simply made RCA's leadership irrelevant. Therefore, although sustainability can be estimated by (1) considering all the changes (environmental forces or competitor actions) that could erode the barriers, and (2) assessing the probabilities of their occurrence over a specified time horizon, there will, of course, always be uncertainty in the estimate.

Case 2. *Competitors could close the capability gap but refrain from doing so.* This situation might occur for any one of four reasons.

a. **Inadequate potential.** A simple calculation may show competitors that the costs of closing the gap would exceed the benefits, even if the possessor of the advantage did not retaliate.

For example, the danger of cannibalizing existing products may preclude effective response. MCI, Sprint, and others were able to create the low-price segment of the U.S. long-distance telephone market largely because AT&T did not choose to respond directly for some time. Most likely it considered that the cost of cutting prices for 100 percent of its customers in order to retain the 1 to 2 percent in the low-price segment was simply too high, and that only when the segment grew to sufficient size would a response become worthwhile.

Other examples of situations where a payoff is not worth the required investment include investing in capacity to achieve "economies of scale" when the capacity required to achieve the required economy exceeds the likely additional demand in the industry; and labor work rules, where the additional compensation demanded by the union in return for such changes would more than offset the potential savings.

The inadequate-potential situation represents a sustainable advantage because the "end game" has already been reached: there are no rational strategic countermoves for competitors to take until conditions change.

b. **Corresponding disadvantage.** Competitors may believe that acting to close the capability gap will open gaps elsewhere (in this or other market segments) that will more than offset the value of closing this one.

---

[2]For example, if the business is a "natural monopoly." A natural monopoly exists where either (1) economies of scale cause marginal costs to decline past the point where production volume equals market demand (that is, where the most efficient economic system is to have only one producer); or (2) the social costs of installing duplicate production/distribution systems outweigh the benefits, a situation usually leading to the establishment of a legal monopoly by government fiat.

For example, a "niche" competitor often relies on this factor to protect him against larger competitors, who (or so he hopes) will reckon that an effective attack on his niche advantage would divert resources (including management time) needed elsewhere, destroy the integrity of their own broader product lines (opening gaps in other segments), or create some other gap.

A "corresponding disadvantage" situation constitutes at least a temporarily sustainable advantage, because for the moment an "end game" has been reached. However, as the attractiveness of competitors' other markets changes, so does their estimate of whether a corresponding disadvantage is present in the niche (as American Motors learned to its cost). In addition, competitors will always be searching for ways to fill the capability gap without creating offsetting gaps. Only if the creation of offsetting gaps is an automatic and inevitable consequence of any such action will the producer's advantage be assured of sustainability in the long run.

c. **Fear of reprisal.** Even though it initially would appear worth doing so, competitors may refrain from filling the capability gap for fear of retaliatory action by the producer. The sustainability of the producer's existing advantage depends, in this case, on the competitors' continuing to exercise voluntary restraint, accepting in effect the producer's position in this market segment.

For example, Japanese steel makers voluntarily refrain from increasing their U.S. market share for fear that American producers can and will persuade the U.S. government to take harsh protectionist measures.

"Fear of reprisal" is probably among the most common strategic situations in business, but it must be considered unstable over time, as competitors' situations and managements shift.

d. **Management inertia.** Finally, there are cases where competitors would benefit from closing the capability gap but fail to do so, either because management has incorrectly assessed the situation or because it lacks the will, the ability, or the energy to take the required action.

For example, Honda's success in dominating the British motorcycle industry is generally attributed to Norton Villiers Triumph's failure to respond to a clear competitive threat until too late.

Psychologists tell us that managers will implement real change only when their discomfort with the status quo exceeds the perceived personal cost of taking the indicated action. This may well explain why competitors often tolerate a performance gap that they could profitably act to close. But it is risky for a producer to rely for long on the weakness or inertia of competitors' management to protect a competitive advantage; by definition, the end game has not been reached.

In all four cases, how long competitors will tolerate capability gaps they are capable of closing depends largely on the relationship between the value of the advantage created by the gap and the cost (to each competitor) of closing it. The worse the cost-to-benefit ratio, the longer the advantage is likely to be sustainable, because greater changes in the environment are required before value would exceed cost. Coupled with an informed view of the rate of environmental change in the industry, this ratio thus allows the analyst to estimate sustainability.

SCA and Strategy

The classic definition of competitive strategy as "an integrated set of actions designed to create a sustainable advantage over competitors" might suggest that possessing an SCA is synonymous with business success—that those producers who have an SCA are guaranteed winners, and that those competitors who lack one should simply exit the business to avoid financial disaster.

This apparently reasonable conclusion is, however, incorrect. Although an SCA is a powerful tool in creating a successful business strategy, it is not the only key ingredient. In fact:

a. Possessing an SCA does not guarantee financial success.

b. Producers can succeed even when competitors possess an SCA.

c. Pursuing an SCA can sometimes conflict with sound business strategy.

Losing with an SCA

Although an SCA will help a producer to achieve, over time, higher returns than his competitors, there are at least three circumstances where its possessor can fail financially:

1. If the market sector is not viable.   In many cases (including most new product introductions), the minimum achievable cost of producing and selling a particular product or service exceeds its value to the customer. In this situation, an SCA will not guarantee the survival of its possessor; it will tend merely to ensure that his competitors will fare even worse.

2. If the producer has severe operational problems.   An SCA can allow management the luxury of focusing more fully on achieving operational excellence, but thousands of companies have failed for operational, rather than strategic, reasons.

3. If competitors inflict tactical damage.   An SCA rarely puts a producer completely beyond the reach of competitor actions such as price cuts and "buying" market share, which may be unrelated to the SCA itself. A producer will be particularly vulnerable to such competitive tactics if the SCA is not very important, either because the depth of the "footprint" described earlier is shallow or because the gap in capability is minor.

In these cases, producers must select their actions very carefully. Actions that can and will be imitated may result only in intensified competitive rivalry. And, where the producer's advantage is unimportant, he will have little cushion against the competitive repercussions. For example, recent airline pricing policies and "frequent flyer" programs have done nothing to contribute to the long-term profitability or competitive positions of their originators. Unimaginative direct cost-reduction efforts (cutting overhead or staffs, for example) may improve profitability in the short term. But if competitors can and will imitate these efforts, the only long-run effect may be to raise the general level of misery throughout the industry.

Competing against an SCA

By definition, not all producers can possess an SCA in a given product/market segment. Other competitors face the prospects of competing (at least for some time) from a handicapped position. Under certain circumstances, however, it is still possible for some to succeed.

Rapidly growing markets constitute one such situation. As long as real market growth over a given period exceeds the additional capacity advantaged competitors can bring on line during that time (due to organizational constraints, risk aversion, and so forth), even competitors can thrive. For example, the booming market for microcomputer software over the past five years has enabled many weak competitors to grow rich. Only when market growth slows or the advantaged competitors increase the rate at which they can grow will true competition begin and the impact of an SCA make itself felt.

In markets where true competition for scarce sales dollars is taking place, the number of disadvantaged competitors who can succeed, the degree to which they can prosper, and the conditions under which they can prosper will vary, depending on the value of the advantage held by the "number-one" competitor.

If the number-one competitor has only a shallow or unimportant advantage, many disadvantaged competitors can prosper for long periods. As noted earlier, each competitor is unique. When all attributes are considered, each will have a competitive advantage in serving some customers. The disadvantaged competitors are more likely to receive lower returns than the number-one producer, but they certainly may be viable.

If the number-one competitor has an important advantage in a given product/market segment, some theorists assert that over the long run there will be only one viable competitor. Others may remain in the segment, but they will be plagued by losses and/or very inadequate returns. If there are six different ways to achieve a major advantage, this reasoning runs, then the market will split into six segments, each ruled by a different competitor, who uniquely excels in the attribute most valued by the customers in that segment.

Be that as it may, in practice other strong competitors may also profitably exist alongside Number One under two conditions:

1. *If the number-one producer's advantage is limited by a finite capacity* that is significantly less than the size of the market; that is, he may expand further, but will not retain his advantage on the incremental capacity. Obstacles to continued advantaged expansion are common: limited access to superior raw materials,

finite capacity in low-cost plants, prohibitive transportation costs beyond certain distances. Antitrust laws also tend to act as barriers to expansion beyond a certain level by number-one competitors.

2. *If the size of the individual competitors is small* relative to the size of the market. In this case, a number of strong competitors can expand for many years without directly competing with each other, by taking share from weak competitors rather than each other.

Weak competitors, of course, are likely to fare badly when competition is intense and the depth of the advantage enjoyed by others is great. Their choices are

a. To leave the business.

b. To endure the situation until the advantage is eroded.

c. To seek to create a new advantage.

If a weak competitor chooses to pursue a new advantage, then he must ensure that it will be preemptive, or that competitors will not notice his move and will fail to respond until he has consolidated his position. Otherwise, his action is virtually certain to be copied and the intended advantage erased.

Pursuing the Wrong SCA

Although its attainment is the goal of *competitive* strategy, sustainable competitive advantage is not an end in itself but a means to an end. The corporation is not in business to beat its competitors, but to create wealth for its shareholders. Thus, actions that contribute to SCA but detract from creating shareholder wealth may be good strategy in the competitive sense but bad strategy for the corporation. Consider two examples.

1. **Low-cost capacity additions in the absence of increased industry demand.** Adding low-cost capacity and recycling the additional profits into product/delivery attributes that attract enough customers to fill that capacity is usually a sound business strategy. However, as industry cost curve analysis has demonstrated, if the capacity addition is not accompanied by increases in industry demand, the effect may well be to displace the high-cost, but previously viable, marginal producer. When this happens, prices in the industry will fall to the level of the costs of the new marginal producer, costs which by definition are lower than the costs of the former marginal producer. Thus, the profit per unit sold of all participants will be reduced.

Depending on the cost structure of the industry, the declines in the profit per unit sold can be dramatic (for example, if all the remaining producers have similar costs). In this case, even the producer who added the new capacity will face declining profitability on his preexisting capacity; in extreme cases his total profit on new and old capacity may fall below the profit he had previously earned on the old capacity alone. While gaining share and eliminating a competitor (good competitive strategy), he has invested *more* to profit *less* (bad business strategy).

2. **Aggressive learning-curve pricing strategies that sacrifice too much current profit.**   Under these strategies, prices are reduced at least as fast as costs in order to buy market share and drive out competitors. The assumption is that the future payoff from market dominance will more than offset the costs of acquiring it. The value of new business, however, is likely to be very sensitive to the precise relationship between prices and costs. This is true particularly in the early stages of the learning curve, when the absolute levels of prices, costs, and margins are relatively high and the profit consequences are therefore greater for any given volume. Especially in high-tech industries such as electronics, where the lifetime of technologies is short, the long-term value of the market share bought by overly aggressive learning-curve strategies can be less than the profit eliminated in the early stages by pricing too close to costs.

The framework for SCA proposed in this article is far from complete. Its treatment of product/delivery attributes and capability gaps (notably organizational strength) is impressionistic rather than detailed. It leaves other aspects of the topic (for example, the sustainability of competitive advantage at the corporate level) unexplored.

But a major concern of the business unit strategist is to determine whether the enterprise (or a competitor's) possesses or is in a position to capture an SCA, and, if so, to examine its strategic implications. The conditions for SCA and the implications of SCA for strategy that have been proposed provide an initial framework for these tasks.

READING 6
FROM WARNING TO CRISIS: A TURNAROUND PRIMER

P. Scott Scherrer

Long before a business fails, warning signals start flashing. But managers often don't notice the red lights, or even ignore them. When they finally do acknowledge something's amiss, some managers will treat the problem as a temporary phenomenon, putting out the fire but not remedying the hazard.

With a bit of education, however, managers can train themselves to perk up and recognize the bad signs, whether they are activated from within the organization or from the outside. Once managers learn the signals, they also can differentiate between the various stages of organizational decline. No matter what phase a company is in, managers need to act—fast.

Following is a turnaround primer that identifies warning signals, categorizes decline phases, and provides a framework to help managers reverse the direction of an organization that may well be on its way to hell in a handbasket.

Influencing Externals

Many managers believe a downward trend will dissipate when bad news from the outside improves. The external elements that cause them trouble range from increased competition to legal/political vacillations (see Exhibit 1).

Among these external, uncontrollable elements are market changes, customer preference changes, foreign competition, capital market movements, legal precedents, and the political climate. Since all businesses in an industry are similarly affected by external elements, each business survives these changes only because of the ability of its management. Some businesses come through external changes with increased market share and profitability; others fail.

A major problem with the uncontrollable elements is their interaction with each other. A cultural/social change, for example, can result in a legal/political change. This, in turn, can affect the economic environment, leading to a shift in technological developments. The rate of technological development affects the status of the competition, which in turn influences the cultural/social environment, and the circle is complete. What managers often do not realize is that they can create a similar chain reaction within their businesses to combat the external elements. Foresight and flexibility will help management safeguard against uncontrollable elements, using tactics such as promotion, education of the consumer, accelerated research and development, product improvements or elimination, changing expansion plans, changing markets, and changing channels of distribution.

Exhibit 1 Nine External Warning Signals

---

1. Economic growth activity gives management an indication of the economic climate and influences expansion plans.
2. Credit availability and money-market activity are barometers of trends in commercial and investment banking that will alter the cost of funds.
3. Capital market activity gives a clear signal to management of investor attitudes toward any given industry and the state of the business climate.
4. Business population characteristics show the numbers of businesses entering and exiting any given industry, signaling market expansion and contraction and the degree of competition within the industry.
5. Price-level changes indicate the rate of inflation and impact production considerations.
6. Changes in the competitive structure of the marketplace affect products, pricing, and marketing/distribution.
7. Breakthrough technology also causes changes in products, marketing/distribution, and production.
8. Cultural/social changes alter consumer preferences or the conditions under which a product can be sold.
9. Legal/political changes can adversely affect the marketplace or have an impact on the production, sale, and distribution of a product.

Consider the tobacco companies. They have known for many years about the external changes taking place in their industry—most importantly, the discovery of smoking's serious health hazards. They have been affected by cultural/social and legal/political changes for the past several decades, and recently experienced severe tests in the court system. To offset declining product sales, they developed new products, such as smokeless tobaccos. They also invested in new businesses: RJR Nabisco, Miller Beer, and other consumer products companies that would use established channels of distribution to gain competitive advantage. The tobacco producers understood the early warning signals of the external, uncontrollable elements and acted to offset them. The ability to cope with external, uncontrollable elements requires that management plans for the unexpected and implements that plan when the unexpected occurs.

Internal Elements

Only 20 percent of business failures are caused by external elements. The other 80 percent are the result of mishandled internal elements. Management is the force that drives the internal functions of finance, production, and marketing/distribution, and yet these elements are at the root of the majority of business failures.

When management does not recognize the internal signals of decline, it pretends that slowdowns are caused by external elements. A shortage of cash is often attributed to poor collections or lack of sales. In fact, the shortage of cash is usually a signal pointing to a deeper problem buried within the firm's management and accounting information systems. It may be that the firm is selling its products or services at a price that does not cover the variable costs of making the product or service. The firm may not have calculated contribution margins, actual product costs, and the direct cost of sales to determine the amount of profitability in the product or service.

Like external forces, the internal elements can interact with each other, and any one of the internal, controllable elements may spark a decline. Production techniques can become antiquated. Marketing/distribution can be in the wrong market with the wrong product. Finance can be unaware that the financial requirements of the other departments have changed. (Poor information flow between departments is another signal of decline.)

Coping with Internal Elements

Management often does not use the managerial tools at its disposal to control internal forces. Many managers do not utilize cash projections, but are only aware of balance sheets and income statements. The heart of any company is the synergy developed between the efficient operations of its various departments. The pulse beat for that synergy is the financial statements. Businesses should run on budgets and cash projections. Budgets are the foundation of financial statements, which reflect the success or failure of the business. For many businesses, however, budgets are mystery stories couched in scenarios that allow managers to hedge their positions. Managers create budgets that cannot be wrong, and consequently they cannot be accurate.

Balance sheets may show adequate working capital even when a company is in decline. When the balance sheet is overly burdened with inventory and accounts receivable that are inaccurate, obsolete, or uncollectable, a company is in trouble. The manager should know the status of accounts receivable. If they are increasing on the financial statements, is it because sales are increasing or collections are slow? If inventory is increasing, is it because sales have decreased and production has not? Managers can reduce a firm's reliance on banks by increasing accounts receivable collections, reducing inventory, and paying accounts payable within the discount period to avoid penalties.

Internal elements require constant monitoring. Since management may be unable to understand the dynamic nature of the internal elements, it is not surprising that declines go unnoticed.

Management often doesn't understand its relationships with stakeholders—the people who work for, live near, invest in, or are affected by a company. Customer service, for example, is often a low priority. In most businesses, 80 percent of sales come from 20 percent of the customers. Often the cost of servicing a customer and the cost of a sale are unknown. Customers are not classified into categories to determine the most favorable customers to the business. Management may perceive that the best customers are those who order the most, although these may be the same people who pay the slowest. In many companies, channels of information—from customers, competition, employees, vendors, and other managers—are not open. Without this information, the business cannot adapt to change. Information and the ability to react to it are the most powerful weapons a business has against decline.

Early Internal Warning Signals

Danger signals can be used by management to begin an internal corporate renewal. There are distinct phases of decline, and the danger signals vary within the stages (see Exhibit 2). Not all of the symptoms of decline will appear; there is sufficient cause to worry if some of them occur.

Also, internal warning signals take on different meaning depending on the company's growth rate. In stabilized companies, managers may continue to manage as if the growth will continue in the near future. When plans are not

---

Exhibit 2 Common Danger Signals and the Stages When They Occur

Early decline
Shortage of cash.
Strained liquidity.
Reduced working capital.
Stretched accounts payable.
Late accounts receivable.
Reduction of ROI by 20 to 30%.
Flat sales.
Several quarters of losses.
Increased employee absenteeism.
Increased employee accidents.
Increased customer complaints (product quality, delivery, back orders, stock-outs.)
Late financial and management information.

Mid-term decline
Increasing inventory.
Decreasing sales.
Decreasing margins.
Increasing expenses.
Increasing advances from banks.
Additional requests for consideration from banks.
Late and unreliable financial and management information.
Eroding customer confidence.
Accelerating accounts payable from vendors.
Overdrafts at the bank.
Delayed accounts receivable from opportunistic customers.
Violation of loan covenants.
Bank used to cover payroll.

EXHIBIT 2 *(concluded)*

Late decline

Little attention paid to decreasing profit.
Staff is cut back without analyzing cause of problems.
Overdrawn bank account substituted for a line of credit.
Cash crisis.
Accounts payable are 60 to 90 days late.
Accounts receivable are more than 90 days late.
Sales decline further.
Employee morale is extremely low.
Company credibility is eroding.
Inventory turnover has decreased excessively.
Supplier restrictions are initiated.
Fewer reports to bank are submitted.
Auditors qualify opinions.
Checks bounce.
Credit is offset.
Accounts receivable continue to age.
Margins decrease further.
Sales volume decreases further.
Uncollectable receivables increase.
No liquidity.
Working capital is depleted.
Lack of funds for payroll.
Ineffective management.
Attempts to convince lenders that company is viable and liquidation is not necessary.

Signals that can occur in any stage

Decreased capital utilization.
Decreased market share in key product line(s).
Increased overhead costs.
Increased management and employee turnover.
Salaries and benefits growing faster than productivity and profits.
Increased management layers.
Losing market share to competition, which is not keeping up with marketplace changes.
Management in conflict with company goals and objectives.
Direction of management and company are different.
Sales forecasts predict company can sell its way out of difficulty.
Poor internal accounting.
Credit advances to customers who do not pay on time.
Nonseasonal borrowing.
Sudden overdrafts.
Increased trade inquiries.

---

modified to address the new situation, the business courts trouble. Many companies religiously draft strategic plans. All too often, however, the plans are carved in granite and are not adaptable to changing situations. When shifts occur (internal, external, or both), the business is unable to cope with them, and instead continues to follow its strategic plan. Managers believe the strategic plan represents the very best of their creative abilities, and therefore are loathe to deviate from it. The strategic plan becomes part of the problem, rather than the solution.

Financial Predictors

Many financial ratios are tip-offs to a downturn, but management often considers them accounting busy work and pays no heed. Five ratios useful throughout all phases of decline and the turnaround process are

1. Working capital to total assets.
2. Retained earnings to total assets.
3. Earnings before interest and taxes (EBIT) to total assets.
4. Market value of equity to book value to total debt.
5. Sales to total assets.

These ratios are especially useful when they are used for at least three years. The business will begin to establish a pattern within the ratios, and deviations from the pattern can be corrected quickly. More mature businesses have long histories, and the ratios should have reached a point where they are consistent annually. A deviation is as good as a red flag.

The ratios noted by turnaround managers generate a picture of the company. They indicate the ability of the business to survive on its own. When they are extremely low, it is time to approach the bank for bridge capital. The bank will not be willing to have any further involvement unless the plan for the turnaround is valid and based on the business's actual ability to support itself after the turnaround.

Double Decline

Often a company suffers a decline thanks to a combination of internal and external elements. Some common signals when both forces are at work include

- Management by exception rather than flexible planning.
- Delegation without inspection, control, feedback, or reinforcement.
- Vertical organization chart, with little if any interaction between departments.
- Managers with responsibility for more than five direct reports.
- Employees with more than one boss.
- Broken chain of command.
- Overreliance on management by objectives.
- Senior managers' abuse of perks.

- Marketing the wrong products.
- Marketing in the wrong markets.
- Inadequate research and development.
- Inappropriate channels of distribution.
- Unresponsive financial information systems.
- Loss of competitive advantage.
- Changing technology.
- Regulatory changes.
- Inadequate understanding of customers' needs.
- Allowing one department or business function to dominate and dictate the mission, goals, and objectives of the business.

Crazy Eddie, Inc., is an example of a company that has suffered from both internal and external problems. Internally, there were too many layers of management, excessive wages, corporate waste, cost overruns, employee morale problems, and information flow deficiencies. The company had almost every signal of decline.

Externally, new competitors entered the market. Since Crazy Eddie's had damaged its relationships with appliance suppliers, it could not receive the necessary merchandise to compete. The company is now undergoing a turnaround; part of the strategy is to cut costs and payroll by a minimum of $25 million. There is also a slump in the company's markets, so revenue has decreased. The internal elements were changed by laying off unnecessary managers, reducing wages, adding a profit-sharing plan, settling the lawsuits on corporate waste, reducing costs, and adding a computer system to prevent selling items below cost. The external elements are being addressed by rebuilding relationships with suppliers, banks, and consumers.

The Turnaround Process

Turnaround managers bring order to chaos, which usually means they must take control of every function in the business. They create budgets from the bottom up and strictly enforce accountability. They analyze products and markets to determine which have the most profitability. Those that generate losses are terminated quickly and permanently, regardless of the company's relationship with the customer or product. The turnaround manager cuts costs, increases the business's adaptability, and saves the profitable products and markets. Actual costs replace standard costing, and product contribution margins are used to determine which products contribute the most to the fixed costs of the business. Cash flow reports are used continually; at first they may be used daily, then weekly, then monthly, and finally semiannually. The reports are used in developing the operating plan. The time line and the amount of cash flowing in will determine how the business can survive.

The classifications of customers and the aging of accounts receivable determine which customers are profitable. The business may have many customers with repeat orders, but they all may be delinquent in paying their accounts. The business cannot afford to carry them any longer. Reviewing accounts receivable is an essential task of turnaround managers. They decide which customers to keep and which to pursue for more business.

Get Everyone Involved

Banks, vendors, customers, employees, boards of directors, and others affected by the decline of the business need to be made part of the solution. Banks and boards of directors are usually the parties that suggest the use of a turnaround manager. Normally, by the time they notice a problem exists, the situation is approaching crisis proportions. This is a common situation because bank executives and boards tend to be chiefly concerned with balance sheets and income statements driven, despite the fact that healthy looking balance sheets and income statements can disguise many problems. Bank managers and board members do not visit the business and review operations. They do not walk the plant floor and talk with employees. They do not review basic financial information, such as accounts receivable and payable. They only learn about employee morale, customer service, equipment condition, and other on-site situations from a report generated by management.

Trade vendors also need to be included in the situation. They are the business's lifeline to its supplies. When payments to them are delinquent, the business is in jeopardy of losing its supply line. Management may argue that it can find other suppliers, but unless the underlying problem causing delinquent payments is addressed, suppliers will evaporate along with the company's credit. New suppliers require credit references, and changing suppliers has substantial switching costs. The new supplier has to produce or acquire the supplies requested, schedule deliveries, and obtain payments. As the business adds new suppliers, the bank will receive credit report requests. This is another signal of decline.

Employee participation is essential in the turnaround process. Turnarounds often require asking for pay concessions. Hours on the job and working conditions may be affected. When employees are part of the restructuring plan, they tend to accept painful concessions with more ease. When the restructuring is complete, management should consider itself indebted to these people and should reward them financially.

SRC, a leveraged buyout from International Harvester, is an example of a turnaround where employee participation was the key ingredient for success. In 1979, the company was losing $2 million a year on sales of $26 million. In 1983, 13 employees of International Harvester bought SRC. They developed a detailed reporting system and a full-blown, daily cash flow statement. In 1986, sales reached $42 million. Net operating income increased to 11 percent and the debt-to-equity ratio has been reduced from 89-to-1 to 5.1-to-1. The appraised value of a share in the company's stock ownership plan has increased from 10 cents to $8.45. Absenteeism and serious workplace accidents have almost disappeared. The company attributes the turnaround to allowing employees to reach their highest potential.

To facilitate a turnaround, union cooperation is essential. It also can greatly influence morale. A turnaround can be accomplished despite the unions, but may require drastic steps such as bankruptcy or massive layoffs. Concessions regarding pay rate, hours, working conditions, raises, vacations, accumulated sick leave, and benefits will be granted only when the union is convinced that the company can survive. That this is possible is indicated by the arrival of the turnaround manager and by the turnaround plan. The cooperation of the other stakeholders also places pressure on the union to cooperate.

Customers must also be taken into account during the turnaround, but businesses in decline tend to forsake customer service. Quality control diminishes, which causes more order returns. This adds expenses to an already strained financial condition. Orders are taken and delivery dates missed, causing loss of credibility with the customers. The inventory, which was a main part of the balance sheet, becomes obsolete and therefore not usable to meet the current demands of the customers. The end result is the loss of the customer base.

Types of Turnarounds and Strategies

A turnaround can take several forms. It can be *strategic* if the business needs to be redefined because of changing markets and products. In the General Nutrition turnaround, for example, the company moved away from its core of vitamins and specialty health foods to the much wider category of health in general. The stores needed items that would make people come to them rather than grocery stores. The company searched for new products and new lines. Brookstone, the specialty gadget store, inspired many of the changes made at General Nutrition. Prior to the turnaround, the stock had plummeted from a high of 29⅝ to a low of 3⅞.

An *operational* turnaround involves changing a business's operations, which could include cost cutting, revenue generating, and asset reduction. In the case of General Nutrition, the turnaround was also focused on the operations of the business. (It is very common for turnarounds to be mounted on several fronts and combine strategies.) At General Nutrition, the management team was strengthened and the company divided into three distinct segments: retailing, manufacturing, and specialty services.

Another example of an operational turnaround is Black and Decker. The company had more than 200 different motor sizes. It had split consumer and professional tools into two separate groups that seldom communicated with each other. This made it easy for the competition to find niches where Black and

Decker did not make tools. To remedy the situation, the company organized plants around motor sizes, reduced product variations, and streamlined manufacturing. The number of plants was reduced from 25 to 19. Excess capacity utilization increased by 75 percent. In addition, the company began producing new products to meet consumer demand.

The *financial* turnaround restructures the financial operations of a business. The object is to utilize the financial strength of the business as an asset. ITT, for example, divested itself of 23 businesses for almost $1.5 billion and increased return on equity from 8 percent in 1979 to 12 percent in 1987. Management slashed expenses by abandoning its lavish lifestyle, renting out full floors at its Park Avenue headquarters, and cutting the work force by two thirds.

Each different type of turnaround may focus on a particular strategy. These include

- *Revenue generating.*   Management tries to increase sales, advertising, and markets while decreasing prices.
- *Product/Markets refocusing.*   Managers analyze products and markets to determine their profitability. Customers are analyzed to determine the nature of their purchases, payment history, and ability to purchase more. Channels of distribution are analyzed to determine their effectiveness. Products are analyzed further to determine their saleability, contribution margins, actual cost of production, cost of sale, cost of distribution, manufacturing efficiency, inventory carrying costs, and cost of customer service. Businesses may have reached the limits of their growth in products and markets, in which case they need to analyze potential moves into other product and market areas.
- *Cost cutting.*   Managers reduce administrative costs, R&D, and marketing.
- *Asset reduction.*   Management removes unnecessary assets that usually look nice on the balance sheet but actually produce only costs of maintenance and no revenue stream.
- The combination of any of the above.

Using the correct strategy is part of the art of successfully turning around a company. As the turnaround progresses, the strategy may change. Cost cutting may be superseded by revenue generating, and so forth. Strategies may be combined and used in various sequences, but using an inappropriate strategy can be a terminal error. Here are four pointers to choosing the correct strategy:

- Mature businesses should use retrenchment and efficiency strategies, not product/marketing refocusing.
- Businesses with low-capacity utilization should pursue cost-cutting strategies.
- Businesses with high-capacity utilization should also pursue cost-cutting strategies.

- Businesses with high market share should pursue revenue-generating strategies and product/market refocusing.

The time frame for a turnaround varies depending upon the business, industry, market, severity of the crisis, cooperation of stakeholders, and turnaround manager. A business that has been in decline for several years cannot expect to be renewed quickly. Its reputation for low credibility will have permeated all of its stakeholders and will take some time to reverse. A business that recognizes signals of decline in the early stage can be renewed more quickly.

In general, turnarounds occur in five stages:

1. Evaluation of the situation, which can take from one week to three months.
2. Creating a plan, which can take from one to six months.
3. Implementation of the plan, which can take from six months to one year.
4. Stabilization of the business, which can take from six months to one year.
5. Return to growth of the business, which can take from one to two years.

Astute managers constantly monitor the health of their businesses and act on the warning signals. Often, managers can see the signals but need outside help to cure the problem. The need to address decline and failure is obvious. The waste of corporate assets and employees' talents that can stem from managerial ignorance can be astronomical. This waste can be minimized if management can notice and address decline in its early stages.

READING 7
STATISTICS ON 185 COUNTRIES AND TERRITORIES

Country or territory	GNP US$000 1990	GNP Real Growth Rate (percent) 1980–90	Population 000 1990	Population Growth Rate (percent) 1980–90	GNP per Capita US$ 1990
Afghanistan[a]	–	–	–	–	–
Albania	–	–	3,255	2.0	–
Algeria	51,585	2.7	25,056	3.0	2,060
American Samoa[b]	–	–	39	1.7	–
Andorra	–	–	50	–	–
Angola	–	8.8	10,011	2.6	–
Antigua and Barbuda	363	5.2	79	0.5	4,600
Argentina	76,491	– 0.5	32,293	1.4	2,370
Aruba[b]	–	–	60	–	–
Australia	290,522	3.2	17,005	1.5	17,080
Austria	147,016	2.1	7,643	0.1	19,240
Bahamas	2,913	3.6	253	1.9	11,510
Bahrain		– 0.1	504	4.1	–
Bangladesh	22,579	3.7	113,188	2.6	200
Barbados	1,680	1.7	257	0.3	6,540
Belgium	154,688	1.4	10,016	0.1	15,440
Belize	373	5.3	189	2.8	1,970
Benin	1,716	2.2	4,741	3.2	360
Bermuda[b]	–	–	58	0.7	–
Bhutan	273	9.7	1,433	2.1	190
Bolivia	4,526	0.0	7,310	2.8	620
Botswana	2,561	9.9	1,254	3.4	2,040
Brazil	402,788	2.7	150,197	2.2	2,680
Brunei[b]	–	–	256	3.3	–
Bulgaria	19,875	2.5	8,991	0.2	2,210
Burkina Faso	2,955	4.1	9,016	2.6	330
Burundi	1,151	4.2	5,470	2.9	210
Cambodia[a]	–	–	–	–	
Cameroon	11,233	2.9	11,941	3.2	940
Canada	542,774	3.3	26,543	0.9	20,450
Cape Verde	331	5.7	371	2.6	890
Central African Rep.	1,194	1.4	3,036	2.7	390
Chad	1,074	5.8	5,679	2.4	190
Channel Islands[b]	–	–	144	1.1	
Chile	25,504	2.8	13,177	1.7	1,940

SOURCE: *The World Bank Atlas* (1991).

Country or territory	GNP US$000 1990	GNP Real Growth Rate (percent) 1980–90	Population 000 1990	Population Growth Rate (percent) 1980–90	GNP per Capita US$ 1990
China	415,884	9.5	1,133,696	1.5	370
Colombia	40,805	3.1	32,843	2.0	1,240
Comoros	227	2.8	475	3.7	480
Congo	2,296	3.2	2,277	3.4	1,010
Costa Rica	5,342	3.0	2,801	2.4	1,910
Côte d'Ivoire	8,920	0.2	12,233	4.1	730
Cuba	–	–	10,626	0.9	–
Cyprus	5,633	6.0	701	1.1	8,040
Czechoslovakia	49,225	1.5	15,680	0.3	3,140
Denmark	113,015	2.1	5,139	0.0	22,090
Djibouti[c]	–	–	427	3.4	–
Dominica	160	4.3	82	1.2	1,940
Dominican Rep.	5,847	1.9	7,140	2.3	820
Ecuador	10,112	1.9	10,559	2.7	960
Egypt, Arab Rep.	31,381	4.7	52,061	2	600
El Salvador	5,767	0.8	5,258	1.5	1,100
Equatorial Guinea	136	–	417	2.0	330
Ethiopia	6,041	1.9	51,183	3.1	120
Faeroe Islands[b]	–	–	47	1.0	
Fed. Sts. of Micronesia	–	–	103	–	–
Fiji	1,326	1.3	749	1.7	1,770
Finland	129,823	3.6	4,979	0.4	26,070
France	1,099,750	2.2	56,453	0.4	19,480
French Guiana[d]	–	–	93	3.5	
French Polynesia[b]	–	–	197	2.3	
Gabon	3,654	0.8	1,135	3.6	3,220
Gambia, The	229	3.0	875	3.3	260
Germany[e]	1,411,346	2.2	77,309	−0.2	22,730
Ghana	5,824	2.8	14,870	3.4	390
Gibraltar[f]	–	–	31	0.0	
Greece	60,245	1.2	10,048	0.4	6,000
Greenland[b]	–	–	56	1.1	
Grenada	199	5.8	94	0.7	2,120
Guadeloupe[b]	–	–	343	0.5	
Guam[b]	–	–	137	2.5	
Guatemala	8,309	0.7	9,196	2.9	900
Guinea	2,756	–	5,718	2.5	480
Guinea-Bissau	176	3.7	981	1.9	180

Country or territory	GNP US$000 1990	GNP Real Growth Rate (percent) 1980–90	Population 000 1990	Population Growth Rate (percent) 1980–90	GNP per Capita US$ 1990
Guyana	293	−2.7	798	0.5	370
Haiti	2,400	−0.4	6,488	1.9	370
Honduras	3,023	2.2	5,119	3.4	590
Hong Kong[g]	66,666	7.0	5,779	1.4	11,540
Hungary	30,047	1.4	10,554	−0.2	2,780
Iceland	5,456	2.4	258	1.2	21,150
India	294,816	5.4	849,510	2.1	350
Indonesia	101,151	6.3	181,580	2.0	560
Iran, Islamic Rep.	139,120	2.7	56,925	3.5	2,450
Iraq[d]	–	–	18,914	3.6	
Ireland	33,467	1.4	3,504	0.3	9,550
Isle of Man[b]	–	–	67	0.0	
Israel	50,866	3.2	4,636	1.7	10,970
Italy	970,619	2.4	57,588	0.2	16,850
Jamaica	3,606	0.7	2,390	1.2	1,510
Japan	3,140,948	4.1	123,503	0.6	25,430
Jordan[h]	3,924	−0.4	3,154	3.6	1,240
Kenya	8,958	4.2	24,368	3.9	370
Kiribati	54	3.6	70	1.9	760
Korea, Dem. Rep.	–	–	21,576	1.7	–
Korea, Rep.	231,132	10.1	42,789	1.1	5,400
Kuwait	–	2.2	2,141	4.4	–
Lao PDR	848	3.7	4,186	2.8	200
Lebanon[d]	–	–	–	–	
Lesotho	832	1.8	1,771	2.7	470
Liberia[a]	–	–	2,560	3.1	
Libya	–	−5.4	4,546	4.1	–
Luxembourg	10,875	4.3	378	0.4	28,770
Macao[d]	–	–	459	3.5	
Madagascar	2,710	0.5	11,620	2.9	230
Malawi	1,662	3.3	8,504	3.4	200
Malaysia	41,524	5.1	17,752	2.6	2,340
Maldives	96	10.0	218	3.5	440
Mali	2,292	3.8	8,461	2.5	270
Malta	2,342	3.1	353	−0.5	6,630
Martinique[f]	–	–	341	0.5	
Mauritania	987	0.6	1,969	2.4	500
Mauritius	2,422	6.4	1,074	1.0	2,250
Mayotte	–	–	73	3.6	–
Mexico	214,500	1.1	86,161	2.0	2,490
Mongolia[c]	–	–	2,124	2.7	
Morocco	23,788	4.3	25,091	2.7	950
Mozambique	1,208	−1.5	15,784	2.7	80

Country or territory	GNP		Population		GNP per Capita
	US$000 1990	Real Growth Rate (percent) 1980–90	000 1990	Growth Rate (percent) 1980–90	US$ 1990
Myanmar[a]	–	–	41,609	2.1	
Namibia[c]	–	–	1,780	3.2	
Nepal	3,289	4.5	19,096	2.6	170
Netherlands	258,804	1.9	14,931	0.5	17,330
Netherlands Antilles[b]	–	–	191	0.9	
New Caledonia[f]	–	–	165	1.8	
New Zealand	43,185	1.4	3,405	0.8	12,680
Nicaragua[c]	–	–	3,853	3.4	
Niger	2,365	– 1.3	7,666	3.4	310
Nigeria	31,285	0.2	117,510	3.4	270
Norway	98,079	3.1	4,242	0.4	23,120
Oman	–	8.6	1,554	1.4	–
Pakistan	42,649	6.3	113,687	3.3	380
Panama	4,414	0.1	2,418	2.1	1,830
Papua New Guinea	3,372	1.9	3,915	2.5	860
Paraguay	4,796	1.9	4,314	3.2	1,110
Peru	25,149	0.2	21,662	2.3	1,160
Philippines	43,954	0.9	61,358	2.4	730
Poland	64,480	1.8	37,966	0.7	1,700
Portugal	50,692	3.0	10,372	0.6	4,890
Puerto Rico	21,346	2.3	3,309	0.3	6,470
Qatar	6,962	– 6.6	439	4.8	15,860
Reunion[f]	–	–	593	1.6	
Romania	38,025	1.5	23,249	0.4	1,640
Rwanda	2,214	1.0	7,113	3.2	310
Saint Kitts and Nevis	133	4.8	40	– 1.2	3,330
Saint Lucia	286	6.3	150	2.0	1,900
Saint Vincent	184	6.9	114	1.0	1,610
Sao Tome and Principe	47	– 1.5	123	2.8	380
Saudi Arabia	–	– 0.8	14,902	4.8	–
Senegal	5,260	3.0	7,428	3.0	710
Seychelles	318	3.2	68	0.7	4,670
Sierra Leone	981	0.9	4,137	2.4	240
Singapore	33,512	7.0	2,722	1.2	12,310
Solomon Islands	187	7.0	324	3.5	580
Somalia	946	1.1	6,284	3.0	150
South Africa	90,410	1.5	35,914	2.4	2,520
Spain	429,404	3.1	39,326	0.4	10,920

Country or territory	GNP		Population		GNP per Capita
	US$000 1990	Real Growth Rate (percent) 1980–90	000 1990	Growth Rate (percent) 1980–90	US$ 1990
Sri Lanka	7,971	3.9	17,002	1.5	470
Sudan[a]	—	—	25,191	2.8	
Suriname	1,365	−2.6	447	2.5	3,050
Swaziland	645	4.5	789	3.4	820
Sweden	202,498	2.1	8,552	0.3	23,680
Switzerland	219,337	2.3	6,690	0.5	32,790
Syrian Arab Rep.	12,404	1.4	12,533	3.6	990
Tanzania[i]	2,779	2.3	24,518	3.1	120
Thailand	79,044	7.6	55,801	1.8	1,420
Togo	1,474	1.8	3,638	3.5	410
Tonga	100	2.1	99	0.5	1,010
Trinidad and Tobago	4,458	−4.3	1,283	1.7	3,470
Tunisia	11,592	3.4	8,175	2.5	1,420
Turkey	91,742	5.5	56,277	2.4	1,630
Uganda	3,814	4.1	17,358	3.2	220
United Arab Emirates	31,613	−3.1	1,592	4.4	19,860
United Kingdom	923,959	2.7	57,483	0.2	16,070
United States	5,445,825	3.2	250,942	1.0	21,700
Uruguay	7,929	−0.3	3,093	0.6	2,560
USSR	—	—	288,734	0.9	—
Vanuatu	167	2.4	157	2.9	1,060
Venezuela	50,574	0.7	19,738	2.8	2,560
Viet Nam[a]	—	—	66,473	2.2	
Virgin Islands (U.S)	—	2.3	110	1.1	—
Western Samoa	121	2.0	165	0.6	730
Yemen Rep.[a]	—	—	11,612	3.0	
Yugoslavia	72,860	−0.2	23,800	0.7	3,060
Zaire	8,117	1.6	35,564	3.1	230
Zambia	3,391	0.7	8,122	3.7	420
Zimbabwe	6,313	2.6	9,809	3.4	640

—Not available.

Note: Figures in italics are for years other than those specified; the number 0 or 0.0 in the table means zero or less than half the unit shown and not known more precisely.

a. GNP per capita estimated to be less than $500. b. GNP per capita estimated to be $6,000 or more. c. GNP per capita estimated to be in the $500–$1,499 range. d. GNP per capita estimated to be in the $1,500–$3,499 range. e. Data for GNP, GNP per capita, and agriculture's share in GDP cover Federal Republic of Germany before unification; other indicators are composites of separate measures previously reported for the Federal Republic of Germany and the German Democratic Republic. f. GNP per capita estimated to be in the $3,500–$5,999 range. g. References to GNP relate to GDP estimates. h. Data for GNP cover the East Bank only. i. Data for GNP and GNP per capita cover mainland Tanzania only. j. GNP per capita estimates for the USSR in 1989 range from $1,780 (*The Economy of the USSR*, 1990, joint report by the World Bank, IMF, OECD, and EBRD) to $9,320 (*Handbook of Economic Statistics*, 1990, U.S. Central Intelligence Agency, using purchasing power parities).

Summary Table

GNP per capita, 1990	Number of Countries	GNP (US$000,000) 1990	Population (000,000) 1990	GNP per Capita (US$) 1990
Less than $500	45	929,000	2,826	330
$500–$1,499	41	499,000	612	820
$1,500–$3,499	38	1,589,000	662	2,400
$3,500–$5,999	11	1,522,000	349	4,360
$6,000 or more	50	16,300,000	846	19,520
World[a]	185	20,839,000	5,295	3,940

a. World Bank staff estimate.

READING 8
SHOPPING FOR COMPANIES

William W. Bain, Jr.

The business press is an avid chronicler of failed mergers and acquisitions. The resulting impression is that an executive who embarks on an acquisition is little better than a compulsive gambler throwing his money away trying to beat the house odds.

There are, of course, significant data supporting this viewpoint. Studies show that a dollar invested in an acquisition has only about a 30 percent chance of creating real economic value—and some who have looked at the record say the success rate is even worse. A craps game offers far better odds of winning.

Yet merger and acquisition activity continues at a high level. American companies laid down some $200 billion last year to make more than 2,500 acquisitions. In Europe, there has been a dramatic increase in M&As. Merchant banks in the United Kingdom, for example, have begun to assume the role of dealmaker first created by U.S. investment banks. The total value of deals there in 1985 was £7.1 billion, the highest total since 1972, adjusted for inflation.

Of course, the M&A gambling analogy does not really hold up. Gamblers are always at the mercy of the house odds, while companies can actually turn the acquisition odds in their favor. A few years ago our firm took a close look at some companies that, through acquisitions, had grown, increased their profitability, and achieved sustainable improvements in their competitive positions. A short list of those that have built substantial corporate value this way would include Heileman Brewing, James River Corporation, Flowers Industries, and the Dun & Bradstreet Corporation in the United States, and such firms as Esselte, BTR, BSN, and Hanson Trust in Europe.

We have attempted to distill out the elements that made these companies successful. Over the past two years, we have assisted clients in some 65 acquisitions in the United States and Europe, working on transactions that involved some $15 billion. Our role is not normally that of dealmaker. Typically, the first phase of our work involves setting strategy, screening acquisition candidates, evaluating them, and helping to determine the value. Structuring the exact terms of the offer and making the legally mandated inspections are areas in which investment bankers, law firms, and accountants have the appropriate expertise. We are often involved in the next stage: helping integrate the new company into the acquirer's strategy. We're still learning, but at this point I believe we do have a set of working principles that serve our clients well.

1. *Weigh an acquisition carefully against all other strategic options for creating long-term shareholder value.* Mobil buys Montgomery Ward to establish a beach

SOURCE: *Across the Board* (July–August 1986), pp. 44–49.

head in a business with faster growth than oil. Coke buys Taylor Wine to get into a fast-growing business in which it can apply its vaunted marketing expertise. Fluor Corporation buys St. Joe Minerals to make good use of extra cash and diversify into a supposedly countercyclical industry.

Each company had plausible justification for making its acquisition. And each now almost certainly wishes it had figured out some other way to achieve its objective.

When an acquisition that looked plausible does not work well, it is usually because the acquisition was not consistent with the buyer's long-range strategic guiding principles. The point is, an acquisition may look like a good opportunity to accomplish some operating goal easily and quickly. But the chances of making the acquisition do what it is supposed to do are minuscule when the acquired company is a poor fit with the parent company's basic corporate strategy. That strategy, carefully thought through and defined, may dictate an entirely different kind of acquisition, or none at all.

The tremendous importance of core strategy is borne out by the experience of most companies that have built value through acquisitions. They have typically done it deliberately, over the long term.

At Dun & Bradstreet, acquisitions accounted for some 80 percent of the company's total revenues in 1984. The revealing figure here is that the acquisitions were made over 25 years. The success of the acquisition strategy at Dun & Bradstreet is seen in such figures as growth of the market-to-book value ratio, which in 1985 was two and a half times greater than that of the Standard & Poor's 400.

At BTR, a British conglomerate, growth in the earnings from base businesses was only 10.2 percent from 1973 to 1983, while acquisitions earnings grew by 22.7 percent. A planned, sequential acquisition program over a period of 16 years strengthened their core businesses and brought them into market leadership in new areas.

The key factor in the success of these and other firms is that they had a clear vision of their corporate strategy, they weighed their options, and they chose acquisition as the means of getting where they wanted to be.

2. *Actively look for a company to buy, rather than trying to save money and time by waiting for a seller to come to you.* The typical merger or acquisition begins with an intermediary, usually an investment bank, approaching several prospective buyers to interest them in a company or a division of a company. Whatever the circumstances, the prospective acquirer is immediately at a disadvantage.

The company that is approached has been targeted by the seller, which probably has only a superficial understanding of the target company's business. Thus, there's a better than even chance that the firm for sale does not fit the prospective buyer's strategy. What is more, the company is for sale for a reason, which almost certainly ensures that an acquirer will be buying a headache of one kind or another.

The acquirer may not mind buying a certain type of headache, but there probably won't be time to make a thorough examination of the company to determine just what that headache is. Bendix, for example, took over Warner & Swasey in a high-pressure white-knight rescue—only to discover later that W&S was lagging far behind the Japanese in product development.

By contrast, if a company has an acquisition strategy, it can seek out the kinds of companies that fit that strategy and take its time in evaluating them. Sara Lee spent 16 months studying Hanes before buying the company—and the combination has been a success.

Even when a firm chooses not to make an active search, the process of setting strategy will give it a head start in making a quick, effective evaluation when an acquisition candidate presents itself.

3. *Invest plenty of effort in screening and establishing priorities among acquisition candidates.* The screening process, done properly, can be a very large project. In a recent search, we began by screening thousands of companies on the basis of the business they were in, their size, and their market value. That left us a list of 219 possible candidates. We assigned each of them a priority on the basis of potential for market growth, profit improvement, and cost sharing; we also did a rough estimate of the probable price versus the net present value of future cash flow. That got us down to 59 companies. A management review and a close look at these companies' businesses left 35 possibilities. Detailed analysis of the companies, including their position versus their competitors, got the list down to 17. Of these, 12 were selected as attractive enough to contact about a possible merger.

That is the short description of the screening process. The "long form" would contain the details, such as a careful analysis of acquisition candidates' technological position, product quality, worldwide cost position, opportunities for cost sharing and profit improvement, and potential "experience-curve" advantages. We would also develop forecasts of costs and prices, capital needs, and future cash flow, and study such factors as the intentions of competitors and the regulatory environment in the particular business.

Of course, many companies do at least some of these analyses before making an acquisition—but too often, the analysis comes after the buyer has already been approached. The company cannot be sure it is looking at the best of all possible candidates, and the time for investigation is limited. Under pressure, the company may skew its basic strategic criteria to fit the acquisition, rather than make certain that the acquisition fits the strategy.

4. *Start with the knowledge that buying an industry leader will be extremely difficult. But don't settle for anything less than a company with a fighting chance to become a leader.* If so many acquisitions run into problems, why not start with the rule, "Buy nothing but the best"? Because the best companies, with rare exceptions, are not for sale. To avoid spending a lot of time and money and winding up frustrated, firms looking for acquisition candidates should include probable availability as a criterion in early screening.

What is implied here, of course, is that the companies evaluated are going to be less than top performers. But that is almost always the case, as we have seen, if a company waits for a deal to come knocking. The advantage in the active approach is that the buyer can choose its problems—and opportunities. The rule of thumb is that a candidate must have a "fighting chance" of becoming an industry leader.

Indications of this fighting chance include one or more of the following: a high-quality product, widespread consumer recognition and acceptance, a strong technological position, clear opportunities to become the low-cost producer, long-term real market growth of at least 10 percent annually, a number of competitors with no one dominant, and a high barrier to market entry. Companies that have relatively low profit rates, despite high relative market share, are particularly good candidates.

5. *When you find a company with undervalued assets but whose business is completely unrelated to yours, think very, very carefully before grabbing this "bargain."* One of the most seductive traps in acquisitions is the "asset bargain," in which a takeover candidate's raw material reserves or other tangible assets can be picked up at a price below the current market. There are two problems with this approach. First, if the market has undervalued a company's tangible assets, there is probably a good reason, and that reason is seldom long in emerging: commodity prices plummet, or the industry runs into manufacturing overcapacity or some other difficulty.

The second problem is that the "undervalued-asset" argument is frequently used when the acquired company's business has no significant relationship to the acquirer's business. This is a problem because one of the key indicators of whether an acquisition will increase shareholder wealth is the degree to which the two companies' businesses are related. In a study of 68 mergers and acquisitions, market value of those involving unrelated businesses had declined by an average of 4 percent two years later.

6. *Make certain all the synergies of an acquisition are firmly based on shared economic systems and can be realized almost immediately.* Our study showed that there was an increase in shareholder wealth when companies' businesses were related, but it was slight. When companies had related businesses and shared economic systems as well, the increase went up by some 3 percent over a two-year period. The seven-point improvement over unrelated acquisitions suggests an enormous improvement in rates of return, given the already large size of most of the acquiring companies.

There are obvious instances of shared economics that produce significant cost reduction. When companies share a customer base or distribution system, for example, functions can be combined to rationalize costs. Some of the most successful mergers, such as those between Nabisco and Standard Brands, and Norfolk & Western and Southern Railway, have been firmly grounded on shared economics. In fact, mergers within industries generally have a high potential for success because of cost sharing. The attractiveness and feasibility of such mergers is greatly increased, of course, under the federal government's current close interpretation of an antitrust law.

The comparatively good prospects for mergers within an industry have been demonstrated in airlines, oil, and other industries that have gone through deregulation. To survive in the newly competitive market, companies are virtually forced into mergers to improve their overall cost structure.

On the other hand, opportunities for good acquisitions within an industry don't always exist—which means that the principles of related businesses and shared economics must be applied creatively. For example, a number of public utilities, faced with slow growth in revenues, have successfully diversified. In one study, we found that the market-to-book value ratio of seven highly diversified utilities was an average of 20 percent higher than those of nondiversified utilities from 1975 to 1985, even though the diversifieds' return on sales and net plant investment was lower. These diversified utilities took advantage of their expertise and existing systems in such areas as monthly billing and crew/fleet scheduling to get into such businesses as transaction processing, time-sharing services, product marketing, fleet management, and energy-maintenance services.

"Shared economics," broadly interpreted, includes combining technology to achieve lower costs. Our own experience in this area has involved, among other things, working with a book publisher to acquire a printing firm whose advanced technology almost immediately resulted in lower costs.

The operative words here are "almost immediately." Convoluted schemes that promise ephemeral cost synergies down the road are not sufficient basis for a good acquisition, as the road often turns out to be a primrose path.

Of course, there are some successful "conglomerates," including several in Britain. Because the British government has raised formidable roadblocks to mergers that increase concentration in an industry, "acquisition houses" have put together groups of essentially unrelated businesses sharing few or no economic systems, and have managed to do it successfully. These companies may be the exception to the rule. But if they enjoy long-term success, it is more likely that they have followed a set of very fundamental principles in assembling their divisions.

7. *Go beyond the minimum "due diligence" by going inside the target to study its strategies and its competitive strengths and weaknesses.* Believe it or not, many buyers never take a thorough look at what they are getting for their money. The typical due diligence study lasts a week or so and may involve only cursory on-site inspections and discussions with the prospect's management personnel.

By contrast, our clients have often asked us to do in-depth internal studies lasting two or three months in order to get a complete understanding of the prospect's strategies, cost position, technical standing, research and development capability, and other characteristics. These "inside studies," done discreetly, can be a first step in a process of friendly acquisition and effective integration. With ample data on the company, the buyer is in a good position to discuss such matters as price and how the company will fit into an overall strategy.

Obviously, an internal study is not possible in all cases, especially in hostile takeovers. But even in those situations, an in-depth analysis can be done from the outside to help size up the target's strategies and competitive position.

8. *Early in your approach to an acquisition candidate, begin talking about your strategy and theirs, and how you intend to fit the two together.* In our experience, the

process of integrating an acquired company should begin early, even before the deal is completed. When the acquired company's management knows what their company's role is to be, and when the acquirer has their feedback on that role, the likelihood of harsh clashes later on is minimized.

Frank discussions at this point also can help smooth the path to a deal that is equitable for all parties. A buyer is unlikely to get a price that is a "steal," but a good relationship with the acquired company can prevent a bidding war.

Having arrived at a price based on information sharing, both companies understand that the price is justified only if the organizations can be integrated smoothly. One of our clients, which has been involved in a number of very successful acquisitions in recent years, adheres to the principle that it will realize the value of the transaction not by buying assets at a bargain price, but by doing a good job of integrating the acquired company.

9. *Determine how much you will pay for a company based on the value created by the merger, and don't get drawn into a bidding war that runs the price up beyond that level.* Simply put, companies tend to pay too much for acquisitions. Between 1970 and 1983, acquiring companies paid premiums normally ranging 40 percent to 50 percent above the actual market value of companies they bought. The combined companies must create a great deal of added economic value to justify such premiums. Few manage to do it.

One reason companies pay too much is that they do not actively seek acquisition candidates, but wait for someone to approach them with a deal. The ensuing process will always maximize the price paid because, after all, the seller or the intermediary representing him is obligated to get the highest possible price for the company on the block. The typical scenario is a bidding war, with the price getting pumped up far above any reasonable level.

By contrast, when a company is an active buyer, it has time and can commit adequate resources to evaluating just what an acquisition is worth. It's not just a matter of valuing corporate assets. In our view, the proper method is to calculate the added value that can reasonably be expected to be achieved by combining the two companies, then use the net present worth of that added value to arrive at a price that gives both buyer and seller a share of the expected benefits.

Walking away when the price gets too high is not easy, but it can be done, as proved by such companies as Hanson Trust, which backed away from at least one acquisition when the price became unjustifiable.

10. *Rather than leave the acquiree alone to get used to the idea of being taken over, begin integrating the company as soon as the ink is dry.* It seems logical: The buyer knows that the acquired firm will have problems because of intensified competition from without and feelings of insecurity from within. So the buyer takes a hands-off attitude, and even issues statements that may exaggerate the degree of autonomy the new subsidiary will have.

Our experience indicates, however, that this approach leads to early sorrow. In a study of 55 acquisitions, we found that 49 did not produce the first-year results that could reasonably have been expected. We believe that the honeymoon is responsible. It simply heightens the anxieties, uncertainties, and inward focus of the newly acquired company. The old corporate culture weakens, and there is nothing to replace it. Suddenly, in the middle of the year or two of grace that the buyer was going to give the acquired company, the problems become so intense that the buyer finds itself jumping in to fight fires, or standing by while the situation deteriorates.

A number of acquisitions have gained dubious distinction that way. Shortly after Midland Bank, of London, took over Crocker National Bank, the latter was reporting sharp losses, which most observers attributed to Midland's hands-off policy. When Prudential Insurance acquired Bache & Company, it reportedly left Bache almost entirely alone, recognizing the potential problems in trying to marry the two companies' vastly different cultures; Bache's early performance was not good. Phibro Corporation, a huge commodities trader, took over Salomon Brothers with the intention of achieving synergy between the two companies, with each operating autonomously under the holding company Phibro-Salomon. From all reports, the synergy did not materialize, and Phibro's subsequent poor performance evidently opened the way for Salomon to turn the tables and gain control of the parent company.

It is more effective—and realistic—to take immediate steps to begin integrating the new company. After all, the buyer has purchased the company as part of its strategy, and the new subsidiary should begin to play its role as soon as possible. Even before the detail is completed, a six-month integration plan should be prepared.

Of course, integrating will mean different things under different circumstances. The buyer may want to give the acquiree a fair degree of autonomy, if that fits the buyer's strategy. For example, the British company Tilling preferred a "light touch" in managing its numerous divisions. That approach seemed to work well until the company ran into problems and was taken over by BTR, which is known for taking a firm hand in managing its acquisitions.

Integrating must be culturally sensitive. Too much interference has been cited as the cause of problems in such cases as Exxon-Vydec and Schlumberger-Fairchild.

But those are simply cautionary tales, and they do not alter the fundamental necessity of making a newly acquired firm understand and follow its role in the buyer's corporate strategy. The acquired company's management and employees may not like the new situation, but at least feelings of uncertainty are laid to rest.

There are some key steps in integrating the new company. One of the most important should be an "audit" to develop an independent data base on such factors as the acquisition's customers, competitors, and costs. This set of facts, agreed to by the buyer and the management of the acquisition, is the foundation for establishing the common goals they will be aiming for. And the plan to reach those goals should be put in motion without delay.

Of course, the most carefully wrought integration plan could turn out to be worthless. Charles A. Lamb, director of planning at Allied-Signal, Inc., has stated the situation succinctly: "No integration process can overcome the problems of an acquisition that was ill conceived in the first place."

The principal reason that so many acquisitions are ill conceived is that most companies who make them are actually assuming a passive stance. The news media's fascination with takeover battles may give the opposite impression—but the fact is, some 85 percent of all acquisitions are initiated by the sellers. The company that makes an acquisition under these circumstances is like the shopper who goes to the supermarket without a grocery list. You spend more money than you intended, and you probably don't get what you need.

III CASES

CASE 1
AB THORSTEN (A)

By late July 1986, Anders Ekstrom waited with a certain amount of impatience for a decision from corporate headquarters in Montreal on his proposal to begin manufacturing XL-4 in Sweden within the next year. After several months of preparation, Ekstrom was anxious to finalize this matter and return his attention to his many responsibilities as president of AB Thorsten, a wholly owned subsidiary of Roget Industries Ltd., a large diversified Canadian company.

Roget's History and Operating Philosophy

Roget Industries Ltd. was one of the largest industrial companies in Quebec. Founded in the 1920s, the company originally produced a simple line of chemical products for sale in Canada. By 1986, it had expanded to produce more than 200 complex chemicals in 21 factories located throughout Canada, the United States, and a few European countries.

André Juvet, chairman of the board and president of Roget, believed that the company's organization (see Exhibit 1) was the result of careful planning:

> Until the mid-1960s, we were organized with one large manufacturing division here in Canada, and one large sales division with a small department devoted to export markets. However, exports grew so fast, and domestic markets became so complex, that we were forced to create three main product divisions, each with its own manufacturing plants and sales organizations.
>
> At first, the United States had been our largest foreign market, but beginning in 1975, we integrated all North American operations into one organization, and gave each division direct responsibility for its international operations. As sales to other markets expanded, each division gradually set up foreign subsidiaries to take over the business in certain areas. For example, in Industrial Chemicals we have two European subsidiaries, one in the United Kingdom serving the EEC markets, and one in Sweden, which serves all Scandinavia. The U.K. and Swedish companies account for 9 percent and 5 percent of divisional sales, about half of which originate in Canada. The domestic department of the Industrial Chemicals Division handles all exports, whether they go to our subsidiaries or to independent agents.
>
> Another thing we achieve in the new organization is individual profit responsibility of all executives at all levels. Mr. Gillot is responsible for profits for all industrial chemicals, Mr. Lambert is responsible for profits from North American operations

This case is summarized from an earlier series entitled AB Thorsten (A) through (C) prepared by Professors Gordon Shillinglaw and Charles Summer, at the International Management Development Institute (IMEDE), Lausanne, Switzerland. Revised with permission, 1988. Copyright © 1969 by IMEDE, Lausanne, Switzerland. The International Institute for Management Development (IMD), resulting from the merger between IMEDE, Lausanne, and IMI, Geneva, acquires and retains all rights. Reproduced by permission. IMD retains all rights.

EXHIBIT 1 Roget Industries Ltd. – Organization Chart

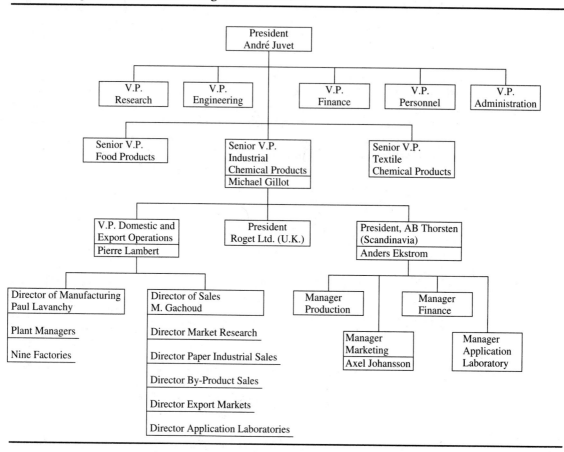

(manufacturing and sales) and from export sales, and Mr. Ekstrom is responsible for profits in Scandinavia from both imported and locally made products. We also utilize a rather liberal bonus system to reward executives at each level, based on the profits of their divisions.

This, together with a policy of promotion from within, helps stimulate managers in Roget to a degree not enjoyed by some of our competitors. It also helps to keep executives in an industry where experience is of great importance. Most of our managers have been in the starch chemicals business all of their lives. It is a complex business, and we feel that it takes many years to learn it.

We have developed certain policies—rules of the game—that govern relationships with our subsidiary company presidents. These are intended to maintain efficiency within the whole Roget complex, while at the same time they provide subsidiary managers with sufficient autonomy to run their own businesses. For example, a subsidiary manager can determine what existing Roget products he wants to sell in his part of the world market. Export sales will quote him the same price as they quote agents in all countries. He is free to bargain, and if he doesn't like the price, he needn't sell the product. Second, we encourage subsidiaries to propose to division management in Montreal the development of new products. If these are judged feasible, we will proceed to manufacture them in Canada for supply to world markets. Third, the subsidiary president can build his own manufacturing plants if he can justify the investment in his own market.

Company Background: AB Thorsten

AB Thorsten was acquired by Roget in 1978. Since that time the same team had constituted Thorsten's board of directors: Michael Gillot, senior vice president in charge of Roget's Industrial Chemical Products Division; Ingve Norgren, a Swedish banker; Ove Svensen, a Stockholm industrialist; and the current president of Thorsten. Swedish corporation law required any company incorporated in Sweden to have Swedish directors, and the Roget management felt fortunate in having found two men as prominent as Norgren and Svensen to serve on the Thorsten Board.

During the first four years of Roget's ownership, Thorsten's sales fluctuated between Skr. 50 and 70 million but hit a low at the end of that period. The board of AB Thorsten decided at that time that the company was in serious trouble and that the only alternative to selling was to hire a totally different management team to overhaul and streamline the whole company. On advice of the Swedish directors, Anders Ekstrom, a 38-year-old graduate of the Royal Institute of Technology, was hired. He had a total of 16 years of experience in production engineering for a large machinery company, as marketing manager of a British subsidiary in Sweden, and, more recently, as division manager in a large paper company. As Ekstrom described his experience:

> Working for the paper company, the European subsidiary of a large U.S. firm, was particularly valuable to me. I knew little of modern financial methods and strategic planning prior to my working with them. As I came into contact with executives who had attended many top U.S. business schools, I came to realize that these were the kind of tools I needed to be successful, those that Sweden needs to operate our industry with maximum productivity. Sure enough, they have been invaluable to me and to Thorsten. A few men in Roget know them, but even there such methods are relatively unknown among managers. One day, everyone here will know these methods, and we will be competitive or even superior to the United States in management. I am proud to have learned such management techniques and they give me confidence in managing Thorsten—for the benefit of the company and for the benefit of Sweden's productive capacity.

Ekstrom had been president of AB Thorsten since early in 1982. During that time, sales had increased to Skr 200 million, and profits had reached levels that Roget's management found highly satisfactory. Both Ekstrom and Norgren attributed this performance to (1) an increase in industrial activity in Scandinavia since the 1982 recession; (2) changes in production methods, marketing strategy, and organization structure made by Ekstrom; (3) the hiring of competent staff; and (4) Ekstrom's own ambition and hard work. Ekstrom's knowledge of modern planning techniques—sophisticated market research methods, financial planning by use of discounted cash flows and incremental analysis, and, as Ekstrom put it, "all those things I learned from my former American employer"—had also contributed to the successful turnaround in Thorsten.

Ekstrom recognized that at the time he joined Thorsten, there were risks:

> I like the challenge of building a company. If I do a good job here, I will have the confidence of Norgren and Svensen as well as of the Roget management in Montreal. Deep down inside, succeeding in this situation will teach me things that will make me more competent as a top executive. So I chose this job even though I had at the time (and still have) offers from other companies.

Initial Proposal for Manufacture of XL-4

In September 1985, Ekstrom informed the Thorsten board of directors that he proposed to study the feasibility of constructing a facility in Sweden for the manufacture of XL-4, a product used in paper converting. He explained that he and his customer engineers had discovered a new way of helping large paper mills adapt their machines at little cost so that they could use XL-4 instead of traditional substitute products. Large paper mill customers would be able to realize dramatic savings in material handling and storage costs, and to shorten drying time substantially. In his judgment, Thorsten could develop a market in Sweden almost as big as Roget's present worldwide market for XL-4. XL-4 was then being produced in Roget's Industrial Chemicals Division at the rate of 600 tons a year, but less than 2 percent of this was going to Sweden. According to Ekstrom, Gillot and the other directors seemed enthusiastic. Gillot reportedly said, "Of course, go ahead with your study and when you have a proposed plan, with the final return on investment, send it in and we will consider it thoroughly." Ekstrom continued:

> During the next six months, we did the analysis. My market research department estimated the total potential market in Sweden at 800 tons of XL-4 per year. We interviewed important customers and conducted trials in the factories of three big companies. These proved that with the introduction of our machine designs, the large cost saving would indeed materialize and would overwhelm the small investment costs associated with making the necessary changes. We determined that if we could sell the product for Skr. 18.50 per kg.,[1] we could capture one half of the market within a three-year period.
>
> At the same time, I called the head of the Corporate Engineering Division in Montreal and asked for his help in designing a plant to produce 400 tons of XL-4 per

---

[1]Throughout this case, figures are given in either metric tons or kilograms (1 ton = 1,000 kg.), where 1 kg. = 2.2 pounds.

year and in estimating the cost of the investment. This is a routine thing. The central staff divisions are advisory and always comply with requests for help. He assigned a project manager and four other engineers to work on the design of factory and machinery and to estimate the cost. At the same time, I assigned three men from my staff to work on the project. In three months, this joint task group reported that the necessary plant could be built for about Skr. 7 million.

Our calculations, together with a complete written explanation, were mailed in early April 1986 to Mr. Gillot. I felt rather excited, as did most of my staff. We all know that introduction of new products is one of the keys to continued growth and profitability. The yield of this investment (15 percent) was well above the minimum 8 percent established as a guideline for new investments by the Roget vice president of finance. We also knew that it was a good analysis, done by modern tools of management. In the covering letter, I asked that it be put on the agenda for the next board meeting.

The board meeting was held in Stockholm on April 28, 1986. The minutes show on the agenda "A Proposal for Investment in Sweden" to be presented by Ekstrom. They also quote from his remarks as he explained the proposal to the other directors:

You will see from the summary table (Exhibit 2) that this project is profitable. On an initial outlay of Skr. 7 million for plant and equipment and Skr. 560,000 for working capital, we get a rate of return of 15.7 percent and a present value of Skr. 2.47 million.

Let me explain some of the figures underlying this summary table. My second chart (Exhibit 3) summarizes the operating cash flows that we expect to get from the XL-4 project. The sales forecast for the first seven years is shown in the first row. The forecast was not extended beyond seven years because our engineers estimated that the technology of starch manufacture will improve gradually, so that major plant renovations will become necessary at about the end of the seventh year. Actually, we see no reason why demand for XL-4 will decline after seven years, as we shall see in a minute.

The estimated variable cost of Skr. 10 per kg. represents the full operating cost of manufacturing XL-4 in Sweden, including out-of-pocket fixed costs such as plant management salaries but excluding depreciation. These fixed costs must of course be included because they are incremental to the decision.

We feel certain that we can enter the market initially with a selling price of Skr. 20 per kg., but full market penetration will require a price reduction to Skr. 18.50 at the beginning of the second year. The variable contribution resulting from these figures is shown on the fifth line. The next two rows list the market development and promotion expenditures that are needed to launch the product and achieve the forecasted sales levels and the resulting net operating cash flows before tax.

The cost of the plant can be written off for tax purposes over a five-year period, at the rate of 20 percent of original cost each year. Subtracting this amount from the before-tax cash flow and multiplying by the tax rate (50 percent) yields the tax payable in row 9. When this is subtracted from the before-tax cash flow, it yields the after-tax cash flow in the last line.

A proposal of this kind also requires some investment in working capital. Our estimate on this element (Exhibit 4) is that we will need about Skr. 800,000 to start

Exhibit 2 AB Thorsten Proposal to Manufacture XL-4 in Sweden; Financial Summary (All figures in thousands of Skr.)

Year	Description	After-Tax Cash Flows*	Present Value at 8 Percent
0	Equipment	−7,000	
	Working capital	−560	
	Total	−7,560	−7,560
1	Cash operating profit	+1,050	
	Working capital	−20	
	Total	+1,030	+954
2	Cash operating profit	+1,600	
	Working capital	−70	
	Total	+1,530	+1,312
3	Cash operating profit	+2,150	+1,708
4	Cash operating profit	+2,150	+1,580
5	Cash operating profit	+2,150	+1,463
6	Cash operating profit	+1,450	+914
7	Cash operating profit	+1,450	
	Recovery value of equipment and working capital	+2,150	
	Total	+3,600	+2,100
	Projected grand total	+6,500	+2,470

Financial Conclusions

Net present value to the corporation	Skr. 2,470,000
Payback period	4 years
Internal rate of return	15.7

NOTE: *From Exhibits 3, 4, and 5.

Exhibit 3 Estimated Operating Cash Flows from Manufacture and Sale of XL-4 in Sweden

Year	1	2	3	4	5	6	7	Total
1. Sales (tons)	200	300	400	400	400	400	400	2,500
Skr. per kg.								
2. Sales price	20.0	18.5	18.5	18.5	18.5	18.5	18.5	
3. Variable costs	10.0	10.0	10.0	10.0	10.0	10.0	10.0	
4. Profit margin	10.0	8.5	8.5	8.5	8.5	8.5	8.5	
Thousand Skr.								
5. Contribution	2,000	2,550	3,400	3,400	3,400	3,400	3,400	21,550
6. Promotion costs	1,300	750	500	500	500	500	500	4,550
7. Before-tax profit	700	1,800	2,900	2,900	2,900	2,900	2,900	17,000
8. Depreciation	1,400	1,400	1,400	1,400	1,400	–0–	–0–	7,000
9. Taxes payable (50%)	(350)	200	750	750	750	1,450	1,450	5,000
10. Net cash flow	1,050	1,600	2,150	2,150	2,150	1,450	1,450	12,000

EXHIBIT 4 Estimated Working Capital Required for Manufacture and Sale of XL-4 in Sweden (Skr. 000)

	Inventory at Cost	Other Current Assets less Current Liabilities	Working Capital (1 + 2)	Change from Previous Year	Tax Credit (30 percent of Change in 1)	Net Funds Required (4 − 5)
Year 0	800	–0–	800	+800	240	560
Year 1	900	−50	850	+50	30	20
Year 2	1,000	−50	950	+100	30	70
Years 3+	1,000	−50	950	–0–	–0–	–0–
Total	1,000	−50	950	950	300	650

EXHIBIT 5 Estimated End-of-Life Value of Swedish Assets (Skr)

Plant...	Skr. 3,000,000	
Less tax on gain if sold at this price	1,500,000	
Net value of plant		Skr. 1,500,000
Working capital..	Skr. 950,000	
Less payment of deferred taxes on special inventory reserves..	300,000	
Net value of working capital		650,000
Net value of Swedish assets after 7 years......		Skr. 2,150,000

with, but some of this can be deducted immediately from our income taxes. Swedish law permits us to deduct 60 percent of the cost of inventories from taxable income. For this reason, and given a tax rate of 50 percent, we can get an immediate reduction of Skr. 240,000 in the taxes we have to pay on our other income in Sweden. We'll need small additional amounts of working capital in the next two years, so that altogether our requirements will add up to Skr. 650,000 (net of taxes) by the end of our second full year of operations.

Now let's come back to the issue of what happens after 1994. Seven years is a very conservative estimate of the life of the product. If we limit the analysis to seven years, we'll be overlooking the value of our assets at the end of that time. At the very worst, the plant itself should be worth Skr. 3 million after seven years (Exhibit 5). We'd have to pay tax on that, of course, because the plant would be fully depreciated, but this would still leave us with a value of Skr. 1.5 million for the plant. The working capital should also be fully recoverable. After paying the deferred tax on inventories, we'd get Skr. 650,000 back on that. The total value at the end of seven years would thus be Skr. 2.15 million.

As I said earlier, however, we have chosen to be conservative in these calculations. It is quite probable that with a small additional investment, the plant could be refurbished and XL-4 sales to Scandinavia could continue for many years.

Ekstrom ended this opening presentation by saying, "Gentlemen, it seems clear from these figures that we can justify this investment on the basis of sales to the Swedish market. Our group vice president for finance has laid down the policy that any new investment should yield at least 8 percent. This particular proposal shows a return of 15 percent. My management and I strongly recommend this project." (The Thorsten vice presidents for production, sales, and finance had been called into the board meeting to be present when this proposal was made.)

Ekstrom told the case writer that while he was making this proposal, he was sure that it would be accepted, and that Gillot had said "that it seemed to him to be a clear case." The minutes of the board meeting show that Gillot asked a few questions, mainly about the longer-term likelihood for more than 400 tons a year, about sales to other Scandinavian countries, and about sources of funds. Ekstrom added:

> I explained that we in Sweden were very firm in our judgment that we would reach 400 tons a year even before one year, but felt constrained to show a conservative estimate of a three-year transition period. If sales to other countries took off in the future, an expansion of the plant's capacity could be undertaken at a fraction of the total costs now envisaged. We also showed him how we could finance any expansion by borrowing in Sweden. That is, if Roget would furnish the initial capital requirements from Canada, and if our 400 tons were reached quickly, any funds needed for further expansion would easily be lent by local banks. The two Swedish directors confirmed this. The board then voted unanimously to approve the project.

Disagreement between Parent and Subsidiary

About a week later, Gillot telephoned Ekstrom. "Since my return to Montreal, I have been through some additional discussions with the production and marketing people here. They think the engineering design and plant cost are accurate but that you are too optimistic on your sales forecast. It looks like you will have to justify this more." Ekstrom related his reaction:

> I pushed him to set up a meeting the following week. This meeting was attended by me and my marketing and production directors, from Sweden, and four people from Canada: Gillot, Lavanchy [director of manufacturing], Gachoud [director of sales], and Lambert [vice president for domestic and export]. It was one of the worst meetings of my life. It lasted all day. Gachoud argued that they had sales experience from other countries and that in his judgment the market potential and our share were too optimistic, that the whole world market for Roget was only 600 tons a year (see Exhibit 6), and that it was inconceivable that Sweden alone could take 400 tons. I told him over and over how we arrived at these figures, but he just kept repeating the overoptimism argument.
>
> Lavanchy then said that the production of this product was very complicated and that he had difficulties producing it in Canada, even with trained workers who had years of experience. I told him I only needed five trained production workers and that he could send me two men for two months to train Swedes to do the job. I impressed on him that "if you can manufacture it in Canada you can manufacture it

Exhibit 6 Estimate of World Market for XL-4 and Current Sales (1985)

	Potential Market (Percent of World Paper Production)	Current Sales of XL-4 (Percent)
Sweden	12	1.7
Finland	7	0.5
Norway	3	0.2
USSR	10	0.0
Rest of Europe	20	8.6
Canada	15	54.8
United States	13	28.5
Rest of the world	20	5.7
Total	100	100.0

for us in Sweden until we learn, that is, if you don't have confidence in Swedish technology." He repeated that the difficulties in manufacturing were great. I stressed that we were prepared to learn and take the risk. Somehow I just couldn't get through to him.

By 6 P.M. everyone was tired. Lambert had backed up his two production and sales officials all day, repeating their arguments. Gillot seemed to me to just sit there and listen, occasionally asking questions. I cannot understand why he didn't back me up. He seemed so easy to get along with at the earlier board meeting in Stockholm—where he seemed decisive. Not so at this meeting. He seemed distant, indecisive, and an ineffective executive.

He stopped the meeting without a solution and said that he hoped all concerned would do more investigation of this subject. He vaguely referred to the fact that he would think about it himself and let us know when another meeting would be held.

Objections from a Swedish Director

Ekstrom returned to Stockholm and reported the meeting to his own staff, and to the two Swedish members of his board. "They, like I, were really disgusted. Here we were operating with initiative and with excellent financial techniques. Roget management had often emphasized the necessity for decentralized profit responsibilities, authority, and initiative on the part of foreign subsidiary presidents. One of my men told me that they seem to talk decentralization and act like tin gods at the same time."

Norgren, the Swedish banker on Thorsten's board, expressed surprise. He went further:

I considered this carefully. It is sound business for Thorsten, and XL-4 will help to build one more growth company in the Swedish economy. Somehow, the management in Montreal has failed to study this, or they don't wish the Swedish subsidiary to produce it. I have today dictated a letter to Gillot telling him that I don't know why the project is rejected, that Roget has a right to its own reasons, but that I am prepared to resign as a director. It is not that I am angry, or that I have a right to dictate decisions for the whole worldwide Roget group. It is simply that, if I spend my time studying policy decisions, and those decisions do not serve the right function for the business, then it is a waste of time to continue.

Ekstrom added, "While I certainly wouldn't bring these matters out in a meeting, I think those Canadian production and sales people simply want to build their empire and make the money in Roget Canada. They don't care about Thorsten and Sweden. That's a smooth way to operate. We have the ideas and the initiative, and they take them and get the payoff."

Further Study

After Gillot received Norgren's letter, he contacted Lavanchy, Gachoud, and Bols [V.P. Finance, Roget Corporate Staff]. He told them that the Swedish XL-4 project had become a matter of key importance for the whole Roget Group, because of its implications for company profits, and for the morale and autonomy of the subsidiary management. He asked them to study the matter and report their recommendations in one month. He also wrote Ekstrom, "Various members of corporate staff are studying the proposal. You will hear from me within about six weeks regarding my final decision."

Report of Roget's Director of Manufacturing

A month after he was asked to study the XL-4 project, Lavanchy gave Gillot a memorandum explaining his reasons for opposing the proposal:

> At your request, I have reexamined thoroughly all of the cost figures that bear on the XL-4 proposal. I find that manufacture of this product in Sweden would be highly uneconomical for two reasons: (1) overhead costs would be higher and (2) variable costs would be greater.
>
> As to the first, suppose that Thorsten does sell 400 tons a year so that our total worldwide sales rise to 1,000 tons. We can produce the whole 1,000 tons in Canada with essentially the same capital investment we have now. If we produce 1,000 tons, our fixed costs will decrease by C$ 218 (Skr. 1200) a ton.[2] That means Skr. 720,000 in savings on production for domestic and export to countries other than Sweden (600 tons a year), and Skr. 1.2 million for worldwide production including Sweden.
>
> Second, if we were to produce the extra 400 tons in Canada, we could schedule longer production runs, have lower set-up costs, and larger raw material purchases, thus allowing mass purchasing and material handling and lower purchase prices. My

---

[2]Total fixed costs in Canada were C$ 327,300, the equivalent of Skr. 1.8 million/year at current exchange rates. Divided by 600, this equals Skr. 3,000 a ton. If it were spread over 1,000 tons, the average fixed cost would be Skr. 1,800 per ton.

Exhibit 7 Estimated Variable Cost of Manufacturing XL-4 in Canada for Shipment to Sweden

Variable costs per ton		
Manufacturing	Skr.	9,300
Shipping from Canada to Sweden		2,500
Swedish import duty		2,000
Total variable cost per ton	Skr.	13,800
Total variable cost, 400 tons to Sweden	Skr	5,520,000

accounting department has studied this and concludes that our average variable costs will decrease from C$ 1.75 to C$ 1.70 (Skr. 9.50 to Skr. 9.30) per kg. as indicated in Exhibit 7. This difference means a saving of nearly C$ 22,000 (Skr. 120,000) on Canadian domestic production or Skr. 200,000 for total worldwide production, assuming that Sweden takes 400 tons a year. Taxes on these added profits are about the same in Canada as in Sweden, about 50 percent of taxable income.

In conclusion, the new plant should not be built. Ekstrom is a bright young man, but he does not know the adhesives business. He would be head over heels in costly production mistakes from the beginning. I recommend that you inform the Thorsten management that it is in the company's interest, and therefore it is Roget policy, that he must buy from Canada.

Report of Vice President of Finance

A few days later, Gillot received the following memorandum from Eric Bols, Roget's financial vice president:

I am sending you herewith a complete economic study of the two alternatives which have been raised for producing XL-4 within the Roget group. The Swedish management has proposed constructing a plant in Sweden, while Messrs. Lavanchy and Lambert on our Canadian staff have proposed producing here in Canada.

First of all, I should state that I agree that this kind of matter must be resolved by highest authority. Industrial chemicals is not the only group within the company which has such location problems, and Mr. Juvet [president of Roget Industries Ltd.] is concerned that any precedent set would also apply to the food and textile divisions.

After thorough analysis by the most advanced financial methods, it is clear that the Roget Group will benefit substantially by producing total world requirements for XL-4 in Canada, including the 400 tons per year which Swedish management estimates it will need over the next seven years. Not only will the Roget group of companies gain the Skr. 170,000 difference between the net present values of both proposals, but the really important factor is that we would have to furnish only C$ 130,000 (Skr. 720,000) in initial capital funds, while in Sweden it would cost Skr. 7.64 million (C$ 1.4 million) to build a new plant and stock it (see Exhibit 8).

The importance of this factor can be demonstrated. The internal rate of return on invested capital is 60 percent for the Canadian project because of the low initial

EXHIBIT 8 Comparison of Economic Gains between Two Alternative Proposals for the Manufacture of XL-4

	Made in Sweden	*Made in Canada*
At 8% discount rate		
Present value of investments	Skr. 7,640,000	Skr. 720,000
Present value of operating profits	8,760,000	2,930,000
Present value of residual assets	1,340,000	420,000
Net present value	Skr. 2,470,000	Skr. 2,643,000
Others		
Payback period	4 years	2.5 years
Internal rate of return	15%	60%
Best economic and financial alternative: Manufacture in Canada		

investment, while it is only 15 percent for the costly Swedish investment. Stated in another way, Sweden is asking us to invest Skr. 6.92 million more than necessary (their required initial investment less ours). If this amount were invested in Eurodollar bank certificates, which have averaged 8 to 9 percent over the last 10 years, it would grow to more than Skr. 12 million after seven years. This shows the opportunity cost of committing needless money in Sweden. Such money is, in effect, wasted, because the internal rate of return is so much lower in Sweden.

Another way to see the importance of initial capital is to look at the payback period. It would take the group four years to get its money back in Sweden but only two and one-half years in Canada. Exhibits 10 through 12 are constructed exactly as Mr. Ekstrom performed his analysis, and provide the subsidiary figures that are summarized in Exhibit 9. They show operating profits, working capital requirements, and the salvage value of assets at the end of seven years, expressed in Swedish kroner at current exchange rates to facilitate comparison. You already have from Paul Lavanchy the variable cost of manufacture and shipping, which are incorporated into Exhibit 10. There is, of course an exchange risk associated with these flows, but one that would apply equally to any future dividends from Sweden.[3]

Finally, I must call attention to my position as compared with that of Mr. Lavanchy. He and I are agreed on the most important issue—that it would be much more profitable to manufacture in Canada. But we differ on one point. He stresses that we would save Skr. 120,000 per year on fixed costs if we manufacture total production here, because our existing plant would produce 400 tons more per year, thus lowering cost per ton and depreciation charges per ton. This is not correct. The plant is already built here. There would be no actual money costs one way or the other for our plant under either of three alternatives: produce in Canada, produce in Sweden, or simply not produce additional XL-4 at all. You will notice, therefore, that I do not include any depreciation cost in my calculations.

---

[3]See Exhibit 13 for historical data on the Swedish kroner/Canadian dollar exchange rates and relative inflation rates in both countries. For simplicity, most calculations in the case have been translated to Swedish kroner at a rate of 5.5 Skr./C$ (prevalent at the time) to facilitate comparisons with the original proposal.

EXHIBIT 9 Roget Industries Ltd. — Proposal for Manufacture of XL-4 in Canada for Export to Sweden and Other World Markets (All figures in thousands Skr.)

Year	Description	After-Tax Cash Flows*	Present Value at 8 percent
0	Working capital	− 540	− 540
1	Cash operating profit	+ 30	
	Working capital	− 100	
	Total	-70	− 65
2	Cash operating profit	+ 390	
	Working capital	− 100	
	Total	+ 290	+ 249
3	Cash operating profit	+ 750	+ 595
4	Cash operating profit	+ 750	+ 551
5	Cash operating profit	+ 750	+ 510
6	Cash operating profit	+ 750	+ 473
7	Cash operating profit	+ 750	
	Recovery value of working capital	+ 740	
	Total	+ 1,490	+ 869
	Projected grand total	+ 4,170	+ 2,643

Financial Conclusions

Net present value to the corporation	Skr. 2,643,000
Payback period	2.5 years
Internal rate of return	60%

NOTE: *From Exhibits 10, 11, and 12.

EXHIBIT 10 Estimated Operating Cash Flows from Manufacture of XL-4 in Canada for Shipment to Sweden

Year	1	2	3	4	5	6	7	Total
Sales (tons)	200	300	400	400	400	400	400	2,500
Skr. per kg.								
Sales price	20.0	18.5	18.5	18.5	18.5	18.5	18.5	
Variable costs	13.8	13.8	13.8	13.8	13.8	13.8	13.8	
Profit margin	6.2	4.7	4.7	4.7	4.7	4.7	4.7	
Thousand Skr.								
Contribution	1,240	1,410	1,880	1,880	1,880	1,880	1,880	12,050
Promotion costs	1,300	750	500	500	500	500	500	4,550
Savings*	120	120	120	120	120	120	120	840
Before-tax profit	60	780	1,500	1,500	1,500	1,500	1,500	8,340
Taxes payable (50%)	30	390	750	750	750	750	750	4,170
Net cash flow	30	390	750	750	750	750	750	4,170

NOTE: *These are savings incurred in sales to other markets due to more efficient purchasing and production scheduling (600 tons × Skr. 200 per ton).

EXHIBIT 11 Estimated Working Capital Required for Manufacture of XL-4 in Canada for Sale in Sweden (Skr. 000)

	Inventory at Cost	Other Current Assets less Current Liabilities	Working Capital (1 + 2)	Change from Previous Year	Tax Credit (30 percent of Change in 1)	Net Funds Required (4 − 5)
Year 0	500	100	600	+600	60*	540
Year 1	550	150	700	+100	–0–	100
Year 2	600	200	800	+100	–0–	100
Years 3+	600	200	800	–0–	–0–	0
Total	600	200	800	800	60	740

NOTE: *Based on finished goods inventory of Skr. 200,000 in Sweden.

EXHIBIT 12 Estimated End-of-Life Value of Canadian Assets

Working capital..	Skr. 800,000
Less payment of deferred taxes on special inventory reserves	60,000
Net value of working capital after 7 years	Skr. 740,000

EXHIBIT 13 Exchange Rates and Relative Inflation — Canada and Sweden (1980–1986)

	Exchange Rates			Inflation Rate Indices (1980–100)	
	Skr./US$	Can$/US$	Skr./Can$	Canada	Sweden
1980	4.23	1.169	3.62	100.0	100.0
1981	5.06	1.199	4.22	112.5	112.1
1982	6.28	1.234	5.09	124.6	121.7
1983	7.67	1.232	6.23	131.8	132.6
1984	8.27	1.295	6.39	137.6	143.2
1985	8.60	1.366	6.30	143.0	153.7
1986 (I)	7.48	1.404	5.28	146.9	158.9
(II)	7.20	1.384	5.20	148.0	159.7

I hope that this analysis is of help to you in formulating a divisional policy on construction of manufacturing plants around the world. It seems to me that it should be the policy of Roget to construct plants whenever and wherever the group as a whole will gain most benefits, taking into consideration worldwide supply and demand, rather than conditions in any one country or one part of the group. That is, we should produce at the point where the cost of production is lowest.

We in Finance have the highest respect for the Swedish management. Mr. Ekstrom, particularly, is an outstanding manager with great financial expertise himself. In this case, he has simply not had the complete information from our total group. I trust that he will understand that this is not a personal rejection, but one that is for the good of the group as a whole—the parent company and Thorsten's sister companies in other countries.

CASE 2
AER LINGUS — ATS (A)

On July 15, 1985, Denis Hanrahan was flying from Dublin to Toronto, as he had many times over the past 11 months, to meet with Klaus Woerner, the owner and president of Automation Tooling Systems (ATS), a robotics firm based in Kitchener, Ontario. Hanrahan's job was to expand the "nonairline" activities of Aer Lingus, and ATS was a company in which he wanted to acquire an equity position.

The negotiations between Denis and Klaus had been friendly but protracted, and it appeared that they were finally nearing an end. The deal, which both sides had agreed to orally, was that Aer Lingus would purchase 75 percent of the shares of ATS and that Klaus would stay on and manage the company. The price that he would receive for his shares would depend on the earnings of ATS in the years ending September 30, 1985 and 1986. If ATS met the profit forecast that Klaus had prepared for it, he would receive a total of $4.6 million in cash and retain a 25 percent interest in the company.

Aer Lingus

Aer Lingus was the Irish international airline, wholly owned by the Irish government. As shown in Exhibit 1, Aer Lingus, like many airlines, had difficulty producing a consistently high level of earnings. The early 1980s in particular were not good years for the airline (nor for any other), and only the consistent profitability of the group's hotels, airline-related businesses (maintenance and overhaul of the other firm's aircraft, training of flight crews, and so on), and financial and commercial businesses kept the company's overall losses in check.

A small group of managers under the leadership of Gerry Dempsey were responsible for managing and expanding Aer Lingus's nonairline activities. Hanrahan, second in command, commented:

> We all recognize that the airline business is a cyclical one, and our goal is to create a stable base of earnings which will see the airline safely through the bottom of the cycles. We have been successful so far so we don't know if the government would bail us out if we did make continued heavy losses, and we don't want to have to find out! The mission of our "ancillary activities" is to increase the group's reported earnings and to strengthen its balance sheet.

Case material of The University of Western Ontario School of Business Administration is prepared as a basis for classroom discussion. This case was prepared by Peter Killing, associate professor. Copyright © 1989, The University of Western Ontario, and the IMEDE Management Development Institute, Lausanne, Switzerland.

Exhibit 1 **Aer Lingus Financial Results — Years Ending March 31 (Millions of Irish Pounds)**

	1985		1984		1983		1982		1981	
	Revenue	*Profit*	*Revenue*	*Profit*	*Revenue*	*Profit*	*Revenue*	*Profit*	*Revenue*	*Profit*
Air transport	281	0.5	270	1.4	244	(2.7)	218	(11.2)	164	(15.9)
Ancillary operations										
Airline related	110	12.7	82	11.1	66	9.0	62	8.6	47	7.5
Hotel and leisure	79	11.7	82	7.7	82	6.0	71	7.8	54	7.7
Financial and commercial	33	5.4	24	4.5	11	3.6	8	2.0	6	1.3
Net profit after head office expenses, interest, tax*	11.6		4.9		(2.5)		(9.2)		(13.6)	

Note: In 1985 the group total assets stood at £285 million. A breakdown of assets employed in each business area was not publicly reported.

*The company earned a positive net profit in each of the four years preceding 1981.

CDN Dollars per Irish Pound
1981: 1.90
1982: 1.75
1983: 1.54
1984: 1.41
1985: 1.44

The financial and commercial results shown in Exhibit 1 include a data processing firm, an insurance company, a helicopter company, a hospital management firm, a land development company, and a 25 percent interest in GPA, formerly Guiness Peat Aviation. Many of these firms, with the exception of the hotels, were founded by former Aer Lingus employees. Although most of the companies were performing well, the undoubted star was GPA. A manager explained:

> In 1975 or so, Tony Ryan, our New York station manager, was transferred back to Ireland and asked to lease out a 747 which we did not need for the winter. In looking at the leasing market, he thought he saw a very good business opportunity, and he convinced us and a related British company to each put up 45 percent of the capital required to start an aircraft leasing company. He kept the remaining 10 percent. As things have developed, he was certainly right about the opportunity. In the 10 intervening years, we have received almost 20 million Irish pounds from that business, and our initial investment was only 2.2 million! We still own 25 percent of the company, and now have firms like Air Canada and the General Electric Credit Corporation as partners. GPA is one of *the* Irish success stories of the past decade.

The Move into Robotics

In 1983 Denis Hanrahan began an informal search for a new area of investment which could provide healthy financial returns to Aer Lingus for at least the next decade. By January 1984, he had concluded that robotics was an extremely interesting field. Robots had been used in Japan since the 1960s but were not adopted in Europe and the United States until the late 1970s. Many analysts expected a robotics boom, with growth rates as high as 30 percent per annum, as Western firms strove to catch up.

Although robot manufacturing appeared to Denis to be an overcrowded field, he was excited about the possibility of becoming a developer of the ancillary technology and components that were required by firms wanting to install robot-based flexible manufacturing assembly lines. His figures suggested that the market value of ancillary systems was at least equal to the value of the robots themselves. Although the volume of business being done in this new area was impossible to quantify with any degree of precision, it appeared to be growing quickly and offer high margins. There were as yet no major companies in the business.

Denis described Aer Lingus' initial entry into the field:

> The first company we looked at was in the United Kingdom. We fairly quickly decided that it was too big, too sexy, and considering its size, depended too heavily on a single supplier of robots. One thing you have to watch out for in this business is guys in very classy suits who know more about doing deals and driving for the initial public offering which is going to make them rich than they do about robotics. It turned out that we were right about that company, as it went bankrupt afterwards.
>
> The company we did buy was Airstead Industrial Systems of the United Kingdom. This is a very small company, much smaller than ATS, but it has the rights to distribute Seiko robots in England. Seiko, in addition to producing products such as watches and Epson computer printers, is a prominent robot manufacturer that was doing very well in some fast growing niches.

After the acquisition of Airstead, Aer Lingus dispatched an analyst to North America to examine six companies that Seiko had identified as the most promising North American robotics systems firms. On August 15, Denis received a telex containing a thumbnail sketch of ATS, indicating that it was the best of the three firms the analyst had seen to date and was worth a closer look. On August 28, Denis was in Kitchener for his first meeting with Klaus Woerner.

Klaus Woerner and ATS

Born in Germany in 1940, Klaus Woerner emigrated to Canada at age 20 after serving an apprenticeship in the tool and die business. He subsequently worked for a variety of manufacturing firms in Canada but, tired of the "hierarchies and rigidities of large corporations," founded ATS in 1978. The new company was not successful, however, until Klaus turned it away from manufacturing and into systems work. The move into robotics was made in late 1981.

By the summer of 1984, ATS had grown to employ 44 people, including 26 tool makers, 15 hardware and software designers, and 3 in sales and administration. Denis was encouraged to see that Klaus was a technically oriented "hands-on" manager whose elegant and creative solutions to systems problems played a major role in the company's success. Klaus, Denis observed, was more at home on the shop floor than talking to accountants, bankers, or lawyers. In his summary of their first meeting, Denis made the following points:

1. Mr. Woerner was an easy individual to get along with, though I would anticipate that he is used to getting his own way. He is the key decision maker in the company, although he does solicit the opinions of his senior colleagues.

2. The company currently turns over approximately $3.5 million per year and expects to double its sales this year after a number of years of relatively slow growth. Woerner reports a current backlog of $3 million.

3. The major financial problem with the business is that there is a significant working capital requirement. I have heard a rule of thumb that suggests 40 percent of turnover is required in this business, but Klaus thought that was far too high. The practical problem is that the final payment of 30 percent of systems cost tends to be delayed for several months after completion of the work while fine tuning is being performed.

4. Mr. Woerner recently came very close to selling ATS to Berton Industries,[1] a major Canadian corporation in the automotive components business. One hundred percent of ATS was to be acquired and, depending on results, it would have been valued at $3 to $4 million. Woerner got very concerned, however, at what he perceived to be the inordinate length of time being taken in detailed negotiations and at the aggressive attitude of the other party's attorneys. In addition, Berton would not give him any assurances about future investment in ATS and apparently Woerner learned that plans had been made to move ATS to another location without any consultation with him. When the president of Berton then ignored Woerner's request that a number of written commitments be made within one week, the deal was off.

5. Mr. Woerner's proposal was that Aer Lingus would take 50 percent of the company for an undetermined amount and that 50 percent of this money would be left in the company and that he would take 50 percent out. I indicated to him that 50 percent would probably be the minimum share that we would require and it could be that we would want considerably more. However, any deal that we would do would be structured in such a way that he and his key people would be committed to staying with the company. He had no difficulty with this point and conceded that he was not wedded to the 50:50 formula, which was clearly an ideal going-in position from his point of view.

---

[1]Disguised name

6. On balance, I found ATS to be very impressive. Although operating in cramped facilities, it does appear to have a real technical depth and undoubtedly has an established customer base. The company appears to be an appropriate size to take over since it is neither so small as to be extraordinarily risky nor so big as to be extraordinarily expensive.

The meeting ended with the two men agreeing to continue discussions and to try to reach a gentlemen's agreement reasonably quickly rather than getting bogged down in protracted technical or legal discussions. Woerner promised to send some financial information as soon as he could get it put together, although he warned that his business plan should not be taken unduly literally as "these things are more exercises than necessarily forecasts of reality."

Subsequent Meetings

Over the next six months, Hanrahan held a number of meetings with Woerner, bringing with him on occasion Gerry Dempsey and Larry Stanley, another of Aer Lingus's ancillary business managers. Both men subsequently supported Denis' view that ATS would be a good acquisition. This positive feedback was also strengthened by comments from Seiko's North American sales manager, who stated that in 10 years ATS would be "one of the top three robot systems integrator firms in North America" if it grew to its potential. The meetings with Klaus also yielded more information about his expectations and the operations of ATS. The following excerpts are taken from Hanrahan's notes and comments on various meetings, all of which were held in Kitchener or Toronto.

Meeting of November 6

Present: G. P. Dempsey, Denis Hanrahan, Klaus Woerner, and Peter Jones,[2] who was Woerner's personal financial adviser and company accountant.

1. Woerner outlined his expectations for growth of the automation and robotics industry and for ATS. It seems clear that they have not done very much forward planning . . . . Woerner quoted Laura Conigliaro of Prudential-Bache as suggesting growth from $250 million in 1984 to $1 billion by 1987, but these figures were not very convincing since they relate to the total industry rather than to the subsegment in which ATS is involved.

2. Woerner stated that he expected ATS revenues to total $4 million for the year ending September 1984, $6 million for 1985 (rather than the $5 million he had earlier been projecting), and to reach $10

---

[2]Disguised name

million in three years' time. He believed that growth to $10 million could be financed through a combination of retained earnings and bank debt.

3. Northern Telecom (a major Canadian multinational firm) apparently accounts for approximately 40 percent of ATS revenues. Woerner indicated that this proportion would fall to one third in 1985 due to the growth of ATS. He stated strongly that in spite of the company's high dependence on Northern Telecom, he could, if necessary, survive a total loss of Northern's business by falling back on traditional nonflexible production line work ("hard" automation). However, he expressed the view that Northern Telecom could not break the relationship with him since they were dependent on ATS for maintenance and software updates.

4. There was an extensive discussion on the subject of control. Woerner's recent negotiations with Berton left him very uneasy about the behaviour of large corporations, and he again expressed his strong preference for a 50:50 partnership. Dempsey responded that our whole approach to subsidiaries was to work in partnership with the management of them and that this approach was not altered whether the shareholding was 2 percent, 50 percent, or 99 percent. Woerner appeared to implicitly accept that we might go to 75 percent or higher of the equity as long as we were concerned only with issues such as overall earnings and growth rather than the detailed operating practices involved. Dempsey suggested that Woerner should write to us in simple nonlegal terms outlining those issues upon which he believed he would require assurance from us. Woerner accepted this suggestion.

5. Woerner also expressed concern that his was a small company and in danger of being "trampled on" by Aer Lingus. While he was happy enough with the people he currently knew in Aer Lingus, he felt that these individuals could change and he could thus find himself exposed to changes of policy or personality. Dempsey responded that we could not fully reassure him on this issue. We had now had a wide range of relationships with subsidiaries over a long period of time and as this had not occurred historically, he saw no reason why it should happen in the future.

6. There were no specific discussions on the matter of price. Dempsey stated on a number of occasions that it was purposeless to discuss price until the financials were available and had been reviewed. Woerner concurred.

7. The meeting ended on a positive and progressive note. It was agreed that we would appoint Peat Marwick to review the affairs of ATS and they would contact Jones as necessary. It was also agreed that Jones would shortly produce a three-year forecast for ATS.

Exhibit 2 ATS Financial Statements (Canadian $000)

	1980	1981	1982	1983	1984
Sales	332	765	1,210	1,753	4,168
Cost of sales	187	491	902	1,450	3,197
Gross margin	145	274	308	303	971
Overheads	58	127	188	243	451
Operating profit	87	147	120	60	520
Interest	2	10	20	26	71
Tax	11	22	4	–0–	18
Net profit	74	115	96	34	431
Balance sheets					
Assets					
Fixed assets	106	211	308	390	517
Current assets	113	282	384	457	1,300
Current liabilities	(35)	(129)	(209)	(252)	(390)
Working capital	78	153	175	205	910
	184	364	483	595	1,427
Funded by					
Share capital	1	6	5	3	3
Revenue reserves	79	114	177	(160)	164
Shareholder's funds	80	120	182	(157)	167
Loan capital	104	244	301	752	1,260
	184	364	483	595	1,427

Meeting of January 10

The next meeting between Klaus and Denis included Bill Harcourt[3] of Peat Marwick Mitchell. During this meeting, the ATS financial statements and projections (see Exhibits 2 and 3) were given to Denis. These were to have been sent to Ireland several weeks earlier.

Denis learned during this meeting that Klaus had not written the promised letter concerning his specific issues of concern because he preferred to discuss them face to face. Further discussion ensued during which Klaus reiterated his general unease at the prospect of being controlled and repeated his desire for a 50:50 deal. While still not raising any specific concerns, Klaus repeatedly referred to the Berton deal and how lucky he was to have avoided it. Denis commented after the meeting:

> All of this was territory that we had covered several times previously with him and we essentially just covered it again. It was clear that as the discussion progressed, Klaus began to get more comfortable and his fears began to recede. I have no doubt that after I depart from Canada he begins to get uneasy again at the unknown. He reiterated that he was quite comfortable working with Mr. Dempsey or myself but that he could naturally have no assurance that we would be around forever.

---

[3]Disguised name

Exhibit 3   Projected ATS Financial Statements (Canadian $000)

	1985	1986	1987	1988
Sales	8,000	11,000	14,000	17,000
Cost of sales	5,920	8,360	10,920	13,260
Gross margin	2,080	2,640	3,080	3,740
Overheads	1,040	1,430	1,750	2,210
Operating profit	1,040	1,210	1,330	1,530
Interest	70	120	200	300
Tax		427	480497	541
Net profit	543	610	633	689
Dividends (projected)	–0–	–0–	250	300

Projected balance sheets	1984	1985	1986	1987	1988
Assets					
Fixed assets	517	680	1,030	1,310	1,860
Development				1,000	1,000
Current assets	1,300	2,417	4,904	5,740	6,580
Current liabilities	(390)	(760)	(1,720)	(1,886)	(2,260)
Working capital	910	1,657	3,184	3,854	4,320
	1,427	2,337	4,214	6,164	7,180
Funded by					
Share capital	3	750	2,000	2,300	2,700
Revenue reserves	164	707	1,317	1,701	2,090
Shareholders' funds	167	1,457	3,317	4,001	3,790
Loan capital	1,260	800	897	2,163	3,390
	1,427	2,337	4,214	6,164	7,180

NOTE: These projections were prepared by Klaus Woerner and Peter Jones.

In the earlier part of the meeting when Klaus was appearing very reluctant, Bill Harcourt asked him directly if he, in fact, wanted to sell ATS. Klaus replied that he didn't really want to—he had devoted all of his time in the last few years in building up the company and wished to continue to do so in the future—but because ATS would not be producing large amounts of cash in the short term he had no choice. He believes that ATS can and must grow very rapidly to forestall the competition—the opportunities are there and if ATS does not take advantage of them, someone else will. In this vein, he mentioned that he had just revised his estimate of the current year's sales from $6 million to $9 million.

The other reason that Klaus feels that he has to sell ATS is that important customers like Northern Telecom are nervous of becoming too dependent on him, as long as he does not have a major corporate backer. Klaus told us in the meeting that

Northern had in fact deliberately cut back their orders to him for this reason, and we independently checked that this was indeed the case.

The meeting ended on a very friendly note with Denis again encouraging Klaus to make up a list of his specific concerns so that they could be addressed, and Klaus inviting Bill Harcourt to visit the ATS plant before the next meeting so that he could develop a better understanding of what they were doing.

Meetings of January 24 and February 20

The meetings of January 24 and February 20 were devoted to discussions of a deal whereby Aer Lingus would acquire 75 percent of ATS stock, with Klaus Woerner holding the remaining 25 percent. At the January 24 meeting, Klaus appeared to accept the idea that he would sell the 75 percent of the company but, apparently as a result of his earlier negotiations with Berton, was adamant that ATS was worth at least $6 million. In the February 20 meeting, Denis finally agreed that ATS could be worth $6 million if the company met Klaus' new projections for it (Exhibit 4) but at the moment it was not. As a consequence, Denis proposed that the amount paid to Klaus should depend on the company's performance in 1985 and 1986. The details, spelled out in a letter from Denis to Klaus following the February meeting were as follows:

1. We propose that a valuation be established for ATS as of September 30, 1986. This valuation will be calculated by taking 3.5 times the pre-tax income for the fiscal year ended September 30, 1985, and adding to it 3.5 times the incremental pre-tax income earned in the fiscal year ending September 1986. By incremental income here I mean the excess of pre-tax income in fiscal 1986 over that earned in fiscal 1985.

2. In determining pre-tax income, research and development costs shall be charged at the rate contained in your financial projections or at a higher rate if so incurred. Profit sharing to employees shall be charged at 10 percent of pre-tax income before profit sharing or such higher rate as may be incurred. In addition, we would require the company to maintain a key-man insurance policy on yourself in the amount of $5 million and the cost of such coverage would be borne as a charge before striking pre-tax income.

3. On the basis of the pre-tax income figures outlined above, the company would have a total value of $6,835,000 as of September 30, 1986.

4. Under the above formula, the maximum value that we would be prepared to put on ATS would be $7 million even if the results are better than projected.

5. It is our view that the company is in need of significant additional funds to allow it to develop to the sales and income levels in your projections. Accordingly, we are willing to inject $2 million into ATS for agreed

EXHIBIT 4 Revised Income Projections (Canadian $000)

	1985	1986	1987	1988
Sales	8,000	14,000	20,000	30,000
Gross margin	2,080 (26%)	3,360 (24%)	4,400 (22%)	6,000 (20%)
General and administration See Schedule 2	862	1,190	1,578	2,159
Income	1,218	2,170	2,822	3,841
Profit sharing	120	217	282	384
Pre-tax income	1,098	1,953	2,540	3,457
Tax @ 45%	494	879	1,143	1,556
After-tax income	604	1,074	1,397	1,901

NOTE: These revisions were dated February 20, 1985. They were prepared by Klaus Woerner, working with Bill Harcourt.

working capital and investment use in the form of a secured debt with a 10 percent interest rate. It would be our intention to make available $750,000 at time of closing, $750,000 at time of completion of the 1985 audit, and the remaining $500,000 as needed by the company on an agreed basis during 1986.

It would be our intention that this loan would be used to purchase treasury stock from ATS at the end of 1986 using the valuation for the company as established by the formula outlined above. In other words, if the company was valued at $6,835,000, the $2 million loan would convert to give us 22.6 percent of the enlarged equity in the company. The attraction of this arrangement from your point of view is that it provides you with the money now to grow but that the shares are ultimately purchased in ATS at the valuation achieved in 1986 rather than at a current valuation.

Depending upon the ultimate valuation of the company, the percentage of its enlarged equity that would be bought by the $2 million referred to above would vary. It would then be our intention to purchase directly from you existing shares held by you in ATS such as would give us 75 percent of the then enlarged equity of the company. In the example quoted above, we would need to purchase 67 percent of your shareholding to give us a total of 75 percent of the enlarged equity. Using the value above, this would cost $4.6 million. In other words, what you would receive would be $4.6 million in cash plus 25 percent interest in the $2 million injected by us, for a total of $5.1 million, which is 75 percent of $6,835,000.

We propose that you would be paid for these shares as follows: on closing $500,000; in March 1986 and March 1987, further payments of $500,000; in March 1988 and March 1989 further payments of $1 million each; the balance payable on March 1990. To the degree that the final value of the company is larger or smaller than the $6,835,000 figure, the above payments would be prorated.

MOVING FORWARD

On March 16, Bill Harcourt phoned Denis to report that he had met with Klaus subsequent to the February 22 meeting. Denis recalled the discussion:

> Apparently Klaus was initially very unhappy with the limit of $7 million that we put on the company, although he is now willing to live with it and in fact has become very positive about doing a deal with Aer Lingus. He appears to have overcome his hesitancy and concern at another party becoming the majority shareholder of ATS. This may be due to the fact that he has taken advice from a friend named Bob Tivey who is the retired president of Monarch Canada.[4] Some minor improvements are required, however.
>
> One of these is that Klaus wants us to increase the $500,000 coming to him on closing so that he can pay employee bonuses—these will come out of his own pocket—and have more for himself. He also wants us to pay interest on the portion of the purchase paid which remains unpaid until the earn-out is completed. Finally, he would like a personal contract which will last five years, and include a good salary plus a bonus that is 2 percent of pre-tax earnings, and a car.
>
> Other news included the fact that Klaus is in the process of hiring a financial person and is considering a second-year registered industrial accountancy student. Bill suggested that he discuss this matter in some detail with us, as it might be advisable to opt for a more high-powered person. Bill also told me that Klaus was facing an immediate decision with respect to new premises for ATS—the major question being whether the company should rent or buy. Purchase cost will be close to $1 million.

Shortly after this phone call, Denis received a letter from Klaus which began, "I wish to advise you that as I am prepared to accept the proposal as outlined . . . subject to the following changes." As expected, the most important of the requested changes were an increased initial payment, the payment of interest on the unpaid portion of the purchase price, and a five-year employment contract.

After some negotiation, Aer Lingus agreed to increase its initial payment to allow Klaus to pay employee bonuses and to increase the initial funds going to his own pocket by approximately 50 percent, which was less than he had requested, but was deemed satisfactory.

In early April, Klaus traveled to Ireland for a meeting with the chief executive of Aer Lingus, and later that month the Aer Lingus board approved the purchase of a 75 percent shareholding of ATS on the terms which had been agreed with Klaus.

---

[4]Disguised name

At the end of April, Denis was once again in Kitchener, where he and Klaus held a most amicable meeting. Denis learned that Klaus and Bob Tivey had prepared a new business plan which they had used to obtain an increase in the ATS credit line. Also, Klaus had decided to proceed with the acquisition, his only objection being that eight board meetings a year was too many. Denis concluded his notes on the meeting with the following:

> We discussed at length the need for ATS management to develop credibility with me and for me to develop credibility on ATS subjects in Dublin, which he seemed to accept. All in all, the discussions were satisfactory and straightforward and have put to rest a significant number of my fears concerning Mr. Woerner's independence and his unwillingness to accommodate the requirements of a major corporate share-holder. In my view, he will accept direction provided that the direction is fast paced and is seen by him as being responsive to ATS's needs.

Due to some apparent foot dragging on the part of Klaus' lawyers and intervening vacations, it was July before Denis arrived in Kitchener to review the drafts of the sale contracts and bring the deal to a conclusion.

The Meeting of July 16

Klaus attended this meeting with Ron Jutras, his new financial controller (who had been hired without consultation with Aer Lingus), and Bob Tivey, who was acting as a consultant to Klaus. Denis recalled the meeting as follows:

> They opened the meeting by tabling a number of requirements which they said were critical to the deal going ahead. These were
>
> 1. A reluctance to hand over control to us before the valuation date of September 1986.
> 2. A five-year guaranteed contract for Klaus, with a 10-year period before we can force him out of share ownership.
> 3. A degree of protection against the possibility that one-off costs may depress 1986 earnings—specifically a *minimum* buy-out price of $6 million!
>
> I was very distressed to find such a total about face on something that we had agreed three months earlier, and when faced with this, Klaus acknowledged that he was changing his mind, but said that he could not afford the possibility of one bad year depressing his buy-out price. As for the contract length, Klaus was very emotional when the possibility of anything shorter than a five-year contract was raised.
>
> The question facing me as I sat in that meeting was how to react. Was it time to give up on this long and apparently fruitless process, or should I continue—and if so, how?

CASE 3
ALCAN ALUMINIUM LTD. (CONDENSED)

> Alcan is determined to be the most innovative diversified aluminum company in the world. To achieve this position, Alcan will be one, global, customer-oriented enterprise committed to excellence and lowest cost in its chosen aluminum businesses, with significant resources devoted to building an array of new businesses with superior growth and profit potential. In the 1990s Alcan will outperform the S&P 400.

In the spring of 1986, David Culver, president and CEO of Alcan Aluminium Ltd, a Montreal-based multinational, was reviewing the above draft of a new mission statement he had been working on for the company (see Appendix A for detailed discussion). Culver had spent the previous months consulting with various managers about the statement, which he felt was nothing less than a "call to arms." The statement crystalized the company's new strategy, which Culver had foreshadowed in the annual shareholders' meeting in 1984. While the company had published a statement of its purpose, objectives, and policies in 1978, it was not as sharply focused as the new mission statement drafted by Culver with the input of a few key senior managers. In particular, the new statement contained a clear financial objective for the 1990s, and Culver wondered what it would take to achieve it.

BACKGROUND

Alcan had just come through a particularly difficult year, suffering an unprecedented $180 million loss in 1985, even higher than the $58 million loss experienced in the major 1981–82 recession, which had represented the first loss in 50 years (see Exhibit 1 for selected financial information). The 1985 loss position was a result of a special charge of $252 million after tax. Approximately one half of this charge reflected a write-down in the value of Alcan's bauxite and alumina assets and most of the other half reflected the cost of a companywide program to reduce management levels and the number of employees. In fact, numbers had been reduced by 3,100 since the end of 1984.

Culver was considering a one-week conference in June 1986 involving Alcan's top 70 managers from around the world. Like Culver, many of these managers had spent most of their working lives with Alcan. The conference

SOURCE: This case was prepared from published records by Professor Mark C. Baetz, School of Business and Economics, Wilfrid Laurier University. It was prepared as a basis for class discussion rather than to illustrate either effective or ineffective handling of an administrative situation. Revised January 1992. Copyright © 1992, Mark C. Baetz.

<u>**Exhibit 1 Selected Financial Information for Alcan Aluminium Ltd.**</u>

Information by Geographic Areas

	Location	1985	1984	1983
Sales and operating revenues to	Canada	$ 921	$1,004	$1,033
third parties (millions of U.S. $)	United States	1,957	1,576	1,358
	Latin America	339	349	298
	Europe	1,756	1,683	1,766
	Pacific	664	709	627
	All other	81	146	126
	Total	5,718	5,467	5,208
	Sales	5,511	5,272	4,969
	Operating revenues	207	195	239
	Total	$ 5,718	$5,467	$5,208
Net income (Loss)	Canada	$ (41)	$ 141	$ 105
	United States	14	17	24
	Latin America	20	39	(11)
	Europe	(7)	51	26
	Pacific	(13)	33	(28)
	All other	—	6	(4)
	Consolidation eliminations*	(153)†	(34)	(39)
	Total	$ (108)	$ 253	$ 73
Total assets at 31 December	Canada	$ 2,476	$2,785	$2,582
	United States	1,110	999	802
	Latin America	705	716	697
	Europe	1,829	1,469	1,652
	Pacific	821	842	845
	All other	268	324	400
	Consolidation eliminations*	(348)	(445)	(378)
	Total	$ 6,861	$6,690	$6,600
Capital expenditures	Canada	$ 152	$ 194	$ 127
	United States	136	45	34
	Latin America	57	37	48
	Europe	161	35	96
	Pacific	61	98	64
	All other	30	18	13
	Total	$ 597	$ 427	$ 382
Average number of employees	Canada	17	18	19
(thousands)	United States	7	5	5
	Latin America	10	10	9
	Europe	20	20	22
	Pacific	14	14	13
	All other	2	3	3
	Total	70	70	71

*Represents intersubsidiary transactions.
†Includes provision against investments in bauxite and alumina operations.

EXHIBIT 1 *(continued)* **Principal Products**

Fabricated products: Since 1982, the company's shipments of fabricated products have increased steadily at an annual average rate of 13 percent, to reach a total of 1,340,000 tonnes in 1985. Over half of this increase has been due to mergers and acquisitions in the United Kingdom and the United States while the balance reflects higher shipments by existing Alcan operations, particularly in the United States. Gross margins on fabricated products declined in 1985 by 24 percent to $437 per tonne from $577 in 1984, compared with $424 in 1983.

Ingot products: In 1985, shipments increased to a record 878,000 tonnes. Increased sales were made principally in the United States and the Far East. Closely following trends in spot metal prices, Alcan's average realizations for ingot products declined by 35 percent from their cyclical peak in the first quarter of 1984 to the fourth quarter of 1985, which was 8 percent lower than the year earlier quarter. Despite steady cost reductions, margins on ingot products averaged $42 per tonne in 1985, as against $293 in 1984 and $200 in 1983.

Other products: In 1985, sales of other products totaled $813 million. The decline in 1985 was due primarily to lower revenues from sales of alumina. Other major contributions to revenues in this category were provided by sales of other metals, particularly stainless steel, magnesium and nickel, and by nonaluminum building products, industrial chemicals, and bauxite.

Operating revenues: In 1985, operating revenues were $207 million, compared to $195 million in 1984 and $239 million in 1983. Tolling (processing of products for third parties for a fee) and sales of surplus power from Canadian and British generating plants, constituted 70 percent of total revenues in this category. The third major component was revenues from third-party ocean freight operations.

Other income: These revenues, consisting principally of foreign exchange items and interest income, totaled $113 million in 1985, $109 million in 1984, and $97 million in 1983.

Revenues by Product
1985 (millions of U.S. $)

		1985	*1984*	*1983*	*1982*	*1981*
36.4%	Flat-rolled products	2,123	2,024	1,826	1,522	1,760
17.9%	Extruded, rolled, drawn	1,042	1,126	996	934	1,067
9.5%	Other fabricated	554	418	373	353	323
	Total fabricated	3,719	3,568	3,195	2,809	3,150
16.8%	Ingot products	979	817	975	867	789
13.9%	Other products	813	887	799	677	793
5.5%	Operating revenues and Other income	320	304	336	356	321

Gross Profit by Product
1985 (millions of U.S. $)

		1985	*1984*	*1983*	*1982*	*1981*
65.8%	Total fabricated products (integrated)	586	700	497	398	627
4.2%	Ingot products	37	169	146	40	166
10.8%	Other products	96	101	85	68	125
19.2%	Operating revenues and other income	171	162	160	153	132

EXHIBIT 1 *(concluded)* **Principal Markets**

Containers and packaging: The increase in consolidated sales to this market was largely due to the acquisition of assets from Arco, which strengthened the company's position in the United States as a supplier of sheet products, especially for beverage containers, and enabled it to enter the foil market for packaging in the United States. Approximately half of the company's total sales for containers and packaging were made in the United States, while one quarter were in Europe, where there is close cooperation among German, British, and Swiss operations in the foil packaging market.
While penetration of aluminum of the U.S. beverage can market is almost complete, efforts continue to develop this market elsewhere. In Canada, the consumption of aluminum for beer cans doubled during 1985, helping to increase the company's shipments to this market. In Germany, the company has been involved in pilot recycling projects to demonstrate some of the benefits from using aluminum for beverage containers, particularly with regards to the disposal of household waste.

Transport: The decline in sales to this market in 1985 was shared by all geographic regions. Approximately 80% of the company's sales were made by German, U.S., British, and Canadian operations. Largely due to the acquisition of assets from Arco, sales to the U.S. automotive industry of fin stock for radiators and air conditioners grew strongly.

Electrical: The United States and Canada accounted for over half of consolidated sales to this market, and declines in these two countries contributed to a reduction in the total. A new wire and cable plant at Shawinigan, Quebec, commenced partial operation in 1985 and will be fully operational in 1986.

Building and Construction: Increased sales in Europe to this market helped to offset reductions elsewhere. Operations in Europe and North America each accounted for approximately 40 percent of total sales. In Europe aluminum applications for building and construction are mostly in the form of extrusions, while in North America the company's sales to this market are made up largely of sheet products, including steel and vinyl, as well as aluminum.

Other markets: The company's sales to the international market for ingot products rose strongly, particularly in the United States and the Far East, and accounted for 17.8 percent of consolidated sales to all markets. The company also sells bauxite, alumina, and other raw materials used to produce aluminum. Sales of other metals and industrial chemicals increased during the year.

Sales by Market
1985 (millions of U.S. $)

		1985	*1984*
20.2%	Containers and packaging	1113	1009
6.7%	Transport	368	432
8.9%	Electrical	490	552
21.0%	Building and construction	1160	1223
43.2%	Other	2380	2056

SOURCE: All information in Exhibit 1 comes from Alcan Aluminium Ltd., *Annual Report*, 1985.

would be held at a secluded hotel in Quebec and its purpose would be to review the draft mission statement which had been prepared. Culver felt such a conference could be an exercise in common understanding as a prelude to coordinated action. Through plenary sessions and 10-person work groups, all conference delegates would have an opportunity to help set Alcan's course for the future. Culver, a 61-year-old Harvard MBA from the 1940s who in 1979 became the third CEO of Alcan, was well aware that the conference he was considering had no precedent in the long history of Alcan.

Production of Aluminum and Alcan's Position in 1986

Producing 1 metric ton of aluminum requires 4 or 5 tons of bauxite, which is one of the most abundant metals in the earth's crust. Bauxite comes from tropical or subtropical regions particularly in the Caribbean, West Africa, and Australia. The bauxite is chemically refined into about 2 metric tonnes of alumina, which is then treated at the smelter using an electrolytic process that consumes between 14,000 and 18,500 kilowatt-hours of electricity. Other metals can then be added to the molten aluminum metal to make aluminum alloys which are then cast into various ingot shapes and sizes, depending on the way the ingot is then to be fabricated.

There were a number of rigidities built into bauxite and alumina production. First, it took several years—between five and six—to build an alumina plant. Second, in order to capture economies of scale, large plants needed to be built; in the 1980s, alumina plants could cost more than $1 billion (U.S.), requiring in some cases consortium approaches. Finally, alumina plants could not be used for other purposes, and, in fact, each plant was locked into certain grades of bauxite.

As of 1986, Alcan's bauxite and alumina operations were expected to provide a geographically diversified supply base sufficient for all the company's smelters and other commitments for more than 50 years. Most of the alumina required for Alcan's smelter operations came from the company's plants in Canada, Ireland, and Jamaica and from related companies in Australia. Bauxite for Alcan's Canadian and Irish alumina plants was purchased mainly from a related mining company in Brazil and a mining company in Guinea in which the company had a minority equity interest. Subsidiaries with smelters in Brazil and India had their own bauxite mining and alumina production facilities.

Alcan owned 17 primary aluminum smelters with a total annual rated capacity of 1.8 million tonnes. Six of these smelters were in Canada: five in Quebec (807,000 tonnes of capacity) and one in British Columbia (268,000 tonnes of capacity). The remaining smelters which were owned either directly or indirectly were in seven other countries.

In Canada, Alcan's smelters obtained virtually all of their power from the company-owned hydroelectric generating plants. These plants were all constructed by 1959. Some of the surplus power from these plants was sold under contract. The power for Alcan's smelters outside Canada was supplied by various sources. The English smelter operated under its own coal-fired plants, those in Australia and India purchased power under long-term contracts from government-owned electric utilities, and those in Brazil and Scotland obtained power from both owned hydroelectric generating plants and outside sources. The German smelter was supplied by a local power authority, and the U.S. smelter purchased power under long-term contract from a financially troubled generating cooperative.

Like many producers of primary aluminum, Alcan was involved in supplying semifabricated and finished products. (There were also many independent fabricators.) In 1986 Alcan was the largest domestic manufacturer of fabricated aluminum products in many countries including Canada, Brazil, India, New

Zealand, and the United Kingdom (see Exhibit 1 for more details on the various products and markets served).

As of 1986, Alcan had bauxite holdings in 7 countries, refined alumina in 7 countries, smelted primary alumina in 8 countries, fabricated aluminum in more than 20 countries, and had sales outlets in more than 100 countries. In addition, the company had research laboratories in Kingston, Ontario; Banbury, England; and Arvida (Jonquiere), Quebec.

History of Alcan's Ownership Structure

In 1901, the Aluminum Company of America (Alcoa) launched a Canadian subsidiary under the name of Northern Aluminum to develop smelting facilities at Shawinigan, Quebec, on the St. Maurice River. As a result of this move, Canada entered the aluminum-producing ingot market 15 years after the United States and Europe first began to produce this versatile metal.

By 1925 Alcoa had smelters in Canada, Italy, and Norway, fabricating plants in England and Germany, and bauxite mines in Yugoslavia and Guyana. Alcoa decided to transfer all the foreign businesses to a new Canadian holding company, Aluminium Ltd., with its former Canadian subsidiary, now renamed the Aluminum Company of Canada (Alcan), being the largest member. Alcoa handed one share in the new company to the Alcoa shareholders for each three they held in Alcoa.

Setting up Alcan solved a personal problem for Arthur Vining Davis. As Alcoa's chairman, he was looking for a new president, and both E. K. Davis, his younger brother, and Roy Hunt, son of a founder, were qualified for the position. He appointed Davis president of Alcan and Hunt president of Alcoa. In 1947, E. K. Davis retired and his son, Nathanael Davis, was appointed president at age 32. In 1979, after 32 years as CEO, Davis retired from active management duties. He remained as chairman of the board until he retired in March 1986.

Although ownership of the Alcan shares had dispersed when Nathanael Davis was appointed president, the U.S. Justice Department believed that Alcan and Alcoa were too intimately connected. In 1950, a judge gave the major shareholders 10 years to sell off their holdings in either Alcan or Alcoa. All but E. K. Davis sold their shares in Alcan.

History of Alcan's Development

In the early 1920s, Alcoa and Northern had set out to develop the power potential of the Saguenay River in Quebec. A new smelter was opened in 1926 at the town of Arvida, named after the then president of Alcoa using the first two letters in each name, Arthur Vining Davis. Nathanael Davis explained the choice of the Saguenay as follows:

> The Saguenay attracted the Americans because of its combination of hydroelectric power and good logistics on deep water. To produce aluminum, you have to bring a tremendous lot of raw materials to the power. Power in the middle of Canada would

have been far less attractive than power on deep water; and the Saguenay was a deep-water port.

At the time, too, Canadian-made aluminum would have had preferential tariffs in Commonwealth countries.

There was probably even more to it than that. I suspect that the risk of other foreign interests moving in led Alcoa to say, "We'd better stake out a position in Canada." The French producers were interested. That power stood there waiting for a user.[1]

Fabrication of aluminum also started at the same time as smelting. A small rod, wire, and cable mill was built beside the original Shawinigan smelter in 1902. Sheet foil and casting followed at several locations.

World War II brought quick growth to the aluminum industry and after a short postwar slump, aluminum became widely used in household items, as well as in paints, cars, and airplanes due to its superior properties of strength and lightness. Much of the use of aluminum came as a result of substitution for other products. For example, aluminum replaced wood and steel in windows and copper in electrical cables.

In the early 1950s, Alcan built the Kitimat hydro and smelting facilities in British Columbia, 400 miles north of Vancouver. The only access to the site was by air or sea. At Kitimat, Alcan was faced with the challenge of creating a whole new community based upon one industry in a remote area with a harsh climate. It also had to construct a deep-water port. With $450 million worth of smelters and generators, Kitimat represented the largest private enterprise undertaking in Canadian history. It was also the world's second largest smelter; the world's largest was Alcan's facility at Arvida.

In the early 1950s, while Alcan's rivals stepped up fabrication to go after the U.S. postwar markets, Alcan basically stuck to its strategy of being the "producer's producer." Alcan's strategy of continuing to produce ingots for fabrication by others meant that they were taking on debt to invest in major hydro and smelting projects. Alcan paid for this nonconformity in the late 1950s when plunging ingot prices caught the company with a high debt load. Up until 1957, the demand for aluminum grew steadily, but in that year it fell sharply. This brought to an end the seller's market that the producing industry had been experiencing, and in 1959 Alcan was forced to temporarily close 34 percent of its Canadian smelting capacity. From 1947 to 1957, the average annual price increase was 6 percent. However, from 1957 to 1972, the industry experienced no price increases. The beginning of this buyer's market occurred three years after the Kitimat operation came on stream. Nathanael Davis commented on Kitimat as follows:

The [Kitimat] decision built up over years of investigation .... With the benefit of hindsight we can see that we miscalculated on costs and in timing. The remoteness factor had been completely misjudged. At the time it put a terrible strain on the

---

[1]*Executive,* November 1979.
[2]*Executive,* December 1979.

company. It ran over budget very significantly and for many years was fairly unproductive.[2]

Revisions to Alcan's Strategy

Too much capacity and declining demand forced the directors of Alcan to revise their strategic direction. Alcan was to forward integrate and to stop being a "producer's producer." This decision committed Alcan to capital expenditures of over $1 billion to develop fabrication plants worldwide. Nathanael Davis explained the significance of this decision as follows:

> It takes a long time to see trends and make a major change in a business such as this. It might take a year or 18 months to make the decision and then you really can't get anything going under five years, so you want to be pretty sure of your ground before you start. All our projects take a lot of capital, and once you start you don't turn back. Like a ship you can change course only fairly slowly.[3]

Between 1955 and 1970, Alcan established new fabrication operations in more than 20 countries. In fact, the company changed from being largely a supplier of primary aluminum to being largely a supplier of fabricated products. In the United States, a market representing one half of the total world market, Alcan teamed up in 1965 with three independent fabricators to build a mill in Oswego, New York. Eventually the independents' share was bought out, but the U.S. subsidiary did not turn a profit until 1973. However, it became the fourth largest U.S. fabricator with 1978 sales of more than $1 billion.

Future efforts at entry into the United States met with resistance. In 1976, Alcan's efforts to buy the Revere Copper and Brass Company's aluminum smelter were stopped by the antitrust regulators. Because Alcan was one of the major players in a concentrated industry, the regulators felt they should not pick up a facility from a smaller company, even though Alcan believed they would have added to competition by strengthening a weak facility. Alcan decided not to pursue the acquisition because of the risks associated with a legal battle.

Alcan in the 1980s

Later, in 1984, Alcan again encountered resistance to its expansion plans in the United States when it attempted to buy the aluminum assets of Atlantic Rich-field Co. (Arco) of Los Angeles. Arco, like many major oil companies that diversified into metals in the 1970s, had become disillusioned with aluminum and found profits hard to come by. U.S. antitrust officials objected to Alcan's desire to buy Arco's ultramodern $450 million rolling mill in Logan County, Kentucky, which produced the aluminum sheet used in beverage cans. Regulators said the purchase of the plant would double Alcan's 7 percent share of the $3.4 billion U.S. market for the product. After 11 months of negotiations, Alcan's lawyers

---

[3]Ibid.

worked out a compromise with the regulators. For $500 million, Alcan would purchase 40 percent of the Kentucky rolling mill, along with 100 percent of Arco's Kentucky-based smelter, two other rolling mills, two foil-producing plants in the United States, and finally Arco's 25 percent interest in an Irish alumina factory. Before the deal was concluded, one report commented on what Alcan's strategy would have been if U.S. antitrust officials were to completely veto the acquisition as they had done in the case of Revere Copper and Brass:

> Alcan President and Chief Executive, David Culver makes it clear that another veto will not deter Alcan from expanding south of the Canadian border. "No one's ever stopped us from building a new plant in the U.S." he says. Adds a former Alcan executive: "They need a facility in the U.S. If they don't buy it from Arco, they're going to build it." Such grit illustrates the change at Alcan under Culver, who became the first Canadian to head Alcan. Before that, Americans held the top job, and—in part because they did not want to raise Canadian hackles—made few bold moves, creating Alcan's long-held reputation for being a "gentleman's club." Says former Alcan executive, Manley S. Schultz: "Visitors said you could fire a cannon in headquarters at five after five and not worry about hurting anybody." No longer. "They're extremely aggressive now," says a rival.[4]

Alcan's aggressiveness was revealed during the recession of the early 1980s, when the company decided to reduce its production much less than its competitors. This move was a break from Alcan's traditional approach to downturns of cutting production at least as much as competitors. Alcan's new strategy was seen as a major blunder by many Wall Street metals analysts and by Alcan's competitors, who saw Alcan's operating rate as exacerbating a price collapse that made the recession worse for all producers, including Alcan.

Two major economic factors important to Alcan were energy and transportation costs. While Alcan had always benefited from low electricity costs, it also had to contend with high transportation costs of both raw materials to its smelters and aluminum ingot to the marketplace; it was hauling bauxite and alumina from the Southern Hemisphere to its Canadian smelters, and then shipping finished or semifinished products to places as distant as the Far East. While the cost of transportation may have offset Alcan's edge in electricity in the past, the two energy price surges in the 1970s clearly put the company among the world's lowest cost producers. A media report in 1983 explained Alcan's position as follows:

> Alcan's power advantage now more than makes up for its shipping-cost penalties . . . . In the last five years the weighted-average electricity costs for smelters in the non-Communist world has doubled from 0.9 cent to 1.8 cents per kwh. As a result, electricity costs now account for about 25 percent, or $300, of the average price of producing a metric ton of aluminum. But the price of power from Alcan's Canadian hydroelectric stations, all of which were built before 1960, has risen hardly at all. It is now just 0.3 cent per kwh, one-sixth of the industry average.

---

[4]*Business Week,* August 27, 1984, pp. 95–96.

Electricity costs Alcan about $50 per metric ton of aluminum. Japan, at the opposite extreme with power from oil-fired generators, faces a cost of 6 cents per kwh, or $990 per metric ton of aluminum. Not surprisingly, most of Japan's smelting capacity is idle and the country is importing most of its aluminum. In the U.S. the Bonneville Power Administration recently jacked up the price it charges aluminum smelters in the Northwest to 2.6 cents, or about $430 per metric ton. . . . Hydropower gives Alcan a peculiar disincentive to cut back in lean times. While other producers' costs vary according to how much electricity they use, Alcan's power costs are fixed. . . . The company lacks a ready market for any surplus (electricity from its hydroelectric plants). "If we shut down our smelters, we go to bed with the electricity that's liberated," says Murray Lester, Alcan's director of energy resources. "If the whole industry had to wind down to the last 2 million tons, and the invisible hand of Adam Smith were working, we'd be the last to go."

High production levels also appear to be part of a company campaign to win labor peace. While its U.S. competitors worked without major disruptions during the 1970s, Alcan was hit with two big strikes, both in years of rising demand. It has been keeping employment relatively high despite the recession and has refrained from fully opening a brand-new, $500-million non-union smelter in Quebec until business improves. "We've tried to maintain our team," Culver says.[5]

Another key part of Alcan's strategy was to ensure that Alcan's shipments of primary aluminum to third parties (i.e., shipments other than to Alcan's own fabricating plants) would not fall below 25 percent of total smelter output. This compared to the U.S. companies that reduced third-party shipments of primary aluminum to 20 percent or less of total shipments. The two major U.S. companies—Alcoa and Reynolds—produced ingot almost exclusively for use in their own fabricating plants. The main rationale for the Alcan strategy was its continuing anticipated power cost advantage in smelting. However, ingots were clearly in a commodity market subject to huge cyclical swings.

Environment in the Mid-1980s

By 1985, Alcan was facing lower world prices for ingot and excess smelter capacity. This was caused by restarts in 1983–84 of previously mothballed smelters, as well as by government-owned aluminum producers outside North America, who ignored low prices and maintained high production levels to protect jobs. Alcan's top managers concluded that the company's economic environment had changed radically. As part of its response to this situation, Alcan adopted a cost-cutting and rationalization program. In addition to cutbacks in the number of production workers, Alcan postponed construction of a major smelter in Laterriere, Quebec, pared investment in Latin America, sold marginal fabricating plants around the world, and withdrew from Africa. It also recognized the impaired economic value of its bauxite and alumina assets arising from significant excess of world production capacity in those areas and took a write-down of these assets in 1985 of approximately $200 million before tax. It also set out to

---

[5]*Fortune*, February 21, 1983, p. 126.

reduce the number of levels of management and rationalize and reduce employee numbers throughout the company, including its head office.

Another response of the company to the environment of the mid-1980s was to increase and redirect R&D expenditures, particularly in the areas of product innovation and exploration (i.e., seeking out entirely new business areas). Alcan's R&D projects included a series of low-density aluminum lithium alloys for aircraft sheet, an integrated manufacturing process for aluminum-structured motor cars, a prototype high-performance light-weight freight rail car, and a revolutionary new packaging system for cooking frozen foods in microwave ovens.

Despite the increase in R&D expenditures, Alcan's efforts remained smaller than competitors, notably Alcoa, which spent $120 million on R&D in 1985 while Alcan spent $77 million. Earlier, in 1979, Davis had described Alcan's R&D efforts as follows:

> In some processes we're leaders but we can't be leaders in everything. Alcoa will lead in certain fields and another company will lead in another field. We're making an effort to have a better interchange of technology, for example with our Japanese associated companies.[6]

In 1984, Alcan's chief scientific officer, Hugh Wynne-Edwards, had described the significance of R&D at Alcan as follows:

> Culver has given us a mandate to be on the cutting edge of technological change. We're in a horse race with the rest of the industry and with manufacturers of other materials. Everybody is trying to out-innovate the other guy.[7]

The president of Alcoa provided the following perspective on the industry's R&D efforts:

> After aluminum replaced steel in the U.S. beverage can market in the 1970s, we somehow let ourselves think that we'd found every practical use for aluminum. Lately, we've realized that aluminum is still a wonder metal and that we have many more mountains to climb.[8]

Despite the various internal efforts by Alcan to deal with lower prices and excess capacity, some observers concluded that the prospects for Alcan heavily depended on uncontrollable external forces. As one analyst even noted: "Alcan is at the mercy of events beyond its control."[9]

The next section covers some of the external forces which were affecting Alcan's prospects.

---

[6]*Executive,* December 1979.
[7]*Canadian Business,* January 1984, p. 16.
[8]Ibid.
[9]*MacLean's,* July 8, 1985.

Competitive Forces

One of the most important structural changes in the aluminum industry to affect Alcan was the increase in the number of competitors. The number of non-Communist aluminum producers grew from 16 in 1950 to more than 80 by 1986, including a number of oil-fired plants in OPEC countries. The dominance of an oligopoly of companies—including Alcan, Alcoa, Reynolds, Kaiser, Pechiney, and Alusuisse—that once controlled up to 80 percent of non-Communist capacity was being undermined.

By the 1980s, a number of the new competitors, lacking a marketing network, turned to middlemen such as metal traders. One metals trader, Marc Rich, controlled a million metric tonnes, the equivalent of half of Alcan's output. Rich reportedly made annual profits in the 1980s of up to $150 million (U.S.) pretax on aluminum-related activities.

Most of Alcan's biggest competitors moved or planned to move their activities downstream, devoting more attention and money to higher value-added activities or diversifying. For example, Alcoa, in an effort to be known as a materials company rather than an aluminum company, hoped to reduce its dependence on aluminum from 85 percent of its sales to 50 percent by 1995. To fulfill this strategy, the company purchased fibre optics, ceramics, and plastic packaging ventures.

One reason for the increase in the number of competitors was that more and more governments, particularly in developing countries, built smelters to create jobs and to earn foreign currency. By 1986, state-owned aluminum producers accounted for about a third of world smelting capacity, up from less than 6 percent in the early 1960s. One observer noted: "Aluminum has changed from an orderly, stable business controlled by more or less like-minded, profit-oriented players into a more chaotic free market."[10]

Impact of Government

Part of Alcan's operations in Quebec almost became state owned. During the 1960s, Rene Levesque, the energy minister in the Liberal government of Jean Lesage, persuaded his colleagues that it would be in the public interest to gather Quebec's hydro resources under the umbrella of a state-owned enterprise. As it turned out, Levesque nationalized 11 utilities and power distribution companies but exempted Alcan's power plants. Some observers saw this as a recognition that Alcan's contribution to Quebec as an aluminum exporter was important and valuable. Nevertheless, the Quebec government took other actions which affected Alcan's competitive environment. In attempting to fulfill its goal of making Quebec an international centre of aluminum production, the Quebec government in 1963 encouraged Reynolds Metals Co. of Richmond, Virginia, to

---

[10]*Fortune*, February 21, 1983, p. 128.

come to Quebec. Reynolds established a wire and cable fabricating plant in Charlevoix and a smelter in Baie Comeau. Similarly, in 1986, Pechiney, a state-owned French metal and chemical conglomerate, encouraged by the Quebec government with favourable power rates, started up a smelter at Becancour on the St. Lawrence River. In this latter case, the Quebec government took a 25 percent equity interest.

Although Alcan had always aimed to retain some emphasis on primary aluminum production, there was on-going pressure on the company by the Quebec government to integrate forward. The government was anxious to see levels of employment maintained. As one former Quebec industry minister noted: "If Alcan rationalized in the primary activity, it must invest in secondary and tertiary activity."

In responding to the pressures, Alcan argued that fabricating plants needed to be close to markets. Nevertheless, Alcan had made investments in Quebec for the fabrication of some commodity products such as coiled sheet and wire bar. These investments employed about 10 percent of Alcan's Quebec work force, which in 1986 amounted to about 10,000 people.

Despite the political pressures, the thrust of Alcan's strategy in Quebec was clearly primary production. One observer provided the following analysis in 1983 of Alcan's relations with the Quebec government:

> Alcan's vitality and political sensitivity have made it extremely popular in Quebec. Provinces that balk at its plans for expansion and exploitation of hydroelectricity have found, to their peril, that Alcan can always come home to Quebec to find room to grow. In 1982 in Manitoba, when politicians began to argue over the merits of an Alcan smelter operation, Alcan cancelled its feasibility studies and promptly exercised an option on 2,000 more acres of land in the Saguenay. As a result about $2 billion worth of modernization will take place there over the next two decades . . . . That is touted by the company and the provincial government alike as proof of the viability of investing in Quebec. In fact, Alcan remains one of the few companies investing money in the province.[11]

Although Alcan may have had generally positive experiences with the Quebec government, this was not always the case with other governments. For example, in 1971, the government of Guyana nationalized Demerarra Bauxite Company, a subsidiary of Alcan. In Norway, Alcan had another frustrating experience with government as described by Davis:

> Norway, with all its hydroelectric power, seemed a very sound place for us. Our company there had very close commercial relationships with a fully owned government company. We provided all its aluminum oxide and took metal in return on a barter basis. So then we thought, "Why not put the two companies together on a 50–50 basis?"
>
> That worked pretty well for a few years but then the government's philosophies and objectives and our objectives started to go in different directions. . . . The

---

[11]*MacLean's,* April 4, 1979.

outcome was that we sold them half our interest. After a few more years we both agreed that the government's objectives and ours were not identical. The government needed to maintain employment in the remote fjords. We were private enterprise-oriented. So we finally sold them the second half.[12]

Davis described the general pressures of government on the company in the following way:

There is constant pressure, not only in Quebec but in Canada, in Norway, in every country we go into; they all feel that, if we don't carry the product one step further locally, then we're not doing right by the host government. This is always a bit of a battle.

But if it's carried too far you could start doing things that are silly and just won't work. These are things that are a little hard for the politician to accept.[13]

Other government-controlled factors affecting Alcan's competitive position were currency and investment controls, withholding taxes, and changes in import duties and restrictions.

Slower Growth

Another external force affecting Alcan was a slowdown in the rate of growth of demand. Annual growth in world demand had slowed from 8 percent in the early 1970s to less than 2 percent by the 1980s. In fact, during the recession in the early 1980s, there was a significant fall in demand and prices, particularly in North America and Europe.

One cause of lower overall growth was increased product sophistication, which meant the reduction in size, gauge, and weight of aluminum materials. Culver estimated that because of lighter, thinner, and stronger versions of existing products in the canning, automotive, and general extrusion markets, aluminum sales in 1983 in the Western world were at least 1 million tonnes a year less than would have been made for the same output of finished product in the mid-70s. Another important factor was significant growth in the recycling of aluminum scrap, primarily in the beverage can area. Culver estimated that this had reduced primary aluminum demand by a further 1 million tonnes a year from the level that would have been required in the mid-70s for the same number of finished units.

Substitute products were another cause of the overall decline in demand growth for aluminum. For example, vinyl had damaged the aluminum siding business, and plastics, benefiting from low oil prices, represented a growing threat. New types of oven-proof cardboard moved into the food packaging market. Another cause of the decline in demand was lack of product

---

[12]*Executive,* December 1979.
[13]Ibid.

innovation. Critics claimed that the industry's last major product innovation was the aluminum can.

The slowdown in demand growth affected prices. Before the 1981–82 recession, ingot spot prices touched $1 a pound, but after a peak in 1983, prices plummeted in 1986 to 52.8 cents a pound. Price movements also became more exaggerated beginning in 1978 when the London Metal Exchange (LME) started trading aluminum contracts. One Alcan manager described the effect of the LME as follows: "The LME reflects a game of paper rather than physical metal. As a result, prices for aluminum have become more volatile."

Alcan's Strategy and Strengths

As Culver considered the new mission statement and the various pressures on the company, he reviewed the five elements of Alcan's strategy he had outlined to shareholders in 1984:

1. Dispersal and sufficiency in our raw material base of bauxite and alumina.
2. Enlargement of our smelter base only where we have our own power, or can expand incrementally, together with a 30-year modernization programme for our Quebec smelter system.
3. Selective growth in fabricating, including finished product businesses which support upstream strengths.
4. Development and application of market-related technology in both existing and new fields.
5. Selective investment in nonaluminum sectors related to our strengths.

Along with the strategy, Culver also reviewed the company strengths as he described them to shareholders in 1983:

Alcan's strengths are people, power, and internationality. . . . Alcan people, individually and collectively, represent an enormous wealth of skills and experience, operating in a decentralized organization in many countries of the world.

Alcan's owned Canadian power position is an undoubted advantage, but one which is needed in our production of primary aluminum, to offset the logistical disadvantages of the distance of our Canadian smelters from both their raw material sources, and their major markets.

Our hydroelectric assets are the result of past investment decisions that were both imaginative and risky, and some of which preempted for many years Alcan's ability to develop in other directions. The benefit of those decisions is, however, increasingly clear and valuable.

Our third major strength, internationality, is also one which is becoming more valuable with time. As the economic geography of both the supply and the demand side of the industry changes, Alcan's ability to deal with the political dimensions, to manage the finances, the technology transfer, and the market development in a truly international industry, is a vital strength.

The June Conference

In contemplating the idea of a June conference to discuss his drafted mission statement, Culver wondered what kind of role the conference and mission statement could or should play in the overall strategic planning process of the company. Under Nathanael Davis, the planning process could be described as reactive. The various subsidiaries around the world submitted annually their plans for the next two years and these were used by head office to allocate scarce resources (usually capital and metal). There were also long-term "strategic plans" where head office asked: "What are your ambitions for the next 7 to 10 years?" These provided the background for the approval of major projects which could dominate the company's capital spending and financing activities for a period of years. In describing Alcan's strategic planning horizon, and the company's future, Nathanael Davis commented in 1979 as follows:

> It's unreasonable to try to look too far ahead. Over a 10- or 15-year span I see the company continuing to grow very much along the same general lines as in the past. We do have opportunities. The demand for aluminum may not grow quite as rapidly as it has—it was extraordinarily rapid growth—and our plans are based on a more modest growth rate. Aluminum is a very useful material that continues to have a good future and our company is fortunate in having the basic materials needed to let us compete effectively over the next decade or longer.
>
> However, we have to keep exploring new technological opportunities to reduce the cost of production and develop new ways of production. Aluminum was long considered a growth industry in financial terms. Profits were growing year by year and aluminum stocks were selling at 20 times earnings. It's no longer considered a growth industry by the financial fraternity; it's considered "cyclical." But in terms of volume it had continued to be a growth industry. Indeed, volume may have been our problem. We produced too much and didn't make a proper return on our investment. Now we're doing much better. . . .
>
> This industry went through many, many years of very low returns. It helped the market of course because aluminum was being sold at very low prices. But the true challenge ahead is to maintain our improved earnings.[14]

With Culver's new mission statement, Alcan's strategic planning process could be seen as more proactive and participative, that is, the senior managers of the company would have an opportunity to help set the company's spending priorities and earnings target, recognizing the constraints and challenges faced by each part of the Alcan Group. The ensuing central decision making would then be in the context of a set of priorities which the CEO had adopted after full discussion.

One issue with the new mission statement was how it might be linked to the statement of Alcan's purpose, objectives, and policies (Appendix B), first published in June 1978. Nathanael Davis, chairman and CEO at that time, explained

---

[14]Ibid.

in the foreword that the statement was for distribution to all Alcan employees in all countries to strengthen their awareness of the basic general principles and policies which had guided the conduct of Alcan's business over the years. This document had emerged from consultation and participation of approximately 200 Alcan managers around the world. The statement was also distributed to Alcan's shareholders and was made available to others on an unrestricted basis.

The statement was reprinted without change in September 1984. In this reprinting, Culver added a foreword which indicated that the 1978 statement had stood the test of time. However, in 1986, Culver felt a new element would have to be added to the "purpose" section of the 1984 statement to make it consistent with the new mission statement. This element would state that the company would concentrate on those chosen aluminum activities in which the company expected to achieve an acceptable rate of return, as well as investment in other businesses, related to company strengths, with better long-term growth and earning prospects. Amending the 1984 statement would require a third printing of the statement.

One issue for Culver with the new mission statement was the likelihood of Alcan outperforming the Standards & Poor's 400[15] in the 1990s. Culver, who beneficially owned 36,500 Alcan shares (trading between 39 7/8 and 48 3/8 in the first quarter of 1986 on the Toronto Stock Exchange) and 13,300 shares subject to options, was aware of criticism of the company's past strategies. One report in 1984 noted:

> The world's major aluminum producers have long envied Alcan Aluminum Ltd. of Montreal its energy self-sufficiency. Until recently they have worked hard to stream-line their plants in order to prevent Alcan—the industry's low-cost producer—from pricing them out of the market. Lately, however, the big U.S. producers have abandoned their attempt to beat Alcan at its own game. Instead they're responding to new and bigger threats: increased Third World production, the substitution of plastic and other materials for aluminum, and recycling. Ironically, they may be better able to cope with these challenges than Alcan, which, some critics suspect, has been blinded by its sizable energy advantage to the need to find new uses for the metal and not just cheaper ways to make it.
>
> As long as aluminum was a commodity business—in which all the players sold pretty much the same products and competed mostly on price—the low-cost producer stood to gain the most. But these days the aluminum industry is becoming heavily oriented toward marketing as well as research and development. . . . Alcoa and Reynolds Metals Co. of Richmond, Va., the No. 2 U.S. producer, have ordered their R&D labs to emphasize new-product innovations over cheaper production methods. . . . But the main factor responsible for altering the way most producers think is recycling. Recycling is both the boon and bane of the industry. "Aluminum wouldn't be a contender for all these new applications if it weren't for its very high recyclability," says Culver. But Culver concedes that recycling has one dreadful and obvious drawback: it reduces demand for the stuff in the first place. Some 56 percent

---

[15]Standard & Poor's is a financial index based on the return on equity of 400 industrial companies.

of all U.S. beverage cans are now recycled;[16] the metal salvaged is equal to the annual tonnage of three large smelters. And if such catchy recycling efforts as Alcoa's "Cangaroo," a vending machine in reverse that pays for used cans, become widespread, the impact on raw-ingot producers such as Alcan could be severe. . . . Recycling is good news for such firms as Reynolds, which depends on used cans and other scrap for a quarter of its annual production. The capital investment required to produce a kilogram of aluminum from recycled materials is about one-10th the investment needed for a kilogram of primary aluminum. Refining recycled aluminum also saves 95 percent of the energy used in producing primary aluminum; this has helped close the power gap between Reynolds and Alcan. "We're not looking to the auto industry only for the increased aluminum that we hope to sell to it," says Reynolds spokesperson, "but also for the huge scrap value an aluminum vehicle would have. We're beginning to think of cars as very large cans."

. . . With aluminum demand likely to crawl along (growing at 4 percent per year, at best, for the next several years), observers feel that the only place to be is in semifinished-product manufacturing. And despite Alcan's heavy commitment to R&D, some feel it isn't moving far enough, fast enough. . . . It's the old Canadian problem of getting caught in the transition from a traditional resource-based company to a competitor selling value-added products in the global market. "Alcan still envisions itself as having a mission to be the raw-ingot supplier to the world," says Stewart Spector, an aluminum analyst with Tsai-Spector Research Associates Inc. of New York. "But the world is rapidly changing, and Alcan will be in serious trouble if it doesn't produce more exclusively for its own plants and cast off the role of being a producers' producer."[17]

Despite the criticism of Alcan, it still represented one of Canada's most formidable Canadian-controlled multinational enterprises. Nevertheless, given the long history and size of Alcan, Culver recognized that setting the company in any kind of new path would require a Herculean effort.

---

[16]The can market represented nearly 20 percent of total aluminum consumption.

[17]*Canadian Business*, January 1984, pp. 16, 19, 20.

Appendix A
Draft of Mission Statement

The Statement is nothing less than a call to arms. It will act as a catalyst for change within the Company. In due course the effects of the action taken as a result of the Statement should touch everyone in the Company. The succinct, strongly worded Mission Statement sums up what Alcan intends to become and how it will get there.

[Following is a sentence-by-sentence review of the new Mission Statement with commentary by Culver about each key word.]

Alcan is **determined** to be the most **innovative diversified** aluminum company in the world.

Determined "The strongest possible commitment to change. Having averaged 9 percent ROE over 30 years and having developed an Alcan style and culture (much of which we are proud of and wish to keep) that has tolerated this mediocre performance, determination is required."

Innovative "This word should be accepted as applying both to our chosen aluminum business and to our new businesses. It does not only mean product and process innovation, which are vital, but also means a new look at the way we solve all our business problems.

"The results of innovation can create some excitement. A reduction in receivables; an increase in recovery; getting by with fewer bodies, etc.—excitement is made of that stuff, just as it is made of new discoveries successfully brought to market. Flawless implementation breeds excitement and excitement breeds flawless implementation. There is excitement in being acknowledged as the most successful aluminum investment. There is excitement in demonstrating how a global enterprise can excel even if based on a commodity!"

Diversified "Aluminum—the metal—is and remains great and growing. It has the qualities that other metals seek and it lends itself to modern living and modern demands for more value to the customer per ton of metal used. We are learning to sell it the way we did after the Second World War. Yes—we intend to be the most exciting *diversified* aluminum company, but not because there is anything wrong with the metal itself! The reason for diversification is the manner in which man has organized himself to make and sell aluminum. What used to be a restricted number of integrated producers has rapidly become a large number of non-integrated producers. This de-coupling of a commodity-based industry has happened before. It changes who our competitors are. It will have much the same impact on our industry as de-regulation has had on the U.S. airlines. All of this restricts Alcan's future ability to achieve earnings growth. We could respond by downsizing—and staying within—our aluminum business. We might achieve a 14 percent ROE on the much smaller business. But we cannot achieve 14 percent ROE plus sustainable growth in earnings per share without diversification."

*   *   *   *   *

To achieve this position, Alcan will be **one, global, customer enterprise** committed to **excellence** and **lowest** cost in its aluminum businesses, with **significant resources** devoted to an **array** of new businesses with superior growth and profit.

One "Splitting Alcan into two pieces would not accomplish our aim of changing Alcan. While there will always be different cultures in Alcan, we must strive for cooperation, mutual understanding and respect between them. In this way we will have a sense of *one* Alcan and not a divided Alcan."

Global "Alcan early on accepted the reality of the global economy. We are increasingly adjusting ourselves to that reality. Some of our best existing businesses are already 'global.'

"We should not confuse the above with the recent departures of Alcan from certain countries. There is no conflict between thinking globally and withdrawing from certain countries where our existing aluminum businesses are not meeting—and seem unlikely to meet—our profitability targets. Alcan never intended 'global' to mean presence in each country for the *sake* of presence."

Customer-oriented enterprise "There is a big difference between *knowing* that we exist to give services and value to our customers, and *living* that way. Those three words are in the Mission Statement to act as a *constant reminder.*"

Excellence and lowest cost "An average of 9 percent over 30 years is not the ROE of a business that is characterized by excellence or uniqueness. To break out of that rut requires the total dedication and commitment of everyone in Alcan to achieving excellence and lowest cost in our cost-driven businesses. In some of our chosen aluminum businesses, as well as in our new businesses, we can also achieve high added value through uniqueness, but, even in these, it is important to have the lowest competitive costs."

Chosen "This is a key word in the Mission Statement. Whereas in the past Alcan fought hard (and expensively!) to grow and to gain market share across a broad spectrum of the global aluminum market, we are now only interested in those specific parts of the total market where we can achieve a minimum of 14 percent ROE. To accomplish this, Alcan will reshape its aluminum activities, concentrating its efforts on the businesses chosen for their sustainable competitive advantage, which should be able to meet the target return on a regular basis. Businesses which show no credible promise of reaching those targets will be sold, or, if that is not possible, closed down."

Significant resources "We mean business—no blowing hot and cold—no stop/go. The status quo is not acceptable. To outperform the S&P 400 in the 1990s, and to provide our shareholders with earnings growth as well as a good ROE, will require significant and sustained diversification effort. This effort will comprise a combination of many small experiments and some big bold moves."

Array "The route we are taking to outperform the S&P 400 in our diversified aluminum business will be to institute a large number of small experiments and a small number of big bold moves. The former requires the acceptance of an admittedly wasteful growth culture in an atmosphere wherein efficiency takes a back seat to experimentation. The latter (big bold moves) requires management courage, an iron will and flawless analysis. There will be some 'market pull' companies as well as some 'technology push' companies. Because these two separate cultures must coexist within one management, that management must be 'bi-cultural.' "There will be many more starters than finishers."

* * * * *

In the 1990s Alcan will **outperform** the S&P 400.

Outperform "For our performance to be acceptable to our shareholders and also attractive to our investors, we need to outperform the S&P 400 over the business cycle, both in terms of ROE *and* sustained growth in earnings per share. It is the latter requirement which dictates our moves into new businesses."

APPENDIX B
ALCAN, ITS PURPOSE, OBJECTIVES, AND POLICIES
1978

Alcan's Purpose

Alcan's purpose is to utilize profitably the risk capital voluntarily invested by the shareholders as a financial base to create productive facilities, employment, and skills devoted to the production and distribution of aluminum and related products to the public on an international scale. This purpose is based on the following convictions:

1. That aluminum possesses superior properties for a large number of uses, is derived from raw materials which are abundant, and, by combining lightness in weight and ease of recycling, incorporates qualities of energy conservation superior to many other materials;

2. That responsible, competitive, private enterprise is the most efficient system for producing and making aluminum available to the public at large. We believe that the role is complementary to the responsibility of governments to develop their own priorities and goals, to set legal and taxation frameworks for corporate enterprises within their jurisdictions and thus to share in the economic benefits of industrialization;

3. That partnerships with national and local governments are on occasion appropriate, provided that our business objectives and their development aspirations are compatible.

Alcan's Objectives

Recognizing that the conduct and effectiveness of an organization is highly dependent upon the quality of the people who comprise it, Alcan's ability to fulfill its purpose and to serve the following interdependent objectives is seen to require a complement of able employees who place a high value not only on the interests of the Company but also on the interests of other individuals and entities with whom they relate both inside and outside Alcan.

These objectives are:

1. To operate at a level of profitability which will ensure the long-term economic viability of the Company by providing a return on the shareholders' investment which compares favourably with other industries of similar capital intensity and risk and will enable the Company to attract capital adequate to support its growth;

2. To maintain an organization of able and committed individuals in the

NOTE: Alcan's "Policies" are not reprinted in this appendix.

many countries in which we operate and to provide opportunities for growth and advancement both nationally and internationally;

3. To strive for a level of operating, technical, and marketing excellence which will ensure a strong competitive position in the various markets which we serve;

4. To recognize and seek to balance the interests of our shareholders, employees, customers, suppliers, and governments and the public at large, while achieving Alcan's business objectives, taking into account the differing social, economic, and environmental aspirations of the countries and communities in which we operate;

5. To maintain high standards of integrity in the conduct of all phases of our business.

CASE 4
AMERICAN SKATE CORPORATION

Introduction

In August 1979 Alan Adams, general manager of American Skate Corporation, and C. Herbert Charlton, president of American Skate's Canadian parent, Dominion Skate and, incidentally, Adams' father-in-law, were reviewing the $2 million financial package put together during the summer of 1979 for the opening of a roller skate plant in Berlin, New Hampshire. The New Hampshire plant was viewed by both men as being a critical element in the Canadian parent's plan for a major U.S. expansion to take advantage of the tremendous roller skating boom in North America. Nonetheless, Alan Adams and Herb Charlton wanted to reconsider all the relevant aspects of the plan before making a final decision to proceed with the Berlin plant. The proposed package involved $1,650,000 long-term debt from various U.S. and New Hampshire development groups, a lease-purchase agreement totalling $500,000 for a 44,000-square-foot plant capable of initially adding 20 percent and, within a year, 200 percent to Dominion's production capacity. All of the debt issued to the subsidiary American Skate was to be guaranteed by both Dominion Skate, which owned all of American Skate's stock, and by Herb Charlton personally.

"Alan, I don't mind going out on the limb if the deal is a good one," Herb told his son-in-law, "but I want you to help me double-check this New Hampshire project in all its aspects. I know I've called the shots pretty much so far, but this will be your baby."

The following paragraphs describe the roller skate industry, the background of both Dominion and American Skate and of their top managements, and the financial package that had been put together during the spring and summer of 1979.

The Roller Skating Industry

Roller skates were first introduced in Holland during the 18th century, and consisted of wooden spools strung on a wooden frame, which was in turn nailed onto the bottom of wooden shoes. These skates were difficult to turn, but this problem was overcome by an American inventor, James Leonard Plympton of New York. In 1863 Plympton put four independent wooden wheels on a shoe,

This case has been prepared by John Barnett, University of New Hampshire (Jonathan Foster, London School of Economics) as a basis for class discussion and is not intended to illustrate either effective or ineffective handling of an administrative situation. ©1985.

making the skate easier to turn. This original pair of Plympton's skates is now housed in the National Museum of Roller Skating in Lincoln, Nebraska, along with pictures of the first roller skating arena, which Mr. Plympton opened in New York a few years later.

The modern roller skate consists of the boot, a base plate, wheels and ball bearings, and the toe stop. The manufacturing process of a complete roller skate includes the following steps: (1) using sets of dies to cut the various parts of the boot from leather or other boot material; (2) machine stitching the various parts of the boot including adding "counters" of reinforcing material in the heel and adding eyelets; (3) stitching the boot together around a mould of a foot, called a *last*; (4) buffing or "roughing" the leather so that it would accept glue; (5) using a combination of glue and staples and a series of machine steps to complete the toe and heel; (6) removing the last; (7) attaching the base plate; (8) securing the wheels and toe stops to the base plate; and (9) inspecting and packing.

Very few manufacturers performed all these steps. Many bought the finished boot from others and attached the base plate, wheels, and toe stop. The manufacturers sold completed skates to sporting goods retailers, distributors, and wholesalers, to chain stores, and to roller skating rinks.

The stimulus for growth in the roller skating industry came from skateboard technology. During the skateboard craze in the mid-1970s, wide polyurethane wheels and precision bearings were perfected that allowed for a quiet ride on pavement. Further, the polyurethane wheels were much more absorbent than earlier metal or hard rubber wheels. As the roller skate manufacturers adopted these wheels and bearings in the late 1970s, the roller skate explosion began as skates moved out of rinks and into the streets and parks.

The roller skating industry just prior to the 1978–79 explosion consisted of a few privately held companies of which Dominion Skate was the only fully integrated major manufacturer. *Time* magazine reported that total industry sales were about a million pairs of skates per year.[1] The major firms included Roller Derby Skate, Chicago Roller Skate, Dominion Skate, and Sure-Grip International, and total dollar sales for the industry were estimated by the casewriters as $25 to $30 million. Roller Derby Skate of Litchfield, Illinois, *Business Week* observed, "dominated U.S. roller skate manufacturing with aggressive pricing of its low-end models."[2]

The roller skate explosion had North America and international repercussions. Exhibit 1 shows *Business Week*'s estimate of 1979 sales by the U.S. leaders.

Keith Parker, the marketing vice president of Nash Manufacturing, described how his company, a major skateboard manufacturer, converted to roller skates in a 60-day period in the fall of 1978. Producing 8,000 pairs a day by the summer of 1979, Parker commented:

---

[1]*Time,* August 6, 1979, p. 66.
[2]*Business Week,* August 27, 1979, p. 120.
[3]Ibid.

EXHIBIT 1 Typical Estimated 1979 Sales

Company	Estimated 1979 Sales in Millions of Dollars
Roller Derby Skate (Litchfield, Illinois)	$ 50–60
Nash Manufacturing (Fort Worth, Texas)	25
Sure-Grip International/RC Sports (California)	20–25
Chicago Roller Skate (Chicago, Illinois)	15–20
Mattel (California)	7–10
Total top five U.S. companies	$117–140
Estimated total U.S. sales	$ 200

SOURCE: *Business Week,* August 27, 1979, p. 120.

The key to our success is that we've expanded much quicker than others. But demand has to hold for another year if we're going to make much profit. . . . The skate business is in such an uproar that we could ship a million pairs tomorrow and still have back orders.[3]

New U.S. manufacturers joined the industry, including Nash and Mattel, the $500 million toy manufacturer that invested over $1 million to begin producing roller skates in March 1979. Further, foreign manufacturers expanded into the North American market. Imports rose from $2 million in 1978 to $30 million in 1979, led by Taiwanese imports. Over 90 factories produced skates in Taiwan, and that nation soon had 85 percent of the U.S. imported market.[4]

The top-of-the-line, premium-priced skates continued to be manufactured in the United States. While children's and low-priced skates might retail from $20 to $50, with adults' prices averaging $60, the well-regarded competition skates produced by the Dayton-based Snyder Skate Company were selling from $110 to $175 a pair. Snyder reports 1979 sales up 30 percent from 1978.

Articles on roller skating appeared in almost every major periodical during 1979, including *Changing Times, The Saturday Evening Post, Popular Mechanics, People, McCalls, Redbook,* and *Glamour.* Skates were endorsed by O. J. Simpson and were worn by Linda Ronstadt on a phonograph album cover. The number of roller skating rinks doubled to over 6,000 during the 1970–78 period—500 new rinks were being added in 1979—and roller disco became a major leisure activity.

Bill Butler, the "Godfather of Roller Disco," looked forward to the opening in the fall of 1979 of his chic New York nightspot, the Roller Ballroom. Butler, who had skated for 38 of his 45 years, had a perspective on skating including a

[4]*The Wall Street Journal,* April 6, 1981, p. 25.

"whole philosophy of life" based on the sport. Nonetheless, *Popular Mechanics* commented:

> New products come on the market so fast nowadays that even the Godfather of Roller Disco has trouble keeping up. Consider, for example, the two cycle, 1.2 HP engine that Motoboard International of Sunnyvale, California, suggests you slip on the back of your skate. For $289 you can zip down the highway at 40 MPH with the wind blowing through your hair and your whole life passing before your eyes.[5]

Sports Illustrated devoted several pages to a guide on buying skates in its October 15, 1979, issue and specifically recommended Reidell and Oberhamer tops for boots ($40 to $90 retail), Chicago or Sure-Grip for the plates and wheels ($20 to $100 retail), and Snyder as the top of the line, with custom skates as high as $400 a pair. Butler commented that his ideal choice was a plate by Snyder, a Reidell boot, and Krypto wheels.

Positive signs for the roller skating industry included a Gallup Poll in early 1979 that showed roller skating fifth in popularity among teenagers, ahead of both tennis and skiing and following basketball, baseball, swimming, and bowling. Both the Girl Scouts and the Boy Scouts gave merit badges for roller skating proficiency.

Fifty percent of the U.S. teenage market would represent about 25 million pairs of skates. The total of North American skaters was estimated at between 30 and 40 million individuals, most of whom skated at rinks where rental skates were available. Chicago Roller Skate was particularly aggressive in skating rink sales.

Many commentators were optimistic. A vice president of Herman's World of Sporting Goods reported a 400 percent increase in skate sales during the first half of 1979 at its 90 stores and noted that "the only thing that is slowing growth is product availability."[6] Mattel's Louis Miraula stated:

> The universe of potential skaters is enormous. Because of the new wheel, people discovered roller skating was an outdoor sport, à la jogging, but a lot more fun. The growth of this industry has a fad quality right now, but there is still that hard-core business that is not going to change substantially.[7]

The optimistic manufacturers predicted $400 million in annual skate sales would be achieved by the early 1980s.

Somewhat more cautious views were expressed in the August 27, 1979, issue of *Business Week* by Chicago Skate, which had concentrated on rink sales:

> An idiot could make money in today's market. I'm walking on tiptoe, trying to gauge whether this is just another fad or has several years of life. [Joseph Sheuelson, *Vice President, Sales, Chicago Skate*]

---

[5]*Popular Mechanics* 151 (June 1979).
[6]*Business Week,* August 27, 1979, p. 120.
[7]Ibid.

by Roller Derby's national sales manager:

The demand is tremendous, but we don't know exactly where it is going. In many ways, what is happening is as new to us as to anybody, although we're the leader in the business. [Kenneth Neidl, *National Sales Manager, Roller Derby Skate*]

and by Sure-Grip/RC Sports:

This is an extremely fast-growing industry, paralleling the sustained demand for bicycles that began 10 years ago. Most manufacturers are now living in a fairy-tale world where demand exceeds supply. In such an atmosphere, those that don't keep their heads could get hurt very badly. [Dennis Lane, *International Marketing Director, RC Sports*]

A more negative view was expressed by a financial analyst:

By its very definition, the "in thing" gets stale after a while. When everyone who is interested in roller skates has a couple of pairs, that's going to be it. [Harold Vogel, *Leisure Industries Analyst, Merrill Lynch*]

Brunswick Corp., the national sporting goods company, sold its small skate division. A skateboard manufacturer, whose 1979 sales were one fifth of 1978's, said he couldn't tell if "roller skates might be like skateboards—here today, gone tomorrow."

Dominion and American Skate

Dominion Skate's Early Years

Herb Charlton had gone to work for his uncle, owner of Dunn's Skate, Ltd., when he was very young. By the time his uncle died in 1946, Herb, then 32, had had substantial experience in all aspects of roller skate manufacture. Not wishing to continue working for his aunt, Herb left Dunn's and began Dominion Skate in the basement of his house near Mississauga, Ontario. Within a few years, Dominion and its three employees overflowed Herb's basement and garage and moved into a vacant school a few doors from the house. In 1958 an older plant facility in Mississauga, a short drive from Herb's house, was leased, giving Dominion a 3,000-square-foot, two-storied building. Additions were made to this plant in 1962, 1970, and 1972. A second plant was leased 15 miles away in Toronto in 1973 and an assembly plant in Mississauga in January 1979. By August 1979 Dominion employed 120 people at three rented locations:

Location	Year Opened	Activity	Square Feet
Mississauga	1958	Manufacturing, assembly	20,000
Toronto	1973	Manufacturing, assembly	20,000
Mississauga	1979	Assembly	10,000

Each plant had a salaried plant manager, each of whom had worked with Herb for some time. Herb Charlton's policy of no layoffs and competitive wages resulted in a hard-working labour force that also had a low turnover rate.

Management

Herb Charlton, 65 years old in 1979, was president and chief financial officer of Dominion Skate and president of American Skate. While Herb made all important decisions, he was assisted by his son Paul, 33, director of plant engineering, his daughter Naomi, 31, office manager, and his son-in-law Alan Adams, 37, production manager and, more recently, general manager of the American subsidiary, American Skate Corporation.

Like Herb Charlton, Alan had dropped out of school and had held several positions as a factory worker and as a printer's apprentice. In 1958 Alan, then 17, went to work for Dominion Skate at the suggestion of Herb's daughter whom Alan was then dating and to whom he was subsequently married.

Dominion sold roller skates, ice skates, and children's double-runner bob skates through a distributor to a small group of retail accounts throughout Canada, ice skates helping offset the seasonality of roller skates. Paul and Alan would occasionally call on these retail accounts, or Herb would infrequently show customers around the Ontario plants. Dominion had a reputation with its customers for a high-quality, medium-priced skate. Dominion had kept pace with industry technology, and its advertisements referred to its "space age skates" with models called "All American Dream" and "Inertia."

U.S. sales were handled by a marketing firm, King R. Lee and Associates, Santa Ana, California. King Lee in turn called on 10 specialty distributors in the United States.

Operations were financed by small working capital loans from local banks, by advances from Herb Charlton, and by trade credit.

Total production capacity was about 285,000 pairs a year. This capacity was based upon one-shift operations. Alan Adams noted that Herb Charlton didn't like to have more than one shift.

> I guess it was partially due to his wanting to be on top of things. Herb relied on personal inspection rather than formal production control systems. This philosophy of personal control extended to stock ownership as well. I had asked him about my owning some stock, so that I could have some security, but even after 20 plus years of working for him, I never got any stock.

Financial Results

Exhibits 2, 3, and 4 present balance sheets, income statements, and related financial statistics for the years of 1976, 1977, and 1978, and the six months ending June 1979.

EXHIBIT 2

DOMINION SKATE CO., LTD.
Balance Sheet
(Canadian $)

	For Six Months Ended June 30, 1979	For the Year Ended December 31		
		1978	1977	1976
Assets				
Current assets:				
Cash, certificates of deposit..........	$ 109,100	$ 239,700	$173,800	$ 22,400
Accounts receivable........................	1,081,300	682,600	464,000	286,300
Net inventory.................................	486,000	461,700	218,300	211,500
Total current assets...............	1,676,400	1,384,000	856,100	520,200
Fixed assets — net:				
Machinery, equipment...................	93,100	103,400	78,100	50,400
Vehicles, leasehold improvements..	23,400	26,700	13,300	4,400
Total fixed assets....................	116,500	130,100	91,400	54,800
Other assets:				
Goodwill..	15,000	15,000	15,000	15,000
Land deposits................................	211,200	211,200	–	–
Total other assets...................	226,200	226,200	15,000	15,000
Total assets............................	$2,019,100	$1,740,300	$962,500	$590,000
Liabilities				
Accounts payable, accruals...............	$ 636,800	$ 706,100	$497,400	$257,600
Taxes payable....................................	173,700	170,200	38,600	12,200
Bank loan..	–0–	50,000	–0–	95,000
Shareholder advances........................	246,600	219,900	101,200	54,800
Total liabilities.......................	1,057,100	1,146,200	637,200	419,600
Equity				
Preferred stock.................................	100	100	100	100
Retained earnings.............................	961,900	594,000	325,200	170,300
Total equity............................	962,000	594,100	325,300	170,400
Total liabilities, equity...........	$2,019,100	$1,740,300	$962,500	$590,000

EXHIBIT 3

DOMINION SKATE CO., LTD.
Income Statement
(Canadian $)

	For Six Months Ended June 30, 1979	For the Year Ended December 31		
		1978	*1977*	*1976*
Sales..................................	$2,655,800	$4,267,100	$3,182,600	$1,518,600
Less: Cost of sales.........................	1,581,900	2,540,500	2,099,900	889,200
Gross profit.................................	1,073,900	1,725,600	1,082,700	629,400
Operating expenses:				
Administrative payroll, sales commissions...........................	410,500	811,800	649,800	445,800
Supplies, freight........................	65,500	137,500	69,300	51,300
Advertising................................	1,100	10,600	3,400	2,400
Insurance....................................	12,200	15,800	9,700	6,800
Professional fees........................	1,800	2,200	1,200	900
Office expenses..........................	4,500	10,500	6,700	4,600
Repairs......................................	3,300	2,700	2,100	500
Rent...	34,300	52,800	42,000	33,800
Telephone, Utilities....................	13,400	20,000	15,400	11,100
Travel..	1,300	1,300	500	200
Vehicle......................................	2,400	2,200	4,100	2,800
Miscellaneous*...........................	27,500	54,400	30,200	16,400
Depreciation..............................	13,600	34,400	24,800	15,000
Bad debt....................................	12,700	21,500	1,000	(5,300)
Total operating expenses........................	604,100	1,177,700	860,200	586,300
Operating profit............................	469,800	547,900	222,500	43,100
Interest expense............................	5,900	5,100	9,200	6,800
Taxes...	180,500	189,300	58,500	17,400
Total.......................................	186,400	194,400	67,700	24,200
Profit after tax.............................	$ 283,400	$ 353,500	$ 154,800	$ 18,900

*Donations (Baptist Church) 1978, 1979 at annual rate of $22,000. Pensions at annual rate of $11,000 (1978), $15,000 (1979). Balance is discounts.

The Financial Package

Berlin, New Hampshire, was considered as a site for U.S. expansion because a Canadian supplier had recently expanded into New Hampshire and had told Charlton that he "got a good deal" in New Hampshire. Northern New Hamp-

EXHIBIT 4 Dominion Skate Co., Ltd. (selected financial statistics)

	1979 (6 months)	1978	1977	1976
Solvency:				
Debt/equity	1.1	1.9	2.0	2.5
Times interest earned	79.6	107.4	24.2	6.3
Liquidity:				
Net working capital	$619,300	$237,800	$218,900	$100,600
Current ratio	1.6	1.2	1.3	1.2
Funds management:				
Days sales in receivables	74	58	53	68
Days cost goods in payables	72	101	87	107
Inventory turnover	5.6	12.6	14.8	
Profitability:				
Return on sales	11%	8%	5%	1%
Return on assets	14	20	16	3
Return on equity	29	60	48	11

shire was less than a day's drive from Toronto and less than half a day's drive from Montreal, where Dominion's Canadian distributor was located. Finally, Berlin development groups had actively pursued Dominion, once its expansion interests were known.

The financial plan put together as of August 1979 included (1) a working capital loan of $1,150,000 from the Economic Development Administration (EDA), a branch of the U.S. Department of Commerce; (2) a loan of $100,000 from a New Hampshire venture capital group; (3) a loan of $400,000 from the Berlin (New Hampshire) Economic Development Council (BEDCO); and (4) a lease-purchase agreement with the Berlin Industrial Development and Park Authority (BIDPA).

Berlin, New Hampshire, about 175 miles north of Boston, had a serious unemployment problem among its population of 13,000. The Converse Rubber Company, a manufacturer of athletic shoes, had closed in early 1979, laying off 400. The only significant employers in Berlin were the James River Paper Company, employing 1,200 to 1,500, and Bass Shoe, employing 250 to 350. Thus BEDCO and BIDPA were anxiously encouraging American Skate to locate in Berlin. BEDCO, directed by a board of business and labour officials and city government representatives, usually lent $5,000 for every job created by a new employer. BEDCO offered American Skate $400,000 at 6 percent annual interest, due in quarterly installments of $10,000, provided that American match its $400,000 with equity.

BIDPA, the developer/administrator of a small industrial park, had a board of directors similar to BEDCO. BIDPA had already built a 44,000-square-foot building, which was vacant and incurring interest charges. BIDPA offered American a 22-year lease-purchase agreement totaling $500,000, with gradually increasing monthly payments. Real estate taxes were waived.

In addition to the Berlin debt, a New Hampshire venture capital group also offered a $100,000 loan at prime (then about 12 percent) plus 1 percent. The state of New Hampshire was, of course, attractive to Charlton and Adams as it had no personal state income, sales, or use taxes and was replacing inventory and similar taxes with a flat 8 percent of net profits tax on businesses.

The EDA offered a 10½ percent $1,150,000 loan, payable over seven years, with gradually increasing monthly payments. Thus, pressure for economic support expressed itself not only from local and state groups but at the federal level as well.

Equipment for the Berlin plant location was available to American Skate for $130,000 from Tiera Footwear of Dover, New Hampshire, which was in liquidation. Tiera's equipment would be sufficient for American's needs.

In trying to determine sales and costs, Herb Charlton and Alan Adams asked King Lee for an estimate of the potential total skate orders from Lee's 10 U.S. distributors for all skate manufacturers. This estimate, totalling 586,500 pairs a year, is reproduced in Exhibit 5. Lee was unsure what percentage of these total orders American Skate might expect to receive.

Dominion Skate estimated its own Canadian sales potential as 312,000 pairs a year. As mentioned above, Dominion's current productive capacity was 286,000 pairs a year. Dominion estimated that the total North American industry sales for all manufacturers would climb from the pre-1979 level of $30 million to over $200 million in the early 1980s, falling to $100 million by 1984.

The Berlin plant would initially produce at an annual level of 65,000 pairs and within one year could be producing as many as 520,000 pairs on a two-shift

Exhibit 5   Estimated Total Skate Orders by Lee's 10 Distributors for All Skates of All Manufacturers

Firm	Annual Volume in Pairs
Gordon & Smith, San Diego, California	93,500
L. Cohen, Los Angeles, California	20,500
Smoothill, San Rafael, California	65,000
West Coast Cycle, Culver City, California	156,000
Bike Factory, Bellevue, Washington	31,000
Donel Distributors, Garland, Texas	31,000
Southeastern Sales, Florence, Alabama	15,500
Tuflex, Ft. Lauderdale, Florida	78,000
A.W.H. Sales, Evanston, Illinois	65,000
Lubins, Watertown, Massachusetts	31,000
Total	586,500

EXHIBIT 6 Cost Estimates for Average Pair of Skates

Selling price		$12.95
Materials:		
Boot	$2.85	
Plate	.77	
Wheels	1.28	
Bearings	1.04	
Toe stop	.14	
Hardware	.35	
Axle	.20	
Box	.19	
Other	.16	
Total materials	6.98	
Labour	.75	
Selling commission	1.56	
Total cost		9.29
Gross profit		$ 3.66

---

basis. Initial employment of 100 should be 300 in two years, if the company's predictions were accurate.

The differential cost of producing a pair of skates was estimated by the company as shown in Exhibit 6. This cost is for an average pair and would be equally true for Ontario or New Hampshire production. New Hampshire administrative salaries would be about $200,000 a year, half of which would be the general manager's salary, and other overhead costs might be an additional $100,000.

Summary

Both Herb Charlton and Alan Adams believed that the financial package available to them now could not be modified further. At a meeting to reach a decision on the Berlin plant, the following dialogue occurred:

    Adams: In addition to liens on all the equipment, you will have to personally guarantee all these loans. But how can you beat $400,000 at 6 percent and $1,150,000 at 1½ percent below prime?

    Charlton: Alan, I believe in growth. Every two or three years we've leased new space or bought new equipment. That cycle means 1979 is a year for more growth. Still, it will be your project to live with. What do you think?

CASE 5
CANADIAN TIRE CORPORATION (CONDENSED)

In November 1981 Dean Muncaster, president and CEO of the Canadian Tire Corporation (CTC), was assessing the position he should take with respect to the takeover of White Stores, Inc., which was headquartered in Wichita Falls, Texas. Since 1977 CTC had been looking for an opportunity to expand to the United States and preferably into the Sunbelt states. For a price that was not to exceed $45 million (U.S.) pending a year-end audit, CTC would acquire White's 81 retail stores, 4 warehouses, trucking fleet, and access to more than 425 independent dealer-owned stores centred in Texas, Louisiana, Oklahoma, and 11 other states. It was now up to Dean Muncaster to decide if he should recommend to the board that Canadian Tire proceed with the purchase.

History of Canadian Tire

In 1922, two brothers, Alfred and John Billes, invested $1,900 and formed Hamilton Tire and Garage Ltd. in Hamilton, Ontario. They dealt primarily in automobile parts and servicing. The firm, renamed Canadian Tire, grew quickly and in 1927 had three stores in Toronto. During the 1930s, the company started supplying other automobile parts and service centres in Ontario. Prior to World War II, six stores existed in Ontario.

The Billes family demonstrated significant innovation during their early years, a trademark that remained as one of the cornerstones to the firm's success. For instance, the first CTC store on Yonge Street in Toronto in 1937 had stockroom clerks on roller skates moving parts to the sales counter for faster customer service time. CTC adopted computer-aided accounting and inventory control procedures as early as 1963. Throughout the 1970s, CTC built one of the most modern distribution networks in the country, utilizing the latest technology in warehousing and inventory control.

By the end of 1981 the firm had grown to 348 retail stores and 83 gasoline stations. The product line had been expanded to include hardware products, lawn-care products, sporting goods, and small household appliances. Internationally, CTC had purchased a 36 percent controlling interest in McEwan's Ltd. of Australia in 1979.

Much of the success of CTC was attributed by some observers to the leadership of Dean Muncaster, age 48, who had been involved with CTC since he was 12 years old. Muncaster had worked in his father's store in Sudbury during

This case was written primarily from published sources by Mark C. Baetz and Ralph Troschke, School of Business and Economics, Wilfrid Laurier University. Copyright © 1986 by Mark C. Baetz; condensed, 1989.

the summers while attending the University of Western Ontario and Northwestern. In 1957 he was hired by Canadian Tire as a financial analyst. Approximately two years later, he left Canadian Tire in Toronto and returned to Sudbury to be the manager of the Sudbury dealership held by his father. He returned to Toronto in 1961 as a vice president and became president in 1966. During his presidency, CTC's sales rose from $100 million to over $1.3 billion (1981), and after-tax net income reached $51.4 million or $4.05 per share. He was well liked and respected by CTC's dealer network and by Canadian financial experts.

Muncaster was faced with managing three divergent groups while steering CTC. The three groups were, first, Alfred Billes and his family; second, the heirs of John Billes headed by John's son, Dick; and, third, the dealer network. The two factions of the Billes family collectively controlled 60.8 percent of the voting shares in the corporation (representing only 8.5 percent of all outstanding shares) and were not always in agreement with one another. For example, Muncaster's decision to enter the Australian market was heavily contested between the two family groups, with Dick Billes in favour and Alfred Billes in opposition. The decision left its scars.

The Billes family was active in the corporation. They managed several stores and held directorships on the board. Their influence was not always evident to the general public as they shunned the limelight and the media.

The Canadian Tire Success Formula

CTC was extremely successful due to the corporation's emphasis on the dealer-run network, advantages incurred from its highly modernized distribution system, and a marketing program that clearly established its desired image in the minds of the consumers. The dealer-manager network was the cornerstone to CTC's success and essential in an understanding of corporate values and strategies.

The dealer-run stores were a type of franchise operation. CTC usually owned the building (87 percent of the time) and acted as the central buyer, distributor, national advertiser, and dealer recruiter. The dealer ran the store as his own business. He would buy all of his goods from CTC (approximately 6,000 of 32,000 products were mandatory), and most operational decisions (for example, personnel, local advertising, and so forth) were his to make. CTC wanted to blend the entrepreneurial spirit with that of a corporate manager. It was hoped that this arrangement would provide individual dealers with enough incentive to turn their stores into a success. The dealers did not have to pay franchise fees but had to invest a minimum of $50,000 into their location. They were free to reap as much profit as they could from their stores.

The corporation was very careful in its selection of prospective dealers. The ability to invest at least $50,000 was not the only criterion. Exhaustive examinations and interviews were utilized to trim the 1,000–1,200 applicants down to the final 50 trainees. The trainees spent three months of in-class training followed by six months of in-store training before posting to a store. Corporate support was always available after the training period on any retailing issue, and dealer-support group meetings were numerous. The system worked so well, in fact, that virtually no dealer failure was encountered by CTC.

The desire for revenues and profits was instilled through the dealer-run network. The advanced distribution system ensured that the parent corporation managed its costs to make its own profit. As well, by having the right merchandise in the right store at the right time, the system ensured customer satisfaction. The key ingredients in this distribution system were three fully automated one-storied warehouses (one in Edmonton and two in Toronto) that utilized robotics, conveyor belts, and computerized cataloguing of parts. The inventory levels of the warehouses, as well as those of individual retail operators, were monitored by computers. Reorder points of the retail and wholesale levels were automatically triggered on a nightly basis. This ensured a maximum delivery time of two days to retail outlets.

The result of CTC's advanced distribution system, from a customer's point of view, was constant availability and selection of thousands of products that CTC carried. This became a trademark of the firm. Inventories were also reduced, increasing CTC's inventory turnover and decreasing its carrying charges. This made profitability easier to attain for CTC and its retailers.

The constant availability and broad selection of numerous products were part of an image that CTC had built for itself through an effective marketing campaign. Consumers also came to know Canadian Tire as a retail outlet offering value with a reputation for low price. This was especially important during 1981 as inflation, interest rates, and unemployment all rose. The value–low price appeal attracted a lot of people who had turned into "do-it-yourselfers" during this period. The average purchase at a Canadian Tire store was $15, and these purchases were said to be interest-rate-proof as they were small "must" expenditures. While the average purchase seemed low, CTC would see approximately 2 million customers per week according to Muncaster.

The typical customer found it difficult to enter the store and buy just one item. Due to the firm's low prices and broad product lines, it was not uncommon to witness the typical customer filling up a shopping basket with various products.

Muncaster identified several additional key factors to CTC's success: (1) CTC became known as a place for "more than just tires," a theme employed in its advertising. Traditionally, 80 percent of CTC's customers had been male, but by 1981, the split was almost even. (2) To lure customers back to the store, the firm employed "Canadian Tire money," which was a form of discount coupons given to customers after each cash purchase. (3) Twice per year, 7 million catalogues listing the entire CTC product line were published and distributed to households across Canada.

These factors led to unusually high growth rates and startling financial successes for CTC. Exhibit 1 highlights the performance of the corporation during this period of high growth and image development. Walter Hachborn, general manager of Home Hardware Stores Ltd., CTC's major Canadian competitor, explained the success of CTC in the following way: "Canadian Tire has

Exhibit 1 Four-Year Review of Performance (dollars in thousands except per share amounts)

	1981	1980	1979	1978	1977
Comparative Income Statement					
Gross operating revenue................	$1,340,764	$1,057,536	$935,753	$798,717	$718,114
Pre-tax income..............................	100,432	72,240	69,583	53,938	52,240
Taxes on income............................	48,966	34,513	33,070	25,163	23,750
Income before extraordinary					
gain..	51,466	37,727	36,513	28,775	28,490
Extraordinary gain.........................	2,212	901	2,195	694	1,000
Net income.....................................	53,678	38,628	38,708	29,469	29,490
Cash dividends..............................	9,936	8,487	7,017	10,435	5,800
Income retained and					
reinvested..................................	43,742	30,141	31,691	19,034	23,690
Comparative Balance Sheet					
Current assets................................		435,183	343,372	312,831	277,894
Investments...................................		44,151	49,371	1,823	1,014
Net property and equipment........		266,854	244,496	235,989	218,209
Other assets...................................		2,213	2,582	3,620	4,026
Total assets....................................		748,401	639,821	554,263	501,143
Current liablities...........................		279,451	211,903	165,040	134,511
Long-term debt..............................		136,387	136,361	138,377	142,317
Deferred income taxes...................		3,599	3,822	3,382	1,512
Shareholders' equity......................		328,964	287,735	247,464	222,803
Per Share Data					
Income before extraordinary					
gain..	4.05	3.07	3.07	2.49	2.50
Net income.....................................	4.22	3.14	3.26	2.55	2.59
Dividends.......................................	.78	.69	.59	.90	.51
Shareholders' equity......................	30.44	26.75	24.20	21.40	19.59
Statistics at Year-End					
Number of associate stores...........		333	319	314	314
Number of gasoline stations..........		71	64	62	61
Number of Class A share-					
holders..		8,665	9,310	10,435	10,035
Number of common share-					
holders..		1,252	1,315	1,450	1,417

Source: For years 1977–80: Canadian Tire annual report, 1980; for 1981: Estimated.

succeeded because of excellent marketing and superior merchandising combined with the fact that they were the first to fill a void in the Canadian retailing market. They happened to come along at the right time and place."

Suppliers to CTC were also impressed with CTC operations. One supplier noted: "We've been impressed by the energy levels exhibited by the CTC head office when negotiating contracts, and although they have pushed the cost of advertising our product in their catalogue on to us, we consider their organization as top-notch."

Despite the phenomenal growth, it was apparent to Muncaster and other senior CTC executives that CTC growth could not be sustained indefinitely. Since 1977 CTC had been following a master plan prepared by Muncaster for future growth. The strategy in 1977 was to blanket the Canadian market by expanding into British Columbia, as yet untapped, and by establishing retail outlets in any community or suburban area that could support a regular-size CTC store. It was estimated in 1980 that 65 percent of Canadians lived within 15 minutes of a Canadian Tire store, and it was felt that by 1985, the maximum penetration of 400 stores would be reached.

The strategy also called for growth into other countries and markets with an English language/cultural component as well as a similar economic base. The Australian entry had taken place in 1979, and the United States was earmarked for entry in 1981. Carrying the CTC concept into these countries was not expected to be difficult, and consumer acceptance was anticipated to be high.

The need to expand was foremost in the mind of Muncaster. Without further expansion, an adverse impact on operating performance was anticipated. Expansion in British Columbia was well underway by 1981, and CTC had attempted to diversify somewhat by getting into gasoline stations and a small automobile engine remanufacturing plant for resale of the engines at its stores. These developments merely held off the inevitable total market saturation by CTC.

The Australian venture into McEwan's, a hardware chain, was intended to allow CTC to enter Australia to gain a foothold, then to expand its operations and to conquer Australia as Canada was conquered. The Australian venture was a small one, involving only a $2.2 million investment for a 36 percent interest. However, McEwan's suffered losses of $1,837,000 (Canadian) in 1980 and $548,000 in 1981. While performance was improving, CTC was disappointed. The Foreign Investment Review Board of Australia had also made it clear that it would prohibit CTC from acquiring a greater than 50 percent share in the Australian firm. CTC decided to sell off the investment in 1982 and use the funds of the sale toward the costs of an entry into the United States.

The Australian experience put some pressure on the president of CTC to seek out a successful expansion opportunity whereby the firm could parachute its Canadian success formula and reap large rewards. The original timetable called for an expansion to the U.S. market. Muncaster had favoured the Sunbelt states as they had exhibited the fastest growth in populations and incomes. Demographic trends from 1973 to 1981 definitely pointed to this area of the United States as a ripening market. Some disagreement existed in CTC management, as some favoured expansion to the northeast, where climatic conditions and automobile models tended to parallel those of the Canadian market more closely.

American/Sunbelt Retail Market Considerations

In its analysis of the Sunbelt area, CTC managers felt that no competitors had a stranglehold on the things that CTC did well. Given the successes in Canada which CTC had enjoyed even when the retailing industry was on a decline, the general consensus among the management in Toronto was that the Sunbelt market was a "sure-fired success." Long-term demographic studies were undertaken, and a heavy reliance was placed on their favourable findings (see Exhibit 2).

It was noted that only six major competitors existed for Canadian Tire in the Texas and Sunbelt markets: Sears Roebuck, Montgomery Ward, K mart, Builders Square, Home Depo, and Handy Dan. The first three competitors did, however, carry a lot of clout within the market. For example, Sears was heavily involved in auto parts and services, and it was not unusual for Sears to have 16 or more auto bays as opposed to 5–6 at White's. Wal-Mart, a potential entrant to this market and a major U.S. retailing force, had chosen at this point in time to forego expansion into the major metropolitan areas in the state of Texas.

On a television documentary, one prominent retail market analyst in Houston described the market characteristics of the United States and, in particular, the Sunbelt states, as follows:

1. In any U.S. market, three markets were at work: a national one, a regional one, and one based on local climate.
2. Retailing in the United States, and more so in the Sunbelt, was highly competitive and dynamic (the rate of change was far greater than in Canada).
3. The Sunbelt market was witnessing an ever-increasing number of retail entrants who were scrambling to get into very specific market niches.
4. Corporate image and advertising had to be slanted to two very different groups: the English- and the Spanish-speaking populations.
5. Promotional campaigns should take into account a high degree of illiteracy and a variety of racial problems (for example, white versus black, white versus Mexican, Mexican versus black).
6. The impact of revenues flowing from oil after 1973 had created a "gold rush" where even poorly run businesses could make money. New people were arriving every day.
7. Every neighbourhood in this area varied due to its ethnic composition.

Exhibit 2   Sample Demographics for Texas

---

1. Texas was the second-largest state in retail sales.
2. Houston was eighth and Dallas was ninth in terms of ranking the size of metropolitan statistical areas.
3. Dallas was expected to increase by 12.9 percent in population from 1980 to 1984; Houston by 14.2 percent; the U.S. average was only 5.2 percent.
4. Mean income (1977):

Dallas	$19,443
Houston	18,340
New York	16,714
U.S. average	17,137

8. Shopping malls predominated since most consumers preferred one-stop shopping.

9. Sunbelt consumers were sophisticated, however, and would visit a variety of shops (usually specialty stores) within one mall to accomplish their shopping needs.

10. Stores in the United States tended to be far larger, especially department stores, where 25,000 square feet would be considered a small area.

11. The U.S. consumer enjoyed a wide option of shopping choices (for example, it would have been typical to see 40 brands of an automotive product available on one shelf).

12. Older downtown areas were considered marginal and these "strip centres" tended to cater to neighbourhood traffic.

13. Hardware and sporting goods stores in Texas were a rarity as every major store sold this kind of merchandise.

14. Some observers considered the Houston area as the toughest market in the United States.

15. Consumers needed to identify with a firm's message (that is, a reason for its existence) in order for it to survive and prosper.

White Stores, Inc.

The White Stores were held by Household International Ltd. of Chicago, which was one of the largest retailers in the United States. At approximately $150 million (U.S.) in annual sales, White's represented only 4 percent of Household's revenues. It was an insignificant holding to this large firm and thus received very little attention from its owners.

Although White's was losing money, CTC felt that if the price was low enough, it could refurbish the units and have them take on a CTC philosophy and market appeal. It was felt that a time frame of two to three years would be necessary before White's could break even and start to contribute to corporate profits. It was felt that the added top management attention and CTC's successful Canadian strategy could turn this firm around and represent a springboard for further U.S. expansion.

With White's, CTC would be acquiring 81 retail outlets, access to supply 425 independent dealer-owned stores, and four warehouses. The chain of stores covered Texas (the majority), Louisiana, New Mexico, and Oklahoma as well as 10 other states. Approximately half of the White-owned outlets were on leased properties, while all of the real estate (that is, land and buildings) of the other half were owned by White Stores. The price tag of a maximum of $45 million (U.S.) seemed reasonable to CTC executives when compared to recent costs of $2.5 million per store to establish new outlets in British Columbia. Exhibit 3 shows a proposed financing scheme for the acquisition.

Exhibit 3 Purchase of White Stores—Financing (Canadian dollars in thousands)

Net working capital to be acquired..		$ 12,134
Property and equipment, including capitalized leases and lease-hold interests...	$35,658	
Long-term portion of capital lease obligations.....................................	(287)	35,371
Other assets..		208
Net assets to be acquired..		$ 47,713
The effect on consolidated working capital is:		
Use of working capital:		
Payment on closing...		$ 15,904
Promissory note due December 31, 1982.......................................		10,603
		26,507
Working capital to be acquired..		(12,134)
Net use of working capital..		$ 14,373

CTC saw other positive factors in the purchase option. The White Stores name was long established, and therefore CTC assumed the name would be a source of loyalty and brand recognition. White's had a store size (approximately 25,000 square feet) that was similar to that of the typical CTC store. As well, like CTC, White's had only a few brands for their products. In general, White Stores did many of the same things that CTC did: automotive service and parts sales; and other broad product lines were available which were similar to CTC except that White's carried furniture as well. This probably would be dropped if the purchase was made. Plenty of warehouse capacity existed. It was estimated that the four warehouses could conduct two to three times their existing volumes without any further capital. The current warehouse utilization rate varied between 30 and 50 percent. The infrastructure for expansion, therefore, was in place.

There were some concerns with an acquisition of White Stores. The locations of many of the stores were not in prime commercial or retail areas but, rather, in local neighbourhoods. In some of these neighbourhoods, the people were Mexican and could not read or understand English. CTC proposed to gradually relocate these by establishing a greater concentration of stores in prime retail space in the lucrative Dallas–Fort Worth market. Further, the 81 stores owned by White Stores were not dealer operated but company owned and operated. CTC felt that this would have to change and become a number one priority in terms of introducing its philosophy and corporate objectives. Although CTC would prefer a dealer network to replicate the strategy in Canada, some of the states containing White Stores locations prohibited exclusive distributor-dealer relationships because of antitrust legislation. Finally, most of the stores were in desperate need of refurbishing. A lot of the outlets were 20 to 30 years old and looked it. CTC did not feel that this would be a problem as it had anticipated having to pour up to an additional $100 million (U.S.) over the following 2½ years into the project.

Other Options

Other growth options had been tossed around CTC's corporate office in Toronto. One option being considered was to access the U.S. market by building a new chain from the ground up and, therefore, not be confined by an existing organization's limitations and problems. However, costs and the time commitment to establish a major foothold made this a difficult option to pursue. Another option was to search out an acquisition in the nearby northeastern U.S. states. One CTC executive who favoured this option noted: "We should expand to a market that is similar to our own—with the same climate, the same autos, and the same kind of products. A place that is close enough, that if there is a problem we can do something about it." But this meant ignoring the fastest-growing segment of the United States, namely, the Sunbelt. A third option involved oil and gas opportunities in Canada. The existing Liberal government in Ottawa heavily favoured Canadian involvement in this industrial sector. The difficulty here was a lack of expertise on the part of CTC's management in this field. A fourth option was vertical integration. The manufacture of CTC products would require a massive capital investment into a field where CTC again had little expertise, and production runs for only CTC dealers would not always prove economical. Furthermore, due to CTC's large size, it already controlled a fair amount of power in distribution channels and could, therefore, already influence prices to some extent. Finally, CTC could turn to real estate sales. The firm had already engaged in some of this type of business and had made a small amount of money at it. Interest rates, however, were unsettlingly high and unstable. Furthermore, the risk involved in a massive venture of this nature might not have been acceptable to CTC shareholders.

Muncaster had a difficult decision ahead of him. Growth in Canada for CTC would peak in approximately three to four years, so the groundwork for a new growth spurt would have to be laid down shortly. Shareholders would not react favourably to a flattening out of earnings per share after 1985. The White Stores acquisition would involve a major refurbishing program to bring the White Stores up to par, and this would create a temporary short-term drain on CTC's earnings.

The Turnaround Strategy

As the president and executive vice president of CTC more closely examined White Stores, they agreed on the following turnaround strategy if they were to acquire White's:

- There would be an aggressive renovation schedule at a cost of $100 million (U.S.) to be completed by the end of 1983. Up to 22 stores would be closed at any one time for up to two months for the renovation.
- CTC dealers would be brought in to run some of the stores with a goal of 81 dealer-run stores by the end of 1983.

Exhibit 4 Typical White's Store/White's Auto Centre

Typical store size in square feet (excluding auto bays):	
Gross area	24,000 sq. ft.
Selling area	14,000
Percent selling area to gross area	58%
Number of auto service bays	5–6
Store focus and sales mix:	
Auto	10–50%
Hardware	15–20
Lawn and garden	15
Sporting goods	15
Housewares	10
Electronics, miscellaneous	5
Percentage of products under promotion discounts	50
Typical inventory (at cost)	U.S. $900,000
Number of products carried	22,000
Final retail gross margin	16–22%
Store sales per year (breakeven point)	U.S. $2.5 million

- The merchandise mix (currently at 23,000 items) would be phased in gradually. (See Exhibit 4 for existing mix and other information on the typical store.)
- More money would be spent on advertising than was spent by the average U.S. retailer in order to develop a clear image. The predominant form of advertising would be flyers.
- The White Stores name would be retained to take advantage of existing customer loyalty.
- In order to gain market share and increase store traffic, White's would use loss leaders.
- In order to help dealers finance their inventories, credit would be given quite freely, although at the prevailing interest rates. If a dealer could not afford a shipment of goods, the price to the dealer would be lowered and the difference added to the notes payable to White's.
- No additional capital would be required to upgrade warehousing facilities since the four warehouses were remaining at 30–35 percent capacity.
- The independent dealer network would be reduced from the existing 425 to 300 stores by cutting off the outlying dealers.

Muncaster summarized the strategy: "We plan to change their [White's] merchandise offering substantially. . . . We believe the appeal will be in a merchandise offering which you see in a Canadian Tire Store." With this strategy, CTC expected White's to break even by the third year.

CASE 6
CANBEC SHOE LTD.

The trip back from Montreal to Actonvale, Quebec, seemed longer than usual for Jean Guy Dufour, president of CanBec Shoe Ltd., who was returning from a meeting with the Banque Nationale de Paris (BNP). The meeting had been relatively successful, but inconclusive. Certainly, the Bank's displeasure had been anticipated as CanBec's financial situation had been deteriorating over the past three years.

This early March 1991 meeting to review the 1990 results was the third in less than two months; although the bank had not formally suggested that it could no longer tolerate the situation, the pressures were unquestionably there. Dufour was fully aware of the fact that CanBec was considered by most banks to be competing in a very difficult industry. The Canadian domestic footwear industry had suffered significantly since the removal of quotas in the men's sector in late 1986 (see Exhibit 1). The good news was that since several of CanBec's domestic competitors had recently gone bankrupt, some market opportunities might open up for CanBec. On the other hand, their demise might be signalling the beginning of the end for the entire industry. For Dufour, the uncertainty of the future was clouded by CanBec's current problems. The BNP wanted corrective action, but how and where to act seemed anything but clear.

Canadian Footwear Industry

The Canadian footwear industry falls into three distinct gender categories including both leather and nonleather segments: men's and boys, women's and girls', and children's and infants'. In addition to these categories were athletic, waterproof, and plastic footwear segments as well as work-type footwear and slippers. Women's footwear was by far the largest category in terms of pairs purchased, followed by the athletic sector. (See Exhibits 2, 3, and 4 for additional details.)

The early and mid-1980s had been relatively good for the entire Canadian footwear industry including retailers, importers, and domestic manufacturers alike. The per capita consumption of footwear remained steady, while the aver-

SOURCE: This case was prepared by Professor James L. Bowey, Bishop's University, and Professor Allen Morrison, The University of Western Ontario, for the sole purpose of providing material for class discussion. Certain names and other identifying information may have been disguised to protect confidentiality. It is not intended to illustrate either effective or ineffective handling of a managerial situation. Any reproduction, in any form, of the material in this case is prohibited except with the written consent of the School.
Copyright 1992 © Bishop's University and The University of Western Ontario

EXHIBIT 1   Canadian Domestic Factory Closings 1985–1991

	Dress Shoes	Casuals	Boots
Bastien, Quebec City		X	X
C.N. Shoes, Toronto	X	X	
Cambrian, Cambridge	X		
Carlaw (men's), Toronto		X	
Corbeil Ltée, Assumption	X		X
Florsheim, London	X		
Greb Inc. Kitchener	X	X	
Grebec, Sherbrooke	X	X	
Jarman, Lachine	X		
Katerina, Quebec City		X	
Montergie, Contrecoeur			X
Nunn Bush	X	X	X
Swing Shoes, Toronto	X	X	X
Remaining Canadian Domestic Factories 1991			
Alfred Cloutier		X	
Bata Shoes, Batawa		X	X
College/Regence, Q.C.		X	X
DeLuca, Montreal	X	X	X
Hart/Dack, Fredricton	X	X	X
Genfoot, Montreal			X
Grenico, Quebec City		X	X
Greb-Kodiak, Actonvale			X
Henri-Pierre, Quebec		X	X
Kaufman	X	X	
Santana		X	X
Susan Shoes (Cougar)	X	X	X
Swing Ltd. (reemized)		X	X
Unico Shoes Ltd.	X	X	X

EXHIBIT 2   Footwear Production in Canada—1984–89 (000 pairs)

Footwear Category	1984	1985	1986	1987	1988	1989	1990	% Change 1984-90
Men's and boys'	7,302	6,216	5,480	4,284	3,472	3,108	2,224	−70
Women's and girls'	17,617	17,295	17,086	15,379	13,127	10,859	8,317	−53
Children's and infants'	2,188	2,326	1,611	1,259	1,138	812	564	−74
Waterproof and plastic	5,061	4,953	5,379	5,395	4,725	2,106	4,106	−19
Work-type footwear	2,935	3,134	3,182	2,670	5,420	5,980	5,769	+97
Slippers	7,082	7,098	7,117	6,427	5,464	5,550	5,532	−22
Athletic	2,378	1,956	1,660	1,777	1,920	3,230	3,191	+34
All other footwear	855	1,306	1,530	1,587	1,311	1,503	1,160	+36
Total	45,418	44,284	43,045	38,778	36,578	33,726	30,863	−32

Exhibit 3   Footwear Imports in Canada—1984–90 (000 pairs)

Footwear Category	1984	1985	1986	1987	1988	1989	1990	% Change 1984-90
Men's and boys'	5,870	6,430	8,653	10,559	7,015	7,476	9,024	+54
Women's and girls	16,898	18,869	20,571	22,293	17,089	22,858	22,647	+34
Children's and infants'	2,826	2,662	2,999	3,823	2,621	4,200	5,036	+78
Waterproof and plastic	11,197	7,918	7,131	5,235	5,952	5,493	5,369	-52
Work-type footwear	245	261	294	263	250	210	283	+16
Slippers	4,238	3,808	7,663	7,902	4,478	5,514	6,153	+45
Athletic	13,414	12,943	20,901	22,243	23,076	22,025	19,791	+48
All other footwear	7,648	6,252	7,246	9,638	10,766	10,798	10,212	+34
Total footwear imports	61,336	59,143	75,458	81,956	71,247	78,574	78,515	+28

Exhibit 4   Apparent Canadian Market—1984–89 (000 pairs)

	1984	1985	1986	1987	1988	1989	1990	% Change 1984-90
Production	45,418	44,284	43,045	38,778	36,578	33,725	30,863	-32
Less: exports	3,403	3,366	3,338	3,791	4,599	2,125	3,066	-10
	42,015	40,918	39,707	34,987	31,979	31,600	27,797	-34
Plus: imports	61,336	59,143	75,458	81,956	71,247	78,574	78,515	+28
Total market	103,351	100,061	115,165	116,943	103,226	110,174	106,312	+3
Import penetration	59.3%	59.1%	65.6%	70.0%	69.0%	71.3%	73.8%	

NOTE: Import figures up to 1987 are based on the old CITC classification system, while those for 1988 are based on the new Harmonized System. Because of this change, the 1987–88 comparison for imports in individual footwear categories cannot be regarded as reliable.

SOURCE: Statistics Canada Catalogues

age price/pair rose significantly versus inflation. Perhaps the only casualty of the past decade had been the once dominant wholesaler.

Wholesalers

Wholesalers had always played an important role in the distribution of footwear, particularly to the independent retailer. Wholesalers would carry many different product lines and cover vast geographic areas with their own dedicated sales force. Wholesalers typically combined orders for an entire territory to provide large volume orders for the domestic factories as well as stocking limited quantities to service the customers who could not meet the manufacturer's minimum order quantities. Although the wholesalers' service reduced some of the risks for both the small independents and the manufacturer, their role was being reduced. Declining sales had forced domestic manufacturers to reduce their minimum order quantities in order to attract additional business. In addition, the combination of high interest rates and improved forecasting skills had discounted the need for intermediary wholesalers. By the end of the 1980s, there remained only a few regional wholesalers.

Faced with diminishing sales, some wholesalers began carrying unbranded imported lines. Competition became extremely tough as traditional wholesalers generally had neither the importing skills nor the sourcing network to compete with previously established importers. New competition, in turn, put added pressure on the unbranded importers who were already facing their own set of challenges. As Canadian shoe quotas were phased out during the mid-1980s, quota ownership was no longer a barrier to entry and the number of small importers skyrocketed. The chains and department stores were also increasingly importing most of their basic items directly. As a result, by early 1991, wholesalers and importers were beginning to take on additional inventory risks and reducing prices at the same time.

Retailers

Unlike wholesalers, the number of retail footwear outlets grew steadily throughout the 1980s. Retailing grew primarily because of the general expansion of new retail concepts and the strong economy. Growth was also enhanced by improving gross margins, quickly increasing average price per pair and a modest decrease in price sensitivity due to market segmentation and new product differentiation strategies. In addition, the retailers' gross margins had improved as a result of lower cost imports, which retailers believed provided better value. Retailers generally did not believe that they had to pass along these savings to the consumer.

In 1976, the Canadian federal government introduced import restrictions through a quota system designed to provide temporary protection against lower cost imports that had rapidly increased market share beyond 60 percent and were believed to be seriously threatening the domestic shoe manufacturers. These protective quotas, combined with the 22.8 percent import duties on leather footwear, were designed to provide domestic manufacturers adequate time to rationalize operations, invest in state of the art technology and accelerate the development of marketing skills. The quota allocations were based on past import history and ownership of the quotas was disbursed to importers, retailers and manufacturers.

Throughout the 1980s, many retailers fought for the removal of quotas. Most retailers, particularly the volume retailers with buying power, believed that import quotas reduced consumer variety, increased consumer prices, and limited the retailers' competitive alternatives. Fortunately for retailers, there were sufficient legal loopholes, and at times, a highly liquid quota market which helped to reduce some of the effectiveness of the quotas.

Interestingly, the smaller independent retailers, who enjoyed virtually no buying power, viewed the removal of quotas as a potential threat. These smaller retailers were unable to buy imports directly like the major retailers and were, therefore, at a competitive disadvantage. They were forced to share gross margins to pay for the services of an importer or to reflect their buying disadvantage with uncompetitive prices.

With the withdrawal of quotas by the end of the 1980s, the independent shoe retailer had clearly lost ground to the major chains, department stores, and even regional mini-chains. Canadian retailing power was being consolidated into the hands of those with buying power. The independent also lacked the much needed leverage to negotiate with the shopping center developers. It was estimated that less than 20 percent of the total market was serviced by the independent retailers.

Manufacturers

Competition between domestic manufacturers had been traditionally regarded as cordial and genteel. The low Canadian dollar during much of the 1980s had offered additional protection against imports; it also provided an opportunity for niche exports to the U.S. However, the past two years became the most devastating period in the entire history of Canadian domestic manufacturing. The removal of import quotas, coupled with a major retail rationalization, and a rapidly rising Canadian dollar completely reversed the fortunes of domestic manufacturers. Total sales from domestic producers of men's and boys' shoes fell 57 percent from 1988 to 1990 to only 29 percent of the market and the looming domestic bankruptcies indicated further market share erosion. A similar pattern was observed in the U.S. where the market share for imports rose to over 80 percent in 1990 as the American domestic shoe manufacturers were exposed to more import competition when the Orderly Marketing Agreements (OMA) were not reinstated in the early 1980s. The OMAs had offered similar protection to the U.S. shoe manufacturers by limiting the quantity of shoe exports to the U.S. on a voluntary basis from individual countries by major exporters such as Taiwan and Korea. Canadian domestic competition had become cutthroat similar to that experienced in the U.S., as volume declined.

Further compounding these problems was the gradual reduction of the tariffs on imports manufactured in the United States. The U.S. tariff rate in accordance with the F.T.A. was 15.96 percent and would continue to decline by approximately 2 percent per year to reach zero by 1999. Not only would the elimination of U.S. tariffs result in additional price pressures, but the domestic manufacturers had difficulty assessing the impact of Canada's general tariff policy which had been in effect since the early 1960s. Recently, the government had begun applying country-specific, temporary tariffs on imports from China (29 percent), Poland (63.2 percent), Romania (35 percent), and Brazil (45 percent), who were being accused of dumping shoes below cost.

By the end of the 1980s, Canadian shoe manufacturing was fragmented, often undercapitalized and normally family owned. Pressures to cut costs and rationalize operations were everywhere. The major retailers bought domestic output only when profitable imports were unavailable or when they wanted to service a particular niche. As one of the men's chain store buyers explained it:

With today's communication and travel facilities, I can easily buy 90 percent of my needs offshore. The prices are lower, my margins are better and the Orient is a lot more exciting to visit than rural Quebec. I save the remaining 10 percent of my business for sudden changes in fashion and for servicing reasons or winter boots and I let the domestics cut each others' throats trying to get those orders.

The Canadian companies that were foreign owned tended to be well managed and could draw on their parent company resources. The major brand names in the men's sector were almost entirely American (i.e., Florsheim, Brown Shoe Co., Nike, Hush Puppies, H. H. Brown). These American brands sourced their raw materials, semifinished uppers, and finished shoes from around the world, providing important sourcing advantages for their Canadian subsidiaries (see Exhibit 5). Major brand names were sold mostly in department stores and by independent retailers. In contrast, the major footwear specialty chain stores (i.e., Agnews, Kinney) tended to avoid branded footwear with the exception of the growing athletic business. Recently, however, a few brand names were beginning to show up in many of the major chain stores.

EXHIBIT 5 Type of Canadian Involvement

	No Canadian Position	Exporting to Canada	Licenced Canadian Distributor	American Owned Manufacturing & Dist. Facilities	Canadian Retailers Position
American Brand Names					
Cole Haan		X			
Florsheim*				X	X
Nunn Bush			X		
Johnston & Murphy	X				
Allan Edmonds	X				
Bostonian		X			
Jarman†	X				
Dexter	X				
Bass			X		
Sebago		X			
Timberland		X			
Sperry Topsider				X	
Rocksport				X	
Hush Puppies				X	
Levis (Brown Shoe)				X	
Street Cars		X			
H. H. Brown				X	
Nike			X		
Reebok				X	
Adidas				X	
Brooks				X	
Converse		X			
Pony			X		

NOTE: *Recently closed the plant
†Recently closed the plant and distribution facilities

Recent Trends

Perhaps the late 1980s were most notable for the extraordinary rise in importance of the athletic footwear category in North America. The expansion of this segment had a dramatic impact on the other segments of the industry. Athletic footwear not only represented nearly 50 percent of the total men's pairs sold, but product technology and styling of both casual and dress categories were heavily influenced by features available in athletic shoes. The popularity of athletic shoes was cited as the principal reason why recent surveys had indicated that comfort had become the most influential factor in purchase decisions of both casual and dress shoes. Athletic footwear technology was at the forefront of that comfort.

As the market for athletic shoes grew, the marketing skills of the major athletic brands were increasingly being aimed at the dress and casual market. These skills and resources were intensifying the competitive pressures of the entire men's footwear industry. Industry experts agreed that the successful market segmentation strategies of the athletic brands were likely to be increasingly focused on the men's dress and casual sectors. As a result, many observers predicted that in the future a greater emphasis would be placed on product innovation, branding and marketing in the high end of the men's dress sector. At the same time, heavy promotional activity and discount pricing in the lower and medium-priced men's dress categories seemed to indicate that this segment had evolved into a commodity type of business.

Despite the highly competitive environment, unit increases were evident in the high-priced men's footwear segment. This resulted in a polarization of prices in Canada with growth at the low end and the high end contrasting with reduced sales volume of medium-priced shoes. At the same time, the improved technical and comfort features of the athletic segment reduced the price sensitivity at the high end of the market. This decreased emphasis on price competitiveness provided domestic manufacturers with new opportunities. However, many observers suggested that Canadian manufacturers currently lacked the marketing skills necessary to be successful in this segment. They believed that brand names were becoming increasingly important to the survival of the domestic supplier as a means of differentiating from the commodity nature of the business and as a significant counterbalance to the extraordinary power of the chain stores.

Many Canadian manufacturers felt that the American men's footwear market had some rather distinct differences that particularly promoted the acceptance of branding in that country. Most branded companies in the United States offered two essential services not normally provided by Canadian companies, that is, excellent in-stock services and a comprehensive size/width assortment. The extraordinary variety of size/width selection was easier to meet in the United States, given the huge size of the domestic market. The majority of the successful American upscale companies also forward-integrated into retail either by developing their own concept stores or through acquisitions. Several companies in New England had expanded the factory outlet concept into a sizeable retail division. The success of factory outlet retailing in the U.S.A. was well understood by both Canadian footwear retailers and consumers.

Exhibit 6 Footwear Imports and Exports, Canada/United States (1986–1990)

	1986		1987		1988		1989		1990	
	Prs. '000	*$M*	*Prs. '000*	*$M*	*Prs. '000*	*$M*	*Prs. '000*	*$M*	*Prs. '000*	*$M*
Canadian exports to the United States	2,590	60.0	2,481	57.8	2,627	58.0	1,534	48.7	2,667	64.1
American export to Canada	2,991	45.1	4,095	57.0	2,236	40.3	2,572	48.9	2,829	49.7
Canada/U.S. trade balance	$14.9		$0.8		$17.7		($ 0.2)		$4.4	

Source: The Shoe Manufacturers' Association of Canada.

The move toward branding at the high end of the industry in Canada clearly benefited the established foreign-owned companies. Branded footwear-accounted for almost 40 percent of the total dress shoe market and nearly 33 percent of the casual market in the United States. Industry sources believed that a similar pattern existed in Canada. Despite the branding advantages enjoyed by foreign-owned companies, Canada remained a net importer of footwear from the United States by 1990 (see Exhibit 6).

Several Canadian boot manufacturers had managed to penetrate the U.S. market during the early 1980s. Most of this success was in the women's segment, although the lower Canadian dollar did help a few men's manufacturers get established. U.S. retailers typically viewed Canada as an excellent supplier of cold weather footwear due to Canada's close proximity, quality image, and natural understanding of the functional requirements of cold weather footwear. In 1990, the Canadian men's boot exports to the United States amounted to approximately 15 percent of the United States market which was estimated at nearly 6.5 million pairs per year. The high-end fashion boot market had been largely ignored by the American domestic manufacturers and most Canadian boot manufacturers were exploring promising niche opportunities.

CanBec Shoe

CanBec Shoe Ltd. was started in 1968 by Gilles Goulet who acquired the Actonvale, Quebec, plant from Bouchard Ltd., where he had worked as the general manager. CanBec, which manufactured men's dress shoes prospered throughout the next 20 years largely due to the efforts of Goulet and his young protege, Jean Guy Dufour. Industry authorities regarded Goulet as one of the most knowledgeable footwear manufacturing experts in the business. Goulet's expertise was sought on many occasions by a variety of American, European, and Canadian manufacturers.

CanBec had grown to become the second largest employer in Actonvale, reaching 185 employees at its peak, but reduced volume and improved technology had forced the relatively young, skilled work force down to approximately 130 including staff by 1991. The plant was spread over an aging, single-level,

35,000-square-foot facility near the centre of Actonvale (population 4,000), approximately 70 kilometres from Montreal. The relatively modest plant was somewhat compartmentalized, which slightly impeded the production flow. However, the technology employed was an excellent combination of modern equipment and some ingenious homemade machines.

CanBec had always prided itself on its manufacturing expertise. It had been a leader in adopting new technologies, particularly in the sole bottoming and finishing processes. Goulet and Dufour had developed an excellent industrywide network in Europe where most of the major technological innovations took place. Their network and production expertise led them to partially backward-integrate into the supply of soles as well as a few other components for CanBec's own consumption. CanBec's philosophy could be summed up as follows: "If we cannot find what we want at the price we need, then we'll make it ourselves."

By the mid-1980s, the company could easily compete with the much-coveted Italian finishing expertise in terms of cost and quality. This advantage was probably one of the primary reasons that CanBec had been able to survive immediately after the removal of quotas in 1986. Furthermore, the company had always enjoyed excellent labour relations with its semicaptive skilled labour force.

Over the years, CanBec had consistently eliminated tedious labour-intensive operations, thereby reducing manufacturing costs. Each individual operation was broken down into standard minutes. Several members of the CanBec team, including Dufour, could estimate the labour costs within a 5 percent deviation for almost any shoe. The necessity for understanding and controlling labour costs was entrenched in the CanBec culture. It further served as an important advantage when senior management worked with major buyers. With an understanding of costs, pricing decisions could be made immediately. This ability to quote prices for large volume orders without the fear of any major profit contribution errors often meant that CanBec would leave the buying offices with confirmed orders.

CanBec had developed an excellent control and management information system that was centered on labour cost control. This tailor-made system provided management with detailed information about any departmental variances so that corrective action could be taken immediately. CanBec had not focused any of its MIS efforts on the marketing side of the business with the exception of some basic sales statistics.

CanBec enjoyed steady sales and profit growth throughout the early and mid-1980s. It was this profitability combined with a desire by Goulet to retire gradually that lead to Dufour's rise to the presidency of the company. The plan which was initiated in the early 1980s to slowly move control of CanBec to Dufour had proceeded without delay throughout the last several years and Goulet gradually reduced his daily involvement.

In spite of the company's success, CanBec was faced with increasing pressure from low cost imports from Brazil, Taiwan, and China. As a result, the company had gradually been forced to reposition itself towards the high-priced end of the market. This new position, although offering higher contribution per unit, had reduced the number of pairs sold per year and thereby increased overhead costs per pair. Compounding this problem was the resistance of Can-Bec's traditional retail customers to accept these new prices. Retail resistance was understandable given that CanBec was not considered a major brand name. In fact, CanBec shoes were often sold under the customer's private label, that is, Eatons, The Bay, and so on.

In addition to the price pressures, CanBec found that its volume was being spread over an increasing number of styles, thereby decreasing the economies of scale which it had traditionally enjoyed. This small lot production had become a major problem that contributed to the decreasing profitability but CanBec, like many domestic suppliers, was forced to provide this type of service to fill up production. The large and medium-volume orders were increasingly going off-shore due to their low-cost labour, which made up between 25 percent and 30 percent of the wholesale selling price. By the spring of 1991, CanBec was running at approximately 60 percent capacity depending upon the labour content of the product line. (See Exhibits 7 and 8 for CanBec's financial statements.)

CanBec Marketing

CanBec spent significant resources on product development. Although CanBec was not considered a market innovator, it was an excellent and relatively fast copier of up-to-date world fashion trends. In 1988, CanBec received a silver award for boot styling from the Canadian Shoe Manufacturers Association at the annual Winter Fashion Show. Most major customers felt that they could rely on

EXHIBIT 7 Income Statement
   (Year Ending December 31st)

	1987	1988	1989	1990	1991 (E)
Net sales	$5,710,499	$5,042,486	$5,139,663	$4,722,398	$5,000,000
Cost of goods sold	4,592,413	4,146,691	4,072,039	3,980,232	4,150,000
Gross margin	1,118,086	895,795	1,067,624	742,166	850,000
Sales expense	320,848	305,022	338,311	297,108	320,000
Administration expense	444,228	404,204	405,781	501,967	480,000
Interest expense	61,148	106,419	170,248	145,586	175,000
	826,224	815,645	914,340	944,661	975,000
Profit before taxes	291,862	80,150	153,284	(202,495)	125,000
Taxes	62,608	8,272	19,155	(58,260)	(40,000)
Net profit (net loss)	$ 229,254	$ 71,878	$ 134,129	($ 144,235)	($ 85,000)
No. of pairs	237,576	184,963	157,359	141,964	138,000

Exhibit 8 Balance Sheet
              (as of December 31st)

	1987	1988	1989	1990	1991 (E)
Assets					
Current assets					
Accounts receivable	$1,527,116	$1,031,016	$1,313,874	$1,287,995	$1,350,000
Taxes receivables				53,356	
Inventory	1,019,095	1,054,570	949,419	855,696	900,000
Prepaid expenses	17,583	9,615	7,214	22,514	10,000
	2,563,794	2,095,201	2,270,507	2,219,561	2,260,000
Fixed assets	185,901	184,469	201,920	188,614	175,000
	$2,749,695	$2,279,670	$2,472,427	$2,408,175	$2,435,000
Liabilities and shareholders' equity					
Current liabilities					
Bank loan	1,022,289	902,638	1,076,967	1,208,996	1,575,000
Accounts payable	468,972	308,711	405,059	479,884	330,000
Taxes payable			20,611		
Current portion L.T.D.	100,000	100,000	100,000	100,000	41,000
	1,591,261	1,311,349	1,602,637	1,788,880	1,946,000
Long-term debt	341,667	241,667	141,667	41,667	0
Taxes on revenue	23,916	21,370	8,710	2,450	0
	1,956,844	1,574,386	1,753,014	1,832,997	1,946,000
Capital and retained earnings					
Capital stock	549,638	429,638	309,638	309,638	309,000
Retained earnings	243,213	275,646	409,775	265,540	180,000
	792,851	705,284	719,413	575,178	489,000
	$2,749,695	$2,279,670	$2,472,427	$2,408,175	$2,435,000

CanBec to provide basic fashion direction and that any specific style could be developed with some modifications from the CanBec product line. CanBec was regarded by the trade as a reliable supplier of good quality footwear with excellent fit and a timely delivery record. The company had never expended nor focused its effort on image or brand-building.

CanBec's quick turnaround time of approximately three to six weeks between order taking and final product delivery was better than the average domestic supplier who took six to eight weeks. Many importers were now matching CanBec's delivery times by providing a limited in-stock service. Volume buyers believed that CanBec's delivery record was a major reason to continue doing some business with it as insurance against delivery problems from offshore sources.

Although CanBec had traditionally done about 75 percent of its business with the major chain stores, the customer mix was being slowly forced toward the

Exhibit 9 Organizational Chart

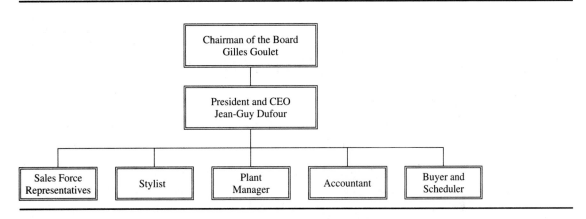

smaller independents where the price pressures were less severe. The independents did not have the buying power to dictate prices, thereby allowing CanBec a higher gross margin. Furthermore, the independent retailers' target market tended to be the higher end segment as they could not compete with the chain stores' low pricing strategy. In March 1991, it was estimated that CanBec serviced 400 of the over 2,000 independent accounts in Canada. Although it was expanding its emphasis on the independents, CanBec had not employed a marketing or sales manager (see Exhibit 9). Instead, Dufour often worked directly with the major buyers and the sales force.

CanBec Product Line

CanBec traditionally had been a dress shoe manufacturer. In 1987, dress shoes represented 229,500 pairs (over 96 percent of total units); however, by 1990 dress shoes accounted for 108,000 pairs (approximately 75 percent of total units), forcing CanBec to diversify its product line to maintain minimum production levels. One of the major problems with adding winter boots and fall casual shoes was the irregular production flow. Retailers insisted that fall dress and casual shoes be delivered by early August and winter boots by early September. As a result, CanBec's recent sales mix caused a major production overflow during June through September and an enormous under-capacity position from November through March. Dufour estimated that the spring business was now less than 30 percent and he expected this trend to continue. CanBec forecasted that winter boots would rise to nearly 26,000 pairs in 1991, while dress shoes were likely to fall to approximately 72,000 pairs (see Exhibit 10).

  CanBec's boot line received encouraging success during the first two seasons it was introduced (1989 and 1990). The gross margins of the boot line were at least 5 percent better than the traditional dress shoe line with an average price of $45. However, the additional interest costs resulting from higher inventory and

Exhibit 10 Product Mix—1987–1991 (in pairs)

	Boots	Casuals	Dress	Total
1991	26,000	40,000	72,000	138,000
1990	19,000	15,000	108,000	142,000
1989	10,000	12,000	135,000	157,000
1988	6,000	15,000	164,000	185,000
1987	0	8,000	229,500	237,500
Average Price/Pair	$45.00	$33.00	$35.00	

longer production lead times did make expansion into the boot market somewhat risky. There were only three major leather boot competitors of any significance in North America (Grenico, Bata, and Cougar). Some nonleather import competition existed but this tended to be at the low-priced end of the market. Price sensitivity for large volume orders was very high in this segment with men's boots rapidly becoming a commodity product. The importance of the brand was much less in the men's boot market than in the men's dress shoe market.

CanBec also supplemented its low capacity periods by periodically doing subcontract work for others such as the American brand, Hush Puppies. The gross margin contributions from contract sales were substantially below the norm. The attraction of this type of business was smoother production flows and it kept skilled labour employed. CanBec was widely regarded as a reliable subcontractor.

CanBec had no "finished shoe" import experience. Following the lead of U.S. subsidiaries, CanBec had attempted to import uppers (the sewn upper portion of the shoe) which were highly labour intensive. This had proven unsuccessful as the small quantities CanBec offered off-shore suppliers severely limited the service attention CanBec needed to maintain its own delivery reputation. CanBec was currently initiating a new program to establish a reliable source of inexpensive uppers from a smaller, more compatible Chinese source. The preliminary prices had suggested that CanBec might benefit more from importing the entire finished product. Dufour felt that a small test program would be a worthwhile learning experience with relatively low risk.

CanBec Sales Organization

CanBec's highly respected sales force was made up of seven representatives who worked entirely on commission. All of the representatives handled nonconflicting product lines for other companies such as women's or children's shoes. Three of these salespeople had just been added to the group and were considered excellent additions as they had worked for competitors who had gone into receivership. The new sales representatives concentrated on the independent accounts in Ontario and the Western provinces. Dufour was considering hiring an additional salesperson to cover the Maritimes exclusively. This territory was currently being handled by the Quebec independent representative.

The possibility of starting a U.S. sales force to handle the CanBec boot line was also being considered. A preliminary study indicated that it would cost approximately $150,000 per year to engage an established representative for New England dedicated to the CanBec product line. This cost would have to be endured for at least three years, until the territory became self-sufficient. Another option was for CanBec to hire several nondedicated sales representatives on a commission basis (8 percent to 10 percent). This alternative would mean that any market penetration would be much slower as the sales representative efforts would be diluted over several other lines. Dufour believed that CanBec's success in the United States would be contained to its boot line, as the American market was unlikely to need another source of unbranded dress high-end shoes.

As an additional option, CanBec had recently approached several American brand names to handle the distribution of the CanBec boots to the United States, while at the same time becoming their exclusive Canadian distributor. The initial response was positive as a couple of the companies were very complimentary about the quality, styling, and value offered by the CanBec boot line. Dufour had very little understanding of the U.S. market and he felt that the wrong intermediary could do irreparable damage to CanBec's export future.

The Future

Dufour, who had spent his entire working life in the Canadian footwear industry, was trying to recall when he had seen such a difficult period. CanBec had weathered many rough storms and its survival capacity coupled with some new opportunities kept him optimistic. Dufour believed that the recent bankruptcies of a few key competitors would likely force some of his customers to work even more closely with the reliable CanBec. Secondly, Dufour thought that although focusing more on winter boots caused some severe cyclical cashflow problems, this strategy might improve margins and reinforce the American market initiative. How and when to introduce a major reorientation such as this would undoubtedly bring with it some implementation challenges. Dufour felt that the bank would probably understand the logic of this opportunity provided he prepared a solid business plan.

The recession, high interest rates and cross-border shopping were taking their toll on Canadian retailers. The downturn had caused CanBec to break several bank covenants, as its inventory and account receivable coverage ratio was now deficient. Despite those concerns, CanBec's backlog of orders was very healthy. Dufour believed that gross margins would likely improve if CanBec continued to emphasize sales to independent retailers. To meet the demands of these retailers, the production scheduling would likely have to be modified slightly and modest increases in inventory and receivables would follow.

The importance of branding was another issue that CanBec would have to address. The Free Trade Agreement with the United States coupled with the emergence of Mexico as a source of cheap labour was not helping the outlook for domestic Canadian manufacturers. In order for CanBec to continue to raise prices on domestically produced shoes, it would have to become more adept at differentiating its product. Dufour was wondering whether licensing an American brand name might be an efficient approach and an acceptable response for the bank. Such a move would bring with it the challenges of developing a full in-stock program and a more comprehensive size/width assortment inherent in the brand business.

Dufour had been impressed by the quality and flexibility of the recent Chinese import initiative that CanBec had been developing. The risks of a small test order seemed minimal, although a letter of credit would add to the cash flow pressure as it would mean that at least $100,000 of borrowing capacity (one container of 3,600 pairs) would be tied up for nearly six months. CanBec's operating loan had consistently stayed at the maximum for the past nine months. Fortunately, CanBec's negligible long-term debt had helped to buffer the reactions of the bank and Dufour felt that these under-leveraged assets were a source of funds for any new strategic initiatives.

In formulating a response to the bank's demand for corrective action, it occurred to Dufour that the bank might insist on additional equity. Dufour was also concerned about CanBec's ability to handle several new strategic moves at once. How much time the bank would provide undoubtedly depended upon the priorities Dufour chose. Clearly, tough decisions were called for, but when and how to act were uncertain.

CASE 7
CARON FURNITURE LTEE.

On May 20, 1987, Yves Richard, president of Caron Furniture Ltee. of St. Jean, Quebec, was assessing Caron's future U.S. export strategy. Caron, one of Canada's larger producers of wood office furniture, currently exported its products via a six-person company sales force and 11 manufacturers' representatives, who in turn serviced 1,700 dealers in the United States. Two options for the U.S. market were being considered: status quo or increased direct investment in showrooms and company sales staff. If the second option was chosen, Richard would have to decide on both the level of investment and the geographic focus. The larger question that loomed was the role the U.S. market should play in Caron's future.

To describe the context in which Richard had to make this decision, information about the North American furniture industry and the history of Caron Furniture Ltee. will be first presented.

The North American Office Furniture Industry

From 1982 to 1985 North American office furniture production increased at an annual rate of 18.7 percent, going from $5.6 to $9.8 billion (Exhibit 1). Growth slowed in 1986, with U.S. production increasing by only 4.4 percent. A 3 percent increase was projected for 1987. Demand for medium-price office furniture was forecasted to grow between 7 percent and 16 percent annually over the next decade.

The North American office furniture industry was highly competitive and fragmented, with some 700 office furniture manufacturers in the United States and 160 in Canada vying for market share. The acknowledged market leader in 1987 was Steelcase with a 21 percent market share in the United States and extensive sales in Canada. Steelcase was a privately held company, with 1986 sales of $1.4 billion (U.S.). Their primary product lines were metal office furniture, storage units, and office systems. Steelcase also produced wood office furniture. Their products were distributed through a wide North American distribution system which included 550 dealers in the United States. Steelcase prided itself on its delivery system which it claimed was 99.5 percent on schedule.

The number two firm, with a 7 percent market share in the United States, was Herman Miller. In 1986, its sales were $531.6 million, with net income of $37.8 million. Like Steelcase, Herman Miller produced both wood and steel

This case was prepared by Jonathan Calof, under the direction of Professor Paul Beamish. Certain names have been disguised; however, essential relationships are maintained. Copyright © 1988, The University of Western Ontario.

products. Known for its marketing innovativeness, Herman Miller had within the past year announced numerous sales incentives including five-year product warranties, trade-in allowances of up to 100 percent, guaranteed delivery dates, and an Office Pavilion dealership program (that provided incentives such as service and management support to dealers in certain locations who enter into partial exclusivity agreements with Herman Miller). As well, Herman Miller planned to hire people for the pavilions who would call on and service small and medium-size businesses.

The office furniture market was composed of two distinct segments: wood and metal. Metal furniture utilised mass-production technologies and was targeted to a broad market. Competition was primarily on the basis of price. In 1985, metal

EXHIBIT 1 The North American Office Furniture Market and North American Furniture Production (1982–1987)

	(Cdn $ millions)					
	1982	*1983*	*1984*	*1985*		
Canada:						
Wood/other	$ 204	$ 323	$ 379	$ 482		
Metal	313	256	321	363		
Total Canada	517	579	700	845		
United States:						
Wood	1,414	1,592	1,942	2,290		
Metal	3,687	4,639	5,640	6,684		
Total United States	5,101	6,231	7,582	8,974		
Total North America	$5,618	$6,810	$8,282	$9,819		

	Selected Furniture Production Segments (Cdn $ millions)*					
	1982	*1983*	*1984*	*1985*	*1986*	*1987 (est.)*
Chairs:						
Wood Canada	14	14	16	22	39	31
Wood United States*	351	432	540	612	711	788
Metal Canada	79	75	85	96	104	140
Metal United States	870	955	1,231	1,537	1,734	1,866
Exports Canada	28	24	23	28	32	38
Desks:						
Wood Canada	46	55	65	80	92	111
Wood United States	314	347	435	468	531	573
Metal Canada	29	30	30	32	34	35
Metal United States	251	252	350	360	406	437
Exports Canada	19	25	39	50	48	52

*1986 and 1987 U.S. figures are estimates, based on 12 years average annual growth. Exchange rate as of December 31 used to convert U.S. sales to Canadian dollars.

SOURCE: *Statistics Canada* 35:006 Quarterly Shipments, Office Furniture Industry. U.S. Commerce Department 85-9633, 87-7411, 83-18541, Office Furniture Industry.

office furniture sales were $7 billion (Exhibit 1), 71 percent of total office furniture sales. Metal sales had increased by 14.5 percent annually over the past 13 years.

Wood furniture was generally targeted to executives and professionals. In 1985, wood furniture production totaled $2.8 billion. Sales of wood office furniture, which 20 years ago had accounted for one fifth of the office furniture market, accounted for 28 percent in 1985 and were expected to increase by 15.8 percent annually over the next 10 years—a rate greater than that of metal. In 1987, wood office furniture production was expected to reach $3.6 billion.

Between 1982 and 1985, many companies in the wood office furniture industry experienced strong gains in both sales and earnings as a result of increased demand and increased production efficiency. Shipments per employee increased by 39 percent in the United States, while in Canada it increased by 13 percent

---

EXHIBIT 2 **North American Wood Furniture Market (Miscellaneous Statistics; 1983–1985)**

U.S. Industry (wood)

	U.S. $ millions		
	1983	*1984*	*1985*
Shipment value	$ 1,167	$ 1,478	$ 1,505
Materials	473.4	586.7	557.4
Total payroll	324.0	406.6	410.5
Production payroll	212.1	272.4	270.0
Employment—000 workers	20.8	24.8	23.7
Production—000 workers	16.6	19.6	18.5
Materials/dollar sale	.406	.397	.370
Payroll/dollar sales	.182	.184	.179
Sales/employee—Cdn $000	69.8	78.8	88.8

Canadian Industry (nonmetal)

	Cdn $ millions*		
	1983	*1984*	*1985*
Shipment value	$256.0	$321.2	$363.3
Materials	108.4	136.4	149.4
Total payroll	68.9	87.2	101.9
Production payroll	50.0	64.1	73.6
Employment—000 workers	3.6	4.2	4.8
Production—000 workers	2.8	3.5	4.0
Materials/dollar sale	.423	.425	.411
Payroll/dollar sales	.195	.200	.202
Sales/employee—Cdn $000	71.3	76.1	75.0

*Exchange rate as of July 31 was used for conversion.
SOURCE: *Predicast* 1987. *Statistics Canada* Cansim matrix 5477—Nonwood Office Furniture Firms.

EXHIBIT 3 Top Markets in the United States

City, and State or Province	Sales (Cdn $000s)*
New York, New York	$156,039
Chicago and area, Illinois	121,661
Houston and area, Texas	58,191
Detroit/Ann Arbor, Michigan	56,313
Dallas/Fort Worth, Texas	53,664
Washington, D.C.	49,372
Cleveland/Akron, Ohio	40,094
Minneapolis/St. Paul, Minnesota	38,635
Atlanta, Georgia	35,895
St. Louis, Missouri	34,663
Seattle/Tacoma, Washington	35,048
Cleveland, Ohio	29,522
Denver/Boulder, Colorado	29,420
Baltimore, Maryland	28,464
Miami and area, Florida	27,447
Denver, Colorado	26,657
Seattle, Washington	26,097
Milwaukee/Racine, Wisconsin	23,174
Cincinnati/Hamilton	22,727
Kansas City, Kansas	22,174
Phoenix, Arizona	21,864
Portland, Oregon	18,508
New Orleans, Louisiana	18,175
Columbus, Ohio	17,595
Indianapolis, Indiana	16,345
Ontario, Canada	49,142
Quebec, Canada	22,850

*Exchange rate as of December 31, 1985, used to convert sales to Canadian dollars. U.S. sales are for 1985; Canadian sales are for 1986.
SOURCE: NOPA study, 1986.

(Exhibit 2). In 1984, the profit margins for the largest U.S. wood manufacturers averaged 10.6 percent.

Wood furniture was usually produced using either batch or job shop technologies. Competition was along the lines of product quality, price, and design. The nature of the product yielded somewhat limited opportunities for automation; thus, capital entry barriers were rather low. This resulted in a proliferation of small firms: over 77 percent of all firms employed less than 50 people. However, due to distribution dynamics which favoured larger, more-established firms, sales were somewhat concentrated. In Canada, five firms accounted for 38 percent of all production activity, while in the United States, eight firms accounted for 40 percent. The major U.S. markets were located in the Eastern United States (Exhibit 3), while in Canada major markets were in

EXHIBIT 4 **1983–1987 Canadian Wood Office-Furniture Market (Shipments of Wooden Chairs and Desks within Selected Markets; Cdn $000s)**

Province or Region	1983	1984	1985	1986	1987 (est.)
British Columbia	$ 3,566	$ 4,128	$ 8,841	$ 7,814	$ 7,520
Alberta	4,516	3,936	4,719	6,958	5,844
Saskatchewan	1,096	1,067	1,220	2,022	—
Manitoba	—	1,107	1,424	1,084	2,247
Ontario	—	23,825	26,232	35,477	39,908
Quebec	11,136	12,834	15,282	22,850	28,401
Atlantic	2,149	2,009	2,261	3,853	3,185

SOURCE: *Statistics Canada* 35:006 Quarterly Shipments, Office Furniture Industry. Figures, 80–85 % of industry production.

Ontario and Quebec (Exhibit 4). Approximately 67 percent of Caron's Canadian sales were in Quebec.

The office furniture market can be further subdivided into the following product categories: chairs, desks, tables, filing and storage units, office systems/ panels, and panel components. Caron's main product lines were wooden chairs and wooden desks which accounted for 80 percent of sales. In 1987, total North American wooden chair production was expected to reach $819 million (Cdn), while wooden desk production was forecast to be $684 million (Exhibit 1).

Wooden Office Furniture Industry: Competition and Distribution

Office furniture firms can be divided into three size classes: large (greater than 500 employees and sales greater than $50 million), medium (100–500 employees and sales up to $50 million), and small (less than 100 employees). In 1985, there were approximately 15 large firms in the United States and one in Canada. These large firms had diversified product lines, with products at multiple price points. As well, they generally diversified either into other industries (e.g., Kimball also produced pianos) or into both the metal and wooden segments of the furniture market. Large firms had national distribution systems and sophisticated marketing and production systems. Due to the high overheads associated with these systems, the large firms' products were usually high priced. A few of the large firms (Herman Miller and Steelcase) were recognized as being among the 100 best-managed firms in the United States.

Large firms distributed their products through the largest and most established dealers. Their size allowed them to exercise significant clout over the distributors and it was not unusual for them to pressure dealers into reducing the number of competitive products which they carried. In recent years, the larger firms had been purchasing medium and small firms as one means of expanding production capacity, line breadth, and line depth.

There were approximately 47 medium-size firms in the United States and 8 in Canada, including Caron. These medium-size firms often concentrated on regional markets close to their manufacturing facilities and distributed their products primarily through independent agents. In recent years many of these firms had started to purchase showrooms and hire their own sales reps.

Small firms usually focused on narrow product lines and relied on economies of specialization. These firms were the most numerous in the industry.

Historically, office furniture was pushed through the dealer channels by the manufacturer. This had started to change. Over the past few years up to 50 percent of sales arose from designers/specifiers and the end-user requesting specific types, brands, and models of furniture—thereby pulling sales through the system. In choosing office furniture, designers usually sought (in order) product aesthetics, construction quality, delivery, and price. Caron had a sales rep in Montreal whose sole job was to contact and service both designer/specifiers and corporations. Although there had been some change in traditional distribution patterns, finding good dealers and then developing and maintaining relationships with them continued to be important. Dealer quality covered a wide spectrum. Quality of a dealer primarily reflected the volume of product moved. To attract top dealers, firms were required to offer, in order of importance, competitive price/price discounts, better than average delivery, good product aesthetics, and quality construction. In addition, it was important that the manufacturer provided showroom support (where the dealer could show customers the manufacturer's products), broad product lines, the ability to service dealers and troubleshoot their problems—and for regional dealers—the ability to offer services to their entire geographic target market.

While dealers, designers, and end-users had different product attribute needs, delivery speed and reliability had begun to emerge as one of the most important attributes for all of them.

In Canada, Caron had exclusively used "A" dealers, while in the United States, Caron's dealers fell into the "B" category (based on the ABC quality classification system). Caron was trying to break into A dealers in the United States; however, this was proving to be difficult, as there were many high-quality producers who had long-term relationships with the A dealers. As well, the high quality of the large firms' products and their clout resulted in their domination of the class A dealers. As a result, many of the medium-size manufacturers were forced to distribute their product through the B dealers.

Company History

Caron was a privately owned company that had been in the wooden furniture business for over 40 years. It was founded in St. Jean in 1935 by Andre Caron to produce and sell wooden residential furniture. During World War II, Caron dropped their residential furniture line and concentrated on producing office furniture for the war effort. The resultant increased volume continued into the early 1950s. The bubble burst when metal office furniture was introduced. Within a few years, metal office furniture captured 75 percent of the market. As a result, Caron's sales dropped in half and profits virtually disappeared. Caron management felt that part of the decline in profits arose from poor labour productivity. In answer to this problem, a piecework incentive program was successfully introduced in 1966. Prior to the incentives, it took 360 minutes to upholster a particular executive chair; after the system was introduced, it took only 86 minutes.

In 1968 Caron weathered its second major crisis. The Canadian government switched to metal furniture, thereby depriving Caron of its single most important source of revenue. Caron responded by upgrading its focus on the business market. This required a reorientation of the firm's marketing and design efforts. The reorientation appeared to succeed. During the 1970s, volume increased: sales in 1970 were $1.2 million, and by 1980 they had reached $10 million. During this period, Caron began exporting to the United States.

Coping with Growth

The increased demand for the firm's products became too great to be handled by Caron's 100-person work force in its old plant on Lavalle Street in St. Jean. In 1980, Caron purchased another furniture plant in neighbouring St. Therese, Quebec.

In 1982, at the suggestion of some of its U.S. representatives, Caron entered the desk market. Caron management felt that the complementary nature of the product in terms of the core market and core production skills made desks a natural extension to the product line. Within three to four years, Caron had one of the largest market shares in the Canadian wood office-desk market.

To cope with increased volume pressure, Caron leased space at the back of a facility on Outremont Drive in St. Jean in 1984. Six months later, the entire facility was bought outright. This served as the new headquarters for Caron as well as its central shipping facility.

With the increased marketing efforts and a broader line, sales doubled between 1980 and 1985, going from $10 to $21 million. As well, the number of product lines increased beyond tables and chairs to include executive and secretarial desks with matching office cabinetry, conference tables, and office systems in order to provide an integrated office line. There were now three plants instead of one, and sales to the United States now accounted for over 40 percent of the firm's volume. The increased complexity of rapid growth during this period made it difficult for the senior managers to operate as they had in the past. Products were shipped late and customer complaints increased. Caron was developing a reputation in the United States for poor delivery, and inventory inaccuracies resulted in production bottlenecks, which in turn led to a mass of partially finished product cluttering up the factories.

By 1985, these factors contributed to a deterioration in profits.

Management realised that there were problems. These included management and control system design, and differences in the core skills and processes required to produce the different products. For example, while it was not a problem for a wooden chair to have scratches as most of the frame would be covered with upholstery, the slightest imperfection on a table or desk surface was readily apparent and lead to customer complaints.

In response to these problems, Caron changed plant layouts and production processes and modified the organization structure. Caron maintained their functional form, but during this growth period added several new positions. At the senior level, Caron created a vice president, production, position. This executive was responsible for plant operations and for the newly formed engineering and quality control departments. Under the treasurer, several new departments were formed, including inventory control, purchasing, and scheduling (Exhibit 5). Prior to the organizational change, these activities were handled in an informal manner by Yves Richard and the plant managers. The modifications resulted in a tripling of the administration staff.

Delivery and production problems were addressed by investment in a computerized manufacturing planning system (MRP II) which was fully integrated by late 1986.

Once delivery systems were improved, Caron developed a quick-ship program that promised a two-week turnaround for 25 percent of Caron's product line with limited product options. For example, although there were over 2,000 choices of material for upholstering chairs (excluding customer material) only 30 fabric choices were offered on the quick-shipment program. By early 1987,

EXHIBIT 5 Caron Furniture Ltee. Organization Chart (March 31, 1987)

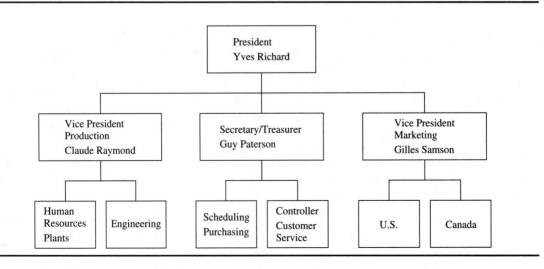

quick-shipment sales accounted for 40 percent of all chair and 60 percent of all desk sales.

With MRP II in place and improved inventory systems, inventory accuracy increased to 95 percent, and production times were reduced for most products. In addition, delivery reliability increased so that 75 percent of the orders were now shipped on time, up from 40 percent; quick-shipment orders were now 98 percent on time.

By the end of 1986, many of Caron's problems had either been solved or were in the process of being solved. Customer complaints had decreased dramatically, delivery time had been reduced, and sales were a record—over $23 million.

For 1987, Caron's 378 employees were expected to generate $28 million in sales, making Caron one of the larger wood office-furniture firms in Canada. Productivity had also improved due to a combination of increased automation, the success of the quality circle program, and improved in-house training programs. However, the adoption of a more complex organization structure, purchase of new plants, the MRP II system, and the high marketing costs in the United States resulted in dramatic increases in fixed costs. In the five years ending 1987, fixed costs were estimated to have increased to $10.8 million from $3.4 million (Exhibit 6). This increased the breakeven point and contributed to a decline in return on sales and return on investment. Organizational problems were emerging; in particular, coordination of the desk, chair, and systems lines was becoming increasingly difficult. The addition of a new metal chair was adding to the complexity.

EXHIBIT 6 Caron Furniture Ltee. (Selected Financial Information; Cdn $000s)

Sales	1983	1984	1985	1986	1987 (est.)
Canadian sales	$ 7,735	$10,201	$11,594	$13,582	$16,496
U.S. sales	5,575	7,902	9,286	9,871	11,235
Total sales	13,332	18,103	20,880	23,050	27,731
Fixed expenses*	3,393	5,085	6,936	8,716	10,763
Increase in sales (percent)	31.3	36.0	15.3	12.2	18.3
Current assets/current liabilities	3.7	1.9	2.2	1.9	1.8
Assets/liabilities	4.4	2.3	2.8	2.6	2.7
Debt to equity (percent)	4.7	26.8	20.6	17.1	12.9
Staff (numbers)	229	338	346	361	378

*Some of the fixed cost is allocated to the cost of goods sold. The gross margin (38 %—in case) excludes other variable costs of transportation, duty, sales discounts and commissions.
SOURCE: Company records.

Involvement in the United States

In 1976, with the domestic market flourishing, consultants were hired to prepare a study of the U.S. wood office-furniture market and suggest the appropriate distribution strategy. They reported that the U.S. market was a viable outlet for Caron, and that the most appropriate form of distribution was through independent representatives. The consultants provided Caron with a list of representatives in the United States. Agents were then appointed throughout much of the United States. It was decided that Caron would manufacture the furniture in its Canadian plant and then ship the product to the United States. Caron entered the market with its existing products of chairs and tables and utilised the same pricing structure that it had in Canada. These prices were comparable to those charged by other U.S. furniture manufacturers.

In 1982, Caron increased its U.S. investment by leasing a showroom facility in Chicago and hiring a regional manager and salesman for Chicago. At the same time, they introduced their new desk line to the U.S. market.

By 1984, U.S. sales increased to $7.9 million (Cdn)—44 percent of sales (Exhibit 6). Caron reevaluated their U.S. distribution strategy and decided to increase their investment in the United States—sales managers were hired for New York and Atlanta.

By 1985, the increased volume in both Canada and the United States had placed a great strain on Caron's resources. Several problems emerged within the United States; there were spotty delivery schedules and product complaints, difficulties in being able to manage the independent agents, and problems in agent reliability. To address the problem of agent reliability, Caron continued to replace weaker agents with either new agents or company salesmen.

By the end of 1986, U.S. sales had reached $9.9 million—42 percent of all Caron sales. At this level of sales and continued growth appearing likely, Caron modified their structure to recognize the importance of the United States. Caron split marketing into Canadian and U.S. divisions and in early 1987 appointed a U.S. national manager, Gerard Thompson, who would spearhead future movements within the United States. Within a few months, Thompson had identified what he perceived to be three major weaknesses in the U.S. operation:

1. *Too many dealers.*   By the end of 1986, Caron was servicing over 2,700 dealers. One of the largest firms in the United States had 225 dealers throughout the entire country. The large number of dealers strained delivery systems and spread both salesmen and agents too thinly.

2. *Too broad a geographical focus.*   The current organization could not effectively cope with a national operation.

3. *Desk design.*   Although Caron products were competitive on price and quality, some additional elements such as line enlarging and additional finishes were needed for the U.S. market.

EXHIBIT 7 Caron Furniture Ltee. (Distribution Arrangements for 1982–1987)

	1983	1984	1985	1986	1987	1988 (est.)
Canadian agents	7	7	7	7	7	7
U.S. agents	16	15	16	15	11	9
Canadian salesmen	3	3	4	4	7	7
U.S. salesmen	0	2	2	3	6	8
Canadian dealers	400	400	375	350	325	315
U.S. dealers	3,500	4,000	3,500	2,700	1,700	1,200

Caron dealt quickly with Thompson's concerns. Involvement in California and in Phoenix, St. Louis, and other West Coast markets was substantially decreased by not replacing unproductive agents. Company salesmen were added in Florida and in Minneapolis and New York. As well, Caron was considering adding more salesmen in Chicago, and the number of dealers was reduced from 2,700 to 1,700 (Exhibit 7). Reactions to desk-design concerns were slower to materialize, as Caron was trying to determine what product characteristics were generally required.

Caron Organization and Management Philosophy

Caron's ownership rested in the hands of a holding company owned by Yves Richard and assorted trusts held by members of the Caron family. The firm was principally run by Richard and three senior executives (Claude Raymond, vice president– production; Gilles Samson, vice president–marketing; and Guy Paterson, secretary/treasurer). All of the top management team were chartered accountants and none had experience in the office-furniture industry prior to joining Caron (Exhibit 8), but together they had over 50 years service with the company. Richard considered that having a background in the furniture business was often less important than having good management skills.

Most strategic decisions were made centrally by Richard. Caron had centralized most aspects of the business including purchasing, engineering, quality control, customer relations, and scheduling. However, they were increasingly giving the plant operating autonomy.

One of Richard's primary concerns was for the welfare of Caron's employees. For example, Caron maintained a no-layoff policy. To maintain this policy, Caron cross-trained employees and had in the past kept workers employed at painting the factory or improving the grounds rather than laying them off when demand was too low to keep the plants operating. Caron had also instituted both profit sharing and stock ownership plans. These personnel philosophies helped create an informal work atmosphere at Caron and was in part responsible for good employee morale and a generally low turnover rate.

Exhibit 8 Caron Furniture Ltee. (Senior Management — Biography)

Yves Richard (President)
Age: 55
Joined company: 1966
Credentials: Honours, Business Administration, University of Western Ontario
             Chartered Accountant designation
Prior work experience: Accounting firm

Gilles Samson (V.P., Marketing)
Age: 42
Joined company: 1973
Credentials: Law degree, C.A., Quebec (1973)
Prior work experience: General, as a lawyer and as an accountant

Claude Raymond (V.P., Production)
Age: 34
Joined company: 1977
Credentials: Honours, Business, McGill (1975)
             Chartered Accountant designation (1977)
Prior work experience: General, as an accountant

Guy Paterson (Secretary/Treasurer)
Age: 40
Joined company: 1980
Credentials: Chartered Accountant designation (1973)
Prior work experience: Two years in construction and work as an accountant

Gerard Thompson (National Manager, United States)
Joined company: 1987
Credentials: Business degree, University of Michigan
Prior work experience: Salesman within the U.S. furniture industry. Worked for
  Hauserman, Herman Miller, and Steelcase

Production

Caron was known in Canada as a producer of high-quality, medium- to high-priced office furniture. Caron maintained a unique mix of human and physical resources from which they developed the ability, somewhat unique in the industry, to work with solid wood.

The importance of product quality led Caron to minimize dependence on outside suppliers for important inputs; 67 percent of all Caron inputs, such as veneer, lumber milling, and wood bending were produced internally. Besides quality, this provided Caron with benefits such as guaranteed supply and lower costs. Few firms in the Canadian industry had integrated to this degree.

Caron's product line included about 60 series of chairs, most of which were upholstered, a dozen series of lounge chairs and sofas, eight types of small tables, conference tables, five series of desks, and office systems (panels). Caron prided itself on offering a broad product line. For example, each desk line had 25 to 30 different basic models. For any model, customers could choose from two wood types and eight finishes. There were 2,000 different table configurations. For chairs, Caron offered over 2,100 types of upholstery, or customers could provide their own material for upholstery.

Production of high-quality wood furniture was difficult. It required experienced craftsmen and consistently high-quality inputs: both were hard to obtain. Getting skilled workers was difficult. However, Caron's reputation for its excellent working environment attracted applicants. In-house training programs were designed to ensure that skill levels were maintained even if fully qualified applicants could not be found. Training ran from six months to over a year, depending on the employees' expertise and the skill requirements of the position.

Difficulty in securing high-quality wood arose from the "living" nature of the inputs. For example, wood could shrink or grow during processing, contained knots, and there could be significant color variations even with the same type of wood. Since there was so much variability with wood, no industry-quality standards or predefined quality levels existed. As a result, input quality was based on supplier quality standards. The importance of final product quality led Caron to establish their own quality standards for wood colouring, knots, and so on.

The production system was built around making the maximum use of piecework methods. For example, batches of chairs or small tables were produced for "white inventory," or storage as completely assembled but unfinished frames. In this way, lots of 50–600 units could be scheduled through the plant independent of customer orders. The batches of parts were moved from station to station on trolleys. Employees worked on batches in efficient, repetitive patterns and were paid on the basis of pieces completed. The frames were then stored until orders were received which called for the specific frame style. The unfinished frames were then moved through the finishing operation, then the upholstery shop (if required), and finally to the shipping department where it would be shipped to the Outremont plant. There the entire client order was gathered.

The piecework system, workflow layout, vertical integration, and especially the product mix resulted in Caron having one of the lowest rates of direct labour and material costs as a percentage of total direct costs of any Canadian furniture manufacturer, and rates which were competitive with U.S. firms.

Caron's production systems and procedures allowed the company to cope with the increased volumes; however, problems still remained. A plant inspection revealed jobs which were one to three months behind promised delivery dates. As well, stock-outs of materials had occurred.

The Current Situation

On May 20, Richard convened a management group meeting to discuss U.S. market options.

Yves Richard: As impressive as our past growth has been, it has been below our growth objective of 26 percent. If we are to attain our objectives and improve profitability, we might have to make changes in our products, prices, distribution arrangements, and markets. The issue that I am bringing forward today is the role that the U.S. market should play in Caron's future.

Gerard Thompson: The U.S. market is our best source for future growth. We are already one of the largest and best-known firms in Canada, so growth in Canada might be somewhat limited, but in the United States, we are barely scratching the surface. However, if we are to be a significant presence in terms of gaining a meaningful market share, then we will have to commit more resources to it. At a minimum, I need to replace some agents with our own sales force. Although agents have connections with dealers, some of them are not committed enough to our products and we cannot really manage them.

Gilles Samson: I would tend to agree with Gerard. Our experience has been that where agents were replaced with company sales reps and showrooms, sales have subsequently increased. For example, over the past five years two salesmen were added in Chicago and additional showroom space was purchased. During that time, sales increased by 552 percent. Although part of the increase might have arisen from other factors such as better personnel, more marketing support, or even improved economic environments, some of it was definitely attributable to the change in our sales approach.

Richard: But what's this going to cost us?

Samson: As near as Gerard and I can figure it in U.S. dollars, a sales rep will cost us $30,000–50,000 a year plus 3 percent commission. Showroom costs are hard to estimate, but for New York it would be $250,000 (U.S.) per year, while in Chicago it would be $200,000 per year. Add in another $200,000 for leasehold improvements, $150,000 for showroom furniture, $30,000 for administration, and another $20,000–30,000 for salesman-related expenses.

Richard: That's rather steep, Gilles. Depending on the extent of our commitment to the United States, the costs could run well into the millions. Besides, as it now stands, although we have been putting more company sales reps into the United States, sales have increased by 20.3 percent per year over the past five years, while Canadian sales have been increasing by 22.6 percent. This might indicate that there is in fact more room for sales growth in Canada. Maybe we should put more resources into Canada and leave the U.S. market as is?

Thompson:	The cost might seem steep, but if we use our own sales force we will save the 8 percent commissions that the agents charge us. Last year alone this amounted to $875,000.
Samson:	As for the total cost, if we increase our investment in the United States, I would not recommend blanketing the entire country with sales reps, agents, and showrooms. Any investment should be limited to the largest potential markets. In fact, over the past two years, we have been reducing our geographic scope to the point that by next year I hope to be limited to the northeastern and north central United States. In line with this focus, showrooms would only be required in what we feel are our major markets. As well, replacing unproductive agents with our own salesmen is the direction we have been heading over the past year, and I would like to see it speed up [Exhibit 7].
Thompson:	My current focus is on Chicago and New York City as they are two of the top markets in North America. I would like large showrooms in each.
Richard:	There is another issue which we should look at. Assuming that the U.S. market materializes for us, do we have the production capacity to cope with the increased volume? It's taken us three years to develop systems for coping with our current volume.
Claude Raymond:	We are hitting capacity constraints in all our plants. But I think that with a change in plant layouts, shifting plant product mixes, and improving some of the production processes, we can add about 30 percent capacity to the Lavalle Street plant and 50 percent to the St. Therese plant. Additional equipment requirements would be minor, but we would need more personnel. As well, I would like to see the Outremont plant's role expanded to include panel and workwall production. The cost for this would be approximately $3 million over four years. The net effect of all these changes would be to increase our capacity to over $60 million. Alternatively, if volume increased dramatically, we could subcontract out some of the less important work or purchase another facility. As for getting more skilled labour, St. Jean College is expanding its wood-working program, so within the next year we will have access to trained craftsmen.
Richard:	What can we expect by way of competitive reaction if we start capturing more market share in the States?
Samson:	Although the U.S. market is significantly more competitive than the Canadian market, I don't expect much reaction

from major competitors as we are not looking to take away much of their business. We are going to go through B dealers, not the major competitors' A dealers, and we are only trying to skim a bit of the market, so we are not going to be a major threat to anyone, yet.

Richard: Is there anything else that any of you would like to add?

Samson: The United States is our biggest source of profits; we charge a similar price for the products, but it is in U.S. dollars, and our only incremental cost besides marketing expenses is a 3.8 percent tariff into the States since our customers pay for shipping. In 1986, the gross profit as a percentage of sales for U.S. operations was 30 percent higher than that for Canadian sales. Most of the incremental profit arose from a 32 percent exchange rate differential. When you consider that our total gross profit last year was 38 percent of sales, you can see how much of an impact the United States has on our operations. Only an improvement of the Canadian dollar vis-à-vis the American dollar can change this. Meanwhile our Canadian market is nicely protected for two reasons: (1) we have an excellent reputation with dealers and designers, who are committed to Caron; and (2) with a 15 percent Canadian tariff for wood office furniture, it is difficult for U.S. firms to export their products into Canada. However, in the event of free trade, this second source of protection will be eliminated. In a worst case scenario—with free trade and a strengthened Canadian dollar—we will be in the throes of the most competitive situation that Caron has ever faced. In all likelihood, our margins throughout North America will be reduced. Within this context, the more competitive we are in the United States, the more competitive we will be under either free trade or an improvement in the exchange rate. This might argue for rethinking our U.S. strategy in order to strengthen ourselves for future competition.

Richard: Exchange rate fluctuations concern me. If the rate had not changed at all over the past five years, we would have lost $1,500,000 from our pretax profits. For each 1 cent increase in the value of the Canadian dollar, we lose $100,000 from our bottom line.

Raymond: Free trade and exchange rate fluctuations are only part of the competitive threat. The Canadian market is going to be more competitive within the next few years as some of our U.S. competitors are starting up operations in Canada.

Thompson: I don't know if we really have a choice. The U.S. market is

getting more and more competitive, with many firms
offering dealers and designers a lot of service support. In
my view, having our own showrooms and sales force is the
price of being in the game—without them our growth will
be limited.

Richard: I think that I have all the information I need. Unless I
hear from any of you with additional information in the
interim, I will get back to you next week with my
recommendation.

Case 8
Currie Construction Limited (A)

In May 1984, Martin Cook, president of Currie Construction Limited, a British Columbia–based road construction and maintenance firm, was contemplating U.S. market entry. Having investigated the opportunity to establish an operation in Houston, Texas, Cook now needed to make his decision.

The B.C. Road Construction and Maintenance Industry

The construction and maintenance of Canada's highways and roads fell under the jurisdiction of the provincial and municipal governments. In British Columbia, for example, the primary government funding agency responsible for the construction and maintenance of the major transportation structures (i.e., highways, roads, bridges) was the Department of Transportation (DOT). As well, each municipal government (e.g., city of Victoria) was also responsible for constructing and maintaining certain roadways in its respective jurisdiction.

The president of the B.C. Road Builders Association, which represented more than 60 road construction/maintenance companies in British Columbia, expressed in a press release his concern about the lack of funding. He noted serious concern about the condition of highways, roads, and bridges on which usage was continually on the increase, while provincial funding for both new construction and maintenance work on the existing system had decreased over the past decade. This view was supported in a series of other recently published reports stating that over half of British Columbia's paved municipal road systems needed either resurfacing or reconstruction over the next five years. This would require over $1.0 billion. As well, one third of the bridges in British Columbia were in need of replacement or rehabilitation within the next five years at an estimated cost of over $150 million. In spite of this real threat to B.C.'s infrastructure, government officials would probably not increase funding significantly within the period.

Competition in the road construction industry was fierce. Exhibit 1 presents market share data and contract value for all road construction work awarded by DOT in 1984. This was only for new construction work awarded by DOT and excluded work tendered by the municipal governments. The industry was fragmented among many competitors.

A tendering process was used by both the DOT and municipal governments to award work to contractors. A tender document was broken down into specific

EXHIBIT 1 1984 Market Share Ranking (DOT)*

Total Contracts 195		Total Value $197,799,506	Total Tonnes 1,259,373	
Rank	Contractor	Contracts	Dollar Value	Market Percentage
1	ARC Holdings Ltd.	13	37,152,682	18.78
2	TCN Construction	4	18,973,518	9.59
3	Arvac Construction	4	11,738,241	5.93
4	Jean Ltd.	2	10,007,533	5.06
5	Pey Ltd.	2	7,028,088	3.55
6	Altas Construction Ltd.	1	6,482,646	3.28
7	RAC Paving	7	6,394,994	3.23
8	Dunn Construction	8	5,876,584	2.97
9	Alden Ltd.	5	5,438,526	2.75
10	Currie Construction	4	5,333,212	2.70
11	Gant Paving Ltd.	1	5,069,375	2.56
12	Lyee Construction Ltd.	3	4,921,515	2.49
13	Rant Construction Ltd.	8	4,815,610	2.43
14	Rome Construction Ltd.	3	4,543,044	2.30
15	Ram Brothers Construction	1	4,100,067	2.07

NOTE: *Figures are disguised.

stages where a cost was assigned for each stage (i.e., stage 1—survey stake out, stage 2—shrubbery removal, stage 3—direct excavation). A unit cost was attached to each stage so that if a cost overrun occurred that was beyond the control of the contractor, then DOT would pay the contractor for the overrun. A contract was awarded on a lowest cost basis among those contractors who prepared a tender for a specific job. There was no limitation on the number of jobs a contractor could bid for as long as the company was qualified (i.e., total dollar value of work the company could do per year) and the qualification associated with each tender call (i.e., assets of company) was satisfied. As a result, in British Columbia often as many as 10 companies bid on one job at a time, thus making it extremely difficult to gain market share.

In order to stay profitable, construction companies had a number of options. The first was to invest in new unproven technology (e.g., recycling) in order to become the leader in this field in developing the B.C. market. This option involved a large amount of risk because DOT and the road construction industry were cautious of new technology claims. The second option was to invest in costly capital equipment. This was critical in this labour-intensive industry because equipment breakdowns were a major reason for cost overruns on a job. A third option was to integrate vertically backwards into the commercial end of the industry. This involved owning an asphalt production plant and/or a sand and gravel operation. Large amounts of money were required as well as a strategic decision to compete in a related industry. The fourth option was to compete in markets other than British Columbia (i.e., the United States, Ontario, Alberta). With this option, the firm risked an incomplete understanding of the market, the competitors, and the customer (i.e., government agencies responsible for road construction/maintenance have varying specifications and methods of doing business in each province or state). The final option was to diversify into an unrelated industry (e.g., concrete, housing, or transportation). This option also involved a great deal of risk because of market unfamiliarity and the large amounts of capital required.

Background Information on Martin Cook

Cook graduated from the University of Manitoba with a bachelor of science degree in 1960 and immediately accepted a job as an asphalt engineer with Shell Canada Limited (SCL). It was in the asphalt division that Cook established a working relationship with David Thomas that would have a significant effect on both their future careers within SCL. By the mid-1960s, Cook was elevated to the position of asphalt sales manager for Western Canada. Not totally satisfied with the constraints of a large corporation, he turned down two excellent promotional opportunities within SCL.

In 1970, Cook and Thomas discussed the possibility of entering into business together in the asphalt-related products market. The business would supply road asphalt and other oil-based by-products to the consumer. On January 1, 1971, Cook and Thomas left SCL and formed a company called Costal Asphalt Limited (Costal). They each contributed their personal savings of $15,000 into this company. As Cook said: "When we left Shell we did not know where we were going. We had to first find a place to set up our plant and then find the necessary financing. However, we knew we had a good idea."

Development of Costal Limited

Cook and Thomas approached the B.C. Development Corporation and the Federal Department of Regional and Industrial Expansion (DRIE) for financial support for Costal. They were turned down because their proposal was determined to be infeasible. The banks also would not provide any financing because Cook and Thomas had no personal assets for use as collateral. However, they were able to get financial support from Mark Currie and Evan Clarry, owners of Currie Construction Limited. The deal was structured so that Currie Construction owned 51 percent of Costal and Cook and Thomas 49 percent. After payment of a $100,000 loan to Currie and Clarry, the equity position would become 50 percent Currie, 25 percent Cook, and 25 percent Thomas. It took one and one-half years to repay the original $100,000 loan.

In 1973, Costal entered into a joint venture with an investor (Jake Garner) to purchase a profitable road construction company, A.A. McLeod Construction Limited (McLeod), in the Queen Charlotte area in British Columbia. Garner was responsible for the day-to-day operations and management of the firm.

From 1973 to 1976, Cook and Thomas concentrated primarily on expanding Costal operations by opening up terminals in Calgary and Edmonton. McLeod continued to be profitable under Garner's direction.

Costal's success to this point was attributed mainly to the dedication of Cook and Thomas. It was not unusual for either partner to work seven days a week, 15 hours a day. During this period, Cook's responsibilities included answering the phone, pouring 425°F asphaltic product into 25 kg containers in the shop, and taking care of financial matters as well as "pounding the pavement to drum up business." This hard work paid off for Cook and Thomas: Costal was profitable from its inception. Over this period, their management skills and business know-how increased enormously.

In 1976, Cook and Thomas wanted to further vertically integrate forward. They attempted to purchase a profitable road construction company in Victoria (similar in size to McLeod), but the deal fell through. At the same time, Currie Construction was offered for sale. Currie and Clarry had received a serious offer from a British-based company to purchase Currie; however, they desired to sell it to Canadian investors if they could be found. Cook and Thomas saw this as an excellent opportunity to become fully integrated in the road construction industry in British Columbia. Because Currie was a major customer for Costal product, a change of ownership could jeopardize this account. Also, the purchase of Currie by another firm could have a negative effect on Costal's operations since Currie owned 50 percent of Costal. Up to this time, Currie and Clarry were silent partners in Costal; they never interfered with the management of Costal, and McLeod and the valuable long-term assets on Currie's balance sheet.

Currie Construction Limited

Currie Construction was one of the oldest and largest road maintenance and construction companies based in British Columbia. Its history dated back to 1919 when Eugene Boyle built the foundations upon which Currie would grow and prosper for the next 60 years. During that time, Currie participated in building such large projects as the Trans Canada Highway and the Alaskan Highway. The company enjoyed enormous success in the 50s and 60s when governments were spending huge amounts of money to build Canada's transportation infrastructure. However, during the late 1960s and early 1970s, Canada's infrastructure was nearing completion and the industry was shifting away from new construction of road systems to reconstruction and maintenance of the existing road networks.

Cook and Thomas decided that with the purchase of Currie Construction, Cook would leave Costal and become president of Currie. There was too much at stake to allow someone else to run the company for them; this was a major acquisition that could cause the collapse of everything they had achieved to date if not managed properly.

On November 15, 1976, Cook took over total control of Currie's operations. During the negotiations to purchase Currie for $10.6 million, Currie had indicated that he expected Currie to make a profit of $1 million for the fiscal year (ending March 31) of 1977. However, much to Cook's surprise, Currie experienced a net operating loss of $1.3 million instead.

Despite the poor performance in 1976, Cook believed that Currie was still a good deal. The company owned valuable pieces of real estate (e.g., two golf courses) whose potential value was enormous. As well, Currie owned and operated asphalt production plants in key strategic locations in the province and owned valuable land north of Vancouver that contained large amounts of aggregate used in the construction process and in the asphalt production plants. Having an asphalt supply was extremely important in the road construction business.

Cook identified some critical problems with Currie's operations initially. A glaring problem was that they were still competing heavily in the highway road construction segment of the market, yet they were losing money. Currie had failed to recognize that the market was undergoing a change from new highway construction to reconstruction and road maintenance. Road construction placed much greater emphasis on earth moving (excavating, drilling, blasting) than road maintenance, where the emphasis was more on grinding and recycling. In addition, Currie's equipment was old and tended to break down. This led to cost overruns and reduced profit margins on all jobs.

Another problem was that Currie was an old company which had old ways of doing business. The majority of the senior-level management had been with the company for over 20 years; in fact, a lot of them had started out as equipment operators and worked their way up into management. Currie lacked fresh "blood" in the organization, the environment was changing dramatically, and management was not able to realize this or keep up with it.

The employees of Currie were very dedicated and loyal to the company. A great majority were immigrants who had worked for Currie for many years. However, Cook noticed that some of the older employees had become comfortable and complacent with their positions and hence their motivation had dropped. As Cook stated: "We had a lot of old employees who were getting late in their years and did not have too much drive. It was imperative that we get their productivity to increase dramatically."

For the next three years, Cook concentrated on restructuring the organization in terms of personnel and operations. The key was to identify those people in management who were able to make the quantum leap from the "old school" to the "new school." Those who were not able to adapt had to retire. Also, Currie had to reorient itself in the market by making the transition from the heavy construction end of the business to the road maintenance end where the profit margins were higher.

By 1980, Cook felt that he had moulded Currie into a more aggressive and stronger competitor in the road construction market. He had removed all the older management that could not adapt to Currie's new environment and, as a result, the senior management staff was much leaner and more aggressive. Secondly, Cook hired two key people to the management staff: one brought valuable experience to the commercial side of the business and the other to the equipment operations area. Finally, Cook had rationalized the operations in some areas and expanded efforts in other areas.

Cook identified six key strategic decisions that were made:

1. Entered into a joint venture operation with a successful and experienced sand and gravel company to develop Currie's 500 acres of gravel deposits north of Vancouver.

2. Made a commitment to become the leader in the pavement maintenance market in British Columbia. This required investing in technology that was new to the industry such as recycling, road surface scarifying, and pavement profiling. Recycling was a process whereby the existing pavement surface was removed (i.e., by grinding machines or by using back hoes to completely tear it up) and used along with virgin aggregate to form a new recycled mix of asphalt. The new mix was then relaid on the roadway using the usual procedures. This process required additional equipment installed in the asphalt production plant. Pavement profiling was a process whereby a machine (i.e., a grinder) with a large rotating drum containing carbide teeth planed the surface of the road to various depths. The material removed from the road could be used in a recycled asphaltic mixture or it could be used as a subgrade material in another project. This process was used to remove surface distress appearing in the pavement. As well, it corrected the pavement profile to allow for proper drainage and to correct curb heights. Road surface scarifying was a process in which a machine heated up the pavement and removed the surface distress. The removed material was treated with an emulsion to rejuvenate its properties and then relaid.

3. Increased Currie's presence in the road calcium segment of the market. Calcium was sprayed on dirt roads to control the amount of dust.

4. Obtained operating authority to transport petroleum products (for Currie and commercially) in Alberta and several surrounding northern U.S. states.

5. Rationalized Currie's operations in Burnaby, moving away from road construction and concentrating on supplying materials (i.e., asphalt and aggregate) and carrying out winter operations (i.e., snow removal and sanding).

6. Purchased a road surfacing company in Alberta. This made Currie one of the dominant firms in this market.

These changes had a positive effect on Currie's income statement. Exhibit 2 presents a financial summary of Currie's performance from 1977 to 1984. Since 1979, Currie had been a profitable company.

A major burden upon Currie's profitability was the interest owing on the $10.0 million loan. The original plan was to repay the bank the entire debt by 1982. However, this was based on an initial interest rate of 8.5 percent, which was adjusted for inflation in the following years. In the early 80s interest rates reached highs of 20 to 25 percent. Consequently, Currie was not able to make any interest payments until 1983. Cook was able to get the bank to agree to capitalize the interest payments over that time.

In 1980, Currie was able to sell some property in order to pay off some of the outstanding debt. As well, the company seemed to be going in the right direction and, as Cook stated: "We were able to see faintly the light at the end of the tunnel."

EXHIBIT 2

CURRIE PAVING LIMITED
Financial Summary (Yearly) ($'000)

Year	Current Assets	Current Liabilities	Long-Term Debt (LTD)	L.T.D. Interest	Revenue	Net Income	Fixed Asset Purchases
March 77*	5,481	4,537	8,974	–	6,899	(1,370)	573
March 78	6,006	5,646	9,725	901	22,380	2,124	–
March 79	6,029	4,323	11,918	1,390	21,159	153	1,337
March 80	5,114	3,970	10,501	1,631	23,433	3,719	1,136
March 81	5,063	2,864	10,280	1,954	23,267	1,025	1,995
March 82	10,478	7,051	11,028	2,095	29,784	2,169	2,082
February 83	9,289	3,588	12,955	2,105	34,702	1,144	1,695
February 84	12,983	8,145	6,827	1,663	40,921	740	2,309

NOTE: *1977 values are for an eight-month period.

The Proposed Houston Division

In the summer of 1983, Cook had business dealings with Brad Carlyle. Carlyle worked for a pipeline construction company in the Calgary area. Prior to this job, he worked in Houston supervising the completion of a rapid transit system. In December 1983, Carlyle arranged to have lunch with Cook. Over lunch, Carlyle told Cook about the opportunities that he saw in the Houston market. Carlyle knew that Currie was looking to expand its operations and he felt that the Houston market was one area that Currie should seriously consider. Currie Construction had previously only worked in the United States as a subcontractor on several road rehabilitation projects.

Carlyle indicated to Cook that he wanted to return to Houston. He believed that he was capable of developing a successful division in this market for Currie. Carlyle had made some valuable contacts within both the government and the construction industry that would be very beneficial. As well, he knew the market and the way it functioned. Cook was impressed with Carlyle's enthusiasm and his belief in the Houston market. Although Carlyle did not have a civil engineering background and was not totally comfortable with road construction techniques, Cook had full confidence in his ability to learn on the job. Cook indicated that he would get back to Carlyle very soon.

As a result of this meeting, Cook and Thomas decided that it would be worthwhile to spend a few days in the Houston market in order to get a better feeling for its potential. None of Currie's senior management people had experience in this market. In mid-January 1984, Cook, Thomas, and Carlyle spent three days in Houston meeting with Department of Transportation officials and touring the area. During this brief stay, a large amount of positive information was gathered about the prospects of entering this market. The DOT officials were excited about Currie entering the market because a recent combines investigation found that a large number of the old established road construction firms were guilty of price fixing and collusion. As a result, they were barred from bidding work for one to two years.

Texas was also experiencing a tremendous amount of growth, and government officials realized that improvements to the infrastructure were required to ensure this growth. As a result, the government had made it a priority to upgrade the highways, bridges, and roadways throughout the state. Cook and Thomas were astonished at the amount of money budgeted to infrastructure upgrading. It was approximately $700 million (U.S.) a year, roughly 4.5 times more than the amount allocated by the DOT in British Columbia.

Even more enticing about this market was the fewer number of competitors compared with the competition in British Columbia. The average number of contractors bidding per job was approximately four.

Further discussion regarding the Houston market took place between Cook, Thomas, and Carlyle. More visits to Houston followed.

The main reason to enter this market according to Cook was because "it offered an opportunity to get better utilization out of our specialized machinery. Instead of having our grinding machines and scarifiers sit idle during the winter months, we could find work for them in Houston. There were no grinders at all in this area of the United States and no one had become involved in recycling."

Cook's orientation for the Houston market was to concentrate primarily on the road maintenance activities of pavement grinding and scarifying operations where Currie was strongest. It was thought that by going in small, Currie could get a better understanding of the market, make some key contacts in government, and develop a good reputation within the industry by doing quality work. Because the road maintenance techniques which Currie possessed were more advanced than those in use in Texas, the company realized it would take a little time to demonstrate their merits to the key government contacts. Currie planned eventually to reproduce its B.C. operations in Texas, where there were no companies totally vertically integrated. Once Currie was established in Texas, it would be able to compete in the nearby surrounding states: Florida, Georgia, North and South Carolina, Tennessee, Alabama, and Louisiana.

The proposed organization chart for the Houston operations is presented in Exhibit 3. Carlyle would report directly to Cook on all matters concerning operations. If the entry took place, Cook planned to spend time overseeing the move to Houston. However, after operations were running, Cook did not plan on spending much time in Houston because Currie did not have much slack in the management ranks. The existing people were all so extended that U.S. entry would have to be delayed if Brad Carlyle, or someone like him from outside existing management, was not available.

EXHIBIT 3   Proposed Organization Chart: Houston, 1984

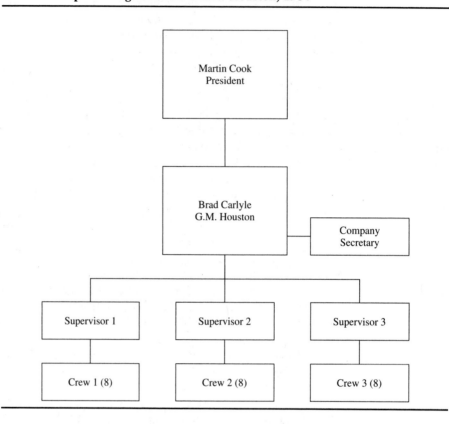

Subsequent Thinking

Although Currie's primary strength was in road maintenance, the decision was made to get involved in the road construction end of the business if Currie entered this market. There were two reasons for this strategy. The first was to generate some cash flow in order to cover the operating expenses until the grinding and scarifying operations picked up. Secondly, according to information provided by Carlyle, the market appeared to be made of gold; it offered easy access to abnormal profits.

Although little public data were available, the competition in this market was primarily family-owned companies. These firms were cash rich and were not accustomed to much competition. As Cook described them, "They are a bunch of old-time southern contractors who are financially very strong and wealthy, primarily from the price fixing that had occurred." One additional key player in the market was ARRON, a subsidiary of Petro Oil, one of the largest corporations in the United States.

EXHIBIT 4

CURRIE CONSTRUCTION LTD.
Cost Analysis for Period Ended

	Cost for Month		Cost to Date		Cost to Complete		Forecasted Final		Planned*		Variance
	Unit	Cost	Unit	Cost	Unit	Cost	Unit	Cost	Unit	Cost	
100 — Contract costs											
110 — Construction costs											
198 — Cost of operations											
200 — Traffic Control											
Quantity											
Man hours											
Labour											
Man hours											
Supervisor											
Permanent materials											
Other construction costs											
Equipment											
Totals											
210 — Erosion control											
Quantity											
Man hours											
Labour											
Permanent material											
Other construction costs											
Equipment											
Totals											
220 — Lump sum construction											
Quantity											
Man hours											
Labour											
Permanent material											
Other construction costs											
Equipment											
Hired equipment and operator											
Hired equipped/operated											
Minority business enterprises											
Totals											

NOTE: *Equals original bid cost

If they proceeded, Cook and Carlyle decided that Currie would buy new equipment since abnormal profits seemed to be present. While Currie would normally lease and/or rent equipment for new operations initially in order to minimize investment in a new market, this would reduce profit margins slightly. It was felt that Currie could be competitive and easily make even more than 4 percent net profit on revenue with new equipment.

Carlyle felt there would be no problem locating supervisors and equipment operators. Due to the large population growth occurring in the southern states and the minor influence of labour unions, Carlyle felt he would be able to hire blue-collar employees at about half the wage rate that Currie was paying its employees in British Columbia. Carlyle would be responsible for hiring all the blue-collar employees; however, he would require Cook's approval in hiring supervisors.

If Currie decided to enter this market, the Houston subsidiary would utilize Currie's existing centralized control systems. In 1982, Currie had paid $15,000 and invested a further $70,000 for a fully integrated job costing/receivable/ledger cost reporting and accounting system which was one of the most comprehensive of any firm in the industry. For each of the 200 active accounts that Currie was working on, it received a monthly cost analysis (see Exhibit 4, for example). This allowed the company to see costs broken down by subcategory on each job for the current month, to date, to complete, and forecasted final—all versus the original plan. For *any* given job, it might be several years before all of the relevant costs had been accounted for and the accounts closed off.

With this background, Cook realized that if he were to enter the U.S. market at all in the next few years, he would have to decide soon.

CASE 9
COOPER CANADA LTD. (CONDENSED)

In late 1982 CCM Canada, a manufacturer of bicycles, skates, and hockey equipment, was put into receivership and the business put up for sale. While CCM's competitors had noted the company's accumulating problems with some satisfaction and relief, they were now faced with new questions: Who would acquire the assets of CCM? What would be the impact on the competitive structure of the industry?

In the meantime, the CCM receiver was pressing for action. John Cooper, vice chairman of Cooper Canada Ltd., one of the interested competitors, described the situation:

> Our people visited the CCM plant and offices last week and they had no sooner returned than the receiver called wanting to know how soon we could make a bid. He said that speed is critical because he expects other bids at any moment and that the creditors want action since CCM's situation worsens every day. We will have to act fast . . . we have a meeting set for next Monday to make an offer if we want to. It is too bad we are under such time pressure but that's the way this deal is.

Cooper was interested only in the skate and hockey equipment part of the CCM business. Here, some elements of the fit between Cooper and CCM's winter goods business were obvious. Cooper could completely outfit a hockey player except for sweaters and skates. CCM's skate line was still one of the most respected in the business. The value of CCM's competing lines of hockey sticks and protective equipment, however, was less clear. The bicycle line was of no interest, but Cooper had made arrangements with another prospective buyer to pick up this part of the CCM operation in a joint bid. The question facing Cooper management, under time pressure, was whether they wished to proceed with their side of a bid and, if so, with what price and conditions.

The Skate and Hockey Equipment Industry

There were four basic product lines in the industry: skates, protective equipment (e.g., helmets, gloves, pads), sticks, and apparel. Cooper management estimated the industry's 1981 value of shipments for these lines was as follows:

	($000)
Ice skates	$78,000
Hockey equipment	31,500
Hockey sticks	29,000
Apparel	27,000

This case was prepared by Professor Donald H. Thain. Copyright © 1985 by The University of Western Ontario.

The overall demand for hockey-related products had grown slowly in the 1970s and little or no growth was expected in the 1980s. Population trends in the prime hockey-playing age groups were not favourable, and participation rates were under pressure. A major problem with participation was the increasing cost of equipping a player: from $100 to $200 for beginners (including used equipment) and up to $1,500 for a professional.

The rapidly changing technology of hockey equipment was one reason for the high cost of equipment. Product innovation was driving toward lighter, safer, and more comfortable gear. As a 1982 article in the Maple Leaf Gardens program described it:

> Space-age hockey equipment is speeding up the game and cutting down on injuries. Technological breakthroughs are sending the NHL where it has never gone before — to lighter, cooler, stronger, tighter-fitting one-piece body protection; aluminum or fibreglass and plastic laminated sticks; and zircon-guarded, carbon-bladed skates encased in ballistic and nylon-wrapped boots.
>
> Leaf trainer Danny Lemelin thinks skates have "changed most dramatically" in the past few years. He points out that most are 4 ounces lighter because of the plastic blade holder and nylon boot. This space-age equipment has speeded up the game and cut down on injuries. And, it's made the felt-and-fibre shin, shoulder, elbow, and pant pads, one-piece ash sticks, and leather tube skates, so popular only a decade ago, obsolete. . . .
>
> The evolution turned revolution in NHL gear is the by-product of by-products. New foams, plastics, nylon, and fibreglass (many invented in Korea during the fifties to keep fighting forces warm and protected) have made things "lighter and stronger," says one long-time equipment manufacturer. All these new inventions have been developed to conform to the game of hockey. . . .

Canadian brands had established an international reputation for product excellence, and exports of hockey equipment had increased from $20 million in 1971 to $41.5 million in 1980. Skates represented the largest export product. The United States was the largest market, but Scandinavia and western Europe were also strong. Japan and Australia were newly developing markets.

The market shares of the major competitors in the industry by-product line are given in Exhibit 1. The skate business was dominated by three firms: Warrington Industries Ltd. (with three brands—Bauer, Lange, and Micron), CCM, and Daoust. Cooper was the primary company in hockey equipment. The stick business was shared by half a dozen significant competitors, of which the largest was Sherwood-Drolet. Cooper and Sport Maska were the two most significant competitors in apparel. A brief description of the companies that Cooper considered interested and capable of bidding for CCM is given in the appendix.

Skates

The demand for skates in Canada had for several years fluctuated between 1 million and 1.3 million pairs. There were two basic types of skate boots, sewn and molded. Leather had been the first boot material and was still used in most high-quality, high-priced skates. Over 90 percent of NHL players wore leather

Exhibit 1 Products, and Estimated Percent Market Shares of Major Competitors in the Canadian Hockey Equipment Market, 1981

Company	Skates	Hockey Equipment	Sticks	Apparel
Cooper		69%	7%	31%
Canadien		7	12	
CCM	25%	7	6	
D & R		7		
Jofa		3		
Koho		2.5	10.5	
Sherwood			25	
Victoriaville			11	
Louisville			6.5	
Titan			11	
Maska				42
Bernard				11
Sandow				10
Bauer*	33			
Lange*	5			
Micron*	13			
Daoust	17			
Orbit	5			
Roos	1			
Ridell	1			
Others		4.5	11	6
	100%	100%	100%	100%
($000,000s)	$78	$31.5	$29	$27

*Brands of Warrington Industries Ltd.

SOURCE: Rough estimates by Cooper product managers.

skates. However, in the 1970s molded boots had entered the market and the low-priced market in particular had become competitive with leather-booted skates.

Information on the total Canadian hockey-skate market and the shares of major competitors segmented by sewn and molded boots is presented in Exhibit 2. Hockey skates could also be segmented by price point as follows:

Range	Retail Price	1982 Estimated Share (units)
High	More than $200	15%
Medium	$120–$180	20%
Low	Less than $90	65%

Exhibit 2   Canadian Hockey Skate Production (000s of pairs)

Year	Sewn	Molded	Total
1977	1,050	50	1,100
1978	775	150	925
1979	1,050	250	1,300
1980	850	300	1,150
1981	970	400	1,370
1982 (forecast)	750	300	1,050
1983 (forecast)	900	350	1,250

1982 Factory Sales and Market Shares of Leading Competitors (000s of pairs)

	Sewn		Molded		Total		Sales		$
	Pairs	%	Pairs	%	Pairs	%	($000)	%	Average of Total
Bauer	305	42.9%	50	13.7%	355	32.9%	$20,265	35.4%	$57.08
Micron	—	—	185	50.5	185	17.2	8,690	15.2	46.97
Lange	—	—	100	27.3	100	9.3	3,280	5.8	32.80
Daoust	205	28.7	—	—	205	19.0	9,780	17.0	47.70
CCM	147	20.6	6	1.6	153	14.2	12,050	21.0	78.76
Orbit	55	7.8	25	6.8	80	7.4	3,205	5.6	40.06
	712	100%	366	100%	1,078	100%	$57,270	100%	$53.13

1982 Hockey Skate Sales by Geographic Market (000s of pairs)

Manufacturer	Canada	U.S.A.	Europe	Far East	Total
Canadian	785	238	67	15	1,105
Non-Canadian	—	312	233	25	570
Totals	785	550	300	40	1,675

Source: Estimates based on industry information and casewriter's estimates.

Industry observers noted that the high- and low-end market shares were increasing and the medium range decreasing. The breakdown of CCM's total unit skate sales in the high-, medium-, and low-price ranges was approximately 60 percent, 25 percent, and 15 percent, respectively, and that of Bauer, the largest brand, was thought to be 20 percent, 30 percent, and 50 percent, respectively.

Skate blades were another factor in the market. They were available from three sources in Canada. The largest manufacturer, the St. Lawrence Company of Montreal, sold mainly to CCM and Daoust. Canpro Ltd., owned by Warrington, sold mainly to Bauer, Micron, and Lange. CCM manufactured their own Tuuk blades and sold some to other skate makers. While blade technology had changed significantly in the late 1970s with the introduction of plastic mounts to replace tubes, the major current change was the trend back to carbon steel, from the newer stainless steel.

Exhibit 3 **Price Ranges for Hockey Equipment**

	Typical Retail Price Range	
Item	*Mens*	*Boys*
Pants	$40–$130	$30–$60
Gloves	50–140	25–70
Helmet	27–45	27–45
Cooperall	115–125	98
Shin pads	20–75	20–75
Elbow pads	19–50	7–25
Shoulder pads	25–70	14–40

Hockey Equipment

Hockey equipment included all items on the list shown in Exhibit 3, which also shows the range of typical retail prices. Continuous research and development was necessary to ensure that these items provided maximum protection and comfort. Cooper dominated the market with a 69 percent share.

Sticks

The composition of sticks was continually changing. What had started out as a one-piece blade and handle developed into a two-piece solid-wood handle and blade, and later a laminated handle and curved blade with fibreglass reinforcement. The most recent development was an aluminum handle with a replaceable wooden blade. Changes were intended to improve strength and passing and shooting accuracy. Sherwood-Drolet led in this market with a 25 percent share.

Apparel

Differences in prices of sweaters and socks were due basically to the material used in the product. The most popular sweater materials were polyester and cotton knits because of their strength and lightness. Designs of sweaters were fairly standard, with lettering and cresting done separately. Socks were a standard product with little differentiation. Sport Maska controlled 42 percent of this market because of its quality product, excellent distribution, and good rapport with dealers.

Distribution

Skates and hockey equipment were sold in a wide range of retail outlets, including specialty, independent, department, discount, chain, and catalogue stores. Although specific numbers were not available, the split of business between these outlets followed a common retail pattern. The specialty independents and chains dominated in the higher-priced items where product knowledge and service were essential. The mass merchandisers were dominant in the lower-priced product areas.

In Canada the most common route from manufacturer to retailer was through distributors who used sales agents. Manufacturers wanted agents who would represent their product aggressively, seek out new orders, and provide them with market feedback. Usually these agents either were, or had been, actively involved in sports. However, since the agents sold multiple lines, it was difficult to control their activities and level and mix of sales. Most companies used a sales force of 10 to 12 reps to cover most of Canada. A few small companies utilized wholesalers to supplement their sales force.

Retail outlets had experienced little real growth in sales and were finding themselves with increasing inventories. Therefore, retailers started carrying shallower stocks, ordering more frequently, and relying on manufacturers or distributors to provide back-up inventories. This trend meant that bargaining power had shifted from the manufacturers to the retailers, who were trying to gain volume discounts and delivery advantages by reducing the number of suppliers.

Promotion

Three types of promotion were used: company and product promotion, media advertising, and trade show participation. Product and image promotion seemed to be the most effective avenue for stimulating sales. Because professional players set industry trends, it was important to get popular players to use and endorse products. To recruit these players, professional "detail men" from sports equipment manufacturers were assigned to players to make sure their equipment fit perfectly and that the player was loyal to the brand. It was also important to get as many players as possible wearing the products so that the brand name would enjoy good exposure during televised games. Therefore, the detail men also tried to work through team trainers to supply most of the team with the brand. While some competitors used financial incentives to push a product, Cooper relied on high-quality, fast service in fitting and repairs and intensive sales efforts, and was not involved with special deals or endorsement contracts.

Media advertising was primarily confined to the larger firms. Print advertising in the concentrated population areas was the most common approach.

Trade shows significantly influenced retail buyers. Many sales took place at the shows, bookings were made for orders, and sales were made on follow-up calls by sales reps. The Canadian Sporting Goods Association organized two shows annually.

Cooper Canada

In 1946, Jack Cooper left Eaton's to join General Leather Goods Ltd., as its first and, until 1951, only salesperson. Subsequently, Cooper and Cecil Weeks bought out the company's original owner and changed the name to Cooper-Weeks. In 1954, Cooper acquired Cecil Weeks' interest, and the company became the exclusive Canadian manufacturer of Buxton Leather goods. In the following years, the company grew through internal development and acquisitions to encompass a wide range of leather and sporting goods products. In 1970, the company changed its name to Cooper Canada Ltd. and went public. By 1981, revenues were almost $63 million, but Cooper experienced its first loss in years. Cooper management expected a return to profitability in 1982 in spite of a recession and high interest rates. Financial statements for Cooper Canada from 1977 through 1981 are presented in Exhibits 4 and 5.

In 1982 Cooper was engaged in two major lines of business; sporting goods (hockey equipment, apparel, golf bags, baseball gloves, inflated goods, etc.) and leather goods and finishing (wallets, carrying bags, etc.). The relative scale and performance of these businesses is illustrated in Exhibit 6. Cooper also had a significant sales and distribution operation in the United States as indicated by the geographic segmentation of the business in Exhibit 6.

Exhibit 4 Consolidated Statement of Income and Retained Earnings, Years Ended December 31 ($000s)

	1981	1980	1979	1978	1977
Net Sales	$ 62,827	$62,183	$55,810	$49,429	$42,803
Less: Operating costs	57,049	55,901	51,844	44,364	38,538
Net before Depreciation, etc.	5,778	6,282	3,966	5,064	4,265
Less: Deprec. & amortization	724	746	748	626	609
Long-term debt interest	1,905	934	1,022	929	778
Other interest	2,933	2,866	2,068	1,138	941
Add: Foreign exchange gain	(105)	369	(107)	216	173
Earnings, discontinued operation	929	—	—	—	—
Less: Income taxes					
Current	14	176	20	525	518
Deferred	208	48	454	21	58
Net Income, Operations	818	1,977	455	2,039	1,650
Add: Extraordinary item	(1,543)	76	—	—	—
Net Income	(725)	2,053	455	2,039	1,650
Shares Outstanding					
Common ($000s)	1,486	1,483	1,483	1,404	1,388
Net income per share	(0.49)	1.38	0.31	1.45	1.18

Exhibit 5 Consolidated Balance Sheet as at December 31 ($000s)

	1981	1980	1979	1978	1977
Assets					
Current					
Short-term bank deposit	—	$ 1,790	—	$ 22	$ 95
Accounts receivable	$ 9,726	10,625	$10,315	9,185	8,340
Inventories:					
Raw materials	6,177	8,792	13,064	5,675	5,535
Work in process	1,593	1,758	1,817	1,006	1,379
Finished goods	15,954	11,669	10,530	10,937	10,839
Prepaid expenses, etc.	580	691	545	886	630
	34,030	35,325	39,271	27,714	26,897
Fixed assets at cost					
Buildings	6,179	6,145	6,145	6,117	6,078
Machines, equipment, etc.	4,191	4,521	4,171	3,354	3,174
Dies, moulds, etc.	235	567	619	435	284
Land	91	91	91	90	90
Less: Accumulated depreciation	5,351	5,104	4,518	4,000	3,712
	5,345	6,220	6,508	5,998	5,914
Investment in nonconsolidated subsidiaries	1,122	—	—	—	—
Deferred income taxes	373	581	533	—	—
	40,870	42,126	46,312	33,713	32,889
Liabilities					
Current					
Bank indebtedness	10,373	15,853	17,423	8,283	6,955
Accounts payable	3,463	3,380	6,380	3,153	3,576
Income and other taxes payable	1,002	695	641	352	314
Long-term debt due	16	233	603	1,134	1,059
	14,854	20,161	25,047	12,924	11,905
Long-term debt					
Bank loans	9,000	4,000	5,375	5,875	6,900
10% sinking funds debs. due 1990	1,582	1,892	1,920	2,053	2,148
6.5% mortgage, due 1992	248	265	273	291	280
Notes payable to shareholders	—	125	437	504	—
Less amount due 1 yr.	16	233	603	1,134	1,059
Deferred taxes	—	—	—	418	397
Shareholders' equity					
Capital Stock					
Common	3,403	3,392	3,392	2,764	2,716
Retained Earnings	11,799	12,524	10,471	10,016	9,600
	$40,870	$42,126	$46,312	$33,713	$32,889

EXHIBIT 6 Cooper Canada Revenues and Profits by Business Segment, 1981 ($000s)

	Industry Segments			Geographic Segments		
	Sporting Goods	*Leather Goods & Finishing*	*Total*	*Canada*	*United States*	*Total*
Revenue	$46,913	$16,076	62,827	$57,122	$11,321	$62,827
Operating profit	7,434	1,678	8,939	7,823	1,289	8,939
Identifiable assets	28,703	8,001	40,870*	30,403	6,301	40,870*

*Includes corporate assets of $4,549.

Management Goals

Jack Cooper, "the chief," and his two sons, John and Don,[1] owned 82 percent of the company's outstanding common stock. Jack Cooper, who retained voting control, was chairman and chief executive officer, and Henry Nolting was president and chief operating officer. John Cooper was vice chairman and deputy chief executive officer. They worked closely together, meeting for frequent discussions daily. The company's organization is shown in Exhibit 7.

Management's immediate concerns were to increase sales and margins; to implement a badly needed information system; to strengthen and control activities in marketing, production, and finance; to reduce short-term bank debt and high-interest expenses; to bring the leather goods division from a loss to a profit; and to iron out troublesome technical and production problems in J. B. Foam, a manufacturer of plastic foam pads and products that had recently been purchased and moved to Cooper's Toronto plant.

Long-term goals called for further development of sporting goods to increase growth and utilize the great strengths of the Cooper name. Additions to the product line were sought through new-product development and/or acquisition. Cooper was also developing more export markets for its sporting goods products.

Performance

Growth had always been foremost among Jack Cooper's goals. Sales had increased continuously since 1969, except in 1975. However, earnings had fluctuated widely over the same period. Earnings dropped in 1979 because of problems in absorbing the purchase of Winnwell Sports. And in 1981, high interest rates, the recession, and the disposal of Cooper's unsuccessful production operations in Barbados all hurt the bottom line. However, interim 1982 figures indicated

---

[1]Don, who had managed the leather goods division for several years, left the company in 1980 and started a women's sportswear retailing company. He remained a director.

EXHIBIT 7 Organization Chart

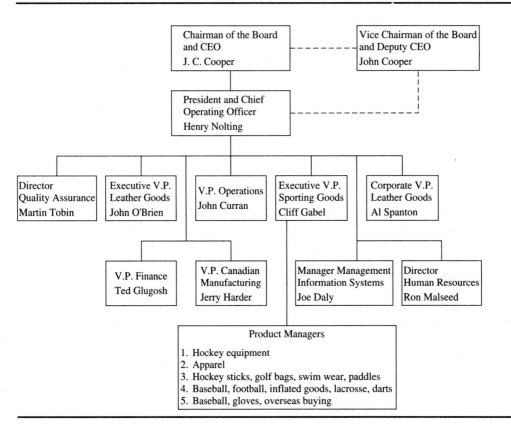

much stronger performance. Although there was little growth in sales, the tight inventory and cost controls implemented by Henry Nolting had helped to increase earnings.

Marketing

Cooper products covered a wide range of quality and price points. In hockey equipment, for example, the Cooper line ranged from high-end items, used by top professional teams around the world, to medium-low for the beginning player. In baseball equipment and supplies, the quality and price covered a medium-high to low range, appealing to younger and more experienced players, but not professionals.

Hockey equipment was the company's major line and future growth area. To keep its competitive edge, Cooper employed eight people to work full time on product development, with a priority on hockey products. The aim was product leadership, giving athletes the best possible effectiveness and protection. An example of the product development work was Cooper's latest product, the Cooperall, an elasticized body garment which held all the protective pads in place. Cooperalls represented a major innovation and had given Cooper a clear lead on competitors who were currently trying to copy the product.

Distribution of Cooper goods was through its 25-person sales force, which provided the most extensive national coverage of any company in the industry. Sales reps were organized on a geographic basis and were paid on a salary-plus-bonus-minus-expenses system, with no upper limit on bonuses. The total customer base was around 1,600. Because Cooper and CCM had been competitive across a wide product line and Cooper accounts usually sold Bauer skates, significant overlap of Cooper and CCM accounts was not extensive. Sales were distributed equally throughout the East, Ontario, and the West. National coverage by its own sales force gave Cooper an advantage over its competitors, few of whom had such coverage. However, a concern was that 90 percent of sales were made to 20 percent of accounts and almost 40 percent of sales were made to only 20 major customers.

Cliff Gabel, executive vice president, sporting goods, reported that the sales force was enthusiastic about adding skates to their line. While no one in the Cooper organization had any in-depth experience in the skate business, Mr. Gabel, who was widely known and highly respected in the industry, had maintained a good relationship with several key marketing managers at CCM, some of whom were now retired. He believed that one man in particular, who had an outstanding reputation as perhaps the "best skate man around," would welcome the opportunity to help Cooper take over and manage CCM should the opportunity arise. A respected and now retired manager from the Bauer Company who was a good friend of John Cooper was also thought to be available.

Cooper was the largest national advertiser in the sporting goods industry and had won awards for the quality of its television and print ads. The latest campaign had featured the Cooperall and was aided during the 1982 Stanley Cup telecasts.

Manufacturing and Distribution

Cooper had two manufacturing facilities. A plant in west Toronto did the bulk of the work but an older woodworking plant in Cambridge produced hockey sticks, baseball bats, and canoe paddles. Each facility manufactured hundreds of separate products that involved thousands of parts, requiring control procedures that were complex and numerous.

There was an excess of relatively expensive manufacturing space in the Toronto plant because it was built larger than necessary in 1976. In addition, several products, previously produced in Canada, had since been contracted to offshore manufacturers at lower costs. These manufacturers were primarily in the Orient and did contract work for most of Cooper's competitors. As a result, Cooper's designs were widely and easily copied by the other companies.

In distribution, Cooper chose to act as a "stockhouse," filling as many customer orders as possible on request. Speedy response was a major factor in maintaining customer loyalty. Cooper had a policy of providing a fill rate of 90 percent in nonpeak seasons and 80 percent in peak seasons. This required substantial working capital, as Cooper's line encompassed over 12,000 stock-keeping units (SKUs). The sporting goods division carried 65 percent to 80 percent of the total company inventory. Sporting goods' finished goods inventory reached as high as $18 million each April for deliveries of fall lines. A company objective was to reduce year-end inventories from $23.7 million in 1981 to a more manageable $18 million by the end of 1982. One manager indicated that a recent reduction in the past company policy of producing 120 percent of forecast sales to a level of 100 percent of forecast sales would be a major factor in reducing inventory.

Information Systems

A monthly report of sales and gross profit for each SKU and product line was available to each product manager. Quarterly reports provided by cost accounting attempted to determine actual margins realized by each division on each product line. Product managers were also provided with a report on the inventory of each SKU. Product managers were expected to make decisions on pricing and provide input on production levels based on the information provided by these reports.

Product managers were evaluated on the basis of sales, market share, and product margins. The market share was expected to be maintained or increased to achieve sales growth. Product line margins were compared to the company average. However, a major argument of the department and product managers, particularly for leather goods, was that allocated overheads were not fair or accurate. The cost accounting department had struggled with this problem for years.

Financing

A bank operating loan and other term loans were the company's major sources of financing. Banking services for Canada were provided by the Canadian Imperial Bank of Commerce (CIBC) and for Cooper International by Marine Midland Bank of Buffalo, New York. The CIBC provided an operating loan to a maximum line of $16 million at 1/4 percent above prime and a term loan at 3/4 percent above prime to be paid in $1 million per year installments in the first five years and $2 million per year thereafter. The bank prime rate was currently 12 percent but had been as high as 20 percent in mid-1982.

A combination of high working capital requirements and high interest rates in the early 1980s had prompted Cooper to seek to minimize capital expenditures without adversely affecting manufacturing or productivity. The payback requirement approval of capital expenditures was 2.5 years or better. Typical annual capital expenditures were additions of new dyes and molds and the purchase of manufacturing equipment.

CCM

Incorporated in 1899 as the Canadian Cycle and Motor Company, CCM was Canada's oldest sporting goods manufacturer. Over its history, CCM had been engaged in three separate businesses: bicycles; automobiles; and skates, hockey sticks, and equipment.

The skate business was entered in 1905 to even out the seasonal sales and production of bicycles. Originally CCM manufactured high-quality blades and riveted them to the best available boots purchased from George Tackaberry of Brandon, Manitoba, to make the skates used by virtually all professional and high-level amateur hockey players. Later, to fill out the line, it purchased lower-quality boots from two small shoe companies in Quebec and its hockey equipment from other manufacturers. By 1967, all winter goods were manufactured by the company in what was then a large, modern, efficient plant, in St. Jean, Quebec.

Through industry-leading product innovation, CCM became the world's premier hockey skate manufacturer. For years, customers in Europe equated Canada with hockey and hockey with CCM.

Performance

Starting in 1961, CCM went through an unfortunate series of ownership and management changes. This resulted at various times in serious labour problems, in inadequate attention to marketing and distribution, and in general to a deterioration of the company's reputation for quality and service. Despite sales growth in recent years, profitability had been erratic and in 1982 devastatingly poor, since an operating loss of $4.3 million was expected.

The company's financial position, as at September 30, 1982, was summarized by the interim receiver as follows:

> CCM owes two secured creditors $33 million—the Royal Bank $28 million and the Enterprise Development Board $5 million—while the liquidation value of the company is $11.6 million less than its total debts of $41 million.
>
> Preferred creditors are owed $1.2 million and product liability claims amount to almost $13 million—$12 million of which rests on the resolution of a New York civil suit lodged by a hockey player who suffered an injury while wearing a CCM helmet.

The financial information available to Cooper on CCM's winter goods operation is presented in Exhibits 8 and 9.

EXHIBIT 8   CCM Inc. Winter Goods Operations ($000s)

	Actual Year Ended						Projected Year Ending Dec. 31/83	
	Sept. 30/80		Sept. 30/81		Sept. 30/82			
Sales								
Skates	$17,148		$16,530		$14,304		$16,500	
Sticks	1,413		2,307		1,445		2,000	
Helmets	1,774		1,814		1,714		2,000	
Protective	3,681		5,047		6,455		6,000	
Sundries	1,250		838		787		1,000	
	$25,266		$26,536		$24,705		$27,500	
Gross margins		%		%		%		%
Skates	$5,985	35.0	$5,604	34.0	$4,577	32.0	$5,940	36.0
Sticks	(230)	(16.3)	(30)	(1.3)	(267)	(18.5)	—	—
Helmets	415	23.4	424	23.4	492	28.7	600	30.0
Protective	482	13.1	934	18.5	1,556	24.1	1,350	22.5
Sundries	381	30.5	262	31.3	215	27.3	300	30.0
	$7,033	27.8	$7,194	27.1	$6,573	26.6	$8,190	29.8
Expenses								
Selling							$1,291	
Administration							661	
Warehouse and distribution			(not available)				1,086	
Financial							618	
							$3,656	
Net before income taxes							$4,534	

SOURCES: 1980–82 from audited financial statements; 1983 projections estimated by CCM management.

Marketing

CCM's world-class strength was in leather skates. Like other leading skate manufacturers, CCM concentrated heavily on supplying skates to professional players because they were the trend setters. Three special pro detail men were employed to sell and service these players, who were often given custom-fitted skates free of charge.

Up to the mid-seventies, when it began to slide, CCM's share of the Canadian and worldwide hockey skate markets had been approximately 60 percent, 30 percent, and 20 percent of the high-, medium-, and low-priced markets, respectively. Because of its domination of the top end of the market, "Supertack," its long-established premium brand name, was better known around the world than CCM. Although skate sales were the largest contributor to fixed costs, they declined from 68 percent of winter goods sales in 1980 to 58 percent in 1982. At

Exhibit 9 Summary of CCM Winter Goods Assets (at cost) October 29, 1982 ($000s)

Inventories		
Finished goods		
Skates	$1,861	
Sticks	407	
Helmets	264	
Protective	1,476	
Sundries	349	
		$ 4,357
Raw material		
Skates	1,264	
Protective	798	
Blades	1,604	
		3,666
Work in process		
Skates	216	
Sticks	250	
Protective	234	
Blades	25	
		725
		$ 8,748
Fixed assets		
St. Jean	1,200	
Hudson	70	
Nylite	867	
		$ 2,137
Total		$10,885

Source: CCM management estimates.

the same time, protective equipment sales roughly doubled from 14 percent to 26 percent, with gross margins of 24 percent. Total gross margin as a percent of sales decreased from 27.8 percent in 1980 to 26.6 percent in 1982.

Distribution

From 1945 to 1982, CCM's dealer network had shrunk from 2,500 to 1,500 and its sales force from 21 to 12. All dealers sold the total CCM line but spent most of their time on winter goods. Up to 1970, the sales reps had been paid salary plus car and expenses and had been encouraged to service dealers and customers. However, industry sources reported that by 1982, the sales reps were strictly on a commission basis and, pressured to get orders through as many dealers as possible, spent little time on service.

Although CCM's reputation for service was suffering, its reputation for quality had been maintained fairly well. A quick survey of a few present or past CCM dealers in November 1982 indicated that approximately one third said they would never carry CCM again; one third would consider carrying CCM again if they could be assured of delivery and service; and one third would stick with CCM through thick and thin because they were enthusiastic about the product and the name.

Manufacturing

Early in November, Henry Nolting, president, and Jerry Harder, vice president of manufacturing of Cooper Canada, Ltd., visited CCM's winter goods plant in St. Jean. Following are excerpts from their reports on the visit:

> The woodworking facility is not modern, looks somewhat like ours as far as equipment and machinery are concerned, and it is not surprising that they do not turn a profit in that part of their operation. The roof in the stick-making facility is leaking and that part of their plant is badly maintained.
>
> The protective equipment manufacturing has nothing in it which we do not know, there is nothing innovative being done and, as far as I am concerned, it is worth very little.
>
> The skate manufacturing operation seems reasonable despite the fact that there are no great innovations. The boot-making part is something which is easily transferable to our location. Jerry feels he would like to have it and can run it. The whole layout seems relatively simple but modern enough and efficient. The equipment is not new but in good repair.
>
> The existing machine shop is old and dirty and there is nothing in it which I would like to buy. They have, at present, approximately 100 people working, but cleaning up work in process. The people are very slow; they seem to be puzzled, unenthusiastic, and listless.
>
> There seems to be a lot of old stock in the finished goods warehouse.
>
> The major lasting machines are leased from United Shoe Machinery which is normal in this trade. They say they have 3,000 plus pairs of lasts (many are specials for individual players) at about $25 per pair. The lasts I saw were in very good repair.
>
> The R&D department has two employees. They have had tremendous problems with their Propacs (copies of Cooperall) and are constantly trying to improve the product. They are working very closely with the Quebec Nordiques in perfecting this product. They have never done any helmet-related work at that facility.
>
> We think their sporting goods division lost approximately $.5 million each year, in 1980 and 1981, sharing equally in the total company loss of $4.3 million at end of September 1982.
>
> The offices are in terrible condition. They are old and in an unbelievable mess.
>
> The president's assessment of the situation is that somebody will buy the assets and he feels that they might go for book value. His opinion is that nobody could pick it up for less.

Not counting raw material storage, we would need at least 25,000 sq. ft., which excludes cutting, to accommodate the skate-making operation. This is equal to 42 of our present 600 sq. ft. bays. To give you another perspective, this area would be slightly larger than the whole area now devoted to apparel. Because of the size, we would have to do major relocations of our existing floors (in Toronto plant). Also, we must be careful of the existing electrical supplies—I would make a cautious estimate of a $25,000 rewiring charge.

Organization

As a result of natural attrition and dim prospects, the CCM organization had shrunk to skeleton status. While it was reportedly limping along, many of the best and most experienced managers had either retired or moved on to better opportunities.

Deciding to Bid

In reviewing a list of possible bidders for CCM (see Appendix), John Cooper felt that the strongest competitive threats would be Warrington and Sport Maska. Both companies had strong management teams, well-established distribution systems, and adequate financial strength. In addition, both companies were Canadian-owned and would not face possible delay and veto of their offer by the Foreign Investment Review Agency. Of further concern was the realization that the St. Jean plant represented up to 200 politically sensitive jobs and that the Quebec government might become involved directly or indirectly in the proceedings. Immediate decisions and actions were essential, however, if Cooper wanted to acquire CCM. Two questions puzzled John Cooper: "If we don't buy CCM, who will? And how will it affect our business?"

APPENDIX

COMPETITORS IN THE SKATE AND
HOCKEY EQUIPMENT INDUSTRY

There were many manufacturers of hockey equipment, helmets, skates, and sticks in Canada. There were seven businesses that Cooper management considered capable and perhaps interested in the CCM winter goods assets.

1. *Canadian Hockey Industries.* CHI was a small company that made high-quality hockey sticks. Its use of fibreglass technology and other materials such as graphite, plastics, laminates, and aluminum had resulted in the most unique stick line in the market. It also marketed a full line of hockey equipment, including a helmet, but no skates or apparel.

Located in Drummondville, Quebec, it had sales of $10 million in 1981, which had been growing rapidly for the past five years. In the factory it employed approximately 120 workers. It was owned by Amer Industries, a Finnish company that also owned Koho.

2. *Koho.* Koho was owned by Amer Industries Finland, and shared marketing, distribution, and some hockey stick manufacturing with Canadian Hockey Industries. It was thought to be the largest hockey stick manufacturer in the world. It also manufactured and marketed hockey equipment and helmets, but no skates or apparel.

Koho had sales of approximately $14 million from about 800 or 900 dealers, serviced by six or seven commission agents who primarily sold Koho and Canadian. Major accounts included large department stores (e.g., Eatons, Simpsons, and Sears), sporting goods chains such as Collegiate Sports, and other stores such as Canadian Tire.

Sticks were manufactured in the Canadian plant in Quebec; sticks and some hockey equipment were manufactured in Finland, and some hockey equipment was purchased in the Orient.

Koho's organization in Canada was headed by a sales manager who reported to a president for North America. The United States also had a sales manager who reported to the North American president. This president reported to the head office of Amer, a very large and profitable Finnish corporation that was involved with shipbuilding, steel, food, and tobacco.

3. *Jofa.* A Volvo-owned company, Jofa manufactured and marketed hockey equipment, hockey sticks, and skates, but not apparel. It had one factory in Sherbrooke, Quebec, and others in Sweden. The rest of its products were purchased in the Orient.

Sales of $10 million were achieved through 700 to 800 dealers and approximately seven commissioned sales agents. Major accounts included large department stores and sporting goods stores and Canadian Tire.

The organization of the company was thin, with one director of marketing responsible for all of North America. Supporting him was a sales manager and a small number of commissioned sales agents.

4. *Sherwood-Drolet.*   Sherwood-Drolet was a Quebec company, 80 percent owned by an American firm, ATO Inc. ATO was the world's largest integrated producer of fire protection equipment and also owned Rawlings and Adirondack sporting goods in the United States.

Sherwood, a producer of high-quality hockey sticks, had been an industry leader in sales and in the introduction of new materials and production processes. It had one of the most automated plants in the industry, enabling it to produce large volumes of sticks of consistent quality. In 1981 its share of the Canadian market was 25 percent.

Sales of approximately $15 million came from approximately 600 dealers. The company's direct sales were aided by 10 sales agents who sold to 300 dealers.

5. *Hillerich and Bradsby.*   Hillerich and Bradsby's head office and manufacturing facility were located in Wallaceburg, Ontario. The company was a wholly owned subsidiary of H & B, Louisville, Kentucky, the world's top baseball bat manufacturer. Besides producing the Louisville hockey stick and being a market leader in brightly coloured goalie sticks, it was making aggressive inroads into the baseball glove and accessory markets. It had also earned a good name for itself in manufacturing golf clubs that were sold primarily through club professionals. The plant employed 62 people.

Sales in 1981 were about $6 million. H & B's distribution system included warehouses in Richmond, B.C.; Dorval, Quebec; Winnipeg, Manitoba; and Concord, Ontario. The sales were achieved primarily by commission sales agents through approximately 400 dealers. Management was reportedly very strong.

6. *Warrington Industries.*   Warrington produced Bauer, Micron, and Lange skates. Bauer had been in the skate business for many years and was CCM's major competitor. This Canadian-owned company was located in Kitchener, Ontario, and produced only skates and shoes. It employed 400 in the skate business and 150 in the shoe business.

Sales of approximately $30 million were generated by 12 to 15 agents through a dealership of 1,200 stores. Warrington was in turn owned by Cemp Investments, a firm representing the interests of the Bronfman family.

7. *Sport Maska.*   Maska was a high-quality hockey-jersey manufacturer. Good distribution resulted in Maska being exclusive suppliers to the NHL. Besides hockey jerseys and apparel, its business consisted of spring and summer

ball uniforms and apparel, soccer jerseys, and leisure wear. The plant in St. Hyacinthe, Quebec, employed approximately 175 people.

Sales in Canada were achieved by approximately nine commissioned agents through 1,200 to 1,500 dealers across Canada. The agents did not carry Maska exclusively. It was distributed coast to coast across the United States through the use of commission agents. Recently, Maska had purchased Sandow, another Canadian athletic apparel company, and had consolidated the manufacturing into its own plant.

Sport Maska was a private company that appeared to be profitable and to have a strong equity base. Industry sources felt that the management team, directed by president Denny Coter, was strong and had good depth.

CASE 10
EDISON PRICE INC.: EVALUATING A LICENSING AGREEMENT

In early 1988, Jeff Shaver, production manager at Edison Price Incorporated, wondered if the USA–Canada Free Trade Agreement (FTA) would provide any new trade opportunities for his company. Edison Price was a New York–based manufacturer of architectural lighting fixtures. The company had made a few sales in Canada over the years but planned to have its Canadian licensee serve the market exclusively in the future. Shaver felt that this decision not to serve the Canadian market directly deserved further analysis.

The Company

Edison Price Incorporated (EPI) manufactured architectural lighting fixtures for the top level of the market. The company was begun in 1952 by Edison Price, a lighting consultant who found he could design and produce lighting products that met higher standards than those of existing manufacturers. Many products were designed by Price as solutions to specific projects. These designs were later adapted to meet general needs. The company pioneered energy-efficient lighting designs in the late 1950s, more than a decade before the energy crisis pushed other manufacturers to develop energy-conscious lighting designs. Quality design and innovation had been the company's great strengths since its inception; most of the industry used design concepts originally developed at EPI.

Throughout the next several decades, due in part to Edison Price's pioneering efforts, architects included lighting designers increasingly as members of their planning teams. By 1980, lighting consultants were routinely involved in construction projects. Currently, the market for top-level architectural lighting continued to grow at a faster rate than the overall lighting industry.

In 1987, there were 167 manufacturers of commercial and institutional lighting fixtures in the United States according to the Department of Commerce; 132 manufacturers were listed for residential fixtures. With sales of just under $14 million, Edison Price was a very small player. Four American lighting manufacturers had sales between $100–$400 million, with another six in the $25–$60 million range.

While Edison Price had achieved state of the art in lighting designs, it had never aggressively pursued growth. Price enjoyed the control that a small

This case was prepared by Jeffrey Shaver, MBA, production manager at Edison Price Incorporated, New York, under the supervision of Dr. Guy Stanley, Institute for U.S.–Canada Business Studies, Lubin Schools of Business, Pace University. This case was written to serve as the basis for class discussion rather than to illustrate either effective or ineffective handling of an administrative situation. Copyright © 1988 Institute for U.S.–Canada Business Studies.

Exhibit 1

EDISON PRICE, INC.
Balance Sheet
As of August 31, 1987

Assets		Liabilities and Shareholders' Equity	
Current assets		**Current liabilities:**	
Cash in bank	$ 113,568	Current portion of long-term debt	$ 311,176
Accounts receivable	2,288,964	Revolving credit arrangement	1,544,400
Royalties receivable	131,401	Accounts payable	737,137
Inventories	1,795,686	Accrued payroll and related taxes	130,440
Federal and state income tax receivable	17,786	Accrued expenses and other current	
Prepaid expenses and other current		liabilities	284,522
assets	61,183	Total current liabilities	3,007,675
Reimbursable costs	45,280	Long-term debt	767,531
		Deferred income taxes	212,589
Total current assets	4,456,268	**Shareholders' equity:**	
Property and equipment	1,763,348	Common stock—par value $0.10/	
Other assets		share, authorized 250,000 shares	
Deposits	30,810	Issued and outstanding, 102,840 shares.	10,284
Cash surrender value of officers' life		Additional paid-in capital	471,368
insurance	91,192	Retained earnings	1,986,253
Sundry receivables	14,512		2,468,005
		Less treasury stock—	
Total other assets	136,514	5,200 shares at cost	99,670
		Total shareholders' equity	2,368,335
Total assets	$6,356,130	Total liabilities and shareholders' equity	$6,356,130

family-run business allowed. There were 29 shareholders, many of them current or former employees. The company's financing needs were met through a revolving bank loan with Bank Leumi of New York. New equipment was financed with capitalized leases.[1] The company's balance sheet appears in Exhibit 1.

Over the years, the company expanded at a modest rate. In 1987, EPI employed 175 people and had plants in Manhattan and Queens, New York. The company planned to increase its manufacturing capacity by more than 50 percent in 1989 when it consolidated its two plants into a single facility located in Brooklyn, New York. This consolidation and the introduction of "just-in-time" production techniques were expected to significantly reduce production costs in the years ahead.

Edison Price products were most often used in museums, galleries, upscale offices and stores, and luxury residences. Lighting fixtures for such projects were

---

[1]A capital lease is a long-term debt contract that transfers tax benefits between the lessor and lessee. In the financial statements, the asset whose use is acquired is valued the same as the present value of the lease obligation. Thus, the capital lease is given a similar treatment as borrowing 100 percent and buying an asset.

usually sold to building contractors through distributors. The building contractors performed or subcontracted the actual installation. Lighting distributors were often limited in their choice of lighting products by job specifications. Usually the architect, lighting consultant, or architectural engineer working on a particular project would specify certain manufacturers whose products must be used, although some job specifications were more flexible than others. An increasing number of specifiers permitted distributors to negotiate changes in manufacturers. Often, especially on large projects, a specification listed alternate manufacturers whose products would be acceptable substitutes. In these cases, the distributor would ask manufacturers to bid on the project. Through the years, EPI had built a network of "stocking distributors" to carry an inventory of popular products.

Edison Price, like most upscale manufacturers, focused its sales effort at specifiers. The company relied on a network of 26 regional sales representatives (reps) across the United States to build relationships with specifiers in their regions and with any specifiers involved in local projects. These sales reps were not salaried employees but earned a commission on each sale. They often represented several other lighting manufacturers in addition to EPI and could be maintained at very little expense to the individual companies. The only costs to EPI, in addition to commissions, were sample fixtures, promotional literature, and occasional advice. Lightolier, the third largest American manufacturer, was the only company that maintained its own national sales force.

LICENSEES

Edison Price's first foreign licensee was Erco Leuchten GmbH of Ludenscheid, West Germany, Europe's largest lighting manufacturer. Erco's president, Klaus-Jurgen Maack, visited several American manufacturers in the early 1970s, hoping to acquire new lighting designs through a licensing arrangement. He chose EPI, believing it to be the most innovative American manufacturer.

Edison Price's Japanese licensee was Yamagiwa Electric of Tokyo, a subsidiary of the Glex Corporation of Yokohama. Associated Lighting Industries of Smithfield, Australia, was another licensee. Both companies were referred to Edison Price after discussions with Erco about lighting design licensing. Erco also referred E. H. Price Ltd. of Winnipeg, Manitoba, to EPI in 1983. However, the licensing agreement was terminated after a year because of a poor working relationship between the two companies.

Edison Price currently had a licensing agreement with Metalumen of Guelph, Ontario, which had stemmed from a single project. Claude Engle, an American lighting consultant with an international reputation, was the consultant for a project at the National Gallery of Canada in Ottawa. Engle wanted to specify EPI for the project but was prohibited by Canadian authorities who insisted on Canadian content for most of the job. Engle interviewed Canadian manufacturers to find one interested in licensing and producing EPI designs for

Exhibit 2 Edison Price Inc., Royalty Income (Fiscal 1983–87)

	1983	*1984*	*1985*	*1986*	*1987*
Erco Leuchen					
West Germany	$203,826	223,308	210,989	328,638	411,072
Yamagiwa Electric					
Japan	71,775	81,293	65,426	73,996	104,299
Associated Lighting					
Australia			10,344	17,216	27,457
Metalumen Mfg.					
Canada					25,727
E. H. Price Ltd.					
Canada	7,645	14,619			
Total	283,246	319,200	286,759	419,850	568,555

the project. Metalumen was chosen by EPI from three candidates. Time constraints on the National Gallery project forced Metalumen to import $48,004 worth of components from EPI. These components were complex parts that Metalumen could not tool for quickly enough. Edison Price also shipped $37,166 worth of similar components to Metalumen to help meet construction deadlines for the Center for Canadian Architecture in Montreal. Since the completion of these jobs in late 1987, Metalumen had tooled for much of the EPI product line.

Arrangements with the four licensees each differed slightly but were essentially the same. Edison Price permitted the licensees to manufacture and sell lighting equipment based on EPI designs, know-how, technology, and patents exclusively in their respective territories. Each licensee agreed to pay EPI a royalty of 2 percent of the licensee's net sales prices for EPI twice a year in U.S. dollars at the prevailing exchange rate. Foreign tax on these royalty payments was credited toward U.S. taxes. Royalty income is listed in Exhibit 2.

The licensing agreements also called for EPI to meet at least once annually with each licensee. These meetings provided the opportunity to discuss product improvements and introduce new designs. See Appendix A for excerpts of the EPI–Metalumen agreement. See Appendix B for a general checklist for license agreements.

The licensees often bought components from EPI. These were usually parts that a licensee had difficulty producing or for which there was only a small requirement.

Export Experience

Edison Price did not export directly. Shipments to foreign licensees were arranged through export brokers. Edison Price provided the broker with carton sizes and weights and an invoice for each shipment to a licensee. Shipments to Metalumen in Canada were also accompanied by a U.S./Canada Uniform Declaration. Edison Price's involvement with this type of shipment ended when the broker picked up the goods at EPI. The broker billed the licensee directly for transportation and export service. Yamagiwa and Associated Lighting used their American affiliates as brokers. Erco used Competent Shipping of New York and Metalumen used Tripar Transport of Toronto.

Exports to areas outside the licensees' exclusive markets were few since Edison Price had no representatives outside the United States. Nevertheless, several international architects and lighting consultants were familiar with EPI products and occasionally specified EPI on overseas jobs.

Edison Price, like many American manufacturers, shipped overseas jobs through American distributors that specialized in export. The largest "international distributor" was Kenclaire Electric of Westbury, New York (or Kenclaire West of Fresno, California). Kenclaire was involved in all EPI overseas jobs.

International distributors handled all correspondence with a foreign project. They determined any product modifications required to meet a country's electrical standards or regulations, set prices while considering exchange rates, and facilitated transportation to the foreign country. Edison Price simply filled the order. Delivery was made to a point within the United States and the international distributor was billed in U.S. dollars.

In 1985, American lighting exports totaled $132 million, while imports totaled $459 million.

Canadian Market

The size of the Canadian economy was 10 percent of the U.S. economy. It seemed reasonable to Shaver that the Canadian lighting industry would be approximately 10 percent of the American lighting industry or U.S. $600 million. Figures available from Statistics Canada showed the value of Canadian lighting fixtures shipped in 1985 equal to C $719,458,000 (1985, U.S. $525,727,430). Figures available at the U.S. Department of Commerce showed that American exports of lighting fixtures to Canada in 1986 were only U.S. $30,795,442. Total Canadian lighting imports (from 28 countries) were only U.S. $39,768,000 in 1986.

Joel Siegel, vice president–sales at Edison Price, preferred the Metalumen license arrangement over selling directly in Canada. In his nine years with Lightolier, Siegel had experienced many barriers to successfully selling in Canada. He had observed a strong commitment on most Canadian projects to have Canadian content. Siegel was surprised to learn that the official Canadian tariff on American lighting fixtures and components was only 11.3 percent. He recalled several experiences where his former company lost sales in Canada because it was unable to be cost competitive with Canadian manufacturers.

Edison Price's current policy was to refer specifiers on Canadian projects to Metalumen and to promote Metalumen among American specifiers who might do Canadian business. Technical support was provided immediately upon request to boost Metalumen's standing among Canadian manufacturers.

Emma Price, controller at EPI, stressed the attractiveness of royalty income. It was cash generated with very little expense. Royalty income was the only reason EPI was able to make a small profit in the early 1980s before production costs were brought under control. The company's income statements appear in Exhibit 3.

It appeared to Shaver that exporting directly to Canada would be simpler than exporting to most countries:

> Several trucking companies already used by EPI had Canadian routes at essentially the same price as domestic service.
>
> Common language and time zones permitted efficient communication with Canadian customers.
>
> Products would not require modification since the Canadian electrical system was identical to the U.S. system. However, EPI products would need to be tested by the Canadian Standards Association (CSA), the Canadian equivalent to Underwriter's Laboratories (UL). CSA and UL requirements were essentially the same.

Metalumen did not have to deviate from any EPI designs to earn CSA approval.

The Free Trade Agreement was intended to reduce tariffs on lighting fixtures 10 percent annually for 10 years beginning January 1, 1989. Rules requiring Canadian content were being changed such that American specifiers would do more business in Canada. There was lively debate on exactly how the FTA would work. Edison Price's agreement with Metalumen was to expire in mid-1991. Shaver still wasn't sure if renewal of the agreement would be the best decision.

EXHIBIT 3   Edison Price, Inc., Statements of Income (Fiscal 1983–87)

	1983	1984	1985	1986	1987
Revenues:					
Net sales	$9,266,870	$11,133,384	$12,892,102	$12,834,475	$13,887,329
Royalty income	283,246	319,220	236,759	419,350	568,555
Miscellaneous	24,022	23,243	45,696	34,200	12,859
Total	9,574,146	11,476,347	13,224,561	13,288,525	14,469,243
Costs and expenses:					
Cost of goods sold	7,524,705	8,864,030	10,106,124	9,958,955	10,560,637
Selling and delivery expense	793,276	1,112,017	1,487,828	1,557,577	2,134,305
General and administrative expense	548,307	713,188	766,360	901,590	880,290
Interest expenses	230,905	209,918	261,479	260,940	223,262
Total	9,097,193	10,899,153	12,621,791	12,759,070	13,856,574
Income before income taxes	$ 476,953	$ 577,197	$ 602,770	$ 529,455	$ 612,669

APPENDIX A
EXCERPTS FROM LICENSE AGREEMENT BETWEEN EDISON PRICE AND METALUMEN

Article I Definitions

Article II Grant of License

A. Licensor hereby grants to Licensee for the term of this Agreement an exclusive license to manufacture and sell Lighting Equipment based on Licensor's Lighting Processes in the Main Territory [Canada].

B. In addition, Licensor hereby grants to Licensee for the term of this Agreement a nonexclusive license to manufacture and sell Lighting Equipment based on Licensor's Lighting Processes in any other part of the world *except* Australia, Austria, Burma, Cambodia, China, Countries of the European Economic Community, Fiji, Finland, German Democratic Republic, India, Indonesia, Japan, Laos, Malaysia, Malta, New Guinea, New Zealand, North Korea, Norway, Papua, Philippines, Portugal, Republic of Korea, South Pacific Islands, Spain, Sri Lanka, Sweden, Switzerland, Taiwan, Thailand, United States of America, Vietnam, and Yugoslavia. Licensee shall pay Licensor for such nonexclusive license a royalty of 1 percent of the net-sales-price on Licensee's sales of Lighting Equipment under the nonexclusive license granted in this Article II (B). This royalty shall not be affected by the provisions of Articles III (B) or VI.

C. Licensor hereby reserves the right to grant an exclusive license to one or more third parties in any part of the world covered by the nonexclusive license granted to Licensee in Paragraph B of this Article II. In such a case, Licensor shall send written notice informing Licensee of its intention to terminate the nonexclusive license for the relevant country or territory by granting an exclusive license to a third party. In those countries or territories in which the Licensee has distributors, as set forth in Schedule B of this Agreement, Licensee's nonexclusive license will end three months after the receipt of the notification . . . .

Article III Exchange of Information; Scheduled Meetings

Article IV First Option for Future Licenses

A. Licensee shall have the first right to apply for a license in the Main Territory on any new Lighting Processes of Licenser within a period of six (6) months after the information on such new Lighting Processes has been supplied to Licensee . . . .

Article V Applications for Patent Protection

[Sets forth rights and obligations with respect to patents obtained by the licensor or, in the licensor's name, by the licensee.]

Article VI Royalty Rates

A. During the period of this Licensee Agreement, Licensee shall pay a royalty to the Licensor of 2 percent of the Licensee's net-sales-prices for Lighting Equipment sold in the Main Territory. Such royalty is subject to modification in accordance with the provisions of Article III. Sales of any electrical fixtures which are designed by Licensee and which do not incorporate any of Licensor's Lighting Processes, in whole or in part, are not subject to royalty payment.

[Provisions set out certain exceptions, including injured sales arising from competition from similar equipment, and in the case of unexpectedly high development costs for adaptation of the equipment for the Canadian market. In such cases, the "parties shall confer and agree upon an appropriate reduction in the royalty rate."]

Article VII Improvements

A. The parties will inform each other promptly of any improvement relating to the Lighting Processes subject to this Agreement.

B. through E.

[Provisions for the negotiation of supplementary agreements concerning improvements.]

Article VIII Sublicenses

[Notification procedures and royalty sharing provisions in the event of sublicensing in Canada. Edison Price would receive 30 percent of all sublicense agreement royalties.]

Article IX Confidentiality

[All information about licensed equipment or processes, or improvements, to remain confidential.]

Article X Licensee's Sales Efforts

Licensee shall exercise all reasonable efforts to market effectively Lighting Equipment based on Licensor's Lighting Processes throughout the licensed countries and territories and to maintain a sales and advertising effort appropriate to the potential market.

Article XI Infringement of Proprietary Rights

[Outlines rights and obligation in the event of infringement by third parties.]

Article XII Term of the Agreement

[July 1, 1986–June 30, 1991, with 12-month notification of termination on that date.]

Article XIII Termination

[90-day notice to terminate in the event of a breach of the agreement.]

Article XVI Modification

[No changes or waivers unless agreed to in writing.]

Article XVII Arbitration

Any disagreements arising under the provisions of the License Agreement will be decided by arbitration in accordance with the Roles for the International Chamber of Commerce Court of Arbitration, with each party appointing an arbitrator and said arbitrators selecting a third. If arbitration is requested by Licensee, the place of arbitration shall be New York City, U.S.A.; if arbitration is requested by Licensor, the place for arbitration shall be Guelph, Province of Ontario, Canada. The arbitration shall be held as promptly as possible at such time as the arbitrators may determine. The decision of a majority of the arbitrators shall be final and binding upon the parties hereto. Judgment upon the award may be entered in the Court having jurisdiction over defendant.

APPENDIX B
CHECKLIST FOR LICENSE AGREEMENTS

Parties
Name of licensor _____
Address _____
Principal office _____
Incorporated in _____
Short title _____
Name of licensee _____
Address _____
Principal office _____
Incorporated in _____
Short title _____

Recitals
Licensor owns inventions _____
 Patents _____ Patent _____
 Applications _____
 Industrial designs _____
 Trademarks _____
 Know-how _____
Licensor represents that it has the right to grant
 a license relating to _____
Licensee represents _____
Licensee desires license relating to _____

Definitions
Define "the products" covered by a limited
 license. If certain types of inventions only are
 covered, define "the inventions." Define
 "patents," "trademarks," "registered designs,"
 "copyrights," "know-how," "net sales,"
 "territory." Adopt other defined terms as
 needed.

Date of agreement
From date hereof _____
From some specific date _____
Effective date _____
When approved by _____

Grant
Patents _____
Trademarks _____
Registered designs _____
Copyright _____
Know-how _____
Existing future improvements by licensor _____
 In licensed inventions or know-how _____
 In same field or for similar applications _____

All rights to use know-how and practice
 inventions ___ and to make, use, and sell
 products _____
Exclusive _____
Exclusive except as to licensor _____
Exclusive for ___ years and nonexclusive
 thereafter
Nonexclusive _____
Irrevocable _____
With right to grant sublicenses _____
 To make (manufacture) _____
 To have made for own use _____
 Unlimited _____
To use _____
To sell _____
To lease _____ rent _____

Nature of know-how
 Invention records
 Laboratory records
 Research reports
 Development reports
 Engineering reports
 Pilot plant design
 Production plant design
 Production specifications
 Raw material specifications
 Quality controls
 Economic surveys
 Market surveys
 Promotion methods
 Trade secrets
 List of customers
 Drawings and photographs
 Models, tools, and parts
 Other (specify)
 Know-how not confidential
 Know-how confidential
  Employees to be bound
  Subcontractors and sublicensees to be bound
 If patents held invalid:
  Know-how payment stops
  Know-how payment continues

Territory
All countries _____ all countries
 except _____ (specify)

Restrictions
Limited to specified field _____
Limited to specified territory _____
Subject to prior license _____
Subject to licensor's right to make _____
    have made ___ use ___ sell _____

Sublicenses
To any other party _____
To nominees of licensor _____
At specified consideration _____
Limitations _____
Consideration to be shared with licensor _____
Copies to be furnished to licensor _____

Term
For _____ years.
Until (specify date) _____
Until some future event (specify) _____
For the life of any patent _____
Until specified notice of termination _____
Extension of term _____
Automatic unless notice of termination _____
Automatic if minimum performance
    achieved _____
Automatic except for terms (e.g., royalty rate)
    to be negotiated or arbitrated _____
Good faith negotiations to
    extend _____

Consideration
Lump-sum payment _____
Single payment _____
Installments _____
Royalty, percent of profits _____
    Gross sales _____
    Net sales, specific amount (specify) _____
    Per unit (specify) _____ other _____
Payment in dollars:
    At then current rate of exchange
    At rate of _____dollars for_____
        (foreign currency)
    If exchange rate decreases or increases by
        5% the payments shall decrease or
        increase by like amount
    Exchange rate shall be that published
        in _____
Payment in currency other than above _____
Stock of licensee (specify)
    Stock of existing company _____
    new company _____
    Value of the shares of stock shall be
        market value at date of agreement _____
        book value _____

Stock shall have full voting rights _____
    nonvoting _____
Stock shall have value not less than $ _____
Stock shall represent not less than _____
    percent of the issued sharesLicensor shall
have the option to acquire
    additional shares at market value _____
    book value _____
Licensor shall have option to appoint
directors:
    With full voting rights _____
    Nonvoting _____

Minimum Royalty
Amount per calendar year _____
    per 12-month period _____
Payable in advance
Payable at end of calendar year _____
    of 12-month period _____
Credited against earned royalties:
    Yes _____   No _____

Inspection of licensee's accounts
Not permitted
Permitted:
    At any time during business hours
    At specified times
    By licensor's authorized representatives
    By accountants

Acknowledgment of licensor's title
Not admitted
Admitted by licensee
If patents held invalid, then:
    Licensee may terminate:
        As to invalid claims _____
        Entire agreement _____

Statements of earned royalty
Quarterly, within _____ days of end of
    quarter
Annually, within _____ days of end of year
Other periods (specify) _____
In writing and certified before notary public
With names and addresses of sublicensees
With copies of sublicenses
Together with payment of royalty accrued

Inspection of licensee's accounts
Not permitted
Permitted:
    At any time during business hours
    At specified times

(continued)

By licensor's authorized representatives
By accountants

Acknowledgment of licensor's title
Not admitted
Admitted by licensee
If patents held invalid, then:
  Licensee may terminate:
    As to valid claims _____
    Entire agreement _____

Improvements by licensee
Not included
Included for products (specify)
  Automatically owned by licensor
  Licensed to licensor automatic
  Licensor's option-free royalty
  For term of agreement _____
    for specified term _____
  First territory of license _____
    for specified territory _____

Diligence by licensee
No obligation
Licensee will use its best efforts
Licensee agrees to:
  Produce _____ or sell _____
    specified units
  Produce _____ or sell _____
    specified products
  Invest specified amounts
  Satisfy demands of trade
  Refuse no reasonable request for
    sublicense
Penalty for lack of diligence:
  License converted to nonexclusive
  Licensor may nominate licensees
  Licensor may terminate upon _____
  days' notice in writing

Infringement
A. Licensed rights
  Past infringement by licensee:
    Forgiven for payment of _____
    Not forgiven _____
  If infringed by others:
    Who will notify
    Who will file suit
    Who is in charge of suit
    Costs: borne by _____
    Divided _____

B. Rights of others
  No indemnity by licensor

Licensor idemnifies licensee
  Who will notify
  Who will defend
  Who will pay costs
    Costs: borne by _____
    Divided _____

C. Damages
  Retained by _____ divided _____

D. Right to settle suit:
  By licensor _____ By licensee _____
  By licensor only with consent
  of licensee _____
Right of inspection
Licensee shall have the right to inspect
  licensor's:
  Research laboratory _____
  Development laboratory _____
  Engineering laboratory _____
  Pilot plant _____
  Production plant _____
  Department relating to product _____
Number of visits permitted per year
Number of persons
Licensor shall have reciprocal rights of
  inspection
Technical personnel
Licensor shall provide technical personnel to
  deliver know-how:
  At licensor's expense _____ At licensee's
    expense _____
  Not more than _____ persons for not
    more than _____ days
At a fee which shall be the salary,
  plus _____ percent.
Travel expenses _____
  Living expenses _____
  Borne by licensor _____
  Borne by licensee _____
Number and duration of stay of technical
  personnel determined by:
  Licensor _____ Licensee _____
  Mutually _____

Confidentiality
No obligation _____ licensee
  Obligated _____ both parties
  Obligated _____
Without limitation as to time _____ life of
  agreement _____
  until published by owner _____
Obligations of confidentiality
  of employees _____ sublicensees _____

Arbitration
No right of arbitration
Parties will use their best efforts
Parties agree to arbitration by:
  Specified body _____
  Three persons, one selected by each party
    and a third by the selected
    persons _____
Appeal from arbitration decision:
  Not permitted, decision final and binding
  Permitted to (specify tribunal)
Termination
By licensor:
  If certain person incapacitated (name)
  If certain person terminated connection with
    licensee (name)
  As specified time
  Only upon breach after _____ days'
    written notice
By licensee:
  At any time upon _____ days'
    written notice
  On any anniversary date
  At any specified time
  Only upon payment of penalty of $ _____
  Only upon breach after _____ days'
    written notice
Upon termination, licensee assigns to licensor:
  Trademarks _____ Patents _____
  Sublicenses _____
As to any specified patent or applications
As to any specified country
Of exclusive license with right to continue as
  nonexclusive
Whenever any essential claim held invalid
Upon bankruptcy of either party

Force majeure
Licensor has right
Licensee has right
Both parties have right
Nature of force majeure
  Natural events: fire, floods, lightning, wind-
    storm, earthquake, subsidence of soil, etc.
  Accidents: fire, explosion, failure of equipment,
    transportation accidents
  Civil events: commotion, riot, war, strike, labor
    disturbances, labor shortages, raw material
    and equipment shortages
  Governmental: government controls, rationing,
    court order
  Any cause beyond control of party
Assignment of agreement and license
Not assignable by either party

Assignable by licensor, without consent of
  licensee _____ with consent _____
By either party:
  Upon merger
  To successor of entire business
  To any company of which a majority of stock
    is owned
  To any company of which a controlling
    interest is owned
Binding upon heirs, successors, and assigns
Most favored licensee clause
Licensor required to notify licensee of similar
  license
License has option to take term of similar
  license
License changed to terms of more favorable
  license
Licensee may terminate

Notices and addresses
By registered air mail
Licensor's legal address for notice
Licensee's legal address for notice
Provision for deemed notice

Integration
This instrument is the entire agreement between
  parties
No modification effective unless written and
  signed by both
This agreement supersedes:
  All prior agreements between the parties   the
  agreement dated
Language
The official language shall be
  English _____ Other _____
  (specify)
Copy in _____ language shall be
  Official _____ Unofficial _____
Law applicable
To be construed according to the laws of

Signatures
For individual:
  "Hand and seal"
For corporations:
  By officer
  Title shown
  Corporate seal

Schedules
Patent list (inventor, number, issue date, official
  title)

(continued)

Patent applications (inventor, serial number, filing date, official title)

Industrial designs (registration number and date)

Copyrights (description, registration number and date)

Trademarks (description, registration, number and date)

Descriptions or copies of official documents, such as sublicenses, assignment, prior license, etc.

Accounting procedures if any for determining sales, net sales, sale value of stock, or other property

Trademark Supplement

If the agreement is to include a trademark license, check the following items:

Licensed trademarks
Trademark application no. and date
Trademark registration no. and date
Classes of goods (specify)
Goodwill of business (specify)

The grant to use
Exclusive _____ Nontransferable _____
Countries trademark registration no.
  Date

  _____
  _____
  _____

Term of license
Consideration
Royalty: % of profits _____ of gross sales
  of net sales _____
Single sum of $ _____ annual minimum
  $ _____
Included in know-how fee _____
  not included _____
Stock of licensee (name company) at market
  value _____ "book value" _____
Product quality control
Mark to be used only on goods (specify)

Made under written specifications:
  Attached to be supplied by
  licensor _____
No other trademarks to be used on same goods
Samples to be furnished upon request:
  quarterly _____ annually _____
Inspection of product manufactured by
  licensor permitted:
  When requested _____
  quarterly _____ annually _____
Liability for misuse:
  Licensor liable _____ Licensee
  liable _____

Trademark use control
Licensor has right to approve, in advance, use
  of mark in:
  Advertising
  Labels
  Containers
  Registration notice
  Exhibits
  Speeches
  Publicity
  Corporate signature

Registration in Trademarks Office
Entire agreement
Separate registered user agreement

SOURCE: *The Licensing and Joint Venture Guide;* reproduced with the permission of The Ontario Government, Ministry of Industry, Trade and Technology.

CASE 11
FISHERY PRODUCTS INTERNATIONAL

In late January 1989, Vic Young, chief executive officer of Fishery Products International (FPI), was considering the future of their new venture in Japan. Following several years of research and development, FPI had launched 11 value-added products in Japan in February 1988, and sales to date had exceeded all expectations. Despite this early success, questions had been raised about FPI's future involvement in Japan, particularly in the light of the dramatically reduced fishing quotas that had just been announced by the Canadian government. As he reviewed an internal report on the profitability of the new venture, Young realized that the company had to decide if it should stay in the Japanese market.

The Canadian East Coast Fishing Industry

There are two main sectors in the east coast fishery: the inshore and the offshore. The inshore fishery is based on independent fishermen who supply fish on a daily basis to primary processing plants. These fishermen own and operate small to medium-size vessels that fish close to the shore. The offshore fishery is serviced by large company-owned trawlers (up to and including factory freezer trawlers), which fish further from shore for periods up to 10 days before returning to unload their catches.

Under the terms of the Northwest Atlantic Fishery Organization (NAFO) convention, the waters off Canada's Atlantic coast are divided into three divisions and 16 individual zones. The government of Canada, as part of its management plan for the Atlantic fishery, uses an enterprise allocation system under which each zone is given an annual allocation, or quota, of fish by species that can be caught during the fishing season.

Three main fish species groupings are used in the allocation system: groundfish including cod, flounder, sole, and redfish; pelagics made up of capelin, mackerel, and salmon; and the shellfish group of crab, shrimp, and lobster. The quota system is subdivided into allocations for the inshore and offshore fishery, with the offshore quota further subdivided into allocations for the various fishing companies.

In the early 1980s, the fishing industry off the east coast of Canada was in a dismal state. Poor fishery management practices, an increase in the number of

This case was prepared by R. William Blake and Diane M. Hogan, Faculty of Business Administration, Memorial University of Newfoundland, with the assistance of Louise Handrigan Jones. It is intended as the basis for classroom discussion rather than to illustrate either effective or ineffective handling of an administrative situation. This case was made possible in part by financial assistance from External Affairs and International Trade Canada. © R. William Blake, 1991.

plant closures, and escalating labour unrest had led to a sharp increase in the number of government bailouts.

As consumer tastes and diets changed, the market had increasingly been demanding a higher-quality fish product. The east coast fishery had been slow to respond to this trend and, despite access to the world's greatest fishing grounds and projections of a continuing increase in cod stocks, had been having difficulty increasing its sales in the Canadian market.

To address these issues, the Atlantic Canada Fisheries Restructuring Act was adopted in November of 1983. This act authorized the minister of fisheries to invest in, and provide financial assistance for, the restructuring of the Atlantic fishery. One of the mandates the government set for the restructuring was that, following the stabilization of the Atlantic fishing industry, it was to move from government control back to the private sector.

In the restructuring, two of the larger independent companies, National Sea Products and Fishery Products, were chosen as the vehicles to create an economically viable and competitive industry. In December of 1984, Fishery Products became the basis for the formation of Fishery Products International Ltd. This new company was formed from 12 individual companies that had been involved in the fishing industry off the Atlantic coast of Canada. In 1986, Fishery Products International was given the largest allocation of fish off the east coast of Canada (Exhibit 1).

Fishery Products International (FPI)

Prior to the creation of FPI, Fishery Products operated six primary processing plants and one small secondary processing plant in Atlantic Canada. After the merger, FPI, from its head office in St. John's, Newfoundland, undertook a major modernization program. Marginal plants were closed and a program of intensive capital investment in processing plants and trawler equipment was implemented. Fourteen of FPI's inshore plants were targeted for sale to independent processors, leaving FPI to own and operate 16 primary and 3 secondary processing plants[1] (Exhibit 2).

To service their plants, FPI operated 58 company-owned trawlers that harvested over 260 million pounds of cod, flounder, sole, perch, haddock, and turbot annually. The company also purchased crab, shrimp, capelin, and herring from some 2,500 independent inshore fishermen in Newfoundland. FPI had traditionally not fully harvested its quotas of underutilized species, such as redfish (ocean

---

[1]Primary processing involves the conversion of raw fish into fillets or blocks for sale as an end product or for transfer for secondary processing. A "block" is an international standard and consists of 16.5 pounds of fish which has been processed and frozen in a freezing frame of exact dimensions. Forty percent of FPI's cod was processed into block, and half of this block was sold to other processors. Secondary processing plants are devoted to the production of value-added finished products, such as fish burgers, fish sticks, and frozen fish dinners for use by the end customer.

EXHIBIT 1 Groundfish Allocations (in thousands of tonnes)

Species		1986	1987	1988	1989
Cod	Inshore	326.7	320.6	309.7	306.9
	Offshore	192.5	193.1	213.7	150.1
FPI quotas		84.6	82.1	86.3	68.0
Percentage of TAC caught		88%	81%	85%	
Haddock	Inshore	19.2	19.2	14.3	11.6
	Offshore	18.0	8.3	10.6	11.5
FPI quotas		1.6	1.6	1.7	4.0
Percentage of TAC caught		94%	3%	4%	
Redfish	Inshore	20.6	22.1	19.7	24.9
	Offshore	119.2	121.2	121.2	108.1
FPI quotas		27.2	26.9	23.7	23.4
Percentage of TAC caught		54%	8%	9%	
American plaice	Inshore	18.9	17.4	17.4	16.4
	Offshore	59.0	53.4	46.5	37.9
FPI quotas		53.0	47.3	38.7	33.0
Percentage of TAC caught		61%	29%	25%	
Yellowtail	Inshore	—	—	—	—
	Offshore	17.6	17.6	17.6	7.8
FPI quotas		13.2	13.1	13.1	4.3
Percentage of TAC caught		80%	13%	10%	
Witch	Inshore	3.0	3.0	2.5	2.5
	Offshore	9.8	9.7	8.1	8.1
FPI quotas		7.7	7.6	6.3	6.3
Percentage of TAC caught		39%	4%	5%	
Flounder	Inshore	5.4	6.4	5.4	6.6
	Offshore	8.4	7.3	8.3	7.1
FPI quotas		0.6	0.5	0.5	0.4
Percentage of TAC caught		53%	0.1%	0.2%	
Greenland halibut (turbot)	Inshore	41.6	45.5	47.2	47.2
	Offshore	30.7	38.7	38.7	28.7
FPI quotas		17.1	17.1	12.0	15.9
Percentage of TAC caught		22%	2.2%	0.6%	
Pollock	Inshore	20.0	23.0	24.5	25.5
	Offshore	20.0	21.5	23.8	22.8
FPI quotas		0.3	0.3	0.6	0.5
Percentage of TAC caught		108%	0.4%	0.5%	

NOTE: Inshore—vessels less than 100 feet; offshore—vessels larger than 100 feet.
TAC—Total allowable catch.

perch) and turbot. Redfish was not as lucrative in its markets as Atlantic cod, and Canadian companies lacked the deep-water-harvesting technology to fully utilize the turbot quotas.

Under the restructuring, FPI became a vertically integrated seafood company, catching and processing fish, developing new seafood products, and marketing them in the international marketplace. Through this process, FPI

EXHIBIT 2 **FPI Plant Locations**

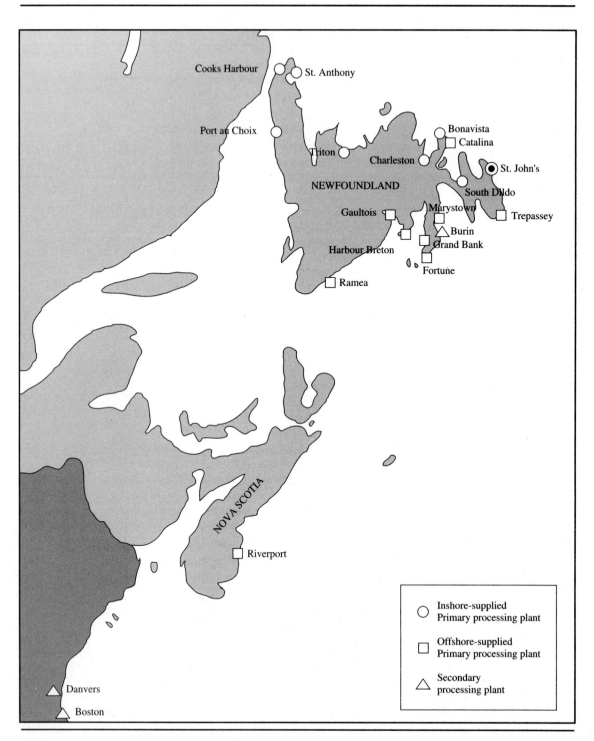

EXHIBIT 3

FISHERY PRODUCTS INTERNATIONAL
Summary of Financial Statement
(thousands of dollars)

	1988	1987	1986	1985
Sales	366,611	395,705	388,664	298,182
Net income (loss)	16,755	57,963	46,596	(20,160)
Cash flow[a]	29,275	71,298	56,731	(8,357)
Working capital	99,467	94,035	55,404	41,192
Long-term debt	38,593	17,487	14,471	24,531
Segmented Information				
Sales				
Canada[b]	338,328	367,051	354,149	252,111
Intercompany[c]	(272,563)	(317,055)	(300,661)	(205,047)
	65,765	49,996	53,488	47,064
United States	264,263	314,342	304,490	231,282
Other[d]	36,583	31,367	30,686	19,836
	366,611	395,705	388,664	298,182
Profit (loss)[e]				
Canada	16,969	58,951	44,757	(15,396)
United States	1,097	7,001	3,945	(4,831)
Other	300	37	(52)	67
	18,366	65,989	48,650	(20,160)
Identified Assets				
Canada	281,662	286,416	238,485	208,516
United States	50,009	56,029	42,085	50,726
Other	9,409	4,626	3,212	5,060
Intercompany accounts	(31,931)	(68,815)	(59,730)	(62,924)
	309,149	278,256	224,052	200,376

NOTE: [a]Cash flow from operations before net changes in noncash working capital balances.
[b]Canadian sales include sales to customers in the United States and other geographic regions.
[c]Transfer pricing: Intercompany sales are at market prices less commissions.
[d]Other includes sales to Europe, Australia, and Japan. Sales to Japan were $3 million of capelin product only.
[e]Profit (loss): Profit is income before provision for profit sharing, income taxes, and extraordinary items.

emerged as a major international player, with sales of $260 million, and a loss of $35 million, in 1984, its first year of operation. Although the company recorded another loss in 1985, it reported healthy profits of $46 million and $58 million in 1986 and 1987, respectively (Exhibit 3). In 1987, Canada accounted for 16 percent of FPI's sales; the United States, 77.6 percent; and other countries (Europe, Australia, and Japan), 6.7 percent.

FPI's approach to the market differed from country to country. FPI was the largest foreign supplier of frozen seafood to the United States and supplied the value-added component of that market from two secondary processing plants in Massachusetts through a subsidiary company, Fishery Products, Inc.

In Europe, FPI principally supplied fish blocks to other processors and finished products to food service companies, using sales offices which employed local people with specific market knowledge in sales and distribution. These subsidiaries were located in West Germany (Fishery Products GmbH) and Great Britain (Fishery Products of Canada Ltd.). The market in Europe was fiercely competitive and Canadian value-added products were subject to high tariffs which made it difficult for them to compete. Marketing and all other related activities for the European operations were handled by headquarters in St. John's.

Prior to the restructuring of the industry, independent fishing companies had placed less emphasis on quality than on increasing the catch. In the light of forecasts of shifting consumer preferences toward higher-quality products, FPI management realized that the company needed to catch and process fish more effectively. The company also needed higher-quality fish for many of the new products being produced in its secondary processing plants.

Improved quality was to be achieved through a capitalization program and an increasing emphasis on quality control. FPI had invested heavily in its fleet and processing facilities. To complement this capitalization program, and to increase productivity and motivation, it had also invested heavily in its work force. This had been accomplished through the implementation of such programs as employee ownership, the use of an FPI newsletter, and employee of the month awards. The company adopted the motto, "Excellence through people, productivity, and profits." It was realized that attempts to increase quality had to be reflected in the employees' attitude, and the employees slowly began to realize that, if they could not produce a higher-quality fish product, their jobs could be lost.

FPI management had become increasingly concerned about the company's financial vulnerability to fluctuations in the exchange rate of the American dollar. Over 75 percent of FPI's sales were in the United States, and management was looking for ways to reduce their reliance on this market. An integral part of the new strategy was to diversify into new markets and to place an increased emphasis on secondary processing.

Fishery Products' expertise prior to the creation of FPI (1984) had been in the supply of both raw and finished products to the food service industry with little emphasis placed on retail sales. The new emphasis on research and development of new value-added products had led to several Canadian awards for innovative products.

To meet its corporate goal of increasing emphasis in the area of secondary processing, FPI had developed a world-class secondary processing capability in its plant in Burin, Newfoundland. The newly modified plant, which reopened in June of 1987, had the capacity to process 15 million pounds of finished product per year. Given the fact that the Canadian market would not immediately utilize the new plant's capacity, part of the company's strategy included steps to explore the Japanese market.

The Japanese Seafood Market

The market development division of FPI had continued the collection of information about the Japanese market that had been started by Fishery Products. As part of their ongoing analysis of the potential of the Japanese marketplace, a team from FPI, including Randy Bishop, director of international marketing sales, participated in a government-sponsored trade mission to Japan in late 1985. During this mission, FPI's representatives learned about the characteristics of the Japanese marketplace and had the opportunity to meet with various seafood marketers. Upon returning to Canada and reviewing their findings, the team concluded that, despite the fact that FPI had been exporting unprocessed capelin, squid, and cod to Japan for years, it knew very little about the Japanese domestic market.

The FPI research found that, on a per capita basis, Japan had the highest fish consumption in the world at 68 kilograms per year as compared to the United States at 7.2 kilograms and Canada at 7 kilograms. Because local resources were insufficient to meet the high demand for fish, Japanese fishing companies used factory freezer trawlers outfitted to fish, freeze, and store while operating worldwide. Historically, Japan had been a major fishing nation, harvesting in excess of 15 percent of the total world fish catch and exporting far more than it imported. Recently, however, the increasingly restrictive policies of many nations had limited access to their fishing grounds, and Japan had become a fish-importing nation (Exhibit 4).

Since World War II, Japan had used very restrictive import policies as a way of developing its economy. Approximately 20 percent of Japanese imports were finished goods, compared to 50 percent for the United States and 40 percent for the European Economic Community. In the fishing industry, a focus on the importation of raw product allowed Japan to continue to utilize the massive fish processing infrastructure developed when it was a major fishing nation.

In recent years, Japan, as a member of the General Agreement on Trades and Tariffs (GATT), had been working at reducing both tariff and nontariff barriers. Despite this trend, companies still found it difficult to enter the Japanese market as government regulations and nontariff barriers were used as

Exhibit 4 Fish Consumption in Japan (in thousands of metric tons)

	1965	1970	1975	1980	1984	1986*
Production	5547	6857	7522	7421	7352	—
Imports	109	294	752	1027	1746	2300
Exports	618	791	755	817	624	—
Apparent domestic consumption	5048	6356	7549	7666	8251	8600
Imports as a % of total market	2.1	4.6	9.9	13.3	21.1	26.7

NOTE: * = Estimated consumption.

deterrents. The quality control standards applied to imports were examples of such nontariff barriers. The FPI team realized during their investigation that there was no central governing body in Japan that it could access to determine product standards. Although there had been a movement to centralize these standards, the process was very slow.

The retail market for frozen seafood in Japan in the large chain grocery stores alone was worth Cdn $1.3 billion annually; in the three major regions of Tokyo, Osaka, and Nagoya, there were 40 of these chains with approximately 2,000 stores. The rest of the retail market, which represented approximately 30 percent of the seafood market, was split among the food sections of department stores and convenience stores with approximately one store per 68 people in the country. Each of these stores had very small sections devoted to frozen food, and there was tremendous competition among brands.

The introduction of new food products in Japan is done very methodically with new releases occurring primarily in February and October. As many as 2,000 new entries will be released each time, of which approximately 300 would be in the frozen food category, the sector FPI would be entering. The success rate for new products was approximately 15 percent, and, in general, new products faced a very short product life cycle, often less than two years.

The Japanese consumer demands high-quality foods and seeks a wide variety of choice in products; as Randy Bishop noted, "the Japanese eat with their eyes." Portion size had to be uniform and be composed of top-quality fish. This would have considerable ramifications for FPI if it decided to enter the market with value-added products. FPI felt that many current top products (as classified by North American and European standards) would not pass the Japanese quality standards for importation.

Japan was becoming more westernized in its tastes and placed a high demand and value on imported products. Once a foreign product was adopted in the domestic market, it usually commanded a high price. Despite the high demand for imported products, FPI realized that the Japanese had very distinct tastes. It was common knowledge that companies such as Nestle and Heinz had entered the Japanese domestic market with their standard products and failed. The experience of such companies had earned Japan the reputation of being a very difficult market to enter successfully.

The distribution network in Japan reflected many characteristics of a hierarchical and closed society. A greatly simplified version of a Japanese distribution chain is provided in Exhibit 5. Imports of raw materials were handled by large trading companies through their import/export divisions. Foreign companies wishing to sell value-added products to the Japanese domestic market would have to do so through the domestic marketing division of the trading company. Given the nature of the trading companies, the import/export division and the domestic marketing division were independent operations. Even though FPI had been exporting raw materials to Japan for years, it had no contacts in the domestic marketing division and, therefore, no access to the domestic retail market or the larger food service market. From its research, FPI realized that

Exhibit 5 Simplified Diagram of the Japanese Distribution Chain for Imported FPI Value-Added Products

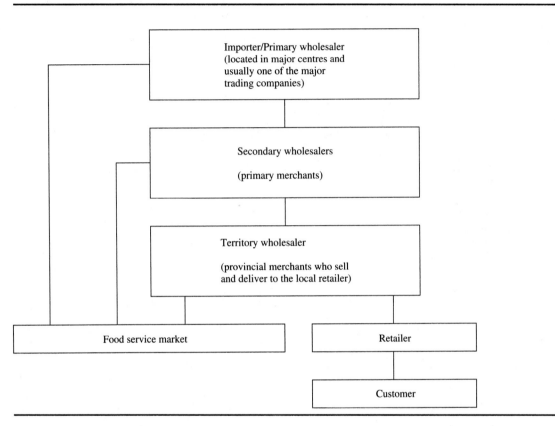

the sale of imported value-added fish products was essentially unknown in these markets.

In addition to increased Japanese demand for foreign products and the potential size of the Japanese market, FPI was encouraged by two other factors; the change in value of the Japanese currency and the Japanese fish consumption pattern. In 1982, the Canadian dollar was worth close to 200 yen, but by 1987 the exchange rate was approximately 100 yen to the dollar (Exhibit 6). This would allow FPI to set prices on its products that would be attractive to the Japanese consumer and generate returns equivalent to its sales in other markets. In terms of consumption, the Japanese were keenly interested not only in cod and sole, but in species such as redfish and capelin, neither of which played a significant part in the North American diet. Exports of fish products from Canada had increased significantly in recent years as Japan actively sought supplies to satisfy its domestic demands (Exhibit 7). This fact was of particular interest to FPI since the quotas for these species were not being fully utilized (Exhibit 1).

Exhibit 6 Average Quarterly Exchange Rate 1980–89 (Japanese yen to Canadian dollar)

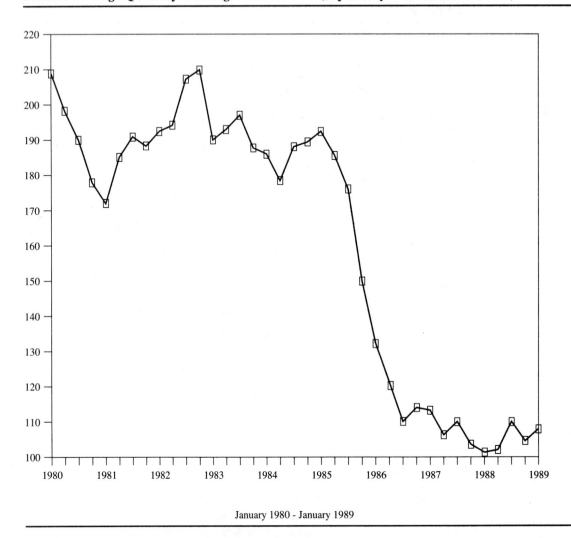

January 1980 - January 1989

The Japanese were very uncomfortable doing business with individuals that they had not known for extended periods of time. They desired to develop "ningen kankei," a sense or feeling of good human relations, before they established any relationship (business or otherwise). Even if FPI was able to establish such relationships, it was recognized that the Japanese would require a high degree of personal contact in order to maintain the relationship. Because of the hierarchical nature of the Japanese culture, these relationships would have to be between individuals at equal levels in the organization (i.e., a Canadian vice president of marketing would not be able to establish such a relationship with a CEO of a Japanese company).

Exhibit 7 **Japanese Fish Imports by Major Suppliers**

			Ranking		
	1985 U.S. $ (millions)	*% Share*	*1985*	*1983*	*1981*
United States	915.0	18.5	1	1	1
Korea	688.4	13.9	2	2	2
Taiwan	578.4	11.7	3	3	3
Canada	269.7	5.5	4	6	8
India	232.7	4.7	5	4	4
Indonesia	226.2	4.6	6	5	5
Australia	198.8	4.0	7	7	7

FPI's experience to date had not taught it to deal with the subtleties of negotiation in Japan. In the past, they had sold capelin, squid, and cod to the Japanese, and more recently they had also been selling some redfish, an underutilized species. If FPI wished to sell excess catches of raw fish, this was done by placing a phone call to the import/export division of a Japanese trading company. FPI management had no experience in negotiating contracts in Japan, although they were aware that Japanese consensus style of negotiating was very different from the North American style. If FPI decided to enter Japan with its value-added products, it would entail significantly more management involvement, money, and long-term commitment to the development of the market.

The Entry Strategy

In considering possible strategies for the Japanese market, three alternatives were considered. The first was for FPI to maintain the status quo by continuing exports of raw materials. This alternative was attractive as the Japanese demand for raw materials was high, the infrastructure was available to process this material, and the price that could be commanded for quality fish would be favourable. Second, FPI could set up an independent sales office in Japan to market its products while maintaining corporate control. The third alternative was to develop a cooperative venture with an existing Japanese seafood marketing company to allow FPI value-added products to be exported to the Japanese market.

After reviewing the alternatives, top management decided to seek an arrangement with one of the larger Japanese seafood marketing firms dealing in both the food service and retail markets. The decision was based on the belief that, despite a lower return on investment, this approach would allow it to penetrate the market more quickly than would be possible if it attempted to set up its own operations in Japan. Through 1986, FPI actively researched Japanese seafood marketing companies, including Toyo, Nippon Su, and Nichiro, in an attempt to identify a potential partner. The analysis led FPI to approach Nichiro

Gyogyo Kaisha (Nichiro), the third largest of the seafood marketing companies, with a proposal for them to market FPI's value-added products in the Japanese domestic market. Nichiro was one of the five Japanese companies purchasing ocean perch and capelin from FPI and was hoping to get exclusive access to FPI's quota for these underutilized species.

After the preliminary meetings of corporate representatives, the CEOs of the two companies met in Boston in September 1986 and agreed that some type of arrangement would be mutually beneficial. The details of the arrangement were to be left to the marketing departments of the companies to complete.

In order to further assess the Japanese market potential, FPI requested that Nichiro provide detailed information on the Japanese distribution system and consumer needs. In addition, a team from FPI, headed by Randy Bishop, made three trips (two lasting a week to 10 days, the other three weeks) to Japan over the following year to become more familiar with the Japanese market and to define the parameters of the agreement. As well, the domestic marketing team from Nichiro visited the FPI plants in Burin, Newfoundland, and Danvers, Massachusetts, to aid in its evaluation of the FPI operations.

In June 1987, Vic Young, CEO of FPI, and Junzo Sasaki, CEO of Nichiro, signed a formal agreement. It was agreed that Nichiro would market FPI's value-added products in Japan and that FPI would provide Nichiro with exclusive access to the purchase of raw fish species traditionally supplied by FPI to the Japanese market.

Development of Product Specifications

In the summer of 1987, FPI's corporate R&D department headed by Nancy Wilson began to develop products for potential release in the Japanese market. In order to maximize effectiveness, research and development into new products was conducted by teams from both partners. The initial contact between the R&D representatives from FPI and Nichiro was a week-long meeting to address product issues, specifications, and consumer demands. Nichiro had advised FPI that a February release date was much preferable to October in the Japanese market. The teams met frequently through the summer in Newfoundland and, although FPI was not obligated by their agreement with Nichiro to produce a specific number of products, eventually 20 were developed for possible release with new Nichiro products in February of 1988. Nichiro typically introduced between 40 and 50 of their own new products at a time.

FPI's first efforts were aimed at producing a bread coating mix specifically for products for the Japanese market. The Japanese deep-fry at lower temperatures than North Americans, a factor which had to be addressed in developing breaded and battered products. FPI already produced breaded products, but the standard coating used did not meet the Japanese requirement of a crunchy look with a soft bite. FPI's initial efforts to develop a new batter to meet Japanese standards were unsuccessful, and it was not until late October 1987 that a suitable coating was developed that met both the needs of the Japanese consumer and FPI production requirements and abilities. Of the 11 products eventually included in the final release, 7 were breaded products.

Packaging requirements presented a number of problems. Japanese package sizes, which averaged 180 grams and contained portion sizes of 20 to 40 grams each, were much smaller than the 300-gram packages FPI was currently producing for its North American and European markets. Product packaging also caused concern as FPI planned to maintain its use of cardboard, a type of packaging that was uncommon in the Japanese marketplace. During the fall of 1987, there was a shortage of cardboard in Canada, which further complicated the production of appropriate packaging. FPI also wanted to ensure that the FPI logo and the Canadian flag were prominent on the package itself. The design of the package was made more difficult because the products to be released in February 1988 were not chosen until October 1987.

Although initial product development was done at FPI's head office, sample production runs were performed at the Burin plant (a four-hour drive from St. John's) to assess the capability of equipment and determine productivity standards. It was also critical to determine whether the stringent Japanese quality standards could be met. The initial sample production runs had reject rates as high as 30 percent, due largely to the Japanese tolerance level of approximately 3 percent on portion sizes compared to a North American standard of approximately 10 percent. All of the rejects from the sample run for the Japanese market would have been considered first quality in the American or European markets.

Concurrent with product development, FPI's marketing department was attempting to determine a pricing strategy for the products to be marketed in Japan. This was complicated by the fact that, although production costing could normally be accurately estimated, the Japanese product would be subject to Japanese quality control standards, the impact of which was impossible to accurately estimate until full-scale production was underway. Moreover, the pricing estimates were to be based on positioning the product as unique and premium in the market, rather than simply on the cost of production. Although contributions appeared to be highest for the cod-based products, cod was relatively unknown to the Japanese consumer. Sole (or flatfish) was well known, and liked, and it was hoped that sole-based products could be used as a part of a "pull" strategy to market the cod products (Exhibit 8).

Most of FPI's previous experience had been in negotiating sales to the food service industry rather than the retail market. It did produce some "house brand" retail packages, but this would be the first significant retail market outside North America that FPI had entered. Japan was perceived as a growth market, particularly for frozen products, although the potential for FPI products in the Japanese market was unknown. Given a per capita fish consumption of 68 kilograms, it was not unrealistic to believe that this market could absorb more of the increased capacity of the Burin plant over time. Conscious of the market potential, FPI priced the product without detailed cost information.

EXHIBIT 8 **FPI Japan—Value-Added Contribution Plan 1988**

Retail Market

Item	Price $/lb.	Direct Cost	Total Cost	Contribution $/lb.
Cod nuggets	2.88	1.97	2.32	0.56
Cod strips	2.84	2.02	2.35	0.49
Sole dinner	2.67	2.18	2.50	0.17
Food Service Market				
Cod nuggets	2.38	1.58	1.91	0.43
Cod sticks	2.42	1.55	1.96	0.46
Scotch sole	2.22	1.86	2.15	0.07
Sole boat	2.72	2.39	2.71	0.01
Sole portion	2.72	2.61	2.89	(0.17)
Fresh-formed sole	2.15	1.51	1.91	0.24
Cod wedge 50 g.	2.23	1.56	1.91	0.31
Cod wedge 65 g.	2.21	1.52	1.87	0.34

NOTE: Cod block raw material costed at U.S. $1.50 rate vs. current price of $1.30.
Direct cost of raw fish based on transfer price.

The Burin Plant

When FPI was created in 1984, the Burin plant was redundant to the needs of the new organization. Although it had once been a productive primary processing plant, it had not been well maintained. However, federal and provincial government money was available to help the community of Burin, and the decision was made to renovate the plant. Because there was inadequate secondary processing capacity in Canada, some value-added products were being imported from the United States at considerable cost. Accordingly, the decision was made to convert the plant to secondary processing. After the renovations, the Burin plant would be able to supply value-added products to the Canadian and international markets. In June 1986, the plant was closed, and renovations to turn it into a state-of-the-art secondary processing facility began. When the renovations were completed in June 1987, staff were recalled and production resumed. During the first two months, production and productivity were low as the plant geared up and the plant workers were trained on the new equipment and production lines, but by October 1987, all 108 people on the seniority list had been recalled.

FPI had contributed approximately $7.3 million of the $11.3 million cost of the Burin plant renovation. While some major equipment, including the deep fryer and cold storage facility, was retained, new equipment, including extensive conveyor equipment, two spiral freezers, and breading lines, was also installed. The renovation increased the plant's capability to process and freeze finished products from 5 million pounds to 15 million pounds annually.

Through the summer and early fall of 1987, R&D efforts at Burin were intensified as products were developed for the Japanese market. In test production runs, wastage of fish continued to be high, as much as 10 percent on certain products, due mainly to products not being shaped properly. It was recognized that until the Burin plant could install additional specialized equipment, part of the processing for some of the Japanese products would have to be transferred to the Danvers plant, since Danvers possessed the only prototype of an acceptable cutting machine in existence.

Staff at the Burin plant were well aware of the importance corporate headquarters was placing upon the new products they were producing. This was illustrated in late 1987 when the decision was made to ship sole, which was then in short supply, to Burin for processing for the Japanese market, rather than supplying traditional customers in the United States. With the pressure to produce a quality product, extra staff had been placed on the breading lines, and the number of quality control personnel was increased. The workers were not accustomed to such strict standards; however, they realized that it was important to produce a quality product, or their jobs and the future of the plant would be jeopardized.

By far the greatest pressure was felt by the management team who had to ensure the coordination of activities so that everything was available in time for production. Because partial processing for some products had to be temporarily carried out at Danvers, management spent considerable time scheduling and coordinating the transfer of fish to the United States, working it into the production schedule at the Danvers plant, and transporting back to Burin for final processing. It was not unusual for the Burin plant to be waiting on a shipment of semiprocessed fish from Danvers and/or packaging materials from Toronto to allow the daily production schedule to be established. There was a considerable amount of time pressure as well, given Nichiro's advice to aim for a February release date.

There was considerable pressure on the Burin workers and management to keep to production schedules and produce a top-quality product, which met the stringent Japanese quality control standards. During the production stage, three quality control specialists from Nichiro worked at the plant on a full-time basis alongside FPI's quality control employees. The groups provided constant feedback to the workers in relation to the control standards.

The first consignments of the 11 products produced at Burin for the February launch into the Japanese market were completed in December and shipped immediately to allow for the six-week lead time. The Burin plant planned to ship products twice a month via Halifax to Japan. Demand for the product was not yet known and neither Nichiro nor FPI was able to predict if these products would be accepted by the Japanese consumer.

With the first shipment of products to Japan completed, management undertook a general assessment of Burin operations, including the production for the Japanese market, and concluded that the plant would have to invest in capital equipment, including the installation of a microwave tempering and block-pressing system, to improve overall productivity. With respect to the Japanese product, Burin management questioned if some of the products currently being produced could be made profitable at the negotiated prices, even with additional equipment.

Release of Products in Japan

The release of value-added products for the Japanese domestic market took place in February 1988 with a press conference and a reception and display of products in Tokyo, jointly hosted by Young and Sasaki. This was followed by similar promotions in six additional cities in Japan during February. All of the products were well received and one, sea strips, was noted by many to be the best product to be produced in the frozen seafood class in the previous 10 years. Demand for the products in Japan through the first six months after the release date was strong.

Review of the Japanese Product Line

A detailed financial review of the Japanese venture was conducted in September 1988 (Exhibit 9). The sales of value-added product to the Japanese market for the period from the February release date to September 3, 1988, were over $4

EXHIBIT 9 FPI Japan—Sales Analysis of Value-Added Products to September 3, 1988

Product	Pounds (000's)	Canadian Dollars (000's)
Retail market		
Nuggets	306.1	$ 830
Sea strips (cod)	324.9	925
Sea dinner (sole)	286.8	765
Total retail	917.8	$2,520
Food service		
Nuggets	99.4	233
Fish sticks	59.4	158
Scotch sole	52.4	116
Fresh formed	140.2	302
Sole boat	190.4	517
Cod boat	31.8	89
Cod loin	24.1	69
Sole portion	104.3	284
Total food service	702.0	$1,770
Total value-added	1,620.0	$4,290

NOTE: The date of September 3 corresponds to Nichiro's fiscal year. FPI uses the calendar year.

million, more than one third of the estimated total sales to Japan for that year and significantly higher than expected.

A contentious issue was the pricing of the raw materials used in the finished product. FPI treated Burin as a profit centre and used open market prices to determine the transfer price charged by its primary production plants to Burin. If, for example, one pound of cod cost $1 on the open market, that was the transfer price used, irrespective of the actual production cost, which might be as low as $.65. Utilizing this cost accounting approach, FPI had determined that certain of the products produced for the Japanese market were marginally profitable or unprofitable for Burin at the prices negotiated in the original arrangements (Exhibit 8). FPI's management knew, however, that when an alternate system of cost allocation was used, some of those products were profitable because production costs were lower than market prices. Despite the oversupply of cod in the market and the resulting buildup in inventory, the determination of the profitability of the Japanese products continued to be based on market pricing.

Management at the Burin plant knew that, although their existing equipment could freeze up to 15 million pounds of fish annually, they could not produce that amount of packaged finished product, particularly for the retail market. With the purchase of $640,000 worth of specialized equipment, Burin would be able to improve its overall productivity, including productivity on the Japanese line and operate independently of the Danvers plant. That investment was expected to yield an annual saving of $195,000 based solely on the projected volumes of sales for 1989 for established Nichiro products.

Because of the innovative nature and high quality of the FPI products, they had been positioned in the premium price range. Although the products had proven to be popular, the fact that the Japanese consumer did not seem to be able to differentiate between premium Atlantic cod and Alaskan pollock, which was being sold for 25 percent less in the ultracompetitive Japanese retail market, had caused some concern.

Conclusion

FPI had made a significant commitment to the Japanese venture and was developing an in-house expertise that would allow it to continue in that market. Although the company realized it was capable of developing products for the Japanese domestic market, it was unsure what its strategy should be, given that not all of its products were profitable. Although the corporate R&D department of FPI continued to research additional new products, the company needed to forecast its long-term opportunity in the Japanese market. The per capita consumption of 68 kilograms of fish was very inviting, but the market share that FPI could realistically hope to achieve was unknown.

On January 30, 1989, the Canadian government announced new fish quotas and allocations, based on research which had shown a major depletion in the cod stock (Exhibit 1). The situation was considered serious, and fisheries experts predicted that further cuts would be necessary in subsequent years. The quota reduction hit FPI hard, and virtually overnight, cod moved from a position of oversupply to undersupply. FPI now had to consider whether it might not be wiser to market its limited resource in traditional markets, rather than attempt to maintain the company's presence in Japan. Foreign exchange markets were also causing some concern. The yen, which had moved from 200 to the dollar to as low as 99 to the dollar in January 1988, had reversed the downward trend. In January 1989, it stood at 109 yen to the dollar, and experts were predicting further increases. Because the prices had been negotiated in Canadian dollars, Nichiro was absorbing the resulting costs, but it was unclear how long they would continue to do so, or what the future financial implications might be for FPI.

As Young again reviewed the report from Randy Bishop, he acknowledged that, although sales to Japan were higher than FPI had anticipated, this had not been achieved without strain on the company. FPI was growing rapidly; in 1986 and 1987, profit had been $22,330,000 and $31,004,000, respectively. Although the company had been successful in Japan, the nature of that market would require the on-going development of new and innovative products and a commitment to the venture which might call for a disproportionate amount of management time. Nichiro was already pushing for the development of new products for October 1989. With currency exchange fluctuations, and a major drop in quotas, Young wondered what the strategy should be for the Japanese market and how it fit with the future growth and direction of FPI.

CASE 12
FORTLAND: THE TENNESSEE DECISION

In June 1990, the members of the executive team of Fortland Manufacturing assembled in their retreat room. They had been in the same room at the same cheap hotel two years previously facing the same problem. The future of the company was at stake. The team knew that a decision on whether to merge the company's primarily auto parts supply operations in Canada with their facility in Tennessee had to be made. They had just lost a second key account to a U.S.–based competitor.

Despite potential savings of up to $10.7 million a year from merging operations, President John Conley wanted to avoid the shutdown of Canadian manufacturing if at all possible. He knew that it meant putting 550 loyal employees out of work in the middle of a recession and requiring at least 23 executives of the management team to uproot their families.

Company Background

Fortland manufactured and distributed products to the automotive original equipment market (OEM) and aftermarket, transportation, and industrial markets. The majority of its business was in the auto parts industry, which had been under a free trade agreement with the United States for 22 years. The products fell into three main categories: polymers, electronic, and mechanical. Polymers included injection molding of windshield wiper structures and extrusion of rubber squeegees. Electronic products included automotive signal flashers and relays. Worm gear hose clamps and other fasteners were in the mechanical products group. Mechanical products represented 50 percent of Fortland's business, and they held the number-one position in the North American market. Polymers represented 37 percent of sales and electrical, 13 percent. Fortland was the third largest firm in polymers and held a strong niche in the flasher market.

On a separate dimension, Fortland's business was divided between 39 percent in the United States automotive aftermarket and industrial market, 25 percent in the Canadian automotive aftermarket and industrial market, 22 percent in the North American original equipment market, and 15 percent in offshore sales.

The company had two Canadian plants, one in Oakville, Ontario (polymer division) and the other in Burlington, Ontario (mechanical and electronic divisions), and a Tennessee facility. The company had been started in Hamilton, Ontario, by the current CEO's father and grandfather in 1925 as the Fortland and Son Stamping Company. The shortened name was assumed in the 1960s. The company was one of the largest producers of plastic windshield wiper blades and hose clamps worldwide.

In the late 1970s, CEO Alex Smithers had a hands-off management style. He hired a management team to run the firm, allowing him to pursue some personal ventures. The company expanded its export sales and offshore operations substantially in the early 1980s. The company embarked on an ambitious global strategy, establishing operations through highly leveraged acquisitions in France, Australia, Denmark, Germany, Singapore, and the United Kingdom.

However, the cost of the expansion and inefficient offshore operations, which were too small, quickly drained the company. In September 1988, the company posted a $2 million loss, the first loss in company history. Further, the increased price competition in all markets was putting the entire company at risk.

Turning Operations Around

The problems prompted Smithers to become actively involved again with the company. Determined to make dramatic changes to stop the losses, the management team was changed, and the new team members developed a vision to save the company. Their vision was to adopt "world-class manufacturing" techniques to bring the company back to profitability.

They started by making major cuts in the unprofitable areas of the firm. Unprofitable offshore operations were sold. They switched away from their complicated and inefficient information system and cut excessive overhead costs by $30 million. These changes, plus the competition, dropped sales from $175 million to $110 million. However, the majority of the lost sales were to customers of the offshore operations, which had been divested.

The team members then started the task of turning the company into a globally competitive operation. They inverted the organization chart, so that management's job was to support the employee teams above. The team also moved managers out on to the floor from their offices. Some managers who could not adapt left on their own; others were replaced.

The executives then met with all the employees and candidly told them the entire financial situation. The family orientation of the company allowed Smithers to maintain the needed trust of the employees. The executive and employees all knew that they had 18 months to turn the company around.

The Fortland community had a goal to create a world-class manufacturing company. Through extensive training and employee participation, it was able to adopt total quality control, line ownership of quality, Kanban, group technology, and team concepts. The adoption and training on the concepts occurred over the next eighteen months. The results were impressive.

Performance Improvements

The Fortland employees and executive made extensive improvements. The younger work force at Oakville adapted quickly. The Burlington work force was slower to adapt, but did improve. The unionized Canadian plants and the union-free plant in Tennessee had similar results. For example, in the polymers division, the molding team's initial systems audit results in August 1988 were at 73 percent, but by April 1990, they were at 93 percent. Systems audits cover whether operating instructions are present, operators are properly trained to do a quality job, check sheets are available for operators to complete, housekeeping is properly carried out, and other areas.

The first quality audit for the molding group showed a 90 percent rating, compared to the improved 98 percent level. The extrusion team was up from 90 percent to 99 percent. Further, scrap and rework dropped to 5.6 percent from 17.6 percent. Also, inventory dropped from four to five weeks down to four hours. Critically, these improvements translated into a $6 million turnaround, before tax, in fiscal 1989 (see Exhibit 1).

Takeover of Fortland

Despite the improvements, Fortland required cash investments to make it competitive in the long term. In January 1989, a friendly takeover was negotiated with Carpar Enterprises. Carpar produced aerospace and defense engineering technology products. It offered the added advantage of being a publicly traded company on the Toronto and Montreal stock exchanges. The takeover gave the previously privately held Fortland access to capital markets.

Carpar took a position of 27 percent of Fortland in January 1990 in exchange for cash and Carpar stock. Carpar was expected to take control of 51 percent of the company in January 1991. Carpar's goal was to take funds out of collapsing defense products and invest them in long-term growth with Fortland. Smithers was to stay on as CEO of Fortland and become vice chairman of Carpar.

Fortland in Trouble

One of President John Conley's greatest fears was that they would be hit with a recession before they could make the changes. However, the changes had been accomplished, and the company restored to profitability. Nevertheless, the success of the company was not long lasting.

Starting in late 1989, the rising exchange rate was causing gradual price increases of Fortland products to foreign customers, primarily in the United States. The modest profitability of 1989 was slipping fast. Further, the market share growth was flat, and customers were looking elsewhere. In January 1990, the executive team was asked to begin to evaluate the business to determine where the problem was located.

Exhibit 1 Non-consolidated Income Statement ($000s)

	10 Months Ended July 31/90	12 Months Ended September 30/89	12 Months Ended September 30/88
Sales	$ 52,350	$ 67,412	$ 66,096
Cost of sales	31,889	42,678	40,820
Gross profit	$ 20,461	$ 24,735	$ 25,276
Production, selling, distribution, and administrative overhead	$ 16,541	$ 18,156	$ 22,054
Muncipal taxes	350	348	340
Provision for depreciation and amortization	2,157	2,523	2,468
Interest on long-term debt	729	1,627	1,095
Other interest	870	1,445	1,485
Research and development	399	199	805
	$ 21,046	$ 24,305	$ 28,247
Dividends received from affiliate	$ 0	$ 150	$ 330
(Loss) Income before income taxes and extraordinary items	− 585	580	− 2,641
Income taxes			
Current (recovery)	0	− 220	− 901
Deferred	− 168	454	− 11
(Loss) Income before extraordinary items	− 417	346	− 1,729
Extraordinary items	1,846	− 3,405	− 5,674
Net income (loss)	$ 1,429	$ − 3,059	$ − 7,403
Retained earnings at beginning of period	$ 10,253	$ 16,959	$ 24,362
Redemption of shares	− 3,105	− 3,647	0
Dividends	− 482	0	0
Net income (loss)	1,429	− 3,059	− 7,403
Retained earnings at end of period	$ 8,095	$ 10,253	$ 16,959
Assets			
Current assets			
Accounts and notes receivable:			
Trade	$ 7,266	$ 11,031	$ 10,417
Subsidiaries and affiliate	2,212	2,839	2,957
Inventories	11,233	10,794	14,652
Prepaid expenses	471	509	539
Income taxes recoverable	0	1,126	1,400
Total current assets	$ 21,182	$ 26,300	$ 29,965
Deferred pension asset	$ 252	$ 795	$ 623
Investment in and advances to subsidiaries and affiliate	1,429	3,813	8,188
Property, plant, and equipment			
Land, buildings, and equipment	38,080	35,489	42,336
Accumulated depreciation	19,912	18,059	16,482
	18,168	17,431	25,853
Total assets	$ 41,030	$ 48,338	$ 64,629

Exhibit 1 *(concluded)* **Non-consolidated Income Statement ($000s)**

	10 Months Ended July 31/90	12 Months Ended September 30/89	12 Months Ended September 30/88
Liabilities and Shareholders Equity			
Current liabilities			
Bank indebtedness	$ 7,987	$11,908	$11,452
Accounts payable and accrued liabilities	6,189	5,816	10,516
Taxes and dividends payable	26	26	26
Principal due within one year on long-term debt	421	287	448
Total current liabilities	$14,623	$18,036	$22,442
Long-term debt	$ 4,991	$ 8,487	$22,091
Note payable to shareholder	1,139	1,139	0
Deferred gain on sale and leaseback	400	2,405	0
Deferred income taxes	1,366	992	1,857
Shareholders' equity			
Capital stock, authorized	9,226	5,810	39
Excess of appraised value of property over cost	1,191	1,217	1,242
Retained earnings	8,095	10,253	16,959
Total liabilities and shareholders' equity	$41,030	$48,338	$64,629

NOTE: Nonconsolidated statements represent Canadian and offshore operations only. The inclusion of U.S. sales would bring sales to approximately $100 million in 1989 and $74 million for the 10 months ending July 31, 1990.

The Marketing Environment

Fortland had a long-standing policy to have the majority of its business from the aftermarket. This policy was set to avoid being overly dependent on one OEM manufacturer, a factor which had destroyed many auto parts companies. This policy forced Fortland to aggressively develop the aftermarket both at home and abroad. However, OEM customers were critical for staying in touch with changes in technology and product requirements.

Fortland was successful in developing its aftermarket customer base. It achieved this primarily through higher product quality and effective market channel management. Fortland had an extremely effective distribution network both in Canada and abroad. Through the distribution network, it sold both branded and unbranded products.

Fortland's Competitive Position

In the late 1970s, Fortland gained market share in the United States through aggressive pricing and selling 70 percent unbranded products. In the early 1980s, Fortland began to be a price leader and to sell branded products to increase profitability. The strategy paid off. Fortland had established a stranglehold on the Canadian hose clamp and wiper markets with a 50 percent and 55 percent respective market share. Fortland also gained a grip on the U.S. market with 30 percent of the hose clamp market and 12 percent of the wiper market. Further, it diversified and captured 10 percent of the electronic flasher market in Canada and 6 percent of the U.S. market.

Competition on the Rise

Despite the solid position of Fortland in the market, its position was beginning to erode. The problem was especially evident in the United States, where the balance of trade deficit was creating political pressure in both the aftermarket and the OEM to buy U.S. products. Fortland had 60 percent of its sales in the U.S. OEM and aftermarket combined, so the impact of the pressure was a serious consideration. Mark Parson, vice president of marketing at Fortland, believed that a U.S. base was worth at least one to two points of market share for patriotic reasons alone.

In addition, Fortland was facing increasing competitive pressure in all three of its divisions. The crisis with the decrease in U.S. automaker's sales, caused mainly by Japanese vehicles, was creating surplus capacity in the auto parts industry. Parson estimated that, across North America, there was 35 percent over capacity in the mechanical market, 20 percent over capacity in polymers, and 15 percent over capacity in electronic. Fortland's traditional U.S. customers' needs were declining, and Japanese firms often brought their suppliers with them. This surplus, in turn, was driving the price of auto parts down in both the aftermarket and the OEM.

Parson felt the profit margins in all markets had been largely squeezed out. It was not unusual for some companies to sell products at below variable cost just to stay in business in the short term. The majority of the players in all three of the markets were experiencing financial troubles. The smaller firms were barely surviving, and some larger firms, like TRICO, were in serious trouble.

Companies such as EPICOR, based in Florida and Mexico, and Wittek, based in Chicago, were aggressively attacking the hose clamp market. ANCO, based in Indiana, and TRICO, based in Mexico and Texas, were attacking the wiper market. Finally, EPICOR and Wagner, both based in Mexico, were pursuing the flasher market.

This cumulative tough price competition was hurting Fortland's market position. Although Fortland's reputation for quality and strong distribution relationships allowed it to hold the majority of its customers, competitors had initiated improvements in their manufacturing operations. Their improved quality and delivery were beginning to show in the marketplace.

Turning Point for Fortland

Fortland's ability to hold the competition off ended dramatically in early 1990. Buick Olds Cadillac (BOC) was one of the major OEM customers of Fortland. Fortland had an excellent long-standing relationship with BOC based on Fortland's quality and delivery reputation. In early 1990, the contract with BOC was open for new competitive bidding. BOC decided that it would not be renewing with Fortland and would be working with one of Fortland's U.S.–based competitors. The $2.5 million contract was a significant loss for Fortland. As a result, Parson decided to investigate the loss personally.

BOC informed Fortland that the competitor had comparable quality and delivery, *and* offered a significant cost savings over Fortland. Parson was shocked by the amount. The competitor had underbid Fortland by $450,000. Parson explained:

> At this level we couldn't make a dime. I checked with our production and finance people to find out how they were doing it. With our cost structure, we determined that their price represented less than our variable and direct costs. Forget contribution, let alone profits. They had to have a lower cost structure, because we knew the health of their firm wouldn't allow them to buy market this way.

This was the clearest example that Fortland had to reevaluate its position as a Canadian manufacturer. It was clear that a thorough investigation of the relative cost structures of different sites needed to be investigated. The executive team was given the task of exploring the Fortland cost structure to make it more competitive.

Options for Change

There were three possibilities that Conley wanted investigated. First, he wanted to know if existing operations could be further improved to obtain the needed savings. Second, he wanted the possibility of rural Canadian sites to be investigated to determine if the cost savings were comparable. Last, he wanted a comparison of U.S. or Mexican sites examined.

The concept of further improvements to the existing operations was quickly eliminated. Ron Zezel, vice president of manufacturing, was certain that nothing could be done internally to achieve the required savings. He stated that "we are still making improvements, but they are in feet and not yards." The only way significant savings could be achieved would be to shut down either the U.S. or Canadian operations. This would allow a reduction in management requirements and other overhead synergies.

However, Matthew O'Roarke, vice president human resources, felt that the Canadian base could be run competitively if all staff not directly required for day-to-day manufacturing, selling, and administration were laid off. This would mean the elimination of R&D activities. He felt the company could survive in the short term, but it would die in the medium to long term without future growth.

The second option was to move the Canadian plants to rural sites in Canada. Sharon Campbell, controller, estimated that a 5 percent saving could be achieved in the base overhead costs at a rural site. However, these savings would be offset by retraining and moving expenses. Further, it would not come close to meeting the savings needs of the firm.

The team felt the firm had either to close the Tennessee facility to reduce executive overhead and run the Canadian operation as a bare bones facility, or to move the firm to the United States. After extensive discussions and inquiries on several American states, the executive team decided to look seriously at moving to Tennessee.

It was felt that Mexico was not an option because the labour force was not perceived to be skilled enough to easily utilize the company's manufacturing techniques. Also, a minimum of 80 percent of the 40-member management, technical, and skilled employees team were needed to make any move successful. This level was not likely to be achieved with Mexico as a destination, because of the cultural differences that the transferees would face.

Preparations for the Meeting

Campbell was one of the coordinators of the financial information for the possible move. She and the management at the existing plant in Smyrna, Tennessee, worked out some comparisons on labour, materials, and overhead costs (Exhibit 2). The move would require two new facilities to be built in Tennessee. (Fortland investigated 38 sites in seven states before choosing Tennessee.) She was able to estimate the cost of these facilities by talking with local officials.

The local and state governments were very interested in bringing Fortland to Tennessee. They had programs that would build and lease the facility to Fortland. Further, the municipality would also give Fortland substantial tax breaks to make the move, and the governments offered to supplement the wages of Fortland's new employees during their training period.

As Campbell worked on the numbers, she realized that Fortland was seriously considering the possibility of moving. Her gut feeling was that the real savings on labour, materials, and overhead was likely to be half of the projected $10.7 million. However, she knew that they had not even looked at tax savings or social program savings.

She was able to account for higher health care costs in the United States by using a fringe rate based on their current operations in Tennessee. This was the only significant higher cost expected from potential new Tennessee operations. The new facilities would require less labour and management personnel due to better equipment and plant proximity synergies. She also noted that the cost of capital was 400 basis points lower in Tennessee at 11 percent.

Campbell also wondered if the cost of the shutdown might be higher than was anticipated. She realized that behind the numbers were a lot of peoples' lives. Personally, she knew that she would not be moving with the company if it went. Her husband's career was well set in Toronto, and a move was not possible. She also knew that many of the other executives were in similar situations.

Ed Finley, vice president of finance, also had concerns about the estimated annual savings. However, he felt that there was duplication between Canada and the United States. He also noted that Carpar would cover the soft costs of a move, and the hard cost could be covered by Tennessee municipal bonds. It was unlikely that his family would agree to the move.

⎯⎯ **Exhibit 2 Potential Annual Savings**
_____

A. Mechanical
  Hourly
  Burlington—Current
    156 employees (assume 22 skilled, 134 operators)
    Current fringe rate 35% (U.S. 53%)
    Current weighted average—operators—13.63/hr.
    Current weighted average—skilled—17.88/hr.
  Annualized current cost
    134 × 13.63 × 2,080 × 1.35 $ 5,128,587
    22 × 17.88 × 2,080 × 1.35 $ 1,104,555
                                                                    ⎯⎯⎯⎯⎯⎯⎯⎯
                                                                     $ 6,233,142
                                                                    ⎯⎯⎯⎯⎯⎯⎯⎯

  Smyrna—Cost of new hires
    91 employees (14 skilled, 77 operators)
    Current rate — operators — 9.04 U.S. @ 0.82 — 11.02 Cdn.
    Current rate — skilled   — 13.00 U.S. @ 0.82 — 15.85 Cdn.
  Annualized cost of new hires
    Operators —77 × 11.02 × 2080 × 1.53 $ 2,700,394
    Skilled   —14 × 15.85 × 2080 × 1.53   706,175
                                                                    ⎯⎯⎯⎯⎯⎯⎯⎯
                                                                     $ 3,406,569
                                                                    ⎯⎯⎯⎯⎯⎯⎯⎯

  Salaried
    1991 salary costs $ 1,544,000
    Deduct cost of new hires—8 @ 41,000   (328,000)
    Budgeted fringes (13.5% × 1,544,000)   208,440
    New hire fringes (26.5% × 328,000)   (86,920)
                                                                    ⎯⎯⎯⎯⎯⎯⎯⎯
    Savings $ 1,337,520
                                                                    ⎯⎯⎯⎯⎯⎯⎯⎯

  Mechanical—1991 budget, building and overhead $ 5,320,000
    Deduct—Salary   (1,544,000)
          —Indirect labour   (896,000)
          —Fringes   (535,000)
          —Environmental   (150,000)
                                                                    ⎯⎯⎯⎯⎯⎯⎯⎯
    Net future savings (annually) $ 2,195,000
                                                                    ⎯⎯⎯⎯⎯⎯⎯⎯

  Mechanical summary
    Current cost—Burlington $ 6,233,142
    Cost of new hires—Smyrna   (3,406,569)
    Salary savings to 1991 budget   1,337,520
    Overhead savings to 1991 budget   2,195,000
                                                                    ⎯⎯⎯⎯⎯⎯⎯⎯
                                                                     $ 6,359,093
                                                                    ⎯⎯⎯⎯⎯⎯⎯⎯

The majority of savings would be realized from combining the Burlington and the Smyrna operations. The synergies in salaried employees, MIS, procurement, and moving costs would be similar at either consolidation site. Finley felt the major annual savings would come from labour cost savings, interest, plant

---

EXHIBIT 2 *(continued)*

B. Polymer (New facility)

Oakville 1991 budgeted hourly employees—230 (current actual 250)—200 operators 30 skilled

    Current rates—operators—11.94/hr.

    Current rates—skilled—18.22/hr.

Cost of operating in Oakville with 230 employees at current rates:

Operators—200 × 11.94 × 2080 × 1.35	$6,705,504
Skilled—30 × 18.22 × 2080 × 1.35	1,534,852
	$8,240,356

New plant—190 hourly employees (162 operators, 28 skilled):

    Operators—7.50 U.S./hr = 9.15 Cdn.

    Skilled—10.00 U.S./hr = 12.20 Cdn.

Cost of operating new facility:

Operators—162 × 9.15 × 2080 × 1.53	$4,717,272
Skilled—28 × 12.20 × 2080 × 1.53	1,087,107
	$5,804,379

Savings – Oakville – new plant		$2,435,977
Assume salary savings @ nil		
Oakville lease (12 mos.)	$564,000	
New plant (100,000 sq. ft.		
@ 3.05)	(305,000)	
	$259,000	$ 259,000
Total polymer savings		$2,694,977

C. Electronics

1991 Budget—74 budgeted employees (65 operators, 9 skilled)

    Burlington—rates—11.58/hr.—operators

    Burlington—rates—16.89/hr.—skilled

    New plant—68 (59 operators, 9 skilled)

    New plant—rates—7.00 U.S. (8.53 Cdn.) and 11.00 (13.41 Cdn.)

Annualized cost old plant (including fringes):

Operators—65 × 11.58 × 2080 × 1.35	$2,113,582
Skilled—9 × 16.89 × 2080 × 1.35	426,844
	$2,540,426

Annualized cost new plant (including fringes):

Operators—59 × 8.53 × 2080 × 1.53	$1,601,606
Skilled—9 × 13.41 × 2080 × 1.53	384,084
	$1,985,960

Hourly labour savings	$ 554,736
Assume salary savings—nil	–0–
Occupancy cost—Burlington 1991	$ 110,000
Lease building (3.25 U.S. – 4.00 Cdn.) × 24,000 sq. ft.	(96,000)
Net savings—Electronics	$ 568,736

EXHIBIT 2 *(concluded)*

D. Procurement savings (annual)

Mechanical—Stainless	$ 500,000
Carbon	90,000
Tooling	50,000
Packaging	100,000
Polymers— Rubber	40,000
Boots	25,000
Duties	40,000
Electronics—All parts (new U.S. vendors)	$ 100,000
Transportation	75,000
Miscellaneous car and equipment leases	50,000
Total savings	$ 1,070,000

Summary

A. Mechanical	$ 6,359,093
B. Polymer	2,694,977
C. Electronic	568,736
D. Procurement	1,070,000
Annualized savings	$10,692,806

NOTE: Above assumes no savings from G & A, MIS, interest costs, state and/or local incentives. There are currently 235 employees in Tennessee: 161 operators, 19 skilled, and 55 administrative and support personnel.

EXHIBIT 3   Estimate of One-time Costs of Move to Tennessee ($000s)

Outplacement	$ 400
Severance	3,900
Moving costs	1,500
Immigration	200
Resettlement incentive*	650
Pension improvements†	1,000
Equipment‡	4,340
Miscellaneous	750
Production inefficiencies§	2,700
Job duplication§	2,000
Utility duplication§	700
	$18,140

NOTE: *For Canadian executives moving to the United States.
†To complete Fortland pension obligation with Canadian work force.
‡Equipment for new plants.
§Costs associated with duplicated facilities during the transition period.

lease expenses, and taxes. There would, however, be significant one-time costs associated with the move (See Exhibit 3).

Other Issues

One of the issues facing Fortland was the grants and loans provided to the company by the Canadian federal and provincial governments. The two governments had invested approximately $17 million in Fortland through various labour and technology programs since the early 1970s. Campbell felt that Fortland's legal obligations with these programs had been mostly met.

However, public and political pressure had forced Firestone Canada to pay back $15 million when they closed their Hamilton plant in 1988. Further, the Canadian government seemed desperate to show that the 1988 Free Trade Agreement with the United States was creating, and not destroying, jobs.

The team was also concerned with the reactions of customers and suppliers to a consolidation move. If Fortland closed the Tennessee facility, it might jeopardize one of their most important OEM customers. Nissan's large car plant in Tennessee was supplied by Fortland. The importance of service and delivery times to Nissan might put the account in jeopardy without a Tennessee facility. Conversely, the closure of the Canadian facilities might jeopardize its strong Canadian market presence. However, Parson thought that Fortland's Canadian distribution network could hold the market.

Lastly, the closure of either the U.S. or Canadian facilities had broader ramifications than those affecting Fortland's employees alone. Fortland had several dedicated suppliers who would be badly hurt by a move. Their employees and families and the whole community would be affected by the decision. Further, the majority of Fortland employees were over the age of 40 and were unlikely to find other jobs easily.

Meeting at the "No-Name Motel"

Conley looked around the room; he knew that the decision they faced was a major one, both professionally and personally. It would not be an easy decision either way. He also knew that he would have to justify the decision to Smithers and to the new parent company.

CASE 13
THE GRAND THEATRE COMPANY

There is no better director than me. Some may be as good, but none better.[1]

In December 1982, the board of directors of Theatre London (see Exhibit 1) were considering a proposal to hire Robin Phillips as artistic director to replace Bernard Hopkins. The hiring decision was complicated by Phillips's ambitious plans for the theatre, which included a change from a subscription theatre to repertory, an increase in budget from $1.9 million to $4.5 million, and even changing the organization's name. The board had to act quickly as plans had to be made and actors hired for the next season.

Theatre in Ontario

Theatre is big business. In Toronto alone (including cabaret, dinner theatre, and opera) some 3.5 million people attended 120 productions in 1982, in 28 locations. There are 24 nonprofit professional theatres in Toronto and 18 in the rest of Ontario.

EXHIBIT 1 The Board of Directors, December 1982

J. Noreen De Shane	President of the Grand Theatre, and president of a stationery firm
Peter J. Ashby	Partner, major consulting firm
W. C. P. Baldwin, Jr.	President, linen supply firm
Bob Beccarea	Alderman and civic representative
Art Ender	Life insurance representative
Ed Escaf	Hotel and restaurant owner
Dr. John Girvin	Surgeon
Stephanie Goble	Representative of London Labour Council
Elaine Hagarty	Former alderman, active in arts community
Barbara Ivey	Active board member of various theatre groups
Alan G. Leyland	Entrepreneur
John F. McGarry	Partner, major law firm
C. Agnew Meek	Corporate marketing executive
Robert Mepham	Insurance company executive
Elizabeth Murray	Board member of theatre groups and Ontario Arts Council
John H. Porter	Vice president and partner, major accounting firm
Peter Schwartz	Partner, major law firm
Dr. Tom F. Siess	University professor
Dr. Shiel Warma	Surgeon

---

[1]Robin Phillips, quoted in *The Globe and Mail,* December 31, 1983, p. E1.

This case was prepared by Dr. Larry M. Agranove from published sources and interviews with numerous people in theatre, government, and arts organizations. Copyright © 1986 by Wilfrid Laurier University.

Virtually all theatre organizations are nonprofit (with rare exceptions such as Ed Mirvish's Royal Alexandra) and are subsidized by local, provincial, and federal grants. Thus, theatres compete for funds with charity, educational, and health care organizations. As shown in Exhibit 2, a third of revenue typically comes from government sources, and half of this comes from the Canada Council. Another 10 percent comes from individual and corporate donors and the balance from the box office. Because of the pressing need for box office revenues, most theatre companies sell subscriptions of five or so plays from October to May.

In 1982–83, audience size was 570,000 for the Stratford Festival, the largest arts organization in Canada, and 268,000 for the Shaw Festival, the second largest theatre company. According to a Stratford audience study, audiences break down into (1) committed theatre-goers (27 percent), who see a number of plays each year and who tend to be older and more educated and live in Ontario; (2) casual theatre-goers (53 percent), who attend a theatre every year or two to see plays of particular interest; and (3) first-timers (20 percent). The challenge for these theatres is to develop these first-timers to be the audience of the future.

Theatre audiences tend to be well educated, with most having university education and slightly over 50 percent having attended a graduate or profes-

---

EXHIBIT 2 The Major Arts Organizations in Canada—Ranked by Size of Total Revenue for 1982–1983

Arts Organization	Total Revenue 1982–1983	Box Office and Earned	Government Grants	Private Donations	Accumulated Surplus/ Deficit End of 1982–1983
1. Stratford Festival	$12,314,300	$9,678,285	$1,405,939	$1,230,076	$(1,731,492)
2. Toronto Symphony	9,480,503	6,020,112	1,893,100	1,567,291	(149,391)
3. National Ballet	7,271,616	3,233,810	2,943,856	1,093,950	(675,096)
4. Orchestre Symphonique de Montreal	7,071,886	4,048,749	2,164,350	858,787	(857,662)
5. Canadian Opera Company	5,969,077	2,668,698	2,029,100	1,271,279	(290,168)
6. Vancouver Symphony	5,189,041	2,488,690	1,784,315	916,036	(818,951)
7. Shaw Festival	4,801,700	3,848,200	586,000	367,500	(45,167)
8. Royal Winnipeg Ballet	4,021,263	1,884,339	1,611,463	525,461	343,639
9. Centre Stage	3,483,020	1,923,312	1,316,000	243,708	(212,108)
10. Citadel Theatre	3,541,911	2,097,096	1,117,733	327,082	(177,821)
.					
.					
.					
.					
18. Grand Theatre	1,990,707	1,277,625	390,000	323,082	0*

*Reduced by Wintario Challenge Fund.

SOURCE: Council for Business and the Arts in Canada.

sional school. Those aged 36 through 50 make up 35 percent of the Stratford audience, and the 21 to 35 and 51 to 64 age groups each make up 25 percent. Visitors from the United States account for 35 percent of box office receipts at the Stratford Festival; Toronto accounts for 25 percent; and the remaining 40 percent come from elsewhere in Ontario. Twice as many women attend as men. It is understood that Shaw's market is similar, with slightly fewer coming from the United States.

A recent study[2] showed that while 42 percent of Ontario residents attended live plays and musicals in 1974, this grew to 55 percent by 1984. Some 24 percent of the Ontario population are "frequent attenders" (at least six times a year). They come from all age groups, but many are "singles," and many are university educated and affluent. In fact, while only 63 percent of Ontarians without a high school education attended live theatre, 94 percent with university degrees have attended live theatre.

There is some price sensitivity: 73 percent said they would attend oftener if tickets were less expensive. However, 77 percent (which included young adults and lower-middle income families) said they would accept a tax increase of up to $25 to support the arts.

The Organization of a Theatre Company

The Board of Directors

The board of directors is fiscally and legally responsible for the theatre. They may determine the theatre's artistic objectives then delegate the fulfilling of these objectives to the artistic director. However, any artistic plan has financial objectives, and the board's responsibility is essentially financial. Artistic directors generally demand, and are generally granted, a great deal of autonomy in such matters as programming and casting; to a large extent the board "bets" on the artistic director's ability to put on a season of theatre, subject to his accountability in meeting budgets and providing an appropriate level of quality.

Board members are typically expected to assist in fund-raising and to set an example by contributing generously themselves.

Board members often have business backgrounds. As a result, they may be—and are certainly often perceived to be—insensitive to the unique needs of an artistic organization. Artistic boards often include lawyers and accountants, who are often recruited to serve a specific function but who tend to remain on long enough to achieve positions of power.

Busy businesspeople serve on boards for a number of reasons. They may perceive their serving as a civic responsibility. Others may see it as an opportunity to wield power at a board level, something they are not allowed to do in

---

[2]Report to the Honourable Susan Fish, the minister of citizenship and culture, Province of Ontario, by the Special Committee for the Arts, Spring 1984.

their own organizations. Membership on a board allows people to widen their social and business contacts; this can be important to lawyers and accountants, who are limited in their freedom to advertise. One common motivation for business people to join arts boards is the opportunity to mingle with luminaries in the arts. Here is one view of their performance:

> It has often been charged that many a hardheaded businessman loses his business sense on entering a meeting of an arts board. Lacking a profit motive to guide the affairs of the organization, businessmen who serve on arts boards sometimes feel unsure of themselves and their expertise. Compounding this problem is the inclination on the part of arts organizations to consider themselves a breed apart, outside the realm of normal business practice. But whether a company manufactures widgets or mounts exhibitions, the basic business concerns remain the same: strategic planning, good marketing, adequate financing, and competent management are essential to any enterprise.[3]

Theatre Management

In addition to the artistic director, whose role and relationship with the board were described above, there is usually a general manager who is responsible for the business affairs of the organization. Since artistic directors strive for maximum quality, which is expensive, and since business managers have to find and account for the money to run the theatre, conflicts often occur. Not surprisingly, boards often side with the business manager because of their similarities of culture and values. Typically, both artistic director and general manager report directly to the board.

Mounting a Production

The theatre company selects "products" to suit its objectives and audiences. For example, a theatre might select a playbill of classics or children's plays. A regional theatre might select a Canadian play (to satisfy government grant-giving agencies), a classic (to satisfy the artistic aspirations of the artistic director), a resounding "hit" from Broadway or England (to help sell the series), and one or more plays that have been successful elsewhere.

Each production requires a producer (who may be the artistic director) to act as the "entrepreneur" to put the show together. He acquires the rights to the play, if it is not in the public domain, for a fee of 7 to 10 percent of the box office revenue. He also retains a director, who may be on staff or who may be a free-lance director retained for the run of the play. In the latter case, minimum scale would be $6,174.80 for a run of three weeks of rehearsal and three to four weeks of performance.

---

[3]"Developing Effective Arts Boards" (Undated publication of the Council for Business and the Arts in Canada), pp. 28–29.

Casting is done, beginning with the major parts, on the basis of a uniform contract, which sets out fees (minimum of $416.27 per week for a major company), starting date, billing, working time, and "perks" (for example, dressing room, accommodation).

Finally, a stage manager is contracted, as are designers for sets, costumes, and lighting. It is essential, of course, that all these people work well together.

The above describes the typical stock, or subscription, company. However, Stratford and Shaw operate as repertory companies, hiring a group of actors for one or more seasons and allocating roles among the members of the company. Repertory companies typically sell tickets for individual plays, while subscription companies sell their series at the beginning of the season with few single ticket sales.

Lead times are considerable; in Stratford, for example, plays that open in May are firmly cast by the previous December, and the entire session is planned by March, when rehearsals begin.

Theatre London

Background

The Grand Opera House was opened in London on September 9, 1901, by Ambrose J. Small, a Toronto theatrical entrepreneur and frustrated producer. It quickly became the showcase of Small's theatrical chain, opening with such attractions as the Russian Symphony Orchestra and later offering such performers as Barry Fitzgerald, Bela Lugosi, Clifton Webb, Sidney Poitier, and Hume Cronyn. Small sold his theatre chain in 1919, deposited a million dollars in his bank, and disappeared. There has been no explanation to this day; however, Small's ghost is said to haunt the Grand.

Famous Players bought the theatre in 1924, tore out the second balcony, and converted the theatre to a cinema. They sold to the London Little Theatre for a token amount in 1945, and the building housed an amateur community theatre till the spring of 1971. The theatre employed professional business management and a professional artistic director, but the actors were all amateurs. Some of London's leading citizens acted in plays, and some even displayed a high level of competence. The theatre was prominent in the social life of the city and attracted one of the largest subscription sales in North America, both as a percentage of available seats and in absolute terms. It also achieved a reputation for a very high level of quality, given that it was essentially an amateur theatre. Articles about the theatre appeared in such magazines as *Life*.

However, there was some concern in the theatre that the level of quality was as high as it was going to get as a company of amateurs and that the community deserved, and was ready to support, a professional theatre. Another local organization, the London Symphony, had engaged a conductor with an international reputation and was changing from an amateur to a professional orchestra. An active art gallery association was formed to work toward providing London with a major art gallery. Although strong objections were raised against the proposal for a professional theatre, particularly because of the increased financial burden, the risk, and the denial to many of the theatre's supporters of an opportunity to participate in their hobby of acting, London Little Theatre changed to Theatre London in 1971 under Artistic Director Heinar Piller. The progressives were vindicated, as theatregoers in London and area were treated to a decade of artistically and financially successful theatre.

Piller was succeeded, at the end of the 1975 season, by William Hutt, who had achieved great success as an actor at Stratford and was well known to Londoners. He served from 1976 to 1978. Bernard Hopkins arrived in 1979 and was artistic director till May 1983.

The Grand was attractively and authentically renovated at a cost of $5.5 million, reopening in the fall of 1978 after being closed for a full season. (The company had a reduced season during that time in small rented accommodations.) During the renovation, seating capacity was reduced from 1,100 to 845, but the Grand emerged from the renovations as one of the finest theatres in Canada.

Theatre London ran successful stock seasons from 1979 to 1982. The 1981–1982 season was particularly successful, operating at 85 percent of capacity. Eighty percent of its tickets were sold through subscription to some 13,431 subscribers. Financial statements are shown in Exhibit 3.

The London Environment

London was founded at the forks of the Thames River in 1793 by Governor Simcoe with the intention of making it the capital of Upper Canada. Instead, it became the cultural and commercial centre of southwestern Ontario. Located on three railroad lines and on Highway 401 that serves the Quebec-Windsor corridor, London also has a major airport served by two airlines. London is two hours away (by car) from Detroit or Toronto; however, it is in a major snow belt. London is a major retail centre, with the second highest per capita retail capacity in North America. It serves as a trading area for almost a million people, although its own population is only 259,000. (See the appendix.) There are four hotels near the core area and motels in outlying areas. Many interesting restaurants had opened with a great deal of excess capacity; a few restaurants closed or changed hands.

There is little heavy industry in London, but there is a major university, a community college, a teacher's college, and two small church-affiliated colleges. Four major hospitals serve a wide area and provide teaching facilities for the university medical school and dental school. In addition to being a retail centre, London is the home of major financial institutions and agribusiness firms, as well as a major brewery.

London is also a major cultural centre. In addition to Theatre London, London has a professional symphony orchestra and a couple of significant choral

EXHIBIT 3

THEATRE LONDON
Condensed Five-Year Operating Results
As of June 30, 1979–1983

	1979	1980	1981	1982	1983 (estimate)
Revenue:					
Productions:					
Ticket sales..................................	$ 551,650	$ 585,938	$ 620,313	$ 664,058	$1,100,000
Sponsored programs..................	26,000	25,000	26,500	9,000	9,000
Program advertising...................	17,283	17,270	19,652	24,241	24,000
Total production revenue......	594,933	628,208	666,465	697,299	1,133,000
Grants:					
Canada Council..........................	145,000	163,000	173,000	185,000	210,000
Ontario Arts Council.................	145,000	152,000	160,000	170,000	180,000
Wintario.....................................	89,254	—	—	—	—
City of London...........................	12,500	—	—	—	—
Cultural Initiative Program.......	—	—	25,000	—	—
Total grants...........................	391,754	315,000	358,000	355,000	390,000
Other:					
Operating fund drive.................	41,222	27,462	182,559	183,188	160,000
Special projects.........................	36,811	36,525	43,881	41,281	65,000
Interest......................................	34,553	50,608	62,128	86,106	80,000
Concessions...............................	33,500	75,073	69,581	62,065	78,000
Theatre school...........................	8,720	17,687	19,481	—	—
Box office commissions.............	3,319	3,721	651	6,142	3,000
Theatre rental and miscellaneous.........................	3,170	—	—	4,704	2,000
Total other revenue..............	161,295	211,076	378,281	383,486	388,000
Total revenue....................	1,147,982	1,154,284	1,402,946	1,435,785	1,911,000
Expenses:					
Public relations............................	179,880	128,502	139,907	177,267	270,000
Administration.............................	91,973	115,798	162,723	167,749	330,000
Production overhead.....................	190,911	237,606	282,270	339,474	350,000
Productions.................................	466,906	414,644	416,440	421,151	780,000
Front of house, box office, and concessions..........................	75,563	123,910	107,617	126,673	140,000
Facility operation.........................	131,445	139,215	152,153	142,061	140,000
Theatre school.............................	9,742	20,832	34,804	—	—
Total expenses........................	1,146,420*	1,180,507	1,295,914	1,374,375	2,010,000
Excess of revenue over expense..	$ 1,562	$ (26,223)	$ 107,032	$ 61,410	$ (99,000)
*Salaries, fees and benefits..............	$ 658,507	$ 754,109	$ 791,954	$ 823,260	$1,000,000†
Supplies and expenses....................	487,913	426,398	503,960	551,115	911,000
	$ 1,146,420	$ 1,180,507	$ 1,295,914	$ 1,374,375	$ 1,911,000

†In addition, development costs for the establishment of a repertory company in the 1983–1984 season could be incurred, which could be largely offset by federal and provincial grants.

Exhibit 3 *(concluded)*

THEATRE LONDON
Condensed Balance Sheets
as of June 30, 1979–1982

	1979	1980	1981	1982
Assets				
Current assets:				
Cash and term deposits....................................	$351,010	$372,868	$325,631	$316,939
Accounts receivable...	3,908	13,957	35,208	10,916
Inventory...	7,463	7,146	6,050	—
Prepaid expenses...	20,257	32,788	46,938	72,471
Total assets..	$382,638	$426,759	$413,827	$400,326
Liabilities and Surplus				
Current liabilities:				
Bank loan..	—	$ 25,000	—	—
Accounts payable...	$ 26,253	24,041	$ 30,112	$ 67,198
Advance ticket sale..	280,431	324,524	319,843	302,983
Advance grants..	1,060	—	15,201	14,805
Payable to Theatre London Foundation.........	—	4,523	—	15,340
Total liabilities.......................................	307,744	378,088	365,156	400,326
Surplus..	74,894	48,671	48,671*	—
Total liabilities and surplus..................................	$382,638	$426,759	$413,827	$400,326

*In addition, there was equity of $453,080 from the Wintario Challenge Fund Program in 1981 and $807,289 in 1982. Under the terms of the program, Wintario will match two dollars for every eligible contributed dollar raised (during the three-year period ending 30 June 1983) in excess of 5.9 percent of the current year's operating expenses. All these matching contributions are placed in a separate investment fund for at least five years, although interest earned on the fund may be used for current operations.

groups. The university has an active program of theatre and music, and the community is a centre for visual artists. There are various commercial art galleries, an art gallery connected with the university, and a major public art gallery located in the city centre. There are several museums, including a unique children's museum and a museum of Indian archaeology. The latter two attract visitors from a wide area.

The Grand Theatre Company

In late 1981, a decade after the company had become professional, concern was again raised in the theatre that the level of quality had stagnated and the theatre would have to move in new directions. Bernard Hopkins was a superb actor and a competent artistic director. With some success he had directed a few plays, rather than have to pay for a free-lance director. However, some members of the board believed that he had taken the theatre as far as he was able, and there was no initiative on either side to extend Hopkins's contract beyond its expiry in May 1983.

A planning committee, under one of the board members, addressed the issue of continuing the growth in quality. They conducted a number of retreats and interviewed experts in professional theatre as well as officers of the Canada Council and the Ontario Arts Council. During the course of the investigation, they interviewed Robin Phillips. Phillips had been artistic director at the Stratford Festival and was well known to Barbara Ivey (who served on both the Stratford and Theatre London boards) and to other Theatre London directors. He also had directed, with considerable artistic success, two productions for Theatre London: *The Lady of the Camellias* and *Long Day's Journey into Night.*

Robin Phillips

Robin Phillips is a highly talented artistic director and a person of incredible charm. (In *all* of the interviews conducted by the casewriter, words like *charm, charisma,* and *talent* abounded.) Actress Martha Henry said, "Once you've worked with Robin, it's almost impossible to work for anyone else."

He came to Canada from England in 1974 to plan the 1975 Stratford season, although he would not direct any specific plays till 1976. His tenure at Stratford has been described as successful but stormy. When he was contracting to direct a production for the Canadian Opera Company in 1976, he said he would not renew his Stratford contract unless he had more evidence of support for his ambition to make Stratford the focus of Canadian theatre, with film and television productions as well as live theatre. He received a five-year contract to run from November 1, 1976; the contract could be terminated with four months' notice.

There was a series of resignations from, and returns to, Stratford starting in July 1978, until Phillips's departure in 1981. In addition to his Stratford activities, Phillips was involved with theatre in Calgary, New York, Toronto's Harbourfront, and Vancouver. He also filmed *The Wars,* a novel by Timothy Findley. It was generally understood that he was seeking a theatre in Toronto to serve as a base for his stage, film, and television ambitions. However, none was available.

The Phillips Plan.   Robin Phillips had a plan for Theatre London and would come only if he had a budget to fulfill his plan and complete artistic autonomy. His plan called for raising Theatre London from 18th place in Canadian theatre to third and changing its name to The Grand Theatre Company.

The plan required a budget of $4.5 million, up from $1.9 million. This included $400,000 of capital cost to improve the Grand's facilities. Box office and concessions would provide 73 percent of the budget; 18 percent would come from donations; 5 percent from the Canada Council; and 4 percent from the Ontario Arts Council. Revenue projections were based on playing to 80 percent of capacity; this was considered feasible because Phillips had surpassed that performance at Stratford, and Theatre London had been operating at 85 percent. The theatre requested a permanent tax exemption from the City of London; the deputy mayor described this request as "cavalier."

Three of the stage productions would be adapted for television and filmed by Primedia Productions of Toronto. This would provide some $100,000 of additional revenue for each production as well as audience exposure.

Robin Phillips strongly favoured a repertory company over a subscription policy. He believed, and often stated, that subscriptions denied audiences a choice, and audiences must learn to discriminate. A change had to be made to make the theatre different, special, and exciting. A repertory company would provide a company of salaried actors who could not be lured away during the season and who would be attracted by steady employment.

Another advantage of the repertory concept is the flexibility afforded patrons who may choose the dates they see a play and their seat locations. In a subscription series, patrons are restricted to the same seat location on the same night for each performance. In repertory theatre, several productions are typically run simultaneously.

The Playbill.   Phillips proposed to offer these plays from October to May on the main stage (in addition to a children's program in a small, secondary theatre):

Godspell by John-Michael Tebelak	A rousing rock musical with audience appeal, especially for younger audiences.
The Doctor's Dilemma by George Bernard Shaw	An established classical "hit."
Waiting for the Parade by John Murrell	A Canadian play, with an all-female cast, showing what women did while their men were fighting World War II.
Timon of Athens by William Shakespeare	A little performed, little-known Shakespearean play, ignored by Stratford.
The Club by Eve Merrian	A musical spoof of men's clubs, with a female cast playing the part of men.
Arsenic and Old Lace by Joseph Kesselring	A well-known classic comedy of American theatre.
The Prisoner of Zenda adapted by Warren Graves	A comedy of political intrigue and romance, set in a mythical Eastern European kingdom.
Hamlet by William Shakespeare	One of his best-known plays.
Dear Antoine by Jan Anouilh	A comedy by a leading contemporary French playwright.

Casting for these plays would not be a problem, as leading actors from Canada, the United States, and England were eager to work with Phillips.

Pricing.   Since the plan envisioned a box office yield of $3.2 million, up from the $1.2 million planned for the 1982–1983 season, revenue would have to be increased in two ways. The number of productions would be increased, with nine productions in the season instead of the previous six. There would be a record 399 performances instead of the 230 performances in the 1982–1983 season. Thus, the plan projected an audience of almost 270,000, compared with the 137,000 planned for the 1982–1983 season. In addition, prices would be increased.

A subscriber in the 1982–1983 season could see five plays for $55 on weekends or $45 on weekdays. This pricing schedule was proposed for the 1983–1984 repertory season:

	Price	
Number of Seats	*Weekdays*	*Weekends*
178	$20.00	$22.50
245	14.50	15.50
422	10.50	12.50

Promotion. Since the theatre would require an expanded audience from a wider area, the plan envisioned a program of investment spending in major area newspapers: the *Toronto Star* and the *Globe and Mail,* the *Kitchener-Waterloo Record,* and the *Detroit Free Press* as well as the *London Free Press.* The advertising would be directed at a first-time audience.

Group sales would be stressed, particularly to schools. Hotel-restaurant-transportation-theatre ticket packages were projected. However, data on expenditures was not available.

The Decision

The directors were impressed by the charm and the reputation of Robin Phillips. The proposal to hire Phillips—and to accept his plan—was supported by some board members who had sound business backgrounds and who had worked in theatre for some years. They had a comfortable, modern theatre, with a recently acquired computer to issue tickets. They had a proven record in selling tickets, as did Robin Phillips.

On the other hand, if Phillips was hired, his artistic strengths might not be matched administratively. There was an administrative director who had been there for only two years and a chief accountant, but no controller. And Stratford, Canada's leading theatre, was less than an hour's drive down the road. Would this summer theatre, located so close to London, be an audience builder or a competitive threat?

APPENDIX

1983 Disposable Income by Census Metropolitan Area

	Income Rating		Per Capita Personal Disposable Income	
	Index	*Rank*	*Amount*	*Rank*
Toronto	117	6	$12,693	7
Montreal	103	11	11,212	14
Vancouver	118	5	12,793	6
Ottawa-Hull	118	5	12,796	5
Edmonton	126	4	13,668	4
Calgary	132	1	14,324	1
Winnipeg	111	8	11,997	9
Quebec	98	14	10,623	18
Hamilton	112	7	12,114	8
St. Catharines	103	11	11,223	13
Kitchener	101	13	10,974	16
London	106	10	11,462	11
Halifax	101	13	10,923	17
Windsor	107	9	11,602	10
Regina	130	2	14,056	2
Saskatoon	129	3	14,021	3
Oshawa	106	10	11,450	12
Thunder Bay	102	12	11,089	15
Canada	100		10,851	

NOTE: This list shows all 18 census metropolitan areas in which the principal city had a population of at least 100,000 in the 1981 Census.

London-Centred Seven-County Market Area Data

	Population June 1/83 (thousands)	10-Year Growth Rate (percent)	Households June 1/83 (thousands)	Wage Earner Average Income 1981	Per Capita Disposable Income 1983	Per Capita Retail Sales 1983
Seven counties	838.5	5.7%	293.7	$14,522	$10,669	$4,238
Canada	24,886.0	12.0	8,335.0	15,141	10,851	4,153

SOURCE: *Canadian Markets,* 1984, and 1981 income tax returns.

CASE 14
GSW WATER PRODUCTS COMPANY

GSW Water Products Company (WPC) was an operating division of GSW Incorporated (GSW), a holding company with investments in various manufacturing enterprises. In early 1989, Roly Thompson, the president and CEO of WPC, was contemplating strategy for the company in light of the recently enacted Canada–United States Free Trade Agreement (FTA). WPC manufactured two basic products, water heaters and water pumps, for the Canadian market. The FTA was forcing Thompson to examine more urgently the possibility of entering the U.S. market with these products.

GSW Inc.

Corporate Structure

GSW was a holding company that held a 20 percent ownership share in Camco, Inc. (Camco), and 100 percent ownership of five distinct operating divisions (see Exhibit 1). Each of the operating divisions was called a *company,* and each was rigorously decentralized: separate assets, income statements, management teams, boards of directors, and strategies. This structure reflected GSW's acquisition-oriented history: it had been built by buying and selling companies. GSW's shares were traded on the Toronto Stock Exchange, but majority control was held by three principal owners: Ralph Barford, Robert Stevens, and George Gardner.

Camco, Inc.

The Camco investment represented a partnership between GSW and GE Canada, which had been formed in 1977. In addition to merging together GSW and GE Canada appliance divisions, Camco also purchased the appliance operations of Westinghouse Canada Ltd. located in Hamilton. The original partnership had seen GE Canada and GSW each with 50 percent of the voting shares, but by the end of 1988, GSW had reduced its position in Camco to 20 percent of the common shares. These holdings amounted to over 4 million shares and had a value on December 31, 1988, of $32,500,000, based on the market price quoted on the Toronto Stock Exchange. A summary of the financial performance of Camco, Inc., for 1987 and 1988 appears in Exhibit 2.

This case was prepared by Steven Cox under the direction of Professor Harold Crookell. Copyright © 1990, National Centre for Management Research and Development, The University of Western Ontario.

Exhibit 1 GSW, Inc., A Profile of the Five Operating Divisions

---

GSW Water Products Company
    Locations: Water heaters: Fergus and Stoney Creek, Ontario (391 employees)
                                  Pumps: Fergus and Bramalea, Ontario (118 employees)
    Products: Water heaters: Domestic water heaters (electric, gas, oil)
                                              Commercial/industrial water heaters
                                                Parts and accessories
                         Pumps: Potable water pumps
                                      Sewage and effluent pumps
                                      Sump and utility pumps
                                      Tanks and accessories related to pumps
    Customers: Water heaters: Plumbing wholesalers
                                              Utilities
                                              Retail distributors
                         Pumps: Plumbing wholesalers
                                      Specialty distributors
                                      Retail distributors

GSW Heating Products Company
    Locations: Hamilton and Nobel, Ontario (140 employees)
    Products: Venting equipment for gas, wood, and oil-fired products
                        Also *sell* wood and gas-burning fireplaces (do not manufacture these
                         products)
    Customers: Installing contractors
                        HVAC distributors
                        Hardware/home centre market

GSW Construction Products Company
    Location: London, Ontario (60 employees)
    Products: Lockers and washroom stall dividers
    Customers: Contractors
                        Institutions

GSW Thermoplastics Company
    Location: Barrie, Ontario (64 employees)
    Product: Vinyl eavestrough systems (Rainware)
    Customers: Retail chains:
                            Home centres
                            Hardware stores
                            Lumber yards

GSW Jackes-Evans
    Location: St. Louis, Missouri (130 employees)
    Products: Stove pipe
                        Stove pipe accessories
                        Fireplace and barbeque accessories
    Customers: Hardware wholesalers
                        Retail chains

Previous American Investment

GSW was no stranger to the U.S. market. Its Heating Products Company had
made an acquisition in 1984 of Jackes-Evans based in St. Louis, Missouri.

Exhibit 2 Camco Financial Highlights

Summary of Operations Year Ended December 31			Summary of Financial Position Year Ended December 31		
(in thousands of dollars)	*1988*	*1987*	*(in thousands of dollars)*	*1988*	*1987*
Sales of products and services	$558,771	$526,053	Cash	$ 20,245	$ 453
			Receivables	78,980	106,854
Operating costs:			Inventories	97,292	77,170
Cost of sales, selling, and administrative expenses before depreciation	508,416	478,016	Other current assets	6,424	5,902
			Total current assets	202,941	190,379
Depreciation	7,386	5,179	Bank borrowings	11,045	18,943
			Other current liabilities	95,065	96,741
Total operating costs	515,802	483,195	Total current liabilities	106,110	115,684
Income from operations	42,969	42,858	Working capital	96,831	74,695
Net interest expense	3,026	1,801	Net fixed and long-term assets	34,045	36,296
Sale of Orangeville property	(8,149)	—			
Plant closure costs—London	—	1,343		130,876	110,991
Income before income taxes	48,092	39,714	Other noncurrent liabilities	10,557	12,316
Income taxes	17,648	17,231		10,557	12,316
Net income for the year	$ 30,444	$ 22,483			
GSW equity interest included in consolidated statement of income	$ 6,091	$ 4,498	Net assets	$120,319	$ 98,675
			GSW interest therein	$ 24,074	$ 19,744

Although Thompson had not been involved in the St. Louis acquisition, he remembered some of its initial difficulties:

> We took the view we knew best—our people, our strategies—would best serve the customers. We tried to superimpose a Canadian culture. Now, St. Louis is run by an American who manages the American market. American companies have also made the same error in reverse when acquiring companies here in Canada.

In addition to initial staffing problems, the St. Louis acquisition had also experienced difficulties in implementing strategies in the marketplace. The Canadians in place didn't appreciate the degree to which American competitors protected their marketplace: "punches, gloves off and no compromise—Americans play hardball, particularly in their home markets."

Financial Performance

GSW's financial statements for the five years ending December 31, 1988, are summarized in Exhibit 3. In an effort to foster financial decentralization, GSW had moved its debt out to the five operating company units. Each company was

EXHIBIT 3

GSW, INC.
Consolidated Balance Sheet
December 31, 1988 ($000's)

	1984	1986	1988
Assets			
Current:			
Cash			4,107
Marketable securities		28,000	12,440
Accounts receivable	15,874	16,253	13,677
Inventories			
Finished goods	9,259	6,579	11,533
Raw materials and work in process	16,823	14,114	15,754
Prepaid expenses	1,038	814	294
Income tax recovery		614	
Total current assets:	42,994	66,374	57,805
Investment in Camco	19,281	16,846	24,074
Fixed:			
Land/building/equipment	22,978	23,677	28,339
Less accumulated depreciation	13,619	15,589	19,014
Total fixed assets	9,359	8,088	9,325
Pension surplus recognized			805
	$71,634	$91,308	$92,009
Liabilities and Shareholders' Equity			
Current:			
Bank indebtedness	1,499	2,273	
Accounts payable	23,098	25,044	25,640
Taxes payable	912	2,437	180
Total current liabilities	25,509	29,754	25,820
Long-term:			
Bank loan	8,000		
Deferred taxes	1,369		2,527
Warranties and other	2,048	2,190	2,165
Total long-term liabilities	10,048	3,559	4,692
Shareholders' equity:			
Share capital	2,298	2,298	2,271
Retained earnings	33,526	55,246	59,552
Foreign currency translation	253	451	−326
Total shareholders' equity	36,077	57,995	61,497
Total liabilities and shareholders' equity	$71,634	$91,308	$92,009

EXHIBIT 3 *(concluded)*

GSW, INC.
Consolidated Statement of Income/Notes to Financial Statements
December 31, 1988 ($000's)

	1984	1985	1986	1987	1988
Sales	$145,615	$142,494	$136,416	$142,040	$ 138,738
Operating costs:					
Cost of sales, selling, and administrative	140,699	136,475	128,496	130,567	129,427
Depreciation	1,872	1,964	1,819	1,789	1,884
Interest	1,978	1,984	1,722	1,176	1,340
Total operating costs	144,549	140,423	132,037	133,532	132,651
Income from manufacturing operations					
before income taxes	1,066	2,071	4,379	8,508	6,087
Income taxes	310	659	2,033	3,671	3,671
Income before the following:	756	1,412	2,346	4,837	3,537
Investment income			999	1,175	1,532
Share of net income in Camco, Inc.	4,794	6,298	4,640	4,498	6,091
Extraordinary items	−1,356	−4,264	12,988		
Discontinued opers.			52		
Net income for the year	$ 4,194	$ 3,446	$ 21,025	$ 10,510	$ 11,160
Retained earnings, beginning	33,556	33,526	35,708	55,246	63,089
Cost, shares cancelled	−2,829			−821	
Dividends	−1,395	−1,264	−1,487	−1,846	−14,697
Retained earnings, end	33,526	35,708	55,246	63,089	59,552
Earnings per common share:					
Before extraordinary	$1.36	$2.07	$2.16	$2.84	$3.04
After extraordinary	$1.02	$0.93	$5.66	$2.84	$3.04
Market value of Camco investment		54,400	48,000	30,000	32,500
(% of common shares)		(34)	(20)	(20)	(20)
Identifiable assets:					
Water products	26,867	28,227	29,349	31,458	30,727
Building products	19,894	19,194	16,057	17,995	20,471
Electronic products	5,082	2,640		discontinued	
Corporate assets	19,791	28,847	45,902	50,002	40,811
Capital expenditures:					
Water products	4,134	2,319	258	550	1,310
Building products	1,151	790	511	1,187	2,360
Sales:					
Water products	70,230	83,353	86,692	94,172	88,860
Building products	50,007	49,954	46,724	47,868	49,878
Electronic products	25,378	9,187		discontinued	
Canadian export sales	10,469	11,794	5,169	3,682	na
Research and development costs included	1,470	1,231	692	706	872
in operating costs					
Operating profit (loss)					
Water products	2,611	4,375	4,712	7,095	5,746
Building products	394	1,767	1,389	2,589	1,681
Electronic products	39	−2,087		discontinued	

expected to finance its own projects from internal resources based on its own capital budgeting processes.

GSW Water Products Company (WPC)

WPC was the largest operating division in the GSW group of companies and accounted for 64 percent of sales, 77 percent of operating profits, but only 60 percent of the assets attributable to the operating divisions. WPC itself had two operating divisions: the Water Heating Company and the Pump Company. The Water Heating Company accounted for roughly 70 percent of WPC sales, while the Pump Company accounted for the remaining 30 percent. However, the Pump Company earned a better overall return. Although the gross margins were similar at the 32 percent range, the Pump Company had lower marketing overheads and hence higher net profits.

Manufacturing Site

The WPC plant was located in Fergus, Ontario, a community of 7,000 located just north of Guelph and about a one-hour drive from Toronto. The company was a key employer in the community, with roughly 500 employees, and one of its corporate objectives was to protect employment in Fergus. The plant facility encompassed 590,000 square feet: 100,000 square feet of administrative offices, 400,000 square feet devoted to the Water Heating Company, and 90,000 square feet used by the Pump Company. The plant had historical roots in the community back to 1911 when it had been the Beatty Pump factory. Over its history, the facility had been used for manufacturing farm implements, appliances, and war munitions, although now it was devoted to water heater and pump manufacturing. The plant's capital cost had been fully paid off. Pump manufacturing did not require a lot of space and hence output was not really constrained by plant size. However, water heaters were constrained by a capacity limit of 500,000 units a year, although with modest investment this capacity could be expanded to accommodate production of 800,000 units.

The GSW plant in Fergus was unionized, and management-labour relations were relatively harmonious. In fact, a former member of the Canadian branch of the Union's international office was on the Water Products Company Board.

Water Heating Company

Production Overview

The manufacturing of a water heater involved the bending, welding, and steel preparation of a cylinder used to heat and store water. The basic equipment used in this metal fabricating process was welding machines (only two suppliers) and furnaces (two suppliers). All water heater products were subject to specifications laid out by the Canadian Standards Association or their numerous provincial and state counterparts.

The technology had undergone major changes in the 1970s when furnaces were upgraded to provide greater energy efficiency and the welding techniques had also advanced. However, in the 1980s, the technology had not changed much. Thompson described the technology used in the manufacture of water heaters as being very narrow, with all nine North American manufacturers using the same basic approach.

Suppliers

The largest cost component in the manufacture of water heaters is steel. Materials and components were supplied by industries with a few concentrated players dominating the field: for example, rolled steel (Dofasco), packaging (Domtar, CPI, and MB), and insulation (Fiberglass). The thermostat control devices were provided by American suppliers.

Key Canadian Customers

As seen in Exhibit 1, there were three major customer groups that the Water Heating Company sold to in Canada:

- Plumbing wholesalers (approximately 50 percent of sales).
- Electric and gas utilities in Ontario[1] only (20 percent of sales).
- Retail distributors such as Home Hardware, Canadian Tire, McLeods (30 percent of sales).

Plumbing wholesalers in Canada were a powerful group, with the five major ones controlling 90 percent of the market. The largest wholesaler, Westburne, was the largest wholesaler in North America.

The company had found that water heater sales were not as cyclical as some other industries that served the housing market—75 percent of its sales were replacement water heaters, and only 25 percent were dependent on new home construction. Water heaters had an average life span of 13 years.

Implications of the FTA

In 1984, GSW began to think about the Water Heating Company in a North American context. The Tokyo Round of GATT negotiations resulted in a 40 percent decrease in the overall level of tariffs between 1983 and 1988. In the

---

[1]The Ontario market was unique in North America for the ownership of water heaters by the major utility companies, who in turn rented them to householders. This concept had never been promoted in Western Canada or Quebec, and was not common practice in the United States due to concern about the monopoly of utilities.

early 1970s, Canadian tariffs on imported water heaters ranged between 17.5 percent and 22.5 percent, but these tariffs had been gradually declining and were expected to continue to decline under the GATT process. However, the reductions were accelerated under the FTA with respect to the United States, and were set to be reduced from an average of 11 percent to zero over a 10-year period. The comparable tariff on Canadian water heater exports to the United States was 4 percent, and this tariff was to be reduced over the same period. In Thompson's view, the die had been cast earlier with the GATT negotiations, and the FTA merely speeded up the process.

A North American Strategy Begins

Thompson had recognized the coming continentalization of the industry and knew that greater aggregate volumes (or "critical mass") were needed by the Water Heating Company to ensure long-term success in the North American marketplace. In 1984, the Canadian market for water heaters was divided roughly as follows:

Company	Approximate Market Share (%)
John Wood	35
GSW Water Products Company	25
Rheem Canada Ltd.*	20
Giant	20

*Rheem Canada Ltd. was a division of Rheem USA, the number-two American water heater company in terms of sales and third or fourth in the United States in terms of unit volume.

At this time, the Water Heating Company more than doubled in size when it acquired the number-one Canadian competitor in the water heater market, John Wood Manufacturing Ltd.

John Wood was a long-time Canadian manufacturer that had been experiencing operational difficulties, and the management of WPC had for several years been continually enquiring about strategic opportunities with them. In 1984, the owners of John Wood finally agreed to sell, and WPC acquired 100 percent control. WPC acquired the employees (all 220 were offered positions in Fergus, but only 25 accepted), the equipment, machines, and tools (which were all stripped from the plant and moved to Fergus), and use of the John Wood product name. The land and buildings were sold separately by the sellers.

The fit was excellent as John Wood and the Water Heating Company served identical markets. The acquisition gave WPC a large increase in overall unit volume and expanded its production capacity from 200,000 units/year to 500,000. Another "hidden value" in John Wood was that the company had been a manufacturer of water heaters in the United States until the 1960s, and there was still some residual brand awareness of the John Wood name in the United

States. Additionally, some buyers still held favourable perceptions of John Wood water heaters with respect to the quality and longevity of the product.

By 1988, the approximate Canadian market shares in the water heater market were as follows:

Company	Approximate Market Share (%)
GSW Water Products Company	44
Rheem Canada Ltd.	22
Giant	22
State Industries (U.S. import)	8
Bradford-White (U.S. import)	3
A.O. Smith (U.S. import)	1

The American Market

The American water heater market was a mature one with annual growth in the 4 to 5 percent range. In contrast to Canada, the American market was split into two almost equal segments with 55 percent sold to roughly 5,000 wholesalers and 45 percent sold to an equally numerous group of retailers. GSW's research had shown that the American market was dominated by agents.

The top managers of the Water Heating Company knew the key players in the American market fairly well and had always made an effort to compare their costs to those of their major American competitors. They knew the approximate size of their major competitors, and had a sense of the competitive threats posed by each one. Most of the American competitors in the water heater market were located in the low-wage south or in the Maquiladora (Mexico) trading area.

The American market was in 1989 served by five manufacturers that accounted for almost 100 percent of the market:

Rank	American Competitor	Ownership	Number of Plants	Estimated Annual Unit Capacity	Approximate Market Share (%)
1	State Industries	Private	1	2,000,000	25
2	Rheem USA*	Public	4	2,000,000	25
3	Mor-Flow	Public	2	1,500,000	20
4	A.O. Smith	Public	2	1,500,000	20
5	Bradford-White	Private/ Australian	1	800,000	10

*Rheem, which is Japanese owned, had a Canadian division that operated out of Hamilton, Ontario.

There was no possibility of the American competitors obtaining further American market share through merger or acquisition as a recent test acquisition case had been turned down by the antitrust department in Washington. For this reason, over the 1984 to 1988 period, three American companies had begun to focus on the Canadian market for increased sales opportunities and had started exporting water heaters to Canada. These three exporters had captured an overall 12 percent share of the Canadian market. Most of the American export market was concentrated in Western Canada, where the American companies had a comparative freight advantage over GSW, which faced the higher cost of Canadian intermodal trailer/rail transport. In Thompson's view, the American competition was becoming increasingly aggressive in Canada, in part encouraged by certain Canadian wholesalers who wanted more competitive choices. In addition, State Industries had some new technology which represented a potential major threat to GSW.   GSW also had an opportunity in the United States in water heaters because of the particular insulation materials used. In the United States, most water heaters were manufactured with foam insulation and there was concern about CFC emission problems from this type of insulation. GSW used only fibreglass insulation, and this would be seen as an advantage from an environmental viewpoint.

Cost Competitiveness

The John Wood acquisition gave the Water Heating Company unit volume, but management knew that their cost structure was not competitive with other U.S. manufacturers south of the border. Thompson decided to undertake a two-year study of the Water Heating Company, its manufacturing process, its suppliers, and markets. This study was completed in 1988.

The study concluded that the Water Heating Company would have to make significant investments in order to become cost competitive. The optimal "critical mass" to be cost competitive was an annual production volume of 750,000 to 800,000 water heaters. While the Fergus physical plant structure could be adjusted to accommodate the volumes of this scale, it was unlikely that WPC would ever get a high enough market share in Canada to sell this kind of volume domestically. It was clear to Thompson that achieving "critical mass" would involve some sort of American market participation.

As part of their study, executives of the Water Heating Company had initiated plant exchange visits and information-gathering meetings with each of their American competitors. They pulled together facts on the American market and the relevant freight costs. The study included an examination of the design and manufacturing processes used in the United States in order to determine where efficiency improvements could be made. The division executives also spent time with the equipment suppliers investigating improvement opportunities.

The study pointed out that if "critical mass" volumes could be achieved, Canadian water heaters would be competitive with U.S. output as long as they were sold within a radius of 500 to 600 miles from Fergus. Within this area, which could be represented by drawing an arc through the U.S. northeast and midwest from Boston to Philadelphia to Washington, D.C., to Chicago, the $3 an hour wage differential would be roughly offset by the freight saving of roughly $1 per 100 miles. In other words, while Canadian wage rates were higher than rates in the southern states, Ontario's proximity to the U.S. Northeast made Fergus a viable production location.

The study concluded that at present volumes, the cost differential between American water heaters and WPC's was approximately $24 a unit. One proposal for eliminating this gap was to seek equal $8/unit cost reductions from three areas: (1) improved product design and engineering, (2) improved purchasing (volume discounts), and (3) increasing labour productivity (by reducing waste/scrap, warranty claims, and by automating certain job functions).

Heating up the United States: Entry Options

One entry option that the Water Heating Company was considering involved locating a "greenfield" operation in the lower-wage South. The study had found a comparative cost disadvantage in wage levels between Ontario (C$12–16/hour) and locations such as Tennessee (US$8–12/hour) and Mexico (US$1–1.50/hour). The company had not yet determined whether sufficient numbers of skilled trades in the areas of electronics, tool and die, and repairs were available in the United States at a competitive cost.

Another option under consideration was acquiring one of the big five U.S. competitors. The company had received a favourable opinion on the legality of pursuing this: "GSW going from a 5 percent continental share to a 20 percent share is not the same as one of our American counterparts going from a 25 percent share to a 45 percent share." As part of the information-gathering process, Thompson and his management team had a fairly close examination of each of the five companies. Several of the competitors had strong technical fits with GSW, but GSW had not proceeded beyond tentative discussions around acquisition or joint venture strategies. Thompson knew an acquisition would be expensive but was unable to quantify the amount at this point.

The third option under examination was pursuing an export strategy to obtain the volumes required to fill the plant. The only American competitor that was located in the northeast was Bradford White, which was located in Michigan. However, Thompson knew that the American market had different standards given the different needs[2] of American consumers. That would mean that the company would have to develop, design, and obtain state-by-state certification on a brand new product since there were differences in volumes (litres versus gallons), tolerances, and electrical and gas requirements. Thompson estimated that investment capital of roughly C$10 million over five years would be required to redesign and retool to American specifications, and another C$5 million needed to increase the plant capacity from 500,000 to 800,000 water heaters.

---

[2]American homeowners preferred tall, skinny water heaters that could be tucked into a kitchen closet as opposed to Canadians, who preferred a more squat model for their basement.

On top of this, a further $700,000 over three years would be needed as part of an operating plan to break into the U.S. market (for personnel, promotion, literature, and trade shows).

Pump Company

GSW's entry into the pump business started with the acquisition of Beatty Pumps in the 1960s, a company that in turn had been founded in 1874.

The Production Process

The manufacturing process basically entailed machining metal components, moulding plastic components, assembling pumps and electric motors, and installing manual or automated control components. The basic structuring of a pump was based on an age-old design technology that had been improved upon in recent years with the advent of more efficient motors and materials (engineered polymers replacing cast iron). In this area, the Pump Company was a world leader, having developed a customized application in 1984 using engineered polymers in the manufacture of pumps, an application over which it held world-wide exclusive rights in association with a large multinational plastics firm. In 1988, WPC used engineered polymers in 15 percent of its pump components, with the remainder using grey iron. Thompson knew that GSW's use of engineered polymers was exclusive and estimated that competitors used grey iron in 80 percent of their components with the remaining 20 percent being made of less durable plastics/PVCs.

Suppliers

Raw materials comprised 60 percent of the final cost of a typical pump. There were many different types of pumps, and the type of pump dictated the choice of materials. The primary material suppliers were mostly American multinationals: motors (General Electric and Franklin), switches (Square D), cast iron (foundries), and polymers.[3]

The GSW–engineered polymer technology produced materials with physical characteristics which are similar to metals and capable of withstanding temperatures up to the 200 to 400 degree Fahrenheit range. The fixed cost investment for engineered polymers (injection moulds that produced a high-precision finished product) cost $10 for every $1 of fixed investment required for grey iron machining equipment (for boring, milling, and tapping). However, the engi-

---

[3]GSW had pursued polymers as a defensive strategy against American incursion into Canada in this area (which never materialized). As the research and development progressed in conjunction with a global plastics multinational, GSW became increasingly intrigued with its opportunities for application and continued to finance further research.

neered polymer was less expensive on an all-in basis since the grey iron components required costly machine labour dependent on volume before assembly could be undertaken, whereas the polymer was ready for assembly after moulding. Dependent upon volumes, the polymer pump had the potential of being cheaper on a per unit basis.

The Pump Company had started integrating polymers into its product line in late 1985, with the eventual goal to replicate the entire line of pumps in polymer form. However, mindful of strong consumer resistance to change, the company planned to operate dual production runs of cast iron *and* polymer lines for the foreseeable future: "Our philosophy is to give the marketplace the choice, not choose for the marketplace." WPC had decided to avoid underpricing as a strategy to launch its new engineered polymer line of pumps, except in a few cases where dealer incentives were offered. The rationale for this strategy was that "if you price low, you stay low, and will never get an increase past dealers above the inflation rate." Polymer-derived pumps were priced at least equal to, or higher than, grey iron pumps and were sold to distributors and customers as a "high-tech" value product (noncorroding material and superior finishes).

For both of its companies, WPC was loyal and committed to its suppliers and expected the same in return. Thompson and his executives made regular forays to meet with each of their suppliers at their world head offices (not necessarily the Canadian subsidiary office) to keep abreast of their developments in engineering, quality, and management. They graded their suppliers under a simple system that was designed to ferret out suppliers who had structural, long-term weaknesses. This process had produced some relationships in which 100 percent of the supply was accounted for by one company (in the case of General Electric).

The Canadian Market and Competition

The Canadian pump market totaled an estimated C$100 million in 1988. Pumps had greater brand awareness than water heaters, but it was relatively minor. Typically, consumers relied heavily on their plumber's advice when it came to purchase decisions in this area. More important was a brand reputation with major plumbers/contractors and distributors, and in these buyers' minds, the Beatty Pump trade name and tradition held great weight. In rural communities, the Beatty name was synonymous with over a century of usage on most farms in Canada.

There were several major competitors selling pumps in Canada, all selling a myriad of varieties of pumps—everything from a cottage-variety shallow well handpump to a metropolis-scale sewage processing model. The five largest Canadian competitors were all foreign-owned: Sta-rite Industries (United States), Gould Pump (the largest in the United States), F.E. Myers Corporation (United States), Marly (Red Jacket) Corporation (United States), and Grundfos (a Danish global pump company with stainless steel technology). Of the above group, only Myers did any Canadian manufacturing. The GSW Pump Company held a dominant Canadian market share of 30 percent, while the remaining big five held 50 percent of the market, in shares ranging from 13 percent to 7 percent.

FTA Tariff Reduction

Under FTA, the cross-border tariffs on Canadian pumps into the U.S. market were to be reduced from an average of 7 percent to 0 percent over a five-year period, while U.S. to Canada pumps would be reduced from 9 percent to 0 percent over the same period.

The U.S. Market

Thompson and his management team utilized the same information-gathering approach as used for the Water Heating Company, arranging plant look-sees and talking to major players in the industry. They hired a consultant to put together an overview of U.S. competitors and found that most of the American competitors were relatively small (compared to WPC), private family-owned businesses operating on a "cash cow" approach to the market. In the areas of engineering and marketing, they had fallen behind GSW because they were not investing in market development or research.

The American market for pumps tended to be regional in terms of product preferences and brand allegiances. In the United States, there were over 40 major competitors scattered across the country, and the smaller players were too numerous to estimate. The U.S. pump industry was dominated by the same top five players as Canada (except for WPC), and their pumps accounted for roughly 50 percent of the American market as well. Each of the top five focused on a different distribution channel—for instance, Gould opted for an exclusive specialty distributor network (granted by zone) and promoted high brand awareness through various product identification strategies (i.e., hats, banners, logos offered to dealers, plumbers, and consumers). The other competitors focused on other exclusive retail or exclusive wholesale channel strategies.

WPC management had found that, in the United States, pump manufacturers competed primarily on price; all pricing changes initiated by manufacturers were started at the dealer level and eventually were pushed down to the consumer.

All the manufacturers claimed to have good quality, and few American dealers or consumers had an awareness of the differences between engineered polymers (strong, last longer, better for environment), plastics/PVCs (cheap and unreliable), and grey iron (tendency to rust and retain pollutants). The only other competitor that offered a unique technology was Grundfos, which had perfected an effective stainless steel pump technology. WPC management realized that the process of enhancing consumer awareness could be an expensive proposition.

Priming the Pump: Entry Choices

In early 1989, the Pump Company was not selling any pumps into the United States. Thompson was considering the same set of options (greenfield, acquisition, or export) for GSW's pump foray into the United States. He was excited about the unique, revolutionary technology his company possessed and wanted to set the American market afire with it.

Decision at Hand

Roly Thompson was also thinking about the possibility of overlapping the U.S. entry strategies for water heaters and pumps because this issue had been considered before in Canada. Pumps and water heaters were usually found in the same warehouses. However, when this had been examined more closely in Canada, it was found that the contractors for each product were fairly unique—pumps were typically installed in the house first, and water heaters were usually installed near the end of the home's completion. As a result, both products were usually installed by different tradespeople.

But Thompson also knew that the American market could be different from the Canadian. Thompson expected that the FTA would lead to real price declines as competitors compressed their prices in response to the reduced duties. He speculated further that some American competitors might even engage in "power marketing" and drop their price 2 percent for every 1 percent drop in duty in an effort to grab market share. His experience told him that most competitors erred in pricing on the downside rather than the high side. In the last increase of the federal manufacturing sales tax to 13.5 percent, Thompson estimated that the industry as a whole had only recaptured 75 percent of this increase.

Thompson knew he would soon have to "put the rubber to the road" and make a decision on how to approach the U.S. market in the context of the new FTA environment—"the FTA is going to be tough, but do-able." He elaborated:

> In many ways, we find ourselves "at the crossroads" faced with critical choices about the future operation of our business. Forces such as the Free Trade Agreement with the United States, continuing tariff reductions under the GATT, and the fluctuating value of the Canadian dollar have placed us in the position of having to react now in order to secure our future. The decisions we make and the manner in which we implement those decisions will determine whether or not GSW Water Products Company will continue to be a strong and viable business in the years to come.

CASE 15
THE HERITAGE GROUP, INC. (CONDENSED)

In October 1985, Henry Beben (pronounced "Beeben"), president and chief operating officer of The Heritage Group, Inc., was preparing for a meeting with Fred Schneider, chairman of the board and CEO. The Heritage Group, one of Canada's largest food processing corporations, had plunged from record earnings in the second half of fiscal 1984 to a first-ever overall loss for fiscal 1985. In his annual address to shareholders in April 1985, Beben assessed the situation as follows:

> This is bitterly disappointing and exasperating. I feel like the little Dutch boy who put his finger in the dike. We solve one problem and another one appears. . . . Five years ago I thought the process [of making a successful transition to a national food products company] would have been finished by now. Now, I'm loathe to predict how long it could take.

Despite his remarks at the annual meeting, Beben recognized he needed to develop a plan for turning things around at Heritage. In the upcoming meeting with Fred Schneider, he planned to present such a plan.

Company Background

In the spring of 1890, John Metz Schneider of Kitchener, Ontario, made sausage in his basement and sold it door to door. After two years, J.M., as he was commonly known, quit his factory job and with $200 in savings went into business for himself.

The initial business was a family operation. Pork sausage was made according to a family homemade recipe. J.M.'s early insistence on quality resulted in steady demand for his sausage products, and his philosophy about quality became a company creed: "Don't use it if you would not eat it yourself or serve it to your family."

Following a strategy emphasizing quality products, the Schneider business enjoyed steady growth and expansion for the next five decades. The company's product lines were broadened during the 1930s to include beef cattle, poultry, eggs, butter, and cheese. In the 1940s, as part of an on-going philosophy of practicality and frugality, production space was built and used as office space until needed for production. J.M. Schneider died in 1942 at the age of 83.

In the 1950s, the company located its creamery and cheese production in Wellesley, Ontario, just outside Kitchener, and numerous building and renova-

---

This case was prepared by Professor Mark C. Baetz with the assistance of Ms. Louise Carroll as a basis for class discussion rather than to illustrate either effective or ineffective handling of an administrative situation.

tion projects continued at the main operation. The 1960s were big expansion years: payroll, customer orders, and internal data reporting needs were handled by computer and data processing equipment: the product line now covered upward of 350 different products; a half-million-dollar primary sewage treatment plant was completed; and expansion of the largely regional market area was encouraged by forays into Quebec and the Maritimes.

In 1965, the company went public and offered shares of stock to prospective buyers outside of the company's employees. In April 1969, Schneider common and preferred shares were listed on the Toronto Stock Exchange for the first time. A stock purchase plan was also set up at the same time for employees.

Members of the Schneider family maintained a controlling number of company voting shares with 70 percent of the common voting shares and 27 percent of nonvoting shares. Of the 70 percent voting shares, 53.7 percent were held by three of the Schneiders (Fred, 21 percent; Herb, 16.5 percent; and Howard, 16.2 percent). Nonvoting shares represented 85 percent of the publicly raised cash invested in the company. Most of these shares were widely held by financial institutions and small investors.

As of 1985, three members of the third generation of the Schneider family held senior management positions: Fred Schneider, chairman of the board and CEO of the Heritage Group, Inc.; Herb Schneider, vice-president, personnel and public relations; and Howard Schneider, vice-president and director of research and development. All three were members of the board of directors.

Relations with the Employees and the Community

A section of "J.M. Schneider, Inc.—A Company History" written in 1985 described the company's relations with its employees:

> The company has always prided itself in treating the employees as members of a large family. . .
>
> In 1944, the Schneider Employees Association was certified by the Ontario Government. The company and the union continue to experience amicable relations. . . . A form of profit sharing was introduced in 1917 for all employees, but [because corporate profits became an increasingly smaller percentage of the total wages paid] the plan was discontinued in 1975.
>
> As far as basic business philosophy is concerned, there is little reason to tamper with an approach which has led to development of an organization that has won: the respect and loyalty of its employees; a high regard for its integrity and efficiency in service among those who do business with it, and a "Famous for Quality" reputation for the products which it offers to its customers.

One top manager who had been with the company for many years described the corporate culture:

> All through the evolution of the company, there has been a family orientation. Not only has the Schneider family played a vital role, but many non-Schneider families with two, three, and four generations of service are employees. A preference has

been given to hire individuals related to existing employees. In many ways it is a "corporation of families." If an employee becomes a problem, family members will go after him! It is really a paternalistic culture.

The Meat Packing and Processing Industry

The meat packing and processing industry transformed livestock, mainly cattle and hogs, into such customer products as sausage and other variety meats. Competition in the meat packing industry was intense. Meat packing was a very low-margin, high-volume business where cost controls were critical. The difference between profit and loss was very small. The squeeze on profitability in the meat packing industry was a result of the following:

1. Retail margins were in the 1 to 2 percent range. Unprocessed meat was considered a commodity and, as a result, the meat packer had little influence on price. However, brand loyalty could be created among consumers of processed meats and, therefore, a degree of control could be regained by manufacturers of processed meat products. Nevertheless, major meat packers such as Heritage were also faced with increasingly powerful customers; beginning in the 1970s, the food chains began acquiring the independent stores, and the independent stores formed buying groups, so that by the 1980s, there were only two to four major buyers of processed meat in any particular region in Canada.

2. Raw materials represented 65 to 80 percent of cost of sales. The sale price for hogs (Schneider's most important raw material) was determined on the basis of grade. Beef cattle sales prices were determined on a live weight basis, a process which introduced some uncertainty for the packer: overestimating the quality or yield of the carcass resulted in reduced profits. Generally the supply and price for raw materials such as hogs and beef cattle was very volatile.

3. Wages paid out to labour represented the second largest cost item at 10 to 20 percent of sales. In the early 1980s, Canadian rates were about $3 per hour above the falling U.S. rate; this represented a differential of almost $5 when fringe benefits were considered. Although the U.S. had imposed countervail duties of 4–5 cents per pound for live hogs to offset Canadian support programs, the border between the United States and Canada was relatively open for the movement of livestock and meat. This made it important that wage rates remained comparable between the two countries after taking into account the exchange rate.

In the 1980s, a nationwide rationalization was taking place in the industry. Despite a rash of plant closings, it was reported in 1984 that the industry still had twice the capacity it needed. Furthermore, even when major packers such as Canada Packers and Burns suffered from labour disruptions, there was little impact on overall industry production because independent packers were able to expand production and fill the demand, sometimes using nonunion labour.

Another concern to meat packers was the existence of marketing boards. Prices were up to 80 percent higher for commodities in Canada controlled by marketing boards which controlled both production and price. Commodities controlled by such boards included eggs, chicken, turkey, and milk. However, products such as pork were controlled by marketing boards without supply management or price controls, and prices for pork products were in some cases lower in Canada than in the United States.

J.M. Schneider, Inc.—National Expansion

In the 1950s, Schneider Corporation made its first attempt at geographic expansion by purchasing a Winnipeg meat packing plant. After the acquisition turned out to be a disaster, the plant was sold. The experience "bloodied our nose," according to Fred Schneider and "made later expansion much more difficult." Nevertheless, primarily through geographic expansion of the product line through the 1970s, J.M. Schneider became a national, rather than solely a regional, meat processor. Supporting the national expansion were a number of acquisitions, some of which were unsuccessful. For example, the company suffered losses approaching $1 million on acquisitions involving dry groceries, frozen food, canned meats, and dry sausage. Because of the losses, these operations were closed in 1975.

During the 1970s, the development of an efficient distribution system consisting of warehouses in Winnipeg and Vancouver, a combination of both company and common carriers, and a number of supplier plants, contributed to the company's progress. However, toward the mid-70s, Schneider slowed its rapid expansion and focused on developing new products and on improving its market position. By stressing sales to the food service market (i.e., hospitals, restaurants, and institutions), Schneider was quick to respond to market trends which indicated that this market was the fastest growing segment in the industry.

During the 1970s, J.M. Schneider, Inc. achieved record sales and profits. Between 1970 and 1979, the company increased its sales from $79.3 million to $374.4 million, an average annual increase of 19.0 percent. Over the same time frame, net earnings increased from $1.4 million to $7.5 million, representing an average increase in profits of 20.6 percent per annum. Despite growing sales and profits, the company suffered at times from declining returns on investment. For example, in 1978, return on capital employed dropped to 16.75 percent from 20.54 percent. The average return over the previous 10 years (1969–78) was 20.73 percent. In order to halt the falling rates of return, capital expenditures on a Vancouver distribution centre were postponed, cost-cutting measures were taken, and part of the outstanding Class B preferred shares were bought back. This quick action, combined with improvements to internal management systems (e.g., upgrade of cost accounting systems, new customer service, and raw material control systems) enabled an increase in the return on capital employed to 23.49 percent in fiscal 1979. Overall, Schneider had been regarded as Canada's most profitable meat processor since 1971. Furthermore, it achieved this status with an extremely conservative debt-equity ratio of 0.24 : 1.

Schneider's performance in the 1970s was all the more significant when considered in the context of the overall industry. The raw materials situation was characterized by frequent shortages and high prices. Changes in consumer economics and preferences meant a decrease in meat consumption, a trend which showed no signs of reversing. In addition, the general economy was poor, resulting in record inflation rates and restrictive government measures (e.g., the Anti-Inflation Board). Despite all this, Schneider grew rapidly in terms of volume of products sold, number of specific product lines offered, capital expansion, and staff size. Not only did it perform well but it resisted the temptation to lower its quality or to cut its prices; the company explicitly recognized that consumers wanted food products of consistently high quality. In 1981, Beben described part of the strategy of the company and results:

> Others in the business thought Schneider was making a mistake by centralizing its meat processing in Kitchener by building a world-scale plant and delivering its production nationally. But the company has found that despite rising energy prices, the economies of scale made possible at the plant more than offset transportation costs and there is nothing on the horizon that suggests this will not continue to be the case. The energy costs of operating a packaging plant are high too.
>
> From being a regional food processor operating basically in the Ontario market 10 years ago, the company has become a major force on the national scene.

Fred Schneider described in 1981 other aspects of Schneider's strategy during the 1970s to which could be attributed the company's success:

> We improved our ability as a marketing company. In particular we improved our selling to the chain stores. . . . At the supermarket, and chain buying level, in addition to a name for quality, you also need the reputation of being able to work with these people successfully, to help them in turn market successfully. You work with them on the kind of deals they require to build volume; you do the kind of things they need done to make sure that the product is rotated properly on the shelves and that it looks good.
>
> [In terms of product mix] we have never put a strong emphasis on the fresh product side of our sales. Unlike traditional packers, we try to cut and slaughter to the market requirements, buying extra cuts when we need them. So we have tended to look on the more perishable side of our product line in a more limited way and have kept that fairly regional.
>
> As we've striven to become national in scope, we have made great strides in increasing the shelf-life of most of our products through better sanitation and better processes in general. . . . This has been, as much as anything, responsible for our ability to market on a national basis from one centralized plant.
>
> In terms of new product introduction, our record of success has been fairly good. (Each year new products account for about 4 percent of the company's business.) Ten or 15 years ago we went to the product management system of marketing,

borrowing from the Procter & Gamble approach. We've applied that system as well as we can in meat packing.

We've always had a very strong new product development department. Currently [1981] it involves 12 or more people, which is probably higher than other companies of comparable size. They work solely with the marketing people, the product managers, through committees on new products.

We make effective use of a consumer panel to make sure we don't make many blunders. However, it's something that you have to continually work at. It's very easy for a meat packer to forget he's in the business of satisfying consumer needs.

Despite the success of the national expansion, the company was concerned that its reliance on the meat segment of the food dollar made it vulnerable. By the close of the decade, J.M. Schneider, Inc., considered itself a food-oriented company and not merely a meat processing organization. With this shift in thinking came the realization that continued growth would require diversification into areas with more dynamic growth than the conventional meat lines. With future growth opportunities in mind in 1979, the chairman of the board, Fred P. Schneider, announced the formation of a new corporate planning group. The group was headed by Beben, senior vice president, corporate development, and its function was to "plan and guide the company into a more balanced product and market grouping and to seek out opportunities for diversification and expansion into food areas other than meat."

The Heritage Group, Inc.—Diversification

Amid great controversy and debate, in 1980, J.M. Schneider, Inc., changed its name to The Heritage Group, Inc. The retired, elder family members felt the Schneider name should stay at the top because the name had become synonymous with quality over the decades. However, 95 percent of the shareholders voted in favour of authorizing the name change and moving the Heritage Group head office to leased space in Waterloo, a few miles away from the Schneider meat division in Kitchener. One manager noted: "It was hoped that physically separating the head office from the meat division would facilitate diversification."

The Heritage Group, Inc., was to act as an "umbrella" corporation under which a group of related, but independent, companies would operate. It would oversee and coordinate the activities of the affiliated companies. The rationale behind the name change included the desire to separate the Schneider name, which was almost exclusively linked to quality meat products, from future forays into other food products. As Beben noted: "We've been promoting J.M. as a master butcher for years. We'd be bending the truth in saying he's a master baker. . . . [Furthermore] consumer research concluded people would resent seeing the image of J.M. Schneider extended to products unrelated to his original butcher shop." It was felt therefore that the name change provided the corporation with the means to grow through product diversification and acquisition. The name change was also regarded as a move to protect one of the company's most valuable assets—the Schneider name—in the event of poor market reception of new product lines. Meat operations were to continue under the subsidiary company name of J.M. Schneider, Inc.

Beben, the major force behind the company's diversification thrust, described the corporate strategy for the 80s as an effort to become Canada's number-one food processor. This goal was expected to be accomplished in two ways: (1) by diversifying to reduce the Heritage Group's dependence on meat and (2) by developing minority interests in suppliers and in areas where the Heritage Group currently lacked expertise. In short, Heritage was looking for opportunities in which the corporation's strengths could be applied to new markets.

Fred Schneider described the rationale and possibilities for diversification:

> We felt we had more or less reached the end of the road for expansion in our traditional processed meat lines. We are either number one or number two in wieners, bologna, and other products right across the country. Once you get to that point it's difficult and very expensive to achieve higher penetrations.
>
> So to continue with the rapid growth we have had, it seemed we would have to branch out and it was logical to do that in areas of food where we have a double advantage. We have marketing experience in working with chain stores and in the food service market as well, so we can use that knowledge and expertise to good effect. In addition, we can use the facilities and knowledge we have in distributing frozen and refrigerated products on a national basis. We have spent a good deal of money and taken a lot of trouble to develop the system which we have in place to do just that.
>
> Using those two advantages, we felt we should get into other areas of food where there was room to grow and where we could use that same frozen distribution system.

Heritage moved quickly in its bid to diversify. In 1980, the corporation held two wholly owned subsidiary companies: J.M. Schneider, Inc., the meat subsidiary, and National Consolidated Food Brands, Inc. (Natco), the newly formed grocery division. By 1981, it had acquired F.G. Bradley, Inc., a major manufacturer and marketer of processed meat products in the food service business. Link Services, Inc., was also established that year; it was responsible for providing transportation and distribution services to all Heritage companies. Finally, in 1984, Heritage established Portage Trade Development to expand the corporation's export trade opportunities.

Each of the five subsidiary companies operated as independent tax-paying corporate entities with a president and slate of officers. Each subsidiary company had its own support services such as computer systems and accounting. The Heritage Group, Inc., was to provide corporate functions along the lines of setting strategic objectives, helping to plan and coordinate the operating objectives of the subsidiary companies, developing business outside the existing businesses, monitoring performance, and obtaining and allocating investment dollars. Heritage was also to provide a personnel function. Each of the subsidiary companies will now be described in greater detail.

J.M. Schneider, Inc.

This company's mandate remained unchanged, that is, Schneider was left to pursue its leadership position in the meat industry. However, the emphasis in the 1980s was threefold: (1) new products which met changing consumer lifestyles and preferences (e.g., the introduction of lite products in 1981), (2) improvements in quality assurance practices (e.g., a shelf-life goal on all products of at least 60 days), and (3) improvements in the company's capacity to deliver products quickly. (This emphasis on distribution ultimately led to the establishment of a distribution subsidiary company, Link Services.)

To minimize the effects of anticipated increased costs in raw materials, supply, and labour, a number of measures were implemented including cost-cutting programs, improved production techniques, increased market penetration, expanded market areas, and the maintenance of a national pricing system. In fact, as the decade unfolded, it became increasingly apparent that the challenge of becoming more competitive in the 80s was to control costs; by 1982, Schneider recognized that efficiency and cost effectiveness were vital and increased efforts to control costs and penetrate markets.

Schneider's volume and profit objectives went unmet after an initial 11 percent increase in sales in 1980. Although prices were raised, prohibitive raw material and labour costs were increasingly responsible for the company's inability to increase its margins. Nevertheless, the increase in profits at J.M. Schneider, Inc., was the primary factor in the doubling of earnings at Heritage from 1982 to 1983, and while other Heritage subsidiaries were losing money, J.M. Schneider remained profitable. According to one top manager, "Reinvesting the profits of J.M. Schneider into other divisions of the company which were losing money had a demoralizing impact on the Schneider employee group."

In terms of facility locations, by 1985, J.M. Schneider, Inc., had a manufacturing plant and distribution centre in Vancouver, a distribution centre in Calgary, two plants and a distribution centre in Winnipeg, the main plant and distribution centre in Kitchener, and a poultry operation in Ayr, Ontario.

In terms of organizational structure, J.M. Schneider had basically a functional organization with vice presidents of human resources, R&D, manufacturing, sales and marketing, plus a controller. In 1983, an executive vice president position was added to groom a new president when long-time president Ken Murray announced his intention to retire.

National Consolidated Food Brands, Inc. (Natco).   Natco began operations in April 1980. Its mandate was to "apply existing corporate strengths to the development of grocery, dairy, and frozen food products." It would draw on the Schneider expertise in such areas as data processing, cost control systems, finance, and distribution of refrigerated products. Natco intended to accomplish its mandate with the development of new and existing products and the acquisition of companies producing complementary products. According to Beben, the decision was made to buy an interest in supplier companies where possible because "if we were to duplicate these facilities, it would take longer and a lot of money." Following this strategy, interests of up to 100 percent were acquired in the following companies: Winchester Cheese (processed cheese), Millbank Cheese and Butter Co. (specialty and cheddar cheese), Dorset Foods (frozen sausage rolls and quiche), and Mother Jackson's Open Kitchens (fruit and meat pies).

Natco's marketing strategy consisted of a quick response to market trends and the innovative development of new products. When Natco was first established, it inherited the Schneider cheese line. Because cheese was considered a "dairy" rather than "meat" item, it was purchased and handled by departments different from meat within retail grocery operations. Therefore, Schneider's cheese products did not always get the marketing attention they deserved. Natco planned to make cheese one of its marketing priorities.

Natco's initial product lines included cheese, shortening, lard, margarine, and Grandma Martin's frozen pastries (tarts, pie shells, quiche). Seven sales reps were employed to secure product listings from the grocery and dairy buyers of major retailers; however, until 1982, the company relied on the Schneider sales force to handle details at the store level, to sell to independents, and to sell Natco products to medium-size and smaller accounts. As the Natco line grew, the Natco direct sales force also grew. One top manager explained the rationale for segregating the grocery and meat sales forces:

> Grocery products are purchased by different buyers from meat products. In addition, with grocery, you can plan your promotional program months ahead but with meat products, program planning does not go beyond a few weeks.

Natco was expected to boost sales to 25 percent of the total Heritage Group sales in 5 to 10 years. During its first full year of operation, Natco had sales of $39 million and earnings were $187,000.

In terms of market development, product listings grew steadily from 225 in 1980 to 875 in 1982. By 1984, Natco had developed manufacturing self-sufficiency and had expanded its direct sales force. But while sales growth was encouraging, earnings were modest, attributed to high start-up costs, particularly advertising and promotional costs associated with new products. Despite the modest earnings, Beben was proudest of the Natco subsidiary, which he described as "the shining light within the corporation." One investment analyst supported this view by noting in 1980: "Schneider's expansion into the highly profitable frozen-grocery-product market is well timed and should result in accelerated growth over the coming decade."

In terms of organizational structure, Natco first started off with a general manager, director of sales, and office administrator/accountant. Natco's equity interests in Winchester Cheese, Mother Jackson's, and Dorset Foods were controlled through individual boards of directors with no direct operating responsibilities for each of these businesses. In 1983, the head of Natco was given the title of president, and the office administrator became controller. Beben assumed leadership of Natco for two years until a president was chosen.

F.G. Bradley, Inc. In February 1981, F.G. Bradley, Inc., was acquired for approximately $12 million, making it Heritage's first major acquisition. With sales approaching $120 million and a work force of 500, Bradley supplied the high-growth food service sector with quality portioned fresh meat products. It was the largest supplier to the fast food chain sector of the market. Bradley contributed three manufacturing plants to the corporation—one each in Toronto, Edmonton, and Winnipeg—thereby opening new markets to both Schneider and Natco.

Various top managers justified the Bradley purchase by noting: (1) it gives access to a larger share of the food service markets, (2) Bradley products will find new markets because of links to the larger Heritage distribution network, (3) Heritage plans to expand Bradley's product line by adapting Heritage lines in meat retail and grocery retail, (4) because Bradley is beef oriented, it will open the door to diversification of Heritage's pork-dominated commodity base, and (5) the acquisition changes the perception that Schneider is not an important part of the food service business.

While Bradley was expected to gain access to Heritage's strengths in the areas of systems, data processing, finance, and some areas of administration and access to other Heritage group products, no change was anticipated in Bradley's marketing and operating concepts. Some of these concepts were different from other Heritage products; for example, while J.M. Schneider always followed a premium-priced strategy, Bradley was not a premium-priced company, due in part to the nature of the food service business. Fred Schneider described in 1981 the key success factors in the food service business in general:

> To be successful in the food service business, price is extremely critical and brand means very little. What counts in food service is how well you can formulate and prepare and process a product to meet the requirements of that particular customer at a price he's willing to pay. There it's loyalty with the trade that you're after. With the hospitality and institutional trade, you have to get a reputation for service, for value, for price.

Growth goals for Bradley were to expand market share with more products in existing markets and with new products in new and existing markets. Projected sales and earnings increases were $24 million and 4.5 percent, respectively, for its first year under the Heritage umbrella. At the time of acquisition, Bradley was experiencing losses.

Bradley failed to meet sales and profit objectives in 1982 and 1983. This poor performance was attributed to a general market decline during the economic recession and to inherited operating deficiencies which took longer to correct than originally estimated. The greatest ongoing problem was unsatisfactory margins. Beben felt the performance of Bradley was especially disappointing because it was a major acquisition that "ended up much poorer than expected." Bradley also suffered from high management turnover. This turnover exacerbated the deficiencies of Bradley's reporting systems. Nevertheless, in conjunction with the Link subsidiary, Bradley lowered costs considerably with a new on-line order entry system and an inventory reporting system. By 1984, Bradley was contributing positively to the earnings of Heritage.

It was originally expected that the J.M. Schneider food service business would be integrated into Bradley. This integration was intended to give a single focus to food service and to increase volume to Bradley to help overcome Bradley's losses. By 1985, this integration had not occurred because of concerns that the Schneider food service business would be lost if it was folded into the Bradley division. In fact, some Schneider processed meat food service business in the west was transferred to Bradley, and within 18 months this business was lost. Bradley's sales force was used to selling fresh red meat and did not feel comfortable selling processed meat. Ultimately, the two food service businesses were kept separate, which meant that two sales forces competed against each other, sometimes selling the same products to the same customer but using different pricing strategies.

In terms of organizational structure, there was a complete reorganization at Bradley in 1982. When Bradley was bought, it had three profit centres—Toronto, Winnipeg, and Edmonton—each with a general manager reporting to the president in Toronto. This was changed to a functional organization. There was now a president, a senior vice president, and four vice presidents: controller, sales and marketing, corporate development and personnel, operations and distribution. Beben assumed the presidency of Bradley until 1985 when a president was appointed.

Link Services, Inc.   Link Services, Inc., was established as a subsidiary company to integrate and provide complete transportation and distribution services for all of the Heritage Group companies. It was set up as a corporate function to be used and paid for by the other subsidiary companies. One of the advantages of Link was that each company would know its exact distribution costs. In addition, Link Services fulfilled three major services: warehousing, administrative services, and transportation.

Progress toward the integration of services was quickly made. Link worked closely with individual companies so that by 1984 it was handling and transporting all Heritage company products. In a number of instances, Link was instrumental in providing new market opportunities for Heritage products. Link's trucks, a combination of owned and common carriers, carried product from all companies to several destinations, a cost-effective measure achieved through rationalization. Finally, Link's administrative services included order processing, order filling, inventory control, and management information reporting. It also worked with companies to develop tailored systems which fulfilled individual system needs and requirements. Link was a corporate service and therefore reported to the senior vice president, corporate services, who reported to the chairman of the board.

Portage Trade Development.   Portage was established in 1983. Its mandate was to expand the corporation's export trade opportunities. To this end and in cooperation with its sister companies, Portage selected a variety of existing products which it felt would appeal to foreign markets. By the end of its first year of operation, Portage had made progress into the Caribbean and the United States. Initial orders from the latter were minimal and as a result, Portage had to rely on Link services to process and deliver smaller quantities. In 1984, Portage recognized that the regional character of the U.S. markets would require different marketing techniques and possibly different products if it were to promote higher volume sales. Therefore, Portage was reassessing its market and product strategy to the United States in an effort to identify new opportunities. The general manager of Portage reported to the president of Heritage Group.

The Current Situation

Beben joined J.M. Schneider, Inc., in 1969, and in 1973 he was appointed vice president marketing, J.M. Schneider Limited, and was elected to the board of directors. Fred Schneider described Beben as "instrumental" in turning Schneider into a national company during the 1970s. According to Schneider, a lot of the growth in the 1970s "could be credited to Henry's aggressiveness." As senior vice president of corporate development and the head of the corporate planning group, Beben was also instrumental in the corporation's diversification strategy which led to the establishment of The Heritage Group, Inc., in 1980. In addition to his responsibilities to the corporate entity, Beben assumed the presidencies of both Natco and F.G. Bradley when they were established. In 1981, he became the executive vice president and chief operating officer for The Heritage Group. Two years later, "in recognition of the high level of his management skills and continuing contribution to the growth of the corporation," Beben was appointed president and chief operating officer.

As a management team, Fred Schneider and Henry Beben were a contrast in styles. Schneider was a "mild-mannered and soft-spoken" person who described his management style as "that of a delegator who likes to keep channels of communication open and be visible both in the office and in the plant." He admitted to not being involved in the business community as he should be. He described himself "as a person who is most comfortable with my personal friends" and one who dislikes large parties. He noted further: "I avoid the limelight. That's the part of the job I like the least."

In contrast, Beben was in the limelight a great deal. Various reports described him as "aggressive," "entrepreneurial," and "immaculately tailored." Beben was the focus of most of the attention that surrounded the company's strategy for the 80s. He was credited with the change in corporate image from a "conservative, traditional company" to a high-growth, dynamic company in tune with major trends in the marketplace. The Heritage Group, with Beben's guidance, was gearing to become a significant player on the world stage in the food industry. Financial analysts and the investment community saw Beben as "the guy who is going to make things happen" at Heritage and characterized the company as "a conservative long-term investment but not one for an investor seeking quick returns." Beben did not object to this description and in fact admitted, "We did not make this [diversification] decision to look good in the short term, but to make good in the long term and to protect our shareholders' interests in the long term." One analyst recommended the purchase of Heritage shares in 1980 because of the company's "strong financial position, strong operating base, national distribution network, and expanding horizons into growing lucrative markets."

Despite corporate enthusiasm and endorsements from the financial community, The Heritage Group's performance since the diversification strategy was adopted had been less than satisfactory (Exhibit 1). Net earnings per share dropped significantly in 1981 to $.73 from the 1980 figure of $2.55; although the EPS had largely recovered by 1984, earnings as a percentage of sales were not commensurate with sales increases. The company failed to maintain or even regain its earnings levels of the 70s and only the Schneider subsidiary was contributing significantly to corporate profits. As the results of the Heritage Group faltered, the senior corporate officers became more involved in the operating decisions of the subsidiary companies.

Employees became increasingly concerned about the rationale for the Heritage Group concept, and this resulted in some strain in management-labour relations. In August 1982, 140 angry poultry workers at the Kitchener plant phoned in sick to protest what they felt was an unsatisfactory contract settlement which gave meat workers raises of $1.25 an hour compared to 50 cents for poultry workers. One report in 1982 put the dispute in the following context:

> Poultry workers and union spokesmen said labour relations at the plant have soured in the last few years, most notably since the creation two years ago of Heritage Group, Inc. They said that instead of being employees of a proud family company, they feel they have become cogs in an impersonal and profit-conscious corporation.
>
> Employee spokesmen said they felt further alienated this summer during contract talks, when management wanted an agreement containing wage gains of less than the industry pattern. The union said efforts to negotiate this summer were "hampered" by Heritage Group announcements in July of a wage freeze and 6 percent pay ceiling for salary personnel.
>
> The company's self-imposed salary cuts came in the face of a profit crunch brought on partly by its aggressive expansion into grocery products and the hotel-restaurant trade.

The company's office workers also felt the company was becoming more impersonal by making decisions without their involvement. Following a unilateral announcement in 1982 by the Heritage corporate office that there would be pay curbs and an increase in prices in the cafeteria, the office workers felt it was "time to protect themselves" and filed for certification with the Ontario Labour Relations Board.

For the first time in the firm's history, there were work disruptions. In 1983, the United Food and Commercial Workers' Union struck the Winnipeg plant. In

EXHIBIT 1 The Heritage Group, Inc.: Ten-Year Statistical Review, Seven-Year Selected Ratios ($000 except where noted)

	1985	1984	1983	1982	1981	1980	1979	1978	1977	1976
Sales	$648,598	$645,558	$590,074	$581,071	$539,364	$391,637	$374,374	$324,675	$262,834	$254,970
Earnings										
Earnings before income taxes and extraordinary items	2,841	10,011	9,494	5,125	3,304	11,535	12,164	7,766	7,544	7,865
Income taxes	832	4,245	4,222	2,238	1,382	4,844	4,620	3,079	2,944	3,288
Earnings before extraordinary items	2,009	5,766	5,272	2,887	1,922	6,691	7,544	4,687	4,600	4,577
As percent of sales	.31	.89	.89	.50	.36	1.71	2.02	1.44	1.75	1.80
Net earnings (loss)	(2,036)	5,766	5,272	2,887	1,922	6,691	7,544	4,687	4,600	3,579
Net earnings (loss) as percent of sales	(.31)	.89	.89	.50	.36	1.71	2.02	1.44	1.75	1.40
Dividends paid	1,167	1,167	1,167	1,162	1,390	1,258	1,088	1,011	824	756
Capital expenditures	6,983	5,254	5,741	3,329	8,486	6,406	4,104	9,389	11,030	5,377
Depreciation and amortization	7,072	5,960	5,978	5,861	5,129	4,725	4,476	3,674	2,652	2,567
Salaries, wages, and employee benefits	126,791	128,316	108,508	100,515	88,924	71,004	61,538	56,501	47,747	42,084
Average number of employees	3,971	3,970	3,827	3,817	3,880	3,327	3,131	3,009	2,874	2,676
Working capital	22,786	24,336	22,487	22,333	18,816	23,842	22,304	17,286	18,984	12,774
Working capital ratio	1.41	1.49	1.51	1.62	1.42	1.89	2.11	1.92	2.44	1.95
Total assets	143,814	136,811	126,867	119,715	126,692	95,537	83,627	76,275	65,057	50,917
Shareholders' equity at end of year	58,780	61,983	57,384	53,279	51,300	50,766	45,364	40,118	36,361	32,287
Percent return on equity at beginning of year	(3.28)	10.05	9.90	5.62	3.79	14.75	18.80	12.89	14.25	12.01
Per share statistics, in dollars										
Earnings before extraordinary items	.76	2.17	1.99	1.10	.73	2.55	2.78	1.73	1.70	1.70
Net earnings (loss)	(.77)	2.17	1.99	1.10	.73	2.55	2.78	1.73	1.70	1.33
Dividends paid	.44	.44	.44	.44	.53	.48	.40	.37	.31	.28
Equity at end of year	22.17	23.38	21.64	20.10	19.56	19.36	17.29	14.77	13.47	11.98
Selected Ratios										
Long-term debt/shareholders' equity	.43	.31	.40	.45	.48	.24	.28			
Total debt/assets	.59	.55	.55	.56	.60	.46	.46			
Inventory/turnover (times)	14.1	14.8	16.7	18.1	17.0	16.2	19.1			
Inventory/Working Capital	2.0	1.8	1.6	1.4	1.7	1.0	.88			

447

1984, the Retail, Wholesale and Department Store Union struck the Winchester plant, and later in the same year a strike was narrowly avoided at the Kitchener plant. Furthermore, in 1984 slowdowns and work-to-rule campaigns prevented the company from picking up market share from strike-prone Canada Packers and Burns. The Schneider Employee's Association struck the Ayr plant in 1985.

A communication program including a 25-minute film was developed in early 1984 to explain to employees and customers the development of the Heritage Group and its subsidiary companies. Nevertheless, Heritage management found itself on the defensive at the 1984 annual meeting of shareholders (see Appendix A for excerpts of Beben's remarks at this meeting).

The faltering performance surprised company observers. One investment analyst noted:

> We are mystified by [these] results as they seem to belie the improving industry and Company trends. . . . As far as industry conditions are concerned, there has been an improving trend in capacity (there is still too much but far less than previously), an apparent end to spiraling labour rates (which have seen Heritage's labour costs rise from 16.5 percent of total costs in 1981 to 20 percent last year), restrictions on hog exports to the United States (which should reduce raw material prices here and permit margin expansion) and, finally, less aggressive pricing by industry leader, Canada Packers (which should also help on the margin front). . . . Internally, Heritage has finally put F.G. Bradley into the black and continues to record improving results from Natco.

In his address to the shareholders on April 24, 1985, Beben reviewed the performance of the various subsidiary companies and then cited a number of factors that continued to contribute to Heritage's lackluster performance including the cost of raw materials, the decline in consumption in meat products, and the steady increase in labour costs (see Appendix B for excerpts of remarks). The local newspaper, the *Kitchener-Waterloo Record,* reported on the annual meeting and on community reaction to Beben's remarks. Headlines in the weeks following the meeting in various newspapers ranged from "Schneider's staff faces tough times" and "Heritage Group finds transition difficult" to "Workers plan Schneider rally" and "Workers angered by 'pay back' comments." Most of the reports concentrated on the part of the address which focused on the role of the employees.

Heritage employees took exception to Beben's remarks and staged a rally outside the J.M. Schneider plant in Kitchener "to send a message to senior management." According to one media report, "Many workers believed the rally is aimed directly at Henry Beben." A statement released at the rally warned, "If the company keeps putting negative pressure on us, the result will be negative pressure from us." Workers rebutted Beben's remarks about their lack of generosity with reminders that employees had accepted a 22-month wage freeze (which was still in effect), that workers had accepted casual labour in the plants, and that production was up. Employees felt that instead of criticizing their workers, management should be thanking them for the sacrifices they have already made.

Beben's Concerns

Beben felt that his remarks were appropriate given the current corporate situation. His comments were directed at all employees, both management and those covered by a collective agreement with the firm. The tension arose from the fact that his statements had been reported out of context. Nonetheless, Beben realized that he would need the cooperation of the employees in order to improve Heritage's overall performance. He wondered what else he could do to ensure better returns.

APPENDIX A
EXCERPTS OF BEBEN'S REMARKS AT 1984 ANNUAL MEETING OF SHAREHOLDERS

The most pressing questions, I suspect, on the lips of many people in this audience is "What has happened to our corporation over the past four and one half years?" "Why have the financial results deteriorated so significantly from our 1979 high?"

What have been our responses to this situation? Many and varied.

We have stayed the course. We continue to believe in our strategic direction. We have not and will not give up our share of the market. We have worked hard at streamlining and making our operations as efficient as possible.

We have strengthened communications with all of our employees so that we all better understand the circumstances facing us.

The results of all these efforts are a matter of public record, a decrease of profits in 1980 followed by an even larger decrease in 1981 and some recovery in 1982 and 1983. The first half of 1984, however, is most disconcerting to your management. We will have to work very hard for the remainder of the year to meet or beat last year's results.

One of our major problems is apparently being in an industry where profit has no meaning or motivation. Unless and until this attitude changes, things will be difficult.

In light of this fact, it will be incumbent upon all of our employees to be extremely cognizant of current circumstance and of our cost structure so that we may be able to produce significantly better results than many of our competitors and it is against this benchmark that we should, as management, judge ourselves. . . .

We've had a long and favourable relationship with our employees at J.M. Schneider in Kitchener and have been able to give them a most respectable and secure standard of living . . . .

In other parts of our corporation we have found, however, that reason and even generosity have failed and this gives rise to much concern. It appears to us that there is uneven access to the minds of our employees and that in many instances good dialogue is impossible.

We have all asked what is wrong with labour relations in Canada. Our view, in part, is that even the most enlightened employer is at a disadvantage in communicating ideas and concerns to his employees. A new equilibrium is necessary if a spirit of labour-management cooperation is to be started and fostered. . . . Our lawmakers have the prime responsibility for beginning the process. . . .

Appendix B
Excerpts of Beben's Remarks at 1985 Annual Meeting of Shareholders

Deja vu seems like an appropriate comment to make as I begin these remarks. . . . Certainly at the end of the last fiscal year and the beginning of this current year, there was every reason to be optimistic about our future results. Yet here we stand in just about the identical position of a year ago.

This is bitterly disappointing and exasperating to your management, particularly, since we feel that fundamental changes have been made that are definite improvements over past practise. . . .

In J.M. Schneider's case there is no doubt that some circumstances difficult to control have contributed to their poor first-half results. In January and February, because of a marketing board decision we were losing 30–40¢ per pound on broiler chickens. . . . In addition we continue to see declining consumption in many of our key product categories.

Given the situation as it is, it's hard to be overly optimistic about Schneider's prospects for the remainder of the year. . . . The task at hand will be to be more proactive in anticipating the required changes in order to maintain current contributions and future prospects. I suspect that many of the adjustments management will have to make will prove to be unpopular. However, it must be understood that they will be absolutely necessary in order to maintain the viability of the company.

I'm certain that it hasn't escaped your attention that our new companies (NATCO, Portage) seem to have picked up momentum and are progressing satisfactorily while the two mature organizations (J.M. Schneider, F.G. Bradley) are experiencing difficulties. These troubles are, in significant part, caused by outside influences that we predicted would occur several years ago. Part of our problem has been that our own people have found it hard to adapt to these fast-changing realities. Some of them simply don't want to believe them even now. This corporation has prided itself on its human relations over many decades. Indeed, it has been exceedingly generous with its employees. I believe, as an employee, that it is now time to begin to pay back to the company some of that generosity as we struggle to come to grips with our changing world. If we display understanding, cooperation, enthusiasm, and willingness to work harder, then the crisis will pass and we will go on to become the truly great company that we can and should be. On the other hand, if we show recalcitrance, sullenness, greed, and idleness, then we doom our collective futures. I believe this company and its employees are far too good to allow that to happen. . . .

In closing, your management is committed to make whatever changes are necessary to protect the investment of the shareholders and the future of the employees in these trying times. I believe we will succeed.

CASE 16
HIRAM WALKER — GOODERHAM & WORTS (A)

In 1985 Hiram Walker—Gooderham & Worts (Hiram Walker) was one of the world's largest and most profitable producers of distilled spirits. Hiram Walker's five key brands—Canadian Club Canadian whisky, Ballantine's Scotch whisky, Courvoisier cognac, and Kahlua and Tia Maria coffee liqueurs were sold internationally and held strong positions in their individual categories. Revenues were steady at about $1.5 billion, yielding consistent after-tax returns of between 15 percent and 16 percent on invested capital. Hiram Walker's recently appointed president and chief executive officer, H. Clifford Hatch, Jr., was pleased with the company's performance and impatient to build on its prosperity: "We have done a great job with profitability . . . but we want to grow, and we have yet to show results in this area. . . . We have to work this out, how are we going to grow?"

The World Distilled Spirits Business

Achieving growth would not be easy. World consumption of distilled spirits had peaked in recent years and was now in slow decline. Shifting consumer tastes and aggressive competitive activity were threatening traditional product and brand positions. Market share had become a major source of growth and power, triggering a consolidation of producer and distributor structures. Observers expected these trends to continue and to create unprecedented opportunities and risks for industry participants.

Demand

From a global perspective, the demand for spirit products and brands was highly fragmented. Product preferences varied widely by country market in relation to local traditions, tastes, and pricing. And within markets, these same factors often led to a broad distribution of brand preferences across local brands, global brands, which may or may not be locally produced (e.g., Smirnoff vodka, Baccardi rum), and global brands with unique national sources (e.g., Scotch whisky, cognac). Statistics for selected spirits by product categories and country markets are presented in Exhibit 1.

In most country markets, domestic demand was served largely by local production. The reasons for this, which varied in importance by market, included unique national tastes, production and distribution economics, and government

This case was prepared by Professor Joseph N. Fry for the purpose of classroom discussion. Copyright © 1989, The University of Western Ontario. R1.

EXHIBIT 1 **Demand for Alcoholic Beverages in Selected Categories and Countries, 1984**
(9 litre case equivalents, 000)

	Canadian Whisky	Scotch Whisky	Bourbon	Cognac	Brandy	Gin	Vodka	Rum	Cordials Liquors	Other Popular	Total Spirits	Total Wine	Total Beer
United States	23,800	19,200	36,700*	1,800	5,200	14,300	31,200	12,220	16,300		179,400	232,900	2,385,300
Growth rate (80/84)	−0.5	−5.7	−4.3	10.0	−1.0	−2.0	0	1.9	4.7		−1.3	4.1	0.7
Canada	6,700	1,200	LV	300	700	1,600	2,500	3,100	2,000		18,800	25,200	212,000
Growth rate (80/84)	−6.2	−3.9		3.5	−1.4	−7.6	−1.0	−2.9	1.7		−3.8	4.0	−1.4
United Kingdom	LV	12,000	LV	1,000	1,000	3,400	3,700	2,100	1,700		25,500	68,700	691,200
Growth rate (79/84)		−3.8		−5.3	3.4	−3.0	1.5	−5.3	3.6		−2.9	4.6	−1.8
West Germany	LV	1,900	500	900	10,600	400	900	5,800	4,000	9,500†	44,000	178,000	985,700
Growth rate (79/84)		−3.7	−7.7	−1.8	−0.8	−2.0	1.8	−3.5	−7.5	.0	−3.7	0.7	−0.1
France	LV	5,300	200	800	1,000	300	300	2,100	NA	12,700‡	30,000	522,000	250,000
Growth rate (79/84)		6.2	6.8	−8.0	−4.6	14.8	9.9	−7.4		−1.4	−0.6	−1.9	−1.6
Italy	LV	3,100	100	200	6,900	300	200	100	3,400		24,800	525,400	119,700
Growth rate (80/84)		2.4	20.0	−1.7	−3.5	15.0	−8.3	−13.0	−3.0		−3.6	−1.9	2.7
Spain	LV	2,000	LV	LV	11,200	6,700	500	2,400	5,200	1,600§	332,800	200,800	251,000
Growth rate (80/84)		1.9			−3.9	1.0	3.4	0.4	−.03	10.4	−1.2	−2.4	2.9
Japan	LV	2,200	LV	500	2,000	200	NA	300	LV	31,700‖	50,800#	10,300	516,200
Growth rate (79/84)		−4.1		10.7	10.6	−2.7		4.8		−0.3	4.0	6.5	0.7
Australia	LV	1,900	LV	LV	800	200	300	800	400		4,900	35,000	204,700
Growth rate (79/84)		3.7			1.5	−2.0	1.3	3.4	−0.5		2.9	5.9	−0.8
World consumption (1982)		65,000		8,900	43,000	59,400	51,800						

NOTE: *Includes straight bourbon and blends.
†Korn, aquavit.
‡Anis, ouzo.
§Spanish whisky.
‖Japanese whisky.
#Totals include sake consumption of 186 million cases.
LV: Low volumes.

453

protection. The residual import volumes, which amounted to about 15 percent of world demand, were still significant, however, and crucial to the exporters of unique source products.

The United States was widely regarded as the most attractive of the world's spirits markets. The U.S. market accounted for about 22 percent of total world spirits demand and about 46 percent of world imports, and it was relatively open to competitive innovation. Thereafter, the opportunities represented by specific markets dropped rapidly in magnitude and became dependent on a wide variety of specific local conditions.

Competition

In spite of on-going consolidation, competitive concentration in the spirits industry was still quite low. In the United States, for example, 30 brands sold over 1 million cases per year, and the top 60 brands, sold by 24 different firms, held only 60 percent of the market. There were very large firms in the industry, of course. Exhibit 2 lists the sales, profits, and growth rates of the top 18 companies. In spite of their scale, however, these firms probably accounted for less than 40 percent of world spirit sales. The balance of business was done by virtually dozens of smaller competitors.

Exhibit 2   Top 18 International Spirits Firms (1985) (U.S. $000,000)

	Sales	*Operating Income*	*Sales Growth Percentage*
Distillers Co. (UK)	$1,600	$293	5.2 (81–85)
Seagram (Canada, U.S.)	2,821	246	0.4 (81–85)
Hiram Walker (Canada)	1,102	213	0.9 (81–85)
Grand Metropolitan (UK)	1,319	181	18.7 (80–84)
Brown-Forman (US)	905	167	4.1 (81–85)
Heublein (US)	NA	152	NA
Bacardia (Bahamas)	950	150	8.0 (80–84)
Moet-Hennessy (France)	597	120	25.2 (80–84)
Allied-Lyons (UK)	1,334*	85	7.1 (81–85)
Pernod-Ricard (France)	581	78	−2.1 (80–84)
Schenley (US)	416	48	−11.7 (80–84)
Arthur Bell (UK)	305	48	5.0 (80–84)
Martell (France)	236	38	18.0 (80–84)
Whitbread (UK)	672	34	NA
National (US)	648	28	−2.8 (81–83)
Wm. Grant (UK)	101	19	7.9 (81–83)
Remy Martin (France)	110	16	11.4 (80–84)
Suntory (Japan)	2,191	NA	−7.4 (83–85)

Estimates for spirits and wine divisions where possible.
*Includes wines, spirits, and soft drinks.
Source: Hiram Walker records.

The emergence of intense competition had been an unsettling development for many participants in the spirits business. They were used to dealing in what was historically known as a gentleman's trade. Now they were engaged in an all-out battle in which the major weapons were aggressive new product and brand marketing, forward integration to control distribution, and acquisitions to balance and expand product portfolios.

Marketing.   The great strength of the multinational firms was in their ability to build and support global brands. Their established premium brands provided very attractive returns and were protected from attack to some degree by traditional tastes and habits and, in most countries, government regulations that limited advertising, sampling, price promotion, and so on. Even when a traditional brand was affected by new developments, its decline was more a matter of erosion than critical failure. There was another side to this, of course. It was very difficult to grow in these mature, competitive markets. New product launches were expensive, time-consuming, and risky. Similarly, campaigns to capture market share by the further penetration of current markets or geographic expansion required long-term thinking and a willingness to make risky investments.

Competitive innovation in the industry was focused on three fronts. The first was the introduction, often by local producers or distributors, of low-priced brands into traditional categories. The second was the search and exploitation of niches as demand in the mature categories fragmented—such as in the promotion of single malt Scotch whiskies. The third was in the pursuit of "new" categories, like those in the liqueur business in the United States, where there was a constant parade of new formulas and flavours—from peach, to kiwi, to root beer. Collectively, these efforts created considerable turmoil in the industry and chipped away at the traditional brand leaders.

Forward Integration.   There were two basic channels of distribution for distilled spirits. In the monopoly markets, which included 18 American states, Canada, and the northern European countries, spirits products were sold by a producer or import agency directly to government distribution organizations. In the open markets, which accounted for the majority of industry revenue, two- and three-tier channel structures were common, involving producer sales companies and/or import agencies, distributors, and retailers.

In the open markets, the proportion of sales through retail chain organizations was increasing. This had stimulated the development of fewer and larger distributors. Producers were facing increasing demands for marketing support, price concessions, and private brands and were finding it more difficult to keep channel attention on marginal brands.

One of the producer responses to increasing channel power was forward integration through the purchase of channel units. There was by no means a consensus in the industry that this was a wise move. It was expensive, took distillers beyond their traditional expertise, and could result in channel conflict. Nevertheless, many of the major firms were moving in this direction.

Horizontal Diversification.   A number of major firms were pursuing acquisitions to diversify and to achieve greater market power. These included steps to diversify (1) outside the alcoholic beverage industry, such as with Seagram's purchase of a major position in DuPont; (2) across the major product classes within the alcoholic beverage industry, such as with Guinness' (a brewer) acquisition of Bell's (whisky) and takeover bid for Distillers (mainly spirits); and (3) across product categories within distilled spirits, such as with Hiram Walker's acquisition of Tia Maria. There was agreement throughout the industry that acquisition activity would accelerate in the coming years.

Hiram Walker Background

In 1856, Hiram Walker crossed the Detroit river from Michigan and built a distillery in the raw timberland on the Canadian side. The company grew and a small community called Walkerville developed around the distillery. In the 1870s, Walker was the first to brand a Canadian whisky, calling his premium product Canadian Club.

Hiram Walker died in 1899 and his family managed the firm for the next quarter century. In 1926, Harry C. Hatch organized the purchase of Hiram Walker from the family and merged its operations with those of the Toronto-based Gooderham & Worts distillery. The new company was in an ideal position to benefit from the prohibition laws in force at the time in the United States. Spirits could not legally be produced or sold in America, but if products made and sold in Canada found their way south, well, so be it.

By the end of prohibition in 1934, Canadian whisky in the U.S. market had become a preferred drink beyond all previous measure. The Canadian distillers such as Hiram Walker and Seagram moved quickly to consolidate their gains and to establish new and now legal distribution and sales organizations.

Over time, Hiram Walker added to its key brand portfolio and broadened its geographic sales coverage. The major brand acquisitions were Ballantine's (1935), Tia Maria (49 percent in 1954, increased to 100 percent in 1984), Courvoisier (1964), and Kahlua (1964). Under Harry Hatch's son, H. Clifford Hatch, who became president in 1964, Hiram Walker developed the potential of these brands, grew profitably, and became a truly multinational operation.

Hiram Walker Resources.   In response to the threat of a takeover, Hiram Walker was merged in 1980 with Consumers Gas and its subsidiary, Home Oil, to form what was ultimately known as Hiram Walker Resources (HWR). The new company encountered some early and serious difficulties with a major resource investment, but by 1985 it had recovered and was regarded as a healthy management company with holdings as outlined in Exhibit 3.

Hiram Walker's Role in HWR.   Hiram Walker was a significant contributor to HWR earnings. Hiram Walker's revenue and profit trends were essentially flat, however, as shown in Exhibit 4. Up to very recently, the company had not been encouraged to grow by acquisition. A new and provisional role statement had opened the acquisition avenue, although Cliff Hatch, Jr. noted that there was no particular pressure from HWR's board to pursue it because "they are more interested in the energy business." HWR's position was that

> Hiram Walker is responsible for all HWR's distilled spirits and wine business. Requiring only small capital expenditures, Hiram Walker provides HWR with high levels of cash flow that can be used for additional investment. Hiram Walker is expected to maintain its relative industry strength with high steady return on invested capital of 16–18 percent from its current brands and assets. In addition, Hiram Walker is expected to capitalize on industry rationalization and propose profitable beverage alcohol acquisitions of at least $250 million within the next five years.

EXHIBIT 3 Hiram Walker Resources Holdings, 1985 ($000,000)

	Identifiable Assets	*Revenue*	*Operating Earnings*
Distilled spirits	$1,511	$1,516	$282
Natural resources	2,052	482	167
Gas utility	1,634	1,767	216
Other investment	551		
Total	$5,748	$3,765	$665

SOURCE: Hiram Walker Resources, Ltd., Annual Report 1985.

EXHIBIT 4 Hiram Walker—Five-Year Performance Summary ($Cdn. 000,000)

	Fiscal Year Ending August 31				
	1985	*1984*	*1983*	*1982*	*1981*
Sales:					
Cases (000)	20,780	20,616	20,575	21,899	22,975
Revenue	$ 1,504.8	$ 1,437.4	$ 1,394.5	$ 1,435.8	$ 1,435.9
Gross margin	695.6	659.2	623.6	623.7	624.1
Percentage	46.2	45.9	44.7	43.4	43.5
Operating income	291.2	294.5	290.3	320.8	294.0
Net (after-tax) operating income	176.4	169.1	175.1	189.6	NA
Invested capital*	1,171.5	1,089.1	1,059.4	1,199.2	NA
Return on average Invested capital (%)	15.6	15.7	15.5	15.6	NA

NOTE: *Invested capital was comprised of current, net fixed, and other assets less nonbank current obligations and deferred income taxes. This is a different concept than "identifiable assets" as used in Exhibit 3. Other smaller accounting differences explain the discrepancies in revenues and income numbers between Exhibits 3 and 4.

SOURCE: Company records.

Hiram Walker's Strategic Position

In 1985, Hiram Walker operations encompassed production plants, marketing units, and investments throughout the world. The company's key brands accounted for over 60 percent of Hiram Walker's revenues and over 70 percent of profit contribution after direct selling expenses. Geographically, the United States accounted for about 60 percent of corporate revenues. The strategic positions of the key brands are outlined below; a summary of sales trends is presented in Exhibit 5.

Canadian Club

Canadian Club was Hiram Walker's historic flagship brand. It was produced and bottled in Canada for domestic and international sale. The brand's primary market was in the United States. There, for years, Canadian Club and its arch rival, Seagram's V.O., had dominated the Canadian whisky business. Of late, however, both brands had been losing ground to lower-priced entries, such as Canadian Mist and Windsor Supreme, that were imported in bulk from Canada. The loss of nearly a million cases of volume each over the past five years had left Hiram Walker and Seagram with significant problems of balancing current production levels and maturing stock inventories. Seagram had to some extent buffered its V.O. sales decline by the successful promotion of its super premium Crown Royal brand. Until 1985, however, there was no Hiram Walker entry in this category.

EXHIBIT 5   **Sales of Selected Hiram Walker Brands in Selected Areas (9 litre case equivalents, 000)**

	Canadian Club	Ballantine's	Kahlua	Courvoisier	Tia Maria
United States, 1984 case sales (000)	2,900	380	1,570	540	130
Market share, point change (84/80)	12.1, –4.9	2.0, –0.3	26.1, –7.4	29.8, –3.3	2.1, –2.7
Canada, 1984 case sales (000)	650	130	210	60	130
Market share, point change (84/80)	9.7, –2.3	10.5, –0.2	18.6, –1.6	21.6, –5.0	11.5, –10.4
United Kingdom, 1983 case sales	LV	90	LV	320	120
Market share, point change (83/79)		1.0, NA		30.0, –2.2	6.8, –3.2
Selected European*, 1983 case sales	LV	1,401	LV	160	LV
Market share, point change (83/79)		13.5, –1.1		8.2, –1.0	
Japan and Hong Kong	LV	130	LV	100	LV
Market share		10.0, NA			
Company shipments, 1985 fiscal year	3,300	3,500	2,200	1,350	683
Percentage change (85/84)	–5.6	–10.3	3.0	1.8	NA

Individual brand/market data based on commercial estimates of wholesalers' depletions known to somewhat overstate actual volumes.
Market share based on category totals (e.g., Canadian Club share of Canadian whisky sales).
LV: Low volume
*France, Italy, West Germany. Excludes duty-free sales.

The strength of Canadian Club was with older, traditional whisky drinkers who, unfortunately, represented a declining market base. To revitalize the brand, Hiram Walker was shifting its marketing focus toward younger, upscale adults. The total advertising approach was being changed, and spending levels were being increased somewhat. Furthermore, a super premium brand, Canadian Club Classic, was being introduced to support and extend the brand range.

Ballantine's

Ballantine's was the world's fourth largest selling brand of Scotch whisky, after Johnny Walker, J&B, and Bell's. Ballantine's was strong in Continental Europe and selected markets throughout the world. It was weak, however, in the United Kingdom and the United States, which together represented about 50 percent of the world's Scotch whisky consumption.

Hiram Walker expected Ballantine's to show volume increases of a little less than 2 percent per year through 1990. To this point, Hiram Walker had not attacked the United Kingdom because of a very competitive and relatively low-profit market environment there. Further, in the United States, Hiram Walker was unhappy with its current distribution arrangements. These were in the hands of an independent distributor who had been under contract since 1938. The company had yet to find a satisfactory resolution for this situation.

Courvoisier

Courvoisier's share of the cognac market had varied over time from a low of 12 percent in 1965 to a high of 21 percent in 1975, at which point it was the leading brand in the industry. Courvoisier's position had fallen more recently to 15.3 percent, placing it third behind Hennessy and Martell. Geographically, Courvoisier was strong in the United Kingdom and United States but relatively weak in Continental Europe and the Far East.

The drop in Courvoisier's share was attributed to product development and marketing spending problems. Courvoisier had been late with new super premium qualities and package formats. This problem was now being addressed. There was a continuing issue, however, with respect to the unprecedentedly high marketing spending of Hennessy and Martell, which Courvoisier, to this point, had been reluctant to match. Striking a trade-off between profit and market share was a key strategic issue for the brand.

Kahlua

Kahlua was Hiram Walker's most profitable brand. It was a premium-priced coffee liqueur produced in Mexico and sold primarily in the United States and Canada.

Hiram Walker's Los Angeles–based Maidstone Wine & Spirits organization had capitalized on Kahlua's versatility to build a strong position in the liqueur market. Kahlua was marketed variously as a traditional liqueur, as a spirit to be used in a mixed drink (e.g., with milk in the Brown Cow or vodka in the Black Russian), or as a flavoring in a host of cooking applications. Kahlua's position was now being challenged directly by low-price imitators and indirectly by the emergence of rapidly changing taste fads for liqueurs and liqueur-based drinks.

In Hiram Walker's view, the major growth opportunities for Kahlua were outside the United States and Canada. Here there were two as yet unresolved positioning issues: whether Kahlua would be sold as a traditional liqueur or as a multiple-use product, and how the potential positioning and distribution overlap with Tia Maria should be handled.

Tia Maria

Tia Maria was a coffee-based liqueur produced in Jamaica. Tia Maria's traditional positioning was as an upscale, imported, classic liqueur product. Its prime markets were the United States, Canada, and the United Kingdom. The brand was faltering in all of these markets, however, as a result, it was thought, of inadequate focus and effort, shifts in liqueur market tastes, and the ambiguity (in the United States and Canada) of positioning and emphasis relative to Kahlua.

The strategic issues facing Tia Maria were those of revitalizing the brand in its key markets and developing distribution in other markets, particularly in Western Europe. The latter efforts would be particularly complicated since Tia Maria, by itself, was in a relatively weak bargaining position in seeking distribution. It needed to be allied with other brands but such natural allies as Ballantine's might not be available if, for example, Ballantine's and Kahlua were combined together in another distribution portfolio.

Hiram Walker's Organization

Hiram Walker was run through a functional management structure of production, marketing, financial, and administrative units (Exhibit 6). This structure reflected a long-standing management philosophy of engaging top management in critical strategic and operating issues. Decisions involving brand strategy, price, image, packaging and labeling, distributor representation, trade practices, production levels, quality assurance, and so on were made at Walkerville.

The top management group at Hiram Walker consisted of Cliff Hatch, Jr., Jim Ferguson, Jim Ford, John Giffen, Steve McCann, and Ian Wilson-Smith. Short biographies of each are given in Exhibit 7. Ferguson, Giffen and Wilson-Smith each headed up functional units as outlined in Exhibit 6. At the time of the case, there was no corporate-level marketing head. This role was being covered by Cliff Hatch, Jr. Ford and McCann were company veterans and were responsible, respectively, for the Courvoisier and Ballantine's supplier companies.

EXHIBIT 6 Simplified Organization Structure

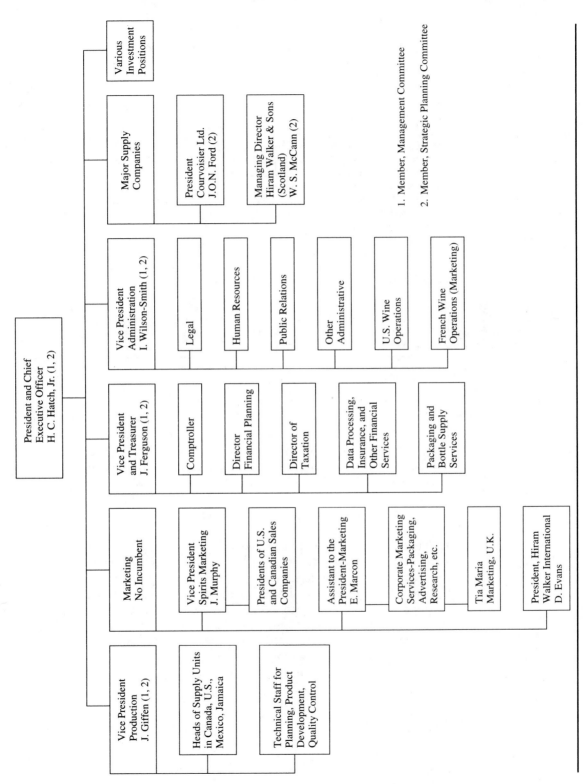

President and Chief Executive Officer
H. C. Hatch, Jr. (1, 2)

Vice President Production
J. Giffen (1, 2)
- Heads of Supply Units in Canada, U.S., Mexico, Jamaica
- Technical Staff for Planning, Product Development, Quality Control

Marketing
No Incumbent

Vice President Spirits Marketing
J. Murphy
- Presidents of U.S. and Canadian Sales Companies
- Assistant to the President-Marketing E. Marcon
- Corporate Marketing Services–Packaging, Advertising, Research, etc.
- Tia Maria Marketing, U.K.
- President, Hiram Walker International D. Evans

Vice President and Treasurer
J. Ferguson (1, 2)
- Comptroller
- Director Financial Planning
- Director of Taxation
- Data Processing, Insurance, and Other Financial Services
- Packaging and Bottle Supply Services

Vice President Administration
I. Wilson-Smith (1, 2)
- Legal
- Human Resources
- Public Relations
- Other Administrative
- U.S. Wine Operations
- French Wine Operations (Marketing)

Major Supply Companies
- President Courvoisier Ltd. J.O.N. Ford (2)
- Managing Director Hiram Walker & Sons (Scotland) W. S. McCann (2)

Various Investment Positions

1. Member, Management Committee
2. Member, Strategic Planning Committee

SOURCE: Derived from company documents.

461

Exhibit 7 **Hiram Walker Senior Management**

H. Clifford Hatch, Jr., 44, was a native of Windsor, Ontario, and a graduate of McGill University and the Harvard Business School. He joined Hiram Walker in 1970 and in 1976 was appointed CEO of Corby Distilleries Ltd. (a Canadian firm in which Hiram Walker held a majority interest). In 1979, he became corporate vice president for marketing of Hiram Walker and became president and CEO in 1983.

James P. Ferguson, 49, was born in Landis, Saskatchewan, and earned a degree from McGill University. He worked for several years with the accountancy firm of Price Waterhouse and joined Hiram Walker in 1974. He was currently corporate vice president for finance and treasurer of the company.

James D.N. Ford, 49, was raised in Glasgow, Scotland, and was a graduate of the University of Glasgow and a chartered accountant. He joined Courvoisier in 1965 and moved to Canada in 1968 as comptroller of Hiram Walker and later vice president. He returned to Courvoisier in 1980 and presently was head of French operations.

John A. Giffen, 47, came from Ingersoll, Ontario, and held B.Sc. (Engineering) and MBA degrees from the University of Windsor. He joined Hiram Walker, becoming corporate vice president for production in 1980.

W. Steve McCann, 64, was a native of Edinburgh, Scotland, where he received his education and became a chartered accountant. He joined Hiram Walker in the Ballantine's organization and became managing director of the Scottish operations in 1971.

Ian M. Wilson-Smith, 52, was born in Middlesex, England, and was a graduate of Cambridge University. His early experience was in production with Harveys of Bristol, England, and later in production and general management positions with other firms in the beverage alcohol business in England and Canada. He joined Hiram Walker in 1980 and was currently corporate vice president for administration.

The Marketing Units. Hiram Walker International and the American and Canadian sales companies were the primary marketing units. They were responsible, within their territories and for assigned brands, for proposing marketing strategies and budgets, building distributor relationships, and achieving sales targets. Special marketing services for legal, packaging, research, and other needs were provided by Walkerville staff groups. Revenues and direct marketing expenses were directly attributable to each of the line marketing units, and further analysis of profitability was possible after allocating product and other costs.

The Supply Units. The supplier units, such as Courvoisier, were responsible for product availability, quality, and cost and, depending on the situation, performed local accounting and administrative functions. The supply unit heads in North America, with the exception of wine operations, reported to John Giffen. Those in Europe reported directly to Cliff Hatch, Jr., although the European units drew on technical assistance from John Giffen's groups. Wine operations, which were relatively small by Hiram Walker standards, reported to Ian Wilson-Smith, who had a special interest and expertise in this area. The supplier units were essentially cost centres, although profitability could be assessed by the attribution of revenues and marketing costs.

Formal Integration

The annual budgeting process was the primary vehicle for tying the marketing and supply units together. Budgets were initiated by the marketing units, reviewed and extended by the supplier units, and approved at the corporate level.

In practice, this was a complicated process. Hiram Walker International, for example, had to deal with forecasts and marketing budgets for a number of brands across a range of countries, distributors, and currencies. Further, as the planning process progressed, Hiram Walker International had to strike agreements with the supplier units, whose interests—in brand progress, capacity utilization, operational stability, and so on—were not always consistent with the marketing view. Finally, all of this had to be assembled by marketing units across suppliers and by supplier units across sales entities for corporate review.

Over the years, the budget process had become increasingly complicated and time-consuming. This was the result of more complex operations and the tendencies of senior managers to micromanage the operating units. John Harcarufka, head of W.A. Taylor in the United States, would note, for example, that he had more autonomy in pricing and promoting Drambuie, an agency brand, than he did for Courvoisier. With the latter, he had to negotiate detailed approvals two ways, as he put it, with both Courvoisier in France and corporate marketing in Walkerville. There was also a strong feeling within the operating units that "Walkerville's" requests for information were too frequent, too detailed, occasionally unrealistic, and often unnecessary.

At the corporate level, the primary formal groups for coordinating the functional units were the Management and Strategic Planning Committees. The Management Committee consisted of Hatch, Giffen, Ferguson, and Wilson-Smith; it met formally on a regular basis to consider corporate issues and to review the proposals and performance of the marketing and supply units.

Informal Integration

A great deal of the burden of coordinating Hiram Walker activities was accomplished informally by old hands working together. Hiram Walker took pride in the long service of its people and in their development and advancement. The company promoted from within whenever possible; most of the top and middle management positions were filled by individuals who had worked their way up from entry-level positions.

The Management Committee members worked together very closely. Their working relationships were strengthened by their long experience in the industry, the traditions of the company, and even by the relatively small size and isolation of corporate headquarters. Formal systems and meetings aside, it was perhaps more important for the running of the company that these managers met casually and frequently in the course of the day, in their offices, at lunch in the executive dining room, and in business and social entertaining.

The members of the Management Committee comprised the first circle of internal influence on corporate affairs. The second level included Jim Ford and Steve McCann, who, in spite of distance, maintained a fairly high level of interaction with the Walkerville group through membership on the Strategic Planning Committee, phone, correspondence, and travel. The second circle might also have included David Evans, the head of Hiram Walker International, except that he had only recently (1981) joined the company from Nestle and had not had the same opportunity to work with the Walkerville executives. The third circle of influence consisted of perhaps 8 to 10 executives, most of whom were marketing unit heads in North America and Europe.

Strategic Planning

Formal strategic planning at Hiram Walker was coordinated by a Strategic Planning Committee consisting of the members of the Management Committee plus Ford and McCann. This committee met annually for two or three days to consider issues of corporate direction and priority and to review progress in specific project areas such as acquisitions. On an informal basis, it served as a sounding board for most corporate initiatives.

For years, Hiram Walker had based its forward planning on five-year rolling forecasts submitted by the operating units. These were discussed with Walkerville, adjusted where necessary, and used as the basis for corporate financial and production forecasts. This forecast system was still in use, although top management was concerned that it placed too much reliance on a projection of the status quo. The February 1985 corporate forecast submitted to HWR projected 1989 revenues from continuing operations of $1,925 million and operating income of $350 million.

To remedy the limitations of existing procedures, the Strategic Planning Committee started in 1982 to introduce a new strategic planning process. The aim was to push strategic thinking as far down the organization as possible; corporate management would be responsible for developing strategic guidelines and conducting reviews, while the unit managers would be responsible for proposing and implementing strategy for their operations. The process was tied to the existing organizational units, but strategy reviews were separated from forecast/budget activities.

The new process was slow to take hold. In spite of adjustments to provide headquarters coordination for new products and "brand champions" to coordinate information on existing brands, the system was not generating clear-cut priorities, commitment, and action. Many of the business possibilities that had been identified remained just that. The terminology that came into use was that "more bite" was needed in the planning process, meaning more definitive guidelines and choices, more resources to back approved programs, and more delegation of authority and responsibility to get ideas implemented.

The Big Issues

As fiscal 1985 closed, very profitably, but still without tangible progress on growth, Cliff Hatch, Jr. was growing increasingly concerned. He had recently asked Ian Wilson-Smith to survey 35 to 40 unit managers to seek their ideas about what the company could do to become more aggressive in the market. Virtually all of the managers polled had responded in writing, often after consulting their colleagues and subordinates, and cumulatively they had offered literally dozens of suggestions. There was a focus, however, on three broad issues: (1) acquisitions, (2) new product development, and (3) organizational refinement. A summary of the views together with comments by members of the top management group follows.

Acquisitions

It was generally agreed that acquisitions were necessary to improve Hiram Walker's growth and competitive position. The sheer volume of suggestions from the management ranks on potential acquisitions and new ventures outnumbered the rest by a wide margin. The major themes were the need to think big rather than small, the desirability of acquiring a few significant "white goods" brands (vodka, gin, etc.), the need to increase Walker's involvement in the wine industry, and a strong interest in beer (especially high-image imports), soft drinks, and mineral waters. The general opinion would have squared with John Giffen's remark that "the pluses and minuses of the existing brand areas add up to really slow growth. . . . Our only avenue for real progress is through acquisition."

The problem in acquisitions, as expressed by several managers, was that Hiram Walker was simply not moving aggressively enough. Jim Ferguson put it bluntly: "Our strategic planning hasn't accomplished very much. . . . We haven't done anything yet!" While this was not strictly true, since the company had made three small acquisitions, it captured the prevailing view that significant action was needed.

Although the formal position of the Strategic Planning Committee was to focus on acquisitions within the spirits industry, there was informal disagreement about this focus within the group. The arguments were classic. Several managers felt that acquisitions should be limited to the business Hiram Walker knew and within this were concerned about availability, cost, synergy, and returns. Other managers cast a wider net, suggesting the spirits industry was in decline and that diversification was necessary, at least into allied fields of prestige products such as perfumes and cosmetics.

There was some feeling that the procedures for screening and pursuing acquisitions were delaying the acquisition process. Currently, various members of the Strategic Planning Committee were asked to follow up on possibilities under the general coordination of Cliff Hatch, Jr. and Ian Wilson-Smith. A count of the assigned projects indicated that most managers on the committee had upwards of five leads to pursue. The formation of a dedicated headquarters unit to screen and analyze acquisitions had been discussed by the committee, but no action had been taken on this matter.

New Product Development

There was an ongoing controversy in the company over what were perceived to be unnecessary delays in bringing new product initiatives (including types, flavors, packaging, labels, etc.) to market. On the one hand, some managers, primarily from marketing positions, argued that more resources and more discretion were necessary to speed up the pace of development. They saw a newly formed product development committee as a dubious solution, as just another corporate hurdle of which there were already too many. Gerry Gianni, who had joined Hiram Walker in 1981 from a large spirits import house and now ran Hiram Walker Incorporated in the United States, commented on the four years that it had taken to bring Canadian Club Classic to market: "A disaster.... The project was mandated from the top, but after that nothing seemed to happen.... The very first thing you should not do is appoint a committee, nor set up a coordinator that will not be around to see the project through.... Politics and bureaucracy set in and the coordinator was forced into a referee's position deciding who should win instead of thinking about benefits for the consumer.... We are still trying to come to grips with packaging."

Other executives argued that checks and balances were necessary to avoid expensive product proliferation, to provide for the orderly development of production facilities, and to ensure that new initiatives were consistent with corporate policy. As one production executive pointed out, "Some of the marketing units seem to change their priorities with the weather.... One moment it's miniatures in plastic for the airlines, the next it's 1.75 litre bottles.... They don't seem to appreciate the supply, inventory, and equipment complications." Furthermore, at the corporate level, the traditional position was reiterated: "We rely on just a few brands and we operate in markets where brand and corporate reputations are crucial factors.... We can't afford to have someone going off half-cocked and creating a quality or public relations problem."

The Organization

Organization suggestions were abundant in the manager responses. The recurring themes were the need to decentralize decision making, adopt a profit centre approach, and set up separate and properly staffed units to handle acquisitions and new products. These comments were echoed by Jim Ford and Ian Wilson-Smith. Ford noted that "Hiram Walker's highly centralized functional management structure is inappropriate for an increasingly competitive environment.... It creates confusion and conflict between the functions and between field and geographical management.... Further, under the present structure I cannot see us developing the well-rounded businessmen we will need in the future.... We will always have to go outside in the crunch." Ian Wilson-Smith was of a similar mind: "We have no adequate framework for the integrated management of our key brands on a worldwide basis or, indeed, of our key markets on a geographical basis; we have succeeded in getting the worst of both worlds and the end result is a further reinforcement of the centralized decision-making process.... We need major structural changes to combine production and marketing activities into manageable business units, integrate the responsibility for our key brands on a worldwide basis, and redefine the role of corporate headquarters."

Other top managers disagreed. They admitted that the organization was not working as well as it should but argued that the current structure was essentially sound. All that was needed were refinements in staffing, policy, and procedures. Jim Ferguson's position was that "you have to understand that our big problem is not in operations. . . . We have strong brands and we are doing well. . . . It is that we haven't gotten on with acquisitions. . . ." [Insofar as current operations are concerned] What we need to do is get a marketing vice president into place and get Cliff out of that role . . . and then use our budgeting and accounting procedures to hold the sales companies more clearly responsible for results. . . . We haven't pushed hard enough." Steve McCann spoke of international operations, "I was involved [in 1965] in the initial conception of HWI and my position then was that the brand-owning companies [e.g., Hiram Walker Scotland] should be complete entities entirely responsible for success and failure. . . . This view was not accepted and HWI was made responsible to Walkerville. While I continue to prefer my original position in principle, I cannot see how HWI can now be unscrambled [whether by returning its functions to the brandowner—in whole or part—or in some other way] without great disruption. And the likely benefits are insufficient to compensate for the disruption. . . . HWI should be allowed to get on with its job without interference from Walkerville, which, in my view, should confine itself to decisions on . . . [elements of brand, strategy, operating policy] . . . the approval of the annual budget and *rigorous* ex post facto examination of HWI's performance." Another top manager put the point bluntly in an informal conversation: "There is *no* way that we are going to reorganize this company."

Action Considerations

Cliff Hatch, Jr. was quite prepared to act, subject to two broad conditions. First, he ruled out major strategic or organization gambles. As he noted, "I have no mandate to wreck this company." Change could and should proceed, but the steps would have to be carefully developed. He was particularly concerned that the disagreements among managers demonstrated that the obstacles to growth were not well understood. As a result, he had tried to this point to keep the options for change open and to avoid the endorsement of specific "solutions." One of the reasons for postponing the appointment of a corporate vice president for marketing, for example, was that this would tend to reinforce past structure and practices.

Second, change would have to respect the corporate values that had helped to build Hiram Walker. "As a company," Hatch said, "we have tried to take the long-term view, to build lasting relationships, and to respect individuals and individual contributions. We have tried to avoid short-term and temporary solutions. I believe these principles will serve us as well in the future as they have in the past."

CASE 17
IKEA CANADA LTD.—1986 (CONDENSED)

Founded as a mail-order business in rural Sweden in 1943, IKEA had grown to more than $1 billion (U.S.) in sales and 70 retail outlets by 1985, and was considered by many to be one of the best-run furniture operations in the world. Although only 14 percent of IKEA's sales were outside Europe, the company's fastest growth was occurring in North America.

Success, however, brought imitators, and in mid-1986 Bjorn Bayley and Anders Berglund, the senior managers of IKEA's North American operations, were examining a just-published Sears Canada catalogue, which contained a new 20-page section called "Elements." This section bore a striking resemblance to the format of an IKEA Canada catalogue (see Exhibits 1 and 2 for sample pages), and the furniture being offered was similar to IKEA's knocked-down, self-assembled line in which different "elements" could be ordered by the customer to create particular designs. Bayley and Berglund wondered how serious Sears was about its new initiative, and what, if anything, IKEA should do in response.

The Canadian Furniture Market

Canadian consumption of furniture totaled more than $2 billion in 1985, an average of well over $600 per household. Imports accounted for approximately 18 percent of this total, half of which originated in the United States. The duties on furniture imported into Canada were approximately 15 percent.

Furniture was sold to Canadian consumers through three types of stores: independents, specialty chains, and department stores. Although the independents held a 70 percent market share, this figure was declining due to their inability to compete with the chains in terms of advertising, purchasing power, management sophistication, and sales support. The average sales per square metre in 1985 for furniture stores of all three types was $1,666 (the figure was $2,606 for stores which also sold appliances) and the average cost of goods sold was 64.5 percent.

While the major department stores such as Eaton's and Sears tended to carry traditional furniture lines close to the middle of the price/quality range, chains and independents operated from one end of the spectrum to the other. At the upper end of the market, specialty chains attempted to differentiate themselves by offering unique product lines, superior service, and a specialized shopping atmosphere.

This case was written by Professor Paul W. Beamish. Condensed by Peter Killing. Copyright © 1988, The University of Western Ontario.

EXHIBIT 1 Sample Page from IKEA Catalogue (1985)

GUTE 126/6

GUTE 87/8

GUTE 126/10

GUTE 87/₄

$98

GUTE 49/2

GUTE 49/6

GUTE 49/2

GUTE 126/6

$130

GUTE 87/4

GUTE. EIGHTEEN DIFFERENT CHESTS   OF DRAWERS TO FIT IN ALMOST ANYWHERE.

GUTE chests of drawers ●möbelfakta White lacquered or pine veneered particleboard, natural or nutbrown stained. W80 cm, D40 cm. QA.
49/2. 2 drawers. H49 cm. White **$94.** Natural or nutbrown **$98.**
49/6. 6 drawers. H49 cm. White **$115.** Natural or nutbrown **$125.**
87/4. 4 drawers. H87 cm. White **$130.** Natural or nutbrown **$145.**

87/8. 8 drawers. H87 cm. White **$170.** Natural or nutbrown **$185.**
126/6. 6 drawers. H126 cm. White **$175.**
Natural or nutbrown **$195.**
126/10. 10 drawers. H126 cm. White **$215.**
Natural or nutbrown **$225.**

EXHIBIT 2 **Sample Page from Sears Catalogue (1986)**

Dressers and chests whose quality and practicality are inherent— in the colors and sizes you want. Assemble them yourself with ease.

Your choice of clear knot-free pine veneer over non-warp platewood core or White baked-on European-quality low gloss enamel on a platewood core.

3 Drawer Units. 38 cm deep, 54 cm high (15 x 21¼").
Wide. 75 cm wide (29½").
012 065 012 DLT – *Pine* Each.**139.98**
012 065 002 DLT – *White* Each.**139.98**
Narrow. 50 cm wide (19½").
012 065 015 DLT – *Pine* Each.**119.98**
012 065 005 DLT – *White* Each.**119.98**

4 Drawer Units. 38 cm deep, 69 cm high (15 x 27¼").
Wide. 75 cm wide (29½").
012 065 011 DLT – *Pine* Each.**159.98**
012 065 001 DLT – *White* Each.**159.98**
Narrow. 50 cm wide (19½").
012 065 014 DLT – *Pine* Each.**139.98**
012 065 004 DLT – *White* Each.**139.98**

6 Drawer Units. 38 cm deep, 99 cm high (15 x 39")
Wide. 75 cm wide (29½").
012 065 010 DLTJ – *Pine* Each.**219.98**
012 065 000 DLTJ – *White* Each.**219.98**
Narrow. 50 cm wide (19½").
012 065 013 DLT – *Pine* Each.**189.98**
012 065 003 DLT – *White* Each.**189.98**

The lower end of the market, on the other hand, was dominated by furniture warehouses that spent heavily on advertising, and offered lower price, less service, and less emphasis on a fancy image. The warehouses usually kept a larger inventory of furniture on hand than the department stores but expected customers to pick up their purchases. Over half the warehouse sales involved promotional financing arrangements, including delayed payments, extended terms, and so on. The major firms in this group, both of whom sold furniture and appliances, were The Brick and Leon's. The Brick had annual sales of $240 million from 15 Canadian stores, and was rapidly expanding from its Western Canada base. With 30 additional stores in California under the Furnishings 2000 name, The Brick intended to become the largest furniture retailing company in the world. Leon's had annual sales of $160 million from 14 stores, and was growing rapidly from its Ontario base. These 14 stores were operated under a variety of names. Leon's also franchised its name in smaller cities in Canada. For part of their merchandise requirements, The Brick and Leon's often negotiated with manufacturers for exclusive products, styles, and fabrics and imported from the United States, Europe, and the Far East. Although both firms had had problems earlier with entry to the U.S. market, each intended on expanding there.

Most furniture retailers in Canada purchased their products from Canadian manufacturers after examining new designs and models at trade shows. There were approximately 1,400 Canadian furniture manufacturers, mostly located in Ontario and Quebec. Typically, these firms were small (78 percent of Canadian furniture plants employed less than 50 people), undercapitalized, and minimally automated. One industry executive quipped that one of the most significant technological developments for the industry had been the advent of the staple gun.

Canadian-produced furniture typically followed American and European styling. It was generally of adequate to excellent quality but was often more costly to produce. The reason for high Canadian costs was believed to be a combination of short manufacturing runs and high raw material, labour, and distribution costs. In an attempt to reduce costs, a few of the larger manufacturers such as Kroehler had vertically integrated—purchasing sawmills, fabric warehouses, fibreboard, and wood frame plants—but such practices were very much the exception in the industry.

The IKEA Formula

IKEA's approach to business was fundamentally different from that of the traditional Canadian retailers. The company focused exclusively on what it called "quick assembly" furniture, which consumers carried from the store in flat packages and assembled at home. This furniture was primarily pine, had a clean European design look to it, and was priced at 15 percent below the lowest prices for traditional furniture. Its major appeal appeared to be to young families, singles, and frequent movers, who were looking for well-designed items that were economically priced and created instant impact.

According to company executives, IKEA was successful because of its revolutionary approach to the most important aspects of the business: product design, procurement, store operations, marketing, and management philosophy, which stressed flexibility and market orientation rather than long-range strategy. Each of these items is discussed in turn.

Product Design

IKEA's European designers, not the company's suppliers, were responsible for the design of most of the furniture and accessories in IKEA's product line, which totaled 15,000 items. The heart of the company's design capability was a 50-person Swedish workshop, which produced prototypes of new items of furniture and smaller components such as "an ingenious little snap lock for table legs which makes a table stronger and cheaper at the same time" and a "clever little screw attachment which allows for the assembly of a pin back chair in five minutes." IKEA's designers were very cost conscious, and were constantly working to lower costs in ways that were not critical to the consumer. The quality of a work top, for example, would be superior to the quality of the back of a bookshelf, which would never be seen. "Low price with a meaning" was the theme.

Although it was not impossible to copyright a particular design or process, IKEA's philosophy was "if somebody steals a model from us we do not bring a lawsuit, because a lawsuit is always negative. We solve the problem by making a new model that is even better."

Procurement

IKEA's early success in Sweden had so threatened traditional European furniture retailers that they had promised to boycott any major supplier that shipped products to the upstart firm. As a result, IKEA had no choice but to go to the smaller suppliers. Since these suppliers had limited resources, IKEA began assuming responsibility for the purchase of raw materials, packaging materials, storage, specialized equipment and machinery, and engineering. What began as a necessity soon became a cornerstone of IKEA's competitive strategy, and by 1986 the firm had nearly 100 production engineers working as purchasers. Together with IKEA's designers, these engineers assisted suppliers in every way they could to help them lower costs, dealing with everything from the introduction of new technology to the alteration of the dimensions of a shipping carton.

Although IKEA sometimes leased equipment and made loans to its suppliers, the firm was adamant that it would not enter the furniture manufacturing business itself. In fact, to avoid control over (and responsibility for) its suppliers, the company had a policy of limiting its purchases to 50 percent of a supplier's capacity. Many products were obtained from multiple suppliers, and frequently suppliers produced only a single standardized component or input to the final product. Unfinished pine shelves, for example, were obtained directly from sawmills; cabinet doors were purchased from door factories; and cushions came from textile mills.

In total, IKEA purchased goods from 1,500 suppliers located in 40 countries. About 52 percent of the company's purchases were from Scandinavia, 21 percent from other countries of Western Europe, 20 percent from Eastern Europe, and 7 percent elsewhere.

Store Operations

IKEA stores were usually large one- or two-storey buildings situated in relatively inexpensive stand-alone locations, neither in prime downtown sites nor in shopping malls. Most stores were surrounded by a large parking lot, adorned with billboards explaining IKEA's delivery policy, product guarantee, and the existence of a coffee shop and/or restaurant.

On entering a store, the customer was immediately made aware of the children's play area (a room filled with hollow multicoloured balls), a video room for older children, and a receptionist with copies of IKEA catalogues, a metric conversion guide, index cards for detailing purchases, and a store guide. The latter, supplemented by prominent signs, indicated that the store contained lockers and benches for shoppers, a first aid area, restrooms, strollers and a baby care area, an "as-is" department (no returns permitted), numerous checkouts, suggestion boxes, and, in many cases, a restaurant. All major credit cards were accepted.

Traffic flow in most IKEA stores was guided so as to pass by almost all of the merchandise in the store, which was displayed as it would look in the home, complete with all accessories. Throughout a store, employees could be identified by their bright red IKEA shirts. Part-time employees wore yellow shirts which read "Temporary Help—Please Don't Ask Me Any Hard Questions." The use of sales floor staff was minimal. The IKEA view was that "salesmen are expensive, and can also be irritating. IKEA leaves you to shop in peace."

While IKEA stores were all characterized by their self-serve, self-wrapping, self-transport, and self-assembly operations, the company's philosophy was that each new store would incorporate the latest ideas in use in any of its existing stores. The most recent trend in some countries was an IKEA Contract Sales section, which provided a delivery, invoicing, and assembly service for commercial customers.

Marketing

IKEA's promotional activities were intended to educate the consumer public on the benefits of the IKEA concept and build traffic by attracting new buyers and encouraging repeat visits from existing customers. The primary promotional vehicle was the annual IKEA catalogue, which was selectively mailed out to prime target customers, which in the Toronto area, for instance, had the following characteristics:

- Income $35,000+.
- Own condominium or townhouse.
- University degree.
- White collar.
- Primary age group 35–44.
- Secondary age group 25–34.
- Husband/wife both work.
- Two children.
- Movers.

With minor variations, this "upscale" profile was typical of IKEA's target customers in Europe and North America. In Canada, IKEA management acknowledged the target market, but felt that in fact the IKEA concept appealed to a much wider group of consumers.

IKEA also spent heavily on magazine advertisements, which were noted for their humorous, slightly off-beat approach. In Canada, IKEA spent $2.5 million to print 3.6 million catalogues, $2 million on magazine advertising, and $1.5 million on other forms of promotion in 1984.

Management Philosophy

The philosophy of Ingvar Kamprad, the founder of IKEA, was "to create a better everyday life for the majority of people." In practice, this creed meant that IKEA was dedicated to offering, and continuing to offer, the lowest prices possible on good quality furniture, so that IKEA products were available to as many people as possible. Fred Andersson, the head of IKEA's corporate product-planning group stated, "Unlike other companies, we are not fascinated with what we produce—we make what our customers want." Generally, IKEA management felt that no other company could match IKEA's combination of quality and price across the full width of the product line.

IKEA also made a concerted effort to stay "close to its customers," and it was not unusual for the general manager of IKEA Canada, for instance, to personally telephone customers who had made complaints or suggestions. Each week an employee newsletter detailed all customer comments and indicated how management felt they should be dealt with.

Another guiding philosophy of the firm was that growth would be in "small bites." The growth objective in Canada, for instance, had been to increase sales and profits by 20 percent per year, but care was taken to sequence store openings so that managerial and financial resources would not be strained.

Internally, the company's philosophy was stated as "freedom, with responsibility," which meant that IKEA's managers typically operated with a good deal of autonomy. The Canadian operation, for instance, received little in the way of explicit suggestions from head office, even in the one year when the budget was not met. The Canadian management team traveled to head office as a group only once every several years. As Bjorn Bayley explained, "We are a very informal management team and try to have everyone who works for us believe that they have the freedom to do their job in the best way possible. It's almost impossible to push the philosophy down to the cashier level, but we try."

IKEA in Canada

IKEA's formula had worked well in Canada. Under the direction of a four-person management team, which included two Swedes, the company had grown from a single store in 1976 to nine stores totaling 75,000 square metres and, as shown in Exhibit 3, predicted 1986 sales of more than $140 million. The sales of IKEA Canada had exceeded budget in all but one of the past five years, and usually by a wide margin. Net profits were approximately 5 percent of sales. Profit and loss statements for 1983 and 1984, the only financial statements available, are presented in Exhibit 4.

IKEA Canada carried just less than half of the company's total product line. Individual items were chosen on the basis of what management thought would sell in Canada, and if IKEA could not beat a competitor's price by 10–15 percent on a particular item, it was dropped. Most of the goods sold in the Canadian stores were supplied from central warehouses in Sweden. To coordinate this process, a five-person stock supply department in Vancouver provided Sweden with a three-year forecast of Canada's needs, and placed major orders twice a

Exhibit 3 IKEA Canada Sales (by store, including mail order; Cdn. $000s)

	1981	1982	1983 (Actual)	1984	1985	1986 (Forecast)	Mail* Order (%)
Vancouver	$12,122	$11,824	$12,885	$19,636	$ 19,240	$25,500	6.8%
Calgary	7,379	8,550	7,420	7,848	9,220	11,500	8.6
Ottawa	5,730	6,914	8,352	9,015	10,119	12,500	1.8
Montreal			8,617	12,623	15,109	22,000†	2.2
Halifax	3,634	4,257	4,474	6,504	7,351	9,000	22.9
Toronto	11,231	13,191	16,249	18,318	22,673	30,500	1.8
Edmonton	6,506	7,474	8,075	8,743	9,986	16,000	15.4
Quebec City		5,057	8,284	9,027	10,037	12,000	6.1
Victoria					2,808	3,500	
Total	$46,602	$57,267	$74,356	$91,714	$106,543	$142,500	6.7%

NOTE: *1984 most recent data available.

†Projected growth due to store size expansion.

EXHIBIT 4 **Statement of Earnings and Retained Earnings (year ended August 31, 1984, with comparative figures for 1983)**

	1984	1983
Sales	$92,185,188	$74,185,691
Cost of merchandise sold	49,836,889	38,085,173
Gross profit	42,348,299	36,100,518
General, administrative, and selling expenses	28,016,473	23,626,727
Operating profit before the undernoted	14,331,826	12,473,791
Depreciation and amortization	1,113,879	1,066,286
Franchise amortization	257,490	257,490
Franchise fee	2,765,558	2,225,571
	4,136,927	3,549,347
Earnings from operations	10,194,899	8,924,444
Rental income	769,719	815,683
Less rental expense	245,803	258,296
	523,916	557,387
Interest expense	2,453,116	3,042,471
Less other income	438,683	65,757
	2,014,433	2,976,714
Earnings before income taxes	8,704,382	6,505,117
Income taxes		
Current	3,789,773	2,716,645
Deferred	(70,400)	175,500
	3,719,373	2,892,145
Net earnings for the year	4,985,009	3,612,972
Retained earnings, beginning of year	5,501,612	1,888,640
Retained earnings, end of year	$10,486,621	$ 5,501,612

SOURCE: Consumer and Corporate Affairs, Canada.

year. Actual volumes were expected to be within 10 percent of the forecast level. As Bayley noted, "You needed a gambler in the stock supply job."

Individual stores were expected to maintain 13.5 weeks of inventory on hand (10.5 weeks in the store and 3 weeks in transit) and could order from the central warehouse in Montreal, or, if a product was not in stock in Montreal, direct from Sweden. Shipments from Sweden took six to eight weeks to arrive, from Montreal two to three weeks. In practice, about 50 percent of the product arriving at a store arrived via each route.

IKEA's success in Canada meant that the firm was often hard pressed to keep the best-selling items in stock. (Twenty percent of the firm's present line constituted 80 percent of sales volume.) At any given time in Canada, IKEA stores might have 300 items out of stock, either because actual sales deviated significantly from forecasts or because suppliers could not meet their delivery promises. While management estimated that 75 percent of customers were willing to wait for IKEA products in a stockout situation, the company nevertheless began a deliberate policy of developing Canadian suppliers for high-demand items, even if this meant paying a slight premium. In 1984, the stock control group purchased $57 million worth of goods on IKEA's behalf, $12 million of which was from 30 Canadian suppliers, up from $7 million the previous year.

As indicated in Exhibit 3, IKEA Canada sold products, rather reluctantly, by mail order to customers who preferred not to visit the stores. A senior manager explained: "To date we have engaged in defensive mail orders—only when the customer really wants it and the order is large enough. The separate handling, breaking down of orders, and repackaging required for mail orders would be too expensive and go against the economies-through-volume approach of IKEA. Profit margins of mail order business tend to be half that of a store operation. There are more sales returns in shipping, particularly because of damages, which can reach 4 percent of shipments. It is difficult to know where to draw the market boundaries for a mail-order business. We don't want to substitute mail-order customers for store visitors."

In 1986, the management team which had brought success to IKEA's Canadian operations was breaking up. Bjorn Bayley, who had come to Canada in 1978, was slotted to move to Philadelphia to spearhead IKEA's entry into the U.S. market, which had begun in June 1985 with a single store. With early sales running at a level twice as high as the company had predicted, Bayley expected to be busy and was taking Mike McDonald, the controller, and Mike McMullen, the personnel director, with him. Anders Berglund, who, like Bayley, was a long-time IKEA employee and had been in Canada since 1979, was scheduled to take over the Canadian operation. Berglund would report through Bayley to IKEA's North American sales director, who was located in Europe.

New Competition

IKEA's success in Canada had not gone unnoticed. IDOMO was a well-established Toronto-based competitor, and Sears Canada was a new entrant.

IDOMO.   Like IKEA, IDOMO sold knocked-down furniture that customers were required to assemble at home. IDOMO offered a somewhat narrower selection than IKEA but emphasized teak furniture to a much greater extent. With stores in Hamilton, Mississauga (across from IKEA), Toronto, and Montreal, IDOMO appeared to have capitalized on excess demand that IKEA had developed but was not able to service.

The products and prices offered in both the 96-page IDOMO and 144-page IKEA catalogues were similar, with IKEA's prices slightly lower. Prices in the IKEA catalogue were in effect for a year. IDOMO reserved the right to make adjustments to prices and specifications. A mail-order telephone number in

Toronto was provided in the IDOMO catalogue. Of late, IDOMO had begun to employ an increased amount of television advertising. IDOMO purchased goods from around the world and operated a number of their own Canadian factories. Their primary source of goods was Denmark.

Sears.   The newest entrant in the Canadian knocked-down furniture segment was Sears Canada, a wholly owned subsidiary of Sears Roebuck of Chicago and, with $3.8 billion in annual revenues, one of Canada's largest merchandising operations. Sears operated 75 department stores in Canada, selling a wide range (700 merchandise lines comprising 100,000 stock-keeping units) of medium-price and quality goods. Sears Canada also ran a major catalogue operation, which distributed 12 annual catalogues to approximately 4 million Canadian families. Customers could place catalogue orders by mail, by telephone, or in person through one of the company's 1,500 catalogue sales units, which were spread throughout the country.

A quick check by Bayley and Berglund revealed that Sears' Elements line was being sold only in Canada and only through the major Sears catalogues. Elements products were not for sale, nor could they be viewed, in Sears stores. In the Fall-Winter catalogue that they examined, which was over 700 pages in length, the Elements line was given 20 pages. Although Sears appeared to offer the same "type" of products as IKEA, there was a narrower selection within each category. Prices for Elements' products seemed almost identical to IKEA prices. One distinct difference between the catalogues was the much greater emphasis IKEA placed on presenting a large number of coordinated settings and room designs.

At least some of the suppliers of the Elements line were Swedish, although it did not appear that IKEA and Sears had any suppliers in common. The IKEA executives knew that Sears was generally able to exert a great deal of influence over its suppliers, usually obtaining prices at least equal to and often below those of its competitors, because of the huge volumes purchased. Sears also worked closely with its suppliers in marketing, research, design and development, production standards, and production planning. Unlike IKEA, Sears tended to purchase completed units. Many lines of merchandise were manufactured with features exclusive to Sears and were sold under its private brand names. There was a 75 percent buying overlap for the catalogue and store and about a 90 percent overlap between regions on store purchases.

Like any Sears' product, Elements furniture could be charged to a Sears charge card. Delivery of catalogue items generally took about two weeks, and for a small extra charge catalogue orders would be delivered right to the consumer's home in a Sears truck. If a catalogue item was out of stock, Sears policy was either to tell the customer if and when the product would be available, or to substitute an item of equal or greater value. If goods proved defective (10% of Sears Roebuck mail-order furniture purchasers had received damaged or broken furniture), Sears provided home pick-up and replacement and was willing, for a fee, to install goods, provide parts, and do repairs as products aged. Sears emphasized that it serviced what it sold, and guaranteed everything that it sold—"satisfaction guaranteed or money refunded." In its advertising, which included all forms of media, Sears stressed its "hassle-free returns" and asked customers to "take a look at the services we offer . . . they'll bring you peace of mind, long after the bill is paid."

In their assessment of Sears Canada, Bayley and Berglund recognized that the company seemed to be going through something of a revival. Using the rallying cry that a "new" Sears was being created, Sears executives (the Canadian firm had 10 vice presidents) had experimented with new store layouts, pruned the product line, and improved customer service for catalogue orders. Richard Sharpe, the chairman of Sears Canada, personally addressed as many as 12,000 employees per year, and the company received 3,000 suggestions from employees annually. Perhaps as a result of these initiatives, and a cut in work force from 65,000 to 50,000 over a several-year period, Sears Canada posted its best-ever results in 1985.

Conclusion

With the limited data they had on Sears, IKEA management recognized their comparison of the two companies would be incomplete. Nonetheless, a decision regarding the Sears competitive threat was required. Any solution would have to reflect Kamprad's philosophy: "Expensive solutions to problems are often signs of mediocrity. We have no interest in a solution until we know what it costs."

CASE 18
INDUSTRIAL EQUIPMENT, INC.

It was a beautiful June evening in 1990, but Jim Costello, president and founder of Industrial Equipment, Inc. of Saint John, New Brunswick, was not able to enjoy it. He was still in his office after another hectic day; supper would have to wait. Jim was considering whether he should try again to buy one of his competitors, Hines Equipment Limited, located in Prince Edward Island. Jim had been in this situation three times before, almost closing deals with Ron Hines; but at the last minute Ron always backed out. This had caused ill will between the two and a rift in the family, as Ron Hines was Jim's father-in-law.

Company Background

Jim Costello established Industrial Equipment, Inc. in 1986 after several unsuccessful attempts to acquire his father-in-law's business. Industrial Equipment sold and serviced a variety of industrial equipment and related products to hospitals, nursing homes, hotels, motels, and various other organizations in the four Atlantic Canadian provinces of New Brunswick, Nova Scotia, Prince Edward Island, and Newfoundland/Labrador.

Products, Services, and Markets

In addition to distributing a broad line of specialized industrial equipment and related products in Atlantic Canada, Industrial Equipment provided design, specification, and planning assistance to architects, builders, and owners designing new facilities or renovating existing operations. Industrial Equipment also installed the equipment it sold. The firm maintained an extensive parts inventory and provided a complete repair and maintenance service for its customers.

Industrial Equipment did not have its own service department; instead it subcontracted the bulk of its repairs, maintenance, and installations throughout Atlantic Canada to Metro Service, a Saint John firm. Occasionally, Industrial Equipment used other, local service firms. This arrangement had permitted Industrial Equipment to grow and offer service to its geographically dispersed customers, something not all of its competitors did, without the expense of a service department. But it was not completely satisfactory. Jim had less control over the service function than he would have liked; especially as he considered

This case was prepared by Robert G. Blunden of Dalhousie University as a basis for classroom discussion, and is not meant to illustrate either effective or ineffective management. Some elements of this case have been disguised. Copyright © 1992 by the Atlantic Entrepreneurial Institute, an Atlantic Canada Opportunities Agency funded organization. Used with permission.

superior service to be one of the keys to long-run success. And while customers called Industrial Equipment for service, when the serviceperson arrived, he was from another firm. Jim knew that Brian Hudson, the owner and commercial service technician of Metro Service, had been soliciting several of Industrial Equipment's customers directly to save the 20 percent discount he offered Industrial Equipment.

Exhibit 1 Industrial Equipment, Inc. Income Statements

	1987	1988	1989	1990
Sales				
Equipment	$261,820	$583,924	$408,619	$ 916,723
Parts	41,341	184,748	119,155	187,199
Service	7,783	64,319	36,434	21,472
Other income	4,772	22,317	13,410	15,562
Total sales	$315,716	$855,308	$577,618	$1,140,956
Cost of sales				
Equipment	186,034	433,482	290,535	714,950*
Parts	28,360	99,538	77,692	109,179
Service	10,687	37,234	30,165	30,099
Total cost of sales	225,081	570,254	398,392	854,228
Gross profit	90,635	285,054	179,226	286,728
Expenses				
Wages	$ 11,237	$ 87,505	$ 60,272	$ 98,213
Management bonus	0	25,000	15,000	23,953
Advertising	8,219	9,892	12,906	8,139
Travel	10,496	5,068	7,159	9,548
Auto expense	5,595	5,162	11,114	24,678
Telephone	6,928	9,782	15,529	17,679
Rent			8,000	9,600
Office supplies	5,877	9,185	7,633	8,233
Insurance	1,045	3,375	3,138	3,218
Interest and bank charges	6,798	16,593	6,998	23,406
Professional fees	2,166	284	1,810	2,809
Install supply	1,299	1,391	4,008	2,411
Depreciation	630	1,967	4,841	9,015
Miscellaneous	2,466	2,754	6,482	9,401
Total expenses	62,756	177,958	164,890	250,303
NIBT	27,879	107,096	14,336	36,425
Income tax	4,181	29,105	3,437	8,433
Net income	$ 23,698	$ 77,991	$ 10,899	$ 27,992

NOTES: Industrial Equipment's fiscal year-end was April 30.
    *Includes about $36,800 of installation expenses.
SOURCE: Audited financial statements.

EXHIBIT 2

INDUSTRIAL EQUIPMENT, INC.
Balance Sheet
April 30, 1990.

Assets

Current Assets		*1990*
Accounts receivable		$116,775
Inventory		129,757
Prepaid expenses		582
Current portion of net investment in lease		19,741
Total current assets		266,855
Fixed assets		40,585
Other assets		
Net investment in lease		64,601
Total assets		$372,041

Liabilities

Current liabilities		
Bank overdraft	58,050	
Accounts payable and accrued liabilities	80,091	
Accrued bonus payable	10,000	
Income tax payable	8,433	
Due to directors	3,538	
Current portion of long-term debt	39,581	
Total current liabilities		199,693
Long-term debt		35,833
Total liabilities		235,526

Shareholders' Equity

Common stock		
Authorized 1,000,000 common shares, no par value		
issued 1 common share	1	
Retained earnings	136,514	
Total shareholders' equity		136,515
Total liabilities and equity		$372,041

SOURCE: Audited financial statements.

Operations

Since its inception in 1987, Industrial Equipment had experienced significant growth in sales and profits (See Exhibits 1 and 2 for the firm's financial statements). Jim expected the growth trend would continue.

This had been accomplished by Jim Costello and a staff of three: an assistant, a secretary, and a combination partsman/dispatcher. Jim was responsible for the day-to-day management of the firm, its long-term direction, and equipment sales. Selling activities required that he spend about half of his time traveling Atlantic Canada. Jim's assistant, his wife Laura, helped him with special projects and handled equipment sales in his absence. Angela Stanbury, the secretary, performed all of the usual reception and secretarial tasks and maintained the accounting records. Ralph Stock coordinated parts and service. He ordered parts, handled parts sales, dispatched service technicians, and maintained the parts inventory.

The organization was small and close-knit; the work atmosphere was friendly and upbeat. They functioned well as a team. Everyone knew much of each other's jobs, and they readily helped each other as necessary. Jim felt the team was a crucial component in Industrial Equipment's success and had recently instituted a bonus plan to help make each team member feel a part of the business and its success.

Strategy

Jim's strategy was to sell quality industrial products at competitive prices and to back those products with prompt, effective service in Atlantic Canada. He saw service as a key strategic variable that differentiated Industrial Equipment from its competitors. Industrial Equipment was the only firm in the region that offered a facility design service. Industrial Equipment and Hines were the only equipment distributors that focused on after sales service as well as equipment sales.

He wanted to see the business grow through expanded operations and selective acquisitions. The desire for growth and concern over his lack of an in-house service operation had led Jim to propose the merger of Industrial Equipment and Metro Service. Jim suspected that Industrial Equipment represented about one-third of Metro's business and that the proportion was growing as Industrial Equipment grew. He also thought that there were significant opportunities to improve the combined operations. Overhead could be reduced as Industrial Equipment could easily absorb Metro's accounting, billing, and dispatching functions, which would eliminate one position in the process. Jim also felt management could be improved at Metro Service. While Brian Hudson, Metro's owner, was an excellent technical person, Jim thought he was a poor manager.

Jim had proposed a deal that he thought offered Brian more personal income for less effort and fewer problems; but Brian did not want to sell. He valued his independence too much. However, to increase the cooperation between the firms and improve customer service, Brian moved Metro Service into the same building as Industrial Equipment, and Jim stocked Brian's service truck with parts at Industrial Equipment's expense.

Jim Costello

Jim had grown up in a family business, owned and operated by his father. Like all the children in the family, Jim began working for the company at an early age. He started doing odd jobs evenings and weekends during high school, and he worked full-time during the summers. After graduating from high school, he pursued a university degree in business but quit in his third year. That night his father offered him a job, and while Jim was proud, he was not too proud to take the job.

Jim's journey into sales was accidental. He was responsible for assembling a display for his father's exhibit at an annual trade show. The company was short staffed, and he was knowledgeable about the products, so he stayed to work in the booth. By the end of the show, he had closed three large deals and decided he enjoyed sales. Soon after, he became a sales representative for the firm.

Jim developed his natural selling ability and eventually left to manage a land development company for the father of his fiancée, Laura Hines. However, the local housing market turned sour, and they closed the business. Still, Ron Hines recognised Jim's sales ability and offered him the position of sales manager at Hines Equipment. Jim moved to Charlottetown, Prince Edward Island, to work for Hines Equipment in May 1981. Shortly after, Jim and Laura were married.

In the years that followed, Jim learned the industrial equipment business and was so successful that by 1985, his sales accounted for over 80 percent of the company's total revenues. His territory was New Brunswick and Newfoundland, but he also assisted part-time representatives in Nova Scotia.

In January 1983, after a serious disagreement with Ron Hines, Jim moved back to Saint John and opened a branch sales office for Hines Equipment at his own expense, working for straight commission. He continued to improve the company's business position by expanding the product line with 25 related products. During the first year of business in Saint John, sales were $240,000; by 1985, sales exceeded $900,000.

The Industry

Market Size, Growth, and Trends

Few hard data were available on industry sales because most distributors were privately held and guarded their performance results carefully. Similarly, most industrial equipment manufacturers were either privately held or were divisions of large diversified firms who did not provide segmented performance results in sufficient detail to determine their sales in the product categories in which Industrial Equipment was active. The matter was further confused by the wide range of industrial equipment, the limited lines distributed by any one firm, and the overlap of lines that existed between firms.

Historically the bulk of Industrial Equipment's sales had been made to hospitals, nursing homes, and hotels, and Jim had collected some data on the approximate sizes of those market segments in Atlantic Canada (see Exhibit 3).

Industry watchers forecast slow overall industry growth roughly in step with population growth trends. Other industry trends included increasingly stream-lined and specialized operations utilizing more equipment and automation to substitute for hard-to-find, expensive labour. Noise reduction and energy conservation were becoming increasingly important equipment issues as well.

EXHIBIT 3 **Beds in Atlantic Canada**

	Hospitals	Nursing Homes	Hotels Motels
Newfoundland	4,115	2,569	4,617
New Brunswick	5,481	4,218	9,010
Nova Scotia	5,899	2,760	9,441
Prince Edward Island	1,037	538	2,988

SOURCE: *Canadian Hospital Directory 1989–90; Directory of Long-Term Care Centres in Canada 1990–91* and 1991 provincial travel guides.

Competition

Industrial Equipment had four main competitors and several smaller competitors in Atlantic Canada. The main competitors were Hines Equipment in Charlottetown, Prince Edward Island; Sam Reid in St. John's, Newfoundland; Québec Équipment Ltée. based in Montreal, Quebec; and Equipment Distributors in Halifax, Nova Scotia.

Hines Equipment was the business owned by Jim's father-in-law, Ron Hines, that Jim was interested in acquiring. It was established in 1961, with its head office in Charlottetown, Prince Edward Island. Hines distributed industrial equipment in the four Atlantic provinces, primarily to hospitals, nursing homes, institutions, and hotels/motels. In many ways, Hines was Industrial Equipment's most direct competitor. Hines and Industrial Equipment both represented the leading industrial equipment manufacturer; they both covered Atlantic Canada, and they both viewed service as a key aspect of their business.

Sam Reid, formerly a sales representative for Hines Equipment, was currently working for himself in Newfoundland. He sold supplies and represented several equipment manufacturers in Newfoundland. Jim thought that Sam had developed a substantial market share in Newfoundland, and he had considered proposing some form of business arrangement to him, but he was uncertain as to whether or not he could work with him.

Québec Équipment, in Montréal, Quebec, sold many of the same lines as Industrial Equipment and Hines Equipment and would occasionally price large orders very aggressively. They could do this in part because they had no local presence or costs and seemed to view Atlantic Canada as incremental business. In addition, Québec Équipment had a broader product line than the Atlantic-based firms. For example, Jim thought they had 60–70 percent of the related industrial equipment market in the food service sector, the next market Jim hoped to penetrate.

Equipment Distributors, a Nova Scotian firm located in Halifax, dominated the lower end of Atlantic Canada's industrial equipment business. Jim felt that much of their success came from the principal product line they represented, which was highly demanded by smaller, cost-conscious customers. This producer only made smaller equipment, but Equipment Distributors also handled some commercial lines, including one represented by Québec Équipement. Jim believed that Equipment Distributors might lose that line because Québec Équipement was pressuring the manufacturer to have only one distributor, and Equipment Distributors was not selling their product line as aggressively as Québec Équipement.

Other competition which Industrial Equipment faced came from two sources. About five smaller distributors in the region offered occasional competition, usually only on certain product categories. Another more serious source of competition came from the centralized purchasing departments of larger hotel chains. They often had direct purchasing arrangements with manufacturers through their U.S. operations. Industrial Equipment had very little control over the purchasing decision in these cases.

The Opportunity

Hines Equipment

Hines Equipment was established in Charlottetown, Prince Edward Island, in 1961 by Ron Hines to distribute industrial and commercial equipment throughout Atlantic Canada. Over the years, the sales level and the sales mix had varied significantly, depending upon the focus and resources of the firm. Ron Hines's primary interest had always been in developing the parts sales and service aspects of the firm, because they had inherently more attractive margins, less competition, and addressed an existing market. Whatever equipment sales he could capture were welcome additional revenue as long as the margins were healthy. However, between 1982 and 1986, Jim expanded the firm's equipment sales dramatically with more aggressive sales efforts and prices. After Jim left Hines Equipment in 1986, equipment sales declined while parts and service revenues regained dominance.

Ron's emphasis on parts and service and Jim's focus on equipment sales were formalized over time as they sorted out the distribution rights to Abbott Equipment, their anchor line of industrial equipment. As soon as Jim had established Industrial Equipment in 1986, he approached Abbott for the rights to distribute their products in Atlantic Canada, the rights that Hines Equipment had had for almost 30 years. Abbott, another family business, did not want to lose Jim's aggressive sales efforts, nor did they want him selling competitors' products, so they made an exception to their standard policy of one distributor to a region. In this case, Hines Equipment and Industrial Equipment would share the region. Jim focused on equipment sales, and Industrial Equipment's equipment sales increased at Hines' expense. In 1988, Ron came to Jim with a deal: Since Ron did not want to compete directly with Jim, Ron suggested that Hines Equipment handle Abbott parts sales and Jim sell Abbott equipment. Jim agreed, and they formalized an arrangement whereby Industrial Equipment bought its parts from Hines while Hines bought its equipment from Industrial Equipment.

Financial data for Hines Equipment (1987-89) are presented in Exhibits 4 and 5.

In 1990, Hines Equipment had five employees. Ron Hines was the company's president, general manager, and sales force. His wife, Lois, was secretary-

EXHIBIT 4 Hines Equipment Income Statements 1987–89

	1987	*1988*	*1989*
Sales	$706,235	$788,163	$481,436
Cost of sales			
Beginning inventory	164,944	164,925	166,255
Purchases and freight	399,667	457,280	205,365
	564,611	622,205	371,620
Ending inventory	164,925	166,255	189,551
	399,686	455,950	182,069
	306,549	332,213	299,367
Expenses			
Wages and commissions	129,796	128,017	139,808
Travel and selling	32,643	30,069	20,491
Advertising and promotion	11,033	8,669	7,146
Telephone	8,898	12,711	14,412
Interest and bank charges	28,446	32,252	37,615
Legal and audit	10,201	7,684	8,079
Installation	—	4,268	—
Office supplies	5,778	6,117	3,300
Rent	15,590	15,258	15,600
Insurance	5,579	8,179	6,220
Civic taxes	1,323	1,104	903
Depreciation	14,836	15,909	13,678
Miscellaneous	3,279	1,416	664
Heat and light	2,334	1,902	712
	269,736	273,555	268,628
Income before below noted	36,813	58,658	30,739
Other income	7,550	11,635	9,942
Income before income taxes	44,363	70,293	40,681
Income taxes	11,887	17,386	9,558
Net income	32,476	52,907	31,123
Retained earnings (beginning)	112,363	124,374	157,219
	144,839	177,281	188,342
Dividends	20,465	20,062	19,513
Retained earnings (ending)	$124,374	$157,219	$168,829

NOTE: Hines Equipment's fiscal year end is August 31.
SOURCE: Audited financial statements

Exhibit 5   Hines Equipment Balance Sheet 1989

		August 31, 1989
Assets		
Current assets		
Cash		$ 50
Accounts receivable		53,584
Inventory		189,551
Work in progress		37,217
Prepaid expenses		2,984
Total assets		283,386
Property and equipment		
Property and equipment	113,169	
Accumulated depreciation	81,086	
Total fixed assets		32,083
Investments		5,010
Receivable from affiliated companies		58,096
Total assets		$378,575
Liabilities		
Current liabilities		
Bank indebtedness		$162,906
Accounts payable and accrued liabilities		16,828
Income taxes payable		9,558
Deferred revenue		—
Principal due within one year on long-term debt		9,600
Total current liabilities		198,892
Long-term debt		10,754
Total liabilities		209,646
Shareholders' equity		
Capital stock		
Authorized		
5,000 Common shares, par value $1 each		
Issued		
100 Shares	100	
Retained earnings	168,829	
Total shareholders' equity		168,929
Total liabilities and equity		$378,575

Source: Audited financial statements.

treasurer to the firm and maintained the business records. Jane Wilson was the secretary and receptionist. Carl Lamont and Frank MacIssac were service technicians and parts salesmen. Normally, one of them was on the road handling service calls while the other staffed the parts desk at the office. This was advantageous to the firm because it meant that most parts orders were handled by a trained service technician who could help the customer over the telephone and yet, when necessary, both men could handle service calls. To ensure that flexibility, both Carl and Frank had fully equipped service vans.

Past Attempts to Buy the Business

Jim had tried to purchase his father-in-law's business several times before. While it had been Ron Hines that initiated the idea of Jim and Laura buying the business, some impediment always prevented the final execution of the sale. Perhaps Ron Hines just could not bring himself to sell the organization he had built.

The first time Jim tried to purchase Hines Equipment was in 1982. At the time, Jim was earning substantial commissions on his growing sales, but he kept them in the business, taking only a regular monthly salary. Nevertheless, Jim did not have enough money to purchase the business outright, so he suggested a payment plan over time. Ron rejected Jim's offer.

In 1984, Jim made a second attempt to purchase Hines Equipment as his relationship with Ron had deteriorated. Unable to finance the purchase himself, Jim approached Québec Équipment, a Montreal-based competitor, and negotiated a deal which would see Québec Équipment provide financing in exchange for 45 percent ownership of the company. Jim would hold 55 percent of the firm and become president. In addition to making it possible for Jim to acquire Hines Equipment, the joint venture had two other advantages. Involving Québec Équipment would reduce competition in Atlantic Canada and Québec Équipment's extensive experience in food service equipment could be transferred to Hines. Before long, Ron was dealing directly with Québec Équipment in an effort to sell them the business. The deal fell through eventually, and Jim realised it was time to leave the company.

In 1983, Jim and Laura decided to move back to Saint John, Jim's home town, but the day before they were to move, Ron asked Jim to stay with Hines Equipment. Jim, willing to give it one more try for the sake of family relations, said that he would stay with Hines Equipment but only under very different terms. The two agreed that Jim would operate a Saint John office, earning a straight commission of 10 percent on his sales and pay all of his own expenses. Jim liked this arrangement because it put some distance between the two men and it also allowed Jim to stay in the industrial equipment industry. This arrangement worked so well that by 1986, Hines Equipment owed Jim $60,000 in commissions as Jim had continued his practice of withdrawing from earnings only what he needed for current expenses.

A third purchase agreement was initiated in 1986, but this time things appeared to be much more serious. Ron wanted $200,000 in cash for the shares of the company with no payment terms. It took Jim eight months, but he eventually arranged complete financing, and an agreement of sale was signed by both parties. But this agreement too was destined to fail. Ron had recently disposed of a company vehicle and at the legal closing of the sale, Jim's lawyer made an adjustment to the agreed-upon purchase price to reflect the vehicle sale since the purchase agreement indicated that there were to be no changes in the assets of the company. This upset Ron, and he left without completing the sale. In desperation, Jim reminded Ron that if he did not return to negotiate, he would have to release all of the commissions Hines Equipment owed him. If he did not pay, Jim said he would take legal action.

Eventually, Jim sued Hines Equipment for $120,000, which represented commissions, lost revenues, and professional fees incurred. Jim won the suit and was awarded $110,000, to be paid in monthly installments over two years. After the court case, Jim offered to settle the matter for an immediate lump-sum payment of $90,000 to put the whole matter behind them. Ron accepted.

Soon after, in 1986, Jim made yet another offer to buy Hines Equipment, this time advising Ron that if he were not able to buy the business, he would start a rival firm. Ron refused to sell and Jim opened Industrial Equipment, Inc.

A Time for Decision

Now Jim was facing a similar situation once again. Ron had approached Jim to buy his business. This time, Jim thought, the deal might just go through. Ron was 63 and ready to retire. Things were different, too, in that Jim's company had taken away much of Hines's business. Hines's 1989 sales had fallen to about $481,000 and 1990 performance appeared to be shaping up similarly; total sales for the first two quarters were about $223,000.

A familiar situation and a familiar question. Jim was not sure how to handle either. Should he ignore the possibility of adding to Industrial Equipment with the acquisition of Hines Equipment, or should he try yet again to strengthen his own company while risking another family quarrel?

CASE 19
JOHNSON & BURGESS LIMITED
(CONDENSED)

On November 4, 1985, Peter Johnson, president of Johnson & Burgess Ltd. (J & B), one of Canada's fastest-growing advertising agencies, faced a complex and potentially explosive situation. Jack Kelly, CEO of the Regal Tobacco Company, a large Canadian cigarette manufacturer, had personally contacted Johnson to request that J & B make a speculative bid for a $5 million piece of Regal's $12 million account.

Since Kelly was a long-time friend, Johnson had been able to probe the reasons for moving the account from the incumbent agency. He concluded that it had gone stale creatively and was experiencing internal problems arising from weak leadership and excessive turnover of account executives.

Over lunch and in a confirming letter, Kelly had stated that his top marketing people were very much sold on J & B because they were aware of the agency's outstanding work and reputation. He had strongly implied that the switch to J & B would be simply a formality if they really wanted the business and the presentation for the Regal marketing management group went as expected. Kelly asked for an answer in three days.

Johnson could not help but be conscious of the irony of his situation. Two weeks previously, he had received an application for employment from a recently graduated MBA, who had asked in her covering letter if J & B handled a cigarette account. He remembered dictating in his reply that J & B did not. Now he was coming to grips with a decision that might change that.

His decision was not as straightforward as it once might have been but was complicated by other recent experiences. In September, while undergoing a routine medical checkup, he and his doctor happened to discuss smoking. In the conversation, his doctor had pointedly mentioned cigarette advertising: "The sooner the government stops these companies from advertising, the better off we'll all be." Johnson would normally have countered with a defensive retort and put the matter out of his mind, but because the doctor was a personal friend and a smoker as well, the statement stuck with him for several days.

Another circumstance disturbed Johnson even more. In mid-October, he learned that a close friend who had been a heavy smoker was dying of lung cancer. In many ways, he was surprising himself with his quandary. "Last year," he thought, "I would have jumped at the chance to take this business. I better put these second thoughts out of my mind and get with it. I'm running an ad agency, not a charitable society." Moreover, he could easily predict what his

This case was prepared by Professor Donald H. Thain with the assistance of Joseph C. Shlesinger.

older partner, Tony Burgess, would say: "Cigarette smoking is legal. It brings people pleasure. Nobody's forcing them to smoke. Therefore, I don't give a damn what effect smoking has on health. If we can make a buck advertising cigarettes, let's go for it!"

He knew that there were mixed feelings about smoking within the agency. It was made a nonsmoking office[1] just six months after a sometimes bitter struggle during which two key creative people threatened to quit. He knew that some of his staff would not really care about the issue, but many, if not most, would. And he also knew that it was his job to think of the agency's future and balance the rights of all his employees to have their personal values respected in such an important decision.

The Advertising Agency Business in Canada

The Canadian advertising scene was characterized by corporate, customer, and geographic concentration. There were about 400 agencies in Canada in 1985. The vast majority were located in Toronto, although Montreal and, more recently, Vancouver were also major centres. Of those 400 agencies, 20 accounted for 48 percent of total industry billings of $2 billion. Moreover, the top 10 advertisers (see Exhibit 1) accounted for nearly one-fifth of industry revenues.

The business was changing. There was a growing tendency for multinational companies to advertise with multinational agencies based in the United States. This was distressing for independent Canadian agencies that were in jeopardy

EXHIBIT 1 Top 10 National Advertisers, 1984

Rank	Company (head office)	Advertising Spending ($millions)
1	Government of Canada (Ottawa)	$ 95.8
2	Procter & Gamble (Toronto)	46.3
3	John Labatt Ltd. (London)	37.6
4	The Molson Companies (Montreal)	35.3
5	Kraft Ltd. (Montreal)	32.5
6	Government of Ontario (Toronto)	32.1
7	Rothmans of Pall Mall Canada (Toronto)	31.0
8	General Motors of Canada (Oshawa)	30.0
9	Nabisco Brands Ltd. (Toronto)	24.5
10	General Foods Inc. (Toronto)	22.9
	Total	$388.0

SOURCE: *Marketing*, May 13, 1985, p. 1.

---

[1]Smoking was prohibited in public areas as a result of a decision voted by employees encouraged by a federal government Department of Health and Welfare–sponsored antismoking program.

of losing U.S. subsidiary accounts as a result of head office decisions beyond their control. At the same time, their opportunity to land such accounts was diminishing. For example, Colgate Toothpaste had just made the decision to advertise in 45 countries with Young and Rubicam of New York, one of the largest worldwide agencies. There was no way an independent Canadian agency could get that type of account.

Competition was stiff in the advertising agency business. As account turnover was a never-ending concern of management, aggressive new-business solicitation was a basic activity in all well-run agencies. New-account selling began with finding potential prospects who could be encouraged to switch agencies. The process developed through building relationships, communicating the competence and value added by the agency, and convincing the marketing people of the potential new client that they should replace the incumbent agency. When this process reached the point of a formal review and appraisal by the client, efforts often reached a fever pitch culminating in a formal presentation selling the agency, its client service team, marketing expertise, advertising ideas, and creativity. While elaborate and costly speculative presentations were frowned upon by the advertising agency association, the final pitch for a major account was usually an elaborate, all-out affair with suggested marketing plans, sample advertisements, and whatever else was thought to be necessary to convince the potential client.

Eroding margins presented another problem. As competition increased, pressures mounted to provide for clients at lower costs more comprehensive services, including marketing planning, marketing and advertising research, sales promotion, and public relations. Although most agencies made a conscious effort to keep salaries below 56 percent of total revenue (see Exhibit 2), agency cost structures generally showed wages at 59 percent of revenue.

Exhibit 2 Agency Cost Structure Target

Revenue (15% commission and fees)			100%
Expenses			
Payroll			
Management	9%		
Client contact	16		
Creative	10		
Other services	20		
Total		55%	
Travel and entertainment		5	
Office facilities		10	
General office expenses		10	
Total expenses			80%
Net profit before tax			20
			100%

SOURCE: Casewriter's estimate.

Although agencies aimed for a 20 percent pre-tax profit, most were closer to 15 percent. Those that got close to 20 percent were generally the smaller agencies. Larger agencies typically had larger clients who were more sophisticated, more bureaucratic, and more demanding. With smaller accounts, it was usually easier and less expensive for the agency to service client needs and get approval of a given ad campaign.

Smoking in Canada

In 1985, 33 percent of Canadians regularly smoked cigarettes, down from 50 percent in 1965. The smoking rate was highest among teenage girls. Industry research indicated that cigarette smoking rates were relatively higher among the following market segments: marital status—separated or divorced; income—low; occupation—blue collar; sex—female; and age—younger and older. One result of the declining market was that manufacturers were, for the first time, initiating and pursuing aggressive price competition. The 8 percent sales decline in 1985 led to major promotional campaigns, with producers sometimes selling products at or below cost. Another outcome was that tobacco growers were being hit hard by falling sales and prices. In 1985, the Canadian federal government allocated $90 million for financial help for tobacco growers to inventory their crop until prices rebounded.

Tobacco industry sales were around $3 billion in 1984, and it was estimated that nearly $6 billion was spent on smoking-related health care. Cigarettes were blamed for 30,000 deaths a year in Canada. In fact, more Canadians died from smoking every 18 months than died in World War II.[2]

Criticism of smoking by the medical profession began in earnest with the 1964 report of the U.S. Surgeon General's Advisory Committee on smoking and health which argued that smoking was a major cause of lung cancer and several other diseases. Recently, *The New York Journal of Medicine* (July 1985) had published a 200-page report stating that the tremendous marketing efforts by cigarette manufacturers to create a strong, favourable image (by sponsoring sporting events and art shows) dwarfed attempts made to combat smoking. It included a report showing that the industry was attracting females by advertising in women's magazines and sponsoring women's tennis tournaments at which samples were often distributed. Other research indicated that smoking posed special health risks for women in their childbearing years, and that babies of women who smoke while pregnant are also affected. For example, babies born to smokers run an increased risk of respiratory problems.[3]

The Canadian Council on Smoking and Health and the Non-Smokers Rights Association had lobbied against tobacco for several years. However, the closest

---

[2] *The London Free Press, Encounter,* May 6, 1985, p. 6.
[3] *Newsweek,* November 25, 1985, pp. 76–77.

the federal government had come to regulating tobacco was in 1969 when a parliamentary committee recommended the elimination of all cigarette advertising. In response to this threat, tobacco manufacturers voluntarily withdrew all television and radio ads.

The only restriction on tobacco marketing was a voluntary code (see Exhibit 3) administered by the Canadian Tobacco Manufacturers Council. Except for political pressure through the Minister of Health and Welfare, the public had no say in the development, enforcement, or interpretation of the code.

EXHIBIT 3 Cigarette and Cigarette Tobacco Advertising and Promotion Code of the Canadian Tobacco Manufacturers' Council

Rule 1. There will be no cigarette or cigarette tobacco advertising on radio or television, nor will such media be used for the promotion or sponsorships of sports or other popular events whether through the use of brand or corporate name or logo.

Rule 2. The industry will limit total cigarette and cigarette tobacco advertising, promotion, and sponsorship expenditures for any year to 1971 levels. The limits will be revised annually to compensate for cost increases or declines.

Rule 3. Advertising of sponsored events associated with a brand or corporate name or logo will be limited to nonbroadcast media and such advertising together with promotional material will not include package identification, product selling line, or slogan, or the words "cigarette" or "tobacco."

Rule 4. No cigarette or cigarette tobacco brand shall be promoted by incentive programs offering to the consumer cash or other prizes. Coupons redeemable for gifts and related gift catalogues will not be advertised.

Rule 5. Direct mail advertising will not be used as a medium to promote the sale of cigarettes or cigarette tobacco.

Rule 6. All advertising will be in conformity with the Canadian Code of Advertising standards as issued in 1967 by the Canadian Advertising Advisory Board.

Rule 7. Cigarette or cigarette tobacco advertising will be addressed to adults 18 years of age or over and will be directed solely to the increase of cigarette brand shares.

Rule 8. No advertising will state or imply that smoking the brand advertised promotes physical health or that smoking a particular brand is better for health than smoking any other brand of cigarettes, or is essential to romance, prominence, success, or personal advancement.

Rule 9. No advertising will use, as endorsers, athletes or celebrities in the entertainment world.

Rule 10. All models used in cigarette and cigarette tobacco advertising will be at least 25 years of age.

Rule 11. No cigarette or cigarette tobacco product will be advertised on posters or bulletin boards located in the immediate vicinity of primary or secondary schools.

Rule 12. All cigarette packages, cigarette tobacco packages, and containers will bear, clearly and prominently displayed on one side thereof, the following words:

"WARNING: Health and Welfare Canada advises that danger to health increases with amount smoked—avoid inhaling.

AVIS: Santè et Bien-être social Canada considère que le danger pour la santé croit avec l'usage—èviter d'inhaler."

(continued)

EXHIBIT 3 *(concluded)*

Rule 13. The foregoing words will also be used in cigarette and cigarette tobacco print advertising. Furthermore, it will be prominently displayed on all transit advertising (interior and exterior), airport signs, subway advertising and marketplace advertising (interior and exterior) and point-of-sale material over 144 square inches in size but only in the language of the advertising message.

Rule 14. Average tar and nicotine content of cigarette smoke from any brand of cigarettes will not exceed, within normal tolerances, 22 milligrams of tar, moisture-free weight, and 1.6 milligrams of nicotine per cigarette.

Rule 15. The average tar and nicotine content of smoke per cigarette will be shown on all cigarette packages and in print media advertising.

Rule 16. Labels carrying the warning noted in Rule 12 are available through the Council to operators of cigarette vending machines. No cigarette brand advertising or corporate symbol except for package facsimiles will appear on cigarette vending machines.

Rule 17. Consumer sampling of cigarettes or cigarette tobacco free of charge will be limited to

new products or existing products in which significant technological changes have been made. Such free sampling will be limited to a period not exceeding 12 months from the date of introduction of the said product in any given area, and the function of sampling limited to those areas in which cigarettes are normally purchased and only to persons who may legally purchase the product and are perceived as in the act of making a purchase. Furthermore, the sampling function will be carried out only by regular employees of the Manufacturer. These restrictions will not preclude free distribution of cigarettes by manufacturers to their employees for their personal use, or to consumers in answer to complaints.

Rule 18. No cigarette or cigarette tobacco brand names will be used on future cigar or pipe tobacco products nor will cigar or pipe tobacco brand names be used on future cigarette or cigarette tobacco products.

Rule 19. The parties to this Code agree that adherence to the Code's provision will be subject to review by a Board of Arbitration and that the Board will have power to impose sanctions on an offending party or parties.

Only two Canadian newspapers, *The Kingston Whig-Standard* and *The Brockville Intelligencer,* had banned cigarette advertising. In May 1985, *The London Free Press* had been pressured by the Non-Smokers Rights Association to drop it but refused to do so. Addressing the issues, Bob Turnbull, the paper's president and associate publisher, wrote:

> The problem here is a medical problem. It has nothing to do with our integrity or anything else. . . . All of these (pressure) tactics are directed, I think, the wrong way. They should be directed at the smoking problem.
> I just can't be convinced that tobacco advertising in daily newspapers would have a significant impact on the medical problem. It is not our role to make these rules.[4]

---

[4]*The London Free Press,* May 29, 1985, p. A3.

To the best of Johnson's knowledge, there were only two Canadian advertising agencies that had an explicit policy of no tobacco advertising. In the case of one, he suspected that it was a matter of "sour grapes" because they had lost a major cigarette account.

A group called Physicians for a Smoke-Free Canada were demanding a ban on all tobacco advertising within two years. Some experts predicted that all forms of cigarette advertising would be banned by the year 2000.

The most threatening trend in the industry, many experts said, was the increasing frequency of cigarette advertising aimed at the youth market. RJR MacDonald Inc., a large Canadian cigarette producer, brought this issue to the forefront with its "Tempo" campaign, which featured young-looking people dressed in the latest fashion for youth. Its apparent focus on the young was accused of being purposely controversial. In response, the Federal Ministry of Health and Welfare—itself a nonsmoking office—began a $1.5 million campaign aimed at the young to counter such advertising. A sample of the kind of media reports currently being read by many J & B employees is presented in Exhibit 4.

Johnson & Burgess Ltd.

J & B was one of the largest Canadian-owned agencies, with commissionable billings of $60 million in 1984. The agency was known for its talented people and had recently won several creative awards. It was considered by many creative people in the industry to be a rising star. J & B had 160 employees, of whom 145 worked in the firm's offices in Toronto and Montreal—both of which were designated nonsmoking.

Over the past 10 years, J & B had grown rapidly. According to Peter Johnson, their strategy had been to "overspend on people so that our creative product and client service are second to none." With strong political connections, a first-class marketing research group, and some widely publicized work in public opinion polling, they had also attracted significant public relations business from three large companies with extensive public affairs activities. Several staff members had worked hard for the PC party in the last federal election. Consequently, they had picked up over $3 million in federal government advertising.

The agency was earning a profit and in good shape financially (see Exhibit 5). However, there was significant slack in certain parts of the organization (as indicated in a comparison of Exhibit 2 and Exhibit 5). The slack was a result of learning curve improvements, particularly on two large accounts the agency had taken over two years previously after fierce competition with several other agencies. Management was concerned about the need to either add more business or reduce salaries and wages in order to keep the creative expenses below the average of most other agencies.

Management also intended at some future point to make a public offering of equity shares in order to build a financial base for diversification into communication ventures. Management shareholdings are outlined in Exhibit 6.

EXHIBIT 4

**Smoking Victims Sue
Tobacco Firms Over Illnesses**

SANTA BARBARA, Calif.—John Mark Galbraith, crippled by heart disease, lung cancer, and emphysema, lived his final years on bottled oxygen.

Yet his widow and children contend he was so addicted after almost one-half century of smoking, he yanked back the oxygen mask to sneak a puff of Camel, Salem, or Winston cigarettes.

This week, Galbraith's life and death will be spotlighted in his survivors' $1-million liability suit in the Santa Barbara County superior court against R. J. Reynolds Tobacco Co. and two stores.

Jury selection began Monday in the suit, the first among about 35 new liability suits against Reynolds to go to trial.

Meanwhile, in Austin, Tex., an elderly couple filed a $58 million lawsuit against three tobacco companies, including R. J. Reynolds, claiming their disabling illnesses were caused by years of cigarette smoking.

The suit claims cigarette manufacturers should be responsible for a percentage of damages even though the Bastrop, Texas, couple—Weldon Carlisle and his wife, Hazel—chose to smoke.

In the Santa Barbara suit, tobacco industry spokesmen and some financial analysts said a win for Galbraith's family could lead to a flood of similar claims against tobacco companies and open the door for liability suits against a wide range of goods, from liquor to fatty foods.

The wrongful death suit filed in 1983 against Reynolds and two stores that sold Galbraith cigarettes claims his 1982 death at age 69 was due to injuries that resulted from cigarette smoking. It claims the cigarettes Galbraith smoked for about 50 years were "defective and unsafe for their intended purpose in that they contained contaminated, adulterated, impure, harmful, lethal and carcinogenic ingredients."

"The heart of the lawsuit is to have an American jury, having heard the medical and scientific evidence presented by both sides, find cigarettes cause human illness and especially, Mr. Galbraith's death," said Paul Monzione, associate to lawyer Melvin Belli, who is handling the case for Galbraith's widow, Elayne, of Stanton, and son and daughter.

Similar suits have been brought before but Reynolds spokesmen say the tobacco industry has never been found liable for damages resulting in death or disease stemming from cigarette smoking.

However, Belli, one of the leading personal injury lawyers in the United States, believes he can win. Belli has brought similar cases against Reynolds and lost them all, the first 25 years ago.

EXHIBIT 4 *(concluded)*

Belli sought out the Galbraith family—a practice prohibited by California law unless the lawyer pledges any proceeds to the public good. Belli says he will donate any income he receives from the case to cancer research.

Unlike previous cases, Belli said this trial will focus on smokers' addiction and on new scientific evidence linking smoking with diseases.

Belli said he will seek out smokers for the jury, since they will better understand his claim of addiction.

Testimony is expected from a University of California professor who contends cigarettes are more addictive than alcohol or heroin.

In the Austin case, Carlisle, 71, said he smoked a pack or two of cigarettes a day since he was 14. He developed throat cancer, forcing doctors to remove his larynx. He speaks through a mechanical voice device that he presses against a hole in his throat.

Mrs. Carlisle, 61, is dying of emphysema, has had a stroke, and is confined to a wheelchair. The Carlisles were joined in the suit, filed in state district court in Austin last month, by the family of Hazel Boatright, a heavy smoker who died of lung cancer and emphysema last March.

Tobacco companies named as defendants in the lawsuit include Philip Morris, Inc., and Liggett & Myers Tobacco. The Tobacco Institute, a tobacco industry lobby group, and Ponca Wholesale Mercantile, an Amarillo, Texas, cigarette distributor, were also named as defendants.

Don Davis, a lawyer representing the Carlisles, said the suit is based on a Texas supreme court ruling involving the crash of a small airplane in which the court ruled pilot error contributed to the accident but that a design flaw in the airplane was partially responsible. The ruling allowed a jury to assign percentages of culpability to the manufacturer.

Davis said if the same doctrine is applied to the Carlisles' case, the tobacco manufacturers could be responsible for 10 percent of the couple's damages.

"This is the first case where people are going in and saying 'we are at fault but so is the tobacco industry,' " Davis said.

The suit seeks $33 million in compensatory damages and $25 million in punitive damages. It charges that tobacco company advertisements suggest cigarette smoking is not only safe but "pleasurable, sophisticated, associated with success and glamour, sports, love and the wholesome outdoors."

Carlisle said he wished he had known the damage cigarette smoking can cause.

"I never would have started," he said.

Reprinted by permission, *The London Free Press*, **November 19, 1985.**

EXHIBIT 5

JOHNSON & BURGESS LTD.
Profit and Loss Statement 1984

Revenues	($000s)	Percent
Gross commissionable billings	$60,000	
Commission	9,000	
Service and other fees	8,000	
Gross revenue	$17,000	100 %
Expenses		
Client contact	3,400	20 %
Management	1,700	10
Creative	1,700	10
TV and radio	1,020	6
Public relations	680	4
Marketing	510	3
Research	340	2
Other	1,530	9
Total	$10,880	64 %
Office Facilities		
Rent	969	5.7%
Amortization/leasehold facilities	51	0.3
Depreciation/furniture, fixtures, and equipment	136	0.8
Heat, light, water	34	0.2
Maintenance and repairs	102	0.6
Municipal taxes	68	0.4
Other	170	1.0
Total	$1,530	9.0%
General Office Expenses		
Postage and courier	$68	.4%
Supplies and stationery	255	1.5
Telephone and telegraph	289	1.7
Donations	136	0.8
Doubtful accounts	34	0.2
Company contribution to pension plan	153	0.9
Group insurance	102	0.6
Unemployment insurance and other benefits	34	0.2
Miscellaneous	289	1.7
Total	$1,360	8.0%
Travel and Entertainment	850	5.0
Total expenses	$14,620	86.0%
Net profit before tax	2,380	14.0
Income tax	1,190	7.0
Net profit	1,190	7.0%
Earnings per share (100,000 shares)	11.90	

NOTE: Johnson & Burgess' profit-sharing plan called for 40 percent of earnings to be distributed to 52 plan participants on a basis proportional to salaries; another 40 percent of earnings was customarily paid out in dividends.

Exhibit 6 Johnson & Burgess Ltd. Shareholders

	Number of Shares	Percent
Tony Burgess	25,000	25%
Peter Johnson	20,000	20
Bill Nugent	12,000	12
Jack Spitzer	10,000	10
Wally Bick	5,000	5
Lou Destino	5,000	5
21 others	23,000	28
	100,000	100%

Shares were valued at six times average earnings per share for last five years plus $33 per share to cover per share portion of earned surplus and deemed good will.

Earnings per share for the past five years had been as follows:

1980	$ 6.80	1983	$11.20
1981	7.10	1984	11.90
1982	10.25		

NOTE: Past 5-year average: $9.45.
1985 EPS forecast: $15.25.

The Key Players

A chart of the J & B organization indicating the main areas of the business and the top managers responsible is presented in Exhibit 7. The six key managers in the agency were described as follows:

Tony Burgess, chairman: Tony was a good advertising-agency man but his greatest asset had always been his friendly, outgoing personality. He had many friends and an amazing network of contacts. For retirement income, he was counting heavily on cashing in his J & B stock, which was currently worth about $2,250,000. He was very much aware that the agency's average five-year earnings-per-share figure could improve rapidly because earnings had been low in 1980 and 1981. Johnson knew that Burgess very much wanted to buy an attractive home in a prime Florida real estate development and that he would not be able to finance it unless the agency did very well in Burgess's remaining two years. A former college rugger player, Burgess had a strong constitution and had smoked since he was a teenager.

Peter Johnson, president: Several industry observers attributed the success of J & B primarily to Johnson's unfailingly pragmatic, open, and positive leadership, his education, training, and experience, his ability to attract and hold good people, and his sincerity and honesty in dealing with clients and staff, alike.

A reformed smoker, he stayed in good shape by jogging the year round and playing in an old-timers hockey league from September to April. While he was

EXHIBIT 7 Johnson & Burgess Ltd. Organization Chart (Age)

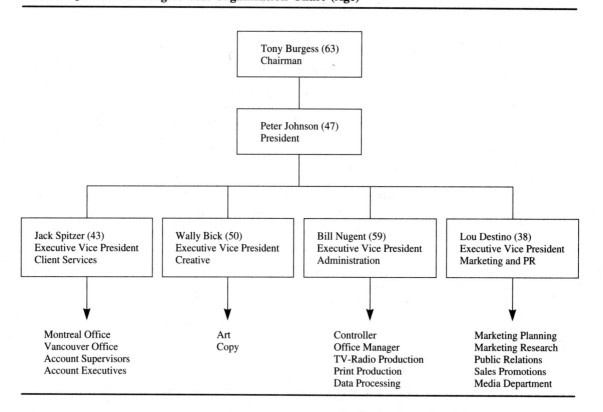

idealistic and socially responsible, he seemed to rationalize easily a wide variety of questionable behaviors as being necessary because advertising agencies were in a competitive, personal service business.

Bill Nugent, vice president, administration: Bill was an unflappable but disorganized workaholic. Of medium height and noticeably overweight, he was a heavy smoker who drank more than his share. Bill was everyone's friend and the confidant of many. His grown children were all married and his wife, the daughter of a once-prominent politician, was involved in many charitable and social activities. Bill worked many evenings, and after working hours his door was always open. Anyone from Tony Burgess to a junior copywriter might be found in his office chatting about personal or business affairs.

Wally Bick, vice president, creative: With an excess of brilliant creative talent, Wally was the key idea man and a driving force of the agency. He was well known as an active member of a large downtown church. A health food devotee, he neither smoked nor drank. On the request of a bishop of his church, he had given many hours of professional help to a group of parents organizing a political action group to fight drunk driving. The creative work for beer and liquor accounts was his general responsibility, but he showed little interest in them beyond seeing that they were handled by top-rated people. Client services personnel, particularly on the beer account, occasionally complained privately to Jack Spitzer that they did not have Bick's full commitment. Johnson hoped that in spite of Bick's condemnation of smoking, he would still see that the creative work on a cigarette account was handled professionally. Johnson worried, however, about what he would tell Kelly if he specifically asked for Bick to be heavily involved on the Regal account. He expected that while Bick would oppose taking a cigarette account, he would stop short of outright action to block the freedom of colleagues to work on what they wished. Bick had in the past mentioned informally that there was no way he would accept any direct or indirect benefits from a cigarette account.

Jack Spitzer, vice president, client services: Pleasant, capable, and efficient, Jack knew and stayed in close touch with client top management personnel and made sure they got what they wanted. Sometimes accused of being too political and pragmatic in giving in to client pressures, he nevertheless was widely respected. Jack had been the hard-driving leader of the agency's new-business campaign and took great personal pride in its growth record. Johnson knew that Jack would be a vociferous and devastating opponent of anyone who raised any barrier to any kind of new business.

Lou Destino, vice president, marketing and public relations: A business school graduate with good training and experience, Lou was the able leader of the marketing and public relations thrust in J & B. Lou did much of the market targeting and planning which guided Jack Spitzer's new business push. Foresighted and strategic in his thinking, he doubted that cigarette business was good for the long term because of falling sales, growing government reaction against tobacco products, medical opposition, and mounting product liability legal claims (none successful) which he was afraid might eventually involve the ad agencies that did cigarette advertising.

However, he had no real personal hangups about working on a cigarette account. While he occasionally smoked cigars and a pipe, he was opposed to cigarette smoking and had told several friends about how happy he had been when his wife, who was a heavy smoker, quit smoking because of the pressure their young children had focused on her. As he recounted the story, the children had appealed to his wife by saying: "Mom, our teacher at school told us that you might die if you keep on smoking."

The Meeting

Since Johnson had to make up his mind immediately regarding his reply to Kelly, he called a special meeting of the Management Committee for the next Saturday morning. Casually dressed, they assembled around the boardroom table. The meeting had been called for 10:00 A.M. and Johnson thought it might take an hour and a half at most. As usual, Nugent and Spitzer smoked throughout. After

Johnson started off by describing Kelly's request and his subsequent meeting, telephone discussions, and letter, he asked for their input to his decision. Excerpts representing the various points of view expressed in what became a no-holds-barred exchange are as follows:

Bick: There is no way we can get around the fact that smoking is just plain bad for everybody and lethal for many. We all know the terrible numbers—10,000 die from lung cancer alone and that's only one of the many possible side effects. And, we all know that's just the beginning—bronchitis, emphysema, cancer of the larynx, bladder, esophagus, mouth, lip, and reproductive systems—you name them, they're all attributable to smoking. There's no way we should take this account. We should all be worried about ourselves for even giving it serious consideration.

Spitzer: Come on Wally, that's a lot of antismoking medical propaganda. The scientists working for the tobacco industry deny those things have ever been proved. For the big majority—must be way over 90 percent—of smokers there's no problem at all. If all that medical crap is really true, how come so many doctors smoke?

Burgess: Regardless of the medical arguments, it's legal and fits in with today's lifestyle. Advertising simply informs people about what they obviously want. We can't make anyone smoke who doesn't want to! And we have no right or responsibility to set ourselves up as judges of what's good for society. That's the job of government. As long as the government raises taxes from cigarettes and openly supports tobacco farmers, how can we be so self-righteous as to make moral judgments against the business?

Spitzer: If we're going to get on a soap box and make public moral "statements," what about some of our other businesses. . . .
Our beer and liquor business is almost $6 million this year. Our automotive business includes a sports car with such incredible performance that four out of five buyers—especially teenagers—are a danger every time they get behind the wheel. Incidentally, yesterday, when I was out at _____ , they told me they've got over $200 million worth of consumer liability legal actions going in North America. We all know that you just can't waste time thinking about this kind of stuff. And why should we? There's no business in the world that's perfect . . .

Nugent: I don't see what harm cigarette advertising does anyway. The tobacco industry says that it's all brand advertising to defend share of market and not to promote primary demand. We all know that cigarette sales are falling in spite of all the advertising that's being done.

Burgess: I think we've got to look at the positive side of this opportunity. It would be the biggest piece of new business we've ever picked up. We'll get some great publication and trade exposure because it will be the biggest account to move this year. That means momentum, reputation, and success. And there's a good chance for a lot more of Kelly's business if we do an excellent job. I'd be less than frank if I didn't admit that it would be a tremendous benefit to me and my wife. I've given my total commitment for 27 years to this team and to making our operation the best. The boost this would give to the price of my stock in a couple of years when I cash out would have to be one of the bigger breaks in my career. Not to speak of what it means in profit sharing for all of us!

Destino: I'm not sure this would be good for us in the longer-term future. Sure, its morally objectionable and it's going to cause internal conflict. But the real problem is the opportunity cost. There is lots of better business out there. If we take this account we'll have no capacity for another big account for quite a while. I wouldn't want to take this at the cost of having to pass on some better business a month or two from now.

Spitzer: Do you have anything specific in mind?

Destino: Not right now.

Spitzer: Well, then, let's take what we can get right now and worry about our next new account when the time comes.

Destino: Yeah, but if we land this account, we might lose some government advertising because of it.

Spitzer: So what if we do? Government can deal with some other agency. They've got too big a bureaucracy anyway—you need client approval at five levels, and it's taking a lot more time than we planned for in our budgets.

Johnson: Okay, but what about the internal consequences? What team will we put on the account?

Spitzer: For an account this size, we'll need eight people: an account supervisor, an account executive, two assistant account executives, two artists, and two copywriters. They would all work for Regal pretty well full time. I'd like to make sure we'd put our best people on this account, since it's so important.

Bick: But some of our best people, like Jim, Marie, and Jan (three of J & B's best copywriters and artists) say they'd have nothing to do with cigarette advertising. In fact, I wouldn't be surprised to find that Jim would quit before we took this account.

Burgess: Look, I can't tell you what to do, but if we don't take this account, someone else will. Then what has our "statement" meant? Only a big loss for us in terms of dollars and exposure. Think about it. Look at what it would mean to our profit-sharing plan. We owe it to all our staff, now and in the future, to go after this account as hard as we can.

Johnson: Maybe we do. But you're making our short-term advances more important than long-term stability. What if we do lose some of our best talent, and don't actually get the account? What effect will that have on our future? Some of these idealistic young people will think we're prostituting the whole agency for a few more bucks. Who'd want to come work for us thinking we cared only about the bottom line? If Kelly's people weren't known to be such a professional and classy organization, it'd be easier to make this decision.

Nugent: Let's put the staff problem in a little perspective. Out of our total of 160 people I'd say only 4 or 5 at the very most would ever quit over this. Another 15 or 20 would be strongly against it and drag their feet or not give their top effort. Another 25 or 30 would be against it but forget about the problem in a week or so. At the other end of the spectrum we would have our 35 to 40 smokers and quite a few nonsmokers who would think we are crazy for even thinking about passing up such a great piece of business. Many of them would think they are being shafted by a bunch of do-gooders.

Finally, after going on for over three hours, the meeting broke up when Lou Destino and Bill Nugent had to leave. Destino's parting comment to Peter Johnson: "You and Tony better take the rest of the afternoon and decide what we should do. I gotta leave. See you tomorrow."

Johnson knew he had to make up his mind quickly. However, after a long talk with Tony Burgess, he was even more confused about what he should do. As he reviewed the file of notes he had accumulated on the problem, he assessed the pros and cons of his options. The organization was strong and cohesive, but he worried that the agency job market was good for experienced, high performers. The tangible costs and benefits were fairly clear, but the intangibles were difficult to assess. The longer he pondered his dilemma, the more he realized there were going to be serious consequences no matter what he decided.

CASE 20
KOLAPORE, INC. (CONDENSED)

In January 1986, Mr. Adriaan Demmers, president and sole employee of Kolapore, Inc., a firm based in Guelph, Ontario, specializing in the importation, processing, and sale of high-quality souvenir spoons, was becoming increasingly frustrated with the pace at which his business was developing. Over a two-year period, Demmers had taken his idea of importing souvenir spoons from Holland to Canada to annual sales of nearly $30,000. He believed the potential existed for well over $100,000 in Canadian sales plus exports to the United States. This success to date had been a strain, however, on Demmers's limited financial resources and had not provided any compensation for the long hours invested. Demmers was beginning to question if he was ever going to have the major breakthrough which he had always believed was "just around the corner."

Recently, Demmers had accepted a full-time position with another firm in an unrelated business. While Demmers realized that he could continue to operate Kolapore, Inc., on a part-time basis, he wondered if he should "face reality" and simply fold up the business or try to sell it. Alternately, Demmers could not occasionally help wondering if he should be devoting himself full-time to Kolapore.

Background

In February/March 1984, Demmers conducted a feasibility study of starting a business to market souvenir spoons. His idea was to offer a high-quality product depicting landmarks, historic buildings, and other unique symbols of the area in which the spoons were to be sold.

There were numerous spoons on the market, but most tended to be for Canada or Ontario rather than local sites of interest and were generally poorly made and not visually appealing. There were few quality spoons, and the ones that did exist were priced in the $15–$40 range.

Sources of spoons were examined and quotations were received from firms in Canada, the United States, and the Netherlands (Holland). The search process for a country from which to source the spoons was a limited one and was settled quickly, thanks to Demmers's Dutch heritage, the existence of a well-recognized group of silversmiths in Schoonhoven, plus a particular company which already had over 40 Canadian specific dies and lower prices.

Demmers felt the key factors for success were good quality product, using designs of local landmarks, and an eye-catching display. He felt displays should

This case was prepared by Professor Paul W. Beamish. Copyright © 1986 by Paul W. Beamish. (Condensed, 1992)

be located in a prominent position in retail stores because souvenir spoons are often bought on impulse.

As part of his feasibility study, Demmers conducted a market analysis (including customer and retailer surveys), a competitive analysis (both manufacturers and distributors), and developed an import plan, marketing plan, and financial projections (including projected break-even and cash flows). Excerpts from this study follow.

Market Analysis

The market for souvenir spoons consists of several overlapping groups—primarily tourists and the gift market. There are also groups interested in spoons for more specialized purposes such as church groups, service clubs, associations, and others. These are very specialized and for special occasions.

A random telephone survey conducted in March 1984 of 50 people in Guelph revealed that 78 percent owned souvenir spoons. Forty-six percent of those people had purchased the spoons themselves, while 54 percent had received them as gifts. In total, almost 25 percent of the people in the sample collected souvenir spoons or had a rack on which to hang them. Retailers indicated that sales occurred primarily during the summer months and at Christmas time. Twelve retail outlets were visited to obtain information regarding quality, sales, and prices. Background on a selection of these retailers is summarized in Appendix A.

There was a high awareness of souvenir spoons in the market, but the product quality was generally at the low end of the market. For example, rough edges on the bowls were common, and the crests on the spoons were often crooked. In fact, one manufacturer's spoon had a picture of Kitchener City Hall which was out of focus and off-center. (Terms concerning souvenir spoons are explained in Appendix B.)

A limited variety of spoons was often available, and few of the spoons were of local points of interest even though these were the spoons that were most in demand. One retailer noted that of a total of 140 spoons sold in 1983, 106 were one variety, a spoon with a relief design in plastic of a Conestoga wagon. This was the only unique spoon Demmers found in the area "other than the cheap picture spoons."

There was no advertising for souvenir spoons due to the nature of the product and the lack of identification with a particular brand.

Souvenir spoons appeared to be a low priority in many producing companies, with little marketing effort made to push the products. Even the packaging was of poor quality; often, boxes were not supplied for gift wrapping.

The sale of spoons was viewed as seasonal by some retailers. Point-of-purchase displays were removed once the summer rush was over in many instances.

Spoons were not prominently displayed in most stores, yet they are largely an impulse item. In several stores, they were kept in drawers and only taken out when requested.

Competitive Analysis

Souvenir spoons essentially serve two customer functions: as gifts or commemoratives. They can be used as gifts for family, friends, or special occasions such as Christmas. They can also serve as a commemorative token of having visited somewhere or for a special anniversary (for example, the Province of Ontario's 200th anniversary). They can be either functional (used for coffee or teaspoons) or may be used for decorative purposes (hung in a spoon rack or put in a cabinet).

Competition comes from all other gift items and all other souvenir items in approximately the same price range.

Demmers identified 11 companies that distributed souvenir spoons in the Southwestern Ontario area and gathered what data he could—much of it anecdotal—on each. This process had provided encouragement for Demmers to proceed. Background on these suppliers is summarized in Appendix C.

Southwestern Ontario contained a number of large urban areas, including Toronto (over 2 million people), Hamilton/Burlington, Kitchener/Waterloo, and London, with over 300,000 people in each—plus many smaller cities, such as Guelph. Guelph was located roughly in the centre of the triangle formed by Toronto, Waterloo, and Burlington and was within an hour's drive of each.

Importing

To import goods into Canada on a regular basis in amounts over $800, an importer number was required. This was available from Revenue Canada, Customs and Excise. Requirements for customs were an advise notice from the shipper and a customs invoice. These were available in office supply stores. A customs tariff number and commodity code were also required to complete the customs B3 form.

Souvenir spoons of either sterling silver or silver plate were listed in the customs tariff under number 42902-1. The Netherlands has Most Favoured Nation status, so the duty was 20.3 percent. On top of the cost of the merchandise (excluding transportation and insurance but including duty), there was a further 10 percent excise tax and 10 percent federal sales tax.

A customs broker could be hired to look after the clearing of goods through customs. Rates were approximately $41 plus $3.60 for every $1,000 of value, duty included.

Insurance on a shipment of less than $10,000 costs a fixed fee of about $150 with insurance brokers. This can be reduced if insurance is taken on a yearly basis, based on the expected value of imports over the year. Freight forwarders charge approximately $2 per kilo regardless of the total weight of the shipment.

The importing can be easily handled without help on small shipments such as spoons. The product can be sent by airmail and insured with the post office. It can also be sent to a small city like Guelph rather than Toronto, and this avoids the busy Toronto customs office and possible delays of several days. The customs office in Guelph can easily clear the goods the same day they arrive.

Marketing Plan

Product.   The proposed souvenir spoons would be a high-quality product with detailed dies made to give them a relief design far superior to any competitive spoons (except for those retailing in the $30 range). These spoons are available in silver plate and alpacca, which makes them similar to jewellery.

Designs would be of specific points of interest. In the Kitchener-Waterloo area, for example, possible subjects would include Seagram Museum, Schneider House, Doon Pioneer Village, university crests, and city crests. Kitchener-Waterloo would be printed under the picture, also in relief in the metal, along with the title of the particular picture.

Price Points.

$2.25	— Metropolitan Supplies: nickel-plated.
$4.50–$6.00	— Breadner Manufacturing: rhodium-plated and silver-plated. Candis Enterprises. Gazelle Importers.
$7.00–$8.00	— Oneida or Commemorative: simple designs with engraved insignia. Appear to be made of a silver alloy.
$10.00–$14.00	— Proposed price range for retail.

      a. Quality comparable to $30.00 spoons, but silver content is lower.
      b. Detailed designs of local landmarks.
      c. Variety of 6–10 spoons in each market.

$30.00 and up — Breadner
      a. Sterling silver.
      b. Fine workmanship.
      c. Very limited variety of designs.

Place.   Because souvenir spoons are purchased on impulse, locations with high traffic are essential. Jewellery stores and gift stores in malls and tourist areas are probably most suitable in this respect.

Due to the price range proposed and the quality of the merchandise, the quality and image of the store has to be appropriate. This would eliminate discount jewellery stores and cheap souvenir shops for the aforementioned reasons. Secondly, it would not please higher-end retailers if the same spoons were sold for less in the same area and would likely restrict distribution in the appropriate channels.

Jewellery stores are perceived by many people as selling expensive, luxury items that are not part of one's everyday needs. For this reason, it would be helpful for these stores to have a window display.

Promotion. Each retail location will carry a minimum product line of six varieties of spoons: one with a Canadian theme, one with a provincial theme, and at least four spoons with designs of local landmarks or points of interest.

The packaging will be suitable for gift wrapping, so will likely consist of a small box with a clear plastic cover.

Each retail location will have an oak countertop display rack. There will be a relatively high cost to the displays initially, but they will attract attention and convey the quality of the spoons. Different sizes can be made depending on the number of spoons for a particular market.

Because souvenir spoons are primarily an impulse purchase, location in the store is important and should be near the entrance or have a window display. This is something which can be controlled only by persuading the retailer that this would increase the turnover and consequently his profits.

Finance

Contribution margin per spoon has been calculated using the most conservative numbers and at a wholesale price of $3.50. Typically, retailers would mark prices up by 100 percent (see Exhibit 1). The contribution margins worked out to $2.05 on alpacca spoons and $1.50 on silver-plated spoons.

The breakeven, assuming costs of $25,250 per year and a contribution margin of $2.05, would be sales volume of 12,317 spoons with sales value of $43,110 (see Exhibit 2). Assuming the spoons would be introduced in the Ontario market and distribution obtained in 100 retail locations, this means sales of 124 spoons per store.

EXHIBIT 1 Forecast Variable Costs and Margins of Spoons

	Alpacca	*Silver Plate*
Quote by Dutch manufacturer (Zilverfabriek) (in guilders) 1 guilder = $.43 Cdn.	2.20 guilders	3.10 guilders
Factory cost in $Cdn.	$0.95	$1.33
Duty @ 20.3 percent	.19	.27
Cost, duty included	$1.14	$1.60
Federal sales tax @ 9 percent	.10	.14
Federal excise tax @ 10 percent	.11	.16
Freight and insurance	.10	.10
Cost	$1.45	$2.00
Contribution margin	$2.05 to $3.55	$1.50 to $3.00
Cost to retailer	3.50 to 5.00	3.50 to 5.00
Retailer markup	3.50 to 5.00	3.50 to 5.00
Retail price	7.00 to 10.00*	7.00 to 10.00

NOTE: *These prices are lower than originally forecast due to Demmers's recognition that a $10 to $14 retail price was too high.

EXHIBIT 2 Forecast Breakeven

Distribution costs (transportation)	$ 4,000
Rent expense (work from home)	—
Salary	15,000
Office supply costs (including telephone)	1,000
Inventory costs	1,000
Merchandising expenses (displays and boxes)	3,000
Investment in dies (10 @ $125 each)	1,250
Total fixed costs	**$25,250**

$25,250/$1.50 = 16,833 spoons
$25,250/$2.05 = 12,317 spoons
$25,250/$3.00 = 8,416 spoons

EXHIBIT 3 Forecast Cash Flow, May–August 1984

	May	*June*	*July*	*August*
Cash	$3,000	$ (750)	$1,000	$ 7,500
Disbursements:				
Moulds	1,250	—	—	—
Purchases	—	7,250	—	7,250
Promotion expenses	2,000	1,000	—	—
Car expenses	500	500	500	500
Total disbursements	3,750	8,750	500	7,750
Net cash	(750)	(9,500)	500	(250)
Receipts:				
Accounts receivable	—	10,500	7,000	10,500
Cash balance (to be borrowed)	$ (750)	$ 1,000	$7,500	$10,250

NOTE: Terms n/30.

Upon graduating from a university business school in April 1984, Demmers planned to devote his efforts to Kolapore. He felt that while there could be a short-term financial drain, his cash balance would be positive at the end of the second month of operation (see Exhibit 3).

Subsequent Events

Soon after graduating in April, it became clear to Demmers that Kolapore was not going to realize forecast sales of $28,000 by September 1984. Due to delays in getting shipments from Holland and difficulty in obtaining distribution in Canada, sales were only $1,830 over the summer. A number of assumptions in the original feasibility study (as described in the first section) had proven incorrect:

1. The number of dies ultimately required (each of which costs $125) was not going to be 10 but closer to 50.
2. The federal sales tax rate had increased to 10 percent from 9 percent.
3. Duty was payable on the dies themselves as well as on the spoons at the rate of 20.3 percent excise tax plus federal sales tax.
4. Delivery time for new dies was closer to six months than the forecast 10–12 weeks (the artist had been ill for several months). Several orders were cancelled during this period as a result.
5. Packaging costs per spoon were closer to 32 cents per unit than the estimated 10 cents.
6. Distribution had been difficult because the large chain stores which dominated the market all had established suppliers.
7. The target market was not nearly as upscale as originally envisioned. Although Kolapore's spoons were readily identifiable as being of superior quality, most customers would only pay a maximum of $7–$8 retail for any spoon. Demmers had estimated the total Canadian souvenir spoon market at about $1.5 million annually. Within that, a very small portion was for sterling silver (where Demmers could not compete), about $450,000 was at the $7 retail price point where Demmers was selling (some of his competitors were promoting similar or poorer-quality spoons at the same price), with the balance of the market reserved for lower-priced/lower-quality spoons.

The goal of 100 stores by September 1984 was still a long way off.

Demmers had also discovered that the chain stores plan all their buying from 6 to 12 months in advance. Because many of the spoons he had designed did not arrive until September 1984, this meant that he had missed much of the tourist season (and nearly all of the Christmas market).

On the positive side, the Dutch guilder had depreciated relative to the Canadian dollar. In September 1984, it cost Canadian $0.39 for 1 guilder rather than $0.43 as forecast. In addition, delivery times for spoons from existing dies required three to four weeks rather than the expected four to six weeks, and the cost of display cases was only about $16 each. These were made of plastic rather than the originally envisioned oak.

Although Kolapore was showing a negative cash balance at the end of August 1984 (see Exhibit 4), sales began to improve in September (see Exhibit 5), growing to nearly $16,000 by the end of the first full year of operation (see Exhibits 6 and 7 for financial statements). A financial loss of $1,800 was incurred for the first year of operation, and this took no account of the countless hours Demmers had invested. Since the business was not yet self-supporting, in September 1984 Demmers had begun to look for other sources of income.

EXHIBIT 4 Actual Cash Flow, 1984

	May	*June*	*July*	*August*
Cash	$2,600	$1,000	$ 950	$ 530
Disbursements:				
Purchases	1,000	550	870	1,460
Expenses	1,000	80	300	300
Total disbursements	2,000	630	1,170	1,760
Net cash	600	370	(220)	(1,230)
Receipts:				
Accounts receivable	400	580	750	1,100
Cash balance	$1,000	$ 950	$ 530	$ (130)

EXHIBIT 5 Actual Sales, 1984–1985

May	$ 400
June	580
July	750
August	1,100
September	2,600
October	2,540
November	1,500
December	1,400
January–March	4,923

Between September 1984 and January 1986, Demmers worked for five months in a fibreglass factory, acquired a house in Guelph in which he was able to live and to rent out rooms, sold Bruce Trail calendars on a commission basis, worked at organizing and selling several ski tours (which did not take place), and opened an ice-cream store in a regional resort area (Wasaga Beach). Due to a low volume of traffic, this latter venture in the summer of 1985 resulted in an $8,000 loss. In the fall of 1985, Demmers accepted a position as production manager for a weekly newspaper in Guelph.

By this time, Demmers was selling direct to retailers in 20 towns and cities in Ontario and through five chains: Simpsons and United Cigar Stores and, to a much smaller extent, Eaton's, Birks, and Best Wishes. Other chains such as The Bay, Sears, and Woolco had been approached but so far without success. Demmers was hoping to find the time so that he could approach the buyers at K mart, Zeller's, Consumer's Distributing, Robinson's, Woodwards, and others.

Kolapore spoons were sold in Simpsons stores from Windsor, Ontario, to Halifax, Nova Scotia, and in 18 United Cigar Store locations in southern Ontario. Four months after Demmers's first delivery to the chain outlets in the

EXHIBIT 6

KOLAPORE, INC.
Balance Sheet
As of March 31, 1985
(Unaudited—See Notice to Reader)

Assets

Current assets:

Cash..$1,708

Accounts receivable.. 1,763

Inventory... 2,873

Total current assets... 6,344

Incorporation expense.. 466

Total assets..$6,810

Liabilities

Current liabilities:

Accounts payable and accruals.. $268

Due to shareholder (note 2, Table 7).. 8,342

Total liabilities... 8,610

Shareholders' Equity

Retained earnings (deficit)...(1,800)

Total liabilities and shareholders' equity..$6,810

NOTE: Notice to reader: These financial statements have been compiled solely for tax purposes. I have not audited, reviewed, or otherwise attempted to verify their accuracy or completeness.

Guelph, Ontario   Chartered Accountant
May 2, 1985

summer of 1985, about half the stores were sold out of Kolapore spoons. Neither chain would reorder stock part way through the year.

To sell direct in some of the smaller cities, Demmers's practice had been to drive or walk through the main shopping areas, stopping at jewellery stores or other likely retail outlets. If he was unable to meet with the store owner, he would usually leave a sample and a letter with some information (see Exhibit 8 for a copy of the letter). Demmers's experience had been that unless he personally met with the right person—which sometimes took three or more visits—no sales would occur. When he was able to meet with the owner, his success rate was over 70 percent. To sell direct in larger centres such as Toronto (where he had 40 customers), Demmers had focused his efforts on hotel gift shops. Having established these customers, he could now visit all 40 customers in Toronto personally in two to three days.

By year-end, Demmers had access to a pool of 89 Canadian-specific dies. Demmers's supplier in Holland had 46 dies in stock which another Canadian

EXHIBIT 7

KOLAPORE, INC.
Statement of Income
Year Ended March 31, 1985
(Unaudited—See Notice to Reader)

Sales		$15,793
Cost of sales:		
Inventory at beginning of year	—	
Purchases	8,453	
Duty and freight	2,288	
Dies	3,034	
	13,775	
Less: Inventory at end of year	2,873	
Cost of sales		10,902
Gross profit		4,891
Expenses:		
Office	657	
Samples	582	
Auto expenses	1,137	
Car allowance	3,900	
Bank interest and charges	139	
Advertising	26	
Accounting	250	
Total expenses		6,691
Net profit (loss) for the year		$(1,800)

NOTES: 1. Significant accounting policies:

KOLAPORE, INC., is a company incorporated under the laws of Ontario on April 6, 1984, and is primarily engaged in the importing and selling of souvenir spoons.

The accounting policies are in accordance with generally accepted accounting principles.

Inventory is valued at lower of cost or net realizable value.

Incorporation expense is not amortized.

2. Due to shareholder is noninterest-bearing and payable on demand.

from Western Canada had had designed. Spoons based on these dies were no longer being sold anywhere as far as Demmers could tell.

For the most part, Demmers was selling spoons based on his own designs. (For those spoons which Demmers had had designed, he had exclusive rights in Canada.) In less than two years, he had 43 more dies made up (see Exhibit 9 for a complete list). In some cases, Demmers had asked a particular company/group to pay the cost of the dies; in others, such as for universities, he had built the die cost into his price for the first shipment; while in others he had simply gone ahead on his own with the hope that he could achieve sufficient sales to justify the investment.

Exhibit 8 **Kolapore, Inc., Letter of Introduction**

Kolapore, Inc.
P.O. Box 361
Guelph, Ontario
N1H 6K5

Dear

   Kolapore, Inc., would like to offer you the opportunity to have your own design on a spoon made up in metal relief, for example, a logo, coat of arms, crest, building, or whatever you would like.

   There is always a large market for souvenir spoons of unique design and high quality. Kolapore Collection Spoons fit this category extremely well and are priced very competitively.

   The spoons are available in silver plate at $3.50 per spoon. This price includes a gift box, federal sales tax, and shipping.

   The minimum order is 100 spoons to get a new design made up, and there is also a one-time die charge of $125.00 to help offset the cost of making the new die. Delivery time is approximately three months if a die has to be made up; subsequent orders will take four to six weeks.

   The dies for Kolapore Collection Spoons are made by master craftsmen in Schoonhoven, Holland, the silversmith capital of the world. The spoons themselves are made in Canada. As a result, the quality of the spoons is exceptional and recognized by the consumer at a glance.

   I trust that this is sufficient information. I look forward to hearing from you. If you have any questions or concerns, please don't hesitate to contact me. Thank you for your time and consideration.

                              Sincerely,

                              Adriaan Demmers
                              President

   There was a wide variability in the sales level associated with each spoon. Sales from his best-seller—the Toronto skyline (which depicted major buildings and the CN Tower)—were about 1,000 spoons a year. Demmers's second-best-selling spoon in Toronto was 300 units of Casa Loma. (For a list of the major tourist sites in Toronto, see Exhibit 10.) This spoon had quickly sold out on site in 10 days. (However, the buyer had been unwilling to order more part way through the year.) Spoons with other Toronto designs were selling less than 50 units a year.

   By December 1985, inventories had increased and Kolapore, Inc., was still showing a small loss (see Exhibit 11). Any gains from changes in the rate of

EXHIBIT 9 Kolapore Collection Spoons—Designs Available

Canada:
Deer
Elk
Caribou
Cougar
Mountain goat
Moose
Bighorn sheep
Grizzly bear
Salmon
Coast Indian
Indian
Coat of arms
Mountie
Maple leaf

Province of Ontario:
✔ Trillium
✔ Windsor, Ambassador Bridge
✔ Sarnia, Bluewater Bridge
✔ Chatham, St. Joseph's Church
✔ London, Storybook Gardens
✔ Woodstock, Old Town Hall
✔ Stratford, swan
✔ Kitchener, Schneider Haus
✔ Waterloo, The Seagram Museum
✔ Waterloo County, Mennonite horse and buggy
✔ Elora, Mill Street
✔ Guelph, Church of Our Lady
✔ Guelph, Credit Union
✔ Guelph, St. Joseph's Hospital
✔ Kitchener-Waterloo, Oktoberfest
✔ Hamilton, Dundurn Castle
✔ St. Catharines, Old Court House
✔ Niagara Falls, Falls, Brock Monument, and Maid of the Mist
✔ Acton, Leathertown (hide with buildings)
✔ Toronto, skyline
✔ Toronto, City Hall
✔ Toronto, St. Lawrence Hall
✔ Toronto, Casa Loma
✔ Kingston, City Hall
✔ Ottawa, Parliament buildings
✔ Collingwood, Town Hall
✔ Owen Sound, City crest

University and community college crests/ coats of arms:
✔ Wilfrid Laurier
✔ Waterloo
✔ Carleton

✔ Guelph
✔ York
✔ Western
✔ Windsor
✔ McMaster
✔ Brock
✔ Fanshawe
✔ Humber

Province of Quebec:
Montreal, skyline
Montreal, Olympic Stadium

Province of Nova Scotia:
Bluenose (schooner)

Yukon Territory:
Coat of arms
Gold panner

Province of British Columbia:
Coat of arms
Prince George
Victoria, Parliament buildings
Victoria, lamp post
Victoria, Empress Hotel
Nanaimo, Bastion
Dogwood (flower)
Totem pole
Kermode Terrace
Smithers
Northlander Rogers Pass, bear
Northlander Rogers Pass, house
Kelowna, The Ogopogo
Okanagan, The Ogopogo
Vancouver, Grouse Mountain/skyride/ chalet
Vancouver, Grouse Mountain skyride
Vancouver, Grouse Mountain skyride/ cabin
Vancouver, Cleveland Dam
Vancouver, The Lions
Vancouver, The Lions Gate Bridge

Province of Alberta:
Banff, Mount Norquay
Banff, Mount Rundle
Banff, Banff Springs Hotel
Calgary, bronco rider
Edmonton, Klondike Mike
Wild Rose (flower)
Oil derrick
Jasper
Jasper sky tram

NOTE: Check mark denotes those made up on Demmers's initiative.

Exhibit 10 Some Major Tourist Sites in Toronto

---

1. Metro Zoo
2. CN Tower
3. Casa Loma
4. Royal Ontario Museum (ROM)
5. Black Creek Pioneer Village
6. Art Gallery of Ontario (AGO)
7. Canada's Wonderland
8. Ontario Place
9. The Ontario Science Centre

---

import duty on spoons (20.3 percent in 1984 to 18.4 percent in 1986) had been negated by changes in federal sales tax (9 percent in 1984 to 11 percent in 1986) and exchange rates. The fluctuating Dutch guilder was at a two-year high relative to the Canadian dollar. From a March 1984 value of Cdn. $0.43, the guilder had declined to $0.36 in February 1985 and climbed to $0.50 by December 1985. Partially due to these exchange fluctuations, during the past eight months, Demmers had also arranged for the spoons to be silver-plated at a cost of 40 cents each in Ontario. This had resulted in a saving of 15 cents a spoon (which varied with the exchange rate). More significantly, because many spoons were purchased as souvenirs of Canada, by adding sufficient value by silver plating in Canada, the imported product no longer had to be legally stamped, "Made in Holland." In fact, the packaging could now be marked "Made in Canada." Demmers was quite optimistic regarding the implications of this change because a number of potential store buyers had rejected his line because it did not say "Made in Canada." Demmers's supplier was upset, however, with the change.

Meanwhile, the feedback he was receiving from many of his customers was positive—in most cases they were selling more of his spoons than any other brand. Some customers, in fact, had enquired about other products. Since he had so far not experienced any competitive reactions to his spoons, Demmers was thinking of investigating the possibility of adding ashtrays, letter openers, key chains, lapel pins, and bottle openers to the product line in 1986—if he stayed in business. Each one of these products could have a crest attached to it. These crests would be the same as those used on the spoons and would thus utilize the dies to a greater extent. The landed costs per metal crest from the same supplier would be 85 cents. Demmers contemplated attaching these crests himself onto products supplied by Canadian manufacturers. However, initial investigations had revealed no obvious economical second product line.

Demmers also planned to phase out alpacca imports—all products would now be silver plated. In fact, Demmers was also wondering if he should acquire the equipment and materials in order to do this silver plating and polishing himself.

With no lack of ideas, many of the original frustrations nonetheless remained. The buyers at major chains such as Eaton's and Simpsons had

EXHIBIT 11

KOLAPORE INC.
Statement of Income
Eight Months* Ending November 30, 1985
(Unaudited)

Sales..	$21,000
Cost of sales:	
Inventory at beginning of year...	2,873
Purchases..	12,000
Duty and freight...	3,500
Dies..	1,950
	20,323
Less: Inventory at end of year...	5,000
Cost of sales..	15,323
Gross profit...	5,677
Expenses...	6,500
Net profit (loss) for the year to date..	$(823)

NOTE: *Annual sales expected to be $30,000.

changed once again, and because they did not use an automatic reorder system, new appointments had to be arranged. This was as difficult as ever. Also, Demmers still had not been able to draw anything from the firm for his efforts. These factors, coupled with his lack of cash and the demands of his new full-time position, had left Demmers uncertain as to what he should do next. With the spring buying season approaching—when Demmers would normally visit potential buyers—he realized that his decision regarding the future of Kolapore could not be postponed much longer.

APPENDIX A:
SURVEY OF SPOONS CARRIED BY LOCAL RETAILERS IN GUELPH AND KITCHENER-WATERLOO REGION

A Taste of Europe—Delicatessen & Gift Store
                    Guelph Eaton Centre
   A selection of spoons from Holland with Dutch designs.
   One with the Canadian coat of arms which looked good.
   Rhodium-plated spoons—$5.98 per spoon.
   Well displayed at front of store.
Eaton's—Guelph Eaton Centre
   Breadner spoons with maple leaf or Canadian flag and "Guelph" stamped in
      the bowl.
   Rhodium-plated—$4.98.
   No display and hard to find.
Pequenot Jewellers—Wyndham Street, Guelph
   Carry Candis spoons, which look cheap and do not sell very well.
   $4.98.
   Poorly displayed.
Smith & Son, Jewellers—Wyndham Street, Guelph
   Do not carry souvenir spoons because they are not in line with the store's
      image. They often get requests for them.
Franks Jewellers—King Street, Waterloo
   Carry Breadner spoons with the Waterloo coat of arms.
   Rhodium-plated spoons—$4.50 per spoon.
   Not on display but kept in drawer.
   Sell less than 12 per year.
Copper Creek—Waterloo Square Mall, Waterloo
   Candis spoons—$5.00 each.
Birks—King Centre, Kitchener
   Carry Oneida and Breadner spoons.
   Rhodium-plated spoons for $5.98.
   Oneida spoons were $8.95 and looked like a silver alloy.
   Sterling silver Breadner spoons for $31.95.
   Displayed in a spoon rack, looked good.
   Birks regency spoons with crest of each province, $12.50.
Eaton's—Market Square, Kitchener
   Breadner spoons, two types for Canada only.
   Rhodium-plated—$4.98 each.
Young's Jewellers—King Street, Kitchener
   Rhodium-plated Breadner spoons, $4.50 each.

Walters Jewellers
   Against chain policy to carry souvenir spoons because of poor quality and low
      turnover.
Peoples Jewellers
   Do not carry souvenir spoons.
Engels Gift Shop—King Street, Kitchener
   Carry Breadner, Oneida, Gazelle, and Metropolitan.
   Altogether about 20 varieties.
   Well displayed near entrance of store; prices range from $2.25 for Metropolitan spoons to $7.98 for Oneida spoons.
   Saleslady said they sell hundreds every year, mostly in the summer.

APPENDIX B:
TERMS CONCERNING SOUVENIR SPOONS

Crest:	Emblem, either metal, plastic, or enamel, that is affixed to a standard spoon.
Picture spoon:	Spoon with a picture under plastic which is heat moulded to the spoon.
Relief design:	Spoon with an engraving or picture which is moulded into the metal of the spoon.
Enamel:	Opaque substance similar to glass in composition.
Plated:	Thin layer of metal put on by electrolysis.
Rhodium-plated:	Shiny "jeweller's metal" which does not tarnish (no silver content).
Silver-plated:	Silver covering on another metal (such as steel).
Sterling silver:	Alloy of 92.5 percent silver and 8.5 percent copper, nickel, and zinc.
Alpacca:	Alloy of 82 percent copper and 18 percent nickel.

APPENDIX C:
SOUVENIR SPOON SUPPLIERS

Name	Location	Retail Price Points	Notes
Breadner	Hull, Quebec	$4.50–$6.00 ($32.00 for Sterling)	National distribution (including catalogue). Have basic design with different crests glued on. Lots of manufacturing capability.
Candis	Willowdale, Ont.	$4.00–$6.50	Good distribution. Have wide selection but quality toward lower end.
Metropolitan	Toronto, Ont.	$1.00–$4.00	Natural distribution includes other souvenirs and novelty items. Low-end spoons.
Gazelle	Grimsby, Ont.	$6.00	Previously imported from Holland. Ontario and Canada general designs. Quality same as Breadner's low end.
Oneida	Niagara Falls, Ont.	$8.00	U.S. subsidiary. High quality but little variety.
Commemorative	Ottawa, Ont.	$7.00–$9.00	Have three basic designs (supplied by Oneida). Often deal with clubs for whom they make up custom spoons.
Parsons-Steiner	Toronto, Ont.	$2.00–$6.00	Lower quality. (Appear to be cast iron with a decal attached.)
Boma	Vancouver, B.C.	$10.00–$20.00	High-quality pewter spoons.
Aalco	Vancouver, B.C.	$2.50–$3.00	National distributor with 300 three-dimensional models of spoons. Also carry numerous other souvenir items.
Souvenir	Downsview, Ont.	$3.00	Operate across North America. Have standardized spoons with crests attached. Have a wide complementary product line.

Case 21
Laval Structures Ltd.
(Revised)

On April 3, 1989, the bankers to Laval Structures Ltd., a Quebec-based home builder, called a meeting with the partners in Laval Structures—Jean and Pierre Montreaux. At this meeting, executives from Roy-Nat, the primary lending company, expressed their dissatisfaction with the company's performance. They wanted to know why the numerous problems had occurred, and what was going to be done about the current crisis. More to the point, they announced that Roy-Nat intended to call its loans in two weeks' time unless the explanation and recovery plan were satisfactory. With this news, the Montreaux hurriedly left the meeting.

Background

Laval Structures Ltd. commenced operations with Jean and Pierre Montreaux, owners and managers of two small companies in Laval, Quebec. The two businesses which they operated were Montreaux and Frere Construction Co., which built small houses under contract and on speculation, and Montreaux Engineering Lumber, which sold building materials and prefabricated chalets and houses. In 1971, they expanded through the purchase of a sand and gravel pit on 130 acres of land located in the area. A new company, Montreaux Gravel Pit Ltd., was formed to develop the gravel and sand business.

In 1974, they decided to expand the gravel pit operations through the purchase of new equipment for sifting and loading sand and gravel. As part of this expansion, they sought and secured a loan for $150,000 from Roy-Nat. The lending company was impressed with the purity of the reserves (estimated at 1 million metres) and the integrity and good credit rating of the owners. The first year of profitability for Montreaux Gravel Pit was in 1978 when it earned $5,000 on sales of $305,000. By using the profits from their other companies, they established a reputation for prompt loan payments and good financial management.

The two other businesses of the partners were conducted through limited partnerships. Montreaux Engineering Lumber was the more profitable and expanding component of the business. In 1978, this firm had sales of $1.7 million and profits of $40,000.

The businesses were short of working capital as a result of the necessity of expanding the facilities and equipment. However, the brothers were anxious to grow and expand. For example, Montreaux Engineering Lumber began to add other prefabricated components to their line of houses and chalets—

This case is adapted from Harold A. Gram, "Laval Structures Ltd." Copyright © Harold A. Gram, 1989.

premanufactured trusses and walls. The company had built facilities in the early years for the manufacture of houses and chalets. The workshop, with the new products, varied in employment from 75 to 150 people. In 1978, the company sold 25 prefabricated houses. The houses represented only one third of sales, while the trusses and prefabricated wall units represented two thirds of sales.

The original chalet model line was expanded by the addition of two standardized houses. One size was 24 feet by 36 feet, and the other was 24 feet by 50 feet. Prices varied between $16,000 to $22,000. The houses were erected by local contractors, who built foundations and installed wiring, plumbing, and heating.

Laval Structures Ltd.

The companies of the brothers were operated in various legal forms. Montreaux Gravel Pit was a limited company, while the other companies were partnerships. Several of the minority partners held various parts of the company through liens and mortgages. When one of the silent partners died, his estate demanded payment of the value of its interests. In order to solve these and other financing problems, in 1980 the various companies were reorganized under the name Laval Structures Ltd. In this new company, Jean Montreaux held 54 percent of the shares, and Pierre held 44 percent. The remaining fraction was used to settle the claims and interests of the various minority partners. Roy-Nat was approached to assist in financing the new company and increased its loan commitment to $235,000. The combined sales and profits of Laval Structures Ltd. is found in Exhibit 1.

By 1980, the company had established itself as a leading producer of prefabricated housing and components. It was estimated that it held 80 percent of the Quebec market. Its only competitor was Alcan. The housing section of the business, which had an excellent reputation as a producer of quality components, and as a quality product, represented 70 percent of the total sales of the corporation.

Expansion and Growth

The major growth of the company began in 1982. In 1983, it formed a joint venture to build 300 houses in a community south of Montreal. This joint venture was planned to last for four years (until 1987). The venture proved very

EXHIBIT 1 Combined Sales and Profits

Year	Sales	Profits ($000)
1979	3,758	95
1980	3,976	25
1981	4,803	3
1982	4,806	35

profitable and assured a steady market of about 75 homes annually. Another hundred houses were sold to a mining company. In order to meet the demand, the company began a move to shift work. The demand for houses was seasonal, and often houses could be transported and erected only during the summer months in northern areas. Nonetheless, the market for prefabricated units appeared very promising. The company, however, was unable to make substantial inroads in Montreal, where more than half of the people lived in rental quarters; its products were sold in the suburbs.

Laval Structures foresaw a rising demand for their products. The period 1982–83 was one of rising increase in the number of housing starts, as shown in Exhibit 2.

In anticipation of increased sales and markets, the plant at Laval was expanded. In 1983, the company was capable of producing 12 houses per week. In 1984, the facilities were expanded further to increase the capability to 20 units per week. A construction company was formed to work in northern Quebec,

Exhibit 2 New Dwelling Starts by Province by Type (population centres of 10,000 and over)*

Year	Atlantic Provinces	Quebec	Ontario	Prairies
		Single Detached		
1981	2,718	9,921	21,245	18,090
1982	2,459	7,410	15,483	8,781
1983	5,310	16,870	29,803	14,348
1984	4,646	15,177	28,320	9,473
1985	5,609	14,803	37,235	11,047
1986	6,091	19,510	48,147	12,374
1987	6,041	26,448	55,022	13,515
		Apartment and Other		
1981	944	10,781	14,160	14,780
1982	1,188	9,078	13,675	15,976
1983	1,520	11,986	14,953	8,025
1984	1,100	15,783	9,100	2,821
1985	2,509	22,823	14,337	3,778
1986	2,436	29,434	15,986	3,875
1987	1,677	35,444	26,587	4,515
		Semi-Detached, Duplex, and Row		
1981	497	2,419	9,994	6,900
1982	649	2,548	6,016	4,676
1983	773	4,790	5,514	2,018
1984	702	4,014	4,900	1,026
1985	1,149	3,778	5,481	702
1986	1,426	3,719	7,780	1,218
1987	1,173	4,865	12,291	1,301

NOTE: *Canadian Housing Statistics, 1987, p. 14.

erecting the prefabricated units. This latter company purchased lots, developed subdivisions, and performed the total installation for the customer. By 1984, Laval Structures Ltd. offered 22 different models of chalets and houses, which ranged in price from $15,000 to $18,000 (F.O.B. Laval).

The Management at Laval Structures

The two brothers who had started Laval Structures Ltd. occupied senior level positions in the company and continued the same management style they had used in the earlier years. Management responsibilities were shared, while the day-to-day operations were carried on by a minority shareholder in the company. A plant manager oversaw the operations of the assembly area. Financial statements were prepared on an annual basis, orders were filled as they were received, and any downturn in orders was accompanied by variations in plant employment. The success which they enjoyed permitted the owners extended southern vacations, and substantially improved their lifestyles.

In 1986, Roy-Nat encouraged the owners to restructure the company. A sales manager was hired along with a controller and a production manager. The first appointee to the position of production manager was fired after only a few months. The lending group encouraged the company to prepare monthly financial reports instead of the previous annual ones and pro forma budgets. The minority shareholder, who had been the effective manager of the operations, purchased the northern Quebec construction company and left the company.

Following this brief attempt to restructure the company, the brothers resumed their past habits. There was to be no director of production or finance and no formal organization structure. The brothers based their operational decisions and their sales efforts on their desire to grow and expand and their familiarity with the market—even though they had no cash controls, cost records, and market analyses.

Laval Structures Ltd. expanded its sales force efforts from Quebec into the Maritimes and the United States. The company noted with pride that its buildings were approved in all 50 states. Structural units for motels, apartments, and schools were added to the product line. Sales of housing units (single-family houses) for the years 1984–87 were as follows: 1984—550 units; 1985—717 units; 1986—601 units; 1987—538 units.

The desire for further expansion led the company into the Ontario market in 1986 through the purchase of a bankrupt construction company in Kingston. The company, along with its assets and liabilities, was purchased for $1 million. The brothers considered this a bargain, since no initial capital investment was required. A manufacturing operation, was established under a general manager. During the first year of operation the company sold 50 houses and secured a contract for an additional 200 houses. Although the company had expected to sell 500 houses, and had built the plant for this level of sales, the Ontario market did not meet their expectations. In 1987, the construction company, along with the facilities for the manufacturing of homes, was sold for a loss of $1,005,000.

The company felt that the general manager had not performed adequately, and he was fired.

By 1987, the construction process had become formalized and highly structured. Houses were built in halves and joined together in the field. Although the houses looked like two trailers, when joined they made an attractive small house. The company had devoted a great deal of their capital to improvements in the facilities and buildings. By early 1987, the plant represented a moderate-size factory with five separate buildings. The plant operated 16 hours per day, 5 days per week in the summer. In winter, production and employment dropped about 50 percent. At capacity, the plant employed 350 people. The major assembly work was conducted in a 65,720-square-foot building. A preassembly building of 21,415 square feet prepared components for the production line. The other buildings were used for a welding shop, storage, and offices.

The company relied upon agents in the field to sell the houses, secure lots, erect the buildings, and install the needed wiring, plumbing, and heating. Ninety agents operated in Quebec, who were often local contractors or building supply companies, price-sensitive to the market demands.

The 1988–1989 Situation

The company's sales were concentrated almost 80 percent in Quebec and 10 percent each in Ontario and the Maritime provinces. There were 25 models of homes, which sold for an average price of $30,000. Since the company began operations in 1980, several other competitors had entered the field. One company was located in Quebec City, and a competitor near Montreal produced similar products. Each of these competitors was small, and had not enjoyed the growth of Laval Structures. The competitors' buildings were also considered inferior in variety of offerings, and in size of plant and facilities. These companies concentrated in the house-building area and did not produce components for schools, motels, and apartment buildings.

In 1987, the company secured a contract for 78 furnished houses as part of a new pulp and paper community in Northern Quebec. The joint venture in the town south of Montreal was also coming to a close.

Since 1986, the company had tried to sell its products abroad to take advantage of the rising demand for housing in Saudi Arabia and countries in South America. The brothers had made several trips abroad in search of these sales, and in late 1987, the company sold 25 houses for a new housing project in Libya, and 50 houses to a South American government. The Libyan contract was expanded in early 1988 by an additional 35 houses.

In late 1987, the company was short of working capital. It requested and received a loan of $600,000 from Roy-Nat, of which $300,000 was for the plant which was built in 1987, and the remainder for the financing of contracts which it had received from abroad. On the basis of its foreign contracts and expected sales in Quebec, the company prepared pro forma financial statements-for 1988 which are included in Exhibits 3 and 4. The order of $2.8 million from Libya, and the $1.2 million order for South America, are included in these figures.

Before the formal year-end financial statements were available for 1988, the company again approached its lending sources. Roy-Nat increased its commitment to $1 million. A chartered bank was approached and made a working capital loan to finance the order. This loan from the chartered bank would ultimately reach $4 million.

In the early months of 1989, the formal statements for Laval Structures became available. Sales of houses had totaled 347, rather than the 825 projected. In the first five months of 1989, the company shipped 91 houses and had total orders for 98 (including the foreign contracts).

EXHIBIT 3

LAVAL STRUCTURES LTD.
Income Statement
($000)

	Year 1985 (historical)	Year 1986 (historical)	Year 1987 (historical)	Year 1988* (pro forma)	11 months 1988 (historical)
Sales	$19,300	$19,300	$21,800	$25,550	$16,730
Cost of goods sold	17,700	17,400	19,800	22,310	12,020
Gross profit	1,600	1,900	2,000	3,240	4,710
Cost of transport and erection	204	275	390	24	2,710
Operating income	1,396	1,625	1,610	3,216	2,000
Income from joint venture	195	71	954	900	–
Total	1,591	1,696	2,564	4,116	2,000
Expenses:					
Sales	306	462	330	305	220
Administration	738	887	1,142	1,037	1,252
Finance	170	181	374	363	508
Loss or gain on sale of assets	15	2	(2)	295	(15)
	1,229	1,532	1,844	2,000	1,965
Income before taxes	362	164	720	2,116	35
Taxes current	96	115	384	996	–
Tax credit	(2)	46	(62)	–	–
Net income	$ 264	$ 95	$ 274	$ 1,120	$ 35

NOTE: *Prepared late in 1987.

Laval Structures manufactured 50 houses for the Libyan order, crated them for shipment, and transported the houses to the Port of Montreal for shipment in the spring of 1989. The Libyan buyers refused to honour the order and refused acceptance. The South American order was not completed.

EXHIBIT 4

LAVAL STRUCTURES LTD.
Balance Sheet
($000)

	Dec. 1985 (historical)	Dec. 1986 (historical)	Dec. 1987 (historical)	Dec. 1988* (pro forma)	Nov. 30, 1988 (historical)
Current assets:					
Cash	$ 22	$ 21	$ 385	$ 464	$ 27
Accounts receivable	2,200	1,200	2,250	2,085	4,468
Notes receivable and deposits	25	10	50	–	835
Joint venture equity	101	103	284	307	65
Inventories	2,500	1,850	3,300	2,236	2,645
Advances to affiliated cos	323	935	–	–	463
Prepaid expense	142	92	9	–	53
Prepaid taxes	92	–	–	–	21
Total	$5,405	$4,211	$6,278	$ 5,092	$ 8,577
Investments/equity in affiliates	16	16	6	400	766
Fixed assets:					
Land and buildings	1,775	1,825	2,303	2,700	2,801
Reserve (depreciation)	(650)	(800)	(903)	(1,000)	(1,011)
	1,125	1,025	1,400	1,700	1,790
Other assets	30	17	284	70	233
Total assets	6,576	5,269	7,968	7,262	11,366
Liabilities:					
Loans	1,700	1,700	830	–	4,038
Checks outstanding	–	177	1,038	200	–
Accounts payable	2,900	1,000	3,300	1,430	2,471
Deposits (for loans and houses)	–	80	77	75	895
Tax payable	197	106	103	1,046	614
Deferred income tax	58	126	476	425	54
Current due on notes	151	205	235	238	234
Total	5,006	3,394	6,059	3,414	8,306
Due directors	88	74	64	64	145
Long-term debt	677	1,064	927	1,120	1,370
Shareholders equity	805	737	918	2,664	1,545
Total	$6,576	$5,269	$7,968	$ 7,262	$11,366

NOTE: *Prepared late in 1987.

In early 1989, the company's working capital was in serious condition. In the first three months, the company lost $770,000. Roy-Nat investigated the financial affairs of the company and discovered that it had more than $1 million in accounts payable that were over 45 days old and had total bank loans and accounts payable of $7,181,623. With this knowledge, Roy-Nat called the meeting for April 3.

CASE 22
LAWSON & JONES LTD. (CONDENSED)

Lawrence (Larry) Tapp, president and CEO of Lawson & Jones Ltd. (hereafter L&J), felt a sense of frustration as he reviewed his last in a long series of requests to B.A.T for increased capital spending. L&J, a major Canadian printing and packaging company, was 75 percent owned by Mardon Packaging International Limited, which was in turn wholly owned by B.A.T Industries plc of the United Kingdom. Tapp felt increasingly uncomfortable with the requirements being imposed upon L&J by its British parent. The following excerpt in a recent (August 17, 1984) letter from a B.A.T board representative described the situation:

> In summary, meeting your trading profit budget for 1984 when a number of key financial figures are unlikely to be achieved will not support your case for a substantial increase in capital spending for 1985. On the other hand, if we see progression on trading profit well up on budget for 1984 and 1985, you will have the credibility to support capital spending for 1985.

Tapp had replied as follows:

> I thought L&J was genuinely earning adequate credibility but you and I seem to differ on this. . . . The capital spending that we are asking for will permit us to meet your objectives—I don't know how to get another $1 million of trading profit this year if our capital spending is delayed.

Tapp felt B.A.T's return objectives were unrealistic for the printing and packaging business, especially without dramatic infusion of capital for acquisitions, equipment, product development, and new technology. He disagreed with the "harvest" strategy emerging from B.A.T's constraints on capital and substantial dividend requirements for L&J. Other aspects of the relationships, the just-in-case somebody asks reporting requirements, and the constantly changing planning system were also annoying, and he believed distracted L&J managers from running their businesses.

Background

L&J was a small part of a large international empire. B.A.T Industries plc had evolved out of the old British American Tobacco Company. During the 1960s and 70s, the company had diversified beyond its core tobacco business and became a multinational conglomerate. From its head office in London, England, B.A.T controlled interests in a portfolio of U.K.– and overseas-based companies. B.A.T Industries was directly involved in activities ranging from its historical base business in tobacco products to retailing, cosmetics, paper, home improvements, and financial products. As Exhibit 1 demonstrates, B.A.T subsidiaries literally covered the globe.

In 1983, B.A.T Industries' sales from consolidated subsidiaries totaled £11,846 million and profits were £651 million. Mardon Packaging International (MPI), B.A.T's principal subsidiary in the printing and packaging business, had sales of £508 million (4.3 percent of B.A.T's total) and profits of £23.9 million (2.8 percent of B.A.T's total). L&J, a 75 percent owned subsidiary of MPI, accounted for 1.2 percent of B.A.T's and 28.3 percent of MPI's sales and 0.8 percent and 32.6 percent of profits, respectively.

B.A.T also held less than majority interests in 13 associated companies in 11 countries, one of which was its 45 percent interest in Imasco Ltd. of Canada, a diversified enterprise in its own right that had emerged from the (Canadian) Imperial Tobacco Company. B.A.T's share of associated companies' profit before tax for 1983 (not consolidated into B.A.T's financial statements) was £125 million. Principal subsidiaries were those in which B.A.T had controlling interests; in associated companies, B.A.T held less than 50 percent of the voting equity.

Performance trends for the last four years are summarized in Exhibit 2. B.A.T's multicountry tobacco products business provided a strong stable base. However, the performance of B.A.T's nontobacco businesses had deteriorated during the 1981–82 recession. Financial reporting at B.A.T was also done by product sector. Tobacco yielded the highest return on assets (20.9 percent), a key measure of performance for B.A.T businesses, printing and packaging the lowest (8.5 percent).

B.A.T provided certain general objectives to all its businesses. These were

- Achieve a 20 percent RONA (*return on net assets*) for U.K. operations and 25 percent overseas.

- Pay dividends according to B.A.T financial guidelines (for MPI £8.0 million in 1984 increasing by £1 million per year to 1989).

Exhibit 1   B.A.T Industries plc, Major Business Sectors

Sector	Subsidiaries	Countries	Sales (£ millions)
Tobacco	49	38	6138
Retailing	8	2	3528
Paper	31	16	1051
Packaging and print	40	9	537
Cosmetics	20	13	
Home improvements	8	3	625
Finance and insurance	8	6	

Source: B.A.T Annual Report 1983.

- Reduce the gearing ratio (D/E) below 60 percent by 1986. (As of December 31, 1984, MPI's was at 74 percent.)
- Generate sufficient cash to finance investment in opportunities for profitable growth as well as improvement of existing businesses, and, where appropriate, expansion.

B.A.T did state that these objectives were for the B.A.T Industries Group as a whole and would not necessarily be directly applicable to individual operating groups and companies. In particular, rates of growth to be aimed for would be determined by the circumstances of the business concerned. B.A.T had the stated objective of increasing (real) dividends paid to its shareholders by a minimum of 4 percent per year.

B.A.T's chairman, Patrick Sheehy, had recently commented on the group's strategy.

> [Our] strategy also imposes its own discipline. Inevitably it involves us in reorganizing, selling or even closing those businesses which do not meet our criteria for long-term growth potential. . .
>
> . . . these moves form part of the unending process of reshaping a very large company to meet the ever-changing conditions of the modern world. But we believe that we have now established a durable framework, made up of two manufacturing businesses—tobacco and paper—and two service businesses—retailing and financial.[1]

Mardon Packaging International (MPI)

Mardon's headquarters were in Bristol, England, with over 80 manufacturing facilities, including 46 in the United Kingdom, 16 in Canada, 8 in the United States, and the remainder in Europe and Central Africa. Over 11,500 people

---

[1] 1983 *Annual Report* of B.A.T Industries. B.A.T had recently acquired a relatively small financial services business.

Exhibit 2 B.A.T Industries—Five-Year Financial Summary

	1980	1981	1982	1983
Sales £ mm	7645	9265	11500	11850
Trading profit (EBIT) £ mm	467	634	783	851
EBIT margin %	6.1%	6.8%	6.8%	7.2%
Net assets £ mm	2894*	3654*	4816	5068
Dividends—ordinary	69	84	100	120
RONA[†] %	16.1%	17.4%	16.3%	16.8%

*Estimated

$$†RONA = \frac{EBIT}{Accounts\ receivable + Investment - Trade\ credit + Net\ fixed\ assets}$$

Source: B.A.T Annual Report 1983; sales include associated companies.

were employed worldwide. A wide variety of packaging and promotional material was produced, including folding cartons, flexible packaging, fibreboard cases, specialist print and labels, and rigid plastic and metal containers. Mardon Packaging was one of the major manufacturers of packaging in the United Kingdom, where it was a market leader in folding cartons, flexible packaging, and calendars.

The origins of this printing and packaging company stretched back to the early nineteenth century. Mardon partially entered the B.A.T empire in 1962 when it became jointly owned by the Imperial Group and B.A.T Industries. Throughout the 1960s and 1970s, Mardon had expanded both internally and by acquisition. By 1983, the Mardon Group's business was concentrated in the United Kingdom (47 percent) and in North America (44 percent).

Mardon became a *wholly* owned subsidiary of B.A.T Industries in 1979. Until 1981, B.A.T's management involvement was limited to having two representatives on the MPI board. At that time John Worlidge, one of the B.A.T executives on the MPI board, replaced John Cornish as managing director of MPI. This was the first time a B.A.T executive became directly involved in the management of MPI. Even this involvement was limited since Worlidge maintained his office at B.A.T headquarters in London and spent most of his time there. Alex Halliday, the current managing director, had succeeded Worlidge at the beginning of 1984. It was widely rumoured that he had been brought in to "clean up" MPI. His early actions, cutting Mardon staff and taking more of a hands-on approach, tended to confirm these suspicions.

Mardon Packaging International had performed between the median and upper quartile for the U.K. packaging industry but had not met B.A.T's financial objectives. There had been a recovery in 1983 from the downward trend begun in 1979. The principal reason for improvement in 1983 was a £2.3 mm profits gain in flexible packaging, the divestment of a company which had lost £2.0 mm in 1982, although its sale caused an extraordinary loss, and the recovery from the recession of 1982.

Mardon had five trading divisions (see Exhibit 3). Flexible packaging in the United Kingdom and Europe was the largest "domestic" business sector, accounting for 18 percent of sales, followed closely by the carton and print division with 17 percent. Although the Overseas Division was reported separately, its activities also included operations similar to those of the major domestic divisions. The Overseas Division, those activities outside the United Kingdom and Europe, made up 42 percent of sales. L&J was the largest single component within Mardon; especially if Mardon Corporation, MPI's holding in the United States, was included. Mardon Corporation was assembled during the 1970s by John Cornish, then MPI's managing director, on his trips to North America. He acquired several small, U.S. printing and packaging companies.[2] Many of these acquisitions proved to be ill considered and the returns from

---

[2]Western Lithograph, one of L&J's U.S.–based companies, had been acquired as part of this process.

EXHIBIT 3

MARDON PACKAGING INTERNATIONAL
Recent Financial Results
(12 months ending Dec 31, 1983)
(£ millions)

Sector	Sales	EBIT	Net Assets	RONA %
Carton and print division	88	2.1	45	4.7
Corrugated division	32	2.0	15	13.0
Flexible packaging division	92	5.1	43	11.9
Rigid plastics and metals	79	4.6	37	12.2
Overseas division				
Lawson & Jones Ltd.	144	7.8	45	17.6
Mardon Corporation (U.S.)	63	1.9	19	9.7
Mardon Printers (Zimbabwe)	8	0.4	8	5.7
Total	508	23.9	212	11.3

SOURCE: MPI Group Plan and Budget, January 1984.

this unit had never been adequate. L&J management had, with B.A.T's support, assumed management responsibility for MPI's American operations in mid-1983. Ownership remained with MPI, at least for the time being.

B.A.T had established performance objectives that would require a continued turnaround in MPI's performance. Critical to achieving these performance objectives was upgrading the competence of the management teams at each of MPI's companies. MPI had developed plans to remedy identified weaknesses in the management group by transfers, recruitment, and management development. The policy of introducing a number of MBAs into U.K. and North American middle management levels was to be continued and graduate recruitment was to be strengthened. A training program to improve the financial awareness of the incumbent general managers had just been completed for the management groups of all U.K. companies. Other key areas for management training were to be addressed by other programs during 1984 and 1985.

Lawson & Jones Limited

L & J was one of Canada's oldest and premier companies in the printing and packaging industries. The company produced a wide range of products and services from magazines, labels, catalogues, and newspaper advertising inserts to folding cartons, flexible packaging, and business forms from 17 plants in Canada and 2 in the United States. In 1982, the corporate head office had been moved

200 kilometres from London, Ontario, to the outskirts of Toronto near the international airport. This had been done at B.A.T's direction and over the objections of the local board.

Background

L&J began in 1882 as a partnership between F.E. Lawson and H.J. Jones in London, Ontario. The partnership's first products were labels and calendars. L&J first sold common shares outside the Lawson family in 1948. By the 1950s, operations in seven cities served the Canadian market for labels and printing. The company entered the business forms market in 1958 and, three years later, acquired its first packaging facility, as well as a printing company, in the United States.

In 1953, the Lawson family learned that Mardon planned to enter the Canadian market and would be a direct competitor with L&J. Ray Lawson knew members of the Mardon management and contacted them to suggest joining forces in Canada. As a result, MPI purchased 50 percent of L&J from the Lawson family, and in 1976 increased its ownership to 75 percent. In 1982, B.A.T had expressed an interest in acquiring the remainder of L&J. However, nothing had come of this indication. Most of the remainder (20 percent) was controlled by Colonel Tom Lawson, grandson of the founder. (Tom Lawson had the rank of colonel in the Canadian armed services during the war and retained this honourary title.) A small number of shares infrequently made available by Colonel Tom had been bought by long-time L&J managers, several now retired, and a few were held by the "public" (approximately 5 percent). Prices for the thinly traded stock were between $300 and $315 per share in early 1984.

Tapp, age 46, joined L&J in 1978 as General Manager of Lawson Graphics Manitoba and was promoted through the positions of division manager – graphics, managing director – packaging, and executive vice president. He assumed the presidency in 1982, being promoted over several incumbent managers with more seniority and industry experience. Prior to joining L&J, Tapp had been vice president of operations for Hallmark Cards (Canada). Tapp commented on the situation at L&J prior to his becoming president:

> In the head office of L&J, at the time, was Tom Lawson, the president, the secretary-treasurer, the accountant, and the internal auditor. There was no detailed oversight of, support for, or coordination of the operating companies. Working capital was not being managed and our operating companies were actually competing with each other for some of the same orders. Mostly, we had good operators running the plants but they had no backup. Furthermore they weren't really concerned about markets, customers, and profits. The measure of success was running the plant at 100 percent capacity.

In 1983, L&J's sales and pre-tax income were C$258.5 million and C$12.5 million, respectively. Growth over the previous 30 years had been achieved in large part by completing 35 acquisitions and expanding to nine new locations. A financial summary, reported in Canadian dollars, for the four years from 1980 to 1983 has been set out in Exhibit 4. Annual performance review sessions were conducted in London, England, by MPI's board of directors with the president of L&J in attendance. Financial reporting at these meetings was done in constant (deflated) pounds sterling.

Results were also reported for the three main divisions: printing (60 percent of sales), packaging (32 percent of sales), and business forms (8 percent of sales). Internal financial reporting was done by product sector.

MPI's Strategic Objectives for L&J

L&J prepared and negotiated an annual strategic plan with MPI. The requirements of the planning process had been changing from year to year. However, an emphasis on strategy, as opposed to simply financial forecasts, had emerged in the last several years. MPI's changing format and content requirements for the plans made developing a consistent approach difficult. Strategic plans were reviewed annually in England. Mardon prepared a 10-year rolling plan for discussion at a meeting with company presidents in attendance. Tapp participated in the detailed annual strategy review sessions for all MPI businesses.

Even though L&J had approved strategies and objectives for each of its businesses, it was unclear to Tapp exactly what this approval meant. Several requests for capital Tapp felt to be consistent with the plan and met hurdle rate requirements had been "delayed to death" by MPI/B.A.T.

EXHIBIT 4

LAWSON & JONES LIMITED
Four-Year Financial Summary

	1980	1981	1982	1983
Sales C$ mm	215.2	234.2	242.1	258.5
Trading profit C$ mm (EBIT)	15.9	16.1	11.9	14.0
EBIT margin %	7.4%	6.9%	4.9%	5.4%
Dividends—common	3.5	3.6	2.4	4.4
Net assets C$ mm	77.9	84.1	82.4	79.6
RONA%	20.4%	19.1%	14.4%	17.6%

SOURCE: L&J annual reports.

Linking Plans to Action

MPI's current plan for L&J was to reshape the group into a smaller number oflarger, core businesses. From 19 companies in 1983, the group would comprise 13 in 1988. The product mix would change as below:

| | Sales C$ million | | | |
	1983	%	1988*	%
Web print	88	34	101	33
Sheet-fed print	26	10	11	4
Labels	41	16	49	16
Cartons	63	24	79	25
Flexible packaging	20	8	27	9
Business forms	20	8	—	—
Rigid plastics packaging	—	—	40	13
	258	100	307	100

NOTE: *Constant 1983 dollars.

The product mix was expected to change. By consolidating production facilities, refining the product mix, and developing exports, web printing was expected to grow substantially. Growth in sheet-fed printing would be limited to maintaining and enhancing L&J's position in labels. Conventional sheet-fed printing was expected to become less significant. The plan called for continued investment in gravure technology and the development of specialized, high-margin products for niche markets in the packaging business. No growth was planned in business forms; indeed, it was a potential divestment candidate.

L&J had included in their plan the intention to enter the rigid plastic container business. This industry in North America contained several attractive segments, such as widemouthed jars, extrusion and injection blow-moulded bottles for toiletries, injection-moulded pails and containers, and closures. MPI already had U.K. manufacturing know-how. L&J planned to enter rigid plastics by making a small acquisition and bringing in technology from a sister company in the United Kingdom. Tapp explained:

> We see this as a very attractive business. The only thing we need is the vehicle, the U.S. base. If we get the go-ahead, this will be the first attempt at a significant technology transfer from the United Kingdom to North America.

Other entry strategies for this business had been explored. In 1982, L&J had been approached by a major Canadian customer about supplying them with widemouthed plastic jars. This proposal had been developed and presented to

MPI. MPI had not moved quickly enough, and the customer had found an alternate supplier.

The move to establish another leg in rigid plastics, probably by acquisition, could logically lead to the purchase of a U.S. business because of the restricted number of suitable opportunities in Canada. The geographical outcome of the other strategies would be a greater concentration in Eastern Canada, given the planned expansion of the web, carton, and flexibles businesses in that area. Most of the business in Western Canada would be divested.

Profit, in real dollar terms, was expected to double over 10 years. The planning document did *not* project detailed sources and applications of funds consistent with the plan.

Larry Tapp believed L&J's strategy as outlined in the plans and agreed to by MPI represented an aggressive, but with appropriate support, achievable outcome. However, several recent events had led him to question whether or not it would ever be realized. In the past six months, two acquisition proposals had been submitted to MPI/B.A.T: one for a business forms operation, the other a plastics container manufacturer, both in the United States. Capital appropriations had been prepared and each met or exceeded MPI/B.A.T return requirements. Each of these had been subject to what Tapp felt were inordinate requests for additional information and interminable delays. Both had eventually been withdrawn by L&J when the opportunities passed. After the last of these, Halliday had shared with Tapp his view that for the foreseeable future, "B.A.T would set strategy and L&J managers should concentrate on running the existing operations." Perhaps even more importantly, constraints on capital for established businesses jeopardized the achievement of the plan.

Organizational Relationships

L&J was composed of 19 separate operating companies. Traditionally, the operating companies had been highly autonomous, often likened to independent fiefdoms. This organizational philosophy was partly the result of growth by acquisition—the owner/operator often became the general manager of the acquired operation—but it also reflected Colonel Tom Lawson's approach to management. Even plants operated as separate entities, managing their own production, marketing, accounting, and sales staff. This approach was believed, by some, to permit quicker response, higher quality, and better service at the customer level. The operating companies were organized into three main divisions, commercial printing, packaging, and business forms.

One of the first things Larry Tapp did in 1982, upon becoming CEO of L&J, was to strengthen the corporate head office.

> I'm not a supporter of big corporate staffs but when I took over we needed a stronger central group for L&J. So I hired Ralph Steedman for finance, Frank Pamenter for human resources, and a planning person. Now we're about two thirds of the way

toward where we should be with the corporate staff group. We still need someone in MIS, banking, and generally some more analytic horsepower to help me do my job better. We're not as far along with the line management. I want to make our operating management more professional; some people are adapting, but I am meeting some resistance.

A typical L&J general manager of an operating company made between C$80,000 and $130,000 base salary with the potential for a bonus of half that much again. The bonus was based upon actual subunit profits against budgeted profits. The system was not perfect. It was strongly suspected by senior L&J managers that at least three subunit managers were manipulating the reporting of results in order to increase their bonus.

Management compensation at L&J had been designed and implemented by the Canadian board but came under scrutiny in 1983 from the Mardon board. B.A.T and Mardon wanted L&J to adopt an approach similar to what they used, keeping total executive compensation the same but to increase base salaries and reduce bonuses. L&J's board preferred to maintain the status quo, believing it was more in line with North American practice and further, even with its problems, the motivation bonuses it gave to its managers had an overall positive effect on results. Currently, alternatives were being assessed by the board.

Tapp wanted to try and improve the strategic thinking of L&J's senior line managers. Many of these managers had "ink in their veins," having begun as printers and risen up through the ranks. A corporate staff planning position was created, and line managers were required to document market and competitive trends, identify opportunities and threats, and propose a strategy for their units. Tapp was assisted in this endeavour by the MPI/B.A.T requirement for formal strategic plans. Quality of the plans naturally varied with the interest and ability of the line managers, but Tapp felt current plans provided a solid informational base upon which to assess L&J's businesses.

Linkages with MPI

The Mardon group was administered by a head office staff of 65 people. Central control was exercised over strategy, finance, and some management development activities. The head office staff provided support for the board in the areas of finance, product and process development, planning, market research, public affairs, management development, and pensions administration.

Each subsidiary company in the Mardon group had a management team comprised of a managing director supported by production, sales, and finance managers. They operated local boards with their own chairmen and had profit responsibility for their operations.

The formal chain of command for L&J was as follows:

Patrick Sheehy   Chairman of B.A.T Industries plc
J. Worlidge   Chairman of Mardon Packaging and executive director of B.A.T Industries plc

A. Halliday	Managing director of MPI
E.H. Webber	Deputy managing director and director of the overseas division (to which L&J belonged)
Dr. D.H. Thain	Nonexecutive chairman of the board of L&J
L.G. Tapp	President and CEO of L&J

The local chairman formally reported to an MPI executive, who in turn reported to Alex Halliday, managing director of MPI. Halliday had just assumed the managing directorship of MPI eight months earlier. He came from the Wiggins Teape group, a B.A.T subsidiary in the paper-making business. Worlidge had been the managing director prior to Halliday, having replaced his predecessor in 1981 after B.A.T had gained complete control of MPI. Except for Worlidge and Halliday, the senior management of MPI was composed of long-service employees without other B.A.T experience. Board members and key officers are described in Exhibit 5.

Informal reporting relationships differed from the formal. Tapp explained:

> Even though Webber and Halliday are in the formal chain of command, I still really report to John Worlidge. He and I came to our positions about the same time. We established a good working relationship and it continues. Of course, this is still an English company and you haven't seen a strict hierarchy in action until you've had lunch at Windsor House.[3] However, I really don't pay much attention to that kind of thing. Perhaps I don't pay enough attention to it.

Thain expanded upon Tapps' comments:

> L&J's relationship with Worlidge has always been cordial but formal. Our disagreement over compensation practices is a good example. Worlidge listens to our arguments for maintaining the current approach, thanks us for our input, and then insists it be done their way. He is a true English gentleman, very cultured but also difficult to warm up to.
>
> Alex Halliday appears to be very different than Worlidge. He comes across as tough, forceful, much more of a hands-on manager. He is numbers oriented and doesn't seem to have much interest in learning about, and coming to understand, the printing and packaging business.

At a lower level, MPI/B.A.T staff often contacted L&J staff directly with requests for information above and beyond that required by normal reporting procedures. Indeed, MPI requests for information were a source of some aggravation. During April 1983, Tapp had informed Worlidge that the equivalent of one person full-time was needed to answer queries on a multitude of financial, marketing, and operational issues not part of the normal reporting required and not necessarily needed by the MPI/B.A.T bureaucracy. Many of these requests originated from the finance director's office at MPI. When asked

---

[3]B.A.T's headquarters in downtown London.

EXHIBIT 5 **Profile of Executives**

MPI Board

Name	Position	Age	Tenure*	Background
E.J. Worlidge	Chairman MPI; director B.A.T.			Oxford graduate
A. Halliday	Managing director MPI	48	24/8 mos.	Wiggins Teape
E.H. Webber	Deputy M.D. of MPI	58	33/2	Oxford graduate; Mardon
J.H.B. Allan	Finance director of MPI	44	13/4	Chartered accountant Deloite, Haskins & Sells
M.B. Edwards	Personnel director of MPI	48	/1	CompAir; Jaguar
R.E. Illingworth	RP & M Division chairman	48	18/1	Illingworth Plastic
K.C. Mardon	Flexibles Division chairman	46	22/?	Mardon
C.E. Muir	Carton & Paint Division chairman	60	13/8	William Thyne Co.
J.P. Dahig	CEO & president Mardon Packaging Corp.	46	/4	
L.G. Tapp	CEO & president Lawson & Jones Ltd.			

Lawson & Jones Board

Outside of Part-Time Appointments

Name	Position	Age	Tenure*	Background
D.H. Thain	Chairman, Lawson & Jones Ltd.	56	1/3	Harvard MBA, DBA U.W.O. Professor
Col. T. Lawson	Honorary chairman of L&J	70	50/3	U.W.O., B.A. 1953–78 president of L&J 1976–82 chairman of L&J
C.D. Parmelee	Vice-chairman of L&J	53	3/3	Pres & CEO of Roman Corp.
E.H. Webber	Deputy M.D. of MPI	58	33/2	Oxford graduate; Mardon

L&J Managers

Name	Position	Tenure*
L.G. Tapp	CEO & president, L&J Ltd.	5
R.B. Steedman	VP finance, L&J Ltd.	2
D.I. Hardie	VP graphics East	12
R.G. Kite	VP graphics West and U.S.	2
M.J. Pilon	VP packaging	<1

NOTE: *The two numbers represent years with L&J / years in present position

why this information was needed, L&J management were given evasive responses but left with the impression they should comply and not ask questions. It was suspected that many of these requests were made "just in case" the staff members' boss might ask for the information.

Another aspect of the relationship was the occasional "inspection tour" B.A.T executives would make to Canada. These visits were taken seriously. Several years ago, after one such trip, a L&J senior manager had been dismissed.

Operating and Capital Budgets

L&J's operating budgets were prepared by the Canadian management teamand submitted to Mardon executives for approval annually. The budgets were to be prepared within the financial guidelines that were established by B.A.T and communicated to L&J through Mardon. Overall estimates of capital budgets were prepared annually. Individual requests were submitted for approval throughout the year.

The harvest strategy that Mardon/B.A.T was apparently imposing on L&J in 1983 and 1984 was conflicting with the selective growth strategy that Tapp hoped to implement, an integrated program of divestiture and growth which would reshape L&J. B.A.T apparently wanted to use the proceeds of divestitures to invest in other units. L&J, on the other hand, wanted to use the proceeds of divestitures within L&J, and had proposed a growth strategy for selected businesses with an accompanying investment program.

Performance Objectives

The annual B.A.T Industries guidelines set specific objectives for return on net assets (RONA). B.A.T considered L&J's performance unsatisfactory because the company consistently failed to meet the target RONA, despite the fact that internal studies showed it performed relatively well within its industry.

B.A.T required each division to pay dividends and set a maximum debt-to-equity ratio. The gearing ratio (debt/equity) was to remain below 60 percent. What was left over after the dividend payout was available to invest either in the business itself through capital spending programs or in another group activity. Currently, L&J had a gearing ratio of 0.45 and theoretically some available debt capacity. However, L&J's statements were consolidated with MPI, which had an overall ratio of 0.77 at the end of 1983.

L&J's dividends had been increased for 1983, from a traditional 50 percent payout level to 60 percent. The L&J board had "expressed its concern and anxieties regarding the [new] dividend rate to the parent company," at a 1983 meeting of the board of directors. Furthermore, MPI/B.A.T wanted L&J's dividends to be C$9.5 million for 1985 and to increase by C$1.2 million every year.

For 1985, L&J was left with a planned discretionary cash flow of C$19 million but had capital spending plans for C$23 million. B.A.T would not authorize the additional C$4 million. Tapp felt this level of expenditures would not allow L&J to maintain its capital base and competitive position and expressed his views on capital constraints to Howard Webber, deputy managing director of MPI:

> We are now looking for additional funds to be allocated to 1985 for the accelerated growth and development that will happen in parallel with the divestment.
>
> Howard, I obviously need your help on this. We can only deal with so much at one time, so the more trust and confidence that you can instill at B.A.T for L&J, the faster we will all get to where we want to be.
>
> Unless I hear from you otherwise, I will include $22–23 million for capital spending in 1985 with the corporate plan and will spell out the justification at that time. Can I count on your support?

The dividend objectives for the printing and packaging business did not leave anything for discretionary capital projects. L&J's capital spending proposals were submitted to B.A.T each year with the intention of improving RONA but had been reduced because past RONA performance did not justify the requested amount.

Mounting Pressures

The relationship between I&J management and B.A.T/Mardon management had deteriorated over the last two years. Printing and packaging appeared not to be a core business for B.A.T. Furthermore, B.A.T apparently had other investment options considered more attractive than L&J's capital expenditure program. Tapp suspected B.A.T had little confidence in those MPI managers not appointed by B.A.T. If this were the case, L&J might be suffering from guilt by association.

Tapp, Steedman, and Thain often discussed the exacerbating aspects of the relationship. They knew B.A.T's strategy for L&J could be implemented by senior executives satisfied with the status quo. However, B.A.T had allowed the formation of an aggressive top management group to replace their predecessors at L&J. Furthermore, L&J had been recruiting young, aggressive, professionally trained managers to corporate staff and middle-level line management positions by describing the challenges that lay ahead. They had participated in the preparation of a tentative growth plan for the Canadian operation. Tapp's credibility would suffer with recently hired managers who might resign if B.A.T's implicit strategy were adopted.

Not all the senior management was as questioning of B.A.T's constraints as Tapp. Many of the old line managers within Lawson and Jones would accept a harvest strategy, some because of their impending retirement and the positive impact it would have on their bonuses; others might view it as an opportunity to ingratiate themselves with B.A.T and undermine Tapp's position.

Tapp felt he had to do something. Personally, he did not find the current situation acceptable.

When I took charge of L&J, the job was really challenging and MPI/B.A.T really gave me the scope to do what needed to be done. It was a positive, productive relationship. In the last year or so, that has changed. I don't really think it would be much fun to manage this business for cash.

Tapp realized that not to take action soon would, given MPI/B.A.T's control on funds, result in the implementation of a harvest strategy for L&J. Once this process began, he felt it would be difficult, if not impossible, to reverse. If he was to take effective action, it must be done soon.

CASE 23
METROPOL BASE-FORT SECURITY GROUP

Pat Haney, president of Metropol Base-Fort Security Group (Metropol), was sitting in his office contemplating the future direction of his company. Metropol, a leading Canadian security firm whose services included the provision of uniformed security guards, mobile security patrols, polygraph testing, insurance and criminal investigations, and a broad range of specialized services, was faced with a number of challenges that threatened its future profitability. "Increasing competition, especially from large multinationals such as Pinkertons, is further reducing already low industry margins," offered Pat. He was also concerned about Metropol's reliance on the commodity-like security guard business for 90 percent of its revenue. "We have to find some way to meaningfully differentiate our services from those of our competitors," Pat observed. "That is essential if we are to achieve the kind of growth we desire."

Company Background

Metropol was founded in 1952 by George Whitbread, a former RCMP officer. In 1975, Whitbread sold the company to former Manitoba premier Duff Roblin. Haney came aboard in 1976 to run the Winnipeg operation, which was then 80 percent of Metropol's business. In the late 1970s and early 1980s, Metropol expanded into Saskatchewan and Alberta. In 1984, it took over the leading Alberta security firm, Base-Fort Security Group, Inc. Pat believed this move offered economies of scale and helped to make Metropol a national company. Of Metropol's $30 million in 1985 revenues, 70 percent were in Western Canada. Offices were maintained in all four western provinces as well as in the Northwest Territories, Quebec, and Newfoundland.

The Security Industry

Security products and services were purchased by individuals and businesses as a means of reducing the risk of loss or damage to their assets. The amount of security purchased depended upon individual risk preferences, their perception of the degree of risk involved, and the value of the assets to be protected. Security, therefore, was very much an intangible product subject to individual evaluation.

This case was written by Stephen S. Tax under the supervision of Professor W. S. Good. Copyright © 1988 by the Case Development Program, Faculty of Management, University of Manitoba. Support for the development of this case was provided by the Canadian Studies Program, Secretary of State, Government of Canada.

The industry offered such services as unarmed uniformed security guards, mobile patrols, investigations, consulting and education, as well as hardware products such as alarms, fences, locks, safes, and electronic surveillance devices (ESDs) and monitoring equipment. Most companies purchased a package combining various services and hardware systems. "It would not make much sense to have 50 television monitors and only one person watching them," Pat pointed out, "nor would it be wise to have 50 security guards roaming around a building which had no locks on the doors."

There were a number of factors which contributed to the competitive nature of the security industry. All a firm needed to enter the business was to open an office. Start-up costs were minimal and no accreditation was required by the company or its employees. Clients considered the cost of switching from one firm to another quite low so the business often went to the lowest-cost provider. Most customers really did not understand the difference in services provided by the various competitors in the security business, which made differentiation very difficult. Pat found in studying the financial statements of the large multinational security firms that most security companies earned pre-tax profit margins of about 4 percent on gross sales.

The 1985 security guard and private investigation markets in Canada were worth about $400 million retail. ESDs and other types of hardware added close to another $400 million to this figure at retail prices.

Growth was expected to continue in the security field for a variety of reasons including a general increase in the level of risk around the world, the rising cost of insurance, economic growth, technological innovation that created new security problems, and an increasing sophistication amongst security system purchasers. The ESD and security guard segments were expected to outpace basic hardware sales growth (Exhibit 1).

On the negative side was the industry's poor reputation for the quality and reliability of its services. This perception threatened to limit growth and provide an opportunity for new competitors to enter the market.

Competition

Metropol's competition came in both a direct and indirect form from a variety of competitors. "We compete with other firms who primarily offer security guard services as well as a number of companies that provide substitute products and services," observed Pat.

There were literally hundreds of security guard businesses in Canada, ranging in size from one or two ex-policemen operating out of a basement to large multinational firms such as Pinkertons, Burns, and Wackenhut. Metropol was the third largest firm in the country with a 7 percent market share (Exhibit 2). It was the leading firm in Western Canada with a 25 percent share of that market.

Hardware products served as the foundation of a good security system. While items such as fencing, lighting, alarms, safes, and locks were to some extent complementary to the security guard business, they also competed with

EXHIBIT 1   Forecasted Market Growth for Security Guard and Private Investigation Services, Electronic Security Devices (ESDs), and Hardware Products in the United States, 1985–1995*

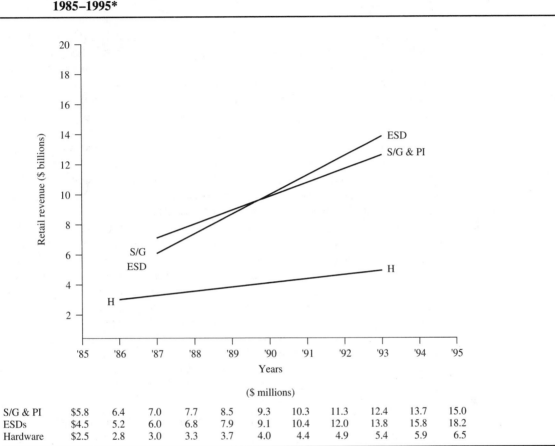

($ millions)

	'85	'86	'87	'88	'89	'90	'91	'92	'93	'94	'95
S/G & PI	$5.8	6.4	7.0	7.7	8.5	9.3	10.3	11.3	12.4	13.7	15.0
ESDs	$4.5	5.2	6.0	6.8	7.9	9.1	10.4	12.0	13.8	15.8	18.2
Hardware	$2.5	2.8	3.0	3.3	3.7	4.0	4.4	4.9	5.4	5.9	6.5

*The Canadian growth rate for each type of service/product was expected to be similar to the U.S. pattern.
SOURCE: Metropol Research.

it—firms could substitute some proportion of either their security guard or hardware expenditures for the other.

Insurance had long been a favorite substitute for security and other loss prevention services. Business spent more on insurance than all forms of security products combined. However, falling interest rates, a series of major disasters around the world, and a trend to more generous damage awards by the courts were making insurance a more expensive alternative. Faced with higher premiums, lower limits, and higher deductibles, businesses were likely to consider spending more on loss-prevention products and services.

The various levels of government also provided some basic protection services to companies (fire, police, etc.). However, their services were geared more to personal than business protection. These government services tended to set the base level of risk in a community. Tight budgets were not permitting these services to keep pace with the growth in crime and the increase in the value of corporate assets. This provided the private security business with an opportunity to fill the void.

Businesses were spending almost as much for ESDs and related services as for security guard services. There were a number of different ESD products, ranging from small electronic gadgets to the very popular central station monitoring systems. ESDs were the fastest-growing segment of the security industry. The principal attribute of these products was that they provided accurate and reliable information to whoever was responsible for responding to a problem situation. Thus, to a large extent, these products were really productivity tools that enhanced the performance of security guards, the fire department, and/or the police force. They did tend to reduce the amount of security guard service needed. Some security-conscious firms with large-scale security needs hired their own internal (in-house) specialists. In most cases, they would also hire guards from companies like Metropol to do the actual patroling.

The primary basis of competition in the security business was price. However, this was as much the fault of small, poorly managed firms and large multinationals trying to purchase market share as it was a fundamental characteristic of the industry. "I've seen companies bid under cost," observed Pat, "and they did not necessarily know they were doing it. It is a very unprofessional business in that sense. If you offer superior service and give a customer what he wants, in most cases you don't have to offer the lowest price. Just recently the Air Canada Data Centre job went to the highest bidder. Lowering your price is very easy but not the way to succeed in this business." However, since price was a key factor in getting jobs, cost control became crucial if profits were to be

EXHIBIT 2 The Largest Security Guard Companies Operating in Canada Ranked by Market Share

Company Name	Canadian Revenue ($ millions)	Employees	Market Share
1 Pinkertons	$ 50	4,600	12.5%
2 Burns	30	4,500	7.5
3 Metropol Base-Fort	30	2,000	7.0
4 Wackenhut	12	2,000	3.0
5 Canadian Protection	12	1,700	3.0
6 Barnes	12	1,500	3.0
7 Phillips	10	1,200	2.5
Canada total	$400	40,000*	100%

*In-house guards could raise this figure by as much as 100 percent. However a better estimate would be 50–60 percent, as in-house accounts use more full-time staff. This means that there are more than 60,000 people working as guards or private investigators at any time. Further, with turnover at close to 100 percent annually, there are over 100,000 people working in this field over the course of a year.

SOURCE: Metropol Research.

made. Pre-tax margins of 4–8 percent quickly disappeared if unanticipated costs occurred.

Market Segments

The market for security products and services could be segmented in a variety of ways, such as by type of service, type of business, geographic location, sensitivity to security needs, government versus private companies, and occasional versus continuous needs. Metropol segmented their customers and the rest of the market, using a combination of the above bases, as outlined below and in Exhibit 3.

Large Security-Conscious Organizations (Private and Public).   The common feature among these companies was that they had the potential for heavy losses if security was breached. They typically had high-value assets, such as computers or other high-tech equipment, or valuable proprietary information, as in the case of research and development firms. These buyers were usually quite

EXHIBIT 3   Security-Guard Service Market Segmentation by Gross Margins and Guard Wages

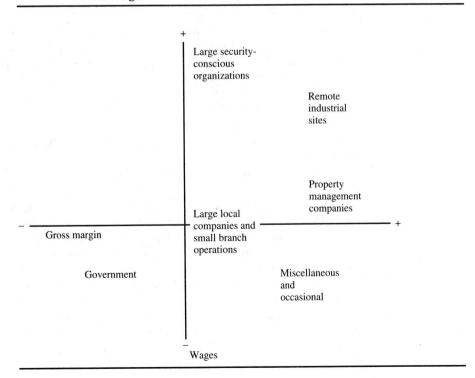

knowledgeable about security and rated quality over price. This group included firms in both local urban and remote, rural locations.

Organizations for Whom Security Was a Low Priority.   This group was dominated by local companies, commercial property management companies, and branches of firms that were headquartered elsewhere. They were less knowledgeable about security and tended to have limited security programs. They were price sensitive and principally utilized low-cost security guards.

Government Organizations.   Government organizations (nonhospital) typically awarded contracts based on a tendered price for a predetermined period of time; usually 1–2 years. The price for these contracts was commonly in the vicinity of the minimum wage plus 5 percent.

Occasional Services.   These included anything from sporting or entertainment events to social or emergency services. For example, this might include seasonal contracts, as with a CFL or NHL sports team, or one-time affairs. Wages paid to the security personnel were usually quite low, but profit margins to the firm were above average.

Buyer Behavior

The buyer of security services was commonly in the stronger position. This resulted from a multitude of firms offering what buyers perceived to be largely undifferentiated products and services, and sellers trying to win business by providing the lowest price. Further, the cost of switching suppliers was low because of the customers' perceived similarity of their services. It was also quite simple for firms to bring the security function in-house if they believed they could achieve substantial cost savings or other improvements in their security programs. In addition, some buyers tended to give security considerations a low priority in their budgeting.

Firms purchasing security products and services had three levels of decisions to make: (1) a general policy on the role and risk-cost framework that security would play in their firm, (2) a decision regarding the types of products and services to be purchased, and (3) the selection of suppliers.

Each decision level involved new groups or individuals within the organization. Policy decisions were generally made at the senior executive level while the product/service and supplier decisions tended to be made at the local level.

Most purchases were straight tender purchases based on a sealed bidding process. Firms with whom security was a low priority, and most government agencies, tended to choose the lowest bidder. Companies who took a greater interest in the quality of their security program considered attributes other than price when deciding upon their security supplier.

As part of a study on the security industry, Metropol surveyed buyers' ratings of the importance of several factors in choosing a security firm. They also had buyers rate Metropol's performance on those performance factors. Among the most significant decision-making criteria identified were consistency and reliability, availability of service representatives, and price. Metropol scored highest on the quality of their representatives and the customers' view of the firm's reputation (Exhibits 4 and 5).

Exhibit 4 Customer Decision-Making Criteria—Survey Results

How important are the following attributes to you when making a decision on security services?

	Not Important			Very Important		Average Score
	1	*2*	*3*	*4*	*5*	
Consistency and reliability	—	—	—	3	14	4.824
Quality of service representatives	—	—	—	5	12	4.706
Price competitiveness	—	—	3	8	6	4.176
Company reputation	1	1	—	7	8	4.176
Emergency services	—	2	4	7	4	3.765
Full range of products and services	—	4	2	6	5	3.706
Consulting services	—	6	6	3	2	3.059
National coverage	4	4	6	2	—	2.375

NOTE: The survey was a convenience sample of Metropol customers.
SOURCE: Metropol Research.

Exhibit 5 Customer Decision-Making Criteria—Survey Results

How would you rate Metropol Security on the following attributes?

	Poor	Fair	Sat.	Good	Excellent	Average Score
	1	*2*	*3*	*4*	*5*	
Consistency and reliability	1	1	5	7	3	3.588
Quality of service representatives	—	2	—	11	4	4.000
Price competitiveness	—	1	4	10	2	3.765
Company reputation	—	—	2	10	5	4.176
Emergency services	1	1	6	7	3	3.556
Full range of products and services	1	2	7	6	1	3.235
Consulting services	—	4	5	5	2	2.944
National coverage	1	—	7	3	—	3.091

Metropol

Metropol organized its operations on a regional (provincial) basis. The Manitoba headquarters developed a centralized policy and operating guidelines procedure that was instituted in all offices. While sales representatives dealt with the day-to-day needs of customers, top management was involved in making sales presentations to large accounts.

Services

Despite Metropol's variety of services, supplying unarmed, uniformed security guards accounted for most of their revenue. Their sales revenue breakdown by service type was

Security guards	90%
Mobile security checks	8
Other (investigation, polygraph testing, retail services, con- sulting, and education)	2
	100%

Providing security guard services involved more than just sending guards to industrial or office sites. Metropol had to train, pay, uniform, and insure the guards. They also had to supervise and dispatch their people as well as provide reports to their clients.

"We have attempted to provide greater value to our customers than our competitors have," stated Pat. "For example, we have a 24-hour dispatch service while all the other firms use an answering service. There is a $100,000 (annual) difference in cost, but we can respond much faster to any situation. Some customers will say they just consider price in their purchase decision but end up liking and buying the extra service."

Metropol also gave their guards special training on the procedures to follow in the case of such emergencies as bomb threats, hostage takings, and fire evacuations. Again, this was an attempt to differentiate their services from those of other security guard companies.

The mobile security business was contracted out to local firms. This market was not considered to be a growth area, and Metropol did not invest a great deal of resources in it.

Investigative and polygraph services were contracted out to a couple of ex-RCMP officers. Metropol had maintained these investigators on its staff at one time but found that demand for these services was not great enough to justify having the high-salaried people as full-time employees.

Education programs were another means Metropol used to create added value and increase switching costs for their customers. Pat explained, "We give seminars on such topics as 'The Protection of Proprietary Information' for our clients and even invite some companies we don't currently serve. We want our clients to realize that if they switch security firms they will be losing something of value."

Metropol did not sell hardware products such as fences, alarms, and locks. However, it could arrange the purchase of such equipment for their clients. It was presently considering working in conjunction with a systems engineer so the company would be able to provide a total security package to their customers.

Costs

Metropol divided its costs into two groups, direct and administrative. A typical job had the following cost characteristics:

Direct costs	83–86%
Selling and administrative costs	8–9%
Pre-tax profit margin	4–7%

Given the above figures, cost control was a key success factor for Metropol and the security industry in general. Metropol's margins were, in fact, higher than the industry average of approximately 4 percent. "We use a job-costing process," volunteered Pat. "Every pay period (two weeks) we look at what we made on each job. We consider and analyze every expense item very closely to see if there was any deviation from what was budgeted."

Direct costs included wages, uniforms, bonding, transportation, and supervision. Metropol did a good job of keeping its costs as low or lower than its competitors despite offering a higher level of service. Some of this was a result of economies of scale in purchasing such items as uniforms, achieved because of their comparatively large size. The company also did a superior job in collecting their outstanding receivables within a two-week period.

Pricing

Prices were determined by identifying the direct costs associated with a job, allowing for a contribution to selling and administrative overhead and providing for a profit margin. Consideration was also given to any particular reason there may be for pricing a bid either particularly high or low. "We once bid at very close to our direct cost for a job in a town where we had no competition in order to discourage other firms from entering that market," noted Pat. He also suggested that it was important to anticipate competitors' likely pricing strategy when bidding on a job as well as recognizing that some projects had greater potential for cost overruns.

Promotion

Metropol individually identified the companies in each of their trading areas that were potential clients and concentrated their promotional efforts on that group. In Manitoba, this "club" amounted to about 500 firms.

Once these firms were identified, strategies were developed to either sell to those potential accounts which presently had no security service or to become the logical alternative for those businesses who were using competitive services. "We want to put pressure on these incumbent firms to perform," explained Pat.

Metropol used, among other things, their educational seminars to stress to their clients that they offered superior service. At times, firms using competing security companies were invited as a means of encouraging them to switch to Metropol.

Employees

Metropol employed almost 2,000 people, 1,900 of whom were security guards and 100 who were selling, administrative, or management personnel.

Security guards came principally from three backgrounds: (1) young people (18–25) who could not find other work, (2) older people (50–65) looking for a second career, or (3) ex-military or police personnel who liked the quasi-military nature of the job.

Annual employee turnover in the security guard industry was very high, estimated to be in the vicinity of 100 percent. Metropol's turnover rate was in the same range. Reasons for the high level included a combination of low wages, generally boring work, and a lack of motivation or support from senior management.

"We have some employees who have been with the company for 15 years," Pat pointed out. "However, the wages we pay are based on our billing rate which often only allows for minimum wages to be paid to our employees." Intense competition and clients who wanted to pay a bare minimum for security guard services forced companies to pay their guards the legal minimum wage. This caused high turnover rates which, evidently, did not bother some clients. Other customers, concerned with employee turnover, specified a higher minimum wage rate which the security company had to pay its guards. Pat liked this attitude because it allowed him to pay his people a higher wage and still be competitive.

Metropol's supervisors and customer service representatives (salespeople) did a good job servicing their accounts and handling any crisis that arose. They helped maintain Metropol's reputation as a competent and reliable security company despite the generally poor reputation of the industry.

The Future

Pat turned his attention to the future. He believed that the way business was conducted in the security guard industry would not significantly change in the near future. He did expect the business to become somewhat more professional with guards being trained in formal, standardized programs. The pressure on profit margins was expected to continue and perhaps even intensify as the larger, multinational firms fought for market share and smaller independents struggled for survival. Pat was thinking about how he could use Metropol's present position and reputation in the security guard sector to expand into more profitable segments of the industry or improve the company's general standing within the guard sector. Some of the opportunities he was considering included

- Geographic expansion.
- A focused strategy.
- Expanding the range of security products and services offered by the company.
- Diversification into other service areas outside the security field.
- Serving the consumer home-security market.

Geographic Expansion. "To be a national company in Canada you need a presence in Southern Ontario," observed Pat. Even though many companies' security needs were handled at the local level, there was considerable potential for a national accounts program. To be involved in providing a national service, a company had to be active in the Toronto area where most national companies' security decisions were made. In addition the Ontario market offered substantial local business. Pat explained, "We handle Northern Telecom's security guard needs throughout Western Canada, but not in Ontario. Northern Telecom has three times the business volume there as it does in all of the western provinces combined."

There were three ways Metropol could enter the Ontario market: (1) by purchasing a local security firm; (2) through merging with another company, or (3) bidding on contracts in Ontario and opening up an office once a contract was obtained.

Pat believed that the merger method was the most appealing since it offered the potential for increased profits with virtually no additional cash investment. He had discussed the possibility with two firms that had head offices in Ontario and were also minor competitors in the Winnipeg, Edmonton, Calgary, and Vancouver markets. The western offices of the merged firm could be closed down, and the business operated under the Metropol name. "The gross margin on their western contracts would go right to the bottom line," suggested Pat. "Because all the current Metropol offices could meet their administrative needs and absorb any incremental expenses."

A restricting factor in this strategy was Metropol's limited product/service line. To provide a "complete" security package for any company on a national basis, it was necessary to offer the hardware and ESD packages in addition to the security guards.

A Focused Strategy.   This alternative was really a continuation of Metropol's current strategy. Following this approach, Metropol's principal objective would be to become the fastest-growing security guard firm in Western Canada, with the highest profit margin and return on equity, the lowest employee turnover, and the most satisfied customers in the business of providing contract, unarmed security personnel. This strategy required an increased emphasis on developing a formal marketing program and increasing the value added of Metropol's security guard and support services. Tighter control of costs and employee motivation would be critical success factors as would be the need to carefully segment the market and identify the most profitable clients.

The strategy would be designed to match the distinct competencies and resources of Metropol with the needs of the marketplace. Pat believed that while the strategy "sounded good," it would be very difficult to implement. "Even if you offer the highest quality service you might not get the job," he offered. "Too many contracts, particularly those involving the government sector and crown corporations, are based solely on price, and simply supplying a higher service level in the provision of security guards is not likely to change that."

Expansion of Security Products and Services.   From the customer's point of view, there was an advantage to having one firm coordinate and provide the complete security coverage required by his business; the security system was more effective and efficient. If the customer had to contract with different firms for guards, fences, locks, lights, alarms, and ESDs, there was likely to be a lot of overlap and, in some cases, gaps in the overall system. Also, it was likely to be more expensive. Pat considered an investment in the production of hardware equipment much too costly, given his firm's limited resources, but he was investigating the possibility of arranging a deal with a large multinational distributor of security hardware and ESD products.

Pat explained, "We would like to have an exclusive relationship whereby they [large multinationals] would provide us, at wholesale, with all the hardware and ESD equipment we needed on a private label basis (Metropol brand) and they would train our people. We could offer them our monitoring services and access to new markets." Metropol would package the system, which would include hardware, software, and people in whatever mix its clients needed. The products would be sold to the client or leased on a five-year arrangement.

The expanded product-line strategy would deliver significant benefits to Metropol. Hardware and ESD equipment offered better margins than security guard services and, in some cases, were subject to becoming obsolete. This provided opportunities to sell up-graded systems. For example, television monitoring devices had already gone through several generations of change despite their relatively recent entry into the security product mix. Service contracts to maintain the equipment would provide another source of additional revenue.

Finally, the need of these systems for close monitoring and servicing increased the dependence of the customer on Metropol. This higher dependence meant that switching costs for the customer were much higher than with security guard services. This would be especially true if the equipment was leased for a five-year period.

Diversification into Other Service Areas.   This alternative would capitalize on Metropol's skills in hiring people for contract-type jobs and administering a payroll. Their current product line could be expanded to include one or all of the following additional services, which could be provided on a contractual basis: secretarial services, nursing care, janitorial services, or landscaping services. The commercial sector would continue to be their primary target market.

Several years ago Metropol got into the commercial cleaning business with poor results. "Businesses such as janitorial and landscaping services are beyond our particular expertise," revealed Pat. "However, we are looking at providing people and handling the payroll for temporary clerical or nursing services. In those cases, we would be taking our established skills to another market." Pat cited Drake International's experience as evidence that the strategy could work. That company went from providing temporary help to the provision of security guards.

The Consumer Market.   Another alternative for Metropol would be to expand into the consumer market for security products and services. The major products of interest to residential customers were locks, supplementary lighting, fences, mobile home checks, house sitting, and alarm systems. This segment was growing slower than the business sector, but still offered substantial opportunity.

Pat was currently exploring Metropol's opportunities as a franchisor of home alarm systems to the numerous small Canadian alarm system dealers. "We would become the Century 21 of the alarm business," Pat suggested.

The alarm business in Canada was made up of a large number of small independent dealers and a few large multinationals. The "small guys" would buy their alarms from wholesalers in small lots which precluded much discounting. They also had to contract out their alarm monitoring to their competition, the large multinationals, because they could not afford the central station monitoring equipment. In most cases, advertising and financing of installations for customers was too expensive to be carried out on a significant basis.

Pat thought a Metropol alarm franchise offered a number of important strategic advantages to independent alarm dealers: (1) by arranging with a large alarm manufacturer to produce a private label Metropol brand alarm line they could pass on volume discounts to their dealers, (2) franchises would have the Metropol name behind them, (3) co-op advertising would provide greater exposure, (4) an arrangement for consumer financing could be established, and (5) Metropol would set up a central monitoring system.

Consideration was also being given to making locksmiths subdealers of Metropol alarm systems. "Normally a customer must call a locksmith and an alarm specialist to secure his home," suggested Pat. "It would be more effective, especially from a selling perspective, if the locksmith could do both."

Conclusion

Pat realized that the alternatives he was considering were not merely incremental changes in Metropol's strategy. In fact, each option represented a distinct direction for the firm's future development. "We have to define our business mission more specifically," Pat thought to himself. "Then we can choose and implement the strategy that best suits that mission."

CASE 24
MICHELIN IN NOVA SCOTIA

In September 1989, the Michelin Group stunned the entire world tire industry by announcing it had reached an agreement to acquire the entire equity interest in the Uniroyal Goodrich Tire Company (UG) for a purchase price of approximately $690 million. Taking into account UG's outstanding debt, the transaction had an overall value of approximately $1.5 billion (U.S.) and with UG's nine plants (five in the United States, two in Canada, and two in Mexico), Michelin would become the world's largest tire company. Before the acquisition could be consummated, Michelin needed to receive the approval of three government agencies: the Antitrust Division of the U.S. Justice Department, the Canadian Bureau of Competition Policy, and Investment Canada. The company now had to decide what case it should make in the submissions to these three government agencies.

Early History of Michelin in North America

A key figure in Michelin's decision to construct plants in North America was Robert Manuge, executive vice president of the Crown Corporation, Industrial Estates Ltd. (IEL), the industrial development agency of the province of Nova Scotia. In 1967 on a flight to New York City, Manuge happened to sit beside the wife of the Canadian president of Citroen, the French car maker. Manuge convinced the woman to introduce him to her husband at the airport. It turned out Citroen wasn't interested in IEL assistance, but Manuge was told that Citroen's parent company, Manufacture Francaises des Pneumatiques Michelin, might be. As a result, Manuge wrote Francois Michelin, the company president, in Clermont-Ferrand near Paris with the following message:

> Unquestionably, the political, economic and labour stability of Nova Scotia have been the underlying factors in motivating so many famous companies to choose our strategically located province as a base of operations. Nova Scotia has the advantage of exceptionally good relations between management and labour.

Manuge offered to meet Michelin in France on 24-hour notice.

It turned out Michelin was considering establishing its first North American plant. At the time, the company had tire sales exceeding $1 billion (U.S.), making it the largest tire producer in terms of sales in Europe and unlike the four U.S. firms—Goodyear, Firestone, Uniroyal, and Goodrich—and unlike its

This case was prepared by Mark C. Baetz, Wilfrid Laurier University, as a basis for class discussion rather than to illustrate either effective or ineffective handling of an administrative situation.

chief European rivals, Dunlop and Pirelli, Michelin had a record of steadily rising profits.[1] Its success was attributed to its emphasis on innovation; in particular, in 1948, Michelin introduced the world to the steel-belted radial tire, which was more expensive than conventional tires but lasted at least twice as long, provided better handling of the car, and improved gas mileage. While radial tires were long popular in Europe, they had made virtually no impact in North America. However, Michelin expected that radials would jump from 5 percent of the market in the United States to 60 percent by 1976. In 1970, Michelin imported 2.5 million tires, representing half of the U.S. radial market. Ford adopted Michelins as standard on certain models,[2] and since 1965, Sears and Roebuck, the world's largest retailer, had been distributing Michelin radials in the U.S. under its own private label.

Michelin's reply to Manuge's letter stated that the company was interested in talking to IEL but all negotiations had to be kept secret. In early 1968, Manuge met with Michelin officials and was surprised to find a head office which was spartan and bare and where top managers worked at desks created by placing a few boards across two filing cabinets. Manuge had now been introduced to what observers called a "bizarre" corporate style. A part of this style was an incredible emphasis on secrecy. Michelin managers required Manuge to use the code name "Project Y" when referring to their discussions, and they initially refused to let Manuge reveal details of the discussions to anyone, including his colleagues at IEL or Nova Scotia government officials. Unknown to Manuge until much later, Michelin even hired a Wall Street lawyer to come to Nova Scotia to check out both IEL and the provincial government under the guise of conducting economic studies on the province for an unnamed client.

Michelin was clearly faced with a decision of whether to establish its first North American facilities in Canada or the United States. The choice was Canada, and the rationale was explained by one Michelin manager as follows:

> Our sales representative [in the United States] argued that we should put our plants in the United States first, say by 1969. But the real pride of our engineers is in the all-steel truck tire. They said, "Let's put our best foot forward." So rightly or wrongly it was decided that Canadian plants would give our people experience with North Americans—with our best product and with less money involved.[3]

One observer of this decision noted: "Since the engineers ruled, the engineers won."[4]

When word leaked out at the end of 1968 that Michelin would build a plant in Nova Scotia, the Quebec government was particularly disappointed. Michelin had been conducting off-again, on-again negotiations with Quebec since 1965, but despite intense pressure from then French President Charles de Gaulle, Michelin was reported to be "opposed to de Gaulle's love affair with Quebec," and concerned about the political volatility in Quebec and the fact that "its labour force was not only unionized but strike-prone to boot."[5] Michelin was particularly concerned about unionization, as noted by one report:

The Michelins are antiunion by instinct and paternalistic by practice. . . . As far back as 1898 when Europe was being beset by large-scale factory strikes, Michelin tried to stem the tide of trade unionism by establishing bonuses for loyal service, and setting up a whole range of services for its employees ranging from company-run food stores to free legal services. Despite that, Michelin's factory in Clermont-Ferrand, along with many others was shut down by French strikes in 1936. . . . Michelin decided as a result of that stoppage "that such strikes should never occur again. . . ." The war between Michelin and unions was born.[6]

In July 1969, IEL announced Michelin's plan of establishing two plants in Nova Scotia: a 500-employee steel-cord plant in the town of Bridgewater (60 miles south of Halifax) and an 800-employee truck-tire factory in the town of Granton (90 miles north of Halifax). The first plant would sell its output to the second.

Michelin's emphasis on industrial secrecy was revealed when the company paid Nova Scotia tradesmen $250,000 to stay away from the construction sites of the new plants while Michelin's own workers installed its proprietary equipment. Some industry analysts also noted that the company decided to build two plants to ensure industrial secrecy rather than economic efficiency.[7]

The two plants were initially publicly announced at $51.4 million, but it was believed the total investment ended up in the order of $85 million. However, extensive financial support from three levels of government minimized considerably Michelin's investment. IEL provided $50 million in long-term loans with an interest rate subsidy calculated to have a net present value of $11 million. IEL also provided $7.6 million in contributions for capital costs and employee training. Granton and Bridgewater reduced municipal taxes for 10 years to 1 percent of assessment from the normal rate of 2.1 percent and 3.7 percent, respectively. This appeared to have represented a total tax saving of approximately $3 million. The town of Bridgewater also donated the site valued at $4,000 based on land values in the region at the time. The federal government provided various kinds of assistance: (1) under regional development legislation, an $8 million contribution; (2) accelerated depreciation on the capital costs of land, buildings, and machinery; (3) under the Machinery Program, duty-free import of manufacturing machinery not produced in Canada; (4) exemption for three years from the normal 17.5 percent duty on imported tires as long as these tires were not produced by Michelin in Canada and as long as the exemption did not disrupt the operations of existing Canadian tire producers (a duty drawback was available for tires reexported to the United States, although such tires would be charged the 4 percent U.S. duty). This duty remission, which was to be made available through a special order-in-council approved by the federal cabinet, allowed long production runs, enabling the Nova Scotia plants to remain internationally competitive. Without the remission, the company might have produced a less efficient product mix in Canada, given Canada's small domestic market.[8] Overall, government officials noted that the assistance given Michelin was well within the contribution levels by governments for projects in that region at that time. Furthermore, Michelin was seen as a real success story compared to other projects which were funded, such as the ill-fated Bricklin car plant and Clairtone plant for stereo equipment and colour television sets.

Michelin also received a different kind of government support in May 1971 when the new premier, Gerald Regan, flew to France to meet with Michelin officials who were concerned about illegal work stoppages at the construction site in Granton. Just over a month later, Regan called a special session of the legislature to pass a law requiring prestart bargaining—a general agreement between the union and construction company before construction begins—at all projects valued over $5 million. The legislation known as the Act for the Stabilization of Labour-Management Relations Affecting Certain Construction Plants also outlawed picketing and forced unions to submit disputes to arbitration after 30 days. Regan admitted the legislation was designed for Michelin but used his experience in labour law and friendships with trade union leaders to avoid a confrontation over the issue.[9]

By the end of October 1971, both of Michelin's plants were in production. The combined plants represented the largest secondary manufacturing investment ever made in the Western Hemisphere by a European company.

The North American Tire Industry

Before Michelin's plants were constructed, the tire industry in Canada consisted primarily of six foreign-owned subsidiaries (five U.S. parents and one European), with 11 plants, 7 in Ontario, 2 in Quebec, and 2 in Alberta. Goodyear Canada was the largest company with 4 plants. The subsidiaries had originally come to Canada because of a high tariff wall (as high as 37 percent) and unlike Michelin, they were producing a full range of tires in Canada. As a result, the companies were faced with short runs, high costs, and low productivity.[10] Some companies were also hit with costly strikes.

There had been a number of unsuccessful attempts to rationalize the Canadian tire industry. On two occasions during the 1960s, there was an unsuccessful attempt to include tires under the Canada–United States Auto Pact, which helped to rationalize the North American car industry. There had also been a threat by Finance Department officials to make the Canadian tire industry more efficient by lowering tariffs on all imports at a faster rate than the gradual lowering of tariffs planned under the General Agreement on Tariffs and Trade (GATT).[11] However, the industry found it difficult to work together to deal with such threats for several reasons. First, the government had successfully sued the companies in 1952 for price-fixing, and this discouraged cooperative efforts. Second, the industry consisted of several foreign-owned subsidiaries, and the variation in the management autonomy of the subsidiary presidents hindered cooperation. Third, there were differences in the corporate strategies among the subsidiaries. For example, Dunlop did not plan to produce radials in Canada, but Firestone was planning to invest in a radial plant in Canada. Such differences in strategies made it impossible to reach consensus on a duty-exemption scheme to rationalize the industry. In fact, federal officials had proposed several schemes to the industry such as duty-free entry of steel-belted radials and possibly equipment when (1) imported by manufacturers of steel-belted radials in Canada or (2) imported by manufacturers of tires generally or (3) imported by any company doing business in Canada. There was also a proposal to reduce the tariff from 17.5 percent to 4 percent on a most favoured nation (MFN) basis. (The MFN rate into the United States from both Canada and France was 4 percent at that time.) While there was no consensus among the various subsidiaries that certain of these proposals were unacceptable, there was no consensus on an acceptable proposal.

As the different companies in the Canadian tire industry struggled to reach consensus on an industry-wide solution to the problem of rationalization, the industry association, The Rubber Association of Canada (RAC), decided in 1969 to meet with the officials in the newly formed Department of Industry, Trade and Commerce (ITC), and it was agreed that the companies would provide the necessary data to ITC for a cost study of the industry. ITC officials were about to meet with each tire company president beginning in 1970 to discuss tire industry rationalization, but these discussions were postponed because of the Michelin deal and because all the companies were in the process of changing their presidents.

In the United States, the industry faced somewhat similar problems as in Canada, such as low productivity, high labour costs, and outmoded production facilities. In addition, a "major marketing disaster" occurred in the mid-1960s when the industry's move to replace conventional four-ply tires with two-plies was rejected by consumers and auto manufacturers.[12] Following this rejection, the industry decided to produce a bias-belted tire, which combined traditional ply construction with a belt under the tread. The U.S. industry switched to the bias-belted tire rather than the radial partly because the conversion costs were so much lower; it was estimated that the U.S. industry would need to spend $600 million to convert to radials. While there was some radial production in limited quantities by U.S. companies, there was no commitment by any U.S. company to the steel-wire belted radial, which had built the Michelin reputation. One report described the position of the U.S. industry as follows:

> The U.S. tire fraternity resisted the radial trend fiercely. Goodyear, for one, pumped millions of dollars into polyester and fiberglass belted tires, a mere modification of the old bias-belted design. Goodyear's goal was to short-circuit the trend to radials for a few more years, if not indefinitely.[13]

Given the difficulties of the tire industry in both Canada and the United States, it was not surprising that tire imports were rising in both countries. In 1970, imports had steadily increased to 10.6 percent of the total U.S. market. The imports would have been even higher in 1971 were it not for a government-imposed temporary 10 percent surcharge on all imports after the U.S. suffered its worst trade deficit ever. In Canada, imports of tires of all types had steadily increased to a level representing over 25 percent of Canadian production in 1970, and exports were only about 5 percent of domestic production. (Domestic production was roughly equivalent to domestic sales.)

Reaction to Michelin in Nova Scotia

Managers in the tire companies in Canada were stunned when they were informed of the package of incentives provided to Michelin in Nova Scotia. They also felt betrayed by the government, which had appeared to be sincere in its efforts to assist in rationalizing the industry. While the government's loans and contributions were available to any company, the duty remission was seen as special treatment for Michelin, which was able to do what the rest of the industry had been unable to do, that is rationalize its product line.

Opposition to the incentives offered to Michelin came on two fronts. First, among the Canadian tire companies, there was a unanimous demand that the package of incentives be rescinded.[14] Second, the United Rubber, Cork, Linoleum and Plastic Workers of America (URW), the certified bargaining agent for the 7,500 tire-production workers in Canada, asked the federal government to rescind the offer of duty remission to Michelin. The URW believed that duty-free entry of Michelin tires would mean fewer workers because of longer production runs with fewer lines of tires produced in Canada. The Member of Parliament for a riding containing several URW members described the fears of his constituents as follows:

> There is no gain to be made for workers in Canada in general, if we create jobs in Nova Scotia . . . at the expense of men and women who are currently employed. All that does is shift unemployment from one part of the country to another, and this at the taxpayers' expense.[15]

In the United States, opposition to the package offered Michelin was based on arguments different from those used in Canada. The Rubber Manufacturers Association (the U.S. equivalent to the RAC) suggested to the U.S. Tariff Commission in late 1970 that "the Canadian government has through its program of concessions and incentives to a foreign producer of tires, in effect subsidized the operation of [Michelin] and has given it an export base from which to further assault the American market." On May 4, 1972, the Nova Scotia government announced that Michelin would be investing at Granton $12 million in a passenger tire plant and at Bridgewater $28.6 million in additional steel cord capacity and another passenger tire plant. The federal Department of Regional Economic Expansion (DREE) had approved a $7.9 million contribution to Michelin in connection with these expansions representing another 1,300 jobs. In addition, IEL agreed to purchase $14.4 million of company bonds, and the local municipalities agreed to extend the tax concessions they had granted in the original investment.

Opposition to the continuation of government assistance to Michelin took an unexpected turn on May 12, 1972, when the U.S. Treasury Department announced that interested parties would have 30 days to submit their views before it would be decided whether countervailing duties were to be applied against Michelin tires from Nova Scotia under the Tariff Act of 1930. The act enabled the United States to levy a duty equal to any government bounty or grant given to promote exports of a product to the United States. The complaint which led to the investigation noted that Canada's government subsidies went to a plant where most (75–85 percent) of the output was destined for the United States. Clearly, the entire federal government regional development program was under attack. In response to the investigation, the Canadian government, Michelin, and the American Importers Association made several arguments including the following:

- Every government, including the United States and state governments, used regional incentive grants, and U.S. corporations were also receiving DREE capital assistance in Canada. (During this period, Goodyear Canada received DREE assistance in Collingwood and Owen Sound, Ontario.)
- Michelin had not yet benefited from duty remission. (In fact in May 1971, the federal government had quietly withdrawn its offer to Michelin to provide duty remission.)
- The Canadian grants to Michelin were not made directly to foster exports. The legislation governing the grants does not distinguish between exporters and local producers.
- The grants and loans offered to Michelin did not offset the losses incurred by Michelin in locating in Nova Scotia compared to elsewhere in Canada. A DREE study found the net additional costs (in $ million) were construction ($+11.4$); land (-2.9); transportation (3.5 per year for 20 years = 60); training, relocating, and recruiting (4.4); and service and supply (1.3 per year for 20 years = 13), totaling $85.9 million, not including nonquantifiable items such as higher inventories and longer lead times on orders.
- Michelin decided to construct new plant facilities in the United States even before the plants in Nova Scotia were established. Ultimately, it is likely that Michelin's Canadian plants will serve mainly Canada, and the United States will be served from U.S. facilities, with some cross-shipping to round out lines.
- The real concern of the U.S. tire companies who launched the complaint "is less over suggested government subsidies for Michelin than the way it has forced the tire industry into producing radial tires sooner than it would otherwise have liked."
- The U.S. balance of payments did not result from alleged government subsidy practices, and a solution to the balance of payments problem should be sought by other means.

On December 5, 1972, Michelin announced its intention to begin constructing a $200 million plant in the United States in early 1973 with production to start within two years. On January 5, 1973, the U.S. Treasury Department announced a 6.6 percent countervailing duty against Michelin tires from Canada, about one fifth the level of duty requested by the U.S. industry. The duty was based on a complicated formula and was justified on the basis that the government assistance given Michelin was a subsidy "which seriously impinges on U.S. jobs and U.S. trade." The Canadian External Affairs Department sent a formal note of protest to the U.S. State Department. While the duty was reduced a few months later to 2.5 percent, Michelin decided to appeal the duty. Ultimately, the U.S. was required to return all the duties it had collected following a ruling under new U.S. trade legislation which required a finding of injury to U.S. companies before countervail duties could be imposed and in this case injury could not be shown.

The "Michelin Bill"

Once the Michelin plants began production, there were a number of attempts to unionize Michelin workers. In 1974, the unions representing the electrical workers and operating engineers signed up a majority of workers in their respective crafts at the Granton plant. However, on the day the Labour Relations Board was to hear the operating engineers' application for certification, the provincial government passed an order-in-council barring craft unions in industrial plants. Later that year, another order-in-council terminated the traditional practice of automatically certifying any union that signed up a majority of a plant's workers. Unlike any other province, from then on in Nova Scotia, a certification vote would be required no matter how many workers a union signed up. The order-in-council was seen by labour as "specifically designed to help Michelin fight a rear-guard action against any successful organizing effort."[16]

A particularly controversial move was made by the provincial government in 1979 when it passed an amendment to the Trade Union Act that required a union seeking certification at companies with interdependent plants to win majority support among the workers in all the interdependent plants. An earlier version of the bill was opposed by some multiplant companies such as fish processors who had both unionized and nonunionized plants and were concerned that the bill would spur unionization in their unorganized plants. As a result of this concern "interdependent" plants were defined as plants which supplied each other. This definition applied only to Michelin and not other companies such as fish processors whose plants did not supply each other. While the bill faced extensive opposition in the Nova Scotia legislature and by labour, which bitterly described it as the "Michelin bill," the Conservative majority government passed the bill during an unprecedented special session between Christmas and New Years, and the bill received royal assent on December 28, 1979.

The timing for passing the bill was particularly important as there had been renewed efforts to unionize Michelin workers. While the URW had its second application for certification of Michelin's Granton plant turned down in early 1979 when only 36.8 percent of the workers voted in favour of the union, during the hearing related to this vote the Labour Relations Board agreed with a union complaint that Michelin had been intimidating its workers by intimating that a union might mean a reduction in wages and benefits. The board ordered the company to cease and desist. Nevertheless, the URW concluded they now had the ammunition for a successful vote. A third certification vote of the 1,600-employee Granton plant was taken in November 1979, and the Labour Relations Board hearing for this vote was set for January 7, 1980. However, the Michelin bill intervened and a retroactivity clause in the bill effectively nullified the November vote, which had not yet been counted. The URW was now faced with the daunting task of signing up 50 percent plus one of the workers in all the Michelin plants within the three-month certification period, and the Bridgewater plant was in a rural area with no union tradition.

The "Michelin bill" was seen to have both positive and negative consequences. On the positive side, the government claimed the legislation would make the province more attractive for business investment. In fact, immediately after the bill was passed, the government announced that Michelin would invest $400 million to construct a third plant at Waterville, a rural (nonunion) area of Nova Scotia and expand its two existing facilities to create 2,000 new jobs by 1982. For this latest investment, the company would receive $56 million in federal and provincial government assistance (but no duty exemption). It was later reported that Michelin offered to make this expansion only if the company could be assured of protection by the Michelin bill.[17]

There were seen to be several negative consequences of the "Michelin bill." The relationship between the provincial government and organized labour deteriorated significantly following the bill's passage. The 70,000-member Nova Scotia Federation of Labour withdrew from all government boards and commissions and refused to communicate with the provincial government. A general strike was threatened, the Canadian Labour Congress (CLC) endorsed a national boycott, and it was suggested that the hostile labour climate might scare off new industry. Echoing the concern of the labour movement, a committee of Oxfam Canada compared the Michelin bill to repressive legislation in Chile and South Africa, and the Roman Catholic church stated that the bill violated the church's social teachings. The CLC, in fact, later tried unsuccessfully to have the bill struck down for violating the Charter of Rights and Freedoms.

The bill was also seen as contradicting previous government decisions. Just months before the bill was passed, the provincial government's own Labour Relations Board decided that each of Michelin's plants, which were 150 miles apart, should be considered as a separate bargaining unit. This bill was also seen as increasing government dependence on foreign companies whose power, such as the threat of job removal, was now increased. Related to this concern was the view that the bill reflected a loss of political control and damage to the reputation of Nova Scotia, whose government was prepared to "turn cartwheels if the price is right."[18] One Nova Scotia labour representative expressed her concern as follows: "I find it really alarming that one multinational company has so much power it can dictate to a provincial government."[19]

A "Memorandum of Understanding"

While Michelin was increasing its plant capacity in North America, the rest of the North American tire industry was going through a major rationalization and restructuring. The various companies began spending the hundreds of millions of dollars required to convert to radial production, sometimes discovering the difficulties of making the conversion. For example, Firestone had to recall almost the entire production of one radial model in 1978 because of flaws. These difficulties supported the claim of one Michelin manager who noted: "Anybody can make a steel-belted radial tire, but to make 100 of them of uniform quality is our secret."[20]

There were also dramatic changes in ownership. For example, in order to meet intensifying foreign competition, long-time rivals Uniroyal, Inc., and B.F. Goodrich merged in 1986 to form Uniroyal-Goodrich Tire Co (UG)., which became the second largest tire manufacturer in North America. Also in 1986, Sumitomo Rubber Industries Ltd. of Japan acquired the European and U.S. tire operations of Dunlop Ltd.

As part of the rationalization process, many plants were closed in the United States from 1973 to 1986. There were also plant closings in Canada, for example, a Firestone tire plant in Calgary, a Goodyear subsidiary (Sieberling) tire plant in Toronto, and Firestone closed the former Dunlop plant in Whitby, Ontario. A significant shutdown occurred in 1986 when Goodyear announced it would close its 69-year-old 1,500 employee plant in west Toronto despite promises of provincial money to keep the facility open. The closure was based on the plant's age, obsolete multistory format, and the $94 million (U.S.) cost to the company of buying back shares to foil a hostile takeover attempt by Anglo-French financier Sir James Goldsmith.

With the dramatic changes occurring in the North American tire industry and the Free Trade Agreement (FTA) between Canada and the United States, the Federal Department of Regional and Industrial Expansion (the department resulting from a merger of ITC and DREE) analyzed the Canadian tire industry and concluded: (1) only Michelin's plants which make truck tires with state-of-the-art technology are truly competitive in a North American free trade context; because of short production runs and small volumes in the six other plants (two UG plants in Kitchener, Ont.; a General Tire Canada plant in Barrie, Ont.; Goodyear plants in Medicine Hat, Alta. and Valleyfield, Que.; and a Firestone plant in Joliette, Que.) are "critically weak" because they lack the economies of scale and productivity to compete on a global basis at a time when the industry is rapidly internationalizing; the average plant in Canada produced 13,500 passenger and truck tires a day compared to 45,000 tires in the average U.S. plant; (2) Canadian plants, except for Michelin's, typically get lower levels of investment and less advanced technology than their affiliates in the United States; they also tend to specialize in declining product lines; for example, the Firestone plant in Hamilton was the last one in Canada specializing in bias-ply tires, a dying part of the market (bias-ply tires averaged 30,000 km compared to

40,000 km for belted-bias and 64,000 km for radials); (3) another weakness of the Canadian industry is the high proportion of tires it sells both to auto manufacturers as original equipment on new cars and to companies that sell them under other brand names (e.g., Canadian Tire or Sears); both these kinds of sales are less profitable for tire manufacturers than tires bearing the manufacturer's own brand names; (4) to revitalize the Canadian tire industry will require investments of hundreds of millions of dollars, but once the 10.7 percent tariff barrier is eliminated under the FTA, there will be little incentive for the foreign companies to inject further capital into Canada, unless federal and provincial governments provide assistance; any new investment has recently been concentrated in the southern United States, where labour is cheaper and low-interest municipal bond financing readily available; (5) corporate return on Canadian tire plants as a whole was only 1.24 percent in 1984 and has edged up only slightly; profit margins are also slim in the United States; return on sales in North America in the past 15 years has been slim, primarily because of the extension of tire life since the introduction of the longer-lasting radial (which slowed market growth to 1 percent from 7 percent in the 1960s) and the growth in imports from Japan, South Korea, and Brazil, which increased by more than 23 percent between 1985 and 1986; imports outside of North America moved from 6 to 9 percent of market share in Canada between 1982 and 1984.[21] Given the evident problems of the Canadian tire industry, the federal government followed a recommendation of the RAC and chose the maximum period allowable under the FTA of 10 years for eliminating the duties on tires entering Canada.

With the apparent need for government assistance to ensure the survival of many of the subsidiaries in the Canadian tire industry, there was renewed interest in industry-government dialogue. In order for the various companies to discuss areas of mutual concern in dialogue with the government and not be charged under the Competition Act, the government used a mechanism known as a "memorandum of understanding," which was signed by all the tire companies and the RAC. This memorandum identified various issues of mutual interest which were to be discussed. Following an initial meeting, it was agreed that one of the tools for assisting the entire Canadian industry was duty remission. Each company interested in participating in duty remission was to submit their five-year business plan to federal officials. The actual formula used in working out the duty remission packages with each company was never made public, but it was reported in the media that the maximum remission was based on $1 payback on the duties charged on foreign-made tires sold in Canada for each $3 the company invested in new plants or equipment.[22] In December 1987, the cabinet approved remission orders totaling up to $124.5 million for three companies: (1) $3.9 million for each of the five 12-month periods beginning October 1987 totaling $19.5 million for UG; (2) $16 million for each of the five 12-month periods beginning October 1987, totaling $80 million for Michelin on most tire imports into Canada (Michelin also received partial sales tax relief to reflect the value of the customs duty remitted on goods); (3) $6.25 million for each of the four 12-month periods beginning

October 1988 for Goodyear with comparable relief in sales tax, totaling $25 million.

There was some controversy associated with the remission orders. First, they were granted by order-in-council, which meant there was no Parliamentary debate before they were granted. One report noted:

> Remission orders, granted under the Financial Administration Act, are normally used to correct tax overpayments. But in recent years they have been used as backdoor policy tools with which cabinet can grant massive amounts of aid without Parliament even knowing about it. . . . A 1985 remission order to give Dome Petroleum up to $400 million in tax relief in connection with the 1981 purchase of Hudson's Bay Oil and Gas Ltd. drew fire from the Auditor General because so much money was given away without the knowledge of Parliament.[23]

A second criticism of the remission orders came from Gord Wilson, president of the Ontario Federation of Labour, who described the orders as "an insult to taxpayers." Wilson noted:

> This shows the sheer lunacy of the FTA that allows U.S. companies open access to the Canadian market with no obligation to produce here. With his trade agreement, Mulroney greased the skids for industry to move south of the border. Now at taxpayers' expense, he's trying to throw sand on the grease.[24]

In response to Wilson's comments, a DRIE official insisted the duty remissions were aimed at addressing the restructuring of the North American tire industry, which was going on before the FTA. It was noted that 31 U.S. tire plants had closed since 1973. DRIE officials and the president of the RAC also noted that Wilson's view was erroneous given that the remission orders encouraged modernization and rationalization in Canada. Wilson also questioned the legality of the remission orders, arguing that it contravened Article 405 of the FTA that prohibits the waiver of custom duties in exchange for performance requirements. However, federal officials responded that the concept of duty remission had been discussed long before the FTA was signed and the remissions would be phased out by 1998 so there was no contravention of the FTA which stated that existing remission programs must be discontinued by 1998.[25] Furthermore, federal officials noted that the remission orders were not given in exchange for performance requirements as defined by the FTA. Such requirements were defined as requiring that (1) a given level of goods or services be exported or (2) domestic goods or services be substituted for imported goods or (3) preference be given to purchasing or producing domestically produced goods or services.

A final criticism of the remission orders was that they did not have much impact. One MP, Patrick Boyer, whose riding was hit by the closure of Toronto's Goodyear plant, concluded that the amounts in the order were inadequate and "there is no criteria for evaluating the impact other than taking what the tire companies have said." Federal officials disagreed with this view, insisting that at least $800 million of incremental investment had been made because of the remission orders. Boyer was also angry because of a public statement from a Goodyear official that Goodyear would have expanded its Canadian facilities with or without the remission order. Boyer speculated that the duty remission to Goodyear was

> a move to silence Goodyear in the United States from making allegations or invoking countervail. It's hush money paid for by the Canadian taxpayers and I find that an unacceptable way to conduct Canadian industrial policy."[26]

UG managers also admitted the remission orders did not have much impact. One manager noted: "We're not going to look a gift horse in the mouth."[27] The president of UG noted that the remissions "will only end up rewarding the Canadian subsidiaries for bringing in more tires that were manufactured in the U.S. without creating new jobs."[28] A federal minister responded to such criticism by stating that the duty remissions were not meant to create new jobs but "to prevent future closures to maintain present jobs." DRIE officials admitted that UG was not in a particularly favourable position to make use of duty remission because of the company's financial problems.

As it turned out, duty remissions combined with grants and interest-free loans from the federal and Ontario governments totaling $56.3 million were not enough to induce an interested purchaser to acquire the 1,300-employee, 66-year old Firestone plant in Hamilton, which was to be closed. A decline in the market for the plant's principal product of bias-ply tires necessitated investment in conversion to radial tires if the plant was to remain open. The federal government had been searching for a buyer of the plant from the spring of 1987 when Firestone agreed to the government's request to delay the plant closure. Cooper Tire and Rubber Co. of Ohio was interested in acquiring the plant and converting the plant to radial production, but the governments decided not to provide the $86 million in assistance desired by Cooper, and the union (URW) refused to accept Cooper's request to ignore seniority provisions in choosing workers from the old Firestone staff. Some government officials felt that a deal was not possible because the URW refused to give concessions. Because a deal could not be consummated, Firestone closed the plant and after disputing its obligation to do so, the company repaid to the government a $13.5 million forgiveable loan given in 1983 to increase and upgrade plant capacity. The loan was forgiveable on the condition that Firestone keep the Hamilton plant open at least until 1992 and spend up to $46 million in new capital expenditures at Hamilton and other plants in Canada. Firestone had already invested $39 million in the plant. This plant closure was the 11th in North America for Firestone since 1980.

Despite the closure of the Firestone plant, there were significant new investments in tire plants. In mid-1988, Goodyear announced its plan to construct a $320 million, 800-employee, state-of-the-art radial tire plant in Napanee, Ontario. The announcement generated controversy because the $32 million loan from the Ontario government and federal duty remissions totaling $63 million (including the $25 million granted earlier) came soon after Goodyear shut down its Toronto plant. A union leader expressed anger over the promised government aid when the company was still embroiled in a dispute with about 200 laid-off workers over severance pay, and none of the 1,300 workers laid off in Toronto were guaranteed jobs in the new plant, which was to be initially nonunion.

Also in mid-1988, Michelin announced a $500 million expansion of its three Nova Scotia plants and planned to create 600 jobs over eight years. The Nova Scotia government provided a $48.3 million loan interest free for 15 years, and the company also received $25 million in federal duty remissions. The announcement was delayed because of a plan by the Canadian Auto Workers (CAW) to unionize the three plants. The company did not want to announce the expansion until the union's plans were made clear so workers would not think they were being bought off. After the union abandoned its plans, the company made the announcement. At this point, there had been several unsuccessful attempts by three different unions to unionize Michelin workers. During the most recent attempt, the CAW surprised everyone by making the first major step of signing up more than 40 percent of the workers at the three plants following a three-month campaign, but the union did not obtain support from 50 percent plus one of all ballots cast during a secret certification vote. During this most recent drive, a business professor at Dalhousie predicted Michelin would shut down its Nova Scotia plants if the vote was successful because the plants would no longer be competitive with Michelin's five nonunion U.S. plants (four plants were in South Carolina and one in Alabama). This was described as "scare mongering" by another professor who suggested that the high value of the U.S. dollar and the fact that auto industry wages in Canada were about $7 per hour lower than in the United States would keep Michelin in the province.

In early 1989, there was another announcement of new investments in tire manufacturing when General Tire Canada, a subsidiary of an American firm which was in turn the largest subsidiary of Continental AG of West Germany, announced a $159 million modernization and expansion of its Barrie plant. The company received from the Ontario government an $11.5 million, 10-year interest-free loan and a $2.5 million training grant, conditional on meeting investment, production, and employment targets.

Michelin's Acquisition of Uniroyal-Goodrich

Michelin's achievements in North America as of 1989 were mixed. The company had become the leader in the North American truck tire market with nearly 50 percent of the market, but had only captured 7 to 8 percent of the passenger car tire market. The company considered the market share in passenger car tires to be insufficient when compared to its main competitor, Goodyear, which held approximately 25 percent of the North American market. (UG had about 9 percent of the North American market.) Observers noted that Michelin's poor showing in passenger car tires could be attributed to the long-established customer relations and lower prices of companies supplying the original equipment market, and Michelin's distribution policies. A manager in a competitor company noted:

> Michelin could have obtained 50 percent market share but they blew their marketing strategy. They could have used exclusive dealers but chose instead to use every dealer in town and then failed to provide a sufficient margin to the dealer to encourage promotion of the Michelin tire. Customers would be drawn to the dealer by the Michelin name but the dealer tended to promote a competitive product and the customer, who could typically be sold off a particular brand, was attracted by the lower price of Michelin's competitors.

One option for increasing the company's market share was to acquire a competitor. In 1988, Michelin and Italy's Gruppo Pirelli were outbid in attempting to acquire Firestone. The large Japanese tire manufacturer, Bridgestone, successfully acquired Firestone for $2.6 billion. At the end of 1988, Clayton and Dubilier, a New York–based private investment firm, which was the principal shareholder of UG, approached Michelin regarding a possible sale of its interest in UG. Following the unsuccessful attempt to acquire Firestone, Michelin had made plans to continue investments in the United States but with the opportunity to acquire UG, the calculations showed that the cost was the same of making new investments compared to making the acquisition. However, the acquisition was seen as more advantageous because of the time factor. Michelin would immediately receive fully operational production facilities and an active sales force. In comparison, the construction of new plants would have delayed Michelin's penetration of a relatively saturated market, it would have inevitably led to an expensive price war, and it would have led to the closure of several competitors' plants with the resulting negative social impact.[29]

It was estimated that the acquisition of UG would make Michelin the world's largest tire manufacturer with 20 percent of the global tire market compared to 17 percent each for Goodyear and Bridgestone.[30] Overall, it was estimated that six companies would have over 80 percent of the global tire market. The other three companies in the top six were Continental, Pirelli Armstrong, and Sumitumo. Several other companies represented the remaining share. Despite the leadership position Michelin would assume, because of the acquisition, the stock price of the company dropped with the announcement. One analyst noted that the acquisition's cost could restrain profits for at least two years and debt would "shoot up" to 175 percent of shareholders' equity, even surpassing the normally heavily indebted Japanese. For example, Bridgestone's debt was 123 percent after its 1988 Firestone acquisition.[31]

In order to complete the acquisition of UG, Michelin had to receive approval from the U.S. Justice Department, the Canadian Bureau of Competition Policy, and Investment Canada. In Canada, the new Competition Act, which came into effect in 1986, had the following purposes: (1) maintain and encourage competition in Canada, (2) promote efficiency and adaptability, (3) expand opportunities for Canadian participation in world markets while recognizing the role of foreign competition, (4) ensure equitable opportunities for smaller-size business, and (5) provide consumers with competitive prices and vehicles. In order to assess whether a merger would be approved under the act, the test that had to be met was whether the merger "prevents or lessens, or is likely to prevent or lessen, competition substantially." This assessment considered any factor relevant to competition in the market while specifically addressing seven criteria: (1) the extent of effective foreign competition, (2) the possibility of failing businesses (i.e., whether a business would have failed on its own), (3) the availability of acceptable product substitution, (4) the existence of barriers to entry, (5) the extent of effective competition remaining in the market, (6) the removal of a vigorous and effective competitor, and (7) the nature and extent of innovation. The act also allowed mergers if the parties could demonstrate that efficiency gains more than offset the effect of lessened competition. Consequently, the legislation explicitly recognized global economics and the restructuring needs of certain industries. The U.S. antitrust legislation was somewhat different from Canada. In particular, there was more focus in the United States on market share and prices in deciding whether a merger should be permitted. Because of U.S. antitrust legislation, Goodyear was advised by its lawyers not to acquire UG.

If the director of investigation and research for the Bureau of Competition Policy decided to challenge a proposed merger, the director could ask for the merger to be restructured or refer the application to the Competition Tribunal, a quasi-judicial body consisting of federal court judges and lay people, such as economists. The tribunal would hold public hearings to decide whether the merger substantially lessened competition and, if so, whether it should be watered down through a forced divestiture of assets or blocked in full. From 1986 to mid-1989, the bureau reviewed 400 proposed mergers and takeovers. Of those, nine were restructured at the bureau's insistence, and seven had gone or were going to the tribunal for a final ruling. This compared with the record of the old Combines Investigation Act under which not one case was successfully contested in the courts in the 70 years it was in force. The director of investigation and research noted:

> The rate of more than 20 contested mergers or takeovers out of the 400 cases considered in the past three years is not significantly dissimilar to that taking place in other industrialized countries today, where antitrust authorities are applying more flexibility and not just basing their analysis on a strict quantitative measure.[32]

Investment Canada, the agency which replaced the Foreign Investment Review Agency in 1985, would also be reviewing Michelin's proposed acquisition of UG because the acquisition was an indirect takeover by non-Canadians involving assets in Canada of more than $50 million. Investment Canada would advise the industry minister if the proposed investment was of "net benefit" to Canada, taking into account the following factors, where relevant: (1) the effect of the investment on the following: the level and nature of economic activity in Canada, productivity, industrial efficiency, technological development, product innovation, and product variety in Canada, competition within any industry, and Canada's ability to compete in world markets; (2) the degree and significance of participation by Canadians in the Canadian business; (3) the compatibility of the investment with national industrial, economic, and cultural policies. The federal cabinet made the final decision. There was no appeal of the decision and there was no opportunity for an applicant to respond to nor be made aware of any submissions made to Investment Canada about the proposed investment.

When the acquisition proposal was announced, a number of points about the deal were reported in the media as follows:

• Michelin's Canadian lawyers indicated that the company intends to expand investment at the two existing UG plants in Kitchener and intends to increase the $500 million, five-year capital investment program of UG and anticipates no layoffs or plant shutdowns. At the same time, an industry analyst noted that the sale of one of the UG plants is still possible because UG's parent in Akron, Ohio, will operate as an autonomous subsidiary of the Michelin Group and the sale of one of the plants may still fit in with its business plan. In fact, UG tried but failed in 1988 to sell its 27-year-old plant in south Kitchener. This plant was a one-story building, unlike the inefficient multistory plant in north Kitchener, but its equipment was not as up-to-date as the north plant.

• The addition of Michelin's technology should make the UG plants better able to compete in the increasingly competitive tire industry. Michelin had consistently spent 5 percent of sales on research and development, ahead of some of its competitors. One of the most recent innovations was the first radial tire for jet planes.

While the president of UG suggested that the Michelin takeover would mean job security for the employees, a few months earlier, the president of the Canadian subsidiary of UG stated publicly during a strike at the 75-year-old north Kitchener plant that this plant ranks "as one of the lowest we have in the North American system in the Uniroyal Goodrich Tire Co. in terms of productivity."[33] Furthermore, investments to improve productivity at the Canadian plants had not been made to the extent possible when a provincial government offer to provide $10 million for plant upgrading was not accepted by the company in 1987 because the company refused to provide job guarantees.

End Notes

1. *Halifax Chronicle Herald,* June 5, 1972.
2. *Business Week,* August 14, 1971, p. 40.
3. *Forbes,* April 15, 1973, p. 56.
4. Ibid.
5. *Financial Post Magazine,* April 26, 1980, p. 36.
6. Ibid., p. 40, 42.

7. David E. Osborn under the direction of Donald H. Thain, "Michelin Tires Manufacturing Co. of Canada Ltd.," Case Study, Western Business School.
8. Ibid.
9. *Financial Post Magazine,* April 26, 1980, p. 42.
10. Osborn, "Michelin Tires."
11. Ibid.
12. *Forbes,* April 15, 1973, p. 55.
13. Osborn, "Michelin Tires."
14. Ibid.
15. House of Commons Debates, May 15, 1972, p. 2259.
16. *Financial Post Magazine,* April 26, 1980, p. 42.
17. Ibid., p. 34.
18. From *Globe and Mail* editorial, as quoted in *Financial Post Magazine,* April 20, 1980, p. 44.
19. Ibid., p. 36.
20. *Forbes,* April 15, 1973.
21. Sections of the DRIE report were quoted in *Canadian Business,* June 1988, p. 56, 58, 243.
22. *Kitchener-Waterloo Record,* January 9, 1988, p. B3.
23. *Kitchener-Waterloo Record,* March 8, 1988, p. B7.
24. *Kitchener-Waterloo Record,* January 9, 1988, p. B3.
25. Ibid
26. *Kitchener-Waterloo Record,* March 8, 1988, p. B7.
27. *Kitchener-Waterloo Record,* January 8, 1988, p. B15.
28. *Globe and Mail,* February 2, 1988, p. B9.
29. Speech by Francois Michelin to annual meeting, 1990.
30. *Globe and Mail,* January 8, 1990, p. B6.
31. Ibid.
32. *Globe and Mail,* June 8, 1989, p. B3.
33. *Kitchener-Waterloo Record,* May 19, 1989, p. B6.

CASE 25
NORTHERN TELECOM JAPAN, INC.

In late May of 1988, Howard Garvey, the newly appointed president of Northern Telecom Japan, Inc. (NTJI), was reviewing the financial projections for the subsidiary's next three years of operation. After two months of studying the operations of the company, Garvey was planning to address a committee, consisting of the presidents of all the Northern Telecom (NT) companies, regarding the current state of NTJI. In his presentation, he would have to either accept the current three-year operating plan or present his proposed revisions. If he accepted the plan, he would be responsible for delivering the forecasted results. If he rejected the plan, he would have to explain why his forecasts differed from those of his predecessors.

With the meeting scheduled to be held in Toronto, Canada, in a month, Garvey decided to review the projections in light of what he had seen during his first six weeks in Japan.

The Telecommunications Industry

The decade of the 80s brought about major changes in the telecommunications industry. Of the approximately 30 major telecommunications manufacturers that had existed in the late 70s, only 15 remained in 1988. The impetus for this change was the rising cost of research required to remain a competitor in this industry. Digital switching, existing only in the minds of engineers at the turn of the decade, had become a necessity for doing business. By 1988, the estimated cost of developing a state-of-the-art digital central office switch was $1 billion.

With the need for greater research dollars came the need for volume. Companies could no longer exist by relying on their national markets alone. Some analysts, extrapolating this trend into the future, were predicting that by the year 2000 only 5 of the current 15 companies would remain, as any one company would need at least a 10 percent share of the world market to continue to compete. Exhibit 1 lists the top eight telecommunications manufacturers in 1988.

By 1988, the major thrust in the industry was on the development of ISDN systems. ISDN was an internationally agreed-upon protocol for an integrated

SOURCE: This case was prepared by Christopher Lane under the supervision of Professor C.B. Johnston for the sole purpose of providing material for class discussion at the Western Business School. Funding for this case was provided by the Pacific 2000 programme operated by the Department of External Affairs, Government of Canada. Certain names and other identifying information may have been disguised to protect confidentiality. It is not intended to illustrate either effective or ineffective handling of a managerial situation. Any reproduction, in any form, of the material in this case is prohibited except with the written consent of the School. Copyright 1992 © The University of Western Ontario.

Exhibit 1 **The Top Eight Manufacturers of Telecommunications Equipment—1988 (revenues in U.S. $ billions)**

1	Alcatel	France	$11.5*
2	AT&T	United States	$11.3
3	Siemens	West Germany	$10.8
4	NEC	Japan	$ 6.5
5	Northern Telecom	Canada	$ 5.2
6	LM Ericsson	Sweden	$ 4.2
7	Hitachi	Japan	$ 3.4
8	Fujitsu	Japan	$ 2.9

*The chart shows only revenues attributed to telecommunications sales. Sales for each company may be significantly higher.

service digital network, a network that would support the simultaneous transmission of data, voice, and image. ISDN technology united the computer, telephone, and television into one network and could eventually devolve these three devices into one.

Northern Telecom

NT first began manufacturing telecommunications instruments in Canada in 1884. The company, then named Northern Electric, began operations as the Canadian subsidiary of the U.S.–based manufacturing giant Western Electric. In 1956, the U.S. Department of Justice passed the AT&T Consent Decree, which forced American Telephone and Telegraph (AT&T) to sever all relationships with firms outside of the United States. The purpose of this action was to prevent the American giant from using its monopoly in the United States to compete unfairly in the rest of the world. Western Electric, as the manufacturing arm of AT&T, was forced to sever its relationship with Northern Electric in the same way that AT&T was forced to sever its relationship with Bell Canada. With this action, NT became a wholly owned subsidiary of Bell Canada.

Historically, both Bell Canada and NT had relied on their parent's research facility, Bell Labs, to keep them at the forefront of the industry. With these relationships now severed, the long-term survival of NT, as a producer of telecommunications equipment, became contingent upon the development of its own research facility. In 1959, NT established an internal research and development division which specialized in designing products for the Canadian market. In 1971, the division was spun off into a jointly owned subsidiary of both NT and Bell. The new company, named Bell Northern Research (BNR), provided research and development for both Bell Canada and NT.

---

[1]The provinces of Ontario and Quebec accounted for 68 percent of the population and roughly 80 percent of the Canadian telecommunications market.

The tricorporate structure provided an ideal environment for the growth of all three companies. Bell Canada, operating as a monopoly in the provinces of Ontario and Quebec,[1] worked closely with BNR and NT to develop the equipment needed to meet its future requirements. While Bell Canada served as the operating telecommunications company (telco) specialist, and BNR as the development specialist, NT provided the manufacturing and marketing expertise.

By the mid-70s, it had become apparent that research and development expenses required to keep NT at the forefront of the telecommunications industry would require revenues greater than those available in Canada alone. NT had to decide to become a small niche player in the industry or to expand its operations globally. In 1976, NT management set themselves an ambitious goal. In an attempt to increase their share of the U.S. market, they focused their research on digital technologies with the hope of becoming the first telecommunications company in the world to offer a complete digital switching system. They thought success in this endeavour would help to springboard them into the world market.[2] In 1976, NT invited executives from North American telephone operating companies to a conference in Disney World, Florida. The Canadian company's announcement that the age of the "Digital World" had arrived through NT's development of the first truly digital switches started the major thrust toward digital switching in North America.

In the early 80s, the U.S. Department of Justice ruled that AT&T would have to be broken up in order to promote greater competition within the U.S. telephone market. In 1984, Judge Green announced the Modification of Final Judgment, which ruled specifically how AT&T would be divided, and ordered that the 22 Bell subsidiaries be grouped together to form seven independent, regional telcos.

This event provided NT with an unprecedented opportunity for growth in the U.S. market. Many of the engineers within these newly formed companies were familiar with the benefits offered by digital switching and were anxious to begin incorporating this technology into their networks. With these companies now free to purchase their equipment from any supplier, not just from AT&T–owned Western Electric, NT was able to make substantial inroads.

By the beginning of 1988, NT had become the world's leading supplier of fully digital telecommunications systems, with sales of $4.85 billion.[3] Bell Canada remained the majority shareholder with a 53 percent holding, while the remaining shares were traded on the New York, Toronto, London, and Tokyo exchanges. On a geographic basis, revenues were derived as follows: 62 percent from Northern Telecom, Inc. (NTI), the U.S. subsidiary; 33 percent from Northern Telecom Canada Ltd.; and 5 percent from Northern Telecom World Trade Corp., the umbrella company which oversaw all international subsidiaries, in-

---

[2]For a more detailed account of this decision, please refer to Western Business School Case number Number 9-83-4031 (REV 10/85), "Northern Telecom (A)".

[3]All dollar figures in this thie case are U.S. denominated.

EXHIBIT 2

CONSOLIDATED FINANCIAL STATEMENTS OF NORTHERN TELECOM LIMITED
For the Year Ended December 31
($U.S. millions)

Earnings and related data	1984	1985	1986	1987
Revenues	3374.0	4262.9	4383.6	4853.5
Cost of revenues	2074.1	2708.9	2730.5	2895.8
Selling, general, and administrative expense	603.2	701.9	764.6	917.8
Research and development expense	333.1	430	474.6	587.5
Depreciation	162.8	203.3	247.3	264.1
Provision for income taxes	120.8	132.8	127.9	141.5
Earnings before extraordinary items	255.8	299.2	313.2	347.2
Net earnings applicable to common shares	243.2	273.8	286.8	328.8
Earnings per common share ($) before extraordinary items	1.06	1.18	1.23	1.39
Dividends per share ($)	0.16	0.18	0.20	0.23
Financial position at December 31				
Working capital	859	933.9	1188.7	570.7
Plant and equipment (at cost)	1458	1737.5	1975.2	2345.6
Accumulated depreciation	591.5	672.4	877.3	1084.2
Total assets	3072.9	3490	3961.1	4869.0
Long-term debt	100.2	107.6	101	224.8
Redeemable retractable preferred shares	293.6	277.5	281	153.9
Redeemable preferred shares	—	73.3	73.3	73.3
Common shareholders' equity	1379.8	164.6	1894.9	2333.3
Return on common shareholders' equity	0.19	0.183	0.163	0.156
Capital expenditures	437.3	457.3	303.8	416.7
Employees at December 31	46,993	46,549	46,202	48,778

SOURCE: Northern Telecom Ltd. Annual Report, 1987.

cluding Japan. (See Exhibit 2 for the consolidated financial statements.) NT was positioned as the fifth largest telecommunications manufacturer in the world with a 6.5 percent share of the global market for telecommunications equipment and related services. NT operated 41 manufacturing facilities worldwide. Of these, 24 were located in Canada, 13 in the United States, 2 in Malaysia, 1 in the Republic of Ireland, and 1 in France. Research was conducted at 24 of these plants as well as at 10 BNR labs including 4 in Canada, 5 in the United States, and 1 in the United Kingdom.

On the technological front, NT was well positioned for competing in the upcoming decade, and NT maintained its lead in ISDN development with a successful test of more than 20 business, government, and residential applications during a trial in Phoenix, Arizona. In addition, NT's SuperNode software technology, which allowed software modules to be added as needed, provided the most powerful and flexible digital switches in the business.

The management of the company chose 1988 to announce to its employees and shareholders Vision 2000, outlining NT's ambitious goal of becoming the world's leading supplier of telecommunications equipment by the year 2000 (see Exhibit 3).

The Japanese Market

The Japanese, impressed by the technological developments that had occurred at Bell Labs in the United States, had modeled their domestic telephone company after AT&T. Their version, Nippon Telegraph and Telephone (NTT), had been

---

EXHIBIT 3   Vision 2000: The Challenge of Leadership

Between now and the year 2000, the global market for telecommunications equipment and associated services is going to explode—from about $75 billion in 1987, to approximately $300 billion, a growth rate unmatched by any other industry.

Northern Telecom's own growth will be equally dramatic. It will be based on the steps we are taking now to ensure the achievements of Vision 2000—our goal of leadership in the worldwide telecommunications marketplace into the next century.

The global information network has already become one of the world's most effective means of increasing productivity. From the remote oil fields of The People's Republic of China, to the financial institutions of the United Kingdom, to the high-tech innovators of California's Silicon Valley, communications provides the advantages for competitive success and improved quality of life.

This is recognized by enlightened governments around the world, which have singled out telecommunications as a major priority for development and modernization.

Traditional voice services and rapidly increasing requirements for data transmission are outstripping the ability of existing networks to meet the competitive pressures of global business needs and the growing demands of society. At the same time, new technologies and new generations of equipment are creating additional demands for services previously only dreamed of.

While new products, services, and technologies are propelling the growth of telecommunications worldwide, we are focusing on markets where the opportunity is greatest. Beyond North America, we are concentrating on such markets as Australia, China, France, Japan, New Zealand, West Germany, and the United Kingdom, where deregulation and growth are creating market opportunities that have already led to strategic sales of our products. In these seven countries alone, the market will grow from $20 billion to $100 billion by the year 2000.

We expect our business outside North America to rise to about 15 percent of our total revenues in the early 1990s and continue to increase through the rest of that decade.

Northern Telecom's vision of the year 2000 involves a number of imperatives. It means continually generating sustainable advantages over our competitors through excellence in creating value for our customers, which in turn enhances their growth and profitability.

It requires our corporation to be global in reach and thinking, while showing flexibility, sensitivity, and good corporate citizenship in diverse markets.

And it demands that Northern Telecom deliver products and systems of the highest quality and reliability, on time, tailored to the varying needs of our customers. We must also provide the highest level of service in the industry.

The conditions of leadership are clear. In a fiercely competitive international marketplace, leadership will go to that corporation with the clearest global vision, the fastest response, the capability, and the commitment to satisfy the ever-more complex market requirements of the future.

Northern Telecom intends to be that corporation.

SOURCE: Northern Telecom Ltd. Annual Report, 1987.

established as a government-owned monopoly with the mandate of providing domestic telecommunications services throughout Japan. Another government-owned company, Kokusai Denshin Denwa (KDD), provided all international long-distance service. NTT's research facility worked very closely with the Ministry of International Trade and Industry, operating more as a national research center than as a corporate research facility. Jointly sponsored research conducted at the lab was largely responsible for helping Japan catch up to the United States in semiconductor technologies.

Unlike AT&T in the United States, NTT did not have any manufacturing facilities. Instead, it relied on four major Japanese suppliers, Nippon Electric Company (NEC), Hitachi, Oki, and Fujitsu, to manufacture its equipment. The "big four" worked closely with NTT researchers to jointly design all of the switches for the Japanese telecommunications network. Under this arrangement, each of them manufactured identical equipment and received roughly a 25 percent share of NTT's business. Through these relationships, Japan was able to build and support a significant manufacturing base for telecommunications equipment.

In 1982, an ad hoc commission of administrative reform was set up by the Japanese government to study ways of introducing competition into the Japanese telecommunications system. In 1985, the committee released a report calling for deregulation of the entire telecommunications industry and the privatization of government-owned NTT. One of the most important results of the report was the establishment of the new common carriers (NCCs). The NCCs were firms that would be licensed to compete in both the domestic and international long-distance telephone markets in a manner similar to Sprint and MCI in the United States. October 1, 1989, was the date set for the beginning of service by the NCCs.

The NCCs presented an opportunity for foreign telecommunications equipment suppliers, as many of these new firms were building their own networks from scratch. Furthermore, these companies didn't have existing relationships with the domestic suppliers and were looking outside of Japan to see how they could gain a competitive advantage over the existing NTT/KDD networks.

In 1988, the Japanese telecommunications market, estimated at $25 billion, was the third largest in the world and one of the fastest growing. The three main segments that made up this market were telcos, corporations, and households.

Telcos

Telcos, providing the network for telecommunications, had needs ranging from wiring and optical fibre to large-scale switching equipment, from underwater cables to satellite or microwave transmission equipment. Sales to telcos were usually made through tenders, often called four to five years in advance of the required installation date. (See the appendix for an explanation of NTT's procurement process.)

Success in this market required not only state-of-the-art hardware but also an extensive service organization. Highly trained servicemen and an inventory of spare parts had to be kept within easy access of all areas of the network, since any problems had to be fixed within hours. In 1988, sales to telcos represented 50 percent of the total Japanese telecommunications market. Sales to NTT represented roughly 90 percent of this segment.

Corporations

As the networking and communications needs of companies grew throughout the 80s, so did the market for private branch exchanges (PBXs). A PBX is the brain of a corporate phone system. It allows companies with only a few outside lines to provide phone service to all of their employees, thus reducing overall telephone costs. PBXs had become increasingly more sophisticated and complex over the years by offering facilities such as voice mail, automatic callback, and direct-inward dialing. Sales of PBX systems were usually made through a tender process.

One factor that distinguished the Japanese market from other world markets, however, was the existence of Keiretsus. A Keiretsu was a group of firms loosely connected through part ownership. (See "A Note on The Japanese Keiretsu," Western Business School Case 9-92-G008, for more information.) These firms had a tendency to purchase equipment from within their group whenever possible. With the big four Japanese competitors all firmly entrenched in their own Keiretsus, the size of the market that was left for NT to compete in was questionable.

Households

In Japan, most individuals purchased their own telephones rather than renting them from NTT. Phones were sold through three primary distribution outlets: department stores, electronics specialty chain stores, and numerous large and small independent electronics stores. Along with the big four, many of Japan's leading consumer electronics companies also manufactured telephones. The resulting market was extremely competitive. (See Exhibit 4 for market data.) Competition among producers tended to occur along three dimensions: product-features, design, and price. In the spirit of "kaizen,"[4] phones were being continually introduced with new features. Many of the best-selling phones were heavily advertised.

The Competition

There were numerous competitors in the Japanese telecommunications market (see Exhibit 5). However, NT faced only four primary domestic competitors in selling to NTT.

---

[4]*Kaizen* is a Japanese word used to describe the Japanese philosophy of continuous incremental improvement.

Exhibit 4 Telephone and PBX Sales in Japan in 1988

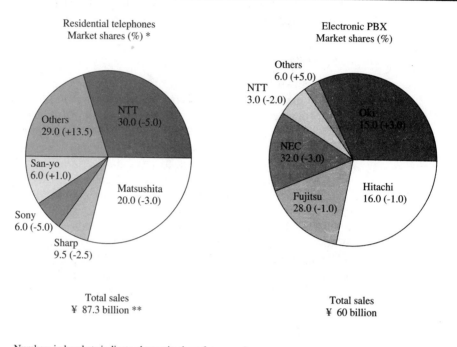

Residential telephones
Market shares (%) *

NTT 30.0 (-5.0)
Others 29.0 (+13.5)
San-yo 6.0 (+1.0)
Sony 6.0 (-5.0)
Sharp 9.5 (-2.5)
Matsushita 20.0 (-3.0)

Total sales
¥ 87.3 billion **

Electronic PBX
Market shares (%)

Others 6.0 (+5.0)
NTT 3.0 (-2.0)
Oki 15.0 (+3.0)
NEC 32.0 (-3.0)
Fujitsu 28.0 (-1.0)
Hitachi 16.0 (-1.0)

Total sales
¥ 60 billion

Numbers in brackets indicate change in share from previous year
** 125 Japanese Yen ▪ $1.00 U.S. (1988)

Source: *Information & Communication in Japan*. Tokyo: InfoCom Research Inc., 1990, p 171.

Nippon Electric Company

NEC, the fourth largest telecommunications producer in the world, reported overall revenues of $22 billion in 1988. The company was organized into four divisions:

1. Communications systems and equipment.
2. Computer and industrial electronic systems.
3. Electronic devices.
4. Home electronic products.

Communications systems and equipment contributed 28 percent of the overall revenue. NEC was well known for the high quality of its hardware. However, adding advanced features to NEC's product was difficult because the company's software was less flexible than NT's.

EXHIBIT 5   Competition in the Japanese Telecommunications Markets

Company	Telephone Sets	PBXs	Digital Switches
Alphone Co., Ltd.	X		
Alcatel NV	X	X	X
Anritsu Corporation	X		
Iwasaki Tsushiniki Co. Ltd.	X	X	
AT&T International Japan	X	X	X
Oidenki Co., Ltd.		X	
Oki Electric Industry Co. Ltd.	X	X	X
Kanda Tsushin Kogyo	X		
Canon, Inc.	X	X	
Kyushu Matsushita	X		
Kenwood Corporation	X		
International Electronics	X		
Sun Telephone Co.	X		
Sanyo Electric Co. Ltd.	X	X	
Siemens K.K.	X		X
Sharp Corporation	X	X	
Shinwa Tsushinki	X		
Sony Corporation	X		
Taiei Manufacturing Ltd.		X	X
Taiko Electric	X	X	X
Takachiho Ltd.	X		
Takamizawa Electric Co.		X	
Omron Electronics Co.	X	X	
Tamura Electric Works Ltd.	X		
Toshiba Corporation	X	X	
Nakayo Telecommunications Ltd.	X	X	X
Nitsuko Corp.	X	X	
NEC Corporation	X	X	X
Victor Company of Japan	X		
Northern Telecom	X	X	X
Pioneer Electronic Corp.	X		
Hitachi Ltd.	X	X	X
Fujitsu Ltd.	X	X	X
Matsushita Corporation Ltd.	X	X	
Mitsubishi Electric Corporation	X	X	
Ricoh Co. Ltd.	X		

SOURCE: *Information & Communications in Japan*. Tokyo: InfoCom Research, Inc., March 1990, pp. 173–178.

Hitachi

With revenues of $40 billion in 1988, Hitachi was the largest overall company of the four competitors. A huge Keiretsu in itself, its product range extended from nuclear power plants to semiconductors. The company was divided into five principal business groups:

1. Power systems and equipment.
2. Consumer products.

3. Information and communication systems and electronic devices.
4. Industrial machinery and plants.
5. Wire and cable and chemicals.

The information and communication systems and electronic devices division encompassed businesses from computers to semiconductors and telecommunications equipment. This division accounted for 33 percent of revenues in 1988. Hitachi was ranked as the seventh largest telecommunications manufacturer in 1988.

In 1987, the company opened a subsidiary to produce PBX units in the United States.

Fujitsu

Fujitsu, IBM's most aggressive worldwide competitor in the mainframe computer market, was divided into four primary business groups:

1. Computers and data processing.
2. Telecommunications.
3. Semiconductors.
4. Components.

Telecommunications represented 12.5 percent of the company's $16 billion in revenue in 1988. The company was strong in all areas of the telecommunications business from fibre optic cable to digital switching equipment. In March 1988, the company released an ISDN system linking computers, word processors, and networks into one package.

Internationally, Fujitsu had formed an alliance with General Electric in the United States to manufacture and market PBX systems.

Oki

Oki, the smallest of the big four Japanese suppliers, was strong internationally in cellular telephones and fax machines. Revenues in 1988 amounted to $3.6 billion with 26.9 percent of this amount resulting from sales of telecommunications systems. The company was divided into three principal groups:

1. Telecommunications systems.
2. Information processing systems.
3. Electronic devices.

Northern Telecom Japan, Inc.

In the early 80s, NT initiated a program whereby senior managers were sent as ambassadors to various telecommunications markets around the world. These managers met with potential customers and assessed the prospects of the market from NT's perspective. Japan, at that time representing the third largest telecommunications market in the world, was selected early as one of the countries to be visited. In 1982, Edward Fitzgerald, president of Northern Telecom Limited, went to Japan as NT's ambassador.

Fitzgerald, although not an expert in doing business in Japan, knew that the Japanese loved baseball as much or more than most Americans. Having owned the Milwaukee Brewers at one point, he was well connected in baseball circles and shared their enthusiasm for the sport. Thinking that it might help, he asked his good friend Buie Khun, the ex-commissioner of major league baseball in the United States, to join him for the trip.

Through Kuhn's connections with Japanese baseball officials and those officials' connections in Japanese business circles, Fitzgerald was able to get a letter of introduction to Dr. Shinto, the president of NTT. Through a combination of his personality, his baseball stories, many gifts of Inuit carvings, and his sincerity in wishing to do business in Japan, he was able to win the respect of his Japanese counterparts, thus laying the groundwork for building NT's relationship with NTT.

While in Japan, Fitzgerald employed the services of a well-known Japanese businessman/consultant to look into NTT's operations and various government and legal issues. The work of the consultant uncovered two significant facts for NT. First, NTT needed to replace a significant number of small community dial office systems in the rural areas of its network. Second, the recent trade friction between the United States and Japan was making the Japanese government very uncomfortable. It seemed very plausible that NTT as a government-regulated monopoly would feel pressure to open up to foreign suppliers, especially to those from the United States.

Armed with this information, NT, acting through its American subsidiary, NTI, prepared an unsolicited proposal for NTT to supply the Japanese company with NT's DMS-10, the world's first fully digital switching system. With a capacity of up to 10,000 lines, the DMS-10 was ideally suited for use as a community dial office. The bid to NTT was made in 1982. At the same time, NT established an office in Japan with the arrival of a single expatriate. Although the bid to NTT was well received, it did not immediately translate into a direct order.

In 1983, NT committed itself to the Japanese market with the legal registration of NTJI. In the latter part of the year, NT received an invitation from NTT to participate in a competitive bid for a single emergency switching system. This switch, which was to be mounted in a trailer, would be used to provide emergency switching capability if an earthquake or other type of disaster left a community without telephone service. Coincidently, the specifications for this switch were very similar to those of NT's DMS-10. The slightly modified DMS-10 was named the KS-2, and NT succeeded in beating the competition to become the first foreign telecommunications company to supply to NTT. Although the one-time sale represented less than $400,000, the associated benefits for NT were far greater. The sale allowed NT to learn more about NTT, its needs, and its methods of doing business. At the same time, the opportunity for NTT to evaluate NT's quality and technology helped to strengthen the relationship that had been developing over time.

In 1984, NTT announced a competitive tender to replace a large number of rural electromechanical community switching exchanges. A decision by NT to bid for this tender would have to include a commitment to establish a full-service network in Japan, as the vendor was required to provide ongoing servicing of the equipment. NT, believing in the long-term potential of the Japanese market, entered a bid, once again featuring the DMS-10.

Designing flexible software systems was one area where North American producers had a competitive advantage over their Japanese rivals. A feature of NT's proposal extended to NTT the right to modify the software operating system of the switch for the purpose of developing market-specific feature applications. This arrangement required NT to provide NTT with documentation on its operating software. AT&T, also bidding on this contract, was reluctant to include this right, fearing that NTT might divulge this information to the four domestic manufacturers.

NT management, after assessing the long-term opportunity of doing business with NTT, determined that the risk was minimal, as the software programs within the switch were reaching maturity. More importantly, however, they wanted to develop a relationship between NT and NTT which was based on reciprocal trust.

On May 19, 1986, Northern's bid was selected by NTT and NT was committed to building and maintaining a subsidiary in Japan capable of installing and servicing 1,500,000 lines over a five-year period, beginning in late 1988. The contract was worth $250 million for NTJI.

The Penetration Strategy

With the establishment of NTJI, NT was committing to a long-term strategy of becoming a supplier of its full line of switching equipment to NTT. Because this relationship would take time to develop, a short-term penetration strategy was also developed for attacking the two other main segments of the Japanese telecommunications market: telephones and PBX units.

Telephones

NTJI entered the Japanese telephone market in 1984 with the launch of its Contempra model, an upscale, "designer" telephone set. Initial sales were encouraging, as the Contempra filled a niche at the top of the market. Unfortunately, when this product was introduced into the middle segment of the market, NT found that the competition was extremely severe. Without the volume of the more standard telephone sets to support the administrative overhead, NT realized that the telephone segment provided little opportunity for profit. As a consequence, efforts were withdrawn on marketing these products.

PBX Unit: The SL-1

NTJI's disappointment in the telephone set segment of the market was not a complete surprise to upper management in Northern Telecom Ltd., as NTI, the U.S. subsidiary, was also experiencing similar stiff competition. What upper management did not anticipate, however, were the problems that NTJI experienced in trying to sell its PBX systems in Japan. The SL-1, NT's digital PBX system, was the world's best-selling PBX system. Because of its successful sales throughout North America, NT had expected that the SL-1 would be a success in Japan as well. When actual sales fell considerably short of forecasts, management decided to investigate.

Examination of this issue highlighted a multitude of miscalculations in NT's marketing approach. First, NT had seriously underestimated the strength of the domestic competition and their Keiretsu relationships. Second, NTJI had not studied how Japanese companies actually used their phone systems and therefore did not realize that its product did not meet the basic needs of the Japanese corporation. To the Japanese, direct access dialing was not a desirable feature, as every call to the company should be answered and greeted by the company's receptionist. She would then call ahead to check if the person was in before either transferring the call or taking a message.

Consequently, NT's highly advanced product offered little advantage to the Japanese customer. Third, the product was being marketed at a premium price. On average, NT's system was priced 20 percent higher than the local competition's product. Finally, all of the promotional materials for the SL-1 were in English, and the product was being sold through a distributor who had been given insufficient product training. Needless to say, the relationship between NT and the distributor became very strained.

Despite the problems encountered in the telephone set and PBX markets, NTJI continued its efforts into the telco market, and in January of 1988, signed an agreement with International Digital Communications (IDC), one of the newly sanctioned NCCs, to provide the switching equipment needed to run their network. IDC chose NT's DMS-250 tandem switching system and DMS-300 international gateway switch. This decision was influenced by NT's previous success in selling these switches to MCI and Sprint in the United States, as NT supplied 50 percent of MCI's and 100 percent of Sprint's switching equipment. IDC was licensed to begin operations on October 1, 1989, and NT was committed to installing a complete network to be ready by that date.

By early 1988, NTJI had grown to employ 87 full-time employees. Of these, roughly 40 were expatriates from NTI and the remaining were local Japanese.

Howard Garvey

Howard Garvey joined NT in 1955 as an installer. He worked his way through the Canadian organization, and after 18 years of service, was appointed assistant to the vice president, sales, of NTI, the U.S. subsidiary. In 1978, he was appointed NTI's first national account manager and subsequently generated the first $50 million supply contract in the United States. In March of 1982, he was appointed vice president, sales, with responsibility for AT&T and the Bell operating companies. This promotion coincided with the beginning of the thrust to market digital systems to the Bell system in the United States, accounting for just under $100 million of NTI's sales.

By 1988, sales in his division were exceeding $1.2 billion, and Garvey was recognized as one of the key people instrumental in achieving NT's success in penetrating the U.S. market. In March of that year, Desmond Hudson, the president of Northern Telecom World Trade (NTWT), asked Garvey if he would do in Japan what he had done so well in the United States. Garvey accepted a three-year posting and was told he had until July to learn all he could about Japan. Shortly afterwards, Fitzgerald, the chairman and CEO of Northern Telecom Limited, upon returning from a trip to Japan, prompted Hudson to accelerate Garvey's assignment. A few weeks later, in April of 1988, Garvey arrived in Japan as president of NTJI.

Garvey's Impressions of NTJI

In commenting on NTJI, Garvey pointed out that:

> In January of 1988, the chairman and several other key executives within Northern Telecom took stock of where the company was in respect to the Japanese market. We had a major contract with NTT to install 1,500,000 lines worth $250,000,000. We had a major contract with IDC with a date staring us in the face that not only meant part of our future but also IDC's future was at stake. If that thing went down then we were dead in Japan. We also had an unprecedented opportunity over here, as we were moving into a new market place with the NCCs.

When they reviewed the NTJI operation, they noticed that there were an increasing number of bypasses around NTJI. The customers, apprehensive about the local organization's ability to service their needs, often dealt directly with North America. It was concluded that the situation required a change in the management of NTJI.

> Because of my background and experience in increasing our market share in the United States, into the Bell system in particular, and because there was such a similarity between the structures of AT&T in North America and NTT in Japan, I was given the opportunity to come and see what needed to be done to make sure that we didn't jeopardize the opportunity that was facing us.

During April and May, Garvey examined the operations of NTJI in an effort to find areas upon which he could improve. The following were his observations:

> The organization that existed in Japan was essentially being run from the United States. Executives in NTI, proud of their accomplishment as one of the few American companies that had successfully broken into the Japanese market, had not been proactive in developing NTJI into a stand-alone subsidiary. There was a sense that

NTI owned NTJI and the practice was that representatives of NTI were continually flying over to Japan to interact with various NTT officials.

As a result, NTJI was still heavily dependent on the United States. This created within Japan an organization very limited in technical, marketing, and management skills, even though the organization had been in Japan for over four years.

There were people in the local management group that were not compatible with Japanese customers. As an example, there was a fellow that was in charge of service, the leading edge in your customer relationship, with a domineering attitude based upon years in the U.S. military . . . he didn't fit very well.

There was a heavy ex-pat presence and that relates back to the dependency on the United States. The ex-pats of course could go back to the United States for anything they wanted. Over and above that, there was no support infrastructure within the Japanese organization. The company was growing with minimum sense of direction, and a complementary management hierarchy was lacking within the company.

Another major shortcoming was that the organization that existed in Japan was facing the United States. In other words, the organization was plugged into the organizational structure that existed in NTI in the United States, into a marketing group in the United States, into a service group in the United States, into a technical support group in the United States, without consideration of turning around and facing the customer and adapting to their organization.

As a result of the existing organization in Japan, engineers in some divisions within NTT would have to interface with two or three different divisions within NTJI (see Exhibit 6). For example, members of NTT's software engineering centre would have to regularly contact people in NTJI's Design, Design Follow-up, and Engineering divisions. Even more troublesome though, managers of NTT regional centres, who managed the outlying areas of NTT's network, would at times have to interface with almost every division within NTJI. This presented great problems for the regional manager, who inevitably called the wrong person within NTJI and spent the rest of the day playing telephone tag with various people before finding the right person to solve his problem.

When we talk about how to succeed in business, we hear more and more these days that you'd better be aware of your customer's needs. You can't have your back to the customer as NTJI did here. The company was structured to do business more conveniently with the United States than with our customers.

An additional problem within the company at the time was that there was a lack of business discipline. For example, local purchasing went virtually uncontrolled. The existing approval system was very loosely monitored. In fact, almost anyone could travel anywhere with minimal approvals.

Because of these factors, there existed a great deal of client apprehension. Customers didn't see any effective marketing, technical, or management support within NTJI. They were justifiably concerned about how NTJI was going to meet the obligations that it had here in Japan, as the company appeared to be run from the other side of the world.

There was also a perceptible split between the ex-pats and the nationals, and I again refer back to trying to do business in Japan and facing the customer. It was to the point where there was minimal reciprocal dialogue between the national employees and the ex-pats. Unfortunately, the ex-pats were predominantly in management positions in NTJI, and many decisions were made without any discussion or involvement with the Japanese employees. They were usually in the situation of "do as we tell you, we know best." Of course, that cost us an awful lot of employee discontent. It carried over into the recognition that we had to start growing some local experienced talent, but our reputation presented further difficulties in trying to recruit people.

There was an inadequate definition of responsibilities within the organization. The nationals particularly did not know what their jobs were. They took day-to-day directions from the ex-pats. Their responsibilities changed because the ex-pats were able to go to any individual, regardless of what his job was, and say "do this" or "go here." It was very unsettling for them. There was a definite lack of defini-

EXHIBIT 6 An Example of Structural Problems in NTJI

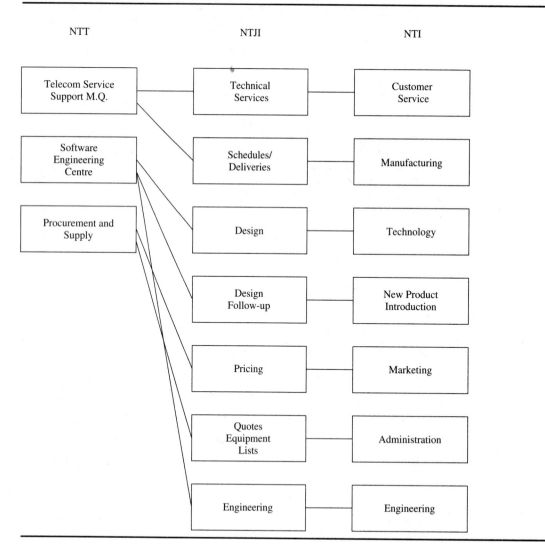

tion of responsibilities, and little sense of belonging to NTJI for the national employees.

Lastly, there was a serious lack of focus on where we were going in NTJI. For example, many of the people required for the installation and maintenance of NTT's contract for DMS-10s had not yet been hired or trained. The company's objectives in Japan and how they were going to be achieved were not communicated well to the employee population.

The Financial Projections

In late May of 1988, Garvey was reviewing the current operating projections for NTJI (see Exhibit 7). He was aware of several developments that had occurred since the original projections had been made in January 1988.

First, NT had received an order from NTT for a single DMS-200. The order was the first central office switch sold to NTT by a non-Japanese vendor. It was commissioned by NTT to be used as an overflow switch to handle the surge in telephone traffic that occurred every year following "golden week."[5] In previous years, NTT had come under severe criticism as its network became jammed with calls and many people could not get through. The DMS-200–based system, to be installed in November of 1989, would eventually contribute $20–30 million in revenue. However, it would also require a similar sized investment in development costs by NT to adapt the DMS-200 to work within the Japanese public network and to develop the necessary supply infrastructure.

Second, it appeared that additional development costs would have to be incurred to modify NT's DMS-250 and DMS-300 for the IDC network. Garvey estimated the costs of these modifications within a range of $10–20 million.

Exhibit 7

NTJI FINANCIAL PROJECTIONS
For the Year Ended December 31
(in U.S. $ millions)

	1988				Totals		
	Q1	*Q2*	*Q3*	*Q4*	*1988*	*1989*	*1990*
Orders					43	126	173
Sales	2.1	2.3	3.0	9.1	16.5	75	130
Earnings					(6)	3	9
Headcount					136	196	232

---

[5]"Golden week," falling in April, is so named because it contains three public holidays within the span of seven days. Many Japanese companies close for the entire week, making this a very popular time for Japanese people to travel.

Furthermore, Garvey had the benefit of being able to compare the first quarter's actual results against the projections. Revenues for the first quarter were slightly lower than projections and costs were slightly higher. From his earlier assessment of the company, he calculated that the forecast seriously underestimated the costs of product development, servicing, and support that companies like NTT demanded. Garvey estimated that over the next two years, an additional $5 million would be needed for increased technical support from the United States, and at least $2 million would be needed for training local personnel.

With these factors in mind, Garvey began planning his presentation for the executive committee.

Appendix
NTT's Procurement Process

Outline of Procedures

Based on the policy of "open, fair, and nondiscriminatory" procurement, NTT procures products required to operate its business following competitive procedures.

At NTT, procurement procedures are divided into five different categories according to the nature of the products to be procured. These are Track I, II, III and II-A, and III-A.

When NTT purchases or hires any products in excess of 130,000 SDR per year (equivalent to 24 million yen[6] for FY 1988), the products are procured according to one of the above-mentioned procedures.

Track I covers the procedures for the procurement of specific products offered to GATT by NTT as items which fall under the "Agreement on Government Procurement." NTT selects suppliers by public tender in conformity with GATT[7] rules.

Track II, III, and Track II-A, III-A cover the procedures for the procurement of products other than those specified for Track I. In addition, NTT procurement procedures are transparent and nondiscriminatory in compliance with the spirit of GATT.

What Is a Track?

Track I.   Track I covers the procedures for the procurement of specific products offered to GATT by NTT as items which fall under the "Agreement on Government Procurement."

As a general rule, NTT issues a public announcement in *Kampo* (the Japanese official gazette) when purchasing Track I products, and product suppliers are selected by tender. Tenders are conducted periodically. Usually, the period is one or two years.

There are two types of Track I tender. One type is the open tender, where tenders are submitted by anyone who desires to participate in the tender, and successful tenderers are selected upon evaluation following tender opening. The other type is the selective tender; for this type of tender, anyone who desires to participate in the tender is required to pass prequalification. Notice of prequalification is provided publicly in advance of the tender notice. Those applicants who have passed the prequalification are eligible to participate in Selective Tender.

---

[6]125 Japanese Yen = $1.00 U.S. (1988).

[7]GATT: General Agreement on Tariffs and Trade.

Tracks II and III.   Tracks II and III cover the procedures for initial procurement of new products other than those procured through Track I.

Track II covers the procedures for initial procurement of such new products produced on a commercial basis or that can be used as is or with minor modification.

NTT selects applicants offering the most attractive proposals to NTT as suppliers for Track II products based on the results of the evaluation of the proposals submitted by the applicants following the instructions provided in the public notice.

Track III covers the procedures for procurement of products that are not produced on a commercial basis and that need to be newly developed. Joint development partners are selected from among the applicants submitting application documents following the instructions provided in the public notice. Joint development partners may be requested to manufacture a prototype for testing to confirm function and performance of the newly developed product.

Track II-A and III-A.   Track II-A and III-A covers the procedures for repeat procurement of the same products already procured previously through Track II and Track III procurement. Track II-A & III-A procedures are also applied to new applicants who have not been qualified but who desire to supply such products. NTT, at all times, welcomes proposals from new applicants. When a new applicant is judged to be superior to a qualified supplier, NTT will also award a contract to such superior applicant as a newly selected supplier.

Products Procured by NTT

NTT procures various categories of products as required to provide telecommunication services:

1. Switching equipment.
2. Transmission equipment.
3. Radio equipment.
4. Data communication equipment.
5. Power supply equipment.
6. Customer equipment.
7. Cables.
8. Others (i.e., office equipment, vehicles, etc.).

Of the products listed above, those that fall under the category of Track I procurement are as follows:

1. Equipment and materials for plants (i.e., vehicles, poles, modems, computers, facsimiles, etc.).
2. Paper and other products for office use including clothing.
3. Equipment for research and development.

4. Equipment for training.

5. Equipment for medical use.

Flow chart diagrams of all procurement procedures were attached to the original document.

SOURCE: "Guide to NTT Procurement Procedures," published by NTT.

CASE 26
NOTE ON THE CANADIAN PLASTICS INDUSTRY

In early 1990, competitors in the Canadian plastics industry could look back on a decade of rapid growth. Throughout the 1980s, growth in the plastics industry consistently outpaced the overall growth of the economy by a factor of two to three. By 1990, the industry was widely considered to be the fastest-growing major manufacturing sector in Canada. It appeared that plastics had become the material of choice, challenging traditional materials in the packaging, construction, automotive, and many other industries. Plastics engineers continued to create innovative, new products to further fuel growth. Projections forecasted continued growth throughout the 1990s in all segments of the plastics industry and rapid growth in a few key sectors.

In spite of these optimistic forecasts, it was expected that many producers would face serious challenges in the 1990s. The Free Trade Agreement with the United States, consumer concern for the environment, high Canadian taxes, a shortage of engineering talent and skilled labour, and other pressures were forcing radical change on the industry. Such pressures suggested that traditional patterns of competition would quickly become outdated. This was particularly true in that relatively few Canadian companies had developed world-class operations. Indeed, much of the success in the industry could be traced to small, highly entrepreneurial firms, protected by high tariffs and an undervalued Canadian dollar. As these protective barriers were dismantled, plastics industry executives were increasingly questioning how best to improve their competitiveness for the decade that lay ahead.

The International Plastics Industry

High growth rates were common to the plastics industries in many countries during much of the 1970s and 1980s. During this period, annual growth of plastics production typically outpaced overall economic growth in most industrialized countries. In the United States, for example, annual production growth of plastics products averaged 9.9 percent from 1982 to 1986. During this same period, production growth averaged 6.7 percent in West Germany and 15 percent in Canada.

The ongoing international growth of plastics-related products could be traced directly to their inherent qualities. Throughout the 1980s, plastics had

This note was prepared by Professor Allen J. Morrison, School of Business Administration, The University of Western Ontario, 1990. Funding was provided by the National Centre for Management Research and Development.

displaced other materials in a broad range of manufacturing sectors. The major factors leading to plastics popularity are summarized below.

Energy Efficiency. It takes less energy to make a product from plastic than any other material. It requires more energy to manufacture a glass bottle than a plastic bottle, aluminum siding than vinyl siding, steel pipe than plastic pipe, and so on.

Processability. Plastics are cost-effective and offer a wide range of properties. In addition, plastic parts can be moulded into the product in one step. Metal parts, on the other hand, usually have to be machined several times.

Lightweight. Plastics are lightweight, resulting in significant transportation cost savings.

Corrosion Resistance. Plastics are replacing traditional materials in many markets because they resist corrosion. For example, plastic pipe and vinyl siding in the construction industry are replacing copper and aluminum.

Industry analysts were expecting that the advantages of plastics would continue to fuel rapid growth in the industry throughout the 1990s. New developments, including conductive polymers, membrane technology, and alloys and blends, were projected to fuel even greater growth. Plastics had traditionally been used as insulators, but newly developed materials could make plastics conductive. Industry experts predicted that the silicon chip would ultimately be a plastics product. Membrane technology would find many applications, especially in medicine. This development could transform kidney dialysis machines the size of a large table to a device the size of a small tube. In the past, plastics scientists have created new plastics materials by manipulating the molecular structure rather than alloying. Research in the late 1980s had shown that alloying and blending various plastics could produce highly desirable characteristics, such as higher resistance to heat and greater strength.

Value-Added Production

Plastics production worldwide was dependent on a variety of value adding processes that commonly started with fossil fuels as building blocks. By feeding petroleum and natural gas feedstocks into reactors and applying heat, pressure, and, in some instances, other raw materials, a variety of petrochemicals could be produced. In Canada, approximately 10 percent of all oil and gas produced was converted into petrochemicals. Through further processing, typically half of this petrochemical stock was upgraded into a variety of monomers (for example, ethylene, styrene, propylene, vinyl chloride). These monomers were then further upgraded into polymers or plastic resins including polyethylene, polystyrene, polyvinyl chloride, ABS, and polypropylene. In Canada, about 60 percent of these resins in total were absorbed by sister industries such as paints, synthetic rubbers, and synthetic fibres. The remainder were used by plastics processors as basic inputs in the manufacture of a wide variety of plastics products (see Exhibit 1).

EXHIBIT 1 The Plastics Industry

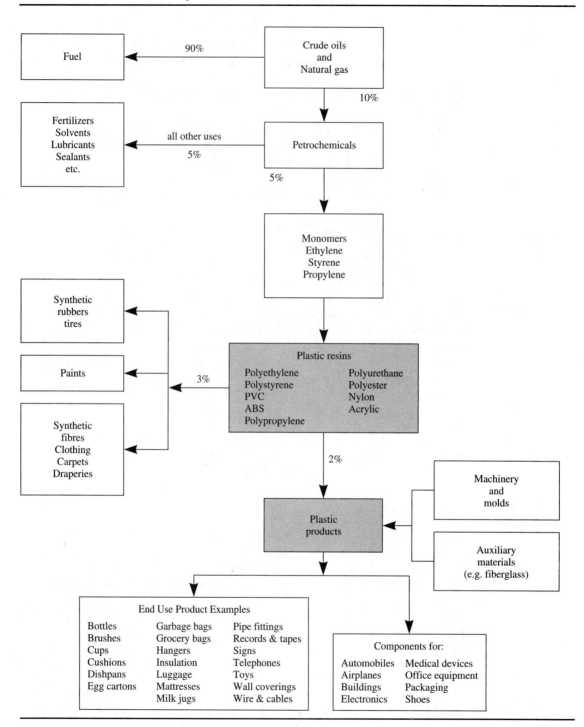

SOURCE: Society of Plastics *Statistical Year Book* 1989.

International Production of Resins. The international production of resins began in the 1920s with basic thermosets (amino and phenol resins). By 1990, the production and consumption of resins were dominated by the industrialized countries of the world. The development of a national plastic resin industry was typically dependent on the availability of petrochemical raw materials, capital, and technology. Technological requirements varied considerably according to the resin but by 1990, most technologies were relatively easy to acquire. Capital requirements also varied according to the type of resin desired and tended to be more problematic. For example, while thermosetting resins could be manufactured efficiently in small plants, thermoplastics (PVC, polystyrene, and polyolefins) were highly sensitive to economies of scale. Huge investments were required to build world-scale thermoplastics plants. As a result, developing countries could manufacture simple phenol resins using small-scale investments, but the bulk of thermosetting and thermoplastic resins were produced by large companies in industrialized countries.

At the close of the 1980s, the international production of thermoplastics was concentrated in the hands of a few huge multinational petrochemical corporations based in the United States (Dow, DuPont, Union Carbide), Europe (BASF, Hoechst, ICI), and Japan (Mitsui Chemical, Asahi Chemical, Mitsubishi Chemical). These companies had extensive research and development facilities, which produced a continued flow of new polymers and polymer applications. To commercialize their new products and applications, they tended to provide customer sales engineers and technicians to assist domestic plastic processors. With this localized service, subsidiaries of multinational corporations have been able to dominate domestic resin sales and production in most host countries.

International Production of Plastics Products. The production of plastics has tended to be strongly influenced by not only the presence of local resin suppliers, but also by the level of a country's economic development and the relative competitiveness of the industries that rely on plastic components. Given the diverse market for plastics products and demands for high levels of customized service, plastic processing industries in most countries have tended to favour smaller, more responsive companies. Low barriers to entry and few potential production economies have also encouraged these small, often entrepreneurial companies. As a result, in most countries, plastics processing had become highly fragmented, with few large players. For example, in 1989 Japan reported over 18,000 plastics processing companies, with average sales of $U.S. 2.3 million; in the United States, there were close to 13,000 processors, averaging sales of $U.S. 4.7 million. See Exhibit 2 for a more complete listing of country-by-country production data.

With small, locally oriented operations, plastics processors in most industrialized countries focused on domestic sales. Processors tended to specialize in either *custom*-moulded or *proprietary* products. Custom-moulded products were produced using moulds owned and designed by customers, with plastics processors acting essentially as subcontractors. In most countries, profit margins were generally healthy for custom processors, reflecting the risk associated with sub-

EXHIBIT 2 **Country-by-Country Plastics Processing**

Country	Number of Companies	Number of Employees (thousands)	Sales Value $U.S.
Australia	2,678	60.0	3,278
Brazil	4,500	220.0	n/a
Canada	2,550	98.5	9,593
France	3,836	122.1	11,074
West Germany	2,138	245.0	24,541
Italy	5,000	104.0	11,678
Japan	18,861	397.2	69,325
Netherlands	366	22.7	3,008
United Kingdom	4,000	180.0	14,476
United States	12,800	605.0	60,206

SOURCE: International Status Report on Plastics for 1988, International Plastics Association Directors.

contract work. This uncertainty, however, encouraged many processors to develop their own moulds and shift production to proprietary products. Processors that concentrated on proprietary products tended to be larger, reflecting the costs associated with the in-house development of moulds and the infrastructure required to support marketing and distribution activities. In many countries, added competition came from *captive* customers which frequently integrated backward through the development of their own processing operations. Companies with large plastics requirements—for example, in the consumer electronics and automotive industries—often moulded more basic products in-house to cut costs and ensure timely delivery. These captive processors, however, tended to rely heavily on custom processors for leadership in product and process technology.

The Canadian Plastics Industry

The Canadian plastics industry was the fourth largest industrial sector in Canada. Shipments by resin manufacturers and plastics processors amounted to almost $16 billion and involved over 110,000 employees in 1989. The plastics industry was also arguably the fastest-growing industry in Canada during the 1980s with an annual growth averaging between two and three times faster than growth in the overall economy. Canada was also a significant player in the world plastics industry. In 1989, Canada produced almost 5 percent of the world's supply of plastics-related products.

Many observers also counted machinery suppliers and mould and die makers as members of the Canadian plastics industry. In Canada, this sector represented just over $800 million in sales in 1989. Of this amount, machinery sales totaled approximately $622 million, with $322 million coming from imports and $227 million generated from exports. It appeared that most customers preferred West German, Italian, and Japanese suppliers for big-ticket machinery purchases;

Canadian suppliers were typically relied upon for materials handling and secondary machinery needs. In contrast, Canada enjoyed a net trade surplus in moulds and dies. Domestic sales amounted to approximately $192 million in 1989, with exports of $231 million and imports of $123 million. With the international adoption of CAD/CAM technologies, Canadian producers were becoming increasingly vulnerable to cost-based competition, exacerbated in early 1990 by the strengthening Canadian dollar. Given the unique competitive pressures on machinery and mould suppliers, this note focuses primarily on the industry dynamics facing resin suppliers and plastics processors.

Resin production and plastics processing were heavily concentrated in Ontario and Quebec. Alberta also had several polyethylene resin plants. Many of these facilities were located near end-use customers or sources of petrochemical feedstock. Ontario and Quebec served as the home base for many of the country's major manufacturers in the packaging, construction, electronics, and automotive industries—key buyers of plastics products. Ontario and Quebec also produced almost 75 percent of petrochemical shipments in Canada, thus providing ample local supply of a wide variety of resins.

Geographic concentration historically facilitated linkages between resin suppliers and plastics processors. With heightened international competition, however, many companies began in the mid-1980s to reassess these traditional relationships. The sections that follow outline the challenges facing Canadian resin suppliers and plastics processors as they entered the 1990s.

Canadian Resin Production

Canadian resin production was highly concentrated and dominated by a few large multinational corporations. In Canada, 15 companies supplied the bulk of resins purchased. Of these, 12 were subsidiaries of foreign-owned multinationals and 3 were Canadian-owned producers: Novacor/Polysar, AT Plastics, and a small manufacturer of polystyrene bead, Plasti-Fab. The location and capacity of major Canadian resin manufacturers are described in Exhibit 3.

In 1988, this sector employed 6,000 people and sold approximately 2.4 million tonnes of resin valued at $3.25 billion. Of this amount, greater than one third of the resins produced (840,000 tonnes) were exported. Over 74 percent of these exports were generated from sales of low-density polyethylene. Canadian companies imported just over 520,000 tonnes of resins, primarily engineering or specialty resins such as polycarbonate. These products were typically not made in Canada because the small size of the Canadian market generally did not justify the investment. More complete industry trade and production information is found in Exhibit 4.

Price Instability.   During much of the 1980s, the demand for resins grew at such rates that a shortage of resin supply on a global basis boosted Canadian prices dramatically. Price increases were also encouraged by the fall in the value of the Canadian and U.S. dollars relative to the Japanese yen and several European currencies. From early 1986 to mid-1987, for example, the yen appreciated 36

Exhibit 3 Location and Capacity of Major Canadian Resin Manufacturers

Resin	Producer	Location	Capacity 000 Tonnes	%LLDPE	Future Capacity	Completion Date
Low-density	AT Plastics	Edmonton	75		15	1990
polyethylene	Dow Chemical	Sarnia	82			
	Novacor	Sarnia	112			
	Petromont	Montreal East	136			
Linear	Dow Chemical	Ft. Sask., Alta.	156	100	20	
low-density	Du Pont	Sarnia	240	40		
polyethylene/	Esso	Sarnia	175	77		
high-density	Novacor	Red Deer, Alta.	340	100	85	
polyethylene		Sarnia	120	15	30	
	Nova/China N'l	Joffre, Alta.		100	200	1992 (Export)
High-density	Dow Chemical	Sarnia	64			
polyethylene						
Total polyethylene			**1500**			
Polypropylene	Himont	Varennes, Que.	127			
	Shell	Sarnia	104			
Total polypropylene			**231**			
ABS	GE Plastics	Cobourg, Ont.	40			
	Monsanto	LaSalle, Que.	30			
Total ABS			**70**			
Polystyrene	Dow Chemical	Sarnia	98			
	Huntsman Russtek	Mansonville, Que.	16			
	Plasti-Fab	Calgary	8			
	Polysar	Cambridge, Ont.	40			
		Montreal	42			
	Scott Styrene	Montreal	6			
Total polystyrene			**210**			
Polyvinyl chloride	Esso	Sarnia	100		30	1990
	B. F. Goodrich	Niagara Falls, Ont.	130		50	1990
		Shawinigan, Que.	60			
		Ft. Sask., Alta.	110			
Total polyvinyl chloride			**400**			

Source: Canadian Plastics *Statistical Year Book* 1989, SPI Canada.

percent against the Canadian dollar; the mark rose a full 28 percent in value. These increases saw overseas demand for cheaper North American resins soar. Benefits from heightened demand were immediate. For the 18-month period ending December 1987, the following price increases were reported:

High-density polyethylene	35%
Crystal polystyrene	83%
Polyvinyl chloride	37%

EXHIBIT 4 Canadian Resin Market ($ billions)

Resin Manufacturers

Year	Shipments	Imports	Exports	Market	Percentage Change
1981	1.90	0.61	0.26	2.25	—
1982	1.80	0.55	0.30	2.05	−8.9
1983	2.11	0.74	0.27	2.58	25.9
1984	2.37	0.85	0.32	2.90	12.4
1985	2.56	0.89	0.43	3.02	4.1
1986	2.69	0.97	0.60	3.06	1.3
1987	2.89	1.08	0.80	3.17	3.6
1988	3.25	1.33*	1.21*	3.37	6.3
1989 (Estimated)	3.36	1.50	1.31	3.53	4.8
				Average growth rate	5.9

*Canada adopted the Harmonized System of Classification in 1988. Comparisons with previous years are therefore not possible.

SOURCE: Canadian Plastics *Statistical Year Book*, 1989, SPI Canada.

Resin prices appeared to peak in 1988. In 1989, new worldwide capacity began to come on stream, attracted in part to the earlier successes in the industry. With the U.S. and Canadian economies beginning to falter, demand also weakened and prices began to slip. Overseas demand also slumped, encouraged in part by rising political problems in China. Nova's Joffre, Alberta, polyethylene plant was particularly hard hit as sales to China crumbled following the Tiananmen Square incident. Overall for 1989, Canadian list prices for polystyrene and polypropylene fell by almost 20 percent; polyethylene prices fell by up to 40 percent.

By the late autumn of 1989, most resin prices had stabilized somewhat, partly the result of accidents at some U.S. production facilities. For example, in Pasadena, Texas, Phillips' high-density polyethylene (HDPE) plant was severely damaged in an explosion, carrying with it about 17 percent of the U.S. production of HDPE. By early 1990, several Canadian polyethylene producers had announced price increases in the 7–8 percent range. Whether this signaled a return to continuous price increases remained uncertain, particularly given ongoing polyethylene overcapacity from U.S. Gulf Coast producers.

Prices for polypropylene, polyvinyl chloride (PVC), and polystyrene also appeared unstable. Oversupply was becoming an increasing concern. Canadian polypropylene production, for example, was expected to increase almost 50 percent by the end of 1990 as Shell Canada added new capacity in Sarnia, Ontario, and Himont opened a new polypropylene composite plant at Varennes, Quebec. PVC production was also slated for significant increases, going up almost 32 percent with the doubling in size of BF Goodrich's Niagara Falls plant in 1990. While no additional capacity was expected at Canada's two major polystyrene plants, prices remained soft given sagging styrene monomer prices.

New Markets.   As many Canadian producers were commodity resin exporters, there was considerable hope that the additional capacity at Canadian plants would be taken up by exports to the United States. The Canada/United States Free Trade Agreement (FTA) had been generally supported by Canadian resin producers, given their size and existing exposure to international market pressures. Pre–FTA tariffs into the United States averaged from 3.0–12.5 percent; Canadian tariffs averaged 5.9–12.0 percent. Tariffs were being phased out over five years, and most Canadian resin producers welcomed the opportunity for greater access to the U.S. market.

In spite of this optimism, U.S. market demand was expected to remain relatively sluggish during most of the early 1990s. Few observers were predicting more than 1–2 percent annual growth in demand from 1990 to 1995. Others were more worried about the wave of capacity additions that were to come on stream in the United States in the early 1990s. Planned increases included over 2.4 billion pounds in new polyethylene capacity, 1.5 billion pounds of polypropylene capacity, 270 million pounds of polystyrene capacity, and 1.3 billion pounds of PVC capacity.

Canadian Plastics Processors

In 1990, there were approximately 2,550 plastics processors in Canada employing nearly 100,000 people. Shipments in 1989 amounted to $12.61 billion, up from $12.0 billion the year earlier. From 1970 to 1990, the annual growth rate of plastics processing in Canada had averaged 2.2 times the growth in GDP. Exhibit 5 provides information on overall industry shipments, including imports and exports.

Exhibit 5   Canadian Plastics Market ($ billions)

Processors

Year	Shipments	Imports	Exports	Market	Percentage Change
1981	6.10	1.38	0.52	6.96	15.0
1982	5.94	1.16	0.61	6.49	−6.8
1983	6.74	1.40	0.71	7.43	14.5
1984	7.78	1.75	0.94	8.59	15.6
1985	8.55	2.15	1.10	9.60	11.8
1986	9.70	2.39	1.45	10.64	10.8
1987	10.80	2.68	1.58	11.90	11.8
1988	12.00	2.38*	1.37*	13.01	9.3
1989 (Estimated)	12.61	2.72	1.42	13.90	6.3
				Average growth rate	9.9

*Canada adopted the Harmonized System of Classification in 1988. Comparisons with previous years are therefore not possible.

Source: Canadian Plastics *Statistical Year Book*, 1989, SPI Canada.

During the 1970s and 1980s, the average return on invested capital for Canadian plastics processors remained consistently in the 20 percent range except for the recessionary period in the early 1980s where returns dipped below 10 percent. Even during the recessionary period, however, the domestic market grew by an average 14.5 percent annual rate. To fuel this growth, total capital spending increased more than twofold to just over $300 million from 1982 to 1986. As the economy pulled out of its recessionary slump, investment accelerated and profits soared. For a review of profitability levels for Canadian plastics processors, see Exhibit 6.

The Canadian Market for Processed Plastics.   Plastics were extensively employed in end-use products throughout the economy. The three major markets for processed plastics in Canada were packaging with 39 percent of resins consumed, building and construction with 27 percent of resins consumed, and automotive with 11 percent of resins consumed. Other identifiable markets included furniture and furnishings, representing 6 percent of resins consumed, and electrical and electronics, representing 4 percent of resins consumed.

Packaging.   During the 1970s and 1980s, the plastics packaging market grew at unexpectedly high rates. In 1990, industry analysts predicted it would continue to grow at 5–7 percent annually through the early 1990s. The leading North American application was food packaging. Polyethylene was the most commonly used resin, combined with polystyrene, polypropylene, and PVC to account for about 95 percent of the packaging market. Film and film-derived products were among

EXHIBIT 6 Profitability—Canadian Plastics Processors

	Return on Investment (%)		Net Profit before Taxes (%)	
	1987	*1988*	*1987*	*1988*
By ownership				
Custom processors	14.2	20.0	5.6	6.5
Propietary processors	31.2	26.0	10.7	6.7
By size				
Sales < $4 million	28.2	22.9	6.5	7.0
Sales $4–10 million	21.5	28.4	7.5	n/a
Sales > $10 million	18.8	20.4	7.9	7.9
By process				
Injection moulding	18.3	24.9	4.7	7.0
Extrusion	18.0	26.7	5.6	5.9
Film extrusion	−2.9	18.1	4.2	7.1
Profile extrusion	23.7	37.8	4.4	4.9
Reinforced products	27.5	8.6	13.5	6.5
Other	32.0	23.4	10.4	6.0
Industry average	21.8	22.8	7.5	6.6

SOURCE: SPI

the few packaging products that could be shipped economically. With heightened international competition in this segment, Canadian processors had for years emphasized economies of scale and had built a substantial capacity to produce economically for export markets. Polyethylene terephthalate (PET) was also becoming increasingly important in the industry. PET was used in plastic bottles and ovenable trays and containers and enjoyed a 20 percent growth rate for the late 1980s. Other markets that analysts anticipated would grow at double-digit rates were thermoformed containers, shrink film, totes, pails and drums, packaging film, and microwave cookware. Multilayer or barrier technology was beginning to open new opportunities for plastics in packaging.

Construction.   The construction market was the second largest market for plastics materials. Although it represented probably the greatest long-term growth potential in the plastics industry, growth had been somewhat less meteoric than optimistic analysts in the 1970s predicted. The entrenchment of traditional building materials was the biggest obstacle faced by processors in this market. PVC siding penetration was the most notable achievement of the 1980s. Between 1981 and 1986, 1,800 million square feet of PVC siding was applied to housing, a 104 percent increase (outpacing aluminum and hardboard by 100 million square feet).

The PVC pipe segment was probably the most mature application. By 1989, it had undergone considerable rationalization and showed signs of continued strong growth in the form of large-diameter pressure pipe for municipal water supplies and smaller diameter PVC–DWV, challenging ABS pipe in Canada. Extruded vinyl windowframes and doors also showed strong growth, having experienced double-digit annual growth for several years.

Automotive.   The automotive sector, composed of automobiles, vans, and trucks, consumed 159 kilo tonnes of resins or about 88 kilograms per vehicle in 1986. Projected growth rates were close to 9 percent. Car interiors were already major plastics users, but interresin substitution was expected to take place in order to reduce costs. The integration of parts for future automotive interiors was predicted to be spurred by the "black-box" subassembly concept. Contracting subassemblies was predicted to provide greater opportunities for exterior, structural, and under-the-hood applications. The market for exterior body panels was expected to accelerate in the early 1990s. Polymer blends and other tailor-made resins were predicted to provide the heat resistance needed to allow increased under-the-hood applications for plastics.

Other Markets.   Slow growth was predicted in the demand for plastics in several other industries. For example, the home and commercial furnishings markets were expecting low growth rates because of an anticipated adverse effect of the FTA on the major appliance market. The communications and electronics market was expected to slow in the early 1990s because production was increasingly being transferred to the Far East. As a result, opportunities for growth were expected to come primarily in the form of innovation. For example, the housewares market could find a growth market in "designer houseware" products to fill the postwar baby boom generation's demand for quality products. The agricultural/environment market had opportunities for growth by developing plastic greenhouses for hydroponically grown food.

Processor Responses to Market Pressures.   Given the extent of buyer fragmentation, processors tended to focus production on particular market segments. This was particularly applicable for the nearly 2,300 custom processors in Canada. The average custom processor was an entrepreneurial, domestically owned, small business which employed 50 people and had annual sales under $4 million. While somewhat larger, proprietary processors were also small firms that were typically operated independently and were run by hands-on managers. The decisions made by both custom and proprietary processors were typically based on short-term commercial imperatives—sales, product, cash flow—in order to keep their companies alive in a fiercely competitive industry sandwiched between powerful raw material suppliers, on the one hand, and concentrated, demanding customers on the other.

Emergence of Major Canadian Processors.   By 1990, a small group of major Canadian custom processors was beginning to emerge. Involving fewer than 20 companies with sales over $75 million, this new class of players had the financial strength to put long-term concerns ahead of short-term cash flow. Long-term perspective allowed these companies to take advantage of the favourable climate in the 1980s to invest in innovative assets to more immediately satisfy their customers' increasingly complex product demands. It also allowed the companies greater freedom to expand geographically—both in Canada and the United States. With financial and technological strength, companies like the Toronto-based ABC Group, which had 23 plants across North America, were often better able to respond to the opportunities brought on by rapidly changing competitive conditions.

FTA Apprehensions.   In spite of the growing confidence of several larger processors, processors as a group were generally apprehensive about the FTA. In 1988, Canadian processors were protected by duties of 13.5 percent. These duties were scheduled for removal over a 10-year period, giving processors some time to adjust. Difficult adjustments were anticipated particularly for processors supplying the packaging market. It was not expected that auto suppliers would be severely affected, given the continuation of the Canada–United States Auto Pact. The fate of processors supplying the construction market was difficult to determine.

Captive Processors.   In addition to the 2,300 custom processors, it was estimated that there were 250 captive processors in Canada in 1990. In-house or captive plastics producers were typically involved in multiple businesses, often making it difficult to define and determine the size of their plastics operations. Some observers estimated that captive producers were responsible for up to 40 percent of the Canadian production of plastics.

Captive processors were scattered throughout many different manufacturing classifications. Companies as diverse as General Motors, Black & Decker, Samsonite, Goodyear, Canada Wire and Cable, Bata Shoes, Irwin Toy, Canadian General Electric, IBM, Bristol Myers, De Havilland Aircraft, and Magna International all produced plastics products or component parts in-house. Captive companies tended to produce in-house because of concerns for cost, quality, and reliable delivery. The increasing internationalization of competition and the recently passed FTA were not expected to have a major impact on captive plastics operations, per se. However, these same pressures were forcing many domestic end-product producers to reconsider the scale and scope of their Canadian operations.

The Challenges Ahead: A View to the Future

In 1990, the plastics industry was facing rapidly changing competitive pressures. In addition to the FTA and the increasing internationalization of competition, many economists were predicting that the Canadian economy would remain sluggish for several years. With the economy weak and markets opening to greater international competition, the future looked cloudy for many Canadian manufacturers. In responding to these uncertainties, Canadian manufacturers recognized that high interest rates and unfavourable taxes would further limit strategic responses.

Beyond these challenges, manufacturers faced two additional concerns: a shortage of trained personnel and the environment. With growing competitive pressures, industry experts recognized that both labour and management skills needed upgrading. The most serious shortage was among process engineers and other skilled operators. In 1989, it was estimated that there was a 22.7 percent job vacancy rate for process engineers, a 10.3 percent vacancy rate for mould and die technicians, and an overall 7.3 percent vacancy rate for skilled personnel. The fragmented structure of Canada's plastics industry tended to exacerbate the situation, particularly for plastics processors. A definite shortage in human resources would be an increasing problem as the industry became more technology dependent. Management skills would also be more highly valued given the added complexities of international competition.

In 1990, the environment was also becoming increasingly important for Canadians. This concern influenced both the supply and demand sides of the plastics industry. On the supply side, resin suppliers were facing mounting costs of meeting ever more stringent environmental regulations. Canada's new Environmental Protection Act was particularly troubling given its stringent pollution guidelines for the introduction of new polymers to the marketplace. Unless the regulations were amended, Canadian resin producers worried that they would be at a severe disadvantage vis-à-vis U.S. and European producers.

On the demand side, concerns over pollution were resulting in growing public hesitance to purchase plastics products. Plastics waste was increasingly singled out as a major threat to the environment. In a 1989 Gallup survey, for example, 72 percent of respondents named plastics as the material which posed the greatest threat to the environment. This growing concern was giving rise to threats of consumer boycotts of nonrecyclable plastics products. These threats appeared to impact most on the packaging market. Here, the National Task Force on Packaging was attempting to develop a national plan to reduce the volume of packaging materials going to landfills by 50 percent by the year 2000. Plastics processors were beginning to feel the heat. On November 1, 1990, McDonald's Corporation announced a timetable for phasing out all polystyrene foam packaging used at its 11,000 outlets around the world. The move, which was widely praised by environmental groups, involved a switch to polyethylene film and paper laminated wrap. While the McDonald's account represented only about 1 percent of all polystyrene sales in the country, its symbolism was not lost on other industry members.

As a result of heightened public concern over the environment, the industry was beginning a number of initiatives. On one front, the industry began a variety of public relations campaigns aimed at educating the public and improving the image of plastics in the marketplace. The McDonald's ban, for example, was widely criticized as a reactionary response to emotional, ill-informed consumers who failed to fairly evaluate the impact of alternative products on the environment. In addition to education, companies began reassessing product lines with an objective of paring back products that were indeed harmful to the environment. Companies such as DuPont took the lead in shutting down production of CFCs, which were shown to have a harmful effect on the earth's ozone layer. Efforts were also underway to move the industry much more rapidly into recycling. Plans were announced in the late 1980s for a number of industry-sponsored recycling projects outside major Canadian urban centres. Some industry experts speculated that recycling would emerge as a major growth sector in the industry during the 1990s.

Beyond responses to environmental concerns, substantial changes in the structure of the Canadian industry appeared inevitable. Experts were predicting several broad trends including consolidation among suppliers, processors, and customers and an increased reliance on R&D alliances. It was also anticipated that FTA and internationalization pressures would result in greater rationalization of operations on a North American basis. The challenge that Canadian managers faced was in determining what strategies their companies would adopt as they entered the 1990s.

CASE 27
PRINCE EDWARD ISLAND PRESERVE CO.

In August 1991, Bruce MacNaughton, president of Prince Edward Island Preserve Co. Ltd. (P.E.I. Preserves), was contemplating future expansion. Two cities were of particular interest: Toronto and Tokyo. At issue was whether consumers in either or both markets should be pursued, and if so, how. The choices available for achieving further growth included mail order, distributors, and company-controlled stores.

Background

Prince Edward Island Preserve Co. was a manufacturing company located in New Glasglow, Prince Edward Island (P.E.I.), which produced and marketed specialty food products. The company founder and majority shareholder, Bruce MacNaughton, had realized that an opportunity existed to present P.E.I. strawberries as a world-class food product and to introduce the finished product to an "up-scale" specialty market. With total sales in the coming year expected to exceed $1.0 million for the first time, MacNaughton had made good on the opportunity he had perceived years earlier. It had not been easy, however.

MacNaughton arrived in P.E.I. from Moncton, New Brunswick, in 1978. Without a job, he slept on the beach for much of that first summer. Over the next few years, he worked in commission sales, waited tables in restaurants, and then moved to Toronto. There he studied to become a chef at George Brown Community College. After working in the restaurant trade for several years, he found a job with Preserves by Amelia in Toronto. After six months, he returned to P.E.I., where he opened a restaurant. The restaurant was not successful, and MacNaughton lost the $25,000 stake he had accumulated. With nothing left but 100 kg of strawberries, Bruce decided to make these into preserves in order to have gifts for Christmas 1984. Early the following year, P.E.I. Preserves was founded.

The products produced by the company were priced and packaged for the gift/gourmet and specialty food markets. The primary purchasers of these products were conscious of quality and were seeking a product which they considered tasteful and natural. P.E.I. Preserves felt their product met this standard of quality at a price that made it attractive to all segments of the marketplace.

This case was prepared by Professor Paul W. Beamish for the sole purpose of providing material for class discussion at the Western Business School. It is not intended to illustrate either effective or ineffective handling of a managerial situation. Any reproduction, in any form, of the material in this case is prohibited except with the written consent of the School. This case was funded in part by a grant from External Affairs, Canada. Copyright 1991 © The University of Western Ontario.

EXHIBIT 1

Operation	Year Opened				
	1985	*1989*	*1990*	*1991*	*1992 Projected*
New Glasgow—manufacturing and retail	X	X	X	X	X
Charlottetown—restaurant (Perfect Cup)		X	X	X	X
New Glasgow—restaurant (Tea Room)			X	X	X
Charlottetown—retail (CP Hotel)				X	X
Toronto or Tokyo?					X

Over the next few years as the business grew, improvements were made to the building in New Glasgow. The sense of style which was characteristic of the company was evident from the beginning in its attractive layout and design.

In 1989, the company diversified and opened The Perfect Cup, a small restaurant in P.E.I.'s capital city of Charlottetown. This restaurant continued the theme of quality, specializing in wholesome, homemade food featuring the products manufactured by the company. The success of this operation led to the opening in 1990 of a small tea room at the New Glasgow location. Both of these locations showcased the products manufactured by the P.E.I. Preserve Co.

In August 1991, the company opened a small (22 sq. metre) retail branch in the CP Prince Edward Hotel. MacNaughton hoped this locale would expand visibility in the local and national marketplace, and serve as an off-season sales office. P.E.I. Preserves had been given very favourable lease arrangements (well below the normal $275 per month for space this size), and the location would require minimal financial investment. As Exhibit 1 suggests, the company had experienced steady growth in its scope of operations.

Marketplace

Prince Edward Island was Canada's smallest province, both in size and population. Located in the Gulf of St. Lawrence, it was separated from Nova Scotia and New Brunswick by the Northumberland Strait. The various levels of government were the major employer in P.E.I. Many people in P.E.I. worked seasonally, in either farming (especially potato), fishing, or tourism. During the peak tourist months of July and August, the island population would swell dramatically from its base of 125,000. P.E.I.'s half million annual visitors came "home" to enjoy the long sandy beaches, picturesque scenery, lobster dinners, arguably the best-tasting strawberries in the world, and slower pace of life. P.E.I. was best known in Canada and elsewhere for the books, movies, and (current) television series about Lucy Maud Montgomery's turn-of-the-century literary creation, *Anne of Green Gables*.

P.E.I. Preserves felt they were competing in a worldwide market. Their visitors were from all over the world and in 1991, they expected the numbers to exceed 100,000 in the New Glasgow location alone. New Glasgow (population

200) was located in a rural setting equidistant (15 km) from Charlottetown and P.E.I.'s best known North Shore beaches. In their mailings, they planned to continue to promote Prince Edward Island as "Canada's Garden Province" and the "little jewel it was in everyone's heart!" They had benefited, and would continue to benefit, from that image.

Marketing

Products

The company had developed numerous products since its inception. These included many original varieties of preserves as well as honey, vinegar, mustard, and tea (repackaged). (Exhibit 2 contains a 1990 price list, ordering instructions, and a product picture used for mail order purposes.) The company had also added to the appeal of these products by offering gift packs composed of different products and packaging. With over 80 items, it felt that it had achieved a diverse product line and efforts in developing new product lines were expected to decrease in the future. Approximately three quarters of total retail sales (including wholesale and mail order) came from the products the company made itself. Of these, three quarters were jam preserves.

With the success of P.E.I. Preserves, imitation was inevitable. In recent years, several other small firms in P.E.I. had begun to retail specialty preserves. Another company which produced preserves in Ontario emphasized the Green Gables tie-in on its labels.

Price

P.E.I. Preserves were not competing with "low-end" products and felt their price reinforced their customers' perception of quality. The 11 types of jam preserves retailed for $5.89 for a 250 ml jar, significantly more than any grocery store product. However, grocery stores did not offer jam products made with such a high fruit content and with champagne, liqueur, or whisky.

In mid-1991, the company introduced a 10 percent increase in price (to $5.89) and, to date, had not received any negative reaction from customers. The food products were not subject to the 7 percent national goods and services tax or P.E.I.'s 10 percent provincial sales tax, an advantage over other gift products which the company would be stressing.

Promotion

Product promotion had been focused in two areas—personal contact with the consumer and catalogue distribution. Visitors to the New Glasgow location (approximately 80,000 in 1990) were enthusiastic upon meeting Bruce, "resplendent in the family kilt," reciting history and generally providing live entertain-

EXHIBIT 2 P.E.I. Preserves Mail Order Catalogue

Prince Edward Island Preserve Co.

Mail Order
Canada

Prince Edward Island Preserve Co.
RR# 2 Hunter River
Prince Edward Island
Canada
C0A 1N0
Tel. (902) 964-2524
Fax. (902) 566-5565

PRODUCTS

Preserves
#	Item	Size	Price
1.	Strawberry & Grand Marnier	250ml	5.69
2.	Raspberry & Champagne	250ml	5.69
3.	Wild Blueberry & Raspberry in Champagne	250ml	5.69
4.	Strawberry, Orange & Rhubarb	250ml	5.69
5.	Raspberry & Peach	250ml	5.69
6.	Blueberry, Lemon & Fresh Mint	250ml	5.69
7.	Black Currant	250ml	5.69
8.	Gooseberry & Red Currant	250ml	5.69
9.	Sour Cherry Marmalade	250ml	5.69
10.	Orange Marmalade with Chivas Regal	250ml	5.69
11.	Lemon & Ginger Marmalade with Amaretto	250ml	5.69
12.	Strawberry & Grand Marnier	125ml	3.60
13.	Raspberry & Champagne	125ml	3.60
14.	Wild Blueberry & Raspberry in Champagne	125ml	3.60
15.	Raspberry & Peach	125ml	3.60
16.	Black Currant	125ml	3.60
17.	Orange Marmalade with Chivas Regal	125ml	3.60

Honeys
#	Item	Size	Price
18.	Summer Honey with Grand Marnier	250ml	5.95
19.	Summer Honey with Amaretto	250ml	5.95
20.	Summer Honey with Grand Marnier	125ml	3.50
21.	Summer Honey with Amaretto	125ml	3.50

Mustards
#	Item	Size	Price
22.	Hot & Spicy Mustard	250ml	3.95
23.	Champagne & Dill Mustard	250ml	3.95
24.	Honey & Thyme Mustard	125ml	3.95
25.	Hot & Spicy Mustard	125ml	2.75
26.	Champagne & Dill Mustard	125ml	2.75
27.	Honey & Thyme Mustard	125ml	2.75

Vinegars
#	Item	Size	Price
28.	Raspberry Vinegar	350ml	5.95
29.	Black Currant Vinegar	350ml	5.95
30.	Peach Vinegar	350ml	5.95
31.	Raspberry Vinegar	150ml	3.50
32.	Black Currant Vinegar	150ml	3.50
33.	Peach Vinegar	150ml	3.50

Specials
34A.	Catharines Hors d'oeuvre & Pasta Sauce	250 ml	6.49
35.	Catharines Hot Antipasto	250 ml	5.69
36.	Catharines Antipasto	250 ml	5.69

Spices (recipes included)
37A.	Bloody Mary, Bloody Caesar Mix	3.95
38A.	Apple Spices - for pies, butters, chutneys	3.95
39A.	Mulling Spices - for wine, cider, or ale	4.95
40A.	Hot Chocolate - rich & tasty, just add hot water	4.95

Tea - *No tea is fresher than ours*
41. a) Monks Blend b) Strawberry c) Raspberry
    d) Earl Grey e) English Breakfast f) Blackcurrant
42. Sachets ...... 50 g 2.95
43. Tea by the Pound, all blends ...... 1 lb 14.95
order tea by # and letter, i.e. 43c is 1 lb. of raspberry tea.

Maple Products
#	Item	Size	Price
44A.	Pure Maple Syrup	100 ml	3.95
45A.	Pure Maple Syrup	250 ml	5.95
46A.	Pure Maple Syrup	500 ml	10.95
47A.	Maple Syrup with Light Rum	250 ml	5.95
48A.	Maple Butter, excellent on pancakes, toast or baking	250 ml	5.95

Coffees - *We think this is the best coffee available*
First Colony - ground coffee, available 8 oz. and 2 oz.
#	Item	Size	Price
49A.	Columbian Supremo	8 oz.	6.49
50A.	Irish Cream 50B. Swiss Chocolate Almond	8 oz.	6.49
50C.	Chocolate Raspberry Truffle	8 oz.	6.49
51A.	Special House Blend	2 oz.	2.25
52.	All flavours available in 2 oz. packs		

(order coffee by # and letter, i.e. 52C is a 2 oz Chocolate Raspberry Truffle)

Teapots - If you've had tea with us, these are the ones!
#	Set	Style	Price
56.	Executive Tea set	Black with Sterling Silver	49.95
57.		Sky Blue with Sterling Silver	49.95
58.		Fern Green with Gold Inlay	49.95
59.		Rust with Gold Inlay	49.95
60.	Romance Tea set	Black with Sterling Silver	59.95
61.		Sky Blue with Sterling Silver	59.95
62.		Fern Green with Gold Inlay	59.95
63.		Rust with Gold Inlay	59.95

1-2 cup teapot / 1 cup & saucer

1-2 cup teapot / 2 cups & saucers

64. Gift Packages - We pack all for long journeys!
A.	P.E.I. Summer House		24.99
B.	Taster's Choice Duo	2-125 ml Preserves Crated	8.25
C.	Taster's Choice Trio	2-125 ml Preserves, 1-125 Honey Crated	11.95
D.	Crated vinegars	2-150ml Fruit Vinegars Crated	7.49
E.	Crated Preserves (2 jars)	250 ml size	12.49
F.	Crated Preserves (3 jars)	250 ml size	17.95
G.	Tea-for-Two	1-125 ml Preserves, Tea, 1-125 ml Honey	11.95
75.	8" Brass Planter - filled with Swiss Chocolate, Hot Chocolate, Chocolate Coffee and more		23.99
76.	6" Brass Planter - 1-125 ml Preserve, 1-125 ml Honey with Liqueur, Honey Dipper and Chocolate		16.50
77.	4" Brass Planter - 125 ml Honey with Liqueur and Honey Dipper		10.95
78.	Wicker House - 2-250 ml Preserves with Liqueur, 1-250 ml Honey with Liqueur, 100 ml Maple Syrup, Irish Cream Coffee, Strawberry Tea		39.95
79.	14" Wicker Hamper - 1-125 ml Preserve, 1-125 ml Honey with Liqueur, 1 Raspberry Tea, 1 Irish Cream Coffee, Honey Dipper		32.95
80.	Hunter Green S M L XL Sweatshirt 87% Cotton, 13% Poly, Preshrunk		29.95
81.	Deep Lavender S M L XL Sweatshirt 87% Cotton, 13% Poly, Preshrunk		29.95

Exhibit 2 *(continued)*

Dear Shopper,

If you have visited our store recently, and wish to purchase an item which is not on this list, please feel free to do so.

On a separate sheet of paper, write a description of the item to the best of your ability, and we will do our best to satisfy your request.

sincerely,

Bruce MacNaughton

For *FAST* delivery call:

(9:00 am to 5:00 pm A.S.T.)

(902) 964-2524
Fax **(902) 566-5565**

*Prices subject to change without notice.

Shipping cost per Address

Value of Order	*Shipping Cost
$ 0. - $30.	5.00
$31. - $40.	6.00
$41. - $55.	7.00
$56. - $65.	8.00
$66. - $75.	9.00
$76. - $100.	10.00
$101. & over	5% of order

All packages are packed well for shipping. We use double strength corrugated boxes and finish the packages with a heavy brown paper wrap.

*Please note that if the postage cost is less than the amount charged to you, we then will charge you the least amount. That is why we prefer if you paid by credit card. Thank you, Bruce.

Gift Wrapping

$3.50 per package

Using the appropriate gift wrap for the season, we'll give your package that little extra. We can supply a small card with your salutation, or if you send us your card with your order, we will include it.

Gift Packaging
Friends, we have many packaging ideas, too many for our catalogue. If you wish us to do up a basket in a certain price range, or any special order for that matter, just give us a call, fax or mail in your request. We are here for you!

Method of Payment [MasterCard] [VISA]

☐ MasterCard ☐ Visa

CREDIT CARD NUMBER

[ ] [ ] [ ] [ ] [ ] [ ] [ ] [ ] [ ] [ ] [ ] [ ] [ ] [ ] [ ] [ ]

Cardholder Name
Please Print

We require a signature

_____ mo./_____ yr.
Expiry Date

① SOLD TO: ☐ Mr. ☐ Mrs. ☐ Ms.

Name _____
Please Print

Address _____

City _____ Prov _____ PostalCode _____
May we have your phone number in case of a question about your order?

Home ( ) _____   Work ( ) _____

Send to me at the above address.

Ship to arrive: ☐ Now ☐ Christmas ☐ Other..........

Prod.#	Quantity	Price Each	Gift Wrap	Total Price
			3.50 ☐	
			3.50 ☐	
			3.50 ☐	
			3.50 ☐	
			3.50 ☐	
			3.50 ☐	
			3.50 ☐	
			Shipping	
			Total Cost	

② Send to: ☐ Mr. ☐ Mrs. ☐ Ms. ☐ Firm

Name _____
Please Print

Address _____

City _____ Prov _____ Postal _____

Greetings from: _____

Ship to arrive: ☐ Now ☐ Christmas ☐ Other..........

Prod.#	Quantity	Price Each	Gift Wrap	Total Price
			3.50 ☐	
			3.50 ☐	
			3.50 ☐	
			3.50 ☐	
			3.50 ☐	
			3.50 ☐	
			3.50 ☐	
			Shipping	
			Total Cost	

EXHIBIT 2 (concluded)

ment. Bruce and the other staff members realized the value of this "island touch" and strove to ensure that all visitors to New Glasgow left with both a positive feeling and purchased products.

Visitors were also encouraged to visit the New Glasgow location through a cooperative scheme whereby other specialty retailers provided a coupon for a free cup of coffee or tea at P.E.I. Preserves. In 1991, roughly 2,000 of these coupons were redeemed.

Approximately 5,000 people received their mail-order catalogue annually. They had experienced an order rate of 7.5 percent with the average order being $66. They hoped to devote more time and effort to their mail-order business in an effort to extend their marketing and production period. For 1991–92, the order rate was expected to increase by as much as 15 percent because the catalogue was to be mailed two weeks earlier than in the previous year. The catalogues cost $1 each to print and mail.

In addition to mail order, the company operated with an ad hoc group of wholesale distributors. These wholesalers were divided between Nova Scotia, Ontario, and other locations. For orders as small as $150, buyers could purchase from the wholesalers' price list. Wholesale prices were on average 60 percent of the retail/mail order price. Total wholesale trade for the coming year was projected at $150,000 but had been higher in the past.

Danamar Imports was a Toronto-based specialty food store supplier which had previously provided P.E.I. Preserves to hundreds of specialty food stores in Ontario. Danamar had annually ordered $80,000 worth of P.E.I. Preserves at 30 percent below the wholesale price. This arrangement was amicably discontinued in 1990 by MacNaughton due to uncertainty about whether he was profiting from this contract. P.E.I. Preserves had a list of the specialty stores which Danamar had previously supplied and was planning to contact them directly in late 1991.

Over the past few years, the company had received numerous enquiries for quotations on large-scale shipments. Mitsubishi had asked for a price on a container load of preserves. Airlines and hotels were interested in obtaining preserves in 28 or 30 gram single-service bottles. One hotel chain, for example, had expressed interest in purchasing 3,000,000 bottles if the cost could be kept under $0.40 per unit. (Bruce had not proceeded due to the need to purchase $65,000 worth of bottling equipment and uncertainty about his production costs.) This same hotel chain had more recently been assessing the ecological implications of the packaging waste which would be created with the use of so many small bottles. They were now weighing the hygiene implications of serving jam out of multicustomer-use larger containers in their restaurants. They had asked MacNaughton to quote on $300,000 worth of jam in two-litre bottles.

Financial

The company had enjoyed a remarkable rate of growth since its inception. Sales volumes had increased in each of the six years of operations, from an initial level of $30,000 to 1990's total of $785,000. These sales were made up of $478,000 from retail sales (including mail order) of what they manufactured and/or distributed, and $307,000 from the restaurants (the Tea Room in New Glasgow, and Perfect Cup Restaurant in Charlottetown.) Exhibits 3 and 4 provide income statements from these operations, while Exhibit 5 contains a consolidated balance sheet.

EXHIBIT 3

P.E.I. PRESERVE CO. LTD. (MANUFACTURING AND RETAIL)
Statement of Earnings and Retained Earnings
Year Ended January 31, 1991
(unaudited)

	1991	1990
Sales	$478,406	$425,588
Cost of sales	217,550	186,890
Gross Margin	260,856	238,698
Expenses		
Advertising and promotional items	20,632	6,324
Automobile	7,832	3,540
Doubtful accounts	1,261	—
Depreciation and amortization	11,589	12,818
Dues and fees	1,246	2,025
Electricity	7,937	4,951
Heat	4,096	4,433
Insurance	2,426	1,780
Interest and bank charges	5,667	17,482
Interest on long-term debt	23,562	9,219
Management salary	29,515	32,600
Office and supplies	12,176	10,412
Professional fees	19,672	10,816
Property tax	879	621
Rent	—	975
Repairs and maintenance	6,876	9,168
Salaries and wages	70,132	96,386
Telephone and facsimile	5,284	5,549
Trade shows	18,588	12,946
	249,370	242,045
Earnings (loss) from manufacturing operation	11,486	(3,347)
Management fees	—	7,250
Loss from restaurant operations—Schedule 2	3,368	—
Earnings before income taxes	8,118	3,903
Income taxes	181	1,273
Net earnings	7,937	2,630
Retained earnings, beginning of year	9,290	6,660
Retained earnings, end of year	$ 17,227	$ 9,290

EXHIBIT 4

P.E.I. PRESERVE CO. LTD.
Schedule of Restaurant Operations
(Charlottetown and New Glasgow)
Year Ended January 31, 1991
(unaudited)

	Schedule 2
	1991
Sales	$306,427
Cost of sales	
Purchases and freight	122,719
Inventory, end of year	11,864
	110,855
Salaries and wages for food preparation	42,883
	153,738
Gross margin	152,689
Expenses	
Advertising	2,927
Depreciation	6,219
Electricity	4,897
Equipment lease	857
Insurance	389
Interest and bank charges	1,584
Interest on long-term debt	2,190
Office and supplies	2,864
Propane	2,717
Rent	22,431
Repairs and maintenance	3,930
Salaries and wages for service	90,590
Supplies	12,765
Telephone	1,697
	156,057
Loss from restaurant operations	$ 3,368

This growth, although indicative of the success of the product, has also created its share of problems. Typical of many small businesses which experience such rapid growth, the company had not secured financing suitable to its needs. This, coupled with the seasonal nature of the manufacturing operation, had caused numerous periods of severe cash shortages. From Bruce's perspective, the company's banker (Bank of Nova Scotia) had not been as supportive as it might have been. (The bank manager in Charlottetown had last visited the facility three years ago.) Bruce felt the solution to the problem of cash shortages

EXHIBIT 5

P.E.I. PRESERVE CO. LTD.
Balance Sheet
As at January 31, 1991
(unaudited)

	1991	1990
Current assets		
Cash	$ 5,942	$ 592
Accounts receivable		
Trade	12,573	6,511
Investment tax credit	1,645	2,856
Other	13,349	35,816
Inventory	96,062	85,974
Prepaid expenses	2,664	6,990
	132,235	138,739
Grant receivable	2,800	1,374
Property, plant, and equipment	280,809	162,143
Recipes and trade name, at cost	10,000	10,000
	$425,844	$312,256
Current liabilities		
Bank indebtedness	$ 2,031	$ 9,483
Operating and other loans	54,478	79,000
Accounts payable and accrued liabilities	64,143	32,113
Current portion of long-term debt	23,657	14,704
	144,309	135,300
Long-term debt	97,825	99,679
Deferred government assistance	54,810	—
Payable to shareholder, noninterest bearing, no set terms of repayment	43,373	49,687
	340,317	284,666
Shareholders' equity		
Share capital	55,000	5,000
Contributed surplus	13,300	13,300
Retained earnings	17,227	9,290
	85,527	27,590
	$425,844	$312,256

was the issuance of preferred shares. "An infusion of 'long-term' working capital, at a relatively low rate of interest, will provide a stable financial base for the future," he said.

At this time, MacNaughton was attempting to provide a sound financial base for the continued operation of the company. He had decided to offer a preferred share issue in the amount of $100,000. These shares would bear interest at the rate of 8 percent cumulative and would be nonvoting, nonparticipating. He anticipated that the sale of these shares would be complete by December 31, 1991. In the interim, he required a line of credit in the amount of $100,000, which he requested to be guaranteed by the Prince Edward Island Development Agency.

Projected sales for the year ended January 31, 1992 were

New Glasgow Restaurant	$ 110,000
Charlottetown Restaurant	265,000
Retail (New Glasgow)	360,000
Wholesale (New Glasgow)	150,000
Mail order (New Glasgow)	50,00
Retail (Charlottetown)	75,000
Total	$1,010,000

Operations

Preserve production took place on site, in an area visible through glass windows from the retail floor. Many visitors, in fact, would videotape operations during their visit to the New Glasgow store, or would watch the process while tasting the broad selection of sample products freely available.

Production took place on a batch basis. Ample production capacity existed for the $30,000 main kettle used to cook the preserves. Preserves were made five months a year, on a single-shift, five-day-per-week basis. Even then, the main kettle was in use only 50 percent of the time.

Only top-quality fruit was purchased. As much as possible, P.E.I. raw materials were used. For a short period the fruit could be frozen until time for processing.

The production process was labour intensive. Bruce was considering the feasibility of moving to an incentive-based salary system to increase productivity and control costs. Because a decorative cloth fringe was tied over the lid of each bottle, bottling could not be completely automated. A detailed production cost analysis had recently been completed. While there were some minor differences due to ingredients, the variable costs averaged $1.25 per 250 ml bottle. This was made up of ingredients ($.56), labour ($.28), and packaging ($.20/bottle, $.11/lid, $.03/label, and $.07/fabric and ribbon).

Restaurant operations were the source of many of Bruce's headaches. The New Glasgow restaurant had evolved over time from offering dessert and coffee/tea to its present status where it was also open for meals all day.

Management

During the peak summer period, P.E.I. Preserves employed 45 people among the restaurants, manufacturing area, and retail locations. Of these, five were managerial positions (see Exhibit 6). The company was considered a good

---

Exhibit 6 Key Executives

Pressident and general manager—Bruce MacNaughton, Age 35

Experience:	Seventeen years of "front line" involvement with the public in various capacities.
	Seven years of managing and promoting Prince Edward Island Preserve Co. Ltd.
	Past director of the Canadian Specialty Food Assocation.
Responsibilities:	To develop and oversee the short-, mid-, and long-term goals of the company.
	To develop and maintain quality products for the marketplace.
	To oversee the management of personnel.
	To develop and maintain customer relations at both the wholesale and retail level.
	To develop and maintain harmonious relations with government and the banking community.

Assistant general manager—Carol Rombough, Age 44

Experience:	Twenty years as owner/operator of a manufacturing business.
	Product marketing at both the wholesale and retail level.
	Personnel management.
	Bookkeeping in a manufacturing environment.
	Three years with the Prince Edward Island Preserve Co. Ltd.
Responsibilities:	All bookkeeping functions (i.e., accounts receivable, accounts payable, payroll).
	Staff management—scheduling and hiring.
	Customer relations.

Production manager—Maureen Dickieson, Age 29

Experience:	Seven years of production experience in the dairy industry.
	Three years with the Prince Edward Island Preserve Co. Ltd.
Responsibilities:	Oversee and participate in all production.
	Planning and scheduling production.
	Requisition of supplies.

Consultant—Kathy MacPherson, Certified General Accountant, Age 37

Experience:	Eight years as a small business owner/manager.
	Eight years in financial planning and management.
Responsibilities:	To implement an improved system of product costing.
	To assist in the development of internal controls.
	To compile monthly internal financial statements.
	To provide assistance and/or advise as required by management.

Store Manager—Natalie LeBlanc, Age 33

Experience:	Fifteen years in retail.
Responsibilities:	To manage the retail store in the CP Hotel.
	Assist with mail-order business.
	Marketing duties as assigned.

---

place to work, with high morale and limited turnover. Nonetheless, most employees (including some management) were with the company on a seasonal basis. This was a concern to MacNaughton, who felt that if he could provide year-round employment, he would be able to attract and keep the best-quality staff.

Carol Rombough was an effective assistant general manager and book-keeper. Maureen Dickieson handled production with little input required from Bruce. Kathy MacPherson was in the process of providing, for the first time, accurate cost information. Natalie Leblanc was managing the new retail outlet in Charlottetown, and assisting on some of the more proactive marketing initiatives Bruce was considering.

Bruce felt that the company had survived on the basis of word of mouth. Few follow-up calls on mail order had ever been done. Bruce did not enjoy partici-pating in trade shows—even though he received regular solicitations for them from across North America. In 1992, he planned to participate in four *retail* shows, all of them in or close to P.E.I.

Bruce hoped to be able eventually to hire a sales/marketing manager but could not yet afford $30,000 for the necessary salary.

The key manager continued to be MacNaughton. He described himself as "a fair person to deal with, but shrewd when it comes to purchasing. However, I like to spend enough money to ensure that what we do—we do right." Financial and managerial constraints meant that Bruce felt stretched ("I haven't had a vacation in years") and unable to pursue all of the ideas he had for developing the business.

The Japanese Consumer

MacNaughton's interest in the possibility of reaching the Tokyo consumer had been formed from two factors: the large number of Japanese visitors to P.E.I. Preserves, and the fact that the largest export shipment the company had ever made had been to Japan. MacNaughton had never visited Japan, although he had been encouraged by Canadian federal government trade representatives to participate in food and gift shows in Japan. He was debating whether he should visit Japan during the coming year. Most of the information he had on Japan had been collected for him by a friend.

Japan was Canada's second most important source of foreign tourists. In 1990, there were 474,000 Japanese visitors to Canada, a figure which was ex-pected to rise to 1,000,000 by 1995. Most Japanese visitors entered through the Vancouver or Toronto airports. Within Canada, the most popular destination was the Rocky Mountains (in Banff, Alberta, numerous stores catered specifi-cally to Japanese consumers). Nearly 15,000 Japanese visited P.E.I. each year. Excluding airfare, these visitors to Canada spent an estimated $314 million, the highest per capita amount from any country.

The Japanese fascination with Prince Edward Island could be traced to the popularity of *Anne of Green Gables.* The Japanese translation of this and other books in the same series had been available for many years. However, the adoption of the book as required reading in the Japanese school system since the 1950s had resulted in widespread awareness and affection for "Anne with red hair" *and* P.E.I.

The high level of spending by Japanese tourists was due to a multitude of factors: the amount of disposable income available to them, one of the world's highest per person duty-free allowances (200,000 yen), and gift-giving traditions in the country. Gift-giving and entertainment expenses at the corporate level are enormous in Japan. In 1990, corporate entertainment expenses were almost ¥5 trillion, more than triple the U.S. level of ¥1.4 trillion. Corporate gift giving, while focused at both year-end (seibo) and the summer (chugen), in fact, occurred throughout the year.

Gift giving at the personal level was also widespread. The amount spent would vary depending on one's relationship with the recipient; however, one of the most common price points used by Japanese retailers for gift giving was offering choices for under ¥2000.

The Japanese Jam Market

Japanese annual consumption of jam was approximately 80,000 tons. Imports made up 6 to 9 percent of consumption, with higher grade products (¥470 or more per kilo wholesale CIF) making up a third of this total. Several dozen firms imported jam and utilized a mix of distribution channels (see Exhibit 7). Prices varied, in part, according to the type of channel

EXHIBIT 7 Jam Distribution Channel in Japan

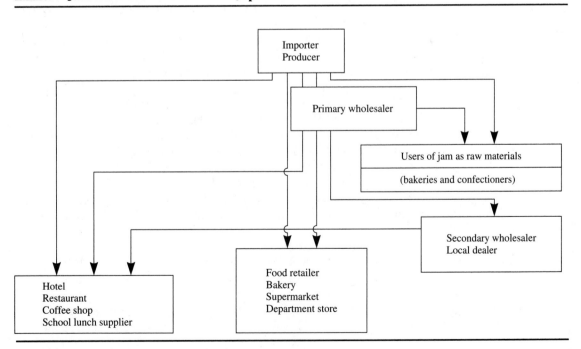

SOURCE: Access to Japan's Import Market, *Tradescope,* June 1989.

structure used. Exhibit 8 provides a common structure. Import duties for jams were high—averaging about 28 percent. Despite such a high tariff barrier, some firms had been successful in exporting to Japan. Excerpts from a report on how to access Japan's jam market successfully are contained in Exhibit 9.

Canadian World

In spring 1990, P.E.I. Preserves received its biggest ever export order; $50,000 worth of product was ordered (FOB New Glasgow) for ultimate shipment to Ashibetsu, on the northern Japanese island of Hokkaido. These products were to be offered for sale at Canadian World, a new theme park scheduled to open in July 1990.

In 1981, Japan's first theme park was built outside Tokyo. Called Tokyo Disneyland, in 1989 it had an annual revenue of $815 million, 14.7 million visitors, and profits of $119 million. Not surprisingly, this success has spawned a theme park industry in Japan. Over the past decade, 20 parks with wide-ranging themes have opened. Another 16 were expected to open in 1991–92.

The idea to construct a theme park about Canada was conceived by a Japanese advertising agency hired by the Ashibetsu city council to stop the city's declining economy. The city's population had decreased from 75,000 in 1958 to 26,000 in 1984, due principally to mine closures.

With capital investment of ¥750,000,000, construction started in mid-1989 on 48 of the 156 available hectares. The finished site included six restaurants, 18 souvenir stores, 16 exhibit event halls, an outdoor stage with 12,000 seats, and 20 hectares planted in herbs and lavender.

The theme of Canadian World was less a mosaic of Canada than it was a park devoted to the world of Anne of Green Gables. The entrance to the Canadian World was a replica of Kensingston Station in P.E.I. The north gateway was Brightriver Station, where Anne first met with Matthew. There was a full-scale copy of the Green Gables house, Orwell School where you could actually learn English like Anne did, and so forth. Canadian World employed 55 full-time and 330 part-time staff. This included a high school girl from P.E.I. who played Anne—complete with (dyed) red hair—dressed in Victorian period costume.

In late August 1991, Canadian World still had a lot of P.E.I. Preserves' products for sale. Lower than expected sales could be traced to a variety of problems. First, overall attendance at Canadian World had been 205,000 in the first year, significantly lower than the expected 300,000. Second, the product was priced higher than many competitive offerings. For reasons unknown to Canadian World staff, the product sold for 10 percent more than expected (¥1200 versus ¥1086).

Exhibit 8 Example of Price Markups in Japan

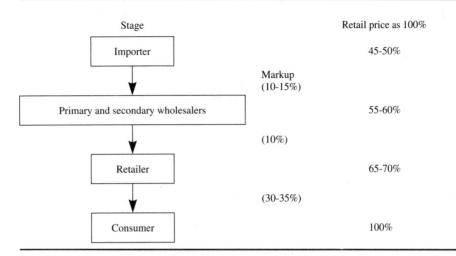

Stage   Retail price as 100%

Importer   45-50%

Markup
(10-15%)

Primary and secondary wholesalers   55-60%

(10%)

Retailer   65-70%

(30-35%)

Consumer   100%

SOURCE: Access to Japan's Import Market, *Tradescope*, June 1989.

Exhibit 9 The Japanese Jam Market

To expand sales of imported jam or to enter the Japanese market for the first time, it is necessary to develop products after precise study of the market's needs. Importers who are making efforts to tailor their products to the Japanese market have been successfully expanding their sales by 10 percent each year. Based on the analysis of successful cases of imported jam, the following factors may be considered very important.

Diversification of consumer preferences: Strawberry jam occupies about 50 percent of the total demand for jam and its share is continuing to rise. Simultaneously, more and more varieties of jam are being introduced.

Low sugar content: European exporters have successfully exported low-sugar jam that meets the needs of the Japanese market. Jam with a sugar content of less than 65 percent occupies a share of 65–70 percent of the market on a volume basis.

Smaller containers: Foreign manufacturers who stick to packaging products in large-sized containers (650g, 440g, 250g), even though their products are designed for household use, have been failing to expand their sales. On the other hand, foreign manufacturers who have developed products in smaller containers (14g, 30g, 42g) specifically for the Japanese market have achieved successful results.

Fashionable items: Contents and quantity are not the only important aspects of jam. The shape and material quality of the containers and their caps, label design, and product name can also influence sales. It is also important that the label not be damaged in any way.

Development of gift items: Sets of various types of imported jams are popular as gift items. For example, there are sets of 10 kinds of jam in 40g mini-jars (retail price ¥2,000) sold as gift sets.

Selection of distribution channel: Since general trading companies, specialty importers, and jam manufacturers each have their own established distribution channels, the selection of the most appropriate channel is of the utmost importance.

SOURCE: Access to Japan's Market Import, *Tradescope*, June 1989.

Wholesale price in P.E.I.	$3.50
Freight ($4.20/kilo, P.E.I. to Hokkaido)	.80
Duty (28% of wholesale price + freight)	1.20
Landed cost in Japan	5.50
Importer's margin (15%)	.83
Price to primary wholesaler	6.33
Wholesaler margin (10%)	.63
Price to retailer	6.96
Canadian World mark up (30%)	2.09
Expected retail price	$9.05
Exchange (Cdn. $1.00 = 120 yen)	¥1086

Third, the product mix chosen by the Japanese buyers appeared to be inappropriate. While it was difficult to locate any of the company's remaining strawberry preserves in the various Canadian World outlets which carried it, other products had not moved at all. Canadian World personnel did not have a tracking system for product-by-product sales. Fourth, the company's gift packs were not always appropriately sized or priced. One suggestion had been to package the preserves in cardboard gift boxes of three large (250 ml) or five small (125 ml) bottles for eventual sale for under ¥2000.

An increasing portion of all of the gifts being sold at Canadian World were, in fact, being made in Japan. Japanese sourcing was common due to the high Japanese duties on imports, the transportation costs from Canada, and the unfamiliarity of Canadian companies with Japanese consumer preferences.

The Tokyo Market

With 10 million residents, Tokyo was the largest city in Japan and one of the most crowded cities anywhere. Thirty million people lived within 50 km of Tokyo's Imperial Palace. As the economic centre of the nation, Tokyo also had the most expensive land in the world—U.S. $150,000 per square meter in the city centre. Retail space in one of Tokyo's major shopping districts would cost $75–160 per square metre or $1,600–$3,400 per month for a shop equivalent in size to that in the CP Prince Edward Hotel. Prices in the Ginza were even higher. In addition to basic rent, all locations required a deposit (guarantee money which would be repaid when the tenant gave up the lease) of at least $25,000. Half of the locations available in a recent survey also charged administrative/maintenance fees (5–12 percent of rent), while in about one third of the locations a "reward" (gift) was paid by tenants to the owner at the time the contract was signed. For a small site, it might amount to $10–15,000.

The Toronto Market

With 3 million people, Toronto was Canada's largest city and economic centre. It contained the country's busiest airport (15 million people used it each year) and was a popular destination for tourists. Each year, roughly 20 million people visited Toronto for business or vacation.

MacNaughton's interest in Toronto was due to its size, the local awareness of P.E.I., and the high perceived potential volume of sales. The company did not have a sales agent in Toronto.

The Toronto market was well served by mass market and specialty jam producers at all price points. Numerous domestic and imported products were available. Prices started as low as $1 (or less) for a 250 ml bottle of high sugar, low fruit product. Prices increased to $2.00–$2.50 for higher fruit, natural brands, and increased again to $3.00–$3.50 for many of the popular branded imports. The highest-priced products, such as P.E.I. Preserves, were characterized by even higher fruit content, highest-quality ingredients, and a broader selection of product offerings.

The specialty domestic producers were from various provinces and tended to have limited distribution areas. The specialty imports were frequently from France or England. The Canadian tariff on imports was 15 percent for most countries. From the United States, it was 10.5 percent and declining.

The cost of retail space in Toronto varied according to location but was slightly lower than that in Tokyo. The cost of renting 22 square metres would be $100 per square metre per month (plus common area charges and taxes of $15 per square metre per month) in a major suburban shopping mall, and somewhat higher in the downtown core. Retail staff salaries were similar in Toronto and Tokyo, both of which were higher than those paid in P.E.I.

Future Directions

MacNaughton was the first to acknowledge that, while the business had been "built on gut and emotion, rather than analysis," this was insufficient for the future. The challenge was to determine the direction and timing of the desired change.

CASE 28
RUSSKI ADVENTURES

On July 15, 1991, Guy Crevasse and Andrei Kakov, the two major partners in Russki Adventures (Russki), contemplated their next move. They had spent the last year and a half exploring the possibility of starting a helicopter skiing operation in the USSR. Their plan was to bring clients from Europe, North America, and Japan to a remote location in the USSR to ski the vast areas of secluded mountain terrain made accessible by the use of helicopters and the recent business opportunities offered by *glasnost.*

During the exploration process, Crevasse and Kakov had visited a number of potential locations in the USSR, including the Caucasus Mountains near the Black Sea, and the Tien Shen and Pamir ranges north of Pakistan in the republics of Kazakistan and Tadzhikistan, respectively. After close inspection of the three areas, and consideration of many issues, the partners had decided upon the Caucasus region.

After almost two years of planning and research, the thought of making a solid commitment weighed heavily on their minds. Their first option was to accept the partnership offer with Extreme Dreams, a French company that had started a small ski operation in the Caucasus Mountains during the 1991 season. Their second option was to enter a partnership with the USSR's Trade Union DFSO and a Russian mountaineer, and establish their own venture in a Caucasus Mountains area made available to them by a Soviet government agency. Their final option was to wait, save their money, and not proceed with the venture at this time.

The Partners

Andrei Kakov, 27, was born in Russia. His family emigrated to Italy and then to Canada when he was 17 years old. After completing an undergraduate degree in economics at the University of Toronto, he worked with Sebaco for two years before enroling in 1989 in the Master's of Business Administration (MBA) program at the University of Western Ontario (Western). Sebaco was a Canadian-Soviet joint venture that, since 1980, had been facilitating business ventures in the Soviet Union by acting as a liaison between the foreign firms and the different levels of Soviet government and industry. This job gave Kakov extensive contacts in the Soviet Union and in many of the firms, such as McDonald's and PepsiCo, which were doing business in the Soviet Union. Kakov was fluent in Russian, Italian, English, and Japanese.

Guy Crevasse, 28, had an extensive ski racing career which began at a young age and culminated in the World Cup with the Canadian National Ski Team. His skiing career took him to many countries in Europe, North America, and South America. During his travels, he learned to speak French, Italian, and some German. After retiring from competitive ski racing in 1984, Crevasse remained active in the ski industry as a member of the Canadian Ski Coaches Federation. He led the University of Western Ontario Varsity Ski Team to four consecutive Can-Am titles as a racer/coach while pursuing an undergraduate degree at Western. Before returning to Western to complete an MBA, Crevasse worked for Motorola, Inc., in its sales and marketing departments, where he worked on key accounts, set up product distribution channels, and developed product programs with original equipment manufacturers in the automobile industry. Crevasse had also worked with a ski resort planning and development firm on a number of different projects.

Overview of the Skiing and Helicopter Skiing Industries

Development of the Ski Resort Industry

In 1990, the worldwide ski market was estimated at 40 million skiers. The great boom period was in the 1960s and 1970s when growth ran between 10 and 20 percent annually. However, the growth stagnation which began during the 1980s was expected to continue during the 1990s. Some of this decline was attributable to increased competition for vacationers' time, the rapidly rising real costs of skiing, and baby-boom effects. The only growth segment was female skiers, who represented 65 percent of all new skiers. The total revenue generated by ski resorts in the United States for 1990 was estimated at $1.5 billion. This figure did not include any hotel or accommodation figures.

Prior to World War II, most skiing took place in Europe. Since there were no ski lifts, most skiing was essentially unmarked wilderness skiing, requiring participants who enjoyed the thrill of a downhill run to spend most of their time climbing. There were no slope-grooming machines and few slopes cut especially for skiing.

The development of ski lifts revolutionized the sport, increased the accessibility to many previously inaccessible areas, and led to the development of ski resorts. After the skiing market matured, competition for skiers intensified and resort operators shifted their efforts away from the risk sport focus toward vacation and entertainment. In order to service this new market and to recover their large capital investments, the large resorts had developed mass market strategies and modified the runs and the facilities to make them safer and easier to ski in order to serve a greater number of customers.

Introduction of Helicopter Skiing

This change in focus left the more adventurous skiing segments unsatisfied. For many, the search for new slopes and virgin snow was always a goal. The rapid rise in the popularity of skiing after World War II, increased demand on existing ski facilities, and thus competition for the best snow and hills became more intense. Those who wanted to experience the joys of powder skiing in virgin areas were forced to either get up earlier to ski the good snow before the masses got to it or hike for hours from the top of ski areas to find new areas close to existing cut ski runs. Hiking to unmarked areas was tiring, time-consuming, and more dangerous because of the exposure to crevasses and avalanches.

This desire to ski in unlimited powder snow and new terrain away from the crowds eventually led to the development of the helicopter skiing industry. The commonly held conception was that powder skiing was the champagne of all skiing, and helicopter skiing was the Dom Perignon. The first helicopter operations began in Canada. From the beginning of the industry in 1961, Canadian operations have been typically regarded as the premium product in the helicopter skiing industry for many reasons, including the wild, untamed mountains in the western regions. For many skiers worldwide, a trip to a Western Canadian heliski operation is their "mecca."

Operators used helicopters as a means of accessing vast tracts of wilderness areas which were used solely by one operator through a lease arrangement with the governments, forest services, or regional authorities. The average area leased for skiing was 2,000–3,000 square thousand kilometres in size, with 100–150 runs. Due to the high costs in buying, operating, maintaining, and insuring a helicopter, the vast majority of operators leased their machines on an as-needed basis with rates based on hours of flight time.

In the 1970s and early 1980s, the helicopter skiing industry was concentrated among a few players. During 1990–1991, the number of adventure/wilderness skiing operators increased from 41 to over 77. The industry could be divided between those operations that provided day-trips from existing alpine resorts (day-trippers) and those operations that offered week-long trips (destination-location).

By 1991, the entire global market for both day-trippers and destination-location was estimated to be just over 23,000 skiers per year with the latter group representing roughly 12,000–15,000 skiers. Wilderness skiing represented the largest area of growth within the ski industry in the 1970s and 1980s. Market growth in the 1980s was 15 percent per year. Only capacity limitations had restrained growth. The addictive nature of helicopter skiing was illustrated by the fact that repeat customers accounted for over 75 percent of clients annually. The conservative estimate of total margin available to the destination-location skiing industry (before selling and administration costs) was U.S. $12.4 million in 1990. Exhibit 1 gives typical industry margin figures per skier for heliskiing.

From a cost standpoint, efficient management of the helicopter operations was essential. Exhibit 2 provides a larger list of industry key success factors.

Exhibit 1 Helicopter Skiing Margin per Skier Week (North America)

Price		$3,500	100%
Costs:	Helicopter*	1,260	36%
	Food & lodging	900	26%
	Guides	100	3%
	Total operating costs	2,260	65%
	Total margin	1,240	35%

*Helicopter costs were semi-variable, but were based largely on a variable basis (in-flight hours). The fixed nature of helicopter costs arose through minimum flying hours requirements and the rate negotiations (better rates were charged to customers with higher usage). On average, a helicopter skier used seven hours of helicopter time during a one-week trip. A typical all-in rate for a 12-person helicopter was $1,800 per flying hour. Hence, the above figure of $1,260 was calculated assuming full capacity of the helicopter using the following: $1,800 per hour for 7 hours for 10 skiers + pilot + guide.

Exhibit 2 Helicopter Skiing Industry Key Success Factors

Factors within management control
• Establishing a safe operation and reliable reputation.
• Developing great skiing operations.
• Attracting and keeping customers with minimal marketing costs.
• Obtaining repeat business through operation's excellence.
• Providing professional and sociable guides.
• Obtaining operating permits from government.
• Managing relationships with environmentalists.

Location factors
• Accessible destinations by air travel.
• Available emergency and medical support.
• Favourable weather conditions (i.e., annual snowfall, humidity, altitude).
• Appropriate daily temperature, sunshine, daylight time.
• Suitable terrain.
• Quality food and lodging.

Combination of Resort and Helicopter Skiing

The number of resorts operating day facilities doubled in 1990. Competition in the industry increased for a number of reasons. Many new competitors entered because of the low cost of entry (about $250,000), low exit barriers, the significant market growth, and the rewarding margin in the industry. The major growth worldwide came mainly from the day operations at existing areas, as they attempted to meet the needs for adventure and skiing from their clientele. The major concentration of helicopter operators was in Canada; however, competition was increasing internationally. Industry representatives thought that such growth was good because it would help increase the popularity of helicopter skiing and introduce more people to the sport.

In Canada, where helicopter skiing originated, the situation was somewhat different. Out of the 20 wilderness skiing operations in Canada in 1991, only two were tied to resorts. However, for the rest of the world, roughly 80 percent of all the operations were located and tied closely to existing ski operations. Both Crevasse and Kakov realized that there were opportunities to create partnerships or agreements with existing resorts to serve as an outlet for their helicopter skiing demand.

Russki's Research of the Heliski Industry

Profile of the Skier

The research that the Russki group had completed revealed some important facts. Most helicopter skiers were wealthy, independent, professional males of North American or European origin. Increasingly, the Japanese skiers were joining the ranks. The vast majority of the skiers were in their late 30s to mid-60s in age. For them, helicopter skiing provided an escape from the high pace of their professional lives. These people, who were financially secure with lots of disposable income, were well educated and had done a great many things. Helicopter skiing was a good fit with their calculated risk-taker image. Exhibit 3 describes a typical customer. It was not unusual for the skiing "addict" to exceed 100,000 vertical feet of skiing in a week. A premium was then charged to the skier.

Buyers tended to buy in groups rather than as individuals. They typically had some form of close association, such as membership in a common profession or club. In most cases, trips were planned a year in advance.

Geographically, helicopter skiers could be grouped into three segments: Japan, North America (United States and Canada), and Europe. In 1991, they represented 10 percent, 40 percent (30 percent and 10 percent), and 50 percent of the market, respectively. There were unique features associated with each segment, and Crevasse and Kakov knew that all marketing plans would need to be tailored specifically to each segment. In general, they felt that the European and North American customers placed more emphasis on the adventure, were less risk adverse, and had a propensity to try new things.

Analysis of the Competition

Crevasse and Kakov had thought that more detailed information on their competitors would help answer some of their questions. During the winter of 1991, they conducted a complete physical inspection of skiing and business facilities of many helicopter skiing operations. As a result of the research, Russki determined that the following companies were very significant: Rocky Mountain Helisports (RMH), Cariboo Snowtours, and Heliski India. RMH and Cariboo Snowtours were industry leaders, and Heliski India was another new entrant

Exhibit 3 **Description of a Typical Helicopter Skiing Addict**

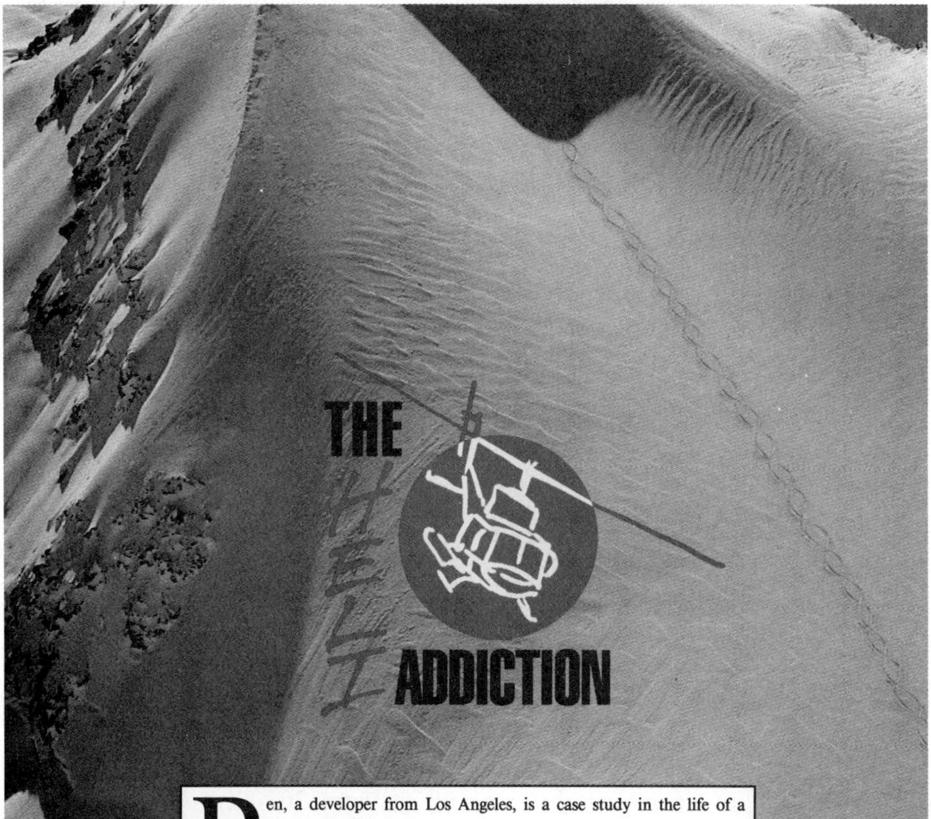

THE HELI ADDICTION

Ben, a developer from Los Angeles, is a case study in the life of a helicopter skiing addict:

It started out innocently enough. As a former racer and lifelong skier, Ben had always dreamed of vast, untracked powder fields where snow billowed overhead on every turn. In all his years of skiing, he'd had good powder days, but never an unlimited, boundless slate for his tracks. His business was doing well, and so, as he reached his mid-30s, he felt his dream deserved to be realized. He committed to a week of heli-skiing in British Columbia.

By the end of four days of fantasy skiing, Ben's group had surpassed the promised 100,000 feet of vertical, and the additional-cost meter was running with every extra foot. But Ben didn't care. If the helicopter went up, he was in it, and he logged close to another hundred grand by the time the week was over. He then committed to another week the following year.

"My wife is going to kill me," he said to himself, "but this skiing, so far from any other human, so wild and untamed and pure, is worth it."

Is helicopter skiing that big a deal? Is it worth the dent in your bank account, the risk of the addiction that snared Ben? Well, take a good, *loooong* look at the photo on this page.

Are there any doubts?

SOURCE: *Powder, The Skier's Magazine,* November 1990.

trying to establish itself in the market. A close analysis had provided Crevasse and Kakov with some encouraging information.

Rocky Mountain Helisports, the first operation to offer helicopter skiing, was started in 1965 in Canada by Gunther Pistler, a German immigrant and the "inventor" of helicopter skiing. In 1991, his operation, servicing 6,000 skiers, represented roughly 40–50 percent of the worldwide destination-location market. He followed a strategy which cloned small operating units at seven different sites in the interior of British Columbia. RMH's strategy was designed to offer a product that catered to a variety of different skier abilities and skiing experiences. The company serviced all segments that could afford the $4,000 price of admission, including introducing less-able skiers to the experience of helicopter skiing. Compared with the revenue of traditional Canadian ski resorts, such as Whistler Resorts in British Columbia, RMH's gross revenue for the 1990 season was larger than any resort in Canada at over $21 million. RMH, which had developed a loyal following of customers in North America and Europe, enjoyed significant competitive advantage because of proprietary client lists, a loyal consumer base, and economies of scale due to its large size.

Cariboo Snowtours, the second largest operation in the world, was established by another German immigrant, Fritz Mogler, at Blue River, British Columbia. In 1991, Cariboo Snowtours served over 2,000 skiers, a number which represented roughly 18 percent of the market. Mogler developed a strategy of one megaoperation and enjoyed economies of scale in the operations area. Similar to RMH, Cariboo Snowtours had a loyal following from North America and Europe and catered to a variety of skiing abilities and price levels.

Heliski India was a new entrant to the helicopter skiing business. In 1990, the first year of operation, the company serviced 30 skiers in a three-week period, increasing to 120 skiers during the 1991 season. Heliski India followed a more exclusive and adventurous strategy aimed at the experienced helicopter skiing enthusiast. To cover the high costs and low volume, the operation charged $5,500.

Russki estimated margins and profit dynamics for these three operations. Exhibit 4 contains the projection for RMH. These projected statements were best guesstimates based on discussions with a wide range of industry experts, managers, and investors. Cariboo Snowtour's total profit was estimated as slightly over $2 million, while Heliski India was projected to turn a small profit. Crevasse and Kakov found these figures very encouraging.

Land Usage and Environmental Concerns in the Industry

The helicopter skiing industry was facing some land use issues which were tough on many operators, but which also created new opportunities on which Russki wanted to capitalize. Of particular concern to many helicopter skiing operations, especially European, were pressures from environmentalists who were concerned that noise from helicopters could adversely affect wildlife habitat and start avalanches.

As a result, severe downsizing or complete shutdown of existing European operations had recently occurred, leaving only eight helicopter skiing operations in continental Europe in 1991. The one Swiss and one Austrian operation were under pressure to close, and a 1992 season for the latter was already doubtful. The six small operations in Italy, which worked in conjunction with existing ski areas, were basically the only helicopter skiing available in Western Europe.

Exhibit 4 Russki's 1991 Projections*: Profit Dynamics of Typical RMH Operation

Revenues						
Ski season duration—Peak	20	wks				
—Regular	0	wks				
Total season duration	20	wks				
Revenue per skier —Peak			$	3500		
Weekly group size (10 skiers + 1 guide × 4)	44	people				
Total season regular revenue (3,500 × 40 skiers × 20 wks)					$2,800,000	
Revenue from skiers exceeding 100,000 vertical feet (10%)					280,000	
Total revenue						$3,080,000
Expenses						
Variable: 9 nights lodging/person/night			$	80	$ 720	
9 days meals/person/day				50	450	
Total variable cost/person/week					$ 1170	
Total annual variable costs (20 wks × 44 × $1,170)						$1,029,600
Contribution margin						$2,050,400
Fixed:						
Helicopter cost/weekly basis (20-week season)			$ 50,000		$1,000,000	
Guides—1 guide per 10 skiers @ $50,000 per guide/year	4	guides			$ 200,000	
Support staff—5 employees @ $20,000 per employee					$ 100,000	
Promotional					$ 250,000	
Total direct fixed costs						$1,550,000
Total margin						$ 500,400
(Revenue − Direct variable costs × Direct fixed costs)						
Annual overhead–Communication			$ 20,000			
–Staff travel			50,000			
–Office branch			20,000			
–Office North America			100,000			
–Insurance @ $5/day/person			50,000			
Total overhead						$ 240,000
Operating profit						$ 260,400
Number of operations	7					
Total operating profit						$1,822,800

*These projected statements were best guesstimates based on discussions with a wide range of industry experts, managers, and investors.

Flying for skiing in France was illegal due to environmentalists' concerns about a negative impact on the limited areas in the Alps. In Sweden, a few companies operated with a shorter season due to the high latitude, and provided less-expensive daily services for visitors who skied within the existing lift systems, but week-long packages were not part of their program.

The North American industry had not been exposed to the same environmental and limited area constraints as the European, mainly because of the vast size of the mountain ranges and good relationships with all interested parties. The American operators, who were associated mostly with the large ski areas, had good working relationships with the forest services, which controlled the areas and issued the working permits.

Canadian operators received their permits from the Ministry of Lands and Forests and the provincial governments. Helicopter skiing had been encouraged because of its ability to bring money into the regions. Due to the vast size of the Canadian mountain ranges and the limited competition for the land use, pressure on the operators in any form had been minimal or nonexistent.

Crevasse and Kakov realized that the environmental and capacity constraints in Europe provided helicopter skiing operators worldwide with significant opportunities. Thus far, it had been mainly the North American operators who had capitalized on this situation, and Russki wanted to find a way to capture unsatisfied demand.

Russian Environment

The Political Environment

Crevasse and Kakov knew that starting a venture in the Soviet Union at this time would be complex. The political situation was very unstable in July 1991, and most expert predictions were not encouraging, including the possibility that the Soviet Union might not exist in the near future. There was a major power struggle going on: the hardliners, most of whom were from the old guard of the Communist party, were trying to hang on to power; and others, such as Russian President Boris Yeltsin, wanted sweeping democratic changes. The new buzz word on the streets was not *glasnost* or *peristroika*, but *razgosudarstvo,* which refers to the breakup of the Soviet state. Secession pressures from many of the republics such as the Baltics tested the metal of the political leaders, *peristroika,* and the strength of the union itself.

On a regional basis, the future status of some of the regions and republics where the physical conditions met the requirements for helicopter skiing, such as Georgia and Kazakhistan, was unknown. However, Crevasse and Kakov were encouraged by the fact that experts predicted that no matter what the state of the whole union, Russia would remain intact and continue to function as a unit. This was one of the many reasons why the Russian Republic was selected for the potential initial location.

The Economic Environment

The economy of the Soviet Union was in dire straits. Confusion, lack of focus, and compromise were crippling the process of change from a government-controlled economy to a market-based one. Real gross domestic product was projected to drop anywhere from 3 to 11 percent or more in 1991. Soviet President Mikhail Gorbachev had been given authority to overhaul the economy. However, what changes he would initiate, and whether he still had the support and power to see the process through to completion, were questionable.

Therefore, developing a helicopter skiing operation in the Soviet Union presented Russki with a difficult business environment. Marshall Goldman, director of Harvard's Russian Research Centre, summed up part of the dilemma facing any new venture in the Soviet Union at this time:

> For those entrepreneurs who think chaos is an ideal environment, this is a perfect time, but for others it is a scary time. The society is collapsing. The economy—both the marketing portion and the planning and administrative sector—is a shambles.

Russki's research indicated that only 20 percent of the 1,300 joint ventures signed since 1987 were operational because of currency exchange problems, bureaucratic delays, and lack of legal framework to make agreements. Also, it had been very hard for the few operational ventures to realize a return on their investment. In 1991, any business in the Soviet Union had to be viewed with a long-term bias in mind. The big question for many businesses was getting hard currency out of Soviet ventures because there was no international market for the Soviet currency, the ruble. Those who were operating business ventures in the Soviet Union suggested to Russki that it was not an area for the fainthearted to tread. PlanEcon's Keith Crane advised that "even after the agreement has been signed it can be very difficult to get down to specifics and venture into working entities. It took McDonald's 14 years to do it." Due to the political and economic realities of the Soviet environment, firms were making deals with republics, with city agencies, directly with Soviet firms or factories, and sometimes with all of them. More and more frequently, firms had to go to the enterprise level to find the right people and partners. Additionally, foreign firms found the business environment difficult because the concept of business that Westerners had was very different from the one that the Soviets had after 70 years of a controlled Marxist economy. The addition of cultural differences made for a demanding business climate. Russki thought long and hard about the fact that doing business in the Soviet Union had never been easy. In 1991, as the nation wrestled with the gargantuan task of restructuring the country, most firms were finding it more confusing than ever. No road map or blueprint for business development existed.

In addition, without the significant financial resources of a highly capitalized firm that could overlook short-term profits for long-term gains, Crevasse and Kakov realized they would be in a more exposed position if they decided to go ahead with the venture. Political unrest or civil war in the Soviet Union, especially in Russia, could destroy their business and investment. Without a steady supply of repeat and new customers, the venture would be finished as an on-going concern. They knew that credibility from an existing operation or established name would make the task of attracting customers to an uncertain environment easier but, in a time of crisis, would guarantee nothing.

The Opportunities

Despite all the negatives, Crevasse and Kakov thought that helicopter skiing in the Soviet Union would be developed on a large scale in the next few years for a number of reasons. The sport was experiencing tremendous growth, environmental pressures were great in Europe, and capacity at all of the good locations was already stretched.

Therefore, a current opportunity existed in the industry. The partners speculated about how fast they could proceed with their business plan and whether they were exposing themselves to too much risk for the return. Would the opportunity still exist in a couple of years? Could a business of this nature function with the future of the Soviet Union being so unstable? The complete answer to these questions was unknown. Crevasse and Kakov felt as if they were doing a case back at business school where someone had left out half the case facts. Regardless, this was a real-life situation, and a decision had to be made on the knowledge available.

After looking closely at their competition and the general environment, they concluded that, despite the instability in the Soviet environment, there were a number of strong points that suggested that they might be able to make a venture of this nature work. On a positive note, the Canadian prime minister, Brian Mulroney, had recently signed the Foreign Investment Protection agreement to ensure stability of Canadian ventures in the USSR. Also encouraging to entrepreneurs wanting to enter the Soviet Union was the new law that allowed for full ownership of Soviet subsidiaries by foreign firms. Experts suggested that these agreements would be honoured by whatever form of government was in place.

The critical factor in the minds of the Russki partners was the fact that they would be taking in all revenue in hard currency. Thus, the absence of profit repatriation risk decreased this business exposure dramatically. Russki would operate all of the sales and administrative tasks outside of the Soviet Union and as a result, all of its revenues would be collected in the West in hard currency, thereby eliminating the currency risk completely. This was a position that would be envied by any firm attempting to do business in the Soviet Union. Also, Russki was attractive to all levels of government because the venture would bring desperately needed hard currency into the country.

Mt. Elbrus, the highest peak in Europe and the Caucasus mountain region, was where Russki had options to locate. It was well known throughout Europe and its high altitudes and warm climate offered ideal skiing conditions. Because a strong allegiance already existed between the European customers and the

Canadian operators, Russki's Canadian background would sit well with customers. In addition, Russki would deliver comparative cost advantage for the Europeans in a Soviet operation, as shown in Exhibit 5, even if Russki charged similar costs for a week of skiing.

The uniqueness of the region and mystique of Russia offered an interesting alternative for tourism. Russia had a 2,000-year history and a rich culture which was reflected in the traditions of the local people and the architecture. Furthermore, the Black Sea area, which was close to the Caucasus Mountains, had been used as a resort area for centuries. The dramatic changes during the early 1990s in the Soviet Union and Eastern Europe had resulted in tremendous interest in these areas.

Since Russki already had the money required for start-up, the company could move quickly without having to take time to raise the capital. The low cost of leasing Soviet helicopters, pilot salaries, service, and fuel as compared with North America was a distinct advantage, and one of the original attractions of Russia. Negotiations with the Russians had shown that this cost advantage was obtainable. The high costs of helicopter operations represented the largest part of the operating costs in helicopter skiing. Lower helicopter costs in Russia would result in cost savings in the range of 50 percent or more in this expense relative to North American competitors.

The Russki management team was strong. Both men were business-school trained individuals with international work experience, language skills, and ski industry background. Additional hard-to-copy assets, including access to the "Crazy Canucks" (a World Cup ski team) and European ski stars as guest guides and Soviet knowledge, would be tough for anyone to match in the short term.

Exhibit 5 Cost Comparison by Geographic Location

North America
Costs for customer to go Heliskiing in North America from different geographic locations

Origin of skier	Trip	Transportation	Total
Japan	$4,000	$2,500	$6,500
Europe	$4,000	$2,000	$6,000
North America	$4,000	$ 750	$4,750

Russia
Cost for customers to go Heliskiing in Russia from different geographic locations

Origin of Skier	Trip	Transportation	Total
Japan	$4,000	$2,000	$6,000
Europe	$4,000	$1,000	$5,000
North America	$4,000	$2,500	$6,500

Conclusion: This comparative analyis of all-in costs to the consumer shows that the Russian operation offers a 20 percent cost advantage to the European customers.

Positioning and Marketing of Russki Adventures

Positioning and Pricing

The Russki team had considered two positioning strategies, a high and low pricing strategy. A premium pricing and service strategy like that of Heliski India at around U.S. $6,000 would require superior service in every aspect of the operation. The lower-priced strategy at $3,500 to $4,000 was $500 below the $4,000 to $4,500 U.S. pricing of Canadian operators like RMH for the initial season. The second positioning strategy would be designed to target a larger market and concentrate on building market share during the first few years, allowing more time and flexibility to move down the learning curve.

Even with parallel pricing of U.S. $4,000, the "all in" (as shown in Exhibit 5) would give a cost advantage to the European and Japanese customers. Crevasse and Kakov knew that this situation would help challenge customers' traditional allegiance to the Canadian operators.

Based on a "best-guess scenario," profit models for the two pricing strategies using conservative sales levels are shown in Exhibits 6 and 7. Though the higher-priced strategy was more lucrative, Crevasse and Kakov felt that they had a higher capacity to execute the lower-price strategy during the first few years of operations regardless of which partner they chose. They were not sure that they could meet the sales volume for the premium strategy as shown in Exhibit 7, regardless of the realization of savings from use of Russian helicopters. (In the unlikely event that the projected helicopter saving could not be realized, the discounted cash flow in Exhibit 6 dropped from $526,613 to $293, and in Exhibit 7 from $597,926 to $194,484.)

These estimates were extremely conservative. One helicopter could service 44 people per week (four groups of 10 skiers and one guide). All projections for the profit dynamics were made with the number of skiers per week below capacity. In addition, the first two years were estimated using 10 and 15 skiers, respectively. In subsequent years, the number of skiers was increased, but never to full capacity, in order to keep estimates conservative. Russki realized that operating at or close to capacity on a weekly basis would increase its efficiency and returns dramatically.

Russki also built in an additional $250 in the variable costs per skier per week for contingent expenses such as the cost of importing all food stuffs.

If Russki proceeded with the lower-priced approach, it would position its product just below the industry standard at $4,000 initially. The intent would be to attack the market as the Japanese automobile manufacturers had done when entering into the North American luxury car market.

Crevasse and Kakov were encouraged by the numbers because the conservative sales estimates using the low-price positioning strategy would allow them to generate a profit in the second year of operations if they could realize the

Ехнiвiт 6 Profit Dynamics Low Price Strategy with Low Helicopter Costs

	Year 1	Year 2	Year 3	Year 4	Year 5
Revenues					
Total season duration	10 weeks	15 weeks	15 weeks	20 weeks	20 weeks
Revenue per skier—Peak	$4000	$4000	$4000	$4000	$4000
Weekly group size	10	15	20	25	25
Total season revenue	$400,000	$900,000	$1,200,000	$2,000,000	$2,000,000
Expenses					
Total variable cost	$100,000	$225,000	$300,000	$500,000	$500,000
(variable cost/skier @$1,000)					
Contribution margin	$300,000	$675,000	$900,000	$1,500,000	$1,500,000
Fixed					
Helicopter cost (Assumes Soviet costs of $10,000/week)	$100,000	$150,000	$150,000	$200,000	$200,000
Guides—1 guide per 10 skiers @ $50,000 per guide/year	$50,000	$75,000	$100,000	$125,000	$125,000
Soviet staff—# employees @ $5,000 per employee	$15,000	$15,000	$15,000	$15,000	$15,000
Promotional	$100,000	$100,000	$100,000	$100,000	$100,000
Total direct fixed costs	$265,000	$340,000	$365,000	$440,000	$440,000
Total margin (Revenues − direct variable costs − Direct fixed costs)	$35,000	$335,000	$535,000	$1,060,000	$1,060,000
Total overhead	$35,000	$115,000	$115,000	$115,000	$115,000
Operating profit	–0–	$220,000	$420,000	$945,000	$945,000

	Year 0	Year 1	Year 2	Year 3	Year 4	Year 5
Investment	− $230,000					
Operating profit		–0–	$220,000	$420,000	$945,000	$945,000
N.A. partner's share: 100%		–0–	$220,000	$420,000	$945,000	$945,000
Taxes @ 30% profit	$ − 230,000	–0–	$154,000	$294,000	$661,500	$661,500
DCF Year 1–5 PV @ 20.00%	$526,613					
IRR	71.86%					

projected savings with Russian helicopters. However, if they didn't, the strategy would still show a profit in the third year. They thought that the return on their investment would be sufficient as far as the internal rate of return was concerned, but they wondered whether the risk of the Soviet environment should increase their demands even more.

Product

Crevasse and Kakov planned to model the Russki product after the RMH operation, which was the best in the industry, by evaluating what RMH had built and improving on its processes. Although Russki wanted very much to differen-

Exhibit 7 **Profit Dynamics Premium Price Strategy with Low Helicopter Costs**

	Year 1	Year 2	Year 3	Year 4	Year 5
Revenues					
Total season duration	5 weeks	10 weeks	10 weeks	20 weeks	20 weeks
Revenue per skier—Peak	$ 6000	$ 6000	$ 6000	$ 6000	$ 6000
Weekly group size	10	10	15	15	20
Total season revenue	$300,000	$600,000	$900,000	$1,800,000	$2,400,000
Expenses					
Total variable cost	$ 50,000	$100,000	$150,000	$ 300,000	$ 400,000
(variable cost/skier @$1,000)					
Contribution margin	$250,000	$500,000	$750,000	$1,500,000	$2,000,000
Fixed					
Helicopter cost (Assumes Soviet costs of $10,000/week)	$ 50,000	$100,000	$100,000	$ 200,000	$ 200,000
Guides—1 guide per 10 skiers @ $50,000 per guide/year	$ 50,000	$ 50,000	$ 75,000	$ 75,000	$ 100,000
Soviet staff—3 employees @ $5,000 per employee	$ 15,000	$ 15,000	$ 15,000	$ 15,000	$ 15,000
Promotional	$100,000	$100,000	$100,000	$ 100,000	$ 100,000
Total direct fixed costs	$215,000	$265,000	$290,000	$ 390,000	$ 415,000
Total margin (Revenues − direct variable costs − Direct fixed costs)	$ 35,000	$235,000	$460,000	$1,110,000	$1,585,000
Total overhead	$ 35,000	$115,000	$115,000	$ 115,000	$ 115,000
Operating profit	–0–	$120,000	$345,000	$ 995,000	$1,470,000

	Year 0	Year 1	Year 2	Year 3	Year 4	Year 5
Investment	$ – 230,000					
Operating profit		–0–	$120,000	$345,000	$ 995,000	$1,470,000
N.A. partner's share: 100%		–0–	$120,000	$345,000	$ 995,000	$1,470,000
Taxes @ 30% profit	$ – 230,000	–0–	$ 84,000	$241,500	$ 696,500	$1,029,000
DCF Year 1–5 PV @ 20.00%		$597,926				
IRR	70.78%					

tiate itself from the rest of the industry, the partners were not sure how far they could go within the constraints of the Soviet environment.

Geographic Distribution

Although Russki would focus on the European and North American markets, the former segment was most important. Both Crevasse and Kakov realized that they would need a strong European operation in marketing and sales if they were going to capitalize on the opportunity available. Developing these functions quickly, especially in Europe, which was not their home turf, was a major concern. They had to decide on the best sales and marketing channels immediately and set them up as soon as possible if they decided to go ahead with the venture.

Promotion

Due to the small size of the target market and promotion budgets, the new company would have to make sure that the promotional dollars spent were directed effectively. Russki would do this by direct mail, personal selling by the owners, travel agents, and free tour incentives to trip organizers and guides. Long-term word of mouth would be the best promotional tool, but it had to be supplemented especially in the start-up phase of the business.

Additionally, Crevasse and Kakov planned to increase the value to customers by inviting business and political speakers to participate in the skiing activities with the groups in return for their speaking services. Celebrity skiers such as Canadian Olympic bronze medallist and World Cup champion, Steve Podborski, would be used as customer attractions. As outlined in Exhibit 8, they budgeted $100,000 for promotional expenses.

Labour

Where possible, Russki planned to employ Russians and make sure that they received excellent training and compensation, thereby adding authenticity to the customers' experience. Providing local employment would also ensure the Canadian company's existence and create positive relations with the authorities.

Currency

Through Kakov's contacts, Russki had worked out a deal to purchase excess rubles from a couple of foreign firms which were already operating in the Soviet Union but which were experiencing profit repatriation problems. Russki would pay for as many things as possible with soft currency.

Exhibit 8 Marketing Promotion Budget—Year 1

Information nights with cocktails @ $1,000/night @ 20 cities	$ 20,000
Travel expenses	10,000
Trip discounts (1 free trip in 10 to groups)	25,000
Direct mail	5,000
Brochures	5,000
Commissions	15,000
Celebrity	20,000
	$100,000

The Partnership Dilemma

During the exploration period, Crevasse and Kakov had well over a dozen offers from groups and individuals to either form partnerships or provide services and access to facilities and natural resources. They even had offers from people who wanted them to invest millions to build full-scale alpine resorts. Many of the offers were easy to dismiss because these groups did not have the ability to deliver what they promised or their skill sets did not meet the needs of Russki. Crevasse and Kakov's inspection and site evaluation helped them to determine further the best opportunities and to evaluate firsthand whether the site and potential partner were realistic. This research gave Russki a couple of excellent but very distinct partnership possibilities. They knew that both options had trade-offs.

Extreme Dreams

A partnership with the Extreme Dreams group had some definite strengths. This French company, located in Chamonix, an alpine town in the French Alps, had been running the premier guiding service in and around Mont Blanc, the highest peak in the Alps, for 11 years. Chamonix was the "avant-garde" for alpinists in Europe and one of the top alpine centres in the world. Extreme Dreams had a 5,000-person client list, mostly European but with some North American names.

What Extreme Dreams had was the operational expertise Russki needed to acquire in order to run the helicopter skiing and guiding side of the business. However, they lacked experience in the key functional areas of business. During the 1991 winter season, it had run a three-week operation servicing 50 skiers in the Elbrus region in the Caucasus Mountains. The Soviet partner facilitated an arrangement with a small resort villa in the area. The facilities, which had just been upgraded during the summer, now met Western standards.

The French company had invested roughly U.S. $100,000, and although it did not have a capital shortage, the partnership agreement that was outlined would require Russki to inject the same amount of capital into the business. The firm would be incorporated in the United States and the share split would be equal amounts of 45 percent of the stock with 10 percent left over for future employee purchase. The Soviet partner, a government organization that helped facilitate the land use agreements and permits, would be paid a set fee for yearly exclusive use of the land.

However, Extreme Dreams lacked experience in the key functional areas of business. Possibly, this situation could be rectified by the partnership agreement whereby the management team would consist of three members. Marc Testut, president of Extreme Dreams, would be in charge of all operations. Guy Crevasse would act as president for the first two years and his areas of expertise would be sales and marketing. Andrei Kakov would be chief financial officer and responsible for Soviet relations.

Extreme Dreams had overcome the lack of some foodstuffs by importing on a weekly basis products not securely attainable in Russia. These additional costs were built into the variable cost in projected financial statements. Russki would do the same if it did not choose Extreme Dreams as a partner.

Trade Union DFSO

The other potential partnership had its strengths as well. The partnership would be with the All-Union Council of Trade Union DFSO, and with a mountaineer named Yuri Golodov, one of the USSR's best-known mountaineers, who had agreed to be part of the management team. Golodov, who had been bringing mountaineers from all over the world to parts of the Soviet Union for many years, possessed valuable expertise and knowledge of the Caucasus area. One of his tasks would be coordination of travel logistics for Soviet clientele. Sergei Oganezovich, chief of the mountaineering department, had made available to Russki the exclusive rights to over 4,000 square kilometres in the Caucasus Mountain Range about 50 kilometres from the area awarded to Extreme Dreams. A small user fee per skier would be paid to the trade organization in return for exclusive helicopter access to the area.

A profit-sharing agreement with Golodov, which would allow him to purchase shares in Russki and share in the profits, was agreed to in principle by Russki, the Trade Union DFSO, and Golodov. Under this agreement, Crevasse and Kakov would remain in control of the major portion of the shares. Capital requirements for this option would be in the $230,000 range over the first two years. The two Canadians would perform essentially the same roles as those proposed in the Extreme Dreams agreement. If Crevasse and Kakov selected this option, they would need to bring in a head guide, preferably European, to run the skiing operations. On a positive note, a small resort centre that met the standards required by Western travelers had been selected for accommodations in the area.

As far as medical care in case of accidents, both locations were within an hour of a major city and hospital. Less than an hour was well under the industry norm. In addition, all staff were required to take a comprehensive first aid course.

After discussions with many business ventures in the Soviet Union and with Extreme Dreams, Russki concluded that having the ability to pay for goods and services with hard currency would be a real asset if the situation were critical. Russki would use hard currency, where necessary, to ensure that the level of service was up to the standard required by an operation of this nature.

Crevasse and Kakov knew that selecting a compatible and productive partner would be a great benefit in this tough environment. Yet they had to remember that a partnership would not guarantee customer support for this venture in the Soviet environment or that the USSR would remain stable enough to function as an on-going concern.

The Decision

Crevasse and Kakov knew that it would take some time for the business to grow to the level of full capacity. They were willing to do whatever it took to make ends meet during the early years of the business. Because helicopter skiing was a seasonal business, they realized that they would need to find a supplementary source of income during the off-season, especially in the start-up phase.

However, they also were confident that, if they could find a way to make their plan work, they could be the ones to capitalize on the growing market. The Soviet Union had the right physical conditions for helicopter skiing, but the business environment would present difficulties. Moreover, the two partners were aware that starting a venture of this nature at any time was not an easy task. Starting it in the present state of the Soviet Union during a recession would only complicate their task further. Yet the timing was right for a new venture in the industry and, in general, they were encouraged by the potential of the business.

Crevasse and Kakov had to let all parties involved know of their decision by the end of the week. If they decided to go ahead with the venture, they had to move quickly if they wanted to be operational in the 1992 season. That night they had to decide if they would proceed, who they would select as partners if they went ahead, and how they would go. It was going to be a late night.

C ASE 29
S ALES AND M ERCHANDISING G ROUP

Introduction

The Sales and Merchandising Group (S&MG) was incorporated in June 1986. Originally, the firm consisted of a partnership between three individuals. Tony LaSorda, the chief executive officer and president, provided the energy, "sweat," and vision necessary for starting a new entrepreneurial company. Michael Preston and Leo Slocombe invested the needed venture capital besides supplying guidance and support.

Before assuming the helm of S&MG, LaSorda spent eight years with Procter and Gamble (P&G). After graduating in 1978 from the University of Windsor with an honours business degree, he joined P&G as a sales representative in the Toronto area. He quickly moved through the ranks, becoming a unit manager for Eastern Ontario, then sales merchandising category manager for Duncan Hines Cookies, later joining the brand management for the Duncan Hines brand, and finally, during his last year with P&G, became Ontario/Atlantic regional manager. In May 1986, at the age of 31, LaSorda left the company to pursue his goal of forming a unique, competitive contract merchandising firm.

By October 1988, the firm had expanded and was catering to the merchandising needs of Toronto-based national firms. S&MG managed merchandising campaigns in Ontario, the Maritimes, and to a limited extent in the western provinces. However, the company had yet to secure a contract to serve clients in the Quebec market. Management felt that in order to meet their ultimate goal of creating a Canadian national firm, S&MG would have to expand its operations both in Western Canada and the Quebec region. LaSorda and Jay Gordon, the vice president of operations, were considering the issues surrounding possible expansion and the timing of such moves.

The Industry and the Competition

At the time of the formation of the company, there existed few North American firms addressing the needs of the sales, merchandising, and promotional segment of the contractual market. Contract merchandising firms provided a reservoir of individuals to carry out specific merchandising tasks on behalf of different clients. These firms supplemented the client's existing sales force, freeing them to devote more time to their area of expertise, while providing a highly motivated

This case was prepared by Stephanie Coyles under the supervision of Professor P. R. Richardson, Queen's University, as the basis for class discussion rather than to illustrate either effective or ineffective handling of an administrative situation. Copyright Queen's University, Kingston, Ontario, 1989.

Exhibit 1 Competition Survey

BLS Retail Resource Group
Services
  Sales blitzes
  Merchandising, in-store merchandising, POS, in-store relaunch
  Research, similar inspection as A. C. Nielson, brand information, lower cost, another source for comparison to Neilson
  Combination short-term and long-term contractual relationship < 2 years
  Located in Montreal (60% of business), remainder in Toronto
History
  Business operational for 2 years
  One partner ex. Steinbergs and one partner ex. packaged goods firm
Employees
  Retired salespeople across Canada, ex. packaged goods firms
  Over 150 sales people nationally
  Average age 45-60
  Recruit through package goods firms' sales departments who contact them when individuals are about to retire
  Experience low turnover because employees put on new products and projects continually (monthly)
  No research done by employees
Competition
  Only company national in scope
  More into selling
Long-term strategy
  Hook up with strong American company from an investment point of view
  See fine line between traditional sales and merchandising and brokerage work
  Focus on Canada as a national broker

---

and skilled merchandising work force at a lower cost than could be done in-house. Typically, contract merchandisers supplied a combination of three basic services: (i) support the sales needs of the client by aiding in new product launches, blitzes, distribution drives, and trade awareness programs; (ii) provide merchandising services such as in-store displays, product relines and planograms, point-of-sale material placement, on-shelf product decal mounting, packaging replacement, product recalls, mystery shoppers, in addition to product sampling and couponing; (iii) information research. Some firms conducted retail audits, market evaluations, or provided overall marketing strategy consultation.

In 1988, there were seven major direct competitors to S&MG operating in Canada. They included Four Seasons Planned Promotions, In-Store Focus, National Features Services, ProToCal Communications, ProTemp Sales, BLS Retail Resource Group, and The Sales Support Company. A profile of the three major competitors is included in Exhibit 1. Most of these firms had been founded by partners with backgrounds from established marketing and merchandising companies such as Colgate, Eli Lilly, Nabisco, Steinbergs, and Procter & Gamble. Most of S&MG's competitors offered a syndicated service, typically assigning one sales representative simultaneously to several different product lines. This sharing resulted in large cost savings to the client.

S&MG also faced competition from their potential clients' established and integrated "in-house" sales and merchandising work force. Although these

Exhibit 1 (concluded)

ProToCal Communications
Services
  2 divisions
    Contract sales service to doctors/dentists/nurses, −5 years old
    Retail merchandising division, 4 years old
  Specialize in drug store merchandising; some department work
  Access over 1,600 stores across Canada
  Selling function somewhat similar to a broker relationship
  Help client develop marketing plans
  Merchandising paid on a per visit basis
History
  Past president of a Canadian drug company (Eli Lilly) and involved in marketing
  Have an accumulated 75 years in the drug store business
Employees
  Have field supervisors, regional supervisors, and divisional managers
  Merchandisers are all women, mostly housewives who are working for supplementary income; typical is between late 30s
    to 50s, average work week 24 hours
  Experience a very low turnover rate, variety of projects
  Employees may work for other companies at the same time but must guarantee they won't work for competitors
The Sales Support Company
Services
  In business of sales and merchandising service
  Offer a temporary/contractual service for packaged goods
  Have both seasonal and long-term relationships
Clients
  Broad range but tend to stick with large companies
  Offer services across Canada, concentration in Ontario
  Referred to through word of mouth
History
  Two partners; extensive backgrounds in packaged goods from Nabisco
  Company formed on December 1, 1986
Employees
  40 employees in field
  Insists people have sales/marketing background to ensure their service is the best possible

groups may not offer the extensive information services provided by the contract merchandisers, their "in-house" work force was usually highly dedicated and likely had extensive knowledge of their own product lines.

S&MG's Competitive Advantages

LaSorda examined the industry in North America and abroad and decided initially to design S&MG's services to reflect those offered by a successful and innovative contract merchandiser operating in England. Since then, S&MG evolved into a unique operation offering two basic products to its clients on a permanent and seasonal basis: the management of field merchandising personnel and the gathering and compilation of information regarding the product's distribution, sales and competition. The management team believed that the firm outperformed its competitors because of its five major strengths:

1. Strong strategic positioning.
2. Company culture.
3. Human resource development.
4. Treatment of information as a resource.
5. International affiliations.

The company's mission statement reflected management's dedication to the continual development and refinement of these strengths:

> S&MG is a profitable, highly entrepreneurial, demonstrably superior sales service organization which, in close partnership with our clients, delivers unique competitive advantages. At S&MG our people make the difference. Our commitment is to the personal growth and professional development of all personnel by encouraging teamwork, continual training and challenge in an environment that is dynamic and fun.
> WE MAKE A DIFFERENCE

Strategic Positioning

Unlike the majority of its competitors, S&MG offered a dedicated and strategic service. The senior management at S&MG worked closely with the client firm to create the appropriate promotional or merchandising plan to meet the client's specific needs. Being able to "value add" was an important competitive advantage. S&MG did not, in principle, accept as a client a firm that was in direct competition with an existing customer.

With its "dedicated" approach, S&MG uniquely assigned a dedicated group of trained field personnel to the client. In contrast, most of S&MG's competitors followed a "syndicated" or "broker" approach, whereby the field personnel worked for several different companies at the same time. While this syndicated approach would be lower cost to the individual client company and more profit for the merchandising firm, S&MG felt that the client company did not receive the same quality of work as a dedicated approach because the field personnel were concerned about the priorities of four or five different companies. With S&MG's dedicated approach, virtually all of the people working on a client's merchandising program worked exclusively for that client, and therefore the client felt an ownership to the merchandising firm and felt very much in control of its priorities. The dedicated approach permitted S&MG to develop a long-term agency partnership with the client, leading to stable contracts similar to an ad agency arrangement with marketing personnel. It also provided a higher degree of operating flexibility than the syndicated approach since field personnel represented an entirely variable cost, which could be managed as circumstances dictated. At the same time, larger clients were required to support the cost of a dedicated service.

Company Culture

Because of their distinct services and strategic positioning, S&MG had been able to foster a strong company culture. All employees, especially those in the field, were encouraged to understand the S&MG philosophy of offering a "cadillac" service to their clients. To this end, the firm took great pride in fostering a professional and entrepreneurial image by hiring outstanding employees and developing appropriate training procedures and follow-up. Furthermore, the location and decor of their office was designed to project the image and reinforce the credibility of the firm. Time and resources were devoted to creating the appropriate interior design. The overall colour scheme, lighting, and modern office furniture were vital components.

Human Resources

As a service firm, the quality of S&MG's product depended heavily on the performance of their employees, whether it be senior management, the full-time employees, or the permanent part-time field personnel.

Management.   The firm prided itself on the expertise it had been able to attract and develop at the management level. By relying on relationships built during his employment at Procter & Gamble, LaSorda was able to recruit key personnel to the point where the majority of senior management were former employees of P&G. They included Michael Foley (vice president, director, sales technology), Jay Gordon (vice president, operations), and Howard Craig (general manager, seasonal sales division). Alison Brown (director of field operations) had experience in training and sales from Revlon International, Clairol, and Elizabeth Arden.

Full-Time Employees.   All employment contracts at S&MG included an explicit clause stating that full-time employees would share in a percentage of any excess profits above a set hurdle rate (approximately 20 percent). The actual allocation was based on seniority, responsibility, and performance, with the lower-level employees receiving priority in the profit-sharing plan.

Quarterly planning and information meetings were held in which all account managers and senior management participated. Ideas on client promotions, training, and short-term strategy revolving around existing business were exchanged. Senior management also provided information on new clients and revenue at these meetings.

Permanent Part-Time Field Personnel.   For its success, S&MG depended on the professionalism of its field personnel since they were the backbone of the service rendered. They executed all the merchandising activities at the store level. This group of individuals was responsible for organizing the store displays and gathering the product information. For this reason, the company developed an extensive recruiting, training, and supervisory plan.

Although recruiting activities were the responsibility of each account coordinator, certain basic steps were followed. Potential candidates were reached through newspaper advertisements, word of mouth, and on-campus recruiting. Most permanent part-time employees tended to be either retirees or homemakers reentering the work force and seeking flexible hours. Seasonal summer employees were most often university students. In some instances, both the client and S&MG were jointly involved in recruitment activities.

Once selection was completed, the recruits underwent an intensive training and orientation program. Training packages for the field personnel were developed by S&MG in cooperation with the client firm. During this period, the field worker was instructed about S&MG and its commitment to professionalism. Client background and extensive product information, as well as detailed job requirements and work methods, were supplied. For the first few weeks, supervisors worked closely with the new recruits.

Field personnel were made to feel like part of the S&MG team through planned meetings and group activities. This form of team building was extremely important because the field personnel had limited day-to-day contact with their supervisors or each other.

Salaries and compensation packages were not uniform. They varied with geographic location, client, product, and employee experience.

Information as a Resource

Senior management believed that the gathering and compilation of data into useful and timely information was one aspect of S&MG's operations that differentiated it markedly from its closest competitors. Although the information supplied could be considered similar to that offered by the larger market research firms such as A.C. Nielson, management viewed their service as complementary. A.C. Nielson's audits were produced on a bimonthly basis and contained an abundance of data, weighted toward high-volume stores, whereas S&MG customized its reports to reflect the specific needs of its client. Summary periodic reports listing distribution, sales, shelf positioning, inventory, sell-through, and competitor information were compiled. The system also produced an exceptions report. These reports were delivered on average every four weeks.

The system ran on an upgraded IBM system 36, model D processor with specifically designed software purchased from a merchandising firm from the United Kingdom. Parts of the software could be tailored to meet the consumer's specific regional and product needs within three days.

This information service was part of the basic merchandising package offered when S&MG accepted a client. The company did not offer the competitive analysis as a separate and distinct service. S&MG's senior management believed that this service helped to retain clients because once a consumer of S&MG's merchandising services realized the value of the information provided, they were

EXHIBIT 2 **International Contract Merchandising Affiliates**

Country	Name	Type
France	AZ Promotions	Syndicated
United Kingdom	Ellert Retail Ops Services Ltd.	Syndicated
	CPM (Counter Products Mktg.)	Dedicated
	TMG (The Merchandising Group)	Dedicated
Germany	PPD (Promotion Product and Display)	Dedicated
Italy	The Promotion Center	Syndicated
Spain	Promotion Y Communicacion S.A.	Syndicated
Australia	Creative Sales	Syndicated

more likely to remain a permanent client. For clients to develop a similar information capability in-house would be expensive and time-consuming.

Foreign Affiliates

One other competitive advantage was S&MG's affiliation with several leading merchandising companies in France, the United Kingdom, Italy, Spain, and Australia (see Exhibit 2). As the sole Canadian representative in the European-based group IPSAS, S&MG benefited from contact with leading edge merchandising companies, and assisted the firm to develop an international reputation. The contract merchandising firms belonging to the IPSAS group were typically smaller, family-run businesses. Senior management from S&MG participated regularly in the annual conferences organized for members of IPSAS.

Current Situation

Since its first year of operation in 1986, S&MG had grown from three managers and 1 field employee to a firm with 63 full-time employees, 175 permanent part-time field personnel, and an additional 180 summer seasonal students. The firm's head office was located in Mississauga, Ontario, within a new corporate development housing similar entrepreneurial businesses, as well as doctors', dentists', and lawyers' offices. This location was selected to properly reflect the company's adherence to quality and professionalism. The office was designed to be visually appealing and to provide S&MG with a suitable environment in which to make presentations to potential clients.

Clients

To date the firm had catered primarily to the needs of corporations with head offices in Toronto. Most clients were solicited through personal contacts and word of mouth, although a direct mail campaign was developed and implemented. The firm's focus was on consumer goods firms because of senior management's extensive knowledge, expertise, and identification with this area (see Exhibit 3).

For the first year or so, the firm's activities were concentrated in Ontario. The firm was now managing clients' operations in eastern Canada. Furthermore, S&MG had been awarded contracts to implement merchandising programs in the western provinces for clients including Minolta, Video One, and Foster Grant. S&MG had not, as yet, managed any programs within the large Quebec market.

S&MG's largest client was the Neilson Cadbury group, part of the specialties division of the George Weston Limited, a conglomerate with diversified interests in food processing, food distribution, and resource operations. Neilson Cadbury produced such well-known brands as Caramilk, the number-one selling chocolate bar in Canada, Crispy Crunch, and Crunchie, as well as a variety of dairy products.

In June 1987, S&MG took over all of Neilson Cadbury's merchandising employees in the Ontario region and began to manage their operations full-time. Neilson Cadbury's employees became S&MG employees although they were still dedicated to merchandising the clients' products. In September 1987, S&MG was awarded a similar contract for the Maritimes. The Neilson Cadbury account was responsible for approximately 40 percent of S&MG's revenue. By

---

EXHIBIT 3   S&MG Clients

Company	Product Category	Trade Channels
S&MG Permanent Year-Round Clients		
B.C. Packers	Frozen entrees/canned fish	Grocery
Fisher-Price	Toys, juvenile products	Department stores, mass merchandisers, toy stores
Foster Grant	Sunglasses/reading glasses	Drug stores, mass merchandisers
Minolta	Photography and video equipment	Department stores, mass merchandisers, camera shops
Neilson Cadbury	Confectionery	Convenience stores, drug stores, grocery
Ontario Milk Marketing Board	Milk promotions	Schools, restaurants
Video One	Prerecorded video cassettes	Mass merchandisers
S&MG Seasonal Clients		
Quaker Oats–Gatorade		
Pepsi-Cola		
Fisher-Price		
Dairy Bureau of Canada		
General Foods		

growing rapidly, S&MG intended to develop its client base to offset its reliance on this client.

Pricing Strategy

S&MG offered a premium-priced product which was justified by management because of the superior quality of services provided by the firm. The price of the service was determined on a cost plus a management fee basis. This approach allowed the client to consult with S&MG whenever it desired at no additional cost, thus fostering loyalty and long-term commitment. Competitors typically charged on a per call basis. Because the services offered by S&MG tended to be higher priced than the competition, most of its clients tended to be larger, well-established firms.

Organizational Structure

Shares in the firm were divided unequally among five individuals. Preston and Slocombe were investors only and did not participate directly in the day-to-day management of the firm. The remaining three individuals shared the operating responsibilities. LaSorda was chief executive officer and president. Foley, vice president, director, sales technology, became a partner in December 1987. Gordon joined the firm in late 1987 to head up a proposed brokerage business (since deferred) and assumed the position of vice president, operations.

   Although information and short-term strategy sessions were held quarterly with the account managers and other senior managers, long-term strategic decision making was limited to the three operational partners and the investors.

   The structure of the company reflected its rapid growth and need for continual reorganization to satisfy the needs of the management (see Exhibit 4). Although the organizational chart was designed to reflect a hierarchy of authority among the permanent employees at head office, management tried to instill a feeling of being part of a team, stressing communication between the employees and vice presidents and president. As a result, the span of involvement of the top management group was much wider than reflected in the direct reporting relationships, on the organization chart.

Other Business Interests

Carts of Canada.   In November 1987, Neilson Cadbury approached S&MG to enquire if the firm was interested in entering into a partnership for street and special event sales of premium quality Haagen-Dazs ice cream bars. This would be an expansion for Neilson Cadbury, who already owned the rights to the

EXHIBIT 4 S&MG Organizational Structure

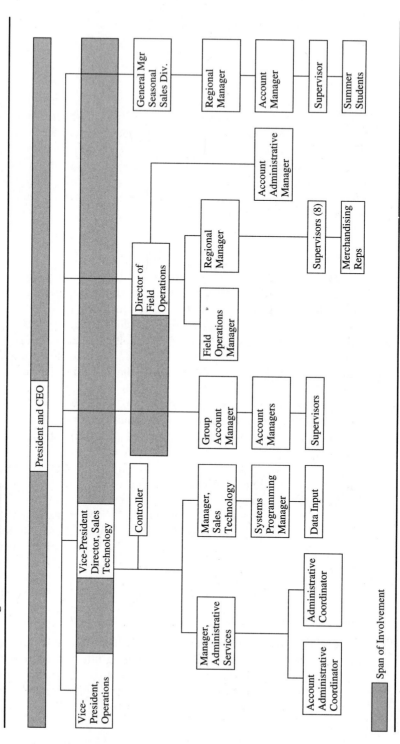

Span of Involvement

in-store sales of the ice-cream bars. S&MG conducted preliminary research in New York and Dallas and, based on the U.S. success rate, concluded that there would be a good market for a similar product in Canada and agreed to form a partnership.

By February 1988, a business plan for this venture was formulated. The product would be marketed through a fleet of "classy" street carts at a premium price of $2.50 per bar. The street carts would be located in downtown Toronto and at special summer events. The initial capital outlay included 15 carts at a cost of $5,000 each (as compared to an average Dickie Dee cart cost of approximately $800) a leased van, one small and one large trailer, and a rented large storage freezer. Instead of young teenagers, first- and second-year university students were employed on a salary plus commission basis. Operations began just prior to the May long weekend.

The partnership encountered many problems. First, licensing regulations governing street sales meant that key downtown street corner locations were "locked up" by other vendors. Second, the summer was hotter than normal and consumers tended not to leave their air-conditioned offices or to buy a product that melted quickly. Third, since demand was not high enough to warrant production in Canada, the product was imported from the United States, incurring an import duty of 27 percent. Furthermore, the firm had to have the Haagen-Dazs bars repackaged in Canada in order to comply with Canadian health regulations. As a result, material costs increased from $.93 to $1.08. Salaries and expenses accounted for an additional 57 percent of sales revenue. By the end of October 1988, the partnership was dissolved and the business disbanded. S&MG recorded a loss of over $86,000 on this failed venture.

Brokerage Activities.   As previously mentioned, Gordon was recruited to head up the brokerage business. A study of the Canadian market had shown that there were only regional brokers and senior management felt that a natural extension of their current business would be to provide brokerage services on a national basis. In this manner, S&MG would become the agent for the manufacturer, serving as a go-between to the wholesalers.

By January 1988, the brokerage idea was shelved indefinitely. A report compiled by a group of MBA students in the spring of 1988 strongly advocated that S&MG remain focused on current business and build on its strengths. Management agreed that S&MG did not want to spread too thin its limited financial, computer, and human resources. It was also believed that there would be inherent contradictions between a dedicated merchandising sales force and a retail sales force. Moreover, the estimated cost of establishing a brokerage business was $500,000.

Financial Position

For 1986, its first calendar year of operation, the firm had total sales of $234,000 and experienced a loss of $97,500. In 1987, S&MG had sales of

EXHIBIT 5

S&MG
Statement of Revenue and Expenses for January 1988 through December 1988

	Jan. 88	Feb. 88	Mar. 88	Apr. 88	May. 88	Jun. 88
Revenue						
Neilson Cadbury	$ 152,375	127,375	134,219	127,375	140,113	145,113
Ontario Milk Marketing Board	10,499	16,900	30,736	27,985	20,358	33,504
Foster Grant		19,075	13,171	17,713	17,826	19,472
Video One		3,000	6,000	13,375	11,216	10,010
Colgate			3,000	6,375	7,025	9,378
Minolta				3,000	6,500	6,795
B C Packers						
Quaker	10,000	30,300	17,879	18,214	88,501	93,500
Communique		14,000	10,000	8,000	71,500	71,500
Dairy Bureau				3,500	24,740	48,099
Pepsi					41,350	64,245
H & PG			1,600			2,500
Fisher Price						
General Food		5,000			10,000	4,300
Miscellaneous	8,400	9,620	(20,000)			
Total Revenue	181,274	225,270	196,605	225,537	439,129	508,416
Field costs						
Field wages & benefits	83,356	91,667	120,420	131,608	191,954	221,537
Field car allowances						
Other direct field expenses	36,256	66,530	9,910	55,447	67,810	91,666
Recruiting/training	2,185	1,279	2,862	3,892	14,584	1,150
Equipment/supplies	1,892	5,057	4,900	3,501	4,186	8,826
Office services						
Data input		2,698	2,720	1,839	3,075	2,294
Set-up costs		2,207	(2,093)			
Total field costs	123,689	169,438	138,719	196,287	281,609	325,473
Central costs						
Admin salaries & benefits	48,763	23,625	33,148	30,489	39,647	45,487
Admin car allowances	3,000	3,000	3,000	3,000	3,000	3,000
Admin business expenses	11,308	3,105	1,265	2,435	2,066	4,037
Admin telephone & communications	1,467	768	798	751	1,273	971
Admin postage & courier	8,903	(3,593)	1,077	596	361	822
Admin office supplies	2,137	5,896	4,344	3,891	3,001	7,685
Building lease & maintenance	9,509	8,380	9,249	8,644	8,978	9,481
Equipment rental & maintenance	238		313	2,213	2,037	7,208
Computer maintenance						
Depreciation expenses					7,574	20,642
Membership & subscriptions		325	486	277	164	2,168
Professional development		1,011	860	260	48	1,360
Recruiting expense						
System special project	2,520	6,000	3,299	3,043	(2,950)	
Insurance		(107)		14	14	14
Legal & accounting	1,854	750	5,000	6,649	12,329	15,519
Promotion expenses				2,482	2,500	2,463
Business taxes & capital taxes			371	370	371	166
Donation						295
Bank charges & interest		2,021	2,265	2,449	2,815	2,928
Shareholder loan interest expense	6,900	4,000	2,900	2,900	2,900	4,295
Miscellaneous expenses		1,163	190	271	303	9,590
Interest & other income				(106)	(572)	(4,166)
Technology service charge-out						
Total central costs	96,599	56,344	68,565	70,628	85,859	133,964
Overhead allocation to Carts of Canada			(8,167)	(8,167)	(8,167)	(8,167)
Profit before income taxes	(39,014)	(512)	(2,512)	(33,211)	79,828	57,146

	Jul. 88	Aug. 88	Sep. 88	Oct. 88	Nov. 88	Dec. 88	Total Jan–Dec. 88
						Projected	
	133,744	146,482	144,081	128,100	136,200	144,104	1,659,281
	25,717	24,010	30,163	31,132	39,121	23,561	313,686
	14,161	20,029	20,820	38,326	21,353	37,765	239,711
	9,555	11,965	16,926	18,655	15,850	12,770	129,322
	13,823	15,140	14,482	16,526	15,583	17,822	119,154
	15,855	17,365	16,610	15,855	12,470	11,550	106,000
		6,532	10,148	10,151	10,635	12,363	49,829
	89,352	63,750	7,246			862	419,604
	68,250	56,784	6,139				306,173
	46,411	45,000	10,643		3,000	5,000	186,393
	74,905	53,675	1,649				235,824
	2,546	20,750	(750)		200		26,846
		23,515	28,327	47,585	45,054	37,423	181,904
		1,610		11,000	16,000	16,000	63,910
				20,456	7,996	2,881	29,353
	494,319	506,607	306,484	337,786	323,462	322,101	4,066,990
	261,583	274,789	148,231	158,470	159,835	192,944	2,036,394
	38,916	48,222	34,800	24,085	23,255	26,184	195,462
	45,388	64,967	44,199	55,732	33,470	35,105	606,480
	750	234	7,603	2,283	5,371	3,202	45,395
	8,110	7,312	6,627	2,778	8,142	3,639	64,970
	2,520	5,758	1,518	5,146	4,016	5,022	23,980
	2,884	1,525	5,444	2,836	980	1,341	27,636
							114
	360,150	402,807	248,422	251,330	235,069	267,437	3,000,430
	52,681	51,068	48,085	50,777	48,050	38,375	510,195
	2,795	2,808	2,513	2,920	3,341	2,262	34,639
	9,353	4,830	9,511	7,636	4,825	6,083	66,454
	501	1,940	892	844	2,236	1,480	13,921
	404	300	135	458	245	193	9,900
	2,693	4,309	4,373	1,862	4,299	4,742	49,232
	9,365	9,065	9,387	9,092	9,054	9,258	109,462
	0	2,820	1,726	2,009	3,113	6,607	28,284
	(367)	338	328	467	358	1,596	2,720
	5,464	5,444	5,444	5,489	5,600	4,035	59,692
	62	424	328	673	959	692	6,558
	0	1,053	19	0	0	448	5,059
	0	0		0	0	0	0
	316	0	613	0	0	0	12,841
	514	514	514	496	842	679	3,494
	2,100	2,300	3,000	2,400	3,500	2,800	58,201
	0	0		160	0	0	7,605
	412	412	412	0	0	0	2,514
	0	0		1,250	0	0	1,545
	2,802	2,983	2,941	2,724	2,616	2,879	29,423
	2,960	3,000	3,000	3,000	3,100	4,166	43,121
	43	0	144	2,328	541	3,539	18,112
	(5,241)	(16,113)	(8,445)	(4,823)	(2,964)	(2,421)	(44,851)
	(1,365)	0	(2,253)	(2,836)	(980)	(1,341)	(8,775)
	85,493	77,495	82,667	86,926	88,735	86,072	1,019,348
	(8,167)	(8,167)	(8,167)	(8,167)			(65,336)
	56,842	34,472	(16,438)	7,697	(342)	(31,408)	112,548

	Partnership loss	(86,781)
	Income before tax, after partnership loss	25,767

$2,340,000 and a loss of $65,000. During the first 10 months of 1988, the firm had total sales of $3,421,427 and profit before tax of $144,298 (see Exhibit 5). Because of the allocation of expenses, S&MG projected a slight loss during the last two months for total sales just over $4.0 million and a profit of just over $25,000.

At the end of September 1988, S&MG had outstanding loans of $260,000 to local banks and $306,000 to the original venture capitalists. Although the company performed better than the shareholders originally anticipated, the company was not in a strong financial position and thus any decisions to expand, grow, or invest had to be carefully evaluated.

Future Interests

As S&MG's senior management looked to the future, their long-term goal was to become an international contract merchandising firm, servicing the needs of its clients in all Canadian provinces as well as the vast U.S. market.

In order to attain these goals, the firm had to expand its current operations to better meet the needs of its western clients and also address the differences in the Quebec market. Operating in these markets would allow S&MG to gain experience outside the familiar Toronto environment. The company could then apply the knowledge to anticipate possible expansion problems before entering the United States. However, management did not wish to undertake projects that would financially endanger the company. The strategic challenge for the company was to decide what advantages there were to a move and when the respective moves should be taken.

Canadian Environment

At the end of October 1988, Canada was poised to return the Conservative government to another four years in power. This would result in the passing of the Canada–United States Free Trade Agreement (FTA), which would increase competitive pressures for Canadian firms such as S&MG. U.S.–based merchandising competitors would be able to offer their services on equal terms to both American and Canadian firms operating in the Canadian market. However, the FTA could also serve to increase the number of potential clients, as U.S. firms looked for a national merchandiser who could handle all their Canadian needs.

Another issue facing the firm was the forecast of an economic slowdown. Even though unemployment figures were dropping, interest rates were on the rise, reaching levels of 11.75 percent in late September, their highest level in two and one-half years. Canada was experiencing record GNP growth, but the Conference Board of Canada was predicting that both the Canadian and the U.S. economies would slow down in 1989. Many economic wizards were forecasting a recession by the early 1990s.

Western Canada

Regionally, provincial unemployment was up in all western provinces except Alberta. The boom that Alberta was experiencing was forecasted to be short-lived if the recovery in oil prices did not remain. Growth was expected to be moderate in Alberta and British Columbia, and Saskatchewan was projected to contract.

S&MG management felt that, although there was potential for growth in the West, the firm was reasonably able to service its clients in this area out of Toronto. In general, most consumer goods companies maintained their Canadian head offices in Toronto, whereas most head offices situated in Vancouver or Calgary were resource based. It was felt that there did not exist the same type of "chez-nous" mentality as in Quebec, and that branch offices in the West were comfortable dealing with a Toronto-based firm. Furthermore, there was limited competition from regionally based merchandisers.

Certain problems arose because of time zone differences and the distance between the account manager (Toronto) and the field workers (western provinces), which limited direct feedback and contact. If business was to continue to grow, however, some form of improved management would have to be developed to increase supervision of an expanded work force in the West.

Quebec

Economic Environment

In the fall of 1988, all economic indicators were forecasting increased activity within the Quebec market. Unemployment in Quebec was down to around 9 percent, still higher than Ontario's 5 percent, but offering a large pool of trained workers. Economic growth was forecast to be 3.5 percent (Ontario 3.6 percent) in 1988 and 2 percent in 1989. The province was poised to benefit from the impending FTA as the number of small entrepreneurial firms continued to grow in number. The federal government had boosted the Quebec economy with large investments since the early 1980s. As Canada's second largest province, Quebec possessed many opportunities for growth.

Competition

Preliminary research conducted by Mike Foley indicated that there was little competition for S&MG at the level of quality of services it provided. Only two other firms operated in the Montreal market. The first, located in an industrial park, was a regional branch of the national firm, ProTemp. It had limited resources, employing five full-time people with access only to a single Macintosh personal computer. It was felt that this firm was more product than service oriented, with very little informational service. The second, BLS Retail Resource

---

EXHIBIT 6 Potential Quebec-Based Clients

Abbott Labs	Corby's	Loto Quebec
Agropour	Culinar	Maple Sugar Producers
Air Canada	Dole Foods	Meagers Distillers
Les Aliments Hygrade	FBI Foods	Medis
Atlantic Promotions (housewares)	Fuller Tools	Merck Frost
Avon Canada	Gattuso	Michelin Tires
Ayerst Laboratories	Gillette	La Brasserie Molson
Banque D'Epargne	Le Group RONA	Reader's Digest
BASF	Hitachi Canada	Reynolds Aluminum
Bell Canada	Imperial Tobacco	Shenley Canada
Bovril Canada (food products)	IPL, Inc. (housewares)	Seagram Quebec
La Brasserie O'Keefe	Johnson & Johnson, Inc.	SICO
Brothers International	Kraft	Sources Monclair
Catelli	Labatts	Via Rail Canada
Clairol Canada	Lactantia	Societe des Alcools
Clouston Foods	Laurential Lab.	Gouvernement du Quebec
Coorch		

Group (Ressource au Detail), was also dismissed as being nonaggressive (see Exhibit 1).

Potential Clients

Even after the mass exodus from Montreal in the mid-70s, many large corporations maintained head offices in Montreal (see Exhibit 6). Furthermore, the regional offices of Canadian companies in Quebec were often relatively independent and operated similar to a head office. Therefore, there existed two different classes of potential clients within Quebec: the provincial operations of existing clients and new Quebec-based clients.

An informal survey was conducted to see if there was interest in the services offered by S&MG. This survey was met with enthusiasm. Most executives questioned felt that there would be a need for merchandising support in their companies.

Montreal Office

In the past, when S&MG had tried to expand its business into the Quebec market, it had often come up against a wall. Senior management believed that the chez-nous mentality limited their potential to make inroads into the market so long as they operated out of the Toronto head office. In order to appeal to Quebec executives, S&MG would have to locate an office in Montreal and would have to appear to be from the province.

There would be definite advantages to locating an office in Montreal. S&MG would be viewed as a truly national company, supplementing its current strategic advantages. Furthermore, it would give the company experience in operating an office in a different environment, in preparation for eventual expansion into the United States. Finally, profit claimed in Quebec is subject to a 5–6 percent lower tax rate than in the province of Ontario.

However, the establishment of an office in Montreal would bring about large financial, opportunity, and resource costs. Management had estimated that the overhead costs for a year of operation would be approximately $320,000, and the initial capital investment would be $75,000. In order to break even, the firm would need to generate sales of over $1.2 million within the first year. If Quebec met these sales objectives, management forecast that in 1989, the company would generate $6.1 million in sales revenue with a net profit of $310,000.

It was essential that management thoroughly examine all issues before committing to the expansion.

First Issue: *Reality of the Chez-Nous Mentality*

Based on their own personal experience, the partners believed that before it could appeal to Quebec-based nationals, it would have to be located in the province. However, S&MG had never targeted Montreal firms with information or presentations. Management felt that it was essential to their credibility to be able to bring potential clients to a well-established, French-speaking, professional office. Although clients such as Foster Grant, Minolta, Fisher Price, and Pepsi/Gatorade had committed in the fall to Quebec programs even without the office, S&MG's major client, Neilson Cadbury, appeared reluctant to give the company its Quebec-based merchandising business until a local office was established. Was there some other way to appeal to the Quebec based executive and market S&MG's services? Would they be best managed out of Toronto or Montreal?

Second Issue: *S&MG's Company Culture and Quebec*

The second issue S&MG's management had to evaluate was how compatible the company's culture was with that of Quebec. Could the firm operate in a French environment? In order to comply with Bill 101, a firm with over 50 employees must operate completely in the French language. For S&MG, this would require the translation of all memos, training manuals, and computer software packages. Communication problems would be intensified, since most Toronto management, especially at the senior level, only spoke English. The smaller national accounts based in Quebec would still be managed from the head office, and they would require overseeing a unilingual French work force. Communication would be further strained by the distance factor. Senior management in charge of the Montreal office would no longer be able to participate in S&MG's informal strategy sessions.

An additional concern was the ability of S&MG to work with Francophone clients to create the appropriate merchandising or promotional campaign. Since the ideas for these modifications often originated from LaSorda and Gordon, both English-speaking Torontonians, management had to decide if it would be able to develop programs that would reflect the French culture.

A further issue centred around the corporate ideals of belonging to "part of a team." Quebec was known for wanting to be independent and original. How would the firm overcome this culture difference? How would the Quebec office "fit" into the existing structure?

Third Issue: Can the Firm Generate the Needed Business?

S&MG was already guaranteed the Quebec contracts for Fisher Price, Foster Grant, Minolta, and Pepsi/Gatorade even without an office in Montreal. If a local office was established, it was understood that these campaigns would be managed through this office. However, these clients would not alone generate the needed $1.2 million. Furthermore, the company would only be shifting their sales revenue, not creating new revenue sources. In effect, the Montreal office would be taking Toronto revenue.

In order for the Montreal office to break even, it was necessary for the company to gain the Neilson Cadbury contract for Quebec (estimated annual revenues of $750,000). Without an office in Quebec, S&MG executives believed they would not receive this key account. Based on their successfully managed Ontario and Maritimes campaign, the firm was confident that with a Montreal office, they could attract Neilson Cadbury's Quebec business. However, there was no guarantee. Should the firm proceed without a guarantee or should it wait? What contingency plans should be developed?

If they should receive the Neilson Cadbury contract, an additional sub-issue would have to be faced. As in the case of Ontario and the Maritimes, S&MG would be taking over a group of employees who did not mesh with their current permanent part-time employee mould. Previously, these employees were used to being relatively unsupervised and independent. S&MG would have to develop a plan to help orientate their newly acquired employees and develop loyalty to S&MG. In so doing, the firm could face an anti-Ontario mentality.

Fourth Issue: How Much Independence Should the Montreal Office Exert?

In order for the firm to operate effectively in the Quebec market, management felt that the office had to be perceived as being Francophone. This created two questions: (1) Should the Montreal office operate under a unique name? (2) Who should head up the new office?

Unique Name. The firm had two obvious options for a Quebec name. It could translate the existing Sales and Merchandising Group name into French or it could adopt a uniquely French title. Direct translation would result in the new firm being able to trade on the goodwill built into the S&MG name. Although not currently operating within the Quebec market, the S&MG logo would be recognizable to most nationally based firms and would lend credence to its search for business. In French the translation was Groupes de Ventes et de Commercialisation.

The alternative was to search for a unique identity. The firm could no longer trade on its reputation, but was more likely to be viewed as a Quebec-based operation. However, this could create conflict with the existing company culture by encouraging the Montreal office to consider itself a separate identity from the Toronto firm.

Manager of the Montreal Office.   Again there were two options available: hire from outside or promote from within. Two potential candidates were identified from outside. Both were French Canadian, had an understanding of the operations within the Quebec market, and had industry expertise and local market contacts. Their skills would complement those lacking within the Toronto senior management. They were both viewed as entrepreneurial and highly skilled.

Management viewed compensation and motivation as potential problems. If S&MG hired from outside the firm, they would have to develop the appropriate incentive program. At the time, the accounting system was not automated. Therefore, in order to calculate bonuses based on Montreal performance, two sets of books and accounts would have to be maintained. This could create a negative form of competition between the two offices. Moreover, senior management did not want to dilute the partnership any further and therefore did not want to offer stock as an incentive.

Another problem was a perceived loss of control over the evolution of the culture of the office. An important task would be to train new Quebec employees in "the S&MG way" right from the birth of the new company. Finally, there was the fear of a loss of security. If an appropriate compensation and motivation plan could not be developed, would the "Quebec lieutenants" ultimately leave and go into direct competition with the firm?

The second option was to staff from within and modify the current corporate structure. The candidate under consideration was Foley, current vice president, director, sales technology. Foley was originally from Montreal, single, had no direct ties to Toronto and was a graduate of McGill University. His supervisory duties in Toronto could be assumed by Tony LaSorda and Jay Gordon. Steve Keech, manager, sales technology was accomplishing most of Foley's information technology–related responsibilities in the Toronto office.

Foley's background with the company was in information technology, but he was perceived to be a very good operations-type manager, possessing the appropriate skills to set up a new business. He was well versed in company culture, possessed an understanding of the Quebec market, and was fluently bilingual. Furthermore, he was already a partner and therefore had a vested interest in the success of the whole company and not just the Montreal office.

If Foley were assigned to Montreal, head office would lose one of its partners. Much of the decision making was already too concentrated. In addition, because he was English-Canadian, he would likely encounter some resistance from potential Francophone clients. This would be further intensified by a possible credibility gap created with clients because of his relatively young age. Finally, he did not have extensive business contacts in Quebec and had limited experience dealing with recruitment of clients.

Conclusion

As LaSorda and Gordon sat finishing their meals and their bottle of wine at their monthly tête-á-tête, they considered how fast and successfully S&MG had grown and prospered within its first three years of operation. However, they realized that the full potential of the Canadian market could not be realized without some form of representation in Quebec and/or the western region. Unfortunately, they were not completely satisfied that this was the correct time for the firm to expand.

CASE 30
SID'S SUNFLOWER SEEDS LTD.

Introduction

In late 1988, Issy Steen, president and owner of Sid's Sunflower Seeds (Sid's) of Regina, Saskatchewan, sat down to assess the results and progress for the year. The assessment was particularly important as Steen had made a major move during the year by signing, in March 1988, an agreement that made Sid's the "official supplier of sunflower seed of Major League Baseball."

Steen had regarded the agreement as a great opportunity but after signing the agreement, he became concerned about certain implications of the decision, such as the need to expand the plant and the availability of raw materials. Steen had to decide how to deal with these concerns, and perhaps even whether he should attempt to withdraw from the agreement.

Company History

Sid's Sunflower Seeds was established in 1938 by Sid Bercovich, who saw an opportunity to capitalize on the growing popularity of sunflower seeds. Bercovich established a small production line in his garage and an office in his house. Sid's manufactured and sold one product: roasted and salted sunflower seeds in the shell. All selling and distribution functions were personally undertaken by Bercovich. This limited growth and initially restricted distribution to Regina.

The post–World War II affluent society and demographics fostered snack and confectionary foods. The market for pet foods also expanded over this period. Bercovich broadened his company's distribution to Saskatoon, Saskatchewan, and points in between with all of the selling still done personally, by Bercovich, or through word of mouth. Orders were filled on an "as available" basis. This nonaggressive approach to marketing and customer service resulted in small but stable growth. Eventually, the business was moved from Bercovich's garage to an older but larger facility in northeast Regina, which allowed for increased storage of raw materials and finished goods.

By the end of 1973, gross sales reached $300,000. Sales were seasonal, peaking in the summer months. During peak production periods, Sid's employed over 50 people. All processing and packaging was done manually from one seed roaster and one packaging line. Seeds were packaged in popcorn-like paper bags

This case was written by C. Brooke Dobni of the University of Saskatchewan as a basis for class discussion rather than to illustrate either effective or ineffective handling of an administrative problem. Some of the financial and other data has been disguised to protect the integrity of the business. Copyright Brooke Dobni and came in two sizes, 200 and 500 grams. After a bag was filled, it was then stapled shut and placed in boxes for shipment.

Market penetration was still confined to Saskatchewan. There was very little competition for sunflower seeds in Saskatchewan, and Bercovich had no desire to expand geographically. Any increase in sales was generally developed and not acquired from the competition.

In 1974, Issy Steen purchased Sid's from Bercovich, who lived in the same apartment building as Steen. By this time, the plant was old and dilapidated. The only significant piece of equipment was the seed roaster. The transition of ownership was also strained by the fact that Bercovich had wanted to back out of the deal at the last minute. Steen refused, so Bercovich pulled all of the corporate records prior to the transfer and refused to introduce Steen to the production process. Steen knew absolutely nothing about the business or related markets and within weeks of the sale, all 50 of the production staff refused to return to work because Steen would not agree to an employment contract. Steen recounts:

> I did not know who I was selling to or who I was buying raw materials from or even how to manage the production process. What I did know, however, was that I had no staff and that the demand for the product appeared overwhelming, so I rolled up my sleeves and began to roast sunflower seeds. I literally destroyed thousands of pounds of seeds before I got the hang of it. Fortunately for me, it was the slow part of the season.

Steen did not make any changes to the production process in 1974. Instead, he wanted to learn more about the business before making any major decisions. He was able to hire new staff in time for the peak season. Even at a rate of one package per minute, production was still a problem as Steen could not meet the demand and his facilities could not accommodate more workers. In fact, Steen estimated that he could only fill one third of his orders.

In 1975, Steen purchased some production and packaging equipment in efforts to increase production efficiency, and soon production outpaced sales. As well, he was able to reduce his staff, allowing him to significantly increase his margins. The next logical step for Sid's was to expand its market presence. For the first time in the company's history, this meant going beyond Saskatchewan's borders.

Throughout the late 1970s and 1980s, Steen continued to improve production efficiency and geographically expand markets through brokers in the northwestern United States, Australia, Europe, the Pacific Rim, and Scandinavian countries. (For market breakdown, see Exhibit 1.) He also broadened the product line to include pumpkin seeds and hulled sunflower seeds. By 1988, Sid's sold more sunflower seeds than any other company in Canada, employed 19 people, and had five seed roasters and an automated production process. In 1988, Sid's sold nearly 3 million kilograms of sunflower seeds.

Sid's built a reputation for product taste and quality. Sid's offered a product that was less salty than competitors and presented it as a nut as opposed to a seed. According to Steen, the production process (particularly roasting and salting), combined with an entrepreneurial spirit, was the secret to the compa-

---

Exhibit 1 Sid's Sales Breakdown by Percentage—Geographic

With MLB Market Penetration (1990–1995 projected)

	1974	1978	1982	1986	1990	1991	1992	1993	1994	1995
Western Canada	100	100	97	92	85	80	70	64	53	40
Eastern Canada*	0	0	0	0	5	7	10	12	15	18
United States†	0	0	2	4	4	6	10	13	18	24
Australia, New Zealand, and Europe ‡	0	0	1	4	6	6	8	8	8	8
Pacific Rim§	0	0	0	0	0	1	2	3	6	10
Total kilograms processed‖ (000)	680	1,181	1,772	2,500	3,540	4,000	4,700	5,400	6,600	8,600

Without MLB Market Penetration

	1974	1978	1982	1986	1990	1991	1992	1993	1994	1995
Western Canada	100	100	97	92	87	83	81	75	71	65
Eastern Canada*	0	0	0	0	3	5	6	8	12	15
United States	0	0	2	4	4	5	5	6	6	8
Australia, New Zealand, and Europe‡	0	0	1	4	6	6	6	8	8	8
Pacific Rim	0	0	0	0	0	1	2	3	3	4
Total kilograms processed‖	680	1,181	1,772	2,500	3,250	3,700	4,100	4,400	4,800	5,200

*Put product into Eastern Canada in 1989 on a test basis.

†The percentage of Sid's sunflower seed sales will increase as Steen signs on more baseball stadiums in the United States.

‡Sid's sell bulk seeds (roasted, salted, but not packaged) to Europe. The seeds are packaged by a producer in Europe and sold under another label. Sid's would like to deemphasize this practice and replace it with their own packaged product.

§Sid's is attempting to capitalize on the popularity of baseball in Japan and Korea. Steen is hoping that the major league baseball logo will help him to do this. By 1995, Sid's hopes to have a strong presence in this market.

‖Total kilograms of all confectionery product processed by Sid's. This includes hulled and dehulled sunflower seeds (bulk and packaged), and pumpkin seeds.

ny's longevity and success. This corporate philosophy remained apparent, and the production process was a proprietary secret.

The Sunflower Seed Industry

The Product and Market

The cultivation and eating of seeds originated in Europe and was brought to North America by early settlers. By 1988, the sunflower was grown mainly for the production of edible oils, though demand for nonoilseed varieties had also grown rapidly. Production of nonoilseed sunflower seeds in the United States and Canada had increased from 24,000 tonnes in 1973 to 276,000 tonnes in 1988, an average annual growth rate of about 17 percent. This was grown in 310,000 hectares concentrated in the midwestern United States and the warmer growing areas of Canada.

About 50 percent of the nonoilseed production was used for confectionary, primarily in two forms. The largest seed (usually 15–25 percent of the nonoilseed crop) was separated, roasted, and packaged whole (i.e., hulled), and sold in the same way as roasted peanuts in the shell. The remainder was dehulled, and the kernels used for confectionaries or in confectionary products, often appearing in roasted form in competition with other packaged shelled nuts. The fraction of the smallest seed (15–20 percent of the nonoilseed crop) was used in the rations for birds and seed-eating pets. Although raw sunflower seed could be stored for an indefinite period of time under the right conditions, it was important to secure top-quality seed to meet production requirements. Unavailability of the proper sizes of seed was often a limiting factor when determining production mix (i.e., hulled versus dehulled).

Food and snack processors bought sunflower seed either from the growers directly by contract or from a seed broker. In order to ensure raw material supply, most processors contracted production for the year, with contracts established in early April just prior to planting. Contracting provided both growers and processors with a predetermined price for specific production levels. However, the amount produced could not be guaranteed due to a number of uncontrollable factors such as weather and insects. Since raw material supply was critical to processors, most spread the risk by contracting with growers in different growing areas.

Human consumption of sunflower seeds in the shell was rather seasonal and often confined to the outdoors. The biggest consumers of sunflower seeds were sports enthusiasts, particularly baseball and football fans, where watching the game and eating seeds had long been considered a "natural" tradition. This tradition contributed to the seasonality of the products. This pattern was slowly changing as market development efforts for sunflower seeds were being directed at more and alternate season sports in the United States.

The status of sunflower seeds as a consumer product was described by Aaron Steen (Issy's brother and sales manager) as follows:

> Sunflower seeds, like other snack foods, are an impulse purchase item. A consumer rarely goes to a store with the intention of buying sunflower seeds. Rather, he or she will notice the product while shopping and then throw it in their basket. This is why product recognition and brand loyalty is important. For example, if they have had Sid's seeds before, say at a sporting event, and enjoyed them, hopefully they will choose our product over the competition the next time they are in the store. Shelf space and displays in strategic positions in as many stores as possible translates into three key marketing variables we rely on: exposure, recognition, and availability. We know our efforts are paying off when retailers tell us that consumers specifically asked for our product when it was not on the shelf.

Distribution and Competition

Confection goods always experienced a great deal of competition, especially as North America's demand for snack foods increased. Securing and retaining shelf space in grocery and convenience stores was tantamount in establishing a competitive edge.

Sunflower seeds had traditionally been considered an add-on to the snack food product lines of potato chips and nuts. This resulted from the seasonality of sales and the lack of effort directed toward market development. Further, sunflower seeds were often only one of a number of products that were processed and marketed by a single company. For example, companies like Old Dutch, Hostess-Frito Lay, and Nutty Club produced and marketed potato chips, pistachios, peanuts, and related products in addition to sunflower seeds. As a result, sunflower seeds were relatively obscure in Eastern Canada and points in the United States.

In Western Canada, confectionary sunflower seeds were considered to be a stand-alone product. This could be credited to the marketing efforts of Sid's and Tasty Flavour. Both Sid's and Tasty Flavour processed and marketed sunflower seeds as their primary product and distributed directly to the retailers without the use of middlemen. Both had embarked on major marketing campaigns in the early 1980s in Western Canada that were directed toward consumer awareness and new market development. As a result of their activity, the consumption of sunflower seeds in Western Canada increased significantly, although this market appeared to be approaching saturation. Both Sid's and Tasty's emphasized the necessity to develop new markets.

Sid's was highly dependent on this Western Canadian market with 83 percent of its sales in this area and only 3 percent in Eastern Canada, 4 percent in the United States, and 6 percent offshore. However, it did hold a dominant position in Western Canada with estimated market shares of 70 percent in British Columbia, 75 percent in Alberta, and 83 percent in Saskatchewan.

Sid's major competition in North America included the following.

Tasty Flavour.   Tasty was Sid's major competitor in Western Canada. Based out of Winnipeg, Tasty's initially concentrated on the Manitoba market where in 1988 it held an estimated 80 percent market share versus Sid's 10 percent. In 1982 (in response to Sid's entry into Manitoba), Tasty began to expand its marketing and distribution efforts outside of Manitoba. Although their efforts had not been as concentrated and aggressive as Sid's, their market share had shown moderate increases in Saskatchewan, Alberta, British Columbia, and Eastern Canada. Of all the competition, Tasty's product was most closely positioned to Sid's, emphasizing freshness and quality. Sunflower seeds represented 85 percent of Tasty's revenues.

Old Dutch.   Old Dutch offered both hulled and dehulled sunflower seeds as a part of their broad product line. The company tended to concentrate on the densely populated Eastern Canadian market. However, their advantages in distribution (using company truck jobbers with sunflower seeds being an extension of their potato chip and nut product line) allowed them to develop markets in Western Canada by supplying more remote areas and capitalizing on existing distribution channels. Old Dutch also benefited from strong brand recognition.

Hostess-Frito Lay.   As a division of General Foods Canada, Inc., Hostess-Frito Lay offered a diversified product line. It focused its activities on Eastern Canada. Like Old Dutch, Hostess seeds were an extension of their potato chip product line. Hostess also took advantage of a comprehensive distribution network, providing them with a competitive advantage, particularly in Eastern Canada.

Other.   Humpty Dumpty, Johnson Nut, Nutty Club, Trophy Nut, Opechee, and David and Sons all offered sunflower seeds as an add-on to potato chips, nuts, and other confection items. These competitors were heavily concentrated in Eastern Canada and the United States while their market presence in Western Canada was minimal due to the lack of population density in the west.

Sid's competition, with the exception of Tasty Flavour, possessed a competitive advantage in their ability to distribute product more effectively and at a lower cost per kilogram. As an add-on product to their mainline confectionary products such as potato chips and nuts, promotion and distribution costs were rationalized. Moreover, competition such as Old Dutch, Hostess-Frito Lay, and Johnson Nut had established shelf space in most stores. Incremental shelf space costs for these companies would be lower than what Sid's would have to pay.

Sid's Operations

Management

The Sid's management group worked informally with a minimum of structure and control. (Exhibit 2 reviews the backgrounds and responsibilities of the top management group.) The team did what had to be done, often covering for each other. In fact, it was not an unusual sight to see Issy or Aaron Steen load a last-minute order for shipment. All of the managers were pressed by the requirements of everyday business. Priority was given to "putting out fires," which often preoccupied one's day. The installation of an information system in late 1986 smoothed out operations, particularly since the plant and the head office were separated.

Marketing

Marketing duties were split between Issy and Aaron Steen. Issy concentrated on identifying and developing growth opportunities in new markets. Aaron was responsible for product line marketing and the maintenance of current accounts. As well, Aaron developed new accounts in existing markets as the opportunities arose. Surprisingly, Aaron Steen knew very little of Issy's developmental efforts.

Sid's employed eight sales representatives (two in British Columbia, two in Alberta, three in Saskatchewan, and one in Manitoba). These reps, who reported to Aaron Steen, made regularly scheduled calls and faxed orders back to the plant on a daily basis. They were paid a wage plus commission, giving them incentive to develop new accounts in their respective territories. Recently, mar-

---

Exhibit 2 Backgrounds and Responsibilities of Top Management Group, Sid's Sunflower Seeds (1974) Ltd.

Issy Steen, Owner/President—Age 42

Degree in Sociology/Psychology—University of Manitoba 1967. Between 1968 and 1974, managed the head office for a family chain of eight restaurants. Purchased Sid's Sunflower Seeds in 1974 and then concentrated his efforts on the general management of this organization. Responsibilities also included contracting of seeds and other major purchases.

Aaron Steen, Sales Manager—Age 35

Joined Sid's Sunflower Seeds in 1986. Prior to coming to Sid's, had worked as a sales representative for Hershey Canada, Inc., a major confectionery company for 12 years. In the last four years of employment with Hershey, was sales manager for Manitoba and Saskatchewan. At Sid's, concentrated on servicing existing accounts and further developing markets in territories where Sid's was already established. Also assumed general management responsibilities when Issy was away for extended periods.

Jerry Cheslok, Controller—Age 48

Bachelor of Administration degree from the University of Regina and a Chartered Accountant (CA) designation. Prior to joining Sid's in 1984, worked for 11 years as a credit officer for SEDCO. At Sid's, responsible for all accounting and credit functions and monitoring relationships with outsiders such as banks and government agencies.

Henry Veenstra—Age 58

Has been production manager with Sid's for over 20 years. At Sid's, responsible for production scheduling, production, maintenance, minor purchases, shipping, and receiving.

---

ket growth in Western Canada had been slowing, and it appeared that the market was approaching saturation.

Sid's marketing philosophy was to market their product to anybody, anywhere provided that a sufficient return could be made without jeopardizing existing accounts. Aaron summed up the market strategy as follows:

> Our target market is anyone with teeth—right from the day that they get them to the day that they lose them. Our product has no legal, cultural, or political barriers; the only thing that we have to be concerned about is getting the product to the customer's place, on time, in a fresh state, and at a cost that will allow us to remain competitive. All product is shipped FOB to the account's doorstep.
>
> We also have to be very careful not to oversell as we do not want to be in the position of having to ration shipments. This could prove devastating to our reputation, especially since the market has become quite competitive.
>
> We are also attempting to capitalize on the health food craze. Within the past two or three years, we have begun to offer roasted, no-salt, hulled, and dehulled sunflower seeds. This, combined with the already low levels of cholesterol associated with seeds, allows us to market it as a health food where necessary. Seeds are great for people who are overweight but like to snack or for people who have just quit smoking and have the sensation to eat.

A key element in Sid's overall marketing program was packaging. In 1976, Sid's converted to a bright red plasticized and laminated foil package that kept the product fresh for up to nine months and added visual appeal with its bright colours. Since the product could sit for some time in the client's stock, freshness had to be guaranteed upon consumer purchase.

Sid's also differentiated its product through price. Their prices were higher across the board, but they were able to maintain this differential by relying on other competitive advantages. Originally, this price differential was necessary to cover higher than average distribution costs. Luckily, it inferred higher product quality, allowing Sid's to be referred to as the "cadillac of sunflower seeds."

Until 1988, Issy had single-handedly developed all of the company's export markets and identified other feasible growth opportunities. The development of new markets had always preoccupied Steen:

> It is costly and difficult to develop new markets. One has to determine how much effort to expend on such tasks. Remember our business relies on volume. When we identify new opportunities, we have to look at areas that will promote volume. When we go into a new market, we have no guarantee that our product will be accepted, or if it is, that the anticipated volume will be guaranteed. We've been burned in the past and that's been costly.

In the continuing effort to develop new markets, Sid's looked to Eastern Canada and the United States. Previous market entry efforts in Eastern Canada were marginally successful, but Sid's was unable to maintain a presence due to excessive costs or other nonmitigating factors. Steen felt that Sid's required a competitive advantage that would allow the organization to sustain a market presence—something that would further differentiate his product from that of the competition. As market growth in Western Canada slowed, the issue of new market development would become even more important. Issy elaborated:

> Trying to get a product established in an already competitive market is both costly and time-consuming. In Eastern Canada, we simply could not compete against the economies of scale possessed by our competition. At that time, nobody there had heard of Sid's sunflower seeds and likely nobody cared. We did an observation study of our product in Fortinos Supermarkets in Toronto. People looked at our product, and even picked it up, but then put it back down in favour of a well-known competitor's product. Quite simply, we did not possess the recognition or loyalty that we enjoyed in the West. Television would have been a natural in an entry campaign, but producing a television commercial would have cost $25,000 or more. Then, of course, air time must be added to this. This would blow our entire advertising and promotional budget. What would that do to our other marketing initiatives?

Promotion

Although Sid's did not develop an explicit marketing plan, the company spent approximately 10 percent of annual revenues on advertising and promotion. At the retail level, campaigns were often aimed at the promotion of eating seeds and outdoor activities. For example, in some of their better retail accounts, a promotion campaign included a canoe and tent giveaway. The in-store static display had two mannequins portraying campers in front of a tent with a canoe filled with bags of Sid's sunflower seeds. With each purchase of a bag of seeds, customers were able to enter their names for a draw to win the canoe and tent. Other promotion activities included sunflower seed give-aways, joint promotions with other products such as Coca-Cola, contests, couponing, other static displays, and print and radio media. Sid's also sponsored a number of sporting events and teams, such as little league baseball tournaments and baseball teams. Many of these activities were done on a test basis and carried a high price tag. After completion of any one campaign, the management team would sit down and attempt to quantify the costs versus the benefits.

Distribution

Sid's emphasized getting the product to the customer on time, in the quantities ordered, and as cheaply as possible. Sid's did not employ truck jobbers, but rather utilized the common carrier system. Under this system, Aaron spent much of his time "tracking" when a shipment became lost in transit.

To reduce shipping costs of less than truckload shipments, Sid's leased a warehouse in Vancouver, British Columbia. Truckload lots were shipped to this warehouse where they were broken down and distributed to various accounts. All of the B.C. accounts and some international accounts were serviced out of this warehouse. All other orders were shipped from the Regina warehouse. Distribution was seen as one area that needed improvement if they were to remain competitive in markets outside of Western Canada.

Sid's took particular pride in being able to deliver their product on time and in the amounts ordered. According to Issy:

> This type of customer service is the basis for our repeat purchases. If the customer can count on us, we can count on them. Not only that, our reputation has been the foundation for much new business. We get calls from all over Western Canada asking if we can immediately supply an order—an order that another producer has failed to supply. Naturally, we jump at the opportunity, providing it will not jeopardize existing accounts. Much of our new business often comes at the expense of a competitor. Once we get a new account, we do our best not to lose it.

Production

Sid's operated an 8,000-square-foot production facility in Regina, Saskatchewan. Raw material was delivered to the plant by the semitrailer load. Once delivered, the raw material was screened and then stored in one of two silos on site. Raw material storage capacity was 30,000 kilograms. There was no room at the production site to build more storage silos, and large capital expenditures would be required to accommodate roof storage.

From bulk storage, the product passed through two more screening areas and one sieve area. Sid's attempted to rid the product of all foreign matter (sticks, rocks, and stems) and ensure proper seed size before roasting. After this process was complete, the seed was stored in clean holding.

Roasting and salting took place on one of five roasting lines. Three lines were dedicated to hulled and unhulled sunflower seeds to be salted. One line was dedicated to pumpkin seeds to be salted while one line processed product that was not to be salted. Sunflower seeds were roasted for approximately 30 minutes at 180 degrees celsius. Salt flour was added while roasting took place. Thus, there were only two raw materials required for production, seeds and salt. From the roaster lines, the product passed through a final screening process before entering one of three packaging lines. Each line was capable of packaging in excess of 60 bags per minute. The product was packaged, boxed, and loaded in a Sid's truck and shipped across town to their office and warehouse. Orders to wholesalers and retailers were filled from the warehouse building and carried by independent truckers. During peak season (April to October), product was processed and shipped daily.

Maximum plant capacity of the existing Regina plant was 5.5 million kilograms annually. This would be realized on three 8-hour shifts, seven days per week (with one portion of a shift being allocated to maintenance). Ideal plant capacity was 4.5 million kilograms annually. The production mix package size for 1988 is presented in Exhibit 3. A percentage breakdown of cost of goods manufactured is presented in Exhibit 4.

Issy Steen had gone a long way to improve the efficiency of the production process. By automating functions and increasing the capacity of equipment, he had decreased production staff from 50 people per shift in 1974 to 6 in 1988, while increasing output from 50 packages per minute in 1974 to 180 per minute in 1988. Obviously, this had decreased the production cost per unit dramatically.

EXHIBIT 3   Sid's Sunflower Seeds, Production Mix 1988

Product	% Production
Hulled sunflower seed	75%
Dehulled sunflower seed	10%
Pumpkin seed	13%
Bird seed	2%

Production Breakdown	% Prod.	Package size					
		45 g	*65 g*	*150 g*	*350 g*	*900 g*	*Bulk 50 lb.*
Hulled sunflower seeds roasted, and salted	72	X	X	X	X	X	X
Hulled sunflower seeds roasted, no salt	3	X	X	X	X	X	X
Dehulled sunflower seeds roasted, and salted	8	X	X				
Dehulled sunflower seeds roasted, no salt	2	X	X				
Pumpkin seed	13	X	X	X			X
Bird seed	2						X

Inventory

During the spring and summer months, scheduled deliveries of raw material arrived at the plant two to three times per week. In the slower winter months, one trailer load per week was received. Sunflower and pumpkin seeds in a raw state can be inventoried for an indefinite period given the right conditions. A major concern was securing the proper size seed at peak production times, which may require holding more inventory than desired at any given time.

All raw inventory (primarily seed product and salt) were stored at the production facility. On a daily basis, finished goods were trucked to the 12,000-square-foot warehouse where the corporate office was also located. In the peak production season, the plant had only enough capacity to store three days' worth of raw material. As a result, coordination of raw material deliveries was of primary importance.

Contracting

All of the sunflower seeds used by Sid's were grown under contract. Every April Steen hooked up his camper trailer to his car and headed to the United States to meet with growers and negotiate contracts. Almost all of the product used by Sid's came from Kansas, Wyoming, and Colorado. To reduce the risk associated with crop failure, Steen established contracts with numerous growers in diverse growing regions and because yields could not be guaranteed, he often contracted for amounts greater than the estimated annual requirements. Only in extenuating circumstances did Steen go to the farmgate to purchase raw material. According to Steen, the price one pays for raw material in any one year can mean the difference between profit and loss, especially in years of poor yields, where demand for material often exceeds supply. Contracts were established FOB the grower, a long-standing industry standard.

EXHIBIT 4 Sid's Sunflower Seeds, Cost of Goods Manufactured Breakdown (percentage basis averaged over a year)

Raw material	
Seeds	28
Salt	2
Freight	
In	12
Out	18
Wages	19
Overhead (including electricity)	21
	100

Finance and Administration

Given its size, the relative simplicity of its operations, and the informal management structure, the company did not have an elaborate management information
system. Although limited use was made of the reports that the management
information system was capable of generating, a monthly report of sales by product
line and area was made available to each manager. Versions of these reports were
then filtered to sales reps and production personnel. Quarterly reports, compiled
manually by accounting, attempted to determine actual margins by product line.

EXHIBIT 5

SID'S SUNFLOWER SEEDS (1974) LTD.
Income Statements
Years Ended September 30
($000s)

	1988	1986	1982	1978	1974	1973
Sales:						
Product	2,136	1,656	1,102	735	406	300
Other	3	3	4	2	—	—
Total sales	2,139	1,659	1,106	737	406	300
Cost of goods sold:						
Direct labour	252	194	127	91	55	42
Direct material	397	305	201	145	89	70
Overhead	278	214	140	101	61	47
Freight	397	306	201	144	87	64
Depreciation	75	61	50	38	12	6
Other	82	66	45	30	6	2
Total cost of goods sold	1,481	1,146	764	549	310	231
Gross profit:	658	513	342	188	96	69
Selling and administrative:						
Wages and fringe	200	180	124	80	45	40
Advertising and promotion	260	175	115	75	27	10
Expenses	60	44	29	15	6	4
	520	399	268	170	78	54
Financial:						
Interest and financial	42	42	50	35	13	—
Other*	—	—	100	—	—	—
	42	42	150	35	13	—
Earnings (loss) before taxes	96	72	(76)	(17)	5	15
Provision for taxes	21.8	10.8	—	—	1.2	3.7
Net income (loss)	74.1	61.2	(76)	(17)	3.8	11.3

*The expense in 1982 can be attributed to an investment by Sid's that failed.

With the exception of a few bad years, the company had been consistently, though not exceptionally, profitable (Exhibit 5). As a result, by the end of fiscal year 1988, net worth was $377,800 and all loan obligations were secured and readily serviceable (Exhibit 6).

Sid's employed a very tough credit policy which helped to limit bad debts. Thirty percent of Sid's customers were well-established national wholesalers representing 70 percent of the company's business. New accounts were screened carefully and often were required to pay COD until credibility could be established. Credit terms were net 30 days with no incentive for early payment. Often, however, it seemed that even the best accounts stretched payments beyond 60 days.

Sid's utilized a $150,000 revolving bank line of credit to finance receivables and inventories. Outstanding term debt had been used for both capital and noncapital purposes. It consisted of commercial bank debt as well as agreements with government agencies, the Federal Business Development

---

EXHIBIT 6

SID'S SUNFLOWER SEEDS (1974) LTD.
Balance Sheet (1973–1988)
As of September 30

	1988	*1986*	*1982*	*1978*	*1974*	*1973*
Assets						
Cash	5,025	3,000	150	150	1,000	500
Accounts receivable	281,749	258,009	175,200	105,751	58,421	40,052
Other current assets	20,351	15,272	1,100	9,872	4,500	–0–
Inventory	250,100	190,350	142,600	89,720	42,100	19,100
Total current assets	557,225	466,631	319,070	205,493	106,021	59,652
Fixed assets	452,350	409,000	310,050	300,192	93,005	100,110
Total assets	1,009,575	875,631	629,120	505,685	199,026	159,762
Liabilities						
Operating loan	153,500	150,000	105,650	71,125	42,120	25,001
Accounts payable	269,269	233,296	136,552	89,747	53,354	50,900
Other current liabilities	33,052	26,756	39,200	12,651	3,052	1,250
Total current liabilites	455,821	410,052	281,402	173,523	98,526	77,151
Term loans	175,950	220,025	244,592	260,000	70,500	0
Total liabilities	631,771	630,077	525,994	433,523	169,026	77,151
Share capital	60,000	60,000	30,000	30,000	30,000	1,500
Retained earnings	317,804	185,554	73,176	42,162	–0–	81,111
Total equity	377,804	245,554	103,176	72,162	30,000	82,611
Total liabilities and owner's equity	1,009,575	875,631	629,170	505,685	199,026	159,762

Bank (FBDB), and the Saskatchewan Economic Development Corporation (SEDCO).

Strategic Planning

Goals, objectives, and strategies were not documented or communicated to employees. Issy felt that the organization was small enough that a formal planning process was still not necessary.

> We have limited resources, both in time and human factors, to formalize this process. I know what I want this company to do over the next five years and how to achieve it. That's good enough for me and so far its worked for us.

One common goal shared by the organization was that of growth; however, the means to achieve this growth was not totally consistent.

Formal planning sessions were limited in scope and held on an ad hoc basis. Issy and Aaron Steen and Jerry Cheslok periodically sat down to analyse accounts in respect to promotion efforts. Changes in promotional strategies were made as necessary.

Issy had a number of reasons for not articulating his strategies. These reasons ranged from industry competitiveness to not wanting to freeze the organization. He was also aware of the dangers associated with not formalizing the organization's strategies. As he said, "If I got struck down by a truck tomorrow, the future plans for Sid's would go with me."

Issy's goals remained quite simple. He wanted the company to remain the number-one producer of seeds in Canada and continue to grow on an incremental basis by exploiting new marketing opportunities. He also wanted the company to continue its growth by expanding its market presence in Eastern Canada and the United States. The idea of building on a reputation of over 50 years while remaining a family-owned and -operated business remained first and foremost in Issy's future plans for Sid's. At the same time, Issy was also very loyal to the city of Regina. He and his wife had lived there for over 20 years, and he felt that both the city and province had been good to him and his business.

The Major League Baseball Agreement

Background

The opportunity to obtain the endorsement of major league baseball came about quite accidentally. Several months after a trade show in New York in May 1987, Issy was contacted by Bart Lewis of the Licensing Corporation of America (LCA). He said that he had enjoyed product samples Issy had sent him and he suggested that sunflower seeds would be ideal for a new promotion that the LCA and Major League Baseball (MLB) were working on. They wanted to change the image of baseball by getting players to switch from chewing tobacco to an alternative product. Lewis asked if Sid's would like to negotiate for the rights to become the official supplier of sunflower seeds to MLB. Steen agreed almost immediately since he saw it as a vehicle for breaking into the eastern market.

The factor underlying MLB's interest was concern with the use of chewing tobacco by players. Chewing tobacco is moist, flavoured tobacco that is chewed instead of smoked. This tobacco is very addictive as the nicotine is highly concentrated. Use of chewing tobacco had been directly linked to mouth, tongue, and lip cancer as well as to chronic halitosis and severely discoloured teeth. Four out of 10 players in MLB used chewing tobacco. In 1988, C. Everett Koop, then Surgeon General of the United States, reported that the use of chewing tobacco had reached epidemic proportions, that over 2 million Americans under the age of 15 were regular users. Since many MLB players were role models for young Americans, the league decided to take positive action to eradicate the use of chewing tobacco. Stopping short of banning its use altogether, these efforts included designating baseball stars such as Nolan Ryan of the Texas Rangers to go on television and speak out against its use to encouraging players to find alternate products to occupy their habits. MLB hoped that sunflower seeds would be one product to provide the natural replacement, allowing the players to set a new example for America's youth.

The Agreement

Sid's and the LCA agreed to terms and signed an agreement in March of 1988. The initial agreement was for five years with a mutually agreed option of renewal for an additional five years. During the agreement period, the LCA could not enter into similar negotiations with competing firms.

The agreement gave Sid's the exclusive right to use the major league baseball logo on packaging and all other advertising and promotion activities. Further, it allowed Sid's to represent their product as the official sunflower seed of MLB. In return, Sid's had to supply sunflower seeds free of charge to players in dugout and clubhouse areas and pay a royalty of $.04 to the LCA on each bag of sunflower seeds sold in major league baseball cities. Any benefits that accrued outside of MLB cities as a result of this agreement would be a bonus to Sid's and of no interest to the LCA. The LCA would in turn pay a royalty to MLB to be divided amongst the 26 teams.

This agreement did not automatically secure concession space in major league baseball stadiums, nor did it exclude the competition from attempting to gain entry to these stadiums. Negotiations, marketing, and promotion efforts to gain entry to each stadium was up to Sid's. After careful consideration, Issy felt that these issues could be mitigated by the very fact that Sid's would be recognized as the official supplier. The potential long-term benefits, in Steen's estimation, appeared to outweigh the short-term costs.

One concern of the LCA was that Sid's maximize its distribution efforts to include all 26 MLB stadiums as soon as possible. Bart Lewis explained:

> Naturally we want to maximize our royalties and get as many players as possible eating seeds. We are in business like anyone else. Initially, Sid's wanted to negotiate for the rights team by team, beginning with the two teams in Canada. I said that this was not acceptable, so we came to an agreement which resulted in Issy taking an option on all 26 teams. He will attempt to penetrate all 26 stadiums and teams by 1995. In 1993, we will review the progress to date before we agree to a renewal. If progress is being made, we will renew.
>
> On several occasions, Issy has made it clear to me that this is a rather aggressive schedule and his concerns about his company's ability to supply are well founded. But we both agreed that the benefits inherent in this opportunity were too significant to overlook. Given Issy's entrepreneurial spirit, we are confident that he can achieve the goals that have been set.

Stadium by Stadium

Stadiums that were homes to MLB teams varied in respect to concession operating policies. For example, in the Toronto Skydome scheduled to open in June 1989, the concessions were to be owned by the Skydome Corporation, which had rigid policies concerning product listing. The Skydome Corporation required a $5 million exclusive listing and partnership fee just to get product into concessions. In contrast, in Olympic Stadium where the Montreal Expos played and owned the concession rights, new products could be listed with no up-front fees. Of the 24 teams in the United States, 12 of the stadium concession rights were owned by the occupying team (see Exhibit 7). It was much easier to penetrate stadiums that had team-owned concessions. In the case where concessions were not team owned, Sid's had to negotiate with both the team and stadium concessionaries.

Soon after signing the agreement with LCA, Steen set out to exercise the options and began negotiating with the Toronto Blue Jays and the Montreal Expos. By the season's end, Sid's was successful in getting their product into Exhibition Stadium and Olympic Stadium. Steen estimated that his company spent $25,000 per stadium to sponsor a Sid's night and another $25,000 in related advertising and promotion expenses. Sid's effort in these two stadiums appeared to be successful. In Montreal alone, the ratio of a bag of seeds per fan increased from 1 to 1,110 up to 1 to 200 by season's end. With the Blue Jays moving to the Skydome, Issy concluded Sid's would not be able to get their product into the concessions because of the prohibitive listing cost.

The stadiums that Sid's could penetrate would be costly. Steen estimated that he would have to spend between $50,000 and $75,000 per stadium for initial endorsement advertising and promotion expenses. He felt that this would be a one-time cost in efforts to establish the product and the name in the ball park. This cost would be exclusive of listing fees, where they were imposed by the concession owners.

EXHIBIT 7 Sid's Sunflower Seeds—Major League Baseball Stadiums

Stadium	Home of (and Division)	Location	Team-Owned Concession
Exhibition Stadium/Skydome*	Toronto Blue Jays (ALE)	Toronto, Ont.	Yes/No
Olympic Stadium	Montreal Expos (NLE)	Montreal, Que.	Yes
Shea Stadium	New York Mets (NLE)	New York, NY	Yes
Yankee Stadium	New York Yankees (ALE)	New York, NY	Yes
Fenway Park	Boston Red Sox (ALE)	Boston, Mass.	No
Memorial Stadium	Baltimore Orioles (ALE)	Baltimore, Md.	Yes
Astrodome	Houston Astros (NLW)	Houston, Tex.	No
Tiger Stadium	Detroit Tigers (ALE)	Detroit, Mich.	Yes
County Stadium	Milwaukee Brewers (ALE)	Milwaukee, Wis.	Yes
Comiskey Park	Chicago White Sox (ALW)	Chicago, Ill.	No
Wrigley Field	Chicago Cubs (NLE)	Chicago, Ill.	Yes
Oakland-Alameda County Coliseum	Oakland Athletics (ALW)	Oakland, Calif.	No
Anaheim Stadium	California Angels (ALW)	Anaheim, Caif.	No
Candlestick Park	San Francisco Giants (NLW)	San Francisco, Calif.	No
Dodger Stadium	Los Angeles Dodgers (NLW)	Los Angeles, Calif.	Yes
Kingdome	Seattle Mariners (ALW)	Seattle, Wash.	No
Arlington Stadium	Texas Rangers (ALW)	Arlington, Tex.	Yes
San Diego Stadium	San Diego Padres (NLW)	San Diego, Calif.	No
Hubert Humphrey Metrodome	Minnesota Twins (ALW)	Minneapolis, Minn.	No
Municipal Stadium	Cleveland Indians (ALE)	Cleveland, Ohio	Yes
Royals Stadium	Kansas City Royals (ALW)	Kansas City, Mo.	Yes
Three Rivers Stadium	Pittsburgh Pirates (NLE)	Pittsburgh, Penn.	No
Veteran's Stadium	Philadelphia Phillies (NLE)	Philadelphia, Pa.	No
Busch Memorial Stadium	St. Louis Cardinals (NLE)	St. Louis, Mo.	Yes
Riverfront Stadium	Cincinnati Reds (NLW)	Cincinnati, Ohio	No
Atlanta-Fulton County Stadium	Atlanta Braves (NLW)	Atlanta, Ga.	Yes

NOTE: Key: ALE—American League East   ALW—American League West
          NLE—National League East   NLW—National League West
*The Toronto Blue Jays planned to move to the Toronto Skydome in mid-season.

Central to Steen's entry strategy was the ability to get key players and personnel of respective teams to act as official Sid's spokesmen and endorse the product. He had done this successfully in Toronto and Montreal where Dave Stieb (starting pitcher for Toronto) and Buck Rogers (manager of the Expos) endorsed the product and undertook promotional activities. Issy remarked:

> Buck Rogers has a box of seeds in the Expos dugout. Before each game, he will go to the opponent's dugout and hand out bags to players and coaches. On one occasion, during a game, he noticed Tommy Lasorda, manager of the Los Angeles Dodgers, eating a competitor's seeds. Between innings Rogers walked over to the Los Angeles dugout and offered him a bag of Sid's. Lasorda took them. This is what I pay Buck Rogers to do.

EXHIBIT 8   Sid's Sunflower Seeds—Total Production in Kilograms (Actual and Projected 1974–1995)

With MLB Penetration

	1974	1978	1982	1986	1990	1991	1992	1993	1994	1995
Kilograms (000) with MLB	680	1,181	1,772	2,500	3,540	4,000	4,700	5,400	6,600	8,600
Manufacturer's level cents/kilogram	.59	.62	.62	.66	.69	.69	.70	.72	.72	.74

Without MLB Penetration

	1974	1978	1982	1986	1990	1991	1992	1993	1994	1995
Kilograms (000) without MLB	680	1,181	1,772	2,500	3,250	3,700	4,100	4,400	4,800	5,200
Manufacturer's level cents/kilogram	.59	.62	.62	.66	.69	.69	.70	.72	.72	.74

NOTE: Total kilograms of all production; hulled and dehulled sunflower seeds, pumpkin seed, and birdseed.

Steen also hoped that promotion activities inside the park would lead to spin-offs outside the park:

> Over 30 million plus fans would be exposed to our product in Shea Stadium. Those fans become consumers when they go back home into their retail stores. It is our hope that they would request and buy Sid's seeds. We would actually be able to make some money, not so much in the stadiums as we will in retail and corner stores and supermarkets in the outlying suburbs around the stadium. Another challenge is to make Sid's seeds available in these stores.

Future Direction—The Next Five Years

Steen and his management were optimistic about the future, particularly as it concerned growth potential. Steen felt that the MLB logo opened the door for tremendous growth opportunities in the United States and the Pacific Rim. Further, it would provide him with the competitive edge required to break away from the competition in Eastern Canada and the United States. This growth was consistent with Steen's preferences to grow in foreign markets.

It was also clear to Steen that both he and his company were feeling stretched. Some significant changes would have to be made to allow Sid's to capitalize on future opportunities. As background to the necessary analysis, Steen developed sales estimates with and without the MLB agreement (Exhibit 8) and their impact on earnings (Exhibits 9 and 10). Further, feeling that the expansion of production capacity would eventually be necessary, he had asked Jerry Cheslok to prepare some cost estimates and financing options for several

EXHIBIT 9

SID'S SUNFLOWER SEEDS (1974) LTD.
Projected Income Statement 1990–1995
Years Ended September 30
($000's)
with MLB Penetration

	1990	1991	1992	1993	1994	1995
Sales:						
Product	2,446	2,760	3,290	3,888	4,752	6,364
Other	3	5	1	1	10	15
Total sales	2,449	2,765	3,291	3,889	4,762	6,379
Cost of goods sold:						
Direct labour	279	326	388	458	559	747
Direct materials	443	517	614	727	884	1,181
Overhead	308	360	428	507	617	825
Freight	438	512	610	723	880	1,177
Depreciation	75	95	115	200	250	300
Other	82	100	110	120	130	150
Total cost of goods sold	1,625	1,910	2,265	2,735	3,320	4,380
Gross profit	824	855	1,026	1,154	1,442	1,999
Selling and administrative:						
Wages and fringe	220	250	300	325	350	375
Advertising and promotion	350	525	600	650	700	900
Expenses	80	100	100	100	120	140
	650	875	1,000	1,075	1,170	1,415
Financial:						
Interest and financial	45	45	180	180	160	110
Other*	40	—	—	—	—	70
	85	45	180	180	160	180
Earnings (loss) before taxes	89	(65)	(154)	(101)	112	404
Provision for taxes	20.2	—	—	—	—	21.8
Net income (loss)	68.8	(65)	(154)	(101)	112	382

*Projected shareholder bonuses and income from operations used for expansionary purposes.
Assumes expansion of plant in Regina (1992).

alternative locations. (See Exhibit 11.) Government assistance was available for financing a new plant. While Sid's had used government programs to develop contacts in the United States and Japanese markets, the company had been generally reluctant to access government funding programs for international market development because of time delays and the restricting conditions attached to the disbursement of funds.

EXHIBIT 10

SID'S SUNFLOWER SEEDS (1974) LTD.
Projected Income Statement 1990–1995
Years Ended September 30
($000's)
without MLB Penetration

	1990	1991	1992	1993	1994	1995
Sales:						
Product	2,250	2,250	2,870	3,160	3,456	3,848
Other	3	3	4	5	6	6
Total sales	2,253	2,553	2,874	3,165	3,462	3,854
Cost of goods sold:						
Direct labour	265	303	334	366	390	442
Direct materials	420	482	530	580	619	700
Overhead	293	335	369	404	432	488
Freight	415	477	525	576	614	695
Depreciation	75	95	115	130	145	150
Other	82	85	85	90	90	95
Total cost of goods sold	1,550	1,777	1,958	2,146	2,290	2,570
Gross profit	703	776	916	1,019	1,172	1,284
Selling and administrative:						
Wages and fringe	220	230	300	300	320	320
Advertising and promotion	280	325	350	400	450	550
Expenses	80	80	90	90	100	100
	580	635	740	790	870	970
Financial:						
Interest and financial	40	40	40	38	36	33
Other*	40	40	40	60	60	60
Total other expenses	80	80	80	98	96	93
Earnings (loss) before taxes	43	61	96	131	206	221
Provision for taxes	9.4	13.4	21.8	28.8	47.9	53.7
Net income (loss)	33.6	47.6	74.2	102.2	158.1	167.3

*Projected shareholder bonuses

EXHIBIT 11 Sid's Sunflower Seeds—State-of-the-Art Processing Facility (Location, Costs and Financing Options)

The cost, sources, and application of funds for a new production facility. Costs are expressed in 1992 Canadian dollars.

Item	Western Canada	Eastern Canada	Midwest United States
Land	$ 0*	$ 250,000	$ 200,000
Infrastructure	300,000	350,000	250,000
Building	1,500,000	1,750,000	1,200,000
Equipment	1,000,000	1,000,000	750,000
Environmental assessment	30,000	30,000	0
Contingency (@ 10%)	283,000	338,000	240,000
	$3,113,000	$3,718,000	$2,640,000
Source of funding (Potential):			
Equity	500,000	500,000	250,000
Debt			
Interest bearing†	1,000,000	3,118,000	790,000
Noninterest bearing‡	1,513,000	0	1,000,000
Income from operations	100,000	100,000	100,000
Grant§	0	0	500,000
	$3,113,000	$3,718,000	$2,640,000

*Would be built on existing land owned by Sid's.

†Projected interest rate average of 12 percent on debt in Western and Eastern Canada. Debt would consist of a combination of bank debt and government institutional funding. Effective interest rate in the United States would be 10 percent.

‡In Western Canada, assumes interest-free Western Diversification Program (WDP) repayable contribution. (WDP was a federal government program aimed at assisting firms with a Western Canada location to penetrate new markets.) In the United States, assumes state industrial revenue bond economic development and relocation assistance (provided Sid's purchases land, constructs a building, and creates jobs in state).

§One-time relocation grant.

CASE 31
SILK ROUTE ORIENTAL RUGS LTD.

In March 1991, eight months after their seven-year-old company, Silk Route Oriental Rugs Ltd., had gone bankrupt, Michael and Sam Hejazi were assessing if (and how) they should reenter the London, Ontario, oriental carpet retail market. Although their accountant and others were advising against trying to reestablish, the brothers' inclination was to find a means of staying in the business. If a new operation was to be started, at issue were questions of product focus, scale, location, and timing.

Brief History of Oriental Rugs

An oriental rug was a hand-knotted or hand-woven rug that originated from an area known as the rug belt. The rug belt was bordered by eastern Europe in the west, China on the east, the southern republics of the ex-Soviet Union to the north, and extended south to include most of India. It was difficult to determine when the first rugs were produced, but the oldest surviving rug, the Pazyryk, was over 2,000 years old.

Rugs were first made to satisfy household needs. As well as cushioning against the cold ground, rugs were used for curtains, canopies, tomb covers, tribute money, gifts, and currency. The rug belt dwellers also exported rugs in exchange for goods that were scarce in their area. The supply of cheap labour and fibre (wool) made it possible for these nations to later start oriental rug industries. Nations to the north of the rug belt had climates that did not support the production of wool (i.e., the raising of sheep), while nations to the south had warmer climates where the need for rugs to provide warmth did not exist.

Trade in oriental rugs began over 500 years ago. Because of Turkey's proximity to Europe, Turkish carpets were being exported to Europe by the 15th century. With the opening of more trade routes in the 16th and 17th centuries, Turkish carpets soon graced the homes of the European elite.

The features which determined a rug's value in the 15th century still determined prices in the 1990s. The quality of the wool or silk used for the pile as well as the quality of the dye was of primary importance. Natural vegetable dyes provided a lustre that increased with age whereas synthetic dyes destroyed the natural oil in wool, making it wear out faster. The number of knots per square inch was another criterion for judging an oriental rug, together with the quality of workmanship. Knots varied from 35 to 800 per square inch. Tighter knotting gave a rug more density and durability. Generally, a good carpet would have at least 200 knots per square inch. Design and colour were also critical in assessing a rug's value. Rugs that were mass-produced using the same designs and colours cost less than those that were more unique. Finally, a rug's value depended on its area of origin and the particular weaving centre within that country. Persian (i.e., Iranian) rugs, for example, because of their history of exceptional quality tended to command a higher price than rugs from other countries. However, with the increased popularity of oriental rugs, traditional designs were no longer made exclusively in the region of origin. The ability to evaluate a rug's quality and origin required great expertise, usually built up over a lifetime.

Oriental Rugs in the Canadian Marketplace

With annual retail sales of over $100 million, Canada was the world's thirteenth largest market for oriental rugs in 1989. Since World War II, oriental rugs had enjoyed tremendous popularity. In 1950, oriental rug imports into Canada totaled only $1.33 million (at wholesale). This low level was attributed to weak distribution channels, a lack of trade promotion to build consumer awareness, and the popularity of wall-to-wall carpeting in both homes and apartments. The 1960s heralded a strong growth in demand for several reasons. First, increased production and export of rugs provided a wider selection for Canadian consumers. Tied to this was a greater responsiveness on the part of manufacturers to change the design and colours to suit North American preferences. Second, a number of Canadian importers and retailers specializing in oriental rugs went into business during this period, enhancing the profile and availability of oriental rugs. Consumer awareness increased as distribution channels improved. Third, a rise in per capita income and expenditure among high income groups increased the demand for good quality, hand-knotted oriental rugs. The main buying reasons included

• Tradition:	most Canadian oriental carpet buyers preferred genuine hand-knotted carpets as floor coverings.
• Durability:	oriental carpets lasted longer than machine-made carpets; area rugs could be taken up easily and moved and were popular with apartment dwellers (home owners preferred wall-to-wall carpeting).
• Colours and designs:	plain wall-to-wall carpeting needed additional decoration to create a warmer atmosphere.
• Status symbol:	oriental rugs conveyed a sense of culture and sophistication.
• Investment:	a fine-quality hand-knotted rug would retain or sometimes increase in value over time.

The strong growth in rug imports came to a halt in the late 1970s as a result of unprecedented price hikes; by 1980, prices had risen 417 percent over 1970 levels. Both supply and demand factors came into play. Soaring prices were caused by fears about the future of the industry given the establishment of the Islamic Republic of Iran. With village life disrupted and the chain of tradition and apprenticeship broken, it was possible that the strong weaving areas would deteriorate. As a result, Western markets placed increasing demand on all rug-producing nations. This coincided with a general belief on the part of the producing nations that prices had been too low and revenues could be easily increased through higher prices.

The recession in the early 1980s prolonged the slow growth of oriental rug imports. However, Canadian demand began to strengthen in 1983, and the next few years saw a significant rise in per capita consumption. From 1986 to 1989, the wholesale value of oriental rugs imported into Canada rose from $30 million to $47 million. Since some importers were known to understate their costs (in order to reduce duties payable) while still maintaining retail margins of twice their actual landed costs, an import level of $47 million translated into a $100 million retail business.

A number of factors explained the increased popularity of oriental rugs. First, the market began to correct itself after the price hikes of the late 1970s. Unfavourable consumer reaction to the sharp price rises had resulted in more exports of lower-quality rugs and rugs from countries where labour was cheaper, thus increasing competition and forcing prices down. Not only were the traditional rug-producing nations exporting more rugs, but other nations such as Egypt and Romania were entering the market. Second, as Canadians became more affluent, they developed more sophisticated tastes in home decor and were spending more money on home furnishings. Third, with the increasing frequency of home moves, there was greater reluctance to purchase wall-to-wall broadloom; area rugs were a financially attractive alternative. Finally, it was rumoured that several countries had dumped carpets into foreign markets as a means of generating foreign exchange. The local government would do this by buying carpets in the local currency and then discounting them in any foreign market for the hard currency.

In 1989, Indian rugs held the largest share of the oriental rug market in Canada at 35.6 percent. Indian rug imports had been on the decline since the early 1970s due, in part, to the Indian government's policy of allowing rugs of any quality to be exported. Canadian consumers began to think that all Indian rugs were of low quality. India subsequently improved its competitive position through active government involvement in production and export promotion. Indian rugs became increasingly better quality at an affordable price. The country's competitive advantage rested on the use of cheap labour and indigenous wool. India had also become a leader in the "programming" of oriental rugs wherein Western importers provided specifications related to design, colours, and knot density which the manufacturers then followed in order to produce a series of rugs.

Chinese rugs held the second largest share of Canada's oriental rug market at 20.7 percent. Imports of Chinese rugs had risen dramatically through the 1980s because of China's use of programming. As well, the need for foreign exchange had led the Chinese government to press for higher production levels in its state-owned factories in the country's weaving centres. Chinese rugs were more expensive than Indian rugs (which had remained the least expensive type of oriental rug) but were also generally of a higher quality. Since Chinese rugs were not always as elaborate in design as rugs from other producing nations, they appealed to Canadian consumers whose tastes ran to area rugs with fewer colours and simpler designs.

With 16.9 percent, Iran held the third largest share of the Canadian oriental rug market. Traditionally the world's largest source of hand-knotted carpets, Iran's competitiveness declined through the 1980s. Iranian labour was more expensive relative to labour in other rug-producing nations and programming had not been adopted as a means to satisfy Western markets. As well, the government, preoccupied with a long war against Iraq, had not played an active role in the production and export of rugs. Although buyers realized that rug production in Iran was continuing under Ayatollah Khomeini, the 1979 takeover of the American Embassy in Tehran had created strong anti-Iranian sentiment. At the same time, Pakistan and India began to produce and export rugs with Persian designs, flooding the market and forcing down the price of authentic Persian rugs.

Pakistani rugs were in fourth position in the Canadian market with 15.2 percent share. The Pakistani country category also included carpets produced by Afghan refugees just inside Pakistan's border. Afghan rugs were never programmed and tended to be red in colour, geometric in design, and lower priced. One oriental rug expert asserted that Canadian consumers were becoming more sophisticated purchasers and were not buying Pakistani (and Turkish) rugs because they were not as good value as rugs from competing nations. According to the president of a major American oriental rug importing firm, "The rug manufacturers in Pakistan tend to be merchants first and rug people second. They produce beautiful rugs but they don't understand colour and design. . . . The weavers and dye houses are much more independent in Pakistan (than in India) so you don't get uniformity of product. You have to be able to order . . . and have it come through in the design, colour, and quality you want. It will probably happen in Pakistan, but I don't see it yet. It took three generations for it to happen in India. I don't see the same evolutionary pattern in Pakistan that I observed in India."

Turkish rugs, with a Canadian market share of 1.9 percent, had been struggling to maintain a presence in the market despite a global market share which made Turkey the world's fourth largest exporter of oriental rugs. In general, Canadians had not been attracted to the rugs because of their perceived poor value. There was speculation, however, that the quality of Turkish rugs would improve in the future because of the government's effort to act as an agent, organizing the production and acquisition of rugs from across the country for

_____

Exhibit 1 Lifestyle Ratings in London, Ontario

Type	Number of Households
Affluent	3,723
Upscale	11,220
Middle class	27,215
Young couples	10,118
Empty nesters	21,480

_____

export. Like the Chinese government, the Turkish government had been encouraging higher exports as a means to obtain foreign exchange.

The London Market

With a population of 300,000, London was the commercial, industrial, financial, and cultural centre in the southwestern part of the province. While the primary trade area for specialty stores consisted of the city of London, the secondary trade area was made up of eight counties with a total population of over half a million people.

The London market was characterized by higher incomes, education, and retail spending levels than the national average. This translated into a personal disposable income level, which was 12 percent more than the Canadian average. Although 11th in terms of population, London ranked 5th in Canada in per capita retail sales. As well, as Exhibit 1 indicates, a disproportionate number of Londoners were among one or more of the target lifestyle groups.

In 1989, the oriental rug market in London was estimated to be about $5 million at the retail level. Purchases were made in specialty oriental rug stores, specialty carpet stores, department stores, antique stores, and at special events and auctions. A history of the competitive situation for oriental carpets in the London area is shown in Exhibit 2.

Silk Route Oriental Rugs Limited

Background on Michael and Sam Hejazi

Michael (32) and Sam (30) Hejazi were born in Canada and attended high school in Windsor. While there, they worked with their father, who had emigrated from Lebanon in 1956 and sold high-end new and antique Persian rugs by referral in the Windsor/Detroit area. Their involvement in the family business included searching for old rugs at antique stores, shows, estate sales, and auctions including those at major auction houses such as Sotheby's and Phillips. They were also involved to a small degree with overseas buying and purchasing

Exhibit 2   History of Local Competition

Postians

Original company opened in 1927 but went bankrupt in 1981. Son Paul reopened in 1982. A fire a little later forced him to close this location and he moved downtown in 1986. Stocked basically Indian Aubussons and Chinese rugs with a limited selection of Indo-Persian, Persian, and Afghan. Owner refused to carry Turkish rugs because he was of Armenian descent. Planned to move to a larger (2,000-square-feet) suburban location in late 1991.

Cyrus Gallery

Operated from 1979 to 1982 in London. Located in 1,250 square feet, next door to where Silk Route operated from 1984 to 1987. Greatest portion of inventory was Persians, with some Afghan. Forced out of business following a major theft for which there was insufficient insurance.

Kashikgians

Located in 1,200 square feet in an industrial park. Established in 1952 as a carpet cleaner but expanded into retail in 1987. Stocked mainly Indian Aubusson rugs with a limited selection of Indo-Persians and Persians.

Registan Rugs

Established in 1987 with 700 square feet of space. Planned to move to 2,000-square-foot location in early 1991. Greatest portion of inventory was Indian Aubussons with a limited selection of Indo-Persians. Since Silk Route closed, Registan has moved into higher-quality decorative and Persian rugs.

Indo-Persian

A Toronto-based company with three large stores in the Toronto area. London store was established in 1990 with 7,000 square feet of space in the London Home and Design Centre. Stocked basically Indian Aubusson rugs with a decent selection of Indo-Persians and a very limited selection of Persians. Known for their heavy advertising.

Alexanians

Two locations and a third planned. Basically a broadloom rug store which placed a reasonable emphasis on oriental rugs. The oriental rugs were mainly Indian Aubussons with a limited selection of Indo-Persians and Pakistani Bokharas. Part of a 22-store chain.

Department Stores

The Bay, Eatons, and Kingsmills all had very small oriental rug departments. Basically carried low-end orientals and machine mades.

Antique Auctions

Auctions presented another opportunity to purchase oriental rugs. London's leading auction house held separate oriental rug auctions as well as general auctions which included rugs. Purchasing rugs through this channel put the onus on the customer to be sufficiently knowledgeable to avoid paying more than the market price.

Hotel Auctions

Eight to 12 times a year, oriental rug sales were held in London hotels and halls. Run by companies that imported and sold oriental rugs at similar events across Canada, these sales had a bad reputation within the trade. Often, the rugs were not good quality, and the prices were not significantly lower than those offered by the city's retailers. Usually, the rugs offered had been rejected by Canadian wholesalers and retailers. Ads often led the consumer to believe that rugs were seized by a bank or Canada customs. Some auctions were stacked with shills, and rugs were falsely described. Many of these auctions had been investigated by Consumer and Corporate Affairs with some charges laid. Local firms found it difficult to clean these rugs because the dyes would run. Irate customers would blame the local businesses and not the firms from which they had initially purchased the rugs. In spite of the problems, these sales were very popular and attracted unsuspecting customers with little knowledge of oriental rugs.

from New York dealers. On a few occasions, they were involved with selling, but that was basically left to their father. As they said: "We had absolutely no experience in retailing, marketing, or finance. We were just knowledgeable about rugs as art!"

In 1982, the brothers came to London to continue their education. Natural rug dealer instincts had them out searching for old rugs in London and the surrounding area. Most of the old rugs they found were profitably sold to New York or European dealers who would retail them. Perceiving that there was no real competition, they decided to open a small showroom to test the London market.

In April 1984, they rented a small 300-square-foot store. After doing some extensive advertising and promoting, they concluded that the London market lacked the knowledge to appreciate antique rugs. At the end of that year, they were trying to decide whether to close or readjust their business focus.

They decided to readjust. They marketed high-quality new Persian, Turkish, and Afghani rugs, not wanting to deal with low-end commercial-quality rugs such as those of Chinese, Pakistani, or Indian origin. Because their present location was too small and not easily accessible to retail traffic, an 800-square-foot store was leased at a more central location with available nearby parking. Suppliers were willing to extend a little credit and to provide a limited quantity of rugs on consignment.

A number of financial institutions were approached at this time for financing but Silk Route was rejected "without serious consideration." Oriental rugs were too alien to financial people to understand and the industry, on the whole, had a "horse trader reputation."

Immediately after opening their new location, there was a dramatic increase in sales. The company went on an extensive campaign of educating their customers. Informative print advertising was conducted and regular (free) lectures were held in the showroom. A hand-washing service was offered (the only one in the area), and a master weaver was brought to Canada to do repair work for the company. Heavy emphasis was placed on providing maximum service to customers.

The showroom was set up like stores in a traditional rug bazaar, with rugs piled shoulder high. While authentic in appearance, it posed problems. Rugs were difficult to show to more than one customer at a time and often customers were unable to view the whole selection. Some customers felt they would be obliged to purchase after generating so much work for company staff, so they would not bother looking. The only solution for this problem would be more space.

The Hejazis also regularly noticed that customers would visit the showroom, acknowledge the beauty of the rugs, but say they were unsuitable for their decor. They would be looking for more decorative types of colours. (During this period, soft pastel shades were in vogue.) The Silk Route's current suppliers did not handle this type of merchandise. The only place they could find decorative colours was in the United States. American wholesalers would set up looms in countries like India and have weavers produce rugs in the latest fashion colours.

The inability to satisfy certain customers' needs prompted another major decision: should they enter the decorative rug market? They decided to dabble a bit in order to see what kind of response they would get. The response was very good for the limited selection they had.

Sourcing

While decorative rugs were being sourced through larger U.S.–based wholesalers, most of the other rugs were obtained through European or Mediterranean-based wholesalers (in the United Kingdom, Germany, Lebanon, Syria, or Turkey) or North American wholesalers from Toronto or New York. On occasion, a European wholesaler would go so far as to send a retailer in North America a plane ticket in order that they could visit. While the least expensive source of carpets was through direct import (see Exhibit 3 for sample calculation), this method required a great deal of time for travel as well as the financial resources to purchase and ship enough carpets to gain the necessary economies. Therefore, most independent retailers, including Silk Route, purchased through an importer/wholesaler. The cost structures for the importing alternatives varied enormously and could sometimes result in customer prices as high as those noted in column 2 in Exhibit 3.

Some wholesalers were willing to provide carpets on consignment to retailers. The decision to extend credit or provide carpets on consignment was based on trust, reputation, and instinct, rather than such things as formal education. As one retailer noted:

> This is not like some businesses where having an MBA carries some weight. In fact, you'll have less chance of getting credit if you are an MBA. None of the suppliers would ever ask you to fill out a credit application. They either trust you, or not.

Further Growth

In 1987, they were approached by one of their customers who was interested in investing in the company. His conditions were that he would receive a "handsome" return on investment, would have first opportunity to purchase (for personal use only) rugs at cost price, and would be able to "hang around." With their past cash flow problems, it was exactly what the company needed. Capital would enable the establishment of new contacts in the United States, while an experienced, credible businessperson could provide guidance to the company and establish them in the community.

At the same time, competition increased. Postians had just reopened, Registan had opened, Kashikgians had expanded their cleaning operation into a full-fledged retail operation, and there were rumours that a major retailer from Toronto was planning to open in London. All these retailers handled low-quality,

---

EXHIBIT 3 Breakdown of Importing Costs for an Average Carpet

	Direct Importing	Purchasing through an Importer
Importer's price (varied according to volume and expertise)	$ 950.00	$ 870.00
+ Agent (15% of price)	142.50	130.50
= Importer's net price	1,092.50	1,000.50
+ Shipping (overland, ocean freight, & bunker charges)	75.20	75.20
+ Insurance	8.00	8.00
= Landed cost	1,175.70	1,083.70
+ Canadian federal goods & services tax	82.30	75.80
+ Customs broker	10.00	10.00
= Importer's cost	1,268.00	1,169.56
= Importer's margin (100% on cost)	50.00	1,169.56
= Retailer's cost	1,318.00	2,339.12
+ Retailer's margin (75% on cost)	988.50	1,754.34
= Retail price	$2,306.50	$4,093.46

Assumptions

1. A single 40-foot container which measured 60 cubic meters held 75 carpets (3 metre × 4 metre) valued at $1,000 per piece for duty purposes.
2. Shipping costs (including overland costs from Teheran and bunker charges) for a nonconference line 40-foot container totaled U.S. $4,800. $1 Cdn = U.S. $0.85.
3. Insurance cost approximately $.80 per $100 value of cargo.
4. A customs broker charged approximately 1% of the value of cargo.
5. The 13.5% federal sales tax was replaced by a national 7% goods and service tax effective January 1, 1991.
6. The importer's margin covered travel expenses, carrying costs, and the importer's profit. Assume $15,000 travel expenses would be incurred to import 300 carpets (i.e., $50/each).
7. With a completed "Form A" which confirms country of origin, no duties are applicable on oriental rugs imported into Canada from "developing" countries such as India, China, Iran, Pakistan, Turkey and Afghanistan. Without "Form A," a 10% duty applies.

---

decorative rugs with, to various degrees, high-end decorative rugs. Also, Alexanians, the Bay, and Eatons were handling the same type of goods.

The Hejazis felt that they had to do something about capturing some of the decorative rug market. They felt strongly that the consumer, properly informed, would pay a bit more for higher quality. A complete line of decorative rugs was added to their traditional goods. With the use of the capital from the investor, the latest fashion colours in the best qualities available were brought in. The response was better than expected. Instead of spending one or two weeks with a customer to sell one or two traditional rugs, customers were coming in with a colour swatch and making a decision to purchase almost immediately. As well, traditional rug sales were not neglected. The brothers worked on building both markets.

EXHIBIT 4

SILK ROUTE ORIENTAL RUGS LIMITED
Statement of Income
For the Year Ended December 31

	1989	1988	1987	1986	1985
Sales	$ 631,686	$ 518,632	$367,950	$299,278	$127,337
Cost of sales	369,747	302,608	233,388	162,371	69,118
Gross profit	261,939	216,024	134,562	136,907	58,219
Expenses					
Advertising	116,345	71,362	28,134	35,400	15,004
Bank charges	4,899	3,062	2,013	1,252	655
Business & capital tax	2,774	1,049	737	874	462
Depreciation	2,614	6,081	3,689	775	591
Insurance	5,366	6,355	3,777	3,176	2,382
Interest on long-term debt	1,152	9,592	4,106	—	—
Legal and accounting	3,314	4,568	2,300	1,400	2,200
Miscellaneous	3,320	344	289	406	2,867
Office	8,548	14,546	15,640	6,846	8,372
Rent	38,634	24,050	12,166	8,470	6,195
Repairs and maintenance	5,388	3,296	4,793	11,630	3,795
Telephone	7,364	12,224	5,781	4,469	3,128
Travel	6,015	5,488	5,829	3,248	5,939
Vehicle	20,172	11,205	4,641	9,763	11,032
Wages and employee benefits	83,964	54,351	39,511	32,387	15,867
	309,869	227,573	133,406	120,096	78,507
Net income for the year	$(47,930)	$(11,549)	$ 1,156	$ 16,811	($ 20,290)

Notes
Almost 10% of sales were from carpet cleaning. Inventory turned on average once per year.

Sales escalated dramatically (see Exhibit 4). However, it became very difficult to work from the small showroom. The Hejazis felt that it was becoming a handicap and that it was time to find a larger location.

In 1988, they leased a 3,500-square-foot showroom in a plaza with three large furniture stores. A warehouse behind the showroom was also leased for the cleaning services. Locating among three furniture stores was ideal for exposing their inventory to consumers who were in the market for home furnishings.

In the summer of 1988, they readied themselves for their move to the new location. They were taking possession of their new location on September 1. They ran a moving sale, which was not a great success. An event struck in August 1988 that they believed eventually led to their bankruptcy.

Our friendly investor turned on us and demanded all his loans due or he would take over our business. Within five days, we raised the funds to repay the loans, but at a devastating cost. Most of our prime inventory had to be listed at or below wholesale. What was worse was the fact that the company was left with no financial backing at a crucial moment in its history. Our closest suppliers backed us up to the best of their ability. But the crucial suppliers of decorative rugs were unable to assist us. These suppliers were located in the United States. Consignment was not practical because of customs duties and offering credit to a Canadian company with a short history was unrealistic. Without the proper inventory that we had planned for our new store, things became a big struggle. The name of the game now was just surviving. Our sales were still increasing, but we had to do so much more advertising to get these sales.

As inventory was sold off, replacing it became more difficult. Suppliers who handled the decorative rugs required major orders, something that they were unable to place. Their financial situation was now starting to deteriorate. Bills were not quickly paid. They tried to counter by advertising more heavily. Sales did increase, but at a heavy price. At the same time, they were seeing the consumer become more hesitant to buy. Especially after the dual budgets of the federal and provincial governments in 1989, traffic slowed to a trickle. They did even more advertising to get people in, and slashed prices even further. Sales during the summer of 1990 dwindled to approximately $10,000 per month. This was when they decided that the only choice was to close.

Several days prior to the closing of the London retail store, Michael Hejazi contacted all of their suppliers to explain that they would be filing for bankruptcy. Those suppliers who had goods on consignment were encouraged to take back their unsold carpets. Where the consigned carpets had already been sold, the suppliers were told that there was not any cash to pay them. The suppliers were surprised and disappointed at the closing of Silk Route. One supplier lost goods with a value of $200,000, with others variously losing $50,000, $30,000, and $12,000 worth of goods. Since supplier margins ranged from as low as 20 percent on low-quality carpets to 100 percent on the finer pieces, the losses to the suppliers were real. Despite this, some of the suppliers seemed to understand the situation and hoped the Hejazis would be back in business at some point.

Subsequent to the closing of the retail store, the Hejazis were left with a large inventory of unsold oriental carpets plus a small warehouse that they rented in another part of the city. This warehouse served as headquarters for a related carpet wholesale company which they had established years earlier. This wholesale operation was known as Silk Route, Inc. (versus Ltd.). It had supplied the Silk Route retail store in London with some of its carpets (using a 20 percent markup to cover overhead and international travel), a franchise affiliate Silk Route store in Windsor (which had been managed by an ex-London store employee and had also now gone out of business), and a small circle of antique dealers and decorators.

With no other source of income, from October 1990 to February 1991, the Hejazis operated a retail operation out of the industrial park warehouse. They felt compelled to conduct a going-out-of-business sale because the oriental carpet industry was rationalizing. Many of the 80 carpet stores in the Toronto area were closing or offering deep discounts. Sales during the five months were roughly equal to what they had been in all of 1989. With lower overhead and limited advertising, this was a profitable period.

While most of the purchasers were repeat customers, the Hejazis were able to add 150 new customers to their mailing list. This list contained 2,200 names, 90 percent of whom had purchased a carpet(s) or had carpets cleaned through Silk Route.

By March 1991, most of the remaining inventory had been either sold on a piece-by-piece basis to individual customers or in larger lots to other wholesalers. At issue now was whether to enter a new line of work or to somehow reestablish some type of oriental carpet business.

CASE 32
TETRA PAK, INC.

In November 1990, Tetra Pak, Inc.'s Environmental Steering Committee, comprised of the president and CEO, the vice president marketing/environment, the vice president finance, the corporate communications manager, and the manager environmental affairs, met to review the company's communications campaign which had been established during the previous fall. The members of the committee were particularly interested in determining whether the campaign had been successful over the past year and what the company needed to do in the future.

A year earlier, Tetra Pak, Inc., of Aurora, Ontario, had obtained consent from the head office in Lausanne, Switzerland, to officially pursue the possibility of recycling its drink boxes. This action was taken to respond to growing Canadian public concern about the contribution of nonrecyclable, nonrefillable packages to solid waste landfill sites. To address these concerns, a manager environmental affairs was hired and, in conjunction with Superwood Ontario Limited, a method of recycling juice boxes by mixing them with plastics to manufacture plastic lumber was implemented. Tetra Pak also carried out an aggressive multifaceted communications campaign, targeting the general public, Tetra Pak customers, the government, and the media. Although the campaign attracted attention to the recyclability of juice boxes, its main objective was to highlight the benefits of the package and its minimal impact on the environment.

The Company

Tetra Pak, Inc. (hereafter Tetra Pak), was the wholly owned Canadian subsidiary of Swiss-based Tetra Pak Rausing SA (hereafter TPR), which was founded in 1951 by Dr. Ruben Rausing, a Swedish scientist. From a small Swedish company with one research facility in Sweden, TPR grew into a highly successful multinational corporation based in Lausanne, Switzerland. Its products were sold in 108 countries around the world. Operations included specialized research facilities in 7 countries and production plants in 30 countries.

In the 1940s, Dr. Rausing developed a new kind of food package that would lock in the nutritional value of perishable beverages without the need for refrigeration or preservatives. His packages were lighter and more compact

This case was prepared by Jennifer McNaughton and Fred Chan under the supervision of John S. Hulland of the Western Business School and by Mark Baetz, with the assistance of Peter Kelly, both of Wilfrid Laurier University. This case was prepared primarily from public sources. Certain information in the case may have been disguised to protect confidentiality. This case was prepared as a basis for class discussion rather than to illustrate either effective or ineffective handling of an administrative situation. Copyright 1992 © The University of Western Ontario and Wilfrid Laurier University.

than existing containers, required fewer resources to manufacture and transport, and generated less waste after their use. Dr. Rausing's vision continued to motivate his company. TPR had remained 100 percent family-owned since its inception and was managed by Dr. Rausing's sons. The company expected 1991 revenues of more than $5 billion from sales of about 60 billion cartons around the world.

TPR obtained its first overseas patent in Canada in 1958. It enjoyed great success with its Canadian entry product, a single-serve coffee cream carton in the shape of a tetrahedron. In the mid 1970s, it set up a sales office near Toronto in order to increase its sales efforts in Canada. In 1985, the company decided to invest roughly $25 million in a state-of-the-art production facility in Aurora, Ontario, just north of Toronto.

In terms of its administration, TPR was a lean organization. The president and CEO of the Canadian subsidiary reported to a senior executive in Switzerland. Tetra Pak had extensive autonomy over its day-to-day operations, with the exception of major capital and operating expenditures. It employed approximately 240 employees across Canada. In Aurora, there were people involved in technical service, production, research and development, and sales administration. In addition, there were sales offices in Vancouver and Montreal.

The Product

TPR's sole business was the manufacture of packaging systems for liquid food products. Research efforts examining packaging for semisolid food such as soup and cheese were under way. However, TPR did not intend to look beyond the food industry for packaging business. For example, it would not consider shampoos, bleaches, and motor oils.

The major product manufactured by the company was the Tetra Brik Aseptic (TBA) carton (commonly known as a juice box). The carton was made of a layer of paper (about 75 percent of the package), four layers of food-grade polyethylene plastic (about 20 percent), and a microthin layer of aluminum (about 5 percent), which was sandwiched between the polyethylene plastic.

The juice box maintained a high level of nutrition and flavour protection while ensuring safety to consumers. These benefits had persuaded many consumers to switch containers. For example, in September 1986, the Institute of Cardiology in Montreal switched from cans to drink boxes for the fruit juice supplied to its new heart recipients. Juice boxes ensured maximum hygiene during the recovery period and were considered easier and safer to use than cans.

The juice box's benefits, both as a product and in terms of its impact on the environment, had been confirmed by various independent studies (Exhibit 1). The first study, which described the marketplace in Germany, was done in 1984–1985 by a Swedish consulting firm. The Netherlands Organization for Applied Scientific Research conducted a similar study in 1990. It examined the

---

EXHIBIT 1 The Inside Story

Outside and in, Tetra Brik cartons were designed to ensure optimum flavour and nutrition protection for a variety of liquid foods, and to use minimal amounts of materials and energy.

The end result is a unique package that reduces demands on the environment.

- Most Tetra Brik paper comes from forests where the growth rate is greater than the fell rate. A renewable resource, paper composes 75 percent of Tetra Brik cartons and uses little or no chlorine in the bleaching process.
- Tetra Brik paper uses 1.5 times less water in the manufacturing process than refillable glass bottles, and 2.5 times less than nonrefillable glass bottles.
- A micro-thin layer of aluminum, about 5 percent of the total, provides an impenetrable barrier against air, light, and bacteria.
- There's less aluminum in a Tetra Brik carton than the lightest of any screw-on bottle cap.
- The small amount of aluminum in a Tetra Brik carton saves more energy than is required to make it, because it allows liquid food to be shipped and stored without refrigeration.
- Pure, food grade polyethylene plastic makes up 20 percent of all Tetra Brik cartons. In all, Tetra Pak cartons seal in the best food quality possible.

A Clean-Air Approach to Packaging
- Manufacturing Tetra Brik cartons creates less air and water pollution than most other kinds of packaging.
- Tetra Brik users indicate that these cartons require half the energy costs to manufacture and deliver products to market than other packaging.
- Tetra Brik cartons comprise less than 3 percent of the total weight of the product. A 1-litre glass bottle comprises 30 percent or more of the product's total weight.

- In June 1989, The Institute of Food Technologists in the United States recognized aseptic packaging as the most significant food science innovation in the past 50 years. The reasons cited were outstanding levels of nutrition and flavour protection, and consumer safety.

Going the Distance for Less
- Less than two standard semitrailers can transport a million unfilled 1-litre Tetra Brik cartons. 52 semi-trailers are needed to haul a million unfilled litre-size glass jars or bottles.
- Filled Tetra Brik cartons take up to 30 percent less energy to ship than glass bottles.
- Tetra Brik cartons produce 12 times less waste than glass bottles for equal product shipments (taking into account Canada's 25 percent recycling rate for glass bottles).

Tetra Brik Cartons Are Recyclable
- Tetra Pak packaging recycles into many useful products including sole shoes, mats, and a durable lumber substitute called "Superwood."
- In June 1990 Tetra Brik cartons were collected for the first time in curbside Blue Box containers in Markham, Ontario.
- Tetra Pak plans to extend recycling programs for drinking boxes into Vancouver and Montreal by the end of 1990, and eventually across all of Canada.

Already, Tetra Pak is minimizing its effect on the environment by greatly reducing its environmental demands during manufacturing and shipping.

Now that it is recyclable, this modern packaging miracle will come full circle in meeting consumers' needs and those of the environment.

---

same parameters considered in the first study but used Dutch data. Deloitte & Touche Management Consultants of North York, Ontario, had undertaken a Canadian study. Results were expected by the summer of 1991.

Production

The packaging cartons (both TBA and nonaseptic) were produced worldwide in seven sizes of varying shapes. Tetra Pak manufactured 250 ml and 1 L boxes and was one of several plants supplying these sizes to TPR's worldwide markets. In late 1990, it was additionally assigned responsibility for the 125 ml carton. Sizes not produced in Canada were imported from plants in other countries to service Canadian customers.

Customers worked closely with Tetra Pak to design the packaging artwork. Tetra Pak then printed the design on offset printing presses. The printed paper was laminated with layers of polyethylene and a microthin layer of aluminum. End-products were then delivered to the customers as rolls of "laminated paper." Due to economies of scale, the minimum purchase order quantity had been set at 250,000 boxes.

The process of sterilizing the paper, filling the packages with liquid food, and then folding the packages into boxes took place at the customers' premises. The juice box was aseptic because the product was sterilized with hydrogen peroxide and the sterilized liquid filling occurred with no air contact. The machines which performed this process cost approximately $1 million each and were leased to customers by Tetra Pak. This allowed Tetra Pak to ensure that regular maintenance was performed and that the high quality standards of the machines were maintained. In 1990, approximately 25 Canadian customers leased these machines. They sold surplus production time to an additional 50 to 60 customers whose volumes did not justify their own capital investment. Tetra Pak's major customers were major juice and fruit beverage producers.

Tetra Pak had operated under stringent internal environmental policies since inception. The company purchased its raw materials (paper, foil, polyethylene granules, and ink) from suppliers which it believed utilized the "best available technology" to ensure minimum impact on the environment. Tetra Pak used nonsolvent organic inks which were cured by electron beam in the offset printing process, again to minimize emissions to the atmosphere.

Sales

Tetra Pak dominated the drink box industry in Canada, with a major share of the approximately 1 billion carton annual market. Combibloc, Inc., was the only other supplier of juice boxes in Canada.

Tetra Pak faced significant secondary competition from glass bottles, cans, gable-top cartons, plastic bottles, polyethylene pouches, and plastic jugs. In 1990, respective shares of these container suppliers for the ready-to-serve juice/drink and nectar market were estimated to be (1) juice boxes, 35 percent; (2) glass bottles, 15 percent; (3) gable-top cartons, 15 percent; (4) plastic bottles, 15 percent; (5) cans, 15 percent; and (6) other, 5 percent.

Events Leading up to November 1989

TPR had not felt a need to actively pursue the possibility of recycling its juice boxes. To a great extent, this view was influenced by the fact that incineration for energy recovery (electricity and steam heat) was a widely accepted method of solid waste disposal in Europe. Fifty to 70 percent of solid waste in Sweden, France, and Germany was incinerated. Landfill sites were not a viable alternative given the population density of European countries.

In Canada, however, there was growing concern over incineration. For example, a 35- to 40-year-old incinerator plant in Toronto, Ontario, had been closed down in 1988 as a result of public outcry against its smoke and other toxic emissions. In this instance, the plant was old and had not been well maintained. New incineration facilities, such as Victoria Hospital's Energy from Waste Plant in London, Ontario, employed sophisticated equipment and stringent emission control technologies. Nonetheless, the public image of incinerators had already been irreversibly damaged by earlier events (Exhibit 2).

Furthermore, there was increasing public concern over capacity problems at landfill sites which were attributed to one-way packaging materials. Between 1991 and 1994, Ontario faced the loss of about 45 percent of its annual landfill capacity. Pollution Probe and other environmental organizations, which echoed "green movements" in Germany, Austria, and Belgium, advocated the use of refillable containers over one-way containers and recycling over incineration. However, such groups did not always take a consistent position. For example, in 1988, Pollution Probe in the United Kingdom issued the original "Green Consumer Guide" in which it stated that Tetra Pak cartons were close-packing, light, and save space and therefore economize on fuel in transport. Pollution Probe in Canada issued a

EXHIBIT 2   NDP Facing 'Environment Test' from Antipollution Activists

NDP
Transition to Power
11 days to Oct. 1

Pollution Probe says the first 18 months of Rae government will indicate how much is going to be done.

**By Gordon Sanderson
and Rob McKenzie**
The London Free Press*

TORONTO—Pollution Probe has set a tough timetable for the new NDP government to deliver on its promise of an environmental cleanup.

"We're looking at the first 18 months as a real test of how much is going to be done," the coalition's Janine Ferretti said Wednesday at Queen's Park. "We will fight for the adoption of the new government's environmental blueprint for Ontario."

INCINERATOR BAN: Among other things, the watchdog group is calling for an immediate ban on new garbage incinerators and, within a year, a plan to shut down existing incinerators, including Victoria Hospital's three-year-old, $32-million energy-from-waste plant, where the bulk of London's household garbage is burned.

Hospital spokesman John Finney said the incinerator is equipped with "state-of-the-art pollution control equipment" and complies with strict rules on pollution. He said it also reduces the hospital's energy bill, freeing up dollars for health care.

Last December, Westminster (nearby London) sued the hospital and London because the city was dumping fly ash from the incinerator at a city-owned landfill in Westminster. Federal tests indicated excesses of toxic metals such as cadmium and lead in the ash.

The hospital stopped dumping the ash in March and began shipping it to a waste company near Sarnia. Westminster dropped the portion of its suit against the hospital and is "not actively pursuing" the portion against the city, says Mayor Dave Murray.

BAN SUPPORTED: Ferretti said Pollution Probe was encouraged by Rae's responses during the election campaign to a questionnaire on the environment.

Rae supported an immediate ban on municipal garbage incineration and endorsed the view that incinerators undermine efforts to reduce waste. (The Liberal government ended the dumping of incinerator fly ash in municipal landfills as of Sept. 1.)

*September 20, 1990. Reprinted by permission

Canadian version in 1989 listing "5 Bad Packages," with Tetra Pak heading the list. When this discrepancy was pointed out to Pollution Probe in Canada, their response was that the two organizations were separate and distinct.

The theme "reduce, reuse, and recycle" was well advertised via radio and newspaper. Notwithstanding the many benefits of the juice box, it became a prime target for environmentalists. Elementary school teachers were writing to parents, asking them not to include juice boxes in their children's lunches. This posed a serious threat to the survival of Tetra Pak. Consequently, Tetra Pak felt strong pressures to respond.

Given the movement toward recycling in Canada, the executives of the company felt that, until juice boxes could be recycled, it would not be possible to effectively convince the Canadian public that Tetra Pak cartons were "environmentally benign." An innovative recycling approach (which involved recycling mixed plastic waste to produce durable synthetic lumber material) developed by Advanced Recycling Technology Ltd. of Belgium, had been available since 1987. Patents to the technology and the equipment had subsequently been transferred to Superwood International (based in Dublin, Ireland), who, in turn, had licensed Superwood franchisees around the world. Superwood Ontario Limited of Mississauga, Ontario, obtained its license in 1989. Tetra Pak, working closely with Superwood International in Ireland, determined that juice boxes, as well as the wrap and straws, could be used as a raw material for this plastic lumber. The juice boxes blended well into the process, and physical testing showed that the incorporation of the paper and aluminum fibres gave the lumber improved strength and stiffness.

Given this development, Tetra Pak requested approval from its head office to sanction the possibility of recycling its products. Approval to "do whatever was deemed necessary" was granted in November 1989. Tetra Pak began by providing financial and technical assistance to Superwood Ontario Ltd., which opened its doors on June 1, 1990. The Ontario and federal government each provided about $200,000 in grants to Superwood. The grants were made available by the Waste Reduction Branch of the Ontario Ministry of the Environment under the Industrial Waste Diversion Program and the federal Department of Industry, Science and Technology under a program to encourage new recycling technologies. Second, the company engaged in an expensive, multifaceted communications campaign to promote its carton's recyclability and minimal environmental impact. In the longer term, some Tetra Pak managers hoped to convince relevant stakeholders that incineration of its packages to create energy was the optimal waste management solution so that recycling would be unnecessary as in many other countries.

Superwood Ontario Limited

Superwood was the result of an innovative plastic extrusion technology. The process combined mixed plastic waste from consumer and industrial sources to produce plastic lumber which could replace wood in a variety of useful applications. At full capacity, Superwood Ontario Limited could process over 3,200 (metric) tonnes of mixed plastic and juice boxes per year. Superwood was a strong, durable, and waterproof material which could be used to produce a variety of products, including picnic tables, park benches, curb stops, planter boxes, and retaining walls.

Several Toronto-area pools had adopted Superwood for benches and storage areas. A mall opening in Scarborough in February 1991 was planning to use 400 curb stops manufactured from Superwood, as well as 48 benches and approximately 100 planter boxes. If acceptance of Superwood continued to grow, environmental concerns regarding juice boxes might be reduced. However, the markets for such recycled products were undeveloped and only a maximum of 15 percent of the volume of the final product contained Tetra Pak materials. The company was working to find a production technology which would incorporate a higher degree of its own material.

Municipal Collection

Of the 27 million tonnes of solid waste produced by Canadians, less than 12,000 tonnes consisted of juice boxes. Because of this low volume, Tetra Pak could not be expected to operate a collection system for its cartons. Instead, the company had to convince municipalities, who were legally responsible for solid waste management, to include juice boxes as part of the plastic stream in their Blue Box programs. The rough breakdown of recyclable materials collected in 1990 was newspapers, 75 percent; glass, 10 percent; steel, 10 percent; and PET/plastics, 5 percent.

The Blue Box collection system had been created under the auspices of a unique business–government cooperative arrangement. In 1985, Ontario Multi-Material Recycling, Inc. (OMMRI), an association of the soft drink industry and its container and container material suppliers, reached an agreement with the Ontario government whereby the costs of the Blue Box program would be shared and nonrefillable containers would be permitted using an initial sales ratio of 60/40 nonrefillable to refillable. The ratio would change to 70/30 when a 50 percent recycling ratio was achieved. Over the period 1986 to 1989, the costs of the Blue Box program were shared as follows: (1) OMMRI, one third of capital costs and some of the promotional costs (OMMRI contributed $20 million over the four-year period); (2) provincial government, one third of capital costs and a declining ratio of operating costs (from 50 percent to zero); (3) municipalities, one third of capital costs and operating costs not covered by the province. In 1989, the Blue Box system was acclaimed by the United Nations Environment Program and the Ontario Ministry of the Environment; the Recycling Council of Ontario and OMMRI were jointly presented with the UN's Environment Award. In the spring of 1990, because of provincial government desires to broaden private sector involvement in waste reduction activities, a new agreement was reached involving more industry groups to expand the Blue Box program. Under the new agreement, six industry sectors agreed to provide $45 million over the five years, 1990 to 1994, to help fund the system which had a mandate to extend the Blue Box network to reach 80 percent of Ontario households and expand the range of materials collected. There was some concern that if provincial governments did not continue to subsidize the Blue Box program, the municipalities would pull out of the program. Overall, it was estimated by Pollution Probe that the soft drink industry was saving up to $80 million annually by being allowed to use nonrefillable containers.[1]

It was not easy to sell municipalities on the idea of collecting juice boxes as part of the Blue Box program. Many did not have the ability to sort or bale the materials nor the capacity to warehouse them once collected. Others simply expressed no interest in the concept. Several municipalities were also reassessing their existing recycling programs. Superwood had three arguments to use in attempting to include juice boxes in municipal recycling programs: (1) significant volumes of materials are diverted from landfills, (2) no sorting of plastics into different types and sorts is necessary, and (3) a guaranteed market exists given that Superwood will sign a contract to buy all their baled postconsumer waste at $60/tonne for a specified period of time.

Tetra Pak's first success with the Blue Box program occurred in Markham, Ontario. In June 1990, coinciding with the opening of Superwood, the town of Markham announced that it would expand a pilot program to include all mixed plastics and, for the first time in Canada and the world, juice boxes. Only those boxes bearing the triangular "Tetra Pak" logo would be accepted. In light of the success of the pilot, the municipality was collecting juice boxes from over 40,000 Markham homes by the fall of 1990. The municipality of Lindsay, Ontario, followed in early October, 1990.

The Eco Logo

In 1988, the federal government announced a new environmental labeling program to help consumers recognize products deemed least harmful to the environment. A black and white maple leaf, made of three intertwined doves, and known as the Eco Logo, was the government's "environmental seal of approval." A 16-member Environmental Choice Board was created to decide whether to give Eco Logos for various product categories and if so, to establish criteria for deciding if an applicant could be licensed (for three years) to use the Eco Logo. The Canadian Standards Association administered the testing. The program was patterned after similar efforts in other countries, particularly the Blue Angel symbol developed in Germany in the late 1970s.

Soon after the Eco Logo program was announced, Tetra Pak made inquiries about using the Eco Logo. Government officials were impressed with the energy efficiency and reduction characteristics of Tetra Pak's product, but stated that politically, granting permission to use the logo would not be appropriate, since

---

[1]*Financial Times of Canada,* February 3, 1992, p. 1.

the product could not be recycled. However, Superwood applied and had been given permission to use the Eco Logo. By the fall of 1990, 26 products had won the right to display the logo, but it was suspected that many more products would be approved. The federal government was planning a multimillion-dollar advertising program to give such products a marketing advantage over competitors.

Manager-Environmental Affairs

In addition to the efforts described above, Tetra Pak's president created a new position, manager environmental affairs, in January 1990. This individual reported to the vice president, marketing/environment, and was given full authority by the Environmental Steering Committee to deal with issues within his or her mandate. This individual's responsibilities included (1) researching new technologies to validate the company's sustainable development efforts, (2) establishing internal recycling programs, (3) developing markets for recycled materials, (4) reducing plant emissions and energy consumption, and (5) responding to concerns of a technical nature from the public, government, and so on. The individual selected for this position possessed a doctoral degree in chemistry and had relevant work experience in the United States and Canada in the management of environmental affairs and government relations.

A National Packaging Protocol

In 1989, in response to demands from consumer groups, environmentalists, and various levels of government, the Canadian Council of Ministers of the Environment (federal and provincial ministers of the environment) decided to explore the feasibility of developing national policies aimed at reducing the amount of waste entering landfill sites. A task force was commissioned, composed of representatives from all relevant stakeholder groups, including the packaging industry, to develop a set of "guiding principles" to achieve the goal of minimizing landfill waste.

During the task force consultations, Tetra Pak strongly recommended that before any further policy development occurred, more research should be conducted to determine the relative environmental impacts of various disposable, recyclable, and refillable containers. The company also made the following points:

1. A "waste efficiency audit" of different packaging systems should be conducted to examine the amount of material used (weight, volume) to deliver an equivalent amount of product. For example, a European study found that a 1 litre Tetra Pak aseptic carton generated 27 grams of waste, as compared to 338 grams for an equivalent volume nonrefillable glass container.

2. An "environmental impact audit" should be conducted to examine the amount of raw materials, water, and energy consumed in producing different types of packages, as well as the amount of pollution created.

3. Municipal officials in Ontario were concerned that the 25 percent interim and 50 percent final reduction goals of the Ontario government for landfill waste, to be achieved by 1992 and 2000, respectively, were too ambitious and unrealistic, particularly in view of the negative stance the provincial government had taken toward municipal incineration. The provincial government provided little financial support to municipalities to meet the reduction targets and to help fund programs like Blue Box collection. As a result, the municipalities were pushing for the return of a bottle deposit system and a ban on all nonreusable or nonrecyclable packages. However, retailers and packaging companies were generally opposed to any form of deposit system.

4. A voluntary set of guidelines, incorporating a monitoring mechanism to ensure reduction targets were met, would be preferred to government-imposed regulations.

Overall, Tetra Pak recommended that reduction be established as the first priority of any waste management strategy. While recycling should be viewed as an important component to reduce the volume of waste diverted to landfills, Tetra Pak felt the packaging industry should be encouraged to develop new technologies and preserve existing ones (such as aseptic cartons), which achieved reductions in the amount of inputs used to produce packaging material.

The final text for the National Packaging Protocol was endorsed in early 1990. The protocol was based on the "3R hierarchy": reduce, reuse, and recycle. Recovery options, such as energy from waste (EFW) and incineration were not encompassed or envisioned in the protocol. The adoption of a 3R hierarchy placed companies like Tetra Pak at a severe disadvantage, inasmuch as aseptic containers were not reusable or easily recyclable, and it was not possible to further reduce the volume of raw material inputs used in manufacturing the container, since such reductions had been incorporated into the original package design. Specific across-the-board waste reduction targets were established in the protocol as follows: Packaging sent for disposal shall be cut to at least 80 percent of the 1988 level by the end of 1992, 65 percent of the 1988 level by the end of 1996, and 50 percent of the 1988 level by the end of 2000.

An independent auditor was appointed to determine the appropriate 1988 base figure for each type of packing material sent to landfills, in order to monitor compliance with these targets. The initial base figure for Tetra Pak had been set at 12,000 tonnes.[2] Given the relatively light weight of the aseptic carton, this 1988 base figure for Tetra Pak was extremely low for the number of litres distributed by that amount of packaging material, even when compared to packages that could be recycled (see Exhibit 3). Tetra Pak was concerned that its

---

[2]Disguised figure to protect confidentiality.

Exhibit 3   Over 500,000 Tonnes of Landfill Saved

- Between 1982 and 1989 inclusive, Tetra Pak sold packaging for a total of approximately 1.6 billion litres of liquid food, using 62,000 tonnes of packaging material (all of which went to landfill).
- If the same volume had been sold in 1.36-L and 284-ml steel cans, the net landfill would have been about 130,000 tonnes (with 50 percent recycling included in the calculations).
- If the same volume had been sold in 1-L and 284-ml glass bottles, total landfill would have been about 625,000 tonnes (with 25 percent recycling included in the calculations).
- The difference in landfill additions between Tetra Pak packaging and glass (563,000 tonnes) is roughly equal to the total amount of landfill produced annually by a city the size of Ottawa.
- Had the same 1.6 billion litres been sold in refillable bottles, making 13 round trips (the average in Europe is 7), the amount of landfill produced by glass bottles would have been about the same as that produced by beverage boxes, but with the added disadvantage of more fossil fuels used in transporting these heavy containers back and forth and more energy used in heating wash water.

These are the assumptions upon which the above comparisons were made:

Weights		*TBA* Volume (1982–1989 inclusive)*	
1-L TBA carton	31.4g	784 million litres	(1-L family size)
1-L glass bottle	400g	853.5 million litres	(250-ml single serve)
1.36-L steel can	166g		
250-mL TBA carton	11g	1637.5 million litres total	
284-mL glass bottle	173g		
284-mL steel can	55g		

Recycling rates (national average)
TBA: 0% (TBA recycling began in 1990)
Glass: 25%
Steel: 50%

---

*TBA refers to Tetra Brik Aseptic cartons.

own base figure of 12,000 tonnes would have to be reduced by 50 percent, but learned from the Packaging Task Force that the 50 percent reduction target was intended to be an across-the-board target rather than a target to be applied equally to each product. In any case, compliance with the targets was entirely voluntary, although various levels of government throughout Canada threatened to implement regulations and even ban products or increase taxes if specified reductions were not achieved voluntarily.

While the National Packaging Protocol could conceivably ensure a consistent approach to regulations for packaging across Canada, different provinces were in fact considering different regulatory approaches. Some provinces were inclined to adopt deposit refillable systems, where industry would be told what to do, while other provinces were considering a "product stewardship model" involving industry self-regulation. The product stewardship model was considered by some observers to be more mature because industry would be responsible for regulating itself, but also more dangerous given the challenges of enforcement and the uncertainty about what financial and other commitments would be made by each company.

Other Tetra Pak Initiatives

Tetra Pak addressed the issue of minimizing the environmental impact of the company's products through a number of initiatives:

1. In Canada, the company provided financial and technical assistance to Superwood, which produced synthetic wood products using, in part, Tetra Pak juice boxes. However, in 1990, the amount of waste diverted to the three plastic lumber companies operating in Canada was small (representing a total of 2,000 tonnes per annum) and synthetic wood, being new to Canada, had a very small market.

2. Pilot programs began on a limited scale in the United States, Germany, and Spain to "repulp" used Tetra Pak cartons. Repulping was a recycling process commonly employed in paper mills whereby wastepaper was shredded, mixed with water in a pulper, and then remanufactured into new paper. Tetra Pak cartons could be repulped in a normal repulping unit outfitted with specially designed screens to remove aluminum and polyethylene particles. These particles could then be recycled along with waste plastics into plastic lumber.

3. In 1990, a pilot project had been launched in Germany to produce chipboard composed entirely of aseptic carton waste. The end product had many of the physical properties of wood and, because of the plastic content, could be thermoformed by placing it in a mould and applying heat. To be economically viable, a chipboard plant required a reliable feedstock supply of approximately 100,000 tonnes per year, which far exceeded the amount of drinking carton waste generated in the Canadian market (12,000 tonnes per annum).

4. A number of extrusion applications were explored. In the extrusion process, aseptic cartons were shredded, heated, and, in some instances, mixed with other inputs to produce a number of different products. Using extrusion, fuel pellets could be produced from cartons to be burned in industrial boilers and cement kilns. These pellets were cheaper than coal and burned cleanly, but tended to cause uneven temperature levels and slagging in boilers, hindering market development efforts. Pallet spacers could also be made using extrusion technology. These spacers were widely used by a variety of industrial firms, including Tetra Pak. However, the end product was heavier than conventional wood pallets.

5. Tetra Pak signed a development contract with BTI of Germany to refine a method of manufacturing low-density rigid board using drink cartons. These boards could be used in products such as wallboard and acoustic panels.

6. Tetra Pak had been able to dramatically reduce the volumes of its own plant waste.

7. In Canada, Tetra Pak funded research to explore the development of other processes which could use aseptic carton waste. These included the use of cartons to replace various quantities of wood chips in the manufacture of medium density fibreboard (used extensively in the construction and furniture industries).

The 1990 Communications Campaign

Tetra Pak structured its 1990 communications campaign around three major target groups: the general public, the company's customers and suppliers, and various levels of government. The overall objectives were to change the perception that laminated plastics could not be recycled and to reinforce the environmental advantage of juice boxes in terms of reductions in waste, energy consumption, and use of raw materials.

General Public

For years, school boards had encouraged students to make nutritious lunch choices in packages that did not break and were safe to use. Juice and milk in Tetra Pak drink boxes seemed to be an obvious choice for many families. However, teachers and parents had developed a negative impression of juice boxes based upon misinformation about their environmental impact.

To kick off the awareness campaign, Tetra Pak worked with a major advertising agency to develop a full-page print ad (Exhibit 4) which appeared in newspapers within Eastern Canada in August and September 1990. The ad stated that the juice box was "a package of environmental solutions" and highlighted reduction of waste, raw materials, air pollution, and energy, as well as the carton's recyclability. Similar advertisements appeared in *Chatelaine, Canadian Living,* and *Macleans* magazines and in several teachers' journals.

With the assistance of a major British Columbia–based advertising firm, Tetra Pak also developed a full colour newspaper insert titled "The Juice Box Story," which appeared in all dailies and some weeklies across Canada during the fall of 1990. Tetra Pak's "very efficient package" (combining the best technology and materials, minimal energy use, minimal landfill impact, and recyclability) was emphasized. Flyers were also distributed to residents whenever their city or municipality began to accept drink boxes in their Blue Box program.

Customers and Suppliers

Tetra Pak took a different approach with its business partners. The company felt it was crucial that its customers and suppliers understood that Tetra Pak was taking a proactive role in managing issues of sustainable development. In early October 1990, Tetra Pak developed the following "Ten-Point Program" for its customers and suppliers: (1) theme: "Good for you, good for the earth," (2) publicity, (3) advertising (consumer/trade), (4) in-store campaign ("shelf talkers"), (5) consumer promotions, (6) educators' program (school kits), (7) recycling (Superwood), (8) government relations, (9) cooperative programs, (10) establishment of the Canadian Beverage Box Council (an association of aseptic packagers, i.e., Tetra Pak, Combibloc, and their customers).

By November, the program had been communicated, via presentations by senior management, to Tetra Pak's major customers. Feedback was positive, with

Exhibit 4 Example of Advertising

THIS IS
A BOX OF SOLUTIONS

The juice box is a package of environmental solutions.

Reduced waste. A juice box is 97% beverage, only 3% packaging. Litre for litre, that's ten times less packaging than glass bottles.

Reduced raw materials. Juice boxes use less raw materials than glass bottles. And 75% of those raw materials come from renewable resources.

Reduced energy. Filled juice boxes are compact and fit together like building blocks with no wasted space, saving energy when storing and shipping them.

Reduced air pollution. Empty juice boxes are light weight and are shipped in compact rolls to food manufacturers for filling. A million empty one-litre packages can be carried in 2 semi-trailers, compared to *50 semi-trailers* for that many one-litre glass bottles.

Recycling. Juice boxes are starting to be recycled. Over 500 Canadian schools already have juice box recycling bins. And some municipalities are leading the way by accepting juice boxes in their regular Blue Box programs.

The right choice. Juice boxes reduce waste, reduce energy use, and conserve resources. They're one of the most healthy and nutritious ways to package liquid food. For these reasons, in 1989, the Institute of Food Technologists named them the most important food science innovation in 50 years.

Juice boxes *are* an environmental solution. For your family, and for your future.

Good for you.
Good for the earth.

For more facts on juice boxes and the environment, call **1-800-263-2228**
or write Tetra Pak Inc., 200 Vandorf Road, Aurora, Ontario L4G 3G8

the general message being "we're glad you're doing something." Tetra Pak also encouraged its customers to be proactive by including "environmental messages" as part of their package design. The company's interaction with its suppliers was still at a preliminary stage.

Government

During his previous work, the manager environmental affairs had established excellent connections with federal and provincial government officials and various committees across Canada. He maintained regular contact with these organizations in his new role at Tetra Pak. For example, Tetra Pak had enjoyed a strong relationship with the Ontario Liberal government, actively participating in committees such as the Ontario Recycling Advisory Council, which represented various business and environmental groups and municipalities. In 1990, a senior manager of Tetra Pak also joined the board of directors of OMMRI.

The company recognized the importance of communicating with government groups on an on-going basis. Recent experiences in the United States had demonstrated the costs of not communicating adequately with government. For example, the state of Maine passed legislation in 1989 which banned the sale of any beverage in aseptic cartons. At that time, aseptic packaging manufacturers were not active in packaging ban lobbying battles. The plastics industry and local retailers did most of the lobbying because plastic packaging was the main target of restrictive bills at that time. The legislators decided that, because they could neither be recycled or reused, aseptic cartons would not fit in with their new law expanding the bottle deposit system to all noncarbonated beverages. Throughout 1989 and 1990, 12 other states either considered some form of multimaterial container bans or formed task forces to look at issues involving multimaterial packaging.

Responding to this threat, aseptic carton makers in the United States, Tetra Pak, and Combibloc formed the Aseptic Packaging Council (APC) and hired a public affairs firm to represent their interests in state capitals. APC started research on recycling pilot programs in early 1990, and by setting up recycling programs, was successful in its lobbying efforts to prevent proposed multimaterial container bans in several states. The APC continued to lobby Maine legislators to lift the aseptic carton ban temporarily in order to facilitate an APC–sponsored pilot-recycling program. Tetra Pak managers in Canada were not involved in APC.

From Tetra Pak's view, the regulatory environment in Canada was both fluid and complex. As a result, the company hired a government relations consulting firm to keep the company informed about what was happening at both the federal and provincial government levels, since each province had to be viewed as a "separate challenge." The consulting firm was not hired to lobby on Tetra Pak's behalf but to gather information about what options the governments were considering, the individuals involved and their backgrounds, and the "key influences" on each government. The consulting firm also provided Tetra Pak with an objective view of the issues and periodically gave advice to the company about possible alliances.

To assist Tetra Pak in communicating its message to governments in Canada, a 12-minute video entitled "A Balanced Environment" was developed with the help of a major public relations firm (see Exhibit 5). The show was initially used in a presentation to the British Columbia government which was

---

Exhibit 5   Communication Video: "A Balanced Environment"

"All of us are in a balancing act between what consumers want and what the environment can take; between what we produce and what we are left with. All packaging is very much under the microscope from an environmental point of view and there is a lot of misinformation out there in the marketplace. We don't have a crisis; we have an opportunity to get a head start on what we throw away. We must reduce by taking less out of the environment when a product is made and when economically and environmentally feasible, we must recycle by putting less back in the environment when the product is consumed. So consumers like to focus on recycle but we've got to be sure that in fostering recycling we don't defeat source reduction. Reduce and recycle—for a truly balanced environment we must strive to do both."

The next segment of the video described the composition of the Tetra Pak aseptic carton.

In the next segment of the video, different individuals representing the Institute of Food Technologists, National Research Council, American Management Association, and Tetra Pak commented on the benefits of the Tetra Pak (TP) carton. An "environmental summary" concluded this segment of the video by flashing the following four points: (1) "No hot water washing/detergents." (The viewer was expected to be aware that reusing glass bottles required hot water washing—which required energy—and the use of detergents—which created water pollution; however, the Tetra Pak carton was never, and could never be, refilled, primarily because health authorities prohibited refilling packages consisting of semipermeable materials, such as paper, wood, and plastic.) (2) "Less aluminum—than screw-on caps." (This point was meant to address concerns that aluminum should not be thrown away but should be recycled.) (3) "Lower energy consumption." (The video noted: "The environmental impact of any package is fundamentally in the areas of energy use, nonrenewable resource use and solid waste creation. When you reduce the weight of a package you reduce the energy required because you reduce the materials.") (4) "Reduced fuel and exhaust emissions." (The video noted: "52 semitransport trailers are needed to transport 1 million empty glass or metal containers. Tetra Pak cartons are shipped in compact rolls. One million cartons require less than two semitrailers reducing fuel consumption and exhaust emissions by over 26 times.) The end of this segment of the video noted: "Tetra Pak environmental policy sums up these facts and figures: To provide *cost effective* packaging systems for liquid food that maximize product *quality and safety* and simultaneously *minimize effects on the environment*" (underlined words were emphasized).

The final segment of the video dealt with the recycling issue and noted the following: "As consumers, we all make choices about the products we consume and their waste. When that waste is an empty Tetra Pak carton, we have two choices: throw it out or recycle it. In either case, because the carton is made with less material in the beginning, there is less waste. The first and best way of dealing with solid waste is to not create it at all—what is called source reduction.... Litre for litre, Tetra Pak cartons produce as little as one-tenth the landfill produced by today's glass bottles and that's after subtracting the bottles that are recycled. Caps and labels off glass bottles are not usually recycled and even they can weigh up to one third of the whole aseptic package.... If we achieved our goal of source reduction to a very high degree, recycling would essentially disappear because there wouldn't be enough material around to recycle."

The segment concluded by describing how Tetra Pak cartons were being recycled into "excellent" particle board and synthetic lumber. It was noted that "the first production plant is in Germany," and "Blue Box collection of TP cartons has already begun in parts of southern Ontario and TP is working to expand this across Canada.... A study by the Grocery Product Manufacturers of Canada states that almost 7 of 10 Canadians are willing to participate in a curbside recycling program.")

The video concluded as follows: "Because it reduces and is now recyclable, we're convinced the Tetra brik aseptic package is a responsible and environmentally sound package. We will cooperate with government, industry partners, and consumers to make it even better. That's our commitment to a world insisting on healthy products and a healthy environment."

considering deposit legislation. Tetra Pak planned to use the show in similar presentations to other provincial governments, the federal government, and a variety of other groups in the educational and recycling fields.

Tetra Pak also developed another 12-minute video entitled "A Box Called Tyler" to educate students about the possible recyclability of the juice box in light of the increasing trend toward "garbageless lunch" programs. In these programs, students were discouraged from bringing nonreusable and nonrecyclable packages for lunch. In addition to the video, the company initiated a pilot school recycling program to collect Tetra Pak packages from the school board in the region of York north of Toronto. Student committees were formed to take responsibility for collecting the packages, and Tetra Pak took responsibility for providing the necessary equipment and collecting and delivering the packages to Superwood for recycling. From this program, the company hoped to gain information about the costs, logistics, and attitudes of school boards, teachers, and children. The Environmental Committee of the Toronto School Board reviewed the program and decided not to participate.

In general, Tetra Pak's approach was "to make itself very available" to participate in packaging or environment-related events or conferences. The company's attitude was that these presented opportunities to communicate accurate messages about the environmental impact of juice boxes.

November 1990

In November 1990, one year after the initiation of their communications campaign, the Environmental Steering Committee felt it was time to review their progress to date. The committee's general feeling was that the communications campaign was "good, but not good enough" and, therefore, members considered changes Tetra Pak could make. To date, advertising efforts had focused on print. The committee wondered if other methods/media should be considered and whether the message should be changed. Members believed that it might be possible for Tetra Pak to do something else to enhance public education and awareness.

Tetra Pak had received some encouraging feedback regarding the newspaper advertisements and inserts. A toll-free telephone number had been established to handle inquiries from the public regarding information in Tetra Pak advertisements. Over 2,000 calls were recorded, more than 85 percent of them positive. However, many people had the perception that Tetra Pak was promoting recyclability, even though the company knew that its product was not being recycled in many municipalities. They complained that the claims meant little to them personally until their communities began to accept juice boxes as part of their local Blue Box programs. Tetra Pak's explanations that municipalities had the prerogative to determine which materials would be recycled and that municipalities often were slow to implement collection programs seemed to fall on deaf ears.

Exhibit 6   NDP's Promise to Outlaw Beverage Boxes 'Shocking'

By John Fox
Financial Post

The pre-election pledge of a senior Ontario New Democrat to ban the use of boxes as beverage containers because they are difficult to recycle is "shocking and shortsighted," says a spokesman for **Tetra Pak Inc.,** the product's maker.

Ruth Grier, a senior NDP MPP rumored to be headed for the environment portfolio in premier-elect Bob Rae's cabinet, promised the ban during a public debate in Toronto a week before her party's election win.

Many environmentalists don't like the containers—used to package everything from wine to milk shakes—because they are not reusable and contain a combination of plastic, paper and aluminum that makes them hard to recycle.

A spokesman for Grier said she would have no comment on the fate of the boxes until after a cabinet has been appointed.

Jaan Koel, a spokesman for the Aurora, Ont. company Tetra Pak, a wholly-owned subsidiary of Swiss-based Tetra Pak Rausing SA, said Grier's opposition to drinking boxes is based on "purely a surface evaluation of the situation" and not on "solid, factual information."

He said the company, with sales of 920 million boxes a year in Canada worth $100 million—and 35% to 40% of sales in Ontario—is launching a recycling program in Lindsay, Ont. and Markham, Ont. in October. Householders will be asked to separate drinking boxes and other plastics from their blue boxes for collection and sale to Superwood Ontario Ltd. of Mississauga, Ont., which will turn them into plastic lumber.

Superwood is also in negotiations with recycling officials in Vancouver and Montreal. Koel said it may take several years to expand the program to the entire Ontario blue box system.

In the meantime, critics of the drinking boxes ignore their environmental and economic advantage, he said.

He said the lightweight packages offer huge savings in transportation costs and the environmental impacts of burning fossil fuels. For example, two million empty drinking boxes can be shipped in two tractor trailers. The same number of empty glass or metal containers would require 52 trucks, Koel said.

Because they are more compact than bottles or cans, he added, they also contribute less to the province's overflowing garbage dumps.

*September 18, 1990
Reprinted by permission

During pre-election speeches, the newly elected NDP government in the province of Ontario had pledged to ban the use of juice boxes (Exhibit 6). The Environmental Steering Committee was uncertain about the impact this would have on the company's business, as policies had not yet been established regarding environmental issues. However, the company was concerned about the role that the new government might play in helping or hindering its activities.

CASE 33
TRANSALTA UTILITIES CORP.

> Very simply, we're making the environment as important as safety, cost and quality
> of service in our decision making.
>
> Ken McCready, CEO & President

As they approached their 1990 strategic planning session, TransAlta's senior
executives confronted a changing business environment. The company's goal had
always been to provide reliable electric service to their customers at the lowest
possible cost. Now, a new variable was entering the picture: the environment and
the question of sustainable development. The 1987 release of the report of the
World Commission on Environment and Development, chaired by Harlem
Brundtland, gave credibility to the concept of sustainable development and
elevated environmental issues on the international agenda.

Canada, having been identified as the biggest consumer of energy per capita
in the world, was under particular pressure to act. The Canadian public had also
taken up the issue. In a recent opinion poll, 25 percent had named the environment as the most important problem in Canada, up from only 2 percent one year
earlier.

There was no doubt in management's mind that TransAlta would be severely
affected by any legislation introduced by the federal government to reduce
emissions. At the same time, the provincial government's highest priority was
diversifying Alberta's economy. It intended to use low-cost electricity to attract
energy-intensive industries to the province. How could TransAlta act to manage
these differing objectives and still secure the interests of its customers and its
shareholders?

Company Background

TransAlta Utilities Corporation was the largest investor-owned electric utility in
Canada, and its shares were widely held. The company operated as a regulated
monopoly and supplied 72 percent of Alberta's electricity needs. In addition,
TransAlta sold electricity to British Columbia and through B.C. Hydro exported
to the U.S. Northwest Power Pool. It had a number of subsidiaries, some
operating in nonregulated industries. These interests included coal mining, en-

ergy systems technology, and oil and gas. Operating statistics appear in Exhibits 1 and 2.

TransAlta was an integrated company with the largest coal mining operation in Canada, producing 21 percent of all coal mined in the country. TransAlta

---

EXHIBIT 1 Financial Record (in millions of dollars unless otherwise noted)

	1988	1987	1986	1985	1984
Statement of earnings					
Electric revenue	950.5	917.3	907.2	833.0	786.7
Other revenue	11.6	7.6	8.3	3.0	0.6
Operating deductions	−615.4	−585.8	−581.1	−524.5	−490.6
Allowance for funds used during construction	33.8	39.2	61.4	75.6	77.3
Investment income	−51.6*	10.9	−110.2*	16.9*	23.0
Interest charges	−148.6	−129.3	−148.1	136.8	−136.2
Preferred share dividend requirements	−61.7	−80.9	−84.0	−86.3	−77.1
Earnings applicable to common shares before extraordinary items	118.6	179.0	53.5	180.9	183.7
Extraordinary items	—	—	—	—	—
Net earnings applicable to common shares	118.6	179.0	53.5	180.9	183.7
Common shareholders' investment					
Average common shareholders' investment (weighted)	1,241.9	1,305.7	1,283.0	1,261.0	1,155.0
% return (before unusual items)	13.6	13.7	13.9	15.2	15.9
Common share information ($/share)†					
Book value (year-end)	9.09	9.90	9.49	9.97	9.42
Earnings before unusual items	1.25	1.33	1.35	1.48	1.44
Dividends declared	0.93	0.92	0.86	0.81	0.74
Interest coverage (times earned before income tax)					
First mortgage bonds	13.84	12.75	11.31	11.01	13.40
All fixed charges	3.99	4.42	4.04	4.12	4.13
Assets and property					
Total assets (year-end)	3,687.3	3,683.9	3,700.1	3,735.6	3,516.9
Property account	3,384.5	3,317.0	3,304.0	3,215.0	3,081.5
Electric utility property in service (year-end)	3,140.0	3,005.3	2,993.4	2,560.5	2,536.0
Additions to property	223.1	170.4	236.5	254.8	306.5
Capitalization (year-end)					
Common shareholders' equity	1,230.1	1,338.4	1,269.8	1,303.0	1,218.8
Preferred shares	678.9	758.7	689.7	741.8	707.8
Long-term debt	1,217.5	946.2	992.3	1,093.9	1,024.6
Preferred shares of a subsidiary	—	124.2	160.0	160.0	120.0
	3,126.5	3,167.5	3,111.8	3,298.7	3,071.2

*Net of unusual items of $50MM, $125MM, and $110MM in 1988, 1986, and 1985, respectively.

†After giving effect to the 2-for-1 stock split February 1, 1988.

Exhibit 2 **Statistical Record**

	1988	1987	1986	1985	1984
Electric energy sales (millions of kWh)					
Residential, general service, & small industry	3,129	2,928	2,854	2,802	2,671
Industrial	9,992	8,789	8,215	7,994	7,205
Cities and towns under wholesale contracts	7,002	6,668	6,522	6,453	6,240
Farms	1,117	1,006	1,006	999	962
	21,170	19,391	18,597	18,248	17,078
Generating capability (nominal net MW)					
Hydro	800	800	800	800	800
Thermal	3,493	3,493	3,493	3,310	3,310
	4,293	4,293	4,293	4,110	4,110
Sources of primary energy (millions of kWh)					
Hydro	1,423	1,444	1,791	1,385	1,420
Thermal—Gas	—	—	—	—	—
—Coal	26,342	24,839	23,813	23,181	21,256
Net purchases and exchanges	−4,619	−4,970	−5,304	−4,610	−3,965
	23,146	21,313	20,300	19,956	18,711
Customers					
Served directly	296,601	292,177	287,758	283,254	279,164
Served indirectly through wholesale contracts	306,327	300,672	296,674	292,538	292,324

produced 94 percent of its electricity (over 25 billion kilowatt-hours) from three wholly owned and one joint venture coal-fired generating plants; the remainder were hydro. This method of generating electricity was very cost effective and allowed TransAlta to become the lowest cost producer of electricity in Canada. A drawback of burning fossil fuels such as coal were the emissions produced, major contributors to acid rain (NO_x and SO_x), and possible contributors to global warming (CO_2). TransAlta used a low sulphur grade of coal; hence, the issue of SO_x emissions was not as significant.

In addition to generation, the company owned almost 80,000 circuit kilometres of operating transmission and distribution lines. It was part of the Alberta Interconnected System (AIS), a province-wide transmission grid linked to B.C. Hydro and the U.S. northwest. Transmission is the process of moving electric power in bulk from the generating plants to local distribution systems. Large transformers step up the voltage to make long-distance cost efficient. As the electricity nears its destination, voltages are reduced or "stepped down" at substations. Electricity is then distributed, by local utilities, to where the customers need it—in homes, stores, industries, and farms.

Provincial Industry Players

There were three principal generators of electricity in Alberta: TransAlta, Alberta Power Ltd. (owned by Canadian Utilities), and Edmonton Power Ltd. (owned by the city of Edmonton).

Alberta Power Limited (APL) was also investor owned and produced approximately 12 percent of Alberta's power requirements by generating electricity through coal-fired plants. APL served the sparsely populated northern part of Alberta, a geographic area similar in size to TransAlta's. Because of the smaller customer base, it was not able to achieve economies of scale, and its costs were approximately 60 percent greater than TransAlta's.

Edmonton Power Ltd. (EPL) was municipally owned and regulated by the city of Edmonton. It produced approximately 18 percent of Alberta's power needs through natural gas and coal-fired plants. Like APL, it was not able to achieve economies of scale, resulting in costs that were estimated to be 22 percent greater than TransAlta's.

Regulatory Bodies

The Public Utilities Board

The Public Utilities Board (PUB) regulated electric, gas, and other utilities in Alberta. By law, the electrical utilities must undergo review by the PUB every three years. In addition, the PUB had public hearings whenever there was an application for a rate change. Interest groups, such as industry associations, agricultural lobby groups, and the city of Calgary would generally challenge some elements of TransAlta's rate case. The hearings were very technical and included a range of customer interest, supported as required by expert witnesses. The PUB arbitrated between the parties based on the evidence brought before it. The main subjects discussed at rate hearings were: (1) forecast demand and revenues, (2) the assets forming the rate base and the expenses incurred in the provision of service, and (3) financial criteria, principally the return on equity that the utility should be allowed to earn.

In principle, rates were set which allowed the utility to make a return on the common equity on those assets currently used to provide electricity that adequately compensated shareholders for their risk. However, there was no guarantee that this rate of return would be earned in any prospective period.

The rate-setting process was not necessarily supportive of environmental expenditures. As one TransAlta manager explained:

> TransAlta is regulated by the PUB. In the past, interveners have made strong representation that TransAlta should not spend money beyond that mandated by government standards. Therefore, unless legislative standards are imposed or, better yet, market mechanisms are put in place to render a value on pollution abatement, it

will be difficult for TransAlta to make expenditures on controlling NO_x, SO_x, or greenhouse gases. Until these expenditures are made, TransAlta's rates will not fully reflect the environmental impact of our operations.

The Electrical Energy Marketing Agency

In 1982, the provincial government introduced the Electric Energy Marketing Agency (EEMA), a nonjurisdictional body, to reduce rate disparities that existed throughout the province. To standardize the rates across the province, EEMA conducted a "paper transaction" by "purchasing" all the electricity generated in the province at a cost determined by the PUB. The electricity was then "pooled," the costs were averaged and then resold back to the utilities at the average cost. The end result was a hybrid alternative to a single electric utility for the province of Alberta. From TransAlta's perspective, they subsidized Alberta Power and Edmonton Power at the expense of their customers, as TransAlta's generating costs were the lowest in the province.

Energy Resources Conservation Board

The Energy Resources Conservation Board (ERCB) approved the construction of transmission lines and generating plants; coal mine developments; service area changes; and interconnection with small power producers. Applications for construction had to be filed with the ERCB months, and often years, before new facilities were required. Environmental and social impact assessments and plans to minimize the impact of utility projects through land reclamation and other programs were presented.

Generation Methods

Alberta's reliance on coal was in contrast to most other provinces in Canada and around the world. Hydro-Quebec and B.C. Hydro primarily utilized hydroelectric generation while Ontario Hydro operated a number of nuclear facilities. Nuclear, hydroelectric, coal-fired, and oil-fired represented the major means of power generation used in developed countries. At a world level, TransAlta's industrial and residential rates were among the lowest when compared to other provinces and industrialized nations (see Exhibits 3 and 4).

Each power generation method had its own set of environmental problems. Burning fossil fuels (coal, oil, natural gas) created local pollution and was believed to impact global warming. Hydroelectric plants drastically altered the local ecosystem during their construction and operation.[1] As yet there was no

---

[1]The primary hurdle in the further development of the James Bay hydroelectric project was federal environmental reviews.

EXHIBIT 3 Canadian Industrial Rates

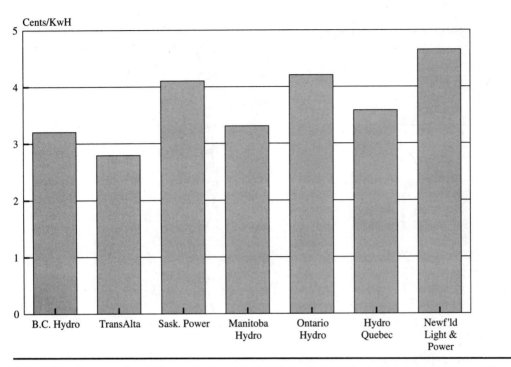

SOURCE: TransAlta survey of electricity rates on December 31, 1989. Based on 5MW loads, 85 percent load factor, and 90 percent power factor.

long-term solution to the problem of disposal of spent nuclear fuel. In addition, the public was very sceptical of the safety of nuclear plants after the incidents at Chernobyl and Three-Mile Island.

Alternate technologies existed for generating electricity, including solar, wind, biomass, and geothermal. However, none of these had been developed to the point where it could match the cost and reliability of the current technologies on a commercial scale. Investment in the development of alternate technologies was curtailed significantly after oil prices dropped in 1986 and government incentive programs were reduced.

External Stakeholders

Customers

As an investor-owned, regulated monopoly, TransAlta was subject to satisfying the conflicting demands of several stakeholders. Their customers, the public, and businesses of Alberta expected low-cost, reliable service. TransAlta invariably

---

EXHIBIT 4 World Rates

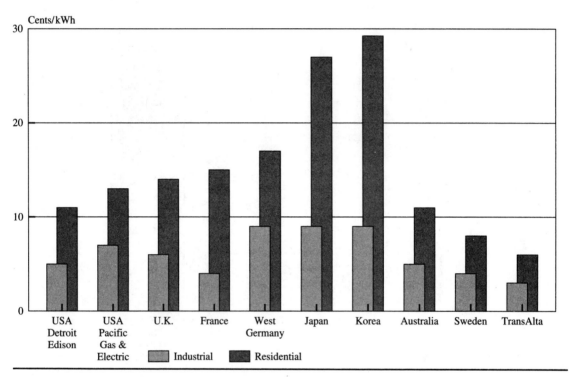

NOTE: Industrial rates are based on 10MW loads, 89 percent load factor, and 95 percent power factor.
      Residential rates are based on an annual consumption of 7,500 kWh.
SOURCE: The Electricity Council—electricity rates as of January 1, 1989.

---

faced strong opposition to any proposed rate increases despite the fact that surveys had shown that customers were very satisfied with the service provided.

Many people felt that the 13–15 percent return allowed TransAlta was excessive and that utilities should be owned by the government. The company pointed out the 13–15 percent return going to shareholders would be shifted to bondholders, as the government would most likely finance these utilities through public debt. The threat of being taken over by the provincial government was always present, especially if there were a change of government. Thus, TransAlta maintained a positive public profile and close relations with the Alberta government.

Provincial Government

Having the lowest electricity rates in Canada made Alberta an attractive place for energy-intensive businesses to invest. The provincial government was concerned with Alberta's reliance upon the oil and gas industry. It was working hard to attract business to Alberta and was using low-cost energy as an incentive. To energy-intensive industries such as pulp and paper, Alberta was becoming more and more attractive, despite the increased shipping distances to major markets. While the government was concerned with the environment, economic diversification and growth appeared higher on its agenda.

Federal Government

The federal government was under pressure internationally and domestically. Environmental groups and the Canadian public had expressed a strong desire for the government to be tougher on environmental issues. Acid rain had long been a difficult issue in Canada's relationship with the United States and was a serious problem in the highly industrialized areas around the Great Lakes. The government had promised to produce a "green plan" in 1990, outlining Canada's environmental strategy, to be followed by legislation. At this stage, the federal government's policy on sustainable development and how to bring it to Canada was still very much in its infancy.

International Organizations

The Montreal Accord on CFCs was a major step, resulting in the first international environmental treaties. The United Nations Committee on the Environment and Development (UNCED), created following the Brundtland Commission, was attempting to get an agreement for action on global warming. Their work would culminate at a conference in Brazil in 1992 and could result in an international agreement to reduce CO_2 emissions.

Shareholders

TransAlta's shareholders were caught in the middle. Through the rate regulatory process, TransAlta was always under pressure to improve productivity and reduce costs. During rate hearings, interest groups would question everything from operating practices, to capacity planning, to capital investments. TransAlta's management wanted to provide shareholders with steady growth in earnings and dividends. The energy marketplace in Alberta did not provide for massive investments in environmental protection and TransAlta needed to find ways to meet its environmental responsibilities at the least possible cost.

Sustainable Development

The Brundtland Commission defined sustainable development as development that improved the standard of living without impairing the ability of future generations to enjoy the same standard of living.

The key elements of sustainable development,[2] as it applied to energy, that needed to be reconciled were (1) sufficient growth of energy supplies to meet human needs, (2) energy efficiency and conservation measures, such that waste of primary resources is minimized, (3) public health, recognizing the problems of risks to safety inherent in energy resources, and (4) protection of the biosphere and the prevention of more localized forms of pollution.

Global Warming

There is little dispute about the increase in atmospheric greenhouse gases. However, there is little or no agreement on the consequences of these increases. The climatic models, which predicted average global temperature increases of 2° to 6° C over the next 50 years, were not reliable. They failed to consider issues such as increase in cloud cover, recapture of carbon by increased plant growth, and so on. In any event, not all the predicted consequences are necessarily negative. Agricultural productivity might actually improve with higher concentrations of CO_2 in the atmosphere.

As CO_2 and other greenhouse gases accumulate in the atmosphere, they create a blanket which insulates the earth. The blanket captures heat radiated from the earth and traps it at the surface, hence increasing the temperature. Although carbon dioxide accounts for almost half of the greenhouse gases, methane, CFCs, nitrous oxides, and others contribute 18 percent, 14 percent, 6 percent, and 13 percent, respectively, and are growing at a more rapid rate.

Carbon dioxide, which comes mainly from the burning of fossil fuels has been, and will continue to be, mankind's greatest contributor to greenhouse gases. (Coal produces the most carbon per unit of heat.)

Acid Rain

Combustion of fossil fuels, particularly coal, contributes more than 80 percent of the SO_2 and most of the NO_x injected into the atmosphere. Almost two thirds of sulphur dioxide emissions come from electric utility plants. Acid rain is created when sulphur dioxides (SO_2) and the oxides of nitrogen (NO_x) are converted to acids when combined with water in the atmosphere. When the environment is not able to neutralize the increased acid deposits of the rainfall, damage occurs.

The acidic rainfall can extend hundreds of miles from the point of emissions. In Eastern Canada, more than half of the acid deposition was believed to originate in the United States; hence, emission reductions were required on both sides of the border.

---

[2]*Our Common Future,* The World Commission on Environment and Development, Oxford University Press, 1990, p. 169.

Incorporating Environmental Effects

National Legislation

Legislation tended to adopt two basic approaches to the reduction of environmentally harmful emissions: (1) command and control (standards) and (2) economic instruments (taxes, incentives, tradeable permits).

Command and Control

Companies emitting pollutants such as sulphur dioxide, nitrous oxide, and/or carbon dioxide would be instructed to use certain technologies and limited to emitting a specified maximum amount of these compounds. If the company exceeded this amount, or if they discharged prohibited pollutants, then penalties or sanctions would be imposed by government.

Concerns with this method include cost effectiveness, impact on coal-burning industries, potential economic dislocation, and lack of incentives for companies to perform better than government standards.

Economic Instruments (Tradeable Permits or Taxes)

Under this type of scheme, the maximum amount of pollutant which could be emitted at an aggregate level in a given region was defined by the government. The amount could be reduced on a regular basis. Permits were allocated to firms, generally on the basis of historical emission or output which would enable the owner to emit a specified type and amount of pollutant. Companies able to reduce their emissions below their limit would benefit from their improved performance by selling unused portions of their permit to other companies unable to meet their own emission limits. If a firm emitted more pollutants than their permits allowed, they would be assessed a severe penalty. Thus, the market was used to allocate emission reductions in the most efficient manner with minimum impact on the economy.

The reduction of lead in gasoline in the United States provided an example of this type of environmental legislation. This approach had also been successful in reducing the use of CFCs at an estimated 50 percent of the cost of the traditional "command and control" approach. Tradeable permits were the centrepiece of the acid rain program of the proposed U.S. Clean Air Act.

Tradeable permits used quantities of emissions as the measure of performance or performance improvement. An alternative economic instrument was based on the price. In this approach, a tax on emissions above the allowed level (or a tax credit for a reduction in emissions below the specified level) allowed the cost of environmental performance to be explicit in the decision making of individuals and corporations.

Global Perspective

CO_2 and the possibility of global warming were truly global phenomena; however, while this presented problems, it also raised opportunities for creative solutions.

In 1989, a U.S. utility, Applied Energy Services, undertook a biotic carbon sequestering program to offset fossil fuel emissions from a 183 MW coal-fired power plant under construction in Connecticut. The basic concept was straightforward. Plants remove carbon from the atmosphere (and release O_2). Therefore, if a utility stimulated net new additions to the biomass of the planet (and kept this carbon sequestered for an appropriate period of time), then on a global basis, there would be zero emissions (of CO_2).

The Connecticut power plant was expected to contribute 15.5 million tons of carbon to the atmosphere over its 40-year life. The utility provided $2 million in support (supplemented by $14 million from various aid agencies) for a 10-year reforestation project[3] in Guatemala. The project was expected to recapture between 18 and 35 million tons of atmospheric carbon. Subtropical areas were attractive for this type of project because of the higher rate of plant growth, low labour costs, and availability of supplemental grants.

TransAlta's Policy Alternatives

Defensive Stance

One option, common in industry during the 1970s, had been to deny the problem or argue that there was insufficient proof of possible negative consequences. The argument had been made that if we want to enjoy our current standard of living, there will be some cost to the environment. Any attempt to protect it would only make our industries less competitive and, in turn, hurt all Canadians. The threat of global warming was still debated in the scientific community and acid rain was not a serious problem in Alberta. Even so, for TransAlta to take up this argument and lobby the federal government against legislation would be risky. While they might succeed in delaying action, it was not thought likely that the issue would disappear. Indeed, management felt strongly that the corporation had an obligation to act, and the company's recent policy statement on the environment called for a more proactive approach (see Exhibit 5).

Investment in New Technology

TransAlta also considered increasing investment in the development of new technologies. In Alberta, additional hydroelectric generation involved higher costs and other environmental issues, and nuclear energy carried its own set of environmental problems, not to mention general fear within the public. Alterna-

---

[3]The project included much more than simple reforestation. It involved a number of species and extensively involved the local population.

Exhibit 5 Environmental Policy Statements

TransAlta is committed to the protection of the environment and to sustainable development. Environmental stewardship is a vital element in our business. We strive to empower all our employees to take initiatives to protect and enhance the environment, based on shared values and the need to satisfy the environmental concerns and expectations of customers, investors and the public.

Our commitments are to:

- Report complete and accurate information on the environmental impact of our business, meet or surpass all environmental standards, and continuously improve our environmental performance.
- Advocate socially responsible environmental standards and the recognition of the economic value of environmental resources.
- Implement conservation and efficiency initiatives for all resources and pursue alternative energy opportunities, both within our own operations and in partnership with others.
- Seek out research opportunities and develop alliances that will improve our environmental performance and make a positive contribution to solving environmental challenges.
- Consult and work cooperatively with those who may be affected by our business and respond to their environmental concerns.
- Recognize and respect the relationship between environment and health in all phases of our business, and use the best knowledge available to protect the health of employees and the public.
- Encourage and develop educational programs and resources, to provide balanced public information and to foster environmentally sensitive attitudes, knowledge and skills.
- Identify and develop business ventures where value can be added to environmental solutions while providing investment opportunities for the corporation and its shareholders.

November 26, 1990

Printed on Recycled Paper

TransAlta Utilities

---

tive energy needed to be nonpolluting in every sense. Solar, wind, and other technologies had been under development around the world for a number of years; however, considerable additional investment in time and money would be required to make any of them viable on a large commercial scale. Any investment TransAlta made in new technology was "noncost-of-service"; hence, there would be no guaranteed returns to the shareholders. Thus, technology development must earn a return sufficient to satisfy shareholders on its own.

TransAlta had been working on developing improved coal burning technology. The overall efficiency of conventional coal-fired thermal generation is 33–35 percent. By improving efficiency, the same amount of energy could be generated with less damage to the environment. TransAlta acquired Low NO_x/SO_x Burner (LNSB) technology from Rockwell International, the U.S. aerospace firm that built the space shuttle. Through the development of rockets, Rockwell became highly knowledgeable in controlled burn technology and maximization of fuel efficiency. LNSB technology was not yet proven to be far superior to previous emission reduction technology such as scrubbers. Scrubbers actually reduced the overall efficiency of the process while reducing SO_x and NO_x emissions, but not

CO_2. LNSB reduced emissions of all pollutants by increasing the efficiency of the process. This technology would be tested in two pilot plants in the United States beginning in 1992.

Conservation & Cogeneration

Demand management measures included efforts to improve the economics of power supply by reducing peak load demands and increasing off-peak sales and payments to customers to encourage the use of efficient equipment. Conservation and especially load management effort were of increasing importance in strategies to encourage the wise use of electricity and to serve customers' electricity needs at the lowest possible cost.

Cogeneration described situations where industrial plants or institutions generated their own electrical power. Typically, these generators were powered by excess energy available as a byproduct of the firm's manufacturing process (thus the term *cogeneration*). These locations were still hooked into the power grid and would not only purchase power to supplement their own needs but also occasionally have excess electricity available for transmission through the grid. Most cogen facilities were powered by fossil fuels, generally natural gas. So reduction in emissions resulted only if the energy was a by-product of another process and/or on-site generation was more efficient (from a fuel consumption standpoint) than generating the power at the utility's plant.

Cogeneration or, more generally, consumer-generated electricity, appeared to be an attractive business in its own right. TransAlta had set up a special unit to pursue this opportunity and currently had two projects (both in Ontario).

Participation in Federal Policy Development

Because federal government policy had not yet been clearly defined, the opportunity existed to influence the process. TransAlta had gained experience dealing with the provincial government, but not as much with the federal government. More, and probably tougher, environmental legislation appeared to be coming. Perhaps TransAlta could be proactive and encourage federal bureaucrats to consider methods that would not harm TransAlta. This would include market mechanisms (such as tradeable permits) used to reduce emissions in concert with Canada's major trading partners.

TransAlta's senior executives felt that it was their responsibility to solve the dilemma in the best way for their customers. While TransAlta did not have any direct competition, their customers did. In essence, the competitiveness of Alberta's economy was dependent on TransAlta's ability to deal with this issue. Ken McCready commented on the broader implications of environmental actions: "Canada cannot act on its own unilaterally to incorporate environmental costs without international agreements. It must press for such agreements if the public demands action in Canada; for to fail to do so would cause a serious loss of competitiveness in international trade."

Deciding upon a course of action to take would be difficult. Influencing public opinion and government policy to implement their strategy would be even tougher.

Case 34
University Hospital— 1987

Finding a better way.[1]

In the fall of 1987, University Hospital (UH) had just completed, with the assistance of outside consultants, an extensive strategy review culminating in a formal strategic plan. The original stimulus for the plan had been to better understand the growth patterns and potential of the hospital's services in order to forecast the need for and justify a significant expansion of the hospital's facilities. However, the final document had gone beyond this original intention, raising questions about the hospital's "service portfolio" and its future potential.

The strategic plan had seven key recommendations (see Exhibit 1), several of which represented significant departures from past practice. As part of the planning process, the hospital's services had been put into different categories, a portfolio approach, with apparent implications for future emphasis and resource allocation. As one UH vice president commented:

> The plan has forced us to establish some priorities for our different services. Not everything we do is, or will be, world class, and the plan will help us allocate our increasingly scarce resources, capital, and operating funds, toward our premier services.

Further, the plan recommended organizing business units around these "service clusters" (or product lines), and continuing the planning process as an ongoing, in-house activity. As Pat Blewett, president and CEO of UH, reviewed the report and its recommendations, he was satisfied with both the process and the results. Blewett was widely recognized as a highly positive, entrepreneurial type of administrator willing to try new ideas and promote innovative services. Results had been impressive. New services had contributed substantially to UH's growth and cash flow. However, the facility was straining within its existing physical space. In addition UH, like other hospitals in the province of Ontario, had to cope with increasing budgetary pressures from the Ministry of Health, while demand for all services continued to grow. Blewett hoped the recommendations from the strategic plan would allow the hospital to deal with these issues while maintaining the institution's innovative and entrepreneurial spirit.

---

[1]UH's motto; attributed to Thomas Edison.

Exhibit 1 Key Recommendations from the Strategic Plan

Recommendation #1: Pursue a Service Cluster Product Line Development Approach
Product line management is a system that organizes management accountability and operations around discrete service or product lines. Service clusters are those groups of services that are provided to distinct market segments. By shifting management focus to product line development, hospitals can increase their market share by improving the efficiency of their services and by tailoring services to specific market needs.

Recommendation #2: Adopt an Appropriate Bed Complement for UH in the 1990s
To facilitate the implementation of a service cluster or product line concept for University Hospital, it will be essential to adopt an appropriate bed complement (for each service).

Recommendation #3: Address Facility Considerations through a Medical Mall Implementation Strategy
The purpose of the medical mall is multifold:

• It compartmentalizes functions and services to allow an optimum level of capital expense by type of service.
• It targets and controls traffic by patient type while ensuring convenience and accessibility.
• It provides a "one-stop" location for multiple levels of inpatient and outpatient support services.

Recommendation #4: Pursue a Networking Strategy as Part of the Role of Tertiary Care
Pursuit of a networking strategy asserts that the role of University Hospital in tertiary care should represent a "hub" within the Canadian and international health care system. As such, options have been developed to ensure University Hospital is able to accept patients who need to be "stepped-up" from community hospitals and outpatient settings and also to "step down" patients who no longer require UH's intensity of services.

Recommendation #5: Adopt a Diversification Strategy
To encourage management to investigate which type of integration makes most sense for UH given its tertiary nature and commitment to research and education. Diversification efforts can be adopted by an institution in basically three ways, through vertical integration, horizontal integration, or geographic dispersion.

Recommendation #6: Implement an Organizational Enhancement Strategy
Due to the complexity and dynamic nature of University Hospital, ongoing strategic planning and administrative support and leadership will be essential. The recommended organizational enhancement strategy has, as its focus, to

• Pursue process planning and implementation by adopting an ongoing planning cycle.
• Assign responsibility/authority for successful ongoing strategic planning.
• Address management/medical staff succession.
• Exploit the benefits of University Hospital's relationship with HCA.

At the heart of this strategy is the need to formalize and integrate current planning mechanisms into an ongoing process.

Recommendation #7: Continue an Aggressive Financial Strategy: Preserve/Enhance Financial Resources
The objectives of this recommendation are twofold:

• To enhance financial resources.
• To preserve financial resources.

Background

While a separate institution, UH was part of a larger health sciences complex of the University of Western Ontario. UH had been an educational and research, as well as a health care delivery, facility since opening in 1972. It was the newest of the three major acute care hospitals in London, Ontario, a community of about 300,000 in southwestern Ontario. UH was established, owned, and operated by the London Health Association (LHA).

Founded in 1909, the LHA's activities had changed dramatically over the years. Originally, it had operated a tuberculosis sanatorium on the outskirts of the city. As the number of tuberculosis patients declined, the LHA made plans to diversify into chest diseases and purchased property adjacent to the university for a new hospital. However, in the decade of the 1960s, the university was growing rapidly, especially in the health sciences, and wanted a full-fledged teaching/research hospital attached to the university. The LHA was persuaded to undertake this more ambitious task but stipulated that their institution would remain administratively separate from the university.

Planning for the new facility began in 1966. An innovative spirit was evident from the outset. Hospitals tend to be very traditional institutions, but the planning group, in its efforts to create an outstanding medical facility, were willing to deviate from conventional practices. The UH motto, "Finding a better way," was applied to facilities design, organizational practice, as well as patient care and research activities. Using a philosophy of form follows function, the hospital layout was guided by an analysis of function. The result was revolutionary with physicians' offices, research areas, inpatient and outpatient departments, and teaching space all on the same floor. Essentially, each of the floors operated as a specialized minihospital sharing support services within a larger hospital setting. UH's deviation from accepted hospital practices were wide ranging from the use of noise-deadening carpeted floors, a hospital blasphemy at the time, to the decentralized organizational structure with an unconventional division of tasks.

The Health Care Environment

Canada's health care system was one of the most comprehensive in the world, providing equal access to all Canadians. The publicly funded system was the responsibility of the provincial governments, although a substantial portion of the funding came from the federal level by way of transfer payments. In Ontario, the Ministry of Health (MOH) was the department concerned with hospitals. Health care costs accounted for 32 percent of the province's $32 billion budget, the single largest category of expenditure with the most rapid growth. As a result, the province was becoming increasingly active in its efforts to contain these costs. Examples included the banning of extra billing by doctors, cuts in the number of medical residency positions, and provision for the MOH to take over any hospital in a deficit position.

Health care funding had evolved in a piecemeal fashion into an extremely complex and often ambiguous system. Basically, the MOH contracted with the hospitals to provide services, in an approved plant, at an approved ("global") budget. Further, the ministry expected each hospital to show an excess of revenue over expenses sufficient to provide for a reasonable accumulation of funds for future capital requirements. Program, service reductions, or bed closures which related directly to patient care required the agreement of the ministry.

However, under pressure to balance budgets, some hospitals were reducing services without the formal agreement of the ministry. Using a universal formula based largely on history, the ministry arrived at a hospital's global operating budget. Most MOH revenues were *not* directly tied to actual expenditures or the provision of services. New programs could be initiated by the hospital, but incremental capital and/or operating costs could be incorporated into the existing global funding base. Additional funds were forthcoming only if approved by the ministry.

In the approval of new programs, district health councils had a prominent voice. They provided the forum for ensuring that changes met the health care needs of the *local* community. The Thames Valley District Health Council (TVDHC) was responsible for the 18 hospitals in the London area. New program proposals submitted to TVDHC were very diverse, ranging from a $400,000 request from UH for a four-bed epilepsy unit, to Victoria Hospital's $94 million expansion request. Evaluating programs on a regional basis, based on local community need, did not allow much consideration of the type of care provided or the referral base they served. UH frequently went outside this process, appealing directly to the ministry, or failing that, by funding projects from their own accumulated surplus.

The government's influence upon hospitals extended well beyond the control of global operating budgets and new programs. It also affected the supply of nurses, residents, and physicians by controlling the number of available positions in nursing and medical schools, by influencing the certification of immigrants, and by limiting the number of hospital residency positions funded. The MOH had recently reduced, provincewide, the number of medical residency positions for physicians doing postgraduate specialty training. Essentially, medical residents learned a specialty while providing patient care in a hospital, freeing physicians to do teaching, research, and other activities. Reduction in residency positions created a gap in the provision of service in larger, teaching hospitals and would ultimately lead to a decline in the number of indigenously trained medical specialists and researchers.

Pressures on the health care system were increasing. Because of an aging population, demand for basic services was expected to increase into the 21st century. Further, increasingly sophisticated and expensive new medical technologies not only improved existing services but also developed new treatments for previously untreatable illnesses; all at a cost, however. While gross measures of productivity, like patient days in hospital per procedure, had been improving, the increasing sophistication of treatments appeared to be increasing costs at a faster rate than offsetting gains in productivity. Further, most gains in productivity came about by requiring fewer personnel to do the same tasks, rather than reducing the number of tasks. The increasing stresses and turnover that naturally resulted were present in all hospital health care professionals but especially evident in the exodus from the nursing profession. Although not as severe in the London area, it was estimated 600 to 800 beds in Toronto hospitals were closed because of lack of nursing staff. Shortages of staff existed in other areas, like occupational and physical therapists, radiologists, and pharmacists.

The province's basic approach to managing demand (and costs) appeared to be by limiting supply. As a result, waiting lists were growing, especially for elective procedures. Certain serious, but not immediately life-threatening, conditions had waiting lists·for treatment of six months to a year and were getting longer.

Social and political expectations also put pressures on the system. Universal, free access to a health care system offering equal, high-quality care to all had become a societal expectation and a political sacred cow. Politically acceptable ideas for fundamentally restructuring the industry were not obvious. There was no apparent way to reconcile increasing demand and costs with the governmental funding likely to be available. As a result, many observers felt that the health care system was out of control. And the ministry was under tremendous pressure to control costs and account for its expenditures, while at the same time providing more, new, and enhanced services. Without an overall approach to the health care situation, it was not clear how the ministry would allocate funds in the future. Choices between high technology, expensive procedures, like heart transplantation and intensive care for premature infants, and basic care for the aged were difficult to make and politically sensitive.

University Hospital

UH was a well-designed and maintained facility. It was located in north London, Ontario. Rising from a three-floor service podium, each of its seven tower floors was divided into two basic components—one an inpatient area, the other an outpatient, office, research, and teaching area. Each inpatient area, except paediatrics, had a corresponding outpatient department for initial assessment and follow up, and the performance of minor procedures. UH had 463 inpatient beds with an average occupancy rate of over 90 percent, which effectively meant 100 percent utilization. The occupancy rate and number of beds had been fairly constant over the past few years. Although space was severely constrained within the hospital, there was a land bank available for future expansion.

In the past, UH had employed some creative solutions to its problem of space constraints. Services had been reviewed to determine whether they could be more effectively provided in one of the other London hospitals, or, as in the case of the Occupational Health Centre, whether they could be better served in an off-site location. Some specialization had already occurred within the city. For example, since another major acute-care hospital specialized in maternity, UH did not duplicate this service. However, UH did have an in-vitro fertilization programme (popularly known as test-tube babies). In a major move during 1986, the Robarts Research Institute (RRI) was opened adjacent to UH. A separate but affiliated institution with its own board, the RRI specialized in heart and stroke research. Moving researchers from UH to this new facility helped to alleviate, at least temporarily, some of the hospital's space pressures. The five-floor, 69,000-square-foot institute housed 35 labs. By the end of 1987, it was expected 80 RRI researchers would be active in conducting basic research into stroke and aging, heart and circulation, and immunological disorders relating to transplantations.

UH housed some of the latest medical technology. For example, a magnetic resonance imaging (MRI) machine costing $3 million was added in 1986. One of the most powerful machines in Canada, the MRI provided unparalleled images of all body organs. Interestingly, neither funding for the total capital cost nor the majority of the ongoing operating costs for this advanced technology instrument was assumed by the ministry. However, this had not deterred Blewett, and UH was considering other high technology equipment like a $3 million gamma knife which would enable neurosurgeons to operate without having to cut the skin surface.

Mission and Strategy

UH's mission involved three core activities: research, teaching, and patient care. And in this way it did not differ from other university-affiliated teaching hospitals. What made it more unique was the emphasis on innovative, leading-edge research. Clinical and teaching activities were expected to reflect and reinforce this focus. This strategy had implications for UH's product/market scope and its service portfolio.

Product/Market Scope

UH attempted to serve the needs of three related, but different markets: teaching, research, and the health care needs of the community. Local community and basic teaching needs generally required a broad base of standard services. On the other hand, research needs argued for focus and specialization of products offered with a physician's clinical activities related to their research and necessarily drawing from a large patient referral base.

With three different markets, service focus was not easy to achieve. The initial design of UH had included only a small emergency service because another hospital in the city specialized in trauma. However, in response to local community pressure, a larger emergency department was incorporated. Balancing the product/service portfolio under increasing space constraints, funding pressure and demand for basic health care services was becoming ever more challenging.

Overall, UH's mix of cases had a high proportion of acute cases, very ill patients requiring high levels of care. UH had approximately 1 percent of the approved hospital beds in Ontario, as well as 1 percent of discharges and patient days in acute-care public hospitals. However, when broken down by the acuity/difficulty of the procedure, UH's tertiary focus was clear (see Exhibit 2).

Geographically, 81 percent of UH's admitted patients came from the primary service area of southwestern Ontario, with one third of all patients originating from the hospital's primary service area of Middlesex County. Fifteen percent of all patients came from the secondary service area, which consisted of

Exhibit 2 Market Share of Ontario Patients by Acuity*

Level I: Primary	0.7%	8,092
Level II: Secondary	1.4%	2,616
Level III: Tertiary	4.2%	2,783
Examples: Heart transplant	66.0%	31
Liver transplant	30.8%	175
Kidney transplant	27.0%	71
Craniotomy (age > 18 yrs)	15.7%	388

*As classified by a scheme developed in the United States designed to reflect intensity of nursing care required.

all parts of Ontario outside the primary region. The remaining 4 percent of patients came from outside the province of Ontario. However, because these cases tended to be more acute than the norm, they accounted for a disproportionate share of patient days, approximately 6 percent, and an even larger proportion of revenues. Exhibit 3 provides a breakdown of current patient origin by service. For the future, the strategic plan had identified transplantation, in vitro fertilization, neurosciences, diabetes, cardiology/cardiovascular surgery, epilepsy, orthopaedics/sport injury, and occupational health care as services with high, out-of-province potential.

To help manage the service/product portfolio, the strategic plan called for the following designation of products: *premier product lines* were designated on the basis of the world-class, cutting-edge nature of the service; *intermediate product lines* represented those services that were approaching premier status or that stood alone as a service entity; *service support clusters* were services that supported the intermediate and premier product lines; *ambulatory/emergency services* included outpatient clinics, emergency services, and regional joint venture arrangements; and *diversification/collaboration ventures* were stand-alone services that generated revenue for UH. The services for premier and intermediate categories are listed in Exhibit 4. A more detailed profile of the premier product lines is provided in Appendix A.

Product Innovation

Developing new and improved leading-edge treatments for health problems was a key element of UH's mission relating to research and teaching. And while the institution, over its relatively brief history, had participated in a number of medical innovations, this success did not appear attributable to formal planning. Rather new programs and services developed at UH in a seemingly ad hoc fashion. As Ken Stuart, the vice president medical observed, "New services happen because of individuals. They just grow. There is some targeted research, but it is not the route of most (activities) because it would stifle people's ideas. They need to fiddle with things and be able to fail." The development of the

Exhibit 3   Patient Origin by Service—1986 (percent)

| | ORIGIN | | | |
| | | | Tertiary | |
Service	Primary (S-W Ont.)	Secondary (Remainder of Ont.)	Canada (except Ont.)	International
Cardiology	71.9	22.3	3.9	1.9
Cardiovascular and thoracic surgery	61.4	28.8	7.8	2.1
Chest diseases	88.1	10.8	0.6	0.5
Dentistry	89.1	10.8	0.0	0.1
Endocrinology	83.2	15.4	0.0	1.5
Gastroenterology	80.1	15.7	2.5	1.0
General surgery	87.5	11.1	0.6	0.8
Gynaecology	70.9	24.4	3.8	1.0
Haematology	92.2	6.8	0.0	1.0
Immunology	90.0	10.0	0.0	0.0
Internal medicine, infectious diseases	85.6	10.1	0.2	2.0
Nephrology	76.8	20.4	0.2	2.5
Neurology	70.0	26.2	2.4	1.4
Neurosurgery	42.6	36.3	2.4	18.6
Ophthalmology	75.9	23.7	0.0	0.4
Orthpaedic surgery	85.6	13.4	0.3	0.7
Otolaryngology	92.2	7.0	0.4	0.0
Paediatrics	42.6	45.0	0.0	12.4
Plastic surgery	86.8	12.4	0.2	0.6
Psychiatry	91.0	6.7	0.3	2.0
Rheumatology	91.9	7.7	0.0	0.4
Urology	92.9	7.1	0.0	0.0

Source: UH Strategic Plan.

Epilepsy Unit, outlined in Appendix B, describes an example of this process. Blewett commented on the development of new programs at UH.

> The fact that the hospital is so small—everyone knows everyone—I can get around. Everyone knows what's going on in the hospital. . . . People just drop in to see me. Someone will come down and tell me that they've found a real winner and they just have to have him/her, and so we go out and get them. There's always room for one more; we find a way to say yes.
>
> When it impacts other resources, Diane [Stewart, executive vice president] becomes involved. She says it's easy for me to agree, but her people have to pick up the pieces. In order to better identify the requirements for new physicians and new programs, Diane came up with the idea of the impact analysis (a study of how new or expanded programs affected hospital staffing, supplies, and facilities). But even when the study is done, we don't use it as a reason to say no; we use it to find out what we have to do to make it happen.

Exhibit 4 Services by Strategic Category

Premier product lines

- Cardiology/Cardiovascular Surgery
  - Arrythmia Investigation and Surgery
  - VAD
- Clinical Neurosurgical Sciences (Neurology/Neurosurgery)
  - Epilepsy Unit
  - Stroke Investigation
  - Multiple Sclerosis
  - Aneurysm Surgery
- Multiple Organ Transplant Centre (Adult and Paediatric)

Kidney	Pancreas
Liver	Small bowel
Heart	Bone marrow
Heart/lung	Whole joint and bone
Other	

- Reproductive Biology
  - IVF Clinic

Intermediate Product Lines

- Chest diseases
- Endocrinology/metabolism
- General internal medicine
- Haematology
- Nephrology—Dialysis unit
- Orthopaedic Surgery
- Paediatrics
- Physical medicine and rehabilitation
- Rheumatology
- Dentistry
- Gastroenterology
- General surgery
- Immunology
- Ophthalmology
- Otolaryngology
- Plastic/reconstructive surgery
- Psychiatry
- Urology

Diane Stewart, the executive vice president, was sensitive to the need for continued innovation. She had stated, "We like to leave the door open to try new things. We go by the philosophy that to try and fail is at least to learn." A UH vice president commented:

> People here are well-read. When ideas break, anywhere in the world, they want them. There is a lot of compromising. But things get resolved. It just takes some time. We haven't learned the meaning of the word "no." But we're at a juncture where we may have to start saying no. We're just beginning to be (in the tight financial position), where many other hospitals have been for several years.

Revenues and Costs

UH's revenues and costs could not be neatly assigned to its major areas of activity. As shown in Exhibit 5a, in 1983 73 percent of UH's sources of funds were a "global allocation" from the MOH; by 1987, this amount had been reduced to 70 percent. For the most part, these funds were not attached to specific activities,

UH Statement of Revenues and Expenses
For the Year Ended March 31
($000s)

	1983	1984	1985	1986	1987
Revenue:					
MOH allocation	$47,067	$51,527	$ 56,329	$ 61,103	$ 69,502
Inpatient services	5,355	7,482	9,986	13,945	14,771
Accommodation differential	1,548	1,624	1,746	2,277	2,537
Outpatient services	1,692	2,069	2,033	2,428	3,135
MOH programs	4,908	5,083	5,405	5,503	5,811
Other revenue	3,626	3,471	4,079	4,510	4,836
	64,196	71,256	79,578	89,766	100,592
Expenses:					
Salaries and wages	35,779	39,480	43,505	47,450	53,581
Employee benefits	3,869	4,441	4,711	4,866	5,628
Supplies and other services	10,312	11,751	13,640	15,289	18,960
Ministry of Health programs	4,978	5,376	5,701	5,976	6,099
Medical supplies	3,679	3,915	4,842	5,506	6,547
Drugs	2,226	2,079	2,871	3,846	5,220
Depreciation	2,444	2,818	3,121	3,398	3,843
Bad debts	192	205	165	197	141
Interest	75	137	144	122	420
	63,554	70,202	78,699	86,650	100,439
Excess of revenue over expenses from operations	642	1,054	878	3,116	153
Add (deduct) unusual items:					
Debenture issue cost					(154)
Gain on asset sale					466
Excess of revenue over expenses	642	1,054	878	3,116	465
Operating statistics					
Inpatient days (000)	137.5	138.5	139.7	140.4	142.0
Inpatient admissions (000)	11.8	11.9	12.5	12.9	13.1
Average inpatient stay (days)	11.7	11.6	11.2	10.9	10.8
Occupancy (percent)	89.5%	89.9%	90.3%	91.0%	90.9%
Outpatient visits (000)	96.5	101.9	108.4	113.1	122.4
Total patients seen	n/a	n/a	221,090	233,688	254,001
Equivalent patient days	n/a	n/a	208,932	214,980	222,137
Bookings ahead:					
Urgent				294	584
Elective				650	724
Number of beds:					
Approved	421	424	424	428	436
Rated	451	451	451	463	463

UH Balance Sheet
As of March 31
($000)

	1983	1984	1985	1986	1987
Assets					
Integrated funds*					
Current:					
Cash and securities	$ 2,795	$ 1,580	$ 1,562	$ 1,799	$ 1,541
Accounts receivable					
Province	3,095	3,341	4,324	6,068	7,508
Other	2,299	3,119	3,742	6,394	7,006
Inventories	1,005	1,147	1,130	1,127	1,064
Prepaid expenses	101	109	99	78	100
Total current assets	9,231	9,296	10,857	15,466	17,219
Funds available to purchase plant,					
property, and equipment	2,099	3,701	3,086	2,764	6,800
Fixed assets:					
Property, plant, and equipment	36,884	37,873	38,511	40,325	48,223
Capital leases	173	144	141	40,249	48,114
	37,057	38,017	38,652	40,325	48,223
	48,387	51,014	52,596	58,555	72,242
Special funds*					
Cash and deposits	19	21	35	40	90
Marketable securities (cost)	4,256	5,042	5,948	7,105	7,187
Accrued interest	57	103	108	123	141
Mortgage receivable	59	56	53	49	46
Advance to integrated fund	1,264	1,004	744	734	1,775
	5,655	6,227	6,888	8,051	9,869
	54,042	57,241	59,485	66,606	82,112
Liabilities and equity					
Integrated funds					
Current:					
Account payable	2,941	4,490	4,153	5,618	6,987
Accrued charges	2,401	2,074	2,580	2,988	3,668
Current portion of leases					
and loans	417	401	400	260	307
Total current liabilities	5,759	6,965	7,133	8,866	10,962

EXHIBIT 5b *(concluded)*

UH Balance Sheet
As of March 31
($000)

	1983	1984	1985	1986	1987
Long-term					
Debentures†					5,629
Advances from special funds	1,265	1,004	744	734	1,775
Capital lease	175	141	95	18	12
	1,440	1,145	839	752	7,417
Less principal due	417	401	400	260	307
	1,023	744	439	492	7,109
Integrated equity	41,605	43,305	45,025	49,196	54,170
	$48,387	$51,014	$52,597	$58,554	$72,241
Special fund‡					
Equity	5,656	6,227	6,888	8,052	9,870
Total equity and liabilities	54,042	57,241	59,485	66,606	82,111

*Revenue and expenses relating to the day-to-day activities of the hospital are recorded in the statement of revenue and expenses and the integrated fund statement of assets. Activities relating to funds made available to the LHA under conditions specified by the donor are recorded in the special funds statement. Most of these monies were donated to the LHA prior to the establishment of the foundation.

†In February 1987, the hospital issued debentures to finance the new parking garage and attached office facility.

‡The hospital has received the following advances from the special fund, repayable with interest:

Year	Amount	Purpose
1983	$1,264,000	New telephone system
1986	$ 250,000	Establishment of Occupational Health Centre
1987	$1,400,000	Finance MRI building

acuity of patients, or outcomes. Over the past few years, UH, like all other hospitals, had simply been getting an annual increase in its global allocation to offset inflation. The stipulation attached to MOH funds was that there could be no deficit.

Some small part of MOH funding was tied to activity levels. Increases in outpatient activity did, through a complex formula, eventually result in increased funding to the hospital. Further, the ministry had established a special "life support fund" to fund volume increases for specified procedures. However, this fund was capped and the number of claims by all hospitals already exceeded funds available, so only partial funding was received. The MOH also funded the clinical education of medical students and interns. This accounted for most of the $5.8 million in revenue from MOH programs (Exhibit 5a).

Approximately 30 percent of UH's revenues did not come directly from the Ministry of Health through its global funding allocation. A large percentage of

UH Statement of Changes in Equity
Year Ended March 31

	1983	1984	1985	1986	1987
Integrated funds					
Balance, beginning of year	$ 40,386	$41,605	$43,305	$45,025	$49,196
Add (deduct) MOH settlements	(1,114)				
	39,272	41,605	43,305	45,025	49,196
Donations and grants	1,692	646	842	1,054	4,509
Excess of revenue over expenses	641	1,054	878	3,117	465
	2,333	1,700	1,720	4,171	4,974
Balance, end of year	$ 41,605	$43,305	$45,025	$49,196	$54,170
Special funds					
Balance, beginning of year	$ 5,044	$ 5,651	$ 6,227	$ 6,888	$ 8,052
Add:					
Donations and bequests	1	1	11	409	835
Net investment income	606	575	650	755	983
Balance, end of year	$ 5,651	$ 6,227	$ 6,888	$ 8,052	$ 9,870
Represented by:					
Nonexpendable funds	$ 492	$ 492	$ 492	$ 492	$ 492
Expendable funds	5,139	5,734	6,396	7,560	9,378
	$ 5,651	$ 6,227	$ 6,888	$ 8,052	$ 9,870

these self-generated revenues originated from servicing out-of-province patients. For patients from other provinces, the MOH negotiated with the paying provinces a per diem charge for services provided. Even so, because out-of-province patients generated incremental revenues, above and beyond the global allocation, they were a very attractive market. For out-of-country patients, UH could set their own price for services provided, thereby ensuring that the full cost of providing health care was recovered. But, as shown in Exhibit 6, the out-of-province and out-of-country revenue appeared to have reached a plateau at around 14 percent of total revenue. There was also a sense the mix of this component was shifting away from out-of-country patients toward out of province.

Additional funds also came from the University Hospital Foundation of London and other entrepreneurial activities. The numerous fund-raising appeals by the foundation included sales of operating room greens in sizes ranging from doll-size through to a small child, and a specially produced record and music video. The foundation was a separate financial entity, and funds flowing to UH appeared as an addition to UH equity (and cash) with no effect on revenues.

Exhibit 6 **University Hospital Revenue Breakdown**

Fiscal Year	MOH Global Base	Other Revenue	Out-of-Province & Out-of-Country
1983	74.6%	25.4%	7.4%
1984	73.7%	26.3%	8.7%
1985	72.1%	27.9%	11.3%
1986	69.3%	30.7%	13.8%
1987	70.5%	29.5%	13.9%

Salaries, wages, and benefits made up the single largest cost category. (The base salary of medical staff, who were employees of the university, were not directly included in this number.) As a proportion of total revenues, these costs had declined marginally over the last five years. Other costs had, however, increased, in particular medical supplies and drugs. Much of this increase was due to the MOH's unwillingness to pay for certain drug therapies. For example, drugs used to prevent rejection of transplanted organs were not paid for by the MOH because the drugs were considered experimental and therefore the cost of these drugs had to be covered under the hospital's global budget. Similar funding limitations had evolved with other drugs and medical apparatus (e.g., implantable defibrillators). The boundary between clinical research and clinical practice was often difficult to draw. Research funding bodies, like the Medical Research Council, would not pay for medical procedures beyond the purely experimental stage. And often the MOH would not immediately step in and fund procedures after research grants expired.

On balance, UH had never recorded a deficit year. However, its operating surplus had been decreasing. See Exhibit 5a. Blewett felt the key to UH's future financial success was reduced reliance on ministry funding. (UH's reliance on ministry funding was already less than most hospitals.) UH was actively pursuing opportunities with the potential to generate funds. One recent development was the Occupational Health Centre (OHC), which opened in 1986 as a separate private, for-profit organization to provide occupational health care services to the business community. By the end of 1987, it had 30 companies with 11,000 employees as clients. However, like most start-ups, the OHC had required an initial infusion of cash and was not expected to generate net positive cash flow for several years.

Not all of the activity undertaken at UH was reflected in its financial statements and operating statistics. Research grants and many of their associated costs were not included in the hospital's statements, even though they were administered by the university and much of the activity was conducted at UH. During 1986–87, UH physicians and researchers were involved in over 200 projects with annual funding of $9.5 million. Exhibit 7 lists the services most involved in research. In an effort to capitalize on the revenue potential of the innovations developed at UH, an innovations inventory was being developed and

Exhibit 7 Clinical Services with Largest Research Budgets

Service	Amount ($000)
Transplantation & Nephrology	$1,979
Gynaecology	1,454
Neurology	1,105
Endocrinology	923
Cardiology	678

Source: *Research Annual Compendium*; does not include the Robarts Research Institute.

the potential for licensing explored. It was expected this activity, if it demonstrated potential, would be spun out into a private, for-profit corporation.

Staffing and Organization

UH was a large and diverse organization employing 2,600 personnel. There were 128 medical clinicians and researchers, 70 residents, 44 interns and research fellows, 875 nursing staff, 140 paramedical, 312 technical, 214 supervisory and specialist, 444 clerical, and 379 service staff.

The relationship with UH's medical staff was especially unique. *All* UH physicians held joint appointments with UH and the university and were technically university employees. As well, they did not have a private practice outside of University Hospital. As a consequence, all patients (except those admitted through the emergency department) were referred to UH by outside physicians. At most other hospitals, physicians were not salaried employees. They had hospital privileges and spent part of their time at the hospital and the rest at their own clinics/offices, usually separate from the hospital. These physicians billed Ontario Health Insurance Plan (OHIP) directly for *all* patient care delivered. At UH, the "GFT"[2] relationship with physicians was very different. They were paid a base salary by the university. Physicians negotiated with the dean of medicine and department chairperson for salaries in excess of this base. This negotiated portion was called the "if earned" portion. UH physicians were expected to make OHIP billings from clinical work inside the hospital at least up to the level of their "if earned" portion. Any additional billings were "donated" to the university and were placed into a research fund. Although arrangements varied, the physicians who contributed their billings usually had some say in the allocation of these research funds.

Because of this GFT relationship, the medical staff at UH generally developed a stronger identification and affiliation with the institution. Even so, retaining medical staff was not easy. Most could make significantly higher incomes if they gave up their teaching and research activities and devoted all their efforts to

---

[2]Geographic full-time.

private practice. While the salary of UH physicians was competitive with similar institutions in Canada, many research hospitals in the United States were perceived to offer higher compensation and often better support for research. To further complicate matters, the available number of university positions in the medical faculty and the dollar amount of the salary had been frozen for several years. As a result, the base salary for any net new positions or salary increases were funded entirely by UH.

Structure

The physicians were by nature highly autonomous and independent. Nominally, at least, medical staff were responsible through their clinical service head (e.g. neurology) or a department head (e.g., neurosciences) to Ken Stuart, vice president medical. The role of service and department head was a part-time responsibility rotated amongst senior clinicians in the particular specialty. The heads of services and departments in the hospital, often, but not always, held parallel appointments in the Faculty of Medicine at the university.

The division of services and departments was in most instances determined by traditional professional practice. However, "product offerings," which crossed traditional departmental boundaries, were common. At UH, the only one with formal organizational recognition was the multiorgan transplant service (MOTS). It had its own medical head, manager, and budget. Other multidisciplinary units, like the Epilepsy Unit, did not have formal organizational status, even though the strategic plan recommended organizing around product lines (or business units).

In general, the hierarchy could best be described as loose and collegial. Although it varied from individual to individual, most physicians, while they might consult with their service and department heads when confronted with a problem or pursuing an opportunity, felt no requirement to do so. Typically, they dealt directly with the persons concerned. Most chiefs of services supported this laissez-faire approach, since they wanted to encourage initiative and did not wish to become overly involved in administration, coordination, and control.

At an operational level, the primary organizational difference between UH and traditional hospitals was its decentralized approach. Each floor acted as a minihospital. A triumvirate of medical, nursing, and administrative staff were responsible for the operation of their unit. In many hospitals, nurses spent much of their time doing nonnursing tasks including administrative duties like budget preparation, coordinating maintenance, and repairs, and so on. At UH, a service coordinator located on each floor handled non-nursing responsibilities for each unit and interfaced with centralized services like purchasing, housekeeping, and engineering. Whenever possible, the allied health professionals, such as psychologists, occupational therapists, and physiotherapists, were also located on the floors. In traditional hospitals, hiring, staff development, quality assurance, and staff assignment of nurses were done on a centralized basis. At UH, a nursing manager, located in each service, handled the nursing supervision responsibilities. A nursing coordinator handled the clinical guidance and supervision of the nurses.

Organizationally, service coordinators and allied health professionals reported through their respective managers to the newly created, and as yet unfilled, position of vice president patient services. Nursing reported through nursing managers to the vice president nursing. In practice, the physicians, nurses, and service coordinators on each floor formed a team which managed their floor. Ideally, integration occurred and operational issues were addressed at the floor level, only rarely referred up for resolution.

Nonmedical personnel working in centralized laboratories and services but not directly involved in patient care reported to the vice president administration. Activities dealing with financial, accounting, and information were the responsibility of the vice president finance. While final hiring decisions for nonphysician positions were decentralized to the units concerned, job description, posting, and initial screening was done in the human resources department. In addition, some employee education and health services were handled through this department. The hiring of physicians, even though technically university employees, was usually initiated within UH. Typically, service or department heads would identify desirable candidates. If the person was being hired for a new position (as opposed to a replacement), then after discussion of the physician's plans, an impact analysis would be prepared identifying the resources required. Generally, Pat Blewett was very involved in the recruitment of physicians.

UH was considered progressive in its staffing and organization, having recorded many firsts among Canadian hospitals. Over the years, they had been one of the first to introduce service coordinators, paid maternity leave, dental benefits, 12-hour shifts, job sharing, workload measurement, and productivity monitoring. The concern for employees was reflected in UH's relatively low turnover, in the 9 percent range. Exit interviews indicated very few people went to another health care job because they were dissatisfied with UH. Aside from normal attrition, the biggest reason for leaving was lack of upward job mobility, a situation caused by UH's flat structure and low turnover amongst its management.

Committees at all levels and often crossing departments were a fact of life at UH and reflected the organization's decentralized and participative approach to decision making. Diane Stewart, for example, was a member of 48 different hospital and board committees. Medical staff were also expected to be involved, as Ken Stuart explained:

> Committee work is not a physician's favourite activity. But it's important they be involved in the management of the hospital. I balance committee assignments amongst the medical staff and no one can continually refuse to do their part. This is a demand UH makes of its GFT physicians that other hospitals do not.

UH's management group had recently undergone a reorganization, reducing the number of direct reports to Pat Blewett from five to three. Now the vice

EXHIBIT 8 Organization Chart

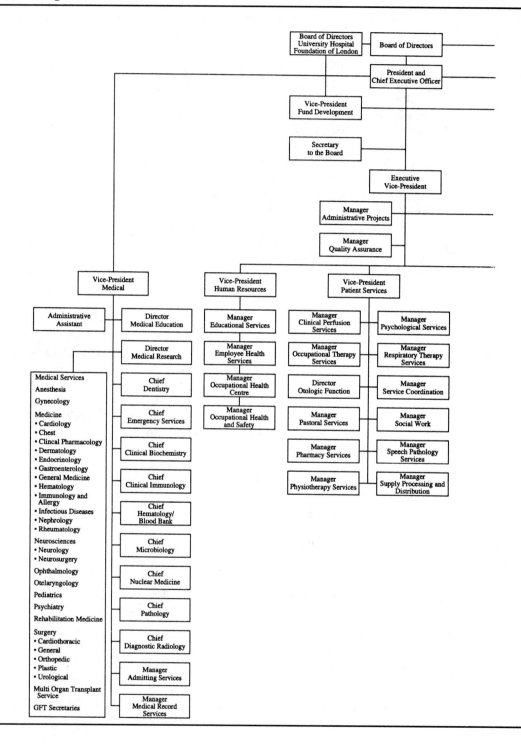

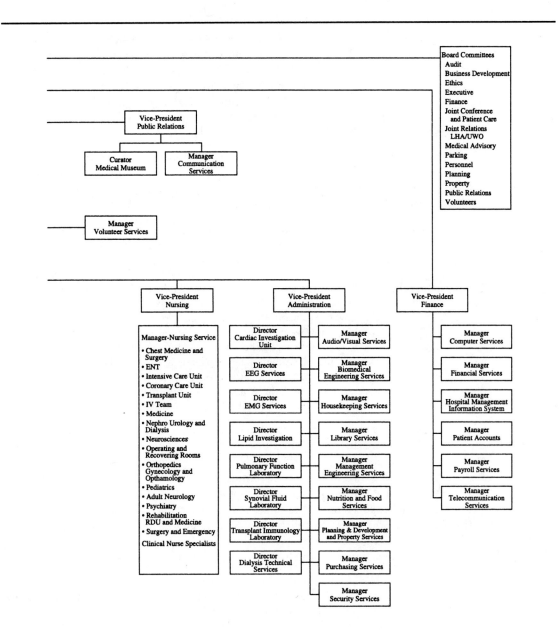

Board Committees
Audit
Business Development
Ethics
Executive
Finance
Joint Conference
  and Patient Care
Joint Relations
  LHA/UWO
Medical Advisory
Parking
Personnel
Planning
Property
Public Relations
Volunteers

Vice-President
Public Relations

Curator
Medical Museum

Manager
Communication
Services

Manager
Volunteer Services

Vice-President
Nursing

Vice-President
Administration

Vice-President
Finance

Manager-Nursing Service

• Chest Medicine and
  Surgery
• ENT
• Intensive Care Unit
• Coronary Care Unit
• Transplant Unit
• IV Team
• Medicine
• Nephro Urology and
  Dialysis
• Neurosciences
• Operating and
  Recovering Rooms
• Orthopedics
  Gynecology and
  Opthamology
• Pediatrics
• Adult Neurology
• Psychiatry
• Rehabilitation
  RDU and Medicine
• Surgery and Emergency

Clinical Nurse Specialists

Director
Cardiac Investigation
Unit

Director
EEG Services

Director
EMG Services

Director
Lipid Investigation

Director
Pulmonary Function
Laboratory

Director
Synovial Fluid
Laboratory

Director
Transplant Immunology
Laboratory

Director
Dialysis Technical
Services

Manager
Audio/Visual Services

Manager
Biomedical
Engineering Services

Manager
Housekeeping Services

Manager
Library Services

Manager
Management
Engineering Services

Manager
Nutrition and Food
Services

Manager
Planning & Development
and Property Services

Manager
Purchasing Services

Manager
Security Services

Manager
Computer Services

Manager
Financial Services

Manager
Hospital Management
Information System

Manager
Patient Accounts

Manager
Payroll Services

Manager
Telecommunication
Services

president human resources and the vice president administration along with the vice presidents of patient services and nursing reported to the executive vice president, Diane Stewart (Exhibit 8). The reorganization centered control of operations around Stewart, allowing Blewett to concentrate on physicians, external relationships, and the future direction of UH.

Budgets

There were five groups that submitted budgets to administration: support services, nursing, allied health, diagnostic services, and administrative services. The annual capital and operating budgetary processes involved a lot of meetings, and give and take. As one manager described:

> The budget of each department is circulated to the other departments within our service. We have a meeting with . . . vice president administration and . . . vice president finance and all the department heads. Although the department heads are physicians, often the department managers will either accompany or represent the department head. In that meeting, we review each department's budget, questioning any items which seem out of place. The department will either remain firm on its budget, back down, or decide to postpone the expenditure to the following year. People do back down. If we can't get our collective budgets within the budget for our service, the vice presidents will either make trade-offs with the other service categories, or speak with the department heads privately to try and obtain further cuts. The majority of cuts are made in the meeting. . . . It works because the department heads are fiscally responsible, and there is a lot of trust between the departments and between the departments and administration.

Operating budgets were coordinated by the service coordinator on each floor but really driven by the plans of the medical staff. Each year, physicians were asked about their activity levels for the upcoming year; these were translated into staffing and supplies requirements, in terms of number of hours worked and the physical volume of supplies consumed. Costs were attached and the overall expense budget tabulated later by the finance department. In the last fiscal year when the overall budget was tabulated, it exceeded the estimated revenues of the hospital by over $10 million, roughly 10 percent. Ross Chapin, vice president finance, explained what happened:

> We went back to each of the clinical services and looked at their proposed level of activity. The hospital had already been operating at 100 plus percent of its physical capacity. Most of the services had not taken this into account in preparing their plans. They had assumed more space and more patient beds would be available. Since this just wasn't going to happen, at least in the short term, we asked them to redo their budgets with more realistic space assumptions. As a result, our revenue and expense budgets came more into line.

While the activity of the medical staff drove the operating expenditures of the hospital, physicians were not in the ongoing budgetary loop. If expenditures were exceeding budget, physicians might not even be aware, and if aware had no incentive to cut expenses and reduce activity levels in order to meet budget. Aside from the number of physicians and the limits of their own time, the major constraint on expenditures was space and the availability of support services. A patient could not be admitted unless a bed was available; an outpatient procedure could not be conducted unless a consultation room was free and the needed support services (e.g., radiology, physical therapy, etc.) could be scheduled.

Because of MOH funding and space constraints, the hospital had a set number of inpatient beds. The allocation of beds amongst services was determined by a committee made up of the manager of admitting, several physicians, and chaired by the vice president medical. Since bed availability affected the activity level of the services and their physicians, this allocation was a sensitive area. Services would often lend an unused bed to another, usually adjacent, service. However, the formal reallocation of beds was done infrequently, and when done, was based on waiting lists (by service) and bed utilization rates.

New Program

While capital and operating budgets for ongoing activities originated with the managers on the floors, the medical staff usually initiated requests for *new* programs and equipment. Money to fund large outlays associated with new or expanded programs would be requested from the MOH or might be part of a special fund-raising campaign. (Private charitable foundations had made significant contributions to the Epilepsy Unit, the MOTU, and the MRI facility.) When proposals for a new program or the addition of a new physician were made, an impact analysis was undertaken. These studies detailed the resource requirement: space, support staff, supplies, and so on, of the initiative and summarized the overall financial impact. The analysis did not, however, identify the availability or source of the required resources should the initiative be pursued. As one vice president explained:

> The impact analysis might show that if we bring on a new orthopaedic surgeon, we'll need two more physical therapists (PTs). But there is no space (and probably no money) for the PTs. Quite often the physician is hired anyway, and the PTs currently on staff have to try and manage the additional work load. We *know* what a new physician will need beforehand, but we don't always ensure it's there before they come on board.

Recently a new physician had arrived after being hired and office space was not available.

Basis for Success

UH attributed its success to several factors. A primary factor was the GFT status of the medical staff, which cultivated a high degree of loyalty and commitment to the hospital and supported the integration of excellence in teaching, research, and practice. The ability of the medical staff to attract out-of-province patients contributed to the hospital's revenues. The strong entrepreneurial orientation of management, its ability to identify and create additional sources of revenue and a widely shared understanding of the mission of UH helped to foster commitment to the organization's goals.

Early in its development, UH had attracted physicians/researchers capable of developing major internationally recognized research and clinical programs: Doctors Drake and Barnett in neurosciences and Dr. Stiller in transplantation. These physicians and their programs had developed international recognition and generated patient referrals from all over the country and around the world.

UH's product portfolio required a delicate balance. It was natural for products to evolve and mature. As innovative procedures became more commonplace, they tended to diffuse to other hospitals. Indeed, UH contributed to this process by training physicians in these procedures (as part of their teaching mission). As a consequence, UH's patient referral base would shrink, and so too would out-of-country, out-of-province revenues from maturing service. UH required a constant inflow of innovative, internationally recognized clinical procedures in order to sustain its out-of-province referral base.

The Strategic Plan

UH did not have an internal ongoing strategic planning process. In 1985, a change occurred. UH signed an affiliation agreement with the Hospital Corporation of Canada (HCC), an affiliate of the Hospital Corporation of America (HCA), a large, publicly owned international health care company, which gave UH access to HCA strategic planning expertise. For UH's existing service portfolio, the consultants assessed underlying demand, UH's share of market, its capability base, and abilities relative to other research and teaching hospitals. They did not specifically consider MOH funding policy.

Senior management wanted a process that would enable people to buy into the emerging plan, so they conducted a series of planning sessions. The first information session was conducted in the fall of 1986, when general information about the health care environment was presented to the chiefs of services and administration. In December, a day-long retreat was held to disseminate information and to provide some education on key strategic concepts such as market share and product life cycle. In January 1987, a second retreat was held. The chiefs of services were asked to come prepared to make a presentation on the direction of their department, resource requirements, and priorities. Blewett commented on the meeting:

> The chiefs did an outstanding job. They really got into it, using business ideas to look at their services and where they are going. They were talking about market share and product life cycles. I believe it gave them a new way to think about things. Really, the chiefs were presenting to each other and they wanted to do a good job and make their best case. A lot of information sharing occurred.

In late February, the consultants' initial recommendations were presented to administration. One of the recommendations was to adopt a portfolio approach to planning. A preliminary designation of products into portfolios of premier, intermediate, and service support clusters was provided. The initial criteria used to determine premier status were: geographic "draw," "leading edge" service, consensus as a priority, and future orientation of its people. Subsequent meetings with the medical staff led to some modifications of these designations. Blewett reflected on the process of identifying the product/service portfolio.

> I never thought we would do it. But when it came down to making the hard decisions, it didn't take that long. I give a lot of credit to the planners and to our administrative person, who kept in close contact with everyone, and made sure that concerns were taken care of. . . . The GFTs are committed to this institution, therefore it's easier to mobilize these people. . . . We also made it clear that services could move between categories, which provides some incentive.

Indeed, sport medicine had not initially been categorized as a premier service, but in the final version of the plan was placed in this category.

The final strategic plan, a 150-page document, was approved by both the Medical Advisory Committee of the hospital and by its board of directors. As Blewett reflected on the process, he was pleased with the results of the effort which had taken over a year to complete. Blewett knew many of his senior managers had applauded the direction the report had taken in providing a more solid foundation on which to make difficult resource allocation decisions. However, he was concerned the plan not be used as a reason to say "no," to stifle initiative and the emergence of new areas of excellence. He wondered how an ongoing planning process would have affected the evolution of the epilepsy unit (described in Appendix B). With this in mind, he was wondering where to go from here. How could the plan, and its recommendations, be used to help guide the hospital?

APPENDIX A
PROFILE OF PREMIER SERVICE CATEGORIES

The premier product lines fell under four categories: cardiology/cardiovascular surgery, clinical neurological sciences, multiple organ transplant, and reproductive biology. More detailed descriptions follow.

Cardiology/Cardiovascular Surgery

The two major programs in cardiology/cardiovascular surgery were arrythmia investigation and surgery and the ventricular assist device (VAD). *Arrythmia investigation* received a major breakthrough when, in 1981, the world's first heart operation was performed to correct life-threatening right ventricular dysplasia. In 1984, UH entered into a collaborative relationship with Biomedical Instrumentation, Inc., a Canadian research and development firm based near Toronto, to produce a sophisticated heart mapping device, which greatly advanced the surgical treatment of patients suffering from life-threatening heart rhythm disorders. The computer-assisted mapping system, which fit over the heart like a sock, enabled doctors to almost instantaneously locate the "electric short circuit" in the hearts of patients afflicted with cardiac arrhythmias. Physicians were then able to more easily locate and destroy the tissue which caused the patient's heart to beat abnormally.

The *ventricular assist device (VAD),* which UH began using in 1987, was functionally no different from some life-support machines, such as the heart-lung machine already in use. In assisting the heart to pump blood, the VAD was used for patients waiting for transplants, those needing help after open heart surgery, and hearts weakened after a severe heart attack. The VAD worked outside the patient's body, carrying out approximately 50 percent of the heart's work. When the patient's heart recovered sufficiently or when a donor organ became available for those who required a transplant, the pump could be disconnected without difficulty. Other than UH, there was only one other hospital in Canada using the VAD.

Clinical Neurological Sciences (CNS)

There were four major programs in CNS: the Epilepsy Unit, Stroke Investigation, Multiple Sclerosis, and Aneurysm Surgery.

The Epilepsy Unit, discussed at length in Appendix B, was one of only a few of its kind in North America. The demand for its services had extended the waiting time for a bed to over a year.

A four-bed *Investigative Stroke Unit* was established at UH in 1983 to improve the diagnosis and treatment of stroke. In 1986, UH, and The University of Western Ontario collaborated in the development of the Robarts Research Institute, which focused its efforts on stroke research.

The Multiple Sclerosis (MS) clinic at UH conducted exploratory research to study the causes and incidence of MS, a chronic degenerative disease of the central nervous system. One study involved 200 MS patients in 10 centres, coordinated by UH, to determine whether cyclosporin[3] and prednisone, either alone or in combination with repeated plasma exchange treatments could prevent further deterioration in MS patients.

Aneurysm surgery became a centre for excellence and internationally renowned early on, when in 1972, Dr. Charles Drake pioneered a technique for surgically treating a cerebral aneurysm. In October of 1979, vocalist Della Reese underwent neurosurgery at UH. She returned to London the following year to give a benefit concert to raise funds for UH.

Multiple Organ Transplant Centre

The first kidney transplant at UH was performed in 1973, followed by its first liver transplant in 1977. In 1979, UH was chosen as the first centre in North America to test the antirejection drug cyclosporin A. In 1981, the first heart

---

[3]Cyclosporin was the drug originally used to minimize the bodies' rejection of transplanted organs. Because of its transplantation experience, UH had a considerable expertise with this drug and immunology in general.

transplant at UH was performed. In that same year, UH became the site of the Canadian Centre for Transplant Studies. In 1984, Canada's first heart-lung transplant was performed at UH.

In 1984, the provincial government announced that they would partially fund a multiorgan transplant unit (MOTU) at UH. The 12-bed MOTU, which opened in 1987, was one of the first units of its kind in the world. With the help of leading-edge computer technology, transplant patients were closely monitored for the first signs of organ rejection. A highly specialized team of transplant experts including surgeons, physicians, nurses, technologists, and physiotherapists joined together in the MOTU to care for transplant patients.

Reproductive Biology

The primary work in reproductive biology was the in-vitro fertilization (IVF) programme. The programme was launched in 1982, with the first birth occurring in 1985. By 1987, the 100th child was born to parents who previously had been incapable of conceiving a child. The pregnancy rate was 27 percent using this method, with a birth rate of 22 percent. These results were comparable to those of well-established clinics worldwide. It was anticipated that with the combination of continually increasing experience together with basic science and clinical research interests in IVF, the success rate in the program would continue to increase. There was a two-year waiting period to participate in the program.

APPENDIX B
THE PROCESS OF INNOVATION AT UH—THE EPILEPSY UNIT

Research and service innovations had been important to UH. This appendix describes how one of these came about.

The Epilepsy Unit probably had its genesis when Dr. Warren Blume, a neurologist, joined Dr. John Girvin, a neurosurgeon at UH in 1972. Girvin had trained under a founding father in epilepsy treatment at the Montreal Neurological Institute (MNI). Blume had done postgraduate work in epilepsy and electroencephalography (EEG)[4] at the Mayo Clinic. Girvin was unique among neurosurgeons in that he had also gone on to obtain a Ph.D. in neurophysiology.

In 1972, the primary treatment for epilepsy was through drug therapy. However, there were many patients whose epilepsy could not be effectively treated this way. For those patients, the only hope was a surgical procedure to remove that part of their brain which caused the epileptic seizure. This required an EEG recording of a patient's seizure to identify the focus of the problem.

---

[4]The mapping of electrical activity in the brain.

There were few individuals trained in the use of EEG to study epilepsy. However, Blume had this expertise. Furthermore, Girvin had the training in neurosurgery to carry out the surgical procedure. Neither physician, however, was recruited specifically to do work in epilepsy. It was an interest they both shared and developed over time.

There were a number of factors that united Blume and Girvin, providing the impetus for the dedicated Epilepsy Unit that was eventually opened in May of 1986. One factor was the integration within UH of neurosurgery and neurology under the umbrella of neurosciences. In most hospitals, the two departments were separate, neurosurgery being part of surgery and neurology being its own service. At UH, they were integrated organizationally and located on the same floor. Many attribute this unique relationship to the leadership and friendship of Doctors Barnett and Drake, the original chiefs of neurology and neurosurgery.

In 1974, a young Italian boy and his father arrived on the doorstep of UH seeking help to control the boy's epilepsy, the precipitating factor that brought Blume and Girvin together to work on their first case experience. It was a complex case, requiring the expertise of both Blume and Girvin. The surgery was successful, and Blume and Girvin realized that by pooling their expertise, they could make a significant contribution to the field. Prior to that time, Blume's efforts had been focused on providing EEG readings for epileptic patients that would either be treated with medication or referred to the MNI for possible surgical treatment. Girvin's efforts had been directed at neurosurgery in general, having no special contact with epileptic patients.

Blume and Girvin began to draw together a team. The technique of removing part of the brain for the treatment of epilepsy was based on the fact that most human functions were duplicated in both temporal lobes of the brain. In the early days of surgical treatment of epilepsy at the MNI, there was no method of ensuring that both temporal lobes were functioning normally. As a result, in some cases where a malfunctioning temporal lobe could not duplicate the function of the part of the brain that had been removed, patients were left with serious brain dysfunction like loss of memory capacity. Later, a procedure was developed whereby neuropsychologists were able to assess the level of function of one temporal lobe, while the other temporal lobe was anaesthetized. It so happened that a neuropsychologist with this expertise was working at UWO's psychology department. She was asked to join the team. For Blume and Girvin, adding a neuropsychologist was essential to their ability to deal with more complex cases. The addition of full-time researchers also served to enhance the team's capability.

Capability was further enhanced, when in 1977, Blume and Girvin were successful in obtaining funding to purchase a computer that would facilitate the recording and reading of the EEG. This was a significant step, since to obtain funding, they positioned themselves as a regional epilepsy unit. This was the first formal recognition of their efforts as an organized endeavour. The computerized monitoring could benefit from a dedicated unit; at the time, beds and staff were still borrowed from other departments as needed. Epileptic patients were scattered around the neurosciences floor.

As the volume of patients increased, it became increasingly apparent that a unit was needed. In order to identify the focus of the brain that triggered the epileptic seizure, it was necessary to record a seizure. As a result, EEG recording rooms were tied up for several hours in the hope that a patient would have a seizure. There were a number of problems with this approach. The patient had to have a seizure while in a recording room, and the patient or technologist had to activate the recorder. It was estimated that over 50 percent of seizures were missed using this method. Furthermore, leaving the patient unattended without the benefit of medication to control their seizures was dangerous. A unit that would provide full-time monitoring in order to get the vital EEG recordings and ensure patient safety was needed.

Blume, Girvin, and the manager of EEG developed a proposal for a four-bed epilepsy unit. The beds that they had been using on an ad hoc basis were the neurosciences overflow beds which "belonged" to paediatrics. Paediatrics was located on the same floor as EEG, so when Blume, who was also a member of the department of paediatrics, heard that paediatrics was downsizing, he had approached the chief of paediatrics to negotiate for four beds. As well, the paediatric nurses, who had been responsible for the overflow beds, had become comfortable with providing care for epileptic patients, and it was agreed that they would provide continued support for the unit. Blume and Girvin approached Blewett with a plan requiring funding of $400,000 for equipment and renovations. There was no provision for an annual budget, since paediatrics was prepared to cover the nursing salaries and supplies.

Blewett and his senior management group supported the plan, and it was submitted as a new program to the TVHC for funding in February 1984. The proposal was ranked 10th, which meant it was not one of the top few submitted to the ministry for consideration. A revised proposal was resubmitted the following February. In the meantime, Blewett, Girvin, and Blume met with the assistant deputy minister of health to make a plea for funding, to no avail. They subsequently received news that the TVDHC had given the proposal a ranking of sixth. Blume and Girvin did not lose hope and were persistent in their efforts to obtain funding. After exhausting all alternatives, Blewett decided to fund it out of the hospital's operating surplus. However, compromises were made in the plans by cutting the budget back as far as possible. The board approved the allocation, and shortly thereafter, the unit was opened.

CASE 35
VICTORIA HEAVY EQUIPMENT LIMITED (REVISED)

Brian Walters sat back in his first-class airline seat as it broke through the clouds en route from Squamish, a small town near Vancouver, British Columbia, to Sacramento, California. As chairman of the board, majority shareholder, and chief executive officer, the 51-year-old Walters had run Victoria Heavy Equipment Limited as a closely held company for years. During this time, Victoria had become the second-largest producer of mobile cranes in the world, with 1985 sales of $100 million and exports to more than 70 countries. But in early 1986, the problem of succession was in his thoughts. His son and daughter were not yet ready to run the organization, and he personally wanted to devote more time to other interests. He wondered about the kind of person he should hire to become president. There was also a nagging thought that there might be other problems with Victoria that would have to be worked out before he eased out of his present role.

Company History

Victoria Heavy Equipment was established in 1902 in Victoria, British Columbia, to produce horse-drawn log skidders for the forest industry. The young firm showed a flair for product innovation, pioneering the development of motorized skidders and later, after diversifying into the crane business, producing the country's first commercially successful hydraulic crane controls. In spite of these innovations, the company was experiencing severe financial difficulties in 1948 when it was purchased by Brian Walters, Sr., the father of the current chairman. By installing tight financial controls and paying close attention to productivity, Walters was able to turn the company around, and in the mid-1950s, he decided that Victoria would focus its attention exclusively on cranes and go after the international market.

By the time of Brian Walters, Sr.'s retirement in 1968, it was clear that the decision to concentrate on the crane business had been a good one. The company's sales and profits were growing, and Victoria cranes were beginning to do well in export markets. Walters, Sr. was succeeded as president by his brother, James, who began to exercise very close personal control over the company's operations. However, as Victoria continued to grow in size and complexity, the load on James became so great that his health began to fail. The solution was to appoint an assistant general manager, John Rivers, through whom tight supervision could be maintained while James Walters' workload was eased. This move was to no avail, however. James Walters suffered a heart attack in 1970, and

This case was prepared by Thomas A. Poynter and Paul W. Beamish, The University of Western Ontario. Case material has been disguised; however, essential relationships are maintained. Copyright © 1986 by The University of Western Ontario. Revised, 1989.

Rivers became general manager. At the same time, the young Brian Walters, the current chairman and chief executive officer, became head of the U.S. operation.

When Brian Walters took responsibility for Victoria's U.S. business, the firm's American distributor was selling 30–40 cranes per year. Walters thought the company should be selling at least 150. Even worse, the orders that the American firm did get tended to come in large quantities—as many as 50 cranes in a single order—which played havoc with Victoria's production scheduling. Walters commented, "We would rather have 10 orders of 10 cranes each than a single order for 100." In 1975, when the U.S. distributor's agreement expired, Walters offered the company a five-year renewal if it would guarantee sales of 150 units per year. When the firm refused, Walters bought it, and in the first month fired 13 of the 15 employees and canceled most existing dealerships. He then set to work to rebuild—only accepting orders for 10 cranes or less. His hope was to gain a foothold and a solid reputation in the U.S. market before the big U.S. firms even noticed him.

This strategy quickly showed results, and in 1976 Walters came back to Canada. As Rivers was still general manager, there was not enough to occupy him fully, and he began traveling three or four months a year. While he was still very much a part of the company, it was not a full-time involvement.

Victoria in the 1980s

Victoria entered the 1980s with sales of approximately $50 million and by 1985, partly as a result of opening the new plant in California, had succeeded in doubling this figure. Profits reached their highest level ever in 1983 but declined somewhat over the next two years as costs rose and the rate of sales growth slowed. Financial statements are presented in Exhibits 1 and 2. The following sections describe the company and its environment in the 1980s.

Product Line

The bulk of Victoria's crane sales in the 1980s came from a single product line, the LTM 1000, which was produced both in the company's Squamish facility (the firm had moved from Victoria to Squamish in the early 1900s) and its smaller plant in California, built in 1979. The LTM 1000 line consisted of mobile cranes of five basic sizes, averaging approximately $500,000 in price. Numerous options were available for these cranes, which could provide uncompromised on-site performance, precision lifting capabilities, fast highway travel, and effortless city driving. Because of the numerous choices available, Victoria preferred not to build them to stock. The company guaranteed 60-day delivery and "tailor-made" cranes to customer specifications. This required a large inventory of both parts and raw material.

Walters had used a great deal of ingenuity to keep Victoria in a competitive position. For example, in 1982, he learned that a company trying to move unusually long and heavy logs from a new tract of redwood trees in British

EXHIBIT 1 Balance Sheet for the Years 1981–1985 ($000 Cdn.)

	1981	1982	1983	1984	1985
			Assets		
Current Assets					
Accounts receivable	$ 8,328	$ 7,960	$ 9,776	$10,512	$10,951
Allowance for doubtful accounts	(293)	(310)	(287)	(297)	(316)
Inventories	21,153	24,425	24,698	25,626	27,045
Prepaid expenses	119	104	156	106	129
Total current assets	29,307	32,179	34,343	35,947	37,809
Advances to shareholders	1,300	1,300	1,300	1,300	1,300
Fixed assets:					
property, plant, and equipment	6,840	6,980	6,875	7,353	7,389
Total assets	$37,447	$40,459	$42,518	$44,600	$46,598
		Liabilities and Shareholders' Equity			
Current Liabilities					
Notes payable to bank	$ 7,733	$ 8,219	$ 9,258	$10,161	$11,332
Accounts payable	9,712	11,353	10,543	10,465	10,986
Accrued expenses	1,074	1,119	1,742	1,501	1,155
Deferred income tax	419	400	396	408	345
Income tax payable	545	692	612	520	516
Current portion of longterm debt	912	891	867	888	903
Total current liabilities	20,395	22,674	23,418	23,943	25,237
Long-term debt	6,284	6,110	6,020	6,005	6,114
Total liabilities	26,679	28,784	29,438	29,948	31,351
Shareholders' Equity					
Common shares	200	290	295	390	435
Retained earnings	10,568	11,385	12,790	14,262	14,812
Total shareholders' equity	10,768	11,675	13,080	14,652	15,247
Total liabilities and share-holders' equity	$37,447	$40,459	$42,518	$44,600	$46,598

Columbia was having serious problems with its existing cranes. A crane with a larger than average height and lifting capacity was required. Up to this point, for technical reasons, it had not been possible to produce a crane with the required specifications. However, Walters vowed that Victoria would develop such a crane, and six months later it had succeeded.

Although the LTM 1000 series provided almost all of Victoria's crane sales, a new crane had been introduced in 1984 after considerable expenditure on design, development, and manufacture. The $650,000 A-100 had a 70-tonne capacity and could lift loads to heights of 61 metres, a combination previously unheard of in the industry. Through the use of smooth hydraulics, even the heaviest loads could be picked up without jolts. In spite of these features, and an

Exhibit 2 **Income Statement for the Years 1981–1985 ($000s Cdn.)**

	1981	1982	1983	1984	1985
Revenue					
Net sales	$63,386	$77,711	$86,346	$94,886	$100,943
Cost and Expenses					
Cost of sales	49,238	59,837	63,996	71,818	75,808
Selling expense	7,470	9,234	10,935	11,437	13,104
Administrative expense	2,684	3,867	5,490	5,795	7,038
Engineering expense	1,342	1,689	1,832	1,949	2,109
Gross income	2,652	3,084	4,093	3,887	2,884
Income taxes	1,081	1,281	1,630	1,505	1,254
Net income	$ 1,571	$ 1,803	$ 2,463	$ 2,382	$ 1,630

optional ram-operated tilt-back cab designed to alleviate the stiff necks which operators commonly developed from watching high loads, sales of the A-100 were disappointing. As a result, several of the six machines built were leased to customers at unattractive rates. The A-100 had, however, proven to be a very effective crowd attraction device at equipment shows.

Markets

There were two important segments in the crane market—custom-built cranes and standard cranes—and although the world mobile crane market was judged to be $630 million in 1985, no estimates were available as to the size of each segment. Victoria competed primarily in the custom segment, in the medium- and heavy-capacity end of the market. In the medium-capacity custom crane class, Victoria's prices were approximately 75 percent of those of its two main competitors. The gap closed as the cranes became heavier, with Victoria holding a 15 percent advantage over Washington Cranes in the heavy custom crane business. In heavy standard cranes, Victoria did not have a price advantage.

Victoria's two most important markets were Canada and the United States. The U.S. market was approximately $240 million in 1985, and Victoria's share was about 15 percent. Victoria's Sacramento plant, serving both the U.S. market and export sales involving U.S. aid and financing, produced 60 to 70 cranes per year. The Canadian market was much smaller, about $44 million in 1985, but Victoria was the dominant firm in the country, with a 60 percent share. The Squamish plant, producing 130 to 150 cranes per year, supplied both the Canadian market and all export sales not covered by the U.S. plant. There had been very little real growth in the world market since 1980.

The primary consumers in the mobile crane industry were contractors. Because the amount of equipment downtime could make the difference between showing a profit or loss on a contract, contractors were very sensitive to machine dependability as well as parts and service availability. Price was important, but it was not everything. Independent surveys suggested that Washington Cranes, Victoria's most significant competitor, offered somewhat superior service and reliability, and if Victoria attempted to sell similar equipment at prices comparable to Washington's, it would fail. As a result, Victoria tried to reduce its costs through extensive backward integration, manufacturing 85 percent of its crane components in-house, the highest percentage in the industry. This drive to reduce costs was somewhat offset, however, by the fact that much of the equipment in the Squamish plant was very old. In recent years, some of the slower and less versatile machinery had been replaced, but by 1985 only 15 percent of the machinery in the plant was new, efficient, numerically controlled equipment.

Victoria divided the world into eight marketing regions. The firm carried out little conventional advertising but did participate frequently at equipment trade shows. One of the company's most effective selling tools was its willingness to fly in prospective customers from all over the world. The company was generous with the use of first-class airline tickets. Victoria believed that the combination of its integrated plant, worker loyalty, and the single-product concentration evident in their Canadian plant produced a convinced customer. There were over 14 such visits to the British Columbia plant in 1985, including delegations from The People's Republic of China, Korea, France, and Turkey.

Competition

Victoria, as the world's second largest producer of cranes, faced competition from five major firms, all of whom were much larger and more diversified. The industry leader was the Washington Crane Company with 1985 sales of $400 million and a world market share of 50 percent. Washington had become a name synonymous around the world with heavy-duty equipment and had been able to maintain a sales growth rate of over 15 percent per annum for the past five years. It manufactured in the United States, Mexico, and Australia. Key to its operations were 100 strong dealers worldwide with over 200 outlets. Washington had almost 30 percent of Canada's crane market.

Next in size after Victoria was Texas Star, another large manufacturer whose cranes were generally smaller than Victoria's and sold through the company's extensive worldwide equipment dealerships. The next two largest competitors were both very large U.S. multinational producers whose crane lines formed a small part of their overall business. With the exception of Washington, industry observers suggested that crane sales for these latter firms had been stable (at best) for quite some time. The exception was the Japanese crane producer Toshio which had been aggressively pursuing sales worldwide and had entered the North American market recently. Sato, another Japanese firm, had started in the North American market as well. Walters commented:

> My father laid the groundwork for the success that this company has enjoyed, but it is clear that we now have some major challenges ahead of us. Washington Cranes is four times our size and I know that we are at the top of their hit list. Our Japanese

competitors, Toshio and Sato, are also going to be tough. The key to our success is to remain flexible—we must not develop the same kind of organization as the big U.S. firms.

Organization

In 1979, a number of accumulating problems had ended Brian Walters' semiretirement and brought him back into the firm full-time. Although sales were growing, Walters saw that work was piling up and things were not getting done. He believed that new cranes needed to be developed, and he wanted a profit sharing plan put in place. One of his most serious concerns was the development of middle managers. Walters commented, "We had to develop middle-level line managers—we had no depth." The root cause of these problems, Walters believed, was that the firm was overly centralized. Most of the functional managers reported to Rivers, and Rivers made most of the decisions. Walters concluded that action was necessary—"We have to change," he said. "If we want to grow further, we have to do things."

Between 1979 and 1982 Walters reorganized the firm by setting up separate operating companies and a corporate staff group. In several cases, senior operating executives were placed in staff/advisory positions, while in others, executives held positions in both operating and staff groups. Exhibit 3 illustrates Victoria's organization chart as of 1983.

By early 1984, Walters was beginning to wonder "if I had made a very bad decision." The staff groups weren't working. Rivers had been unable to accept the redistribution of power and had resigned. There was "civil war in the company." Politics and factional disputes were the rule rather than the exception. Line managers were upset by the intervention of the staff VPs of employee relations, manufacturing, and marketing. Staff personnel, on the other hand, were upset by "poor" line decisions.

As a result, the marketing and manufacturing staff functions were eradicated with the late-1985 organization restructuring illustrated in Exhibit 4. The services previously supplied by the staff groups were duplicated to varying extents inside each division.

In place of most of the staff groups, an executive committee was established in 1984. Membership in this group included the president and head of all staff groups and presidents (general managers) of the four divisions. Meeting monthly, the executive committee was intended to evaluate the performance of the firm's profit and cost problems, handle mutual problems such as transfer prices, and allocate capital expenditures among the four operating divisions. Subcommittees handled subjects such as R&D and new products.

The new organization contained seven major centres for performance measurement purposes. The cost centres were

1. Engineering; R&D (reporting to Victco Ltd.).
2. International Marketing (Victoria Marketing Ltd.).
3. Corporate staff.

Exhibit 3 Victoria Organization Structure, 1979–1983

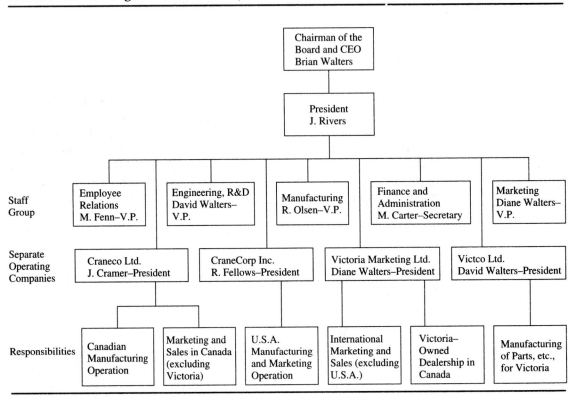

The major profit centres were

1. CraneCorp., Inc. (U.S. production and sales).
2. Victco Ltd. (supplying Victoria with components).
3. Craneco (Canadian production and marketing).
4. Victoria-owned Canadian sales outlets (reporting to Victoria Marketing Ltd.).

The major profit centres had considerable autonomy in their day-to-day operations and were motivated to behave as if their division were a separate, independent firm.

By mid-1985, Brian Walters had moved out of his position as president, and Michael Carter—a long-time employee close to retirement—was asked to take the position of president until a new one could be found.

Walters saw his role changing. "If I was anything, I was a bit of an entrepreneur. My job was to supply that thrust but to let people develop on their own

Exhibit 4 Victoria Organization Structure, Late 1985

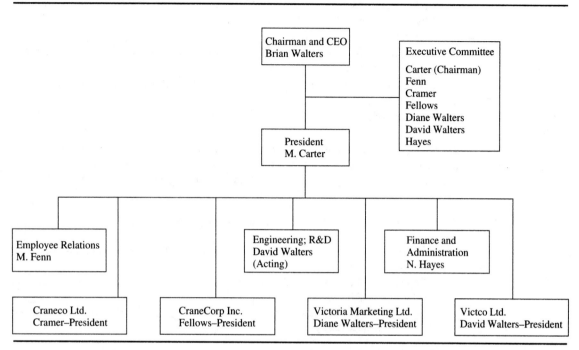

accord. I was not concerned about things not working, but I was concerned when nothing was being done about it."

In the new organization, Walters did not sit on the executive committee. However, as chairman of the board and chief executive officer, the committee's recommendations came to him and "they tried me on six ways from Sunday." His intention was to monitor the firm's major activities rather than to set them. He did have to sit on the product development subcommittee, however, when "things were not working . . . there was conflict . . . the engineering group (engineering, R&D) had designed a whole new crane and nobody including me knew about it." Mr. McCarthy, the VP of engineering and R&D, called only five to six committee meetings. The crane his group developed was not to Walters' liking. (There had been a high turnover rate in this group, with four VPs since 1983.) Recognizing these problems, Walters brought in consultants to tackle the problems of the management information system and the definition of staff/line responsibilities.

In spite of these moves, dissatisfaction still existed within the company in 1986. The new organization had resulted in considerable dissension. Some conflict centred around the establishment of appropriately challenging budgets for each operating firm, and even more conflict had erupted over transfer pricing and allocation of capital budgets. In 1985–86, even though requested budgets were cut equally, lack of central control over spending resulted in overexpenditures by several of the profit and cost centres.

The views of staff and the operating companies' presidents varied considerably when they discussed Victoria's organizational evolution and the operation of the present structure.

Diane Walters, the president of Victoria International Marketing, liked the autonomous system because it helped to identify the true performance of sections of the company. "We had separate little buckets and could easily identify results." Furthermore, she felt that there was no loss of efficiency (due to the duplication of certain staff functions within the divisions) since there was little duplication of systems between groups, and each group acted as a check and balance on the other groups so that "manufacturing won't make what marketing won't sell." Comments from other executives were as follows:

> The divisionalized system allowed me to get closer to my staff because we were a separate group.
>
> We ended up with sales and marketing expertise that was much better than if we had stayed under manufacturing.
>
> If you (run the firm) with a manufacturing-oriented organization, you could forget what people want.
>
> In a divisionalized system there was bound to be conflict between divisions, but that was not necessarily unhealthy.

Some executives saw the decentralized, semiautonomous operating company structure as a means of giving each person the opportunity to grow and develop without the hindrance of other functional executives. Most, if not all, of the operating company presidents and staff VPs were aware that decentralization brought benefits, especially in terms of the autonomy it gave them to modify existing practices. One senior executive even saw the present structure as an indicator of their basic competitive stance: "Either we centralize the structure and retract, or we stay as we are and fight with the big guys." With minimal direction supplied from Brian Walters, presidents were able to build up their staff, establish priorities and programs, and, essentially, were only held responsible for the bottom line.

Other executives believed that Victoria's structure was inappropriate. As one executive put it, "The semi-independence of the operating companies and the lack of a real leader for the firm has resulted in poor coordination of problem solving and difficulty in allocating responsibility." As an example, he noted how engineering's response to manufacturing was often slow and poorly communicated. Even worse, the executive noted, was how the priorities of different units were not synchronized. "When you manufacture just one product line all your activities are interrelated. So when one group puts new products first on a priority list while another is still working out bugs in the existing product, conflict and inefficiencies have to develop."

The opposing group argued that the present organization was more appropriate to a larger, faster-growing, and more complex company. As one senior executive put it, "We're too small to be as decentralized as we are now. All of this was done to accommodate the 'Walters kids' anyway, and it's now going to detract from profitability and growth." Another of these executives stated that rather than being a president of an operating company, he would prefer to be a general manager at the head of a functional group, reporting to a group head. "If we had the right Victoria Heavy Equipment president," he said, "we wouldn't need all these divisional presidents." Another continued,

> Right now the players (divisional presidents and staff VPs) run the company. Brian Walters gives us a shot of adrenaline four or six times a year but doesn't provide any active leadership. When Brian leaves, things stop. Instead, Brian now wants to monitor the game plan rather than set it up for others to run. As we still only have an interim president (Carter), it is the marketplace that leads us, not any strategic plan or goal.

The New President

Individual views about the appropriate characteristics of a new president were determined by what each executive thought was wrong with Victoria. Everyone realized that the new president would have to accommodate Brian Walters' presence and role in the firm and the existence of his two children in the organization. They all generally saw Brian as wanting to supply ideas and major strategies but little else.

All but one of Victoria's executives agreed that the new president should *not* get involved in day-to-day activities or in major decision making. Instead, he should "arbitrate" among the line general managers (subsidiary presidents) and staff VPs and become more of a "bureaucrat-cum-diplomat" than an aggressive leader. As another put it, "The company will drive itself; only once in a while he'll steer a little."

The 1986 Situation

Industry analysts predicted a decline of 10 percent in world crane sales—which totaled 1,200 units in 1985—and as much as a 30 percent decrease in the North American market in 1986. Victoria's sales and production levels were down. Seventy-five shop floor employees had been laid off at Squamish, bringing total employment there to 850, and similar cuts were expected in Sacramento. Worker morale was suffering as a result, and the profit sharing plan, which had been introduced in early 1985 at Walters' initiative, was not helping matters. In spite of the optimism conveyed to workers when the plan was initiated, management had announced in October that no bonus would be paid for the year. Aggravating the problem was the work force's observation that while certain groups met their budget, others did not, hence all were penalized. This problem arose because each bonus was based on overall as well as divisional profits.

Many of the shop-floor workers and the supervisory staff were also disgruntled with the additions to the central and divisional staff groups, which had continued even while the work force was being reduced. They felt that the paperwork these staff functions created was time-consuming and of little benefit. They noted, for example, that there were four or five times as many people in production control in 1986 as there were in 1980 for the same volume of production. In addition, they pointed out that despite all sorts of efforts on the part of a computer-assisted production control group, inventory levels were still too high.

Brian Walters commented on the 1986 situation and his view of the company's future:

> What we are seeing in 1986 is a temporary decline in the market. This does not pose a serious problem for us, and certainly does not impact on my longer term goals for this company, which are to achieve a 25 percent share of the world market by 1990, and reach sales of $250 million by 1999. We can reach these goals as long as we don't turn into one of these bureaucratic, grey-suited companies that are so common in North America. There are three keys for success in this business—a quality product, professional people, and the motivation for Victoria to be the standard of excellence in our business. This means that almost everything depends on the competence and motivation of our people. We will grow by being more entrepreneurial, more dedicated, and more flexible than our competitors. With our single product line we are also more focused than our competitors. They manage only by the numbers—there is no room in those companies for an emotional plea, they won't look at sustaining losses to get into a new area, they'll turn the key on a loser . . . we look at the longer term picture.

"The hazard for Victoria," Walters said, "is that we could develop the same kind of bureaucratic, quantitatively oriented, grey-suited managers that slow down the large U.S. competitors. But that," he said, turning to his audience, "is something I'm going to watch like a hawk. We need the right people."

CASE 36
WAYSIDE INDUSTRIES LTD.

Wayside Industries, located in Saint John, New Brunswick, was a producer of noncorrugated boxes for the fisheries industry. In March 1990, Bob Snodgrass, the owner and president of the company, was faced with a crucial decision regarding the firm's future direction. He had just received the results of a major marketing study done by a firm of outside consultants. Their report highlighted many of Bob's concerns and provided detailed marketing data to supplement his own information.

Bob was assessing several alternatives: to invest in a new plant, thereby increasing productivity; to upgrade production equipment, thereby expanding into new markets; to do both; to wait for another year before reaching a decision; or to investigate divestment opportunities. The facility and equipment expansion projects were of comparable size, and both appeared attractive, but Bob had to be realistic about his firm's available resources. His decision had to be ready for the capital budget meeting in April.

Background

The $15 million Atlantic Canadian market for noncorrugated cardboard packaging was almost evenly divided into institutional and consumer segments. The institutional market segment was a low-margin, low-technology commodity business dominated by regional producers. Half of the institutional segment was in the fish industry, with the balance in miscellaneous near markets. The higher margin, higher technology consumer market was dominated by nonregional producers, principally from Ontario. The regional institutional market was under pressure, while the nonregional consumer market showed a bright future.

Wayside was a successful company within the institutional market segment, with an account base that was primarily composed of fish-processing plants. The company had established itself as the market leader in New Brunswick and Nova Scotia for 5–20-lb. wax-coated noncorrugated institutional fish boxes. However, dependence on this market segment presented some inherent difficulties to Wayside:

- The fish-processing business was seasonal. Several profitable months of positive cash flow were followed by several months of negative cash flow.
- The fish-processing business was in crisis, with demand expected to decline. Dependence on the small independent processors increased the risk to receivables.

This case was prepared under the direction of Professor Paul W. Beamish by Kerry McLellan as a basis for classroom discussion rather than to illustrate either effective or ineffective handling of an administrative situation. © 1990. The University of Western Ontario.

The fishing industry had always been cyclical, but the latest downturn appeared to be different. There were signs that years of overfishing, principally by foreign trawlers operating just outside the 200-mile limit, had severely depleted fish stocks. In response, domestic quota cuts of 30 percent or more in some species had been announced. The supply problem would not improve until the issue of foreign overfishing had been dealt with. Negotiations were likely to take years, and it would be years after that before stocks recovered. This industry downturn was expected to be particularly severe and long lasting.

Wayside's production facility and equipment seriously limited entry into other packaging market segments. At the peak of the fish season, the production of boxes for the current fish customers required all of the company's existing capacity. Thus, it would not be able to meet the orders of new nonfish customers. In addition, Wayside printing equipment was inadequate to produce the quality graphics required on packaging in the consumer market segment.

Assessment of Manufacturing Capabilities

Wayside's present facility had evolved through a progression of technological and process upgrades. Coupled with the creative use of low-cost labour, they had transformed an antiquated plant into a viable production business. Wayside had compensated for a lack of technical productivity by improving raw material (paper board) quality, by installing the capability to handle paperboard rolls instead of sheets, and by targeting at quality-sensitive rather than price-sensitive business. The firm depended on two-colour technology, unsuitable for consumer packaging. The existing machinery was inefficient and labour intensive.

The production plant had expanded from the original building which had been a wartime aircraft hangar to an amalgamation of three separate buildings, connected at different levels, with varying ceiling heights. Because the facility was located in a residential area, further expansion and truck access would be restricted. Material handling was difficult, and there was only a limited amount of improvements that could be made to the process flow.

A new 50,000-square-foot building, in a well-located industrial park, would cost $38 per square foot to construct. The present facility, plus associated real estate, had a realizable market value of approximately $700,000. The new building would provide a 20 percent productivity increase as a result of layout and material-handling improvements. This saving would be incremental to any other changes. For the 1989 year-end, such productivity gains were estimated at $85,000. Annual operating and maintenance savings of $40,000 could also be achieved. In addition, Bob recognized that the present facility would require $150,000 in repairs, including a new roof, within the next few years. There was a possibility that an associated company, A. T. Snodgrass Co. Ltd. (ATSCO Sales), would locate in the building for a saving of $100,000 for that firm. Bob's preliminary investment analysis for the new facility decision showed the project to be very attractive.

The fish business was seasonal with Wayside's peak demand period running from early spring to late fall. Given the very high uncertainty associated with the fish business and the customized nature of the products, Wayside found it very difficult to smooth production rates using forecasted demand planning. The work force fluctuated from a low of 20 in January to a peak of 50 or more in the summer. This fluctuation made it difficult to hold on to skilled operators. However, since much of the work required only unskilled labour, this was not as serious a problem as it could have been. During the summer months, the plant operated 21 hours per day, 7 days per week, on a two-shift basis. Most workers put in large amounts of overtime. During 1989, the average was 18 hours overtime per week for each worker during the peak period.

The existing machinery was serviced by a firm in Chicago. Historically, there had been only a couple of service calls required each year as Wayside had been very careful with its preventive maintenance program. The U.S. firm had provided excellent service (24-hour response) and would be able to service any equipment contemplated in a modernization. This assurance was necessary due to the unavailability of local trained service personnel.

The key liability of the current Wayside facility was its lack of ability to produce consumer packaging because of limited productivity and capacity. To exploit the market opportunities outside of the fish industry, Wayside had to improve graphics capabilities, lower the variable cost of production, and increase volume capacity.

Assessment of Graphics Capabilities

Addressing new markets required colour graphics capabilities beyond Wayside's current scope. Wayside did "double pass" printing to get limited colour graphics capability. This process had serious quality implications, restricting entry into consumer packaging markets. To exploit the consumer market, a technological leap would be required in equipment and manpower skills.

Assessment of Productivity

Plant layout and work flow, unskilled labour, and specific production equipment represented areas where improvement was needed. Plant improvements would have to incorporate a reorganization of the work flow, specifically the loading and staging area (which was inadequate and at the furthest point from the inventory). The best solution for most of the productivity problems would be a new facility. The die cutter was inefficient and had quality control problems. This problem represented a barrier to competitive entry to specific near markets.

Assessment of Plant Capacity

The printing capacity would appear to have been the limiting factor on production capacity. However, two bottlenecks in the manufacturing process, die cutting and gluing, meant that existing printing capacity was not being fully used.

A recently released interfirm comparison of paper box manufacturers in Eastern Canada, prepared by Peat Marwick Stevenson & Kellogg for the Department of Industry, Science and Technology confirmed Bob's own findings and made several other observations. The report noted that Wayside's location provided it with a relatively inexpensive source of labour, but that the effectiveness of the labour was eroded by a very high level of practical capacity utilization, poor plant layout, difficult material handling, and outdated equipment. The consultants recommended that the firm review the impact of any changes in production volume on its product mix and cost structure. Because the manufacture of a more complex product would create new bottlenecks, production scheduling and sequencing would become more costly. Wayside processed more rush orders than most industry participants and used a significant amount of overtime in doing so.

Assessment of Management

Guy Richard was Wayside's plant manager, vice president, and partial owner. Although only 29, Guy had worked in the institutional paperboard packaging industry since he was 14. This practical experience was complemented by university exposure to engineering and business administration courses. In 1983, when Bob Snodgrass purchased the company, he appointed Guy as plant manager. By 1990, he was handling most of the day-to-day functions, including production planning, maintenance scheduling, and inventory managing.

Ownership of Wayside was a factor in the expansion decision. Bob Snodgrass owned the industrial distribution firm of ATSCO Sales, several other business concerns, and 80 percent of Wayside. Guy Richard owned the remaining 20 percent. Bob considered Guy to be the major strength of the company. Guy viewed his minority ownership position as an important part of his compensation package and felt challenged to make it meaningful through increased profitability. Bob was concerned that Guy might become dissatisfied if the firm's future was threatened by lack of response to the decline in fishing activity. He believed that Wayside's demise would be greatly hastened if Guy left the firm to pursue other challenges. He was also aware that Guy was apprehensive about diluting his ownership position. Bob had expressed a willingness to sell further shares in the business, provided his majority ownership position was not threatened. However, Guy had just purchased a new home and had limited additional resources to invest. A $250,000 expansion in Wayside's equity base would reduce Guy's ownership to 7.5 percent unless an arrangement could be negotiated.

Larry O'Neill, the company controller, was involved in the implementation of a new computer system which would integrate manufacturing and accounting, allowing a 100 percent increase in business without requiring additional management staff. As the designer of the previous system, Larry, a young graduate of the CMA program who had been with Wayside for more than five years, was familiar with the industry and the cost information required to manage effectively. Guy had been slowly transferring operating responsibilities to Larry and had found Larry competent.

Dave Short was the director of sales for Wayside. He had been in industrial sales with the Snodgrass group for more than 20 years. Largely due to his efforts, Wayside had come to dominate the fisheries market. Dave seemed less than enthusiastic about pursuing market opportunities outside the fishery, indicating that within that sector more work could be done. Dave's experience was with the industrial and institutional market segments, which were very different from the consumer packaging segment. Dave had been a loyal, productive employee and had a strong personal relationship with Bob Snodgrass.

Hazen Douglas was plant superintendent, responsible for production and worker supervision. He had proven skills for achieving productivity from low-skilled labour and antiquated machinery. Bob was confident that Hazen would be able to manage in an upgraded environment.

Wayside and the other companies within the Snodgrass group of firms were expected to operate as self-financing units. The small management group of four at Wayside enjoyed complete operating autonomy; however, capital budgeting decisions were usually dealt with at the annual planning meeting.

Assessment of Marketing Capabilities

Wayside relied on its sister distribution company, ATSCO, for its sales and marketing efforts, paying 5 percent of the gross sales for the services provided. ATSCO's 12 sales representatives provided complete coverage of the Atlantic Canada region. The provinces of New Brunswick, Newfoundland, and Prince Edward Island were serviced by the nine sales representatives based out of the Saint John head office. This territory contained a population base of 1.5 million. The province of Nova Scotia was serviced by three sales representatives in a branch office located in Halifax and responsible for a territory containing a population of 800,000. This arrangement was a cost-effective solution for Wayside and useful in terms of intercompany revenue allocations.

ATSCO was divided into two specialized groups for packaging and office supplies. New hires into sales were well educated (bachelor-level graduates) with good communication skills. An old-style sales approach with an aversion to new marketing direction was still evident, though slowly disappearing as new hires made an impact.

One area of concern for Wayside, with respect to the marketing capabilities of ATSCO, was the absence of a packaging expert with a good understanding of the consumer packaging market. Helping clients improve design and presentation of their packaging was critical to successful penetration of the consumer market. ATSCO was not fully capable of operating as the sales arm of Wayside, in the sophisticated consumer packaging market, without this expertise. In consumer packaging, the packaging supplier could contribute considerably in the final design of the package, and packaging represented an important value-added component of the product (as opposed to the institutional market, where it was just a box).

Bob was aware that the structure of the sales and marketing firm, as well as its relationship to Wayside, were becoming of concern to Guy. In the past, Wayside's simple products and market focus, as well as its small size, had lent efficiency arguments to the arrangements between the two firms. However, the rapid growth in the firm's sales and the modernization plans had left Guy with doubts as to whether the arrangement would be appropriate in the future. Since ATSCO Sales was 100 percent owned by Bob Snodgrass, the relationship with Wayside had been very lucrative for ATSCO.

Market Analysis

In order to decide upon his recommendations to the capital budget meeting, Bob has to study the analysis of Wayside Industries, which had been recently completed by the firm of outside consultants. Exhibit 1 presents their analysis of the fish market, near market, and consumer market segments. The fish segment data had been of no surprise to Bob; however, the extent of the opportunities in the other segments had been a pleasant revelation. Each segment was analyzed in terms of product examples, product requirements, key purchasing criteria, the percentage of Wayside's business contributed by the segment, market outlook, estimated size, and market share potentially available to Wayside.

The *fish market* refers to the fish processors who use 5–20-lb. wax-coated boxes. This has been Wayside's primary market.

The *near markets* consist of other types of business with packaging needs which are within Wayside's existing production capability. Examples of this include garment boxes, dairy packaging, and bakery boxes. This segment represents immediate market opportunities for Wayside, which could be addressed with the firm's existing technology.

The *consumer market* refers to the market for consumer-oriented packaging such as six-pack beer cartons, frozen food boxes, and boxes for confectionary

Exhibit 1 Segmentation of Maritime Markets for Noncorrugated Box Cartons

	Fish Market	*Near Markets*	*Consumer Market*
Product examples	Wax-coated boxes (tops and bottoms)	Weiner and sausage boxes, creamer trays, novelty boxes for dairy products pie boxes, cake boxes plain shipping cartons salt cartons, sugar cartons flower boxes	Local six-pack beer cartons National Sea seafood dinner boxes Frozen food packages Chocolate boxes Irving tissue boxes
Product requirements	Basic wax-coated carton At most, 2-colour print required Focal point of Wayside's existing product line	Basic noncorrugated cardboard carton 2-colour print required Pie boxes (windows) and salt boxes (spouts) are only products beyond Wayside's current production capabilities	Require offset litho capabilities High-level graphics (4-6 colours) Beyond Wayside's current production capabilities
Key purchasing criteria ranked	Delivery time Price Product quality	Price Quality Delivery time	Quality Price Delivery time
% of Wayside's existing business	85%	15%	Nil
Market competitors	Wayside (60%)—competes on quality, delivery Price Wilson (20%)—Montreal—competes on price Ellis Paperboard (15%)—Maine, USA—competes on price Ling Industries (3%) Royal Print (2%)-Dartmouth, N.S.-quality, price	Royal Print (45%)—loyal Nova Scotia base Ling Industries (30%)—strong price competitor Price Wilson (15%)—no obvious competitive advantages Wayside (10%)—New Brunswick base—some quality problems Emphasizes service	Royal Print (52%)—focus on small runs—monopoly position in this niche Ontario Suppliers (48%)-Lawson Marden Ltd. Somerville Packaging and low cost producers—only interested in very large volume accounts
Segment outlook	Declining volumes Reduced margins Increasingly price competitive	Potential to displace nonbio-degradable packaging Moderate growth segment	High-growth segment Free Trade Agreement has resulted in tremendous growth in packaged food processing Ontario Suppliers have poor service record and long delivery times Potential to displace nonbiodegradable packaging Inadequate service by Royal Print
Total market size	$3,500,000	$3,500,000	$8,000,000
Amount available to Wayside	$2,200,000	$2,000,000 (primarily N.B. and P.E.I.)	$4,000,000 (primarily N.B. and P.E.I.)

items. These were mass-produced products requiring a high-level graphics capability that was beyond Wayside's current production capabilities.

Equipment Upgrade Requirements

Offset Lithography—The Ideal Technology

In view of the market opportunities, offset lithography represented the best technological option. The versatility and the ability to do small runs was the real asset of offset litho. Plate-making equipment would also be required to implement this technology. A mechanical control system would be adequate to address market needs (no need for CAD/CAM user interface).

As alternatives, Bob and Guy had investigated rotogravure and flexograph processes. These processes had much lower costs of production. However, minimum run sizes were so large that there would be few opportunities to use this potential efficiency in Atlantic Canada.

Debottlenecking—Costly but Necessary

There were two weak links in the production process that had to be addressed in order to take advantage of the offset litho's capacity: die cutting and gluing. A large-capacity die cutter, capable of trimming, would be required to increase the production capacity. However, a new die cutter cost three times as much as the cost of an offset litho. Also, an additional gluing machine would be needed to accommodate growth objectives.

The new production levels would require an efficient and productive plant flow, particularly for materials. A new roll handling system would be needed to improve material handling.

The overall cost required to bring plant production capacity up to that of the desired printing technology (offset litho) would be almost four times that of the printing technology itself. This was not as ironic as it appeared, since the most significant improvements to packaging technology during the past three decades had been in production rates. These productivity gains had come as a result of the application of advanced technology to previously simplified mechanical processes.

Modest Infrastructure Requirement

There would be some modest improvements required in the current plant's infrastructure to accommodate the modernization. These included structural reinforcement of the floor for new production equipment, minor roof modifications, additional electrical and plumbing work, a new loading dock, and a modern staff services facility.

Capital Equipment Requirement

Three primary pieces of equipment:	
4 Colour offset litho	$100,000
Die cutter	300,000
Gluer	100,000
Additional equipment (including: plate making, electric pallet system, roll handling system)	95,000
Infrastructure (including: electrical, floor work, roof repairs, loading dock, washroom facilities)	228,500
Allowance for overruns	76,500
Total estimated expenditures—modernization	$900,000

The installation of the equipment could take place in the existing facility although Bob recognized that many productivity gains would have to be forgone. Construction work and installation of the equipment would take a total of five months to complete. Late spring to fall represented the company's busiest and most profitable months. Movement of the production process to a new facility would cost $150,000 to $200,000.

Operating Requirements

The major impact of the capital equipment changes would be a shift in the work force skills required. Although Wayside would not become a "high-tech" producer, manual functions would be automated, with workers responsible for the operation of more sophisticated equipment. To aid worker adjustment, Guy had proposed initially using the new equipment to manufacture only the company's existing product line and products which were close to the existing product line. As time progressed, it would become possible to use the new equipment to expand the product offerings and penetrate more sophisticated markets.

Other work force changes included the elimination or reduction in seasonal workers and overtime and the addition of four new full-time positions. As a consequence, labour costs would be reduced by $72,000. The increased productivity of the company's labour force would result in an improved competitive position for the firm. Also Wayside would probably be able to keep the balance of the staff securely employed on a more year-round basis.

Another operating change would be the firm's need to provide creative graphics services to customers in the consumer packaging sector. This service, expected of packaging suppliers, was an important means of tying customers to the firm. Wayside did not possess this skill in-house. Also, Saint John had no graphics firm with extensive expertise in the areas required by Wayside. There were several good local graphics companies, but the nearest firm with the required specific experience was in Halifax, Nova Scotia. At the present time, it was unknown whether a local firm would be interested in acquiring the necessary expertise.

Sales Growth Forecast with Equipment Modernization

The plant modernization would permit Wayside to expand its annual sales from $2.6 million to $4.3 million or more. The question facing management was whether sales growth of $1.7 million could actually be achieved in the consumer packaging market. An external consultant had prepared a forecast of Wayside's potential sales volume in the consumer packaging market. The consultant had been optimistic that the numbers were attainable but realization was going to take some effort.

	Five-Year Growth in Sales (Dollars)				
	Year 1	Year 2	Year 3	Year 4	Year 5
Incremental	497,540	402,460	300,000	200,000	300,000
Cumulative	497,540	900,000	1,200,000	1,400,000	1,700,000

Market opportunities had been identified that would reduce the firm's dependence on the fishing industry. However, realization of these opportunities required radical changes to the company in terms of capital equipment and operations.

Financial Analysis and Feasibility

The information in Exhibits 2 to 4 was compiled to show an investment analysis of the new equipment and the new facility, based on a differential cash flow during the first five years of operation. The analysis highlighted the modernization plan's very strong positive cash flow and significant return on investment because of the potential for large increases in revenue without notable increases in the fixed costs of the company. In other words, after the modernization, virtually all of the incremental gross margin would accrue to the net income of the company. At the same time, annual labour savings of $72,000 per annum ($60,000 in wages and $12,000 benefits and employee related expenses) would

Exhibit 2 Investment Analysis of New Equipment—Differential Cash Flow Only ($000s)

	Year 1	Year 2	Year 3	Year 4	Year 5
Capital investment	900				
Initial working capital required	65				
Amount of incremental equity	290				
Amount to be financed	675				
Incremental revenue	497	900	1,200	1,400	1,700
Variable cost of goods sold	368	666	888	1,036	1,258
Contributions from incremental revenue	129	234	312	364	442
Labour savings	36	72	72	72	72
Production cost increases	(5)	(10)	(10)	(10)	(10)
Incremental income before financing	160	296	374	426	504
Interest (including operating loan)	98	114	114	111	109
Incremental income before tax	62	182	260	315	395
Economic return					
Return on incremental equity	21.3%	62.9%	89.8%	108.6%	136.2%
Return on investment	16.6%	30.7%	38.8%	44.1%	52.2%
5-year average ROE	83.7%				
5-year average ROI	36.5%				

NOTE: 1. ROE calculations used incremental income before tax.
2. ROI calculations used incremental income before interest and tax.
3. Potential tax liabilities were ignored in calculations. Maximum exposure was estimated to be less than 25 percent.

be achieved. While the first 13 months of construction and operation would not be as profitable, they would, nevertheless, generate a positive incremental cash flow and a strong return on investment.

No Investment—No Future

After an analysis of the firm's situation, Bob had determined that, without investment, operations would remain marginally profitable for the next three years, after which revenues would decline enough to put the company into a loss position. While it might be possible to mitigate the losses to some extent by reducing staffing levels and taking other cost-cutting measures, the eventual outcome would, nevertheless, be the same: the company would go out of business. There was also possibility that the business might be sold as a viable concern to one of the existing competitors in this oligarchic industry. However, Bob was not certain that there would currently be any interest in the business and what price could be expected. In a wind-up scenario, Bob expected that the firm's fixed assets might yield $800,000 to $900,000.   The existing business was in decline and the company required strategic investment in order to survive. The equipment modernization could provide the means to breathe new life into the operations of Wayside by shifting its revenue dependence away from the declining fishing industry toward a more diverse and stable client base.

Capital Requirements

The first 6 to 12 months of the modernization project would be the most capital intensive. Once in operation, the business would begin to generate sufficient cash to meet ongoing working capital requirements. The company's incremental cash equity requirements would reach a peak in the first 13 months of about $290,000, an amount in excess of what the operating line of credit would be able to provide. The excess amount of $290,000 would arise from several sources

EXHIBIT 3   Investment Analysis of New Facility—Differential Investment Only ($000s)

Investment	
Capital cost	1,900
Less: Value of present facility	(700)
Net capital cost	1,200
Less: Avoidance of major repairs	(150)
Less: Avoidance of required infrastructure improvements	(200)
Net additional capital investment	850
Plus: Moving costs	150
Net investment for new facility	1,000
Expected savings	
Expected annual operating and maintenance savings	40
Savings on ATSCO Sales Office	100
Expected productivity improvement (direct labour, transportation, etc.)	85
Total immediate benefits	225

Return on investment/incremental equity
1. As a stand-alone project the ROI was 22.5% while ROE was 42%.
Assumptions and additional considerations
1. Productivity improvement will increase in proportion to sales.
2. Interest rate is assumed to be 14%.
3. 75% project financing is assumed.
4. ROI calculations used incremental savings before interest and tax.
5. Potential tax liabilities were ignored in calculations. Maximum exposure was estimated to be less than 25%.

related to the start-up of the newly expanded operations: the residual amount of the $900,000 modernization costs (only $675,000 in financing could likely be expected), interest on the interim construction loan totals over $39,000, and other start-up/construction factors contributing to the excess including interest on the interest, reduced production capacity due to construction activities, and start-up related training.

EXHIBIT 4 Investment Analysis of Upgraded Equipment and New Facility—Differential Cash Flow Only ($000s)

	Year 1	Year 2	Year 3	Year 4	Year 5
Equipment					
Equipment capital investment	900				
Less: Renovations	250				
Net equipment investment	650				
Initial working capital required	65				
Total	715				
Equity	227				
Financed	507				
Building					
Incremental investment for new building	850				
Moving cost	150				
Total	1,000				
Equity	250				
Financed	750				
Incremental revenue	497	900	1,200	1,400	1,700
Variable cost of goods sold	368	666	888	1,036	1,258
Contribution from incremental revenue	129	234	312	364	442
Labour savings	36	72	72	72	72
Production cost increases	(5)	(10)	(10)	(10)	(10)
Production Increase due to new facility	95	103	109	113	119
ATSCO office savings	100	100	100	100	100
Reduce operation and maintenance	40	40	40	40	40
Incremental income before financing	395	449	523	679	763
Interest (Including operating loan)	203	219	219	216	214
Incremental income before tax	192	230	304	463	549
Economic Return					
Return on incremental equity	40.2%	48.3%	63.7%	97.0%	114.9%
Return on investment	22.8%	25.9%	30.1%	39.1%	44.0%
5-year average ROE	72.8%				
5-year average ROI	32.4%				

NOTE: 1. ROE calculations used incremental income before tax.
2. ROI calculations used incremental income before interest and tax.

EXHIBIT 5

WAYSIDE INDUSTRIES (1983) LTD.
Income Statement
1985–1989
($000s)

	1989	*1988*	*1987*	*1986*	*1985*
Gross sales	2,626	2,259	1,991	1,776	1,624
Cost of goods sold					
Materials	1,252	1,065	981	822	788
Direct labor	283	251	216	199	183
Other	596	517	465	397	387
Total cost of goods sold	2,131	1,833	1,662	1,418	1,359
Gross profit	495	426	329	358	265
Expenses					
Selling	148	126	93	98	89
Administrative	182	156	130	132	107
Financial	109	91	81	72	58
Total expenses	439	373	304	302	254
Taxes	6	–0–	–0–	–0–	–0–
Net income	50	53	25	56	11

The financing issue concerned Bob, but discussions with local banks had assured him that 75 percent financing could be expected because Snodgrass companies had a very good record with regard to their financial obligations (Exhibit 5). This financing would be secured by the new facility/equipment. Bob accepted the likelihood that financing guarantees would have to be provided for Wayside's project by one of his other larger, more established firms. Bob was looking at several other attractive investments, outside Wayside, and had determined that the maximum cash investment he could infuse into the firm was $250,000. He was willing to sell additional shares to outside investors but he saw many problems that would have to be overcome if he was to pursue this option.

Bob recognized that the modernization and new facility project were critical to the future of Wayside Industries. The project could yield a return on investment in excess of 36 percent and provide the strategic redirection that would be needed for the welfare of the company in the long run. The new facility project, with a return on investment of 23 percent, would improve the firm's long-term efficiency. A combined project, with an estimated ROI of 32 percent, offered the benefit of avoiding some investment costs. To Bob, the issue was not whether Wayside should move forward with the proposed projects but whether the firm

EXHIBIT 5 *(concluded)*

WAYSIDE INDUSTRIES (1983) LTD.
Balance Sheets
As of November 30, 1989
($000s)

	1989	1988
Assets		
Cash	–0–	–0–
Receivables	556	549
Inventory	350	347
Prepaids	25	34
Total current assets	931	930
Sundry	49	21
Land	119	117
Net building, machinery, furniture	366	424
Total fixed assets	534	562
Total assets	1,465	1,492
Liabilities		
Bank	405	315
Payables	184	303
Other	89	79
Total current liabilities	678	697
Long-term liabilities	405	459
Loans from shareholders	225	229
Total liabilities	1,308	1,385
Preferred shares	100	100
Common shares	1	1
Retained earnings	56	6

had the resources to undertake both of them. If not, which one should be chosen and at what pace should the firm proceed? Should the projects be delayed? Or should Bob begin to investigate the possibility of selling the business? Bob was not certain of the best strategy, but he knew the decision would determine the firm's future.